Organizational Behavior

Human Behavior at Work

Fourteenth Edition

John W. Newstrom, Ph.D.
University of Minnesota Duluth

ORGANIZATIONAL BEHAVIOR: HUMAN BEHAVIOR AT WORK, FOURTEENTH EDITION

Published by McGraw-Hill Education, 2 Penn Plaza, New York, NY 10121.

Some ancillaries, including electronic and print components, may not be available to customers outside the United States.

This book is printed on acid-free paper.

4 5 6 7 8 9 0 QVS/QVS 1 0 9 8 7

ISBN 978-0-07-811282-9
MHID 0-07-811282-6

Senior Vice President, Products & Markets: *Kurt L. Strand*
Vice President, Content Production & Technology Services: *Kimberly Meriwether David*
Managing Director: *Paul Ducham*
Brand Manager: *Michael Ablassmeir*
Development Editor: *Laura Hurst Spell*
Marketing Manager: *Elizabeth Trepkowski*
Director, Content Production: *Terri Schiesl*
Content Project Manager: *Jessica Portz*
Buyer: *Susan K. Culbertson*
Media Project Manager: *Shawn Coenen*
Cover Design: *Studio Montage, St. Louis, MO*
Cover Image: © *Lawerence Manning/Corbis RF*
Compositor: *Cenveo® Publisher Services*
Typeface: *10/12 Times LT Std Roman*
Printer: *Quad/Graphics*

Library of Congress Cataloging-in-Publication Data

Newstrom, John W.
Organizational behavior : human behavior at work / John W. Newstrom, Ph.D., University of Minnesota Duluth. — 14 Edition.
pages cm
ISBN 978-0-07-811282-9
1. Organizational behavior. 2. Industrial sociology. I. Title.
HD58.7.D36 2013
302.3'5—dc23 2013039478

www.mhhe.com

This edition is dedicated to my grandchildren—Ruth, Axel, and Pearl—whose admirable qualities (innocence, inquisitiveness, careful observation, hunger for learning, enthusiasm for life, unconditional love, and all-around sweetness) give me great confidence for the future. My hope is that our families will enjoy many more special "cabin moments" together at our Finnish-heritage "Hevosenkenkä Jarvi Tupa" (Horseshoe Lake Cottage) in northern Minnesota.

About the Author

John W. Newstrom *University of Minnesota Duluth*

John W. Newstrom is a respected teacher, widely published author, and consultant to organizations in the areas of training and supervisory development. He is a Professor Emeritus of Management in the Management Studies Department of the Labovitz School of Business and Economics at the University of Minnesota Duluth (UMD). While there, he taught courses in managing change, training and development, organizational behavior and management, and interpersonal and group relations for nearly 30 years. He was previously on the faculty at Arizona State University (ASU), and he also worked at Honeywell Company. He holds bachelor's, master's, and Ph.D. degrees from the University of Minnesota. He has conducted training programs on a wide range of topics for organizations in the health care, steel, taconite mining, consumer products, gas transmission, public utility, and paper products industries as well as for city governments and federal agencies.

Dr. Newstrom has published more than 60 professional and practitioner articles in periodicals such as *Academy of Management Executive, Academy of Management Journal, Workforce, Personnel Journal, Human Resource Planning, Business Horizons, Training and Development, Journal of Management Development, California Management Review, S.A.M. Advanced Management Journal, Training, Supervisory Management, Journal of Management, Journal of Occupational Behavior,* and *Supervision.* He has served on the editorial review boards for several management journals, and he is the co-author of more than 45 books in various editions and languages, including *The Manager's Bookshelf, Organizational Behavior, Supervision, Transfer of Training, Games Trainers Play, Leaders and the Leadership Process, The Big Book of Team Building Games, Leading with a Laugh,* and his newest, *The Fun Minute Manager.*

His administrative experiences include being chairperson of UMD's Business Administration Department, director of the Center for Professional Development, acting director of ASU's Bureau of Business and Economic Research, and chairperson of the Management Education and Development (MED) division of the Academy of Management. He has also served on (or as a strategic consultant to) the boards of directors of several organizations, such as the American Society for Training & Development, St. Louis County Heritage and Arts Center, United Developmental Achievement Center, Duluth-Superior Community Foundation, Riverwood Healthcare Center, Riverwood Foundation, and Arrowhead Food Bank. He has held memberships in the Academy of Management, Organizational Behavior Teaching Society, and the Society for Advancement of Management.

Dr. Newstrom has received many awards in recognition of his innovative teaching and dedicated service to students and the community. He was the recipient of an Outstanding Reviewer Award from the MED division of the Academy of Management, the Outstanding Faculty Award from the UMD Student Association, the campus Outstanding Adviser Award, and several "favorite professor" recognition awards at UMD. His highest honor occurred when he was named a recipient of the Horace T. Morse–University of Minnesota Alumni Association Award for Outstanding Contributions to Undergraduate Education. Dr. Newstrom is also a member of the University of Minnesota's prestigious Academy of Distinguished Teachers.

On the personal side, John is married (to Diane, for 50 years!) and is the father of two college graduates (Scott and Heidi). He loves to hunt, work crossword puzzles, bake Scandinavian pastries, play with his grandchildren, drive his red sportscar, play golf and pickleball, maintain contact with former students, play practical jokes, conduct genealogical research, work outdoors at his cabin in northern Minnesota, spend quality time with family members, play cribbage with friends, and vacation in sunny climates. His favorite community service activities have included being a frequent blood donor, certified pickleball trainer and referee, co-leader of a Paint-A-Thon team for painting the houses of low-income persons, hospice volunteer, and "big brother" to a young boy. John has also sung bass in several barbershop quartets. He and his wife divide their time between Aitkin, Minnesota, and The Villages, Florida, where he practices the fine art of "neoteny" (energetic and joyful living).

Contents in Brief

Contents

Chapter 3
Managing Communications 52

Chapter 4
Social Systems and Organizational Culture 84

PART TWO
MOTIVATION AND REWARD SYSTEMS 113

Chapter 5
Motivation 114

Chapter 6
Appraising and Rewarding Performance 146

PART THREE
LEADERSHIP AND EMPOWERMENT 177

Chapter 7
Leadership 178

Chapter 8
Empowerment and Participation 204

PART FOUR
INDIVIDUAL AND INTERPERSONAL BEHAVIOR 229

Chapter 9
Employee Attitudes and Their Effects 230

Chapter 10
Issues between Organizations and Individuals 258

PART SEVEN
EMERGING ASPECTS OF ORGANIZATIONAL BEHAVIOR 435

Chapter 16
Organizational Behavior across Cultures 436

PART EIGHT
CASE PROBLEMS 461

Preface

A ROADMAP FOR READERS: INVITATION TO A JOURNEY OF BEHAVIORAL LEARNING

Have you had at least part-time experience in some form of business or voluntary organization? If so, you have quickly learned that not all behavior—whether your own, your manager's, or that of your associates—is entirely rational. And you may have pondered a series of questions about what you saw and felt:

- Why do people behave as they do at work?
- How can individuals, groups, and whole organizations work together more effectively within the increasing pace of corporate change, dramatic restructurings and downsizings, global recessions, and intense competition?
- What can managers do to motivate employees toward greater levels of performance?
- What responsibility do managers have for ensuring employee satisfaction?
- What can you learn from theory, research, and the experiences of other managers to help you become an effective future manager?

These and many other questions provide the background for this fourteenth edition of *Organizational Behavior: Human Behavior at Work.* In the next few paragraphs I will guide you on your journey through this book by providing you with a "roadmap"—an introduction to some of the key topics and methods that form the critical pathway for your learning journey.

Great progress has been made in the field of organizational behavior (OB) in recent years. One long-time observer, after conducting an extensive study, concluded that "a consensus regarding the theoretical knowledge possessed by the field seems to be emerging."[1] New theories have appeared on the scene, others have been validated, and some have begun to fade into oblivion. Organizational behavior, while recording great progress, still faces many questions and opportunities for improvement. This book pulls together the best and most current knowledge and provides rich insights into people at work in all kinds of situations and organizations.

One criticism of the OB field is that it has largely ignored the needs of practitioners. By contrast, this book makes a major effort to include numerous examples of real-life work situations, and dozens of these are identified by name. In addition, the chapter-closing "Advice to Future Managers" sections provide extensive lists of practical suggestions that can guide managers for years into the future. The book is characterized by its *applied orientation,* including a variety of end-of-chapter experiential approaches that encourage readers to reflect on what they have read and engage in self-examination. The text is designed to be kept as a reference guide, and it includes **160 action prescriptions** for practical guidance (see the summary of managerial prescriptions in Appendix B).

These rules form one powerful basis for a critical managerial skill—that of *deductive reasoning*. Once you grasp the rule and understand the underlying rationale (theory) for it, you can then derive useful observations and conclusions in a specific situation on your own. (This is a process of moving from the general to the particular.) You can also develop the complementary skill of *inductive reasoning,* which is combining an observation of an event with a relevant explanation to infer new rules (action prescriptions) for yourself. (This is a process of moving from the particular to the general.) These scientific processes are aided by four skills, as discussed below.

FOUR LIFELONG SKILLS

This book is written in part to encourage and promote the development of four distinct but complementary thought processes by students—insights, causal analysis, critical thinking, and reflection.

Insights are basically those "Ah-ha!" moments when the metaphoric light bulb goes on in your brain and you reach a meaningful conclusion (new perception) about something. You are asked to search for and generate these via the "Generating Organizational Behavior (OB) Insights" exercise at the end of each chapter.

A second major objective is to encourage you to think about logical and research-based connections between relevant variables. This **causal thinking** involves the capacity to identify an independent factor that, when present or introduced, results in a predictable consequence (good or bad).

Business leaders continually admonish younger managers to engage in **critical thinking**[3]—to ask penetrating questions, examine underlying assumptions, search for probable unintended consequences, detect inconsistencies in arguments, be sensitive and alert to the agendas and motivations of others, objectively appraise the merits of positions held by others, balance the needs of different stakeholders, and even challenge the mental models and theories espoused by others. Useful practice in critical thinking can be gained while reading this book as you search for behavioral insights, derive conclusions from material read, and challenge the utility of various concepts.

Reflection suggests pondering an idea, probing its meaning, reconsidering a position, or engaging in careful thought. Despite its possible connotation as a passive process, it is best viewed as an active mental activity in which you think deeply about something, relate it to previous experiences or relevant material, explore reasons for observed phenomena, review and analyze what you have encountered, and reach new insights into the material. Reflection requires that you open your mind and become receptive to the new ideas and different perspectives offered by others.[4] Throughout this book, I encourage you to develop your critical thinking and reflection skills by asking many "Why?" and "How" questions. You are given an opportunity to demonstrate these skills in the end-of-chapter exercises, "Nurturing Your Critical Thinking and Reflective Skills."

Earlier editions of this book have been tested on the firing line in university classrooms and in organizations for many years, and revised substantially over time to reflect new developments. Many ideas—both for additions and deletions of material—offered by long-time users of previous editions and other insightful reviewers are incorporated into this new edition. Many topical ideas, figures, and applied examples have been provided by professors and managers from around the country and around the world. I actively solicit comments to help make this book even more useful in the future. I listen, I care about your input, and I strive to produce a high-quality, well-documented, useful product. I invite you to contact me via the Internet (jnewstro@d.umn.edu) with any comments, ideas, or questions you may have.

THE AUTHOR'S ROLE

How is a book like this created and updated? I begin by continuously immersing myself in the thinking, research, and practice of organizational behavior to gain an in-depth understanding of hundreds of concepts. I keep abreast of new developments by regularly reading dozens of journals and books, as well as interacting with managers in a variety of organizations. Then, I develop a logical and engaging organizational framework and proceed to identify the most important elements for inclusion. Finally, I organize and present the information in ways that will help readers learn and retain the ideas.

My primary objective is to produce a book that is accurate, useful, up-to-date, and engaging. Content and substance are emphasized, and I present the material in an organized and provocative fashion that will enable readers to integrate the various parts of this discipline into a whole philosophy of organizational behavior. The fourteenth edition has been upgraded with thorough citations to recent research and practice, which indicate the basis for my conclusions and advice.

Where appropriate, I include alternative viewpoints on a subject or express the weaknesses inherent in a particular model or concept. There are no simple answers to complex behavioral issues. I encourage readers to do their own thinking and to integrate a variety of perspectives. Consequently, I believe this book will serve as a valuable foundation of behavioral knowledge. I hope it will stimulate readers to enrich their understanding through continued study of organizational behavior. Many prior students have chosen to retain their copy of *Organizational Behavior,* and they refer to it as a valuable reference manual when they encounter real-world problems and issues.

FEATURES OF THE BOOK

Many features of *Organizational Behavior: Human Behavior at Work* stand out in the eyes of its users. The most notable is its **careful blending of theory with practice,** so that its basic theories come to life in a realistic context. Readers learn that concepts and models do apply in the real world and help build better organizations for a better society. The ideas and skills learned in organizational behavior can help readers cope better with every aspect of their lives.

Another popular feature is the large number of **examples of real organizational situations.** These real-life vignettes show how actual organizations operate and how people act (sometimes unexpectedly!) in specific situations. Most of the major concepts in this book are illustrated with one or more of these true examples.

A feature highly appreciated by both faculty and students is the book's **readability.** I have maintained a moderate vocabulary level, manageable sentence length, and a readable style to present a complex field in understandable language. Variety—provided by figures, practical illustrations, margin notes, and research results—enhances the readability by presenting a refreshing change of pace from content discussions. I have also woven into the text a wide variety of rich analogies (e.g., "People are like snowflakes; no two are alike") to help you "see" a concept from a more common perspective.

Other features of the book include:

- A detailed table of contents to locate major topics
- Provocative quotes at the beginning of each chapter to stimulate thought and in-class discussion, and margin notes to highlight key concepts
- A "Facebook" page provides a glimpse into the chapter topics via the exchanges between two or more students
- Chapter-opening illustrations preceding every chapter to engage the reader in a real-life issue
- "Engaging Your Brain" questions get you to think about some of the chapter material before you have even read the content.
- A widely accepted, and specially updated, presentation of five models of organizational behavior that provides an integrating framework throughout the book
- Strong, and early, coverage of employee communication
- A comprehensive chapter on motivational theories and another on their application to reward systems in organizations

- A chapter on empowerment and participation that is unique among organizational behavior books in capturing this highly contemporary approach
- Discussion of international issues in organizational behavior so students can later examine how selected concepts might require adaptation to other cultures
- A unique discussion of the limitations of organizational behavior to provide yet another balanced perspective
- At least one behavioral incident for analysis and one experiential exercise to involve students in their own learning, at the end of every chapter
- A comprehensive glossary of terms at the end of the book, providing a concise definition-at-a-glance for about 400 key organizational behavior terms
- A 16-chapter structure that accents the issues of greatest importance in organizations today—motivation, leadership, conflict and power, groups and teams, and the nature of change and its effects
- Substantial coverage of teams—their organizational context, factors that make them successful, and team-building processes that help members work together more effectively
- A distinctive in-chapter exercise, called "Critical Thinking Exercise," that encourages students to identify the likely positive and negative effects of a variety of behavioral concepts
- A unique feature, called "What Managers Are Reading" that provides concise summaries of recent best-selling books related to the chapter content
- Boxes within each chapter that focus on ethical questions in organizational behavior or real company examples
- Special emphasis on practicality, as evidenced by the inclusion of "Advice to Future Managers" to guide managers toward improved practice of organizational behavior
- An end-of-chapter exercise, "Nurturing Your Critical Thinking and Reflection Skills," designed to facilitate your development in this area
- The inclusion of Appendix A, which encourages students to insert their scores from the "Assess Your Own Skills" exercise, compare their own assessments with those of others, and develop a personalized self-improvement plan
- The development of a "Generating OB Insights" exercise at the end of each chapter, in which students are encouraged to review the text material and create a set of 10 key insights gained that will help them build a strong base of OB knowledge

You are about to embark on a journey of learning about key behavioral concepts that have been proven to be useful to managers at every level of an organization. I sincerely hope this "roadmap" helps you get started and guides you successfully to your chosen destination!

John W. Newstrom

Preface for Instructors

I encourage you to read my open "letter" to students in the preceding four pages, and to embrace and reinforce the themes I have presented there. Now I will briefly highlight the learning aids I have used in this book, the instructional aids available to you, and provide well-earned acknowledgments to a variety of people.

Major features included in each chapter are chapter objectives, introductory quotations and incidents, a chapter summary, terms and concepts for review, and true case incidents for analysis in terms of chapter ideas. All chapters contain thorough and both classical and up-to-date references that provide a rich source of additional information for the interested reader. These come from a wide variety of sources, covering both academic and practitioner-related publications, to demonstrate that useful knowledge and illustrations can be found in many places. I encourage students to refer to these references regularly, since they not only indicate the source of information but often provide an interesting historical perspective on an issue or a counter vailing viewpoint. There are also numerous discussion questions, many of which require thought, encourage insight, or invite readers to analyze their own experiences in terms of the ideas in the chapter. Other questions suggest appropriate group projects. Each chapter also contains an experiential exercise to involve students in the application of a chapter concept.

A wide array of new material is incorporated into the fourteenth edition of this book. New topics covered include sustainability, paradigm shifts, transparency, work–family conflict, countercultures, reverse mentoring, high-energy (vs. fatigued) workers, positive contagion, perceptual distortion, workplace bullying, face time, emotional contagion, employee engagement, social screening, care and compassion, incivility/abusive supervision, social norms, crowdsourcing, red-teaming, shared mental models, champions, accelerators of change, nonwork stressors, and mindfulness.

INSTRUCTIONAL AIDS

Online Learning Center

The following supplements for instructors are available from the Online Learning Center: *www.mhhe.com/newstrom14e.*

The Instructor's Manual is designed to save instructors time. It includes sample assignment sheets for quarter and semester schedules; chapter synopses; teaching suggestions; a detailed analysis for each of the end-of-chapter case incidents; and suggested answers to the end-of-chapter discussion questions and cases in the last part of the text.

The Test Bank contains multiple-choice and true-false questions for each of the text's chapters, with solutions for each.

PowerPoint slides are available to help instructors demonstrate key principles and concepts during their lectures. Slides consist of key points and figures from the text.

Student Resources are also available from the Online Learning Center, including practice quizzes and chapter review material. Access to the Manager's Hot Seat Videos (www.mhhe.com/mhs) can also be purchased through a link on the website.

Organizational Behavior Video DVD, Vol. 2

Videos are available for instructors to enhance their lectures.

ACKNOWLEDGMENTS

Keith Davis, a former president and fellow of the Academy of Management and recipient of its Distinguished Educator award, was the creator of the predecessor to this book. It was originally called *Human Relations at Work: Dynamics of Organizational Behavior,* and he was the sole author through the first six editions as he laid a powerful foundation for its subsequent evolution and development. Keith was my admired co-author, gentle coach, and thoughtful friend who gave me the opportunity and assistance vital to establishing a highly successful book-publishing career. I am deeply grateful for his many contributions and the opportunity to continue in his successful publishing footsteps.

Many other scholars, managers, and students have contributed to this book, and I wish to express my appreciation for their aid. In a sense, it is their book, for I am only the agent who prepared it. I am especially grateful for the thorough, insightful, and highly useful review of the book by Dr. Kristina Bourne (my first-ever undergraduate student to obtain her Ph.D.!), who also provided useful assistance in revising Chapter 16. Dr. Bourne's comments and suggestions have been carefully studied, found to be of substantial merit, and incorporated into the text wherever possible.

Many of my academic associates at the University of Minnesota Duluth and elsewhere have directly or indirectly provided valuable insights, collegial support, and ongoing encouragement, and for that I wish to thank them. In particular, Jon L. Pierce—my wise academic mentor, highly productive co-author on other writing projects, and long-time close personal friend—has provided wise counsel, intellectual stimulus, and staunch support across three decades of collaboration. I also appreciate the help and support of the many McGraw-Hill employees—especially Michael Ablassmeier and Laura Spell—who took a sincere and professional interest in improving the quality of the book. Last (but certainly not least), my wife (Diane) has provided unwavering strength, support, freedom, encouragement, and love in the pursuit of my interests, goals, and dreams. I am extremely grateful to her.

John W. Newstrom

Part One

Fundamentals of Organizational Behavior

Chapter One

The Dynamics of People and Organizations

A primary goal of management education is to develop students into managers who can think ahead, exercise good judgment, make ethical decisions, and take into consideration the implications of their proposed actions.

Jane Schmidt-Wilk[1]

(Management students) must develop systemic thinking skills that will enable them to develop a richer understanding of the complexity they will face on a daily basis.

J. Brian Atwater, et al.[2]

CHAPTER OBJECTIVES

AFTER READING THIS CHAPTER, YOU SHOULD UNDERSTAND

1–1 The Meaning of Organizational Behavior
1–2 The Key Goals and Forces with Which It Is Concerned
1–3 The Basic Concepts of Organizational Behavior
1–4 Major Approaches Taken in This Book
1–5 How Organizational Behavior Affects Organizational Performance
1–6 The Limitations of Organizational Behavior

Facebook Page 

Student A: Hey, I just registered for this college course.

Student B: What's it called?

Student A: Something like "Organizational Behavior," or OB for short.

Student C: I didn't think organizations behaved. What's OB about?

Student A: The course description says OB is "the systematic study and careful application of knowledge about how people—as individuals and as groups—act in organizations, and how they can do so more effectively."

Student B: Sounds interesting, but a bit intimidating.

Student C: What do you think you'll learn?

Student A: By the end of the first chapter, I'm expected to understand Organizational Behavior, know its goals and some forces it's concerned about, identify some basic concepts in OB, understand the four major approaches taken in the book, see how OB affects organizational performance, and also recognize the limitations of OB.

Student C: That's a mouthful. I think you'd better get started right now, dude.

Student D: Like.

Student A: I'm on it already. Wait until you hear some of the new terms I'm expected to learn—behavioral bias, contingency approach, evidence-based management, law of diminishing returns, selective perception, and more.

Student B: What ever happened to one- and two-syllable words?

Chris Hoffman graduated from college and was excited to begin her new job as a sales representative with IBM. The first few months at work were extremely hectic for her. She attended numerous formal training sessions, learned about the wide array of products she was to sell, and tried hard to understand the complex and fluid nature of her new employer.

Returning to her home late one night, she was too confused to fall asleep immediately. Many questions raced through her mind, based on her observations at work in recent weeks: "Why are some of my colleagues more successful than others? How can we act as a team when we are working out of our homes and interacting primarily through our laptop computers? How will I ever learn to handle the stress of meeting my sales quotas? Why doesn't my colleague Carrie cooperate with me when I ask her for assistance? Why does my manager ask me for suggestions, and then go ahead without using my input? How is the new 'IBM culture' different from the old one? And why is it constantly changing, anyway?"

Chris is already learning some key facts about life at work. *Organizations are complex systems.* If Chris wishes to be an effective employee and later a manager, she'll need to understand how such systems operate. Organizations like IBM effectively combine people and science—humanity and technology. With the rapid discoveries and improvements that science has provided in the past century, mastering technology itself is difficult enough. When you add people to the mix you get an immensely complex sociotechnical system that almost defies understanding. However, the progress of society in the twenty-first century depends heavily on understanding and managing effective organizations today.

Engaging Your Brain

1. Do you think that most managers, upon studying OB, will likely use that knowledge for the benefit of employees, the organization, or themselves?
2. You hear a lot about the need for increased productivity in the economy. What important factors do you think lead to productivity?
3. Do you think it is likely that managers will become overly biased toward the use of OB knowledge to guide their efforts?

Chris also sees that *human behavior in organizations is sometimes unpredictable.* The behavior of her colleagues, manager, and customers arises from their deep-seated needs, lifetime experiences, and personal value systems. However, *human behavior in an organization can be partially understood* by studying and applying the frameworks of behavioral science, management, and other disciplines. Exploring the various facets of such behavior is the objective of this book. *There are no perfect solutions to organizational problems,* as Chris will soon discover. However, employees can increase their understanding and skills so that work relationships can be substantially upgraded. The task is challenging, but the results are worthwhile.

Organizational behavior is needed

On occasion, Chris may become so frustrated that she will be tempted to withdraw from her job. The uncooperative colleague may limit Chris's effectiveness; the behavior of her manager may sometimes be difficult to understand. Whether she likes the behavior of these individuals or not, Chris does not have the luxury of *not* working with or relating to other people. Therefore, it is imperative that she learn about human behavior, explore how to improve her interpersonal skills, and begin to manage her relationships with others at work. These are areas where knowledge of organizational behavior can make a significant contribution to her effectiveness.

UNDERSTANDING ORGANIZATIONAL BEHAVIOR

To provide an understanding of what goes on at the workplace, it is useful to begin with the definition, goals, forces, and major characteristics of organizational behavior (OB). Later in the chapter we introduce the key concepts that OB deals with, lay out the four basic approaches taken in this book, and identify some factors that limit or even undermine the success of OB.

Definition

Organizational behavior is the systematic study and careful application of knowledge about how people—as individuals and as groups—act within organizations. It strives to identify ways in which people can act more effectively. Organizational behavior is a scientific discipline in which a large number of research studies and conceptual developments are constantly adding to its knowledge base. It is also an applied science, in that information about effective practices in one organization is being extended to many others.

Five levels of analysis

Organizational behavior provides a useful set of tools at many levels of analysis. For example, it helps managers look at the behavior of *individuals* within an organization. It also aids their understanding of the complexities involved in *interpersonal* relations, when two people (two co-workers or a superior–subordinate pair) interact. At the next level, organizational behavior is valuable for examining the dynamics of relationships within small *groups,* both formal teams and informal groups. When two or more groups need to coordinate their efforts, such as engineering and sales, managers become interested in the *intergroup* relations that emerge. Finally, organizations can also be viewed, and managed, as *whole systems* that have interorganizational relationships (e.g., mergers and joint ventures).

Goals

Four goals of OB are to describe, understand, predict, and control human behavior at work

Most sciences have four major thrusts, and these are also the **goals of organizational behavior.**

- The first objective is to *describe,* systematically, how people behave under a variety of conditions. Achieving this goal allows managers to communicate about human behavior at work using a common language. For example, one benefit from the study of this book is the acquisition of a new vocabulary about organizational behavior (see, for example, the Glossary at the end of this book).
- A second goal is to *understand* why people behave as they do. Managers would be highly frustrated if they could only talk about the behaviors of their employees and not understand the reasons behind those actions. Therefore, inquisitive managers learn to probe for underlying explanations.
- *Predicting* future employee behavior is another goal of organizational behavior. Ideally, managers would have the capacity to predict which employees might be dedicated and productive or which ones might be absent, tardy, or disruptive on a certain day (so that managers could take preventive actions).
- The final goal of organizational behavior is to *control,* at least partially, and develop some human activity at work. Since managers are held responsible for performance outcomes, they are vitally interested in being able to make an impact on employee behavior, skill development, team effort, and productivity. Managers need to be able to improve results through the actions they and their employees take, and organizational behavior can aid them in their pursuit of this goal.

Some people may fear that the tools of organizational behavior will be used to limit their freedom, manipulate their thoughts and actions, and take away their rights. Although that scenario is possible, it is not likely, for the actions of most managers today are subject to intense scrutiny. Managers need to remember that organizational behavior is a human tool for human benefit. It applies broadly to the behavior of people in all types of organizations, such as businesses, government, schools, and service organizations. Wherever organizations are, there is a need to describe, understand, predict, and control (better manage) human behavior.

Forces

Four key forces

A complex set of forces affects the nature of organizations today. A wide array of issues and trends in these forces can be classified into four areas—people, structure, technology, and the environment in which the organization operates. Each of the four forces affecting organizational behavior, and some illustrations of each, is considered briefly in the following sections.

People People make up the internal social system of the organization. That system consists of individuals and groups, and large groups as well as small ones. There are unofficial, informal groups and more official, formal ones. Groups are dynamic. They form, change, and disband. People are the living, thinking, feeling beings who work in the organization to achieve their objectives. We must remember that organizations should exist to serve people, rather than people existing to serve organizations.

The human organization of today is not the same as it was yesterday, or the day before. In particular, the workforce has become a rich melting pot of **diversity,** which means that employees bring a wide array of educational and ethnic and cultural and religious and gender and economic backgrounds, talents, and perspectives to their jobs. Occasionally, this diversity presents challenges for management to resolve, as when some employees express themselves through alternative dress or jewelry, while others present unique challenges through their unique lifestyles and recreational interests. Other employees have examined their values and are determined to put their personal goals ahead of total commitment to the organization. Managers need to be tuned in to these diverse patterns and trends, and be prepared to adapt to them.

> Some of the changes in the labor force are as follows: There has been a decline in the work ethic and a rise in emphasis on leisure, self-expression, fulfillment, and personal growth. The automatic acceptance of authority by employees has decreased, while desires for participation, autonomy, and control have increased. At the same time, several major factors are affecting the workforce. Skills become obsolete as a result of technological advances, and manual workers must either be retrained for knowledge-oriented jobs or be displaced. Security needs become foremost in the minds of millions of workers (and loyalty diminishes) because of the threat or the reality of downsizings and outsourcings. And even in eras of controlled inflation, the absence of meaningful salary growth for many employees has placed renewed emphasis on money as a motivator.

Indeed, a new labor force has emerged, and management's leadership practices must change to match the new conditions. These fast-moving developments have given new emphasis to leadership ability. Some companies are discovering that demonstrating a sense of caring, really listening to employees, and being concerned with both competence and relationships are among the keys to motivating the present workforce. Other companies are urging their managers to respond to a diverse workforce by building pride without devaluing others, empowering some without exploiting others, and demonstrating openness, confidence, authentic compassion, and vulnerability.[3]

Structure Structure defines the formal relationship and use of people in organizations. To accomplish all of an organization's activities, different jobs are required, such as managers and employees, accountants and assemblers. These people must be related in some structural way so their work can be effectively coordinated. These relationships create complex problems of cooperation, negotiation, and decision making.

Technology Technology provides the resources with which people work and affects the tasks they perform. The great benefit of technology is that it allows people to do more and better work, but it also restricts people in various ways. It has costs as well as benefits. Examples of the impact of technology include the increasing use of robots and automated control systems in assembly lines, the dramatic shift from a manufacturing to a service economy, the impressive advances in computer hardware and software capabilities, the widespread use of the Internet, and the need to respond to societal demands for improved quality of goods and services at acceptable prices. Each of these technological advancements, in its own way, places increased pressure on OB to maintain the delicate balance between technical and social systems.

Environment Environments can be internal or external, and all organizations operate within them. Any organization is part of a larger system that contains many elements, such as government, the family, and other organizations. Numerous changes in the environment create demands on organizations. Citizens expect organizations to be socially responsible; new products and competition for customers come from around the globe; the direct impact of unions (as measured by the proportion of the labor force that is unionized) diminishes; the dramatic pace of change in society quickens. All these factors—but especially the rapid globalization of the marketplace, whose impact on OB is discussed in Chapter 16—influence one another in a complex system that creates a dynamic (even chaotic) context for a group of people. The external environment influences the attitudes of people, affects working conditions, and provides competition for resources and power. It must be considered in the study of human behavior in organizations.

Positive Characteristics of the Organizational Behavior Field

Interdisciplinary

One major strength of organizational behavior is its *interdisciplinary* nature. It draws from the fields of *psychology* (the study of cognitive functions and behaviors), *sociology* (the study of human society and institutions), *social psychology* (the study of how people's thoughts, feelings, and actions are influenced by the presence of others), *group dynamics* (the study of behaviors within or between groups), and *anthropology* (the study of the evolution of humans and their cross-cultural relationships). OB integrates relevant knowledge from these behavioral science disciplines with other social sciences that can contribute to the subject. It applies from these disciplines any ideas that will improve the relationships between people and organizations. Its interdisciplinary nature is similar to that of medicine, which applies knowledge from the physical, biological, and social sciences into a workable medical practice.

Another strength of organizational behavior is its emerging base of *research knowledge, theories, models, and conceptual frameworks.* The field of organizational behavior has grown in depth and breadth, and it will continue to mature. The keys to its past and future success revolve around the related processes of theory development, research, and managerial practice.

Three keys to success

Theories (see additional arguments for theories in What Managers Are Reading) offer explanations of how and why people think, feel, and act as they do. Theories identify important variables and link them to form tentative propositions that can be tested through research. Good theories are also practical—they address significant behavioral issues, they contribute to our understanding, and they provide guidelines for managerial thought and action.[4] You will be introduced to several practical and interesting theories in this book, presented in a straightforward fashion.

Research is the process of gathering and interpreting relevant evidence that will either support a behavioral theory or help change it. Research hypotheses are testable statements connecting the variables in a theory, and they guide the process of data collection. Data are generated through various research methods, such as case studies, field and laboratory experiments, and surveys. The results of these research studies, as reported in various journals, can affect both the theory being examined and future managerial practices.

Research is an ongoing process through which valuable behavioral knowledge is continually uncovered. Examining a stream of research is like exploring the Mississippi River from its gentle source in northern Minnesota to its powerful ending in the Gulf of Mexico. Just as a trip down the entire river allows us to better appreciate its growth and impact, so does a review of research help us better understand how the major ideas in organizational behavior evolved over time. Consequently, the highlights of dozens of relevant research studies are briefly presented to you in appropriate places in this text.

Neither research nor theory can stand alone and be useful, however. Managers apply the theoretical models to structure their thinking; they use research results to provide relevant guides to their own situations. In these ways, theory and research form a natural and healthy foundation for **practice,** which is the conscious application of conceptual models and research results in order to improve individual and organizational performance at work. This is similar to the application of **evidence-based management,** which asks managers to set aside some of the things they think they know (conventional wisdom) and become totally committed to a rigorous collection of facts and combine these with relevant research. Evidence-based management depends heavily on the explicit use of four pillars

What Managers Are Reading 

LEARNING TO BECOME GOOD CONSUMERS OF THEORY

Two best-selling authors and Harvard Business School professors argue that executives should care deeply about management theory (causal connections between variables). Despite the widespread misconception that theories are impractical, they are shown to be valuable in two key ways: They help make predictions, and they help interpret and understand present situations and explain why they occurred. As social psychologist Kurt Lewin once said, "There's nothing so practical as a good theory."

Since every action that managers take and every decision they make is based on some theory (implicit or explicit; valid or not), accepting and embracing theory, using it constructively, and helping improve it are important for managers. Managers are strongly urged to learn which theories will help them most and to differentiate between good and bad theories. In essence, managers should learn to become discerning *consumers* of theory.

Source: Clayton M. Christensen and Michael E. Raynor, *The Innovator's Solution*, Cambridge, MA: Harvard Business School Press, 2003.

of information: (1) immersion in, and critical evaluation of, existing research evidence on "best organizational practices"; (2) in-depth information unique to the organization and its local context; (3) input and reactions from various persons affected by it (similar to the patient in a clinical setting); and (4) the wisdom, expertise, and practiced judgment of the manager. This, needless to say, is a rather monumental task.[5]

Managers also have a vital role to play in the other direction—the testing and revision of theory and conducting research. Feedback from practitioners can suggest whether theories and models are simple or complex, realistic or artificial, and useful or useless.

Organizations serve as research sites and provide subjects for various studies. As shown in Figure 1.1, there is a two-way interaction between each pair of processes, and all three processes are critical to the future of organizational behavior. Better models must be developed, theory-based research must be conducted, and managers must be receptive to both sources and apply them to their work.

FIGURE 1.1
The Interaction of Theory, Research, and Practice in Organizational Behavior, and Sample Sources for Each

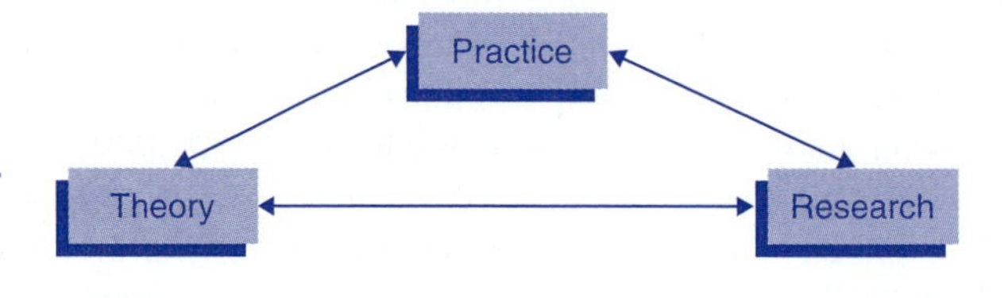

Sample Sources		
Theory Information	**Research Information**	**Practice Information**
Academy of Management Review	*Academy of Management Journal*	*Sloan Management Review*
Human Relations	*Journal of Applied Psychology*	*Organizational Dynamics*
Administrative Science Quarterly	*Journal of Management*	*Harvard Business Review*
Psychological Bulletin	*Organizational Behavior and Human Decision Processes*	*Business Horizons*
Annual Review of Psychology	*Journal of Organizational Behavior*	*California Management Review*
	Academy of Management Discoveries	*Workforce Management*

Increased acceptance

Researchers have identified key questions, designed appropriate studies, and reported the results and their conclusions. Others have examined related studies, and used them to construct models and theories that explain sets of findings and help guide future studies. As a result, organizational behavior has progressed substantially, and will continue to be vitally important throughout the twenty-first century. Sample sources of OB theory, research, and practice information are shown in Figure 1.1.

FUNDAMENTAL CONCEPTS

Every field of social science, or even physical science, has a philosophical foundation of basic concepts that guide its development. In accounting, for example, a fundamental concept is that "for every debit there will be a credit." The entire system of double-entry accounting was built on this equation when that system replaced single-entry bookkeeping many years ago. In physics, a basic belief is that elements of nature are uniform. The law of gravity operates uniformly in Tokyo and London, and an atom of hydrogen is identical in Moscow and Washington, D.C. Even though such uniformity cannot be applied to people, certain basic concepts regarding human behavior do exist.

As shown in Figure 1.2, organizational behavior starts with a set of fundamental concepts revolving around the nature of people and organizations. These concepts are the enduring principles that form a strong foundation for OB. A summary of these ideas follows, and they are woven into later chapters.

The Nature of People

Six basic concepts exist in regard to people: individual differences, perception, a whole person, motivated behavior, desire for involvement, and the value of the person.

Individual Differences People have much in common (they become excited by an achievement; they are grieved by the loss of a loved one), but each person in the world is also individually unique. The idea of **individual differences** is supported by science. Each person is different from all others, just as each person's DNA profile is different. And these differences are usually substantial rather than meaningless. Think, for example, of a person's billion brain cells and the billions of possible combinations of connections and bits of experience stored there. All people are different, and this diversity should be recognized and viewed as a valuable asset to organizations.

Law of individual differences

The idea of individual differences comes originally from psychology. From the day of birth, each person is unique (the impact of *nature*), and individual experiences after birth tend to make people even more different (the influence of *nurture*). Individual differences mean that management can motivate employees best by treating them differently. If it were not for individual differences, some standard across-the-board way of dealing with employees could be adopted, and minimum judgment would be required thereafter. Individual differences require

FIGURE 1.2
Fundamental Concepts of Organizational Behavior

The Nature of People	The Nature of Organizations
• Individual differences	• Social systems
• Perception	• Mutual interest
• A whole person	• Ethics
• Motivated behavior	
• Desire for involvement	
• Value of the person	

that a manager's approach to employees be individual, not statistical. This belief that each person is different from all others is typically called the **law of individual differences.**

Perception People look at the world and see things differently. Even when presented with the same object, two people may view it in two different ways. Their view of their objective environment is filtered by **perception,** which is the unique way in which each person sees, organizes, and interprets things. People use an organized framework that they have built out of a lifetime of experiences and accumulated values. Having unique views is another way in which people act like human beings rather than rational machines.

Selective perception

Employees see their work worlds differently for a variety of reasons. They may differ in their personalities, needs, demographic factors, and past experiences, or they may find themselves in different physical settings, time periods, or social surroundings. Whatever the reasons, *they tend to act on the basis of their perceptions.* Essentially, each person seems to be saying, "I react not to an objective world, but to a world judged in terms of my own beliefs, values, and expectations." This way of reacting reflects the process of **selective perception,** in which people tend to pay attention to those features of their work environment that are consistent with or reinforce their own expectations. Selective perceptions can not only cause misinterpretations of single events at work but also lead to future rigidity in the search for new experiences. Managers must learn to expect perceptual differences among their employees, accept people as emotional beings, and manage them in individual ways.

A Whole Person Although some organizations may wish they could employ only a person's skill or brain, they actually employ a whole person rather than certain characteristics. Different human traits may be studied separately, but in the final analysis they are all part of one system making up a whole person. Skill does not exist apart from background or knowledge. Home life is not totally separable from work life, and emotional conditions are not separate from physical conditions. People function as total human beings.

> For example, a supervisor wanted to hire a new telemarketer named Anika Wilkins. She was talented, experienced, and willing to work the second shift. However, when Anika was offered the job, she responded by saying that she would need to start a half hour late on Wednesdays because her child care service was not available until then. Also, since she had a minor handicap, her workstation required a substantial adjustment in height. So her supervisor had to consider her needs as a whole person, not just as a worker.

Better person

When management applies the principles of organizational behavior, it is trying to develop a better employee, but it also wants to develop a better *person* in terms of growth and fulfillment. Jobs shape people somewhat as they perform them, so management must care about the job's effect on the whole person. Employees belong to many organizations other than their employer, and they play many roles inside and outside the firm. If the whole person can be improved, then benefits will extend beyond the firm into the larger society in which each employee lives.

Motivated Behavior From psychology, we learn that normal behavior has certain causes. These may relate to a person's needs or the consequences that result from acts. In the case of needs, people are motivated not by what *we* think they ought to have but by what *they* themselves want. To an outside observer, a person's needs may be unrealistic, but they are still controlling. This fact leaves management with two basic ways to motivate people. It can show them how certain actions will increase their need fulfillment, or it can threaten decreased need fulfillment if they follow an undesirable course of action. Clearly, a path toward increased need fulfillment is the better approach, and this illustrates that motivation is essential to the operation of organizations.

Desire for Involvement Many employees today are actively seeking opportunities at work to become involved in relevant decisions, thereby contributing their talents and ideas to the organization's success. They hunger for the chance to share what they know and to learn from the experience. Consequently, organizations need to provide opportunities for meaningful involvement. This can be achieved through employee empowerment—a practice that will result in mutual benefit for both parties (see Chapter 8).

Value of the Person People deserve to be treated differently from other factors of production (land, capital, technology) because they are of a higher order in the universe. Because of this distinction, they want to be treated with caring, respect, and dignity—and they increasingly demand such treatment from their employers. They refuse to accept the old idea that they are simply economic tools or a "pair of hands." They want to be valued for their skills and abilities, be provided with opportunities to develop themselves, and be given reasonable chances to make meaningful contributions—now.

The Nature of Organizations

The three key concepts of organizations are that they are social systems, they are formed on the basis of mutual interest, and they must treat employees ethically.

Social Systems From sociology, we learn that organizations are social systems; consequently, activities therein are governed by social laws as well as psychological laws. Just as people have psychological needs, they also have social roles and status. Their behavior is influenced by their group as well as by their individual drives. In fact, two types of social systems exist side by side in organizations. One is the formal (official) social system, and the other is the informal social system.

The existence of a social system implies that the organizational environment is one of dynamic change rather than a static set of relations as pictured on an organization chart. All parts of the system are interdependent, and each part is subject to influence by any other part. Everything is related to everything else.

The idea of a social system provides a framework for analyzing organizational behavior issues. It helps make organizational behavior problems understandable and manageable.

Superordinate goal

Mutual Interest Organizations need people, and people need organizations. Organizations have a human purpose. They are formed and maintained on the basis of some **mutuality of interest** among their participants. Managers need employees to help them reach organizational objectives; people need organizations to help them reach individual objectives.[6] If mutuality is lacking, trying to assemble a group and develop cooperation makes no sense, because there is no common base on which to build. As shown in Figure 1.3, mutual

FIGURE 1.3
Mutual Interest Provides a Superordinate Goal for Employees, the Organization, and Society

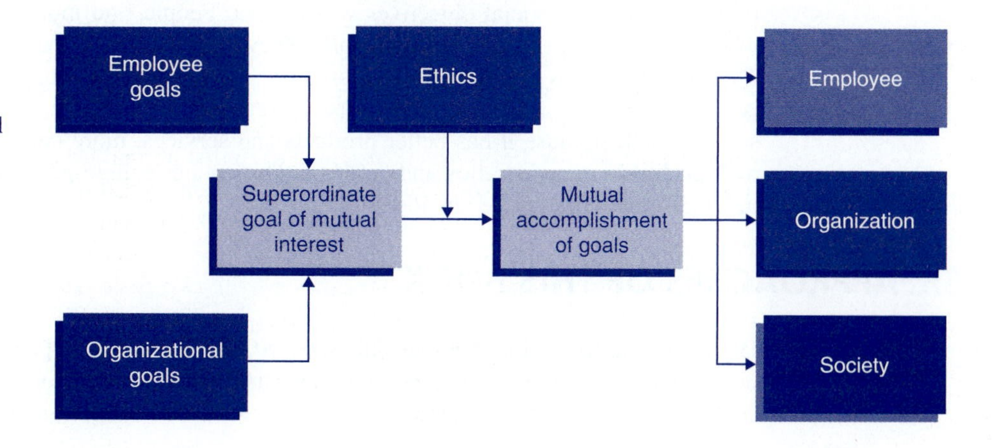

What Managers Are Reading 

THE FOUR ELEMENTS OF MORAL INTELLIGENCE

Two management consultants, Doug Lennick and Fred Kiel, define moral intelligence as "the ability to differentiate right from wrong as defined by universal principles." A combination of behavior and smarts, moral intelligence builds on universal virtues to help leaders achieve personal and business goals. The authors argue that behaving morally is not only right, but also good for business.

With a premise that people are "born to be moral," Lennick and Kiel suggest that four key elements underlie moral intelligence:

- Integrity (acting consistently with one's values)
- Responsibility (willingness to accept accountability for the consequences of our actions and admit mistakes and failures)
- Compassion (caring about others)
- Forgiveness (recognizing that others will make mistakes, and accepting them)

These four elements can become competencies if managers proceed through a three-step process encompassing self-awareness, self-disclosure, and the discovery of strengths and weaknesses in others.

Source: Doug Lennick and Fred Kiel, *Moral Intelligence: Enhancing Business Performance and Leadership Success,* Philadelphia: Wharton School Publishing, 2005.

interest provides a superordinate goal—one that can be attained only through the integrated efforts of individuals and their employers.

Ethics is the use of moral principles and values to affect the behavior of individuals and organizations with regard to choices between what is right and wrong

Ethics In order to attract and retain valuable employees in an era in which good workers are constantly recruited away, organizations must treat employees in an ethical fashion. More and more firms are recognizing this need and are responding with a variety of programs to ensure a higher standard of ethical performance by managers and employees alike. Companies have established codes of ethics, publicized statements of ethical values, provided ethics training, rewarded employees for notable ethical behavior, publicized positive role models, and set up internal procedures to handle misconduct. They have begun to recognize that since organizational behavior always involves people, ethical philosophy is involved in one way or another in each action they take. (See, for example, the argument for moral intelligence in "What Managers Are Reading.") Because of the importance of ethics, this theme will be addressed periodically throughout the text.

When the organization's goals and actions are ethical, it is more likely that individual, organizational, and social objectives will be met. People find more satisfaction in work when there is cooperation and teamwork. They are learning, growing, and contributing. The organization is also more successful because it operates more effectively. Quality is better, service is improved, and costs are reduced. Perhaps the greatest beneficiary is society itself, because it has better products and services, more capable citizens, and an overall climate of cooperation and progress. This creates a three-party win–win–win result in which there need not be any losers.

BASIC APPROACHES OF THIS BOOK

Organizational behavior seeks to integrate the four elements of people, structure, technology, and environment. It rests on an interdisciplinary foundation of fundamental concepts about the nature of people and organizations. The four basic approaches—human

FIGURE 1.4
Basic Approaches of This Book

Human resources (supportive)	Employee growth and development are encouraged and supported.
Contingency	Different managerial behaviors are required by different environments for effectiveness.
Results-oriented	Outcomes of organizational behavior programs are assessed in terms of their efficiency.
Systems	All parts of an organization interact in a complex relationship.

resources, contingency, results-oriented, and systems—are interwoven throughout subsequent chapters (see Figure 1.4).

A Human Resources (Supportive) Approach

The **human resources approach** is developmental. It is concerned with the growth and development of people toward higher levels of competency, creativity, and fulfillment, because people are the central resource in any organization and any society. The nature of the human resources approach can be understood by comparing it with the traditional management approach of the early 1900s. In the traditional approach, managers decided what should be done and then closely controlled employees to ensure task performance. Management was directive and controlling.

The human resources approach, on the other hand, is supportive. It helps employees become better, more responsible people, and then it tries to create a climate in which they may contribute to the limits of their improved abilities.[7] It assumes that expanded capabilities and opportunities for people will lead directly to improvements in operating effectiveness. Work satisfaction also will be a direct result when employees make fuller use of their abilities. Essentially, the human resources approach means that better people achieve better results. It is somewhat illustrated by the ancient proverb that follows:

> Give a person a fish, and you feed that person for a day; Teach a person to fish, and you feed that person for life.

Supportive approach

Another name for the human resources approach is the **supportive approach,** because the manager's primary role changes from control of employees to active support of their growth and performance. The supportive model of organizational behavior is more fully discussed in Chapter 2.

A CONTINGENCY APPROACH

Traditional management searched for principles to provide "one best way" of managing. There was presumed to be a correct way to organize, to delegate, and to divide work. The correct way applied regardless of the type of organization or situation involved. Management principles were considered to be universal. As the field of organizational behavior developed, many of its followers initially supported the concept of universality. Behavioral ideas were supposed to apply in any type of situation. One example was the belief that employee-oriented leadership should consistently be better than task-oriented leadership, whatever the circumstances. An occasional exception might be admitted, but in general early ideas were applied in a universal manner.

On the Job: U.S. Navy

The diminishing returns associated with various incentives for enlisting in the U.S. Navy were studied in interviews with 1,700 civilian males. Substantially different levels of incentives were offered: $1,000 versus $3,000 bonuses, two years versus four years of free college, and 10 versus 25 percent of base pay for exceptional performance. None of the three larger incentives produced more favorable dispositions to enlist. In fact, the respondents found the 10 percent bonus more attractive, leading the researchers to conclude that not only is more not necessarily better but it "can be worse."[11]

The Law of Diminishing Returns

Can there be too much of a good thing?

Overemphasis on a valid organizational behavior practice may produce negative results, as indicated by the **law of diminishing returns.**[12] It is a limiting factor in organizational behavior the same way it is in economics. In economics, the law of diminishing returns refers to a declining amount of extra outputs when more of a desirable input is added to an economic situation. After a certain point, the output from each unit of added input tends to become smaller. The added output eventually may reach zero and even continue to decline when more units of input are added.

How does the law of diminishing returns work in organizational behavior?

The law of diminishing returns in organizational behavior works in a similar way. It states that at some point, increases of a desirable practice produce declining returns, eventually zero returns, and then negative returns as more increases are added. The concept implies that *for any situation there is an optimum amount of a desirable practice,* such as recognition or participation. When that point is exceeded, a decline in returns occurs. In other words, the fact that a practice is desirable does not mean more of it is more desirable. *More of a good thing is not necessarily good* (see "On the Job: U.S. Navy").

Why does the law of diminishing returns exist? Essentially, it is a system concept. It applies because of the complex system relationships of many variables in a situation. When an excess of one variable develops, although that variable is desirable, it tends to restrict the operating benefits of other variables so substantially that net effectiveness declines. For example, too much security may lead to less employee initiative and growth. Although the exact point at which an application becomes excessive will vary with the circumstances, an excess can be reached with nearly any practice. This relationship shows that *organizational effectiveness is achieved not by maximizing one human variable but by combining all system variables together in a balanced way.*

Unethical Treatment of People and Use of Resources

A significant concern about organizational behavior is that *its knowledge and techniques can be used to manipulate people unethically as well as to help them develop their potential.* People who lack respect for the basic dignity of the human being could learn organizational behavior ideas and use them for selfish ends. They could use what they know about motivation or communication in the **manipulation of people** without regard for human welfare. People who lack ethical values could use people in unethical ways.

The *philosophy of organizational behavior is supportive* and oriented toward human resources. It seeks to improve the human environment and help people grow toward their potential. However, the *knowledge and techniques of this subject may be used for negative as well as positive consequences.* This possibility is true of knowledge in almost any field, so it is no special limitation of organizational behavior. Nevertheless, we must be cautious so that what is known about people is not used to manipulate them. The possibility of manipulation means that people in power in organizations must maintain high ethical and moral integrity and not misuse their power. Without ethical leadership, the new knowledge

Ethical managers will not manipulate people

learned about people becomes a dangerous instrument for possible misuse. **Ethical leadership** will recognize such principles as the following:

- *Social responsibility* Responsibility to others arises whenever people have power in an organization.
- *Open communication* The organization will operate as a two-way open system, with open receipt of inputs from people and open disclosure of its operations to them.
- *Cost-benefit analysis* In addition to economic costs and benefits, human and social costs and benefits of an activity will be analyzed in determining whether to proceed with the activity.

As the general population learns more about organizational behavior and becomes more vigilant, it will be more difficult to manipulate people, but the possibility is always there. That is why society desperately needs ethical leaders. On a topic related to social responsibility (but more comprehensive), the ideas of global stewardship, conservation, and responsible management and consumption of resources have rapidly emerged in recent years. **Sustainability**—the capacity of a system to endure across time—presents a difficult challenge to organizations, which must balance environmental, social, and economic demands. These demands are often referred to as the three P's of the **triple bottom line**—or *planet, people, and profit.* Through the pressure from Greenpeace International and others, many organizations have initiated efforts to operate in a more environmentally friendly manner. Some firms have cut energy consumption, used renewable power, developed recycling programs, used green building materials, or switched to sustainable agriculture. For example, Walmart has cut its energy use, McDonald's and Cargill have helped to stop the widespread cutting of Amazon rainforests, and Hewlett-Packard (HP) has made its computers 100-percent recyclable. These examples illustrate that it is possible—and good business—to be sensitive to societal values and ecological needs.[13]

CONTINUING CHALLENGES

Seeking Quick Fixes and Using Old Solutions

Immediate expectations are not realistic

One problem that has plagued organizational behavior has been the tendency for business firms to have short time horizons for the expected payoff from behavioral programs. This search for a **quick fix** sometimes leads managers to embrace the newest fad, to address the symptoms while neglecting underlying problems, or to fragment their efforts within the firm. In the early twentieth century, managers often searched for the "holy grail" of simplicity in the mistaken belief that they could identify universal prescriptions for their practice. Consequently, when they found something that appeared to work for them once, they clung to it tenaciously and attempted to repeat their success. However, you may have heard the tongue-in-cheek definition of insanity, which is doing the same thing over and over and expecting different results—especially as conditions change (and they do). Noted business author Clay Christensen has concluded that "If you only do what worked in the past, you will wake up one day and find that you've been passed by."[14] The emergence of organizational development programs that focus on systemwide change (see Chapter 14) and the creation of long-term strategic plans for the management of human resources has helped bring about more realistic expectations concerning employees as a productive asset.

> Some management consultants and writers have even been labeled "witch doctors" because of their blind advocacy of a single approach as a way to solve an entire organization's problems. Some of the management concepts that have been blindly

Advice to Future Managers

1. Remember that your managerial actions have implications at one or more levels of OB: individual, interpersonal, group, intergroup, and whole system. Therefore, try to increase your skills by *predicting the results and monitoring the consequences of your decisions.*
2. Discipline yourself to read at least one item from the literature in OB theory, research, and practice each month. *Search for applications from each.*
3. Create an inventory of the observed differences you see across your employees, and then *state the implications of those differences.* (How will you treat them based on what you know about them?)
4. *Identify the ethical issues* you face. Share these with your employees so they understand them.
5. Analyze the organizational results you are currently responsible for. *Identify which of the major contributing factors* (knowledge, skill, attitude, situation, or resources) *is most under your control,* and develop a plan for improving that one.
6. Examine a potential change you are considering making. *Identify its costs and benefits,* both direct and indirect, and use that information to help determine your decision.
7. When an employee problem or issue emerges, discipline yourself to focus briefly on *describing the undesirable behavior* before attempting to understand it or change it.
8. Force yourself to *take a systems approach to organizational problems* by rigorously differentiating the consequences of actions as positive versus negative, intended versus unintended, and short-term versus long-term.
9. As your study of OB progresses, create an inventory of your favorite behavioral concepts and practices. Then, *caution yourself to avoid becoming overly biased* in favor of these approaches.
10. When the pressure for rapid solutions to complex problems rises, *resist the tendency to search for quick fixes or to blindly repeat old solutions.*

promoted by one or more authors are management by objectives, job enlargement, sensitivity training, quality circles, visioning, and strategic planning. Unfortunately, these quick fixes have often been promoted on the basis of only interesting stories and personal anecdotes. Managers are urged to be cautious consumers of these perspectives.[15]

Varying Environments

Can organizational behavior adapt to change?

Another challenge that confronts organizational behavior is to see whether the ideas that have been developed and tested during periods of organizational growth and economic plenty will endure with equal success under new conditions. Specifically, the environment in the future may be marked by shrinking demand, scarce resources, and more intense competition. When organizations stagnate, decline, or have their survival threatened, there is evidence that stress and conflict increase. Will the same motivational models be useful in these situations? Are different leadership styles called for? Will the trend toward participative processes be reversed? Since these and many other questions have no easy answers, tremendous room for further development of organizational behavior still clearly exists.

Definitional Confusion

Organizational behavior, early in its history, experienced some difficulty emerging as a clearly defined field of study and application. There was a lack of consensus regarding its *unit of analysis* (individual, group, or total organization), its greatest *need* (as a source of empirical data and integrating theory, or as a basis for applied information), its major *focus* (micro or macro issues), and its major *contributions* to date. This lack of clear definition was compounded by the multiple criteria that can be used to assess its effectiveness. Issues here include identification of the relevant stakeholders, short or long time frames to wait for results, and reliance on soft or hard data (perceptions or records). All these issues have subsequently received useful attention and clarification.

Summary

Organizational behavior is the systematic study and careful application of knowledge about how people—as individuals and groups—act in organizations. Its goals are to make managers more effective at describing, understanding, predicting, and controlling human behavior. Key elements to consider are people, structure, technology, and the external environment. Organizational behavior has emerged as an interdisciplinary field of value to managers. It builds on an increasingly solid research foundation, and it draws upon useful ideas and conceptual models from many of the behavioral sciences to make managers more effective.

Fundamental concepts of organizational behavior relate to the nature of people (individual differences, perception, a whole person, motivated behavior, desire for involvement, and value of the person) and to the nature of organizations (social systems, mutual interest, and ethics). Managerial actions should be oriented to attain superordinate goals of interest to employees, the organization, and society. Effective management can best be attained through the understanding and use of the human resources, contingency, results-oriented, and systems approaches.

A behavioral bias, the law of diminishing returns, and unethical use of behavioral tools can all limit the effectiveness of organizational behavior. Managers must guard against using OB as a quick fix, using old solutions, and failing to recognize the impact of different environments. If these factors are overcome, OB should produce a higher quality of life in which harmony within each person, among people, and among the organizations of the future is enhanced.

Speaking OB: Terms and Concepts for Review

Behavioral bias, *17*
Contingency approach, *14*
Cost-benefit analysis, *16*
Diversity, *5*
Ethical leadership, *19*
Evidence-based management, *7*
Goals of organizational behavior, *5*
Human resources approach, *13*
Individual differences, *9*
Law of diminishing returns, *18*
Law of individual differences, *10*
Manipulation of people, *18*
Mutuality of interest, *11*
Organizational behavior, *4*
Perception, *10*
Practice, *7*
Productivity, *14*
Quick fix, *19*
Research, *7*
Results orientation, *14*
Selective perception, *10*
Supportive approach, *13*
Sustainability, *19*
Systems approach, *15*
Theories, *7*
Triple bottom line, *19*

Discussion Questions

1. Define organizational behavior in your own words. Ask a friend outside of class or a work associate to do the same. Identify and explore the nature of any differences between the two definitions.
2. Assume that a friend states, "Organizational behavior is selfish and manipulative because it serves only the interests of management." How would you respond?
3. As you begin to understand organizational behavior, why do you think it has become a popular field of interest?
4. Consider the statement "Organizations need people, and people need organizations." Is this assertion true for all types of organizations? Give examples of where it is and where it probably isn't true.
5. Review the fundamental concepts that form the basis of organizational behavior. Which concepts do you think are more important than the others? Explain.

6. Select one of your work associates or friends. Identify the qualities that make that person substantially different from you. In what ways are you basically similar? Which dominates, the differences or the similarities?
7. Discuss the major features of the social system in an organization where you have worked. In what ways did that social system affect you and your job performance, either positively or negatively?
8. Review the four approaches to organizational behavior. As you read this book, keep a list of the ways in which those themes are reflected in each major topic.
9. Examine the formulas leading to effective organizational productivity. Which factors do you think have the greatest potential for making a difference between organizations? What can be done to affect the other ones?
10. Are behavioral bias and diminishing returns from organizational behavior practices the same or different? Discuss.

Assess Your Own Skills

How well do you understand organizational behavior?

Read the following statements carefully. Circle the number on the response scale that most closely reflects the degree to which each statement accurately describes you. Add up your total points, and prepare a brief action plan for self-improvement. Be ready to report your score for tabulation across the entire group.

	Good description								Poor description	
1. I thoroughly understand the nature and definition of organizational behavior.	10	9	8	7	6	5	4	3	2	1
2. I can list and explain the four primary goals of organizational behavior.	10	9	8	7	6	5	4	3	2	1
3. I feel comfortable explaining the interaction between theory, research, and practice in organizational behavior.	10	9	8	7	6	5	4	3	2	1
4. I am fully aware of the ways in which people act on the basis of their perceived world.	10	9	8	7	6	5	4	3	2	1
5. I believe that most employees have a strong desire to be involved in decision making.	10	9	8	7	6	5	4	3	2	1
6. I feel comfortable explaining the role of ethics in organizational behavior.	10	9	8	7	6	5	4	3	2	1
7. I can easily summarize the basic nature of the contingency approach to organizational behavior.	10	9	8	7	6	5	4	3	2	1

8. I can list and explain each of the factors in the formula for producing organizational results.	10	9	8	7	6	5	4	3	2	1
9. I can explain why a systems approach to organizational behavior is appropriate.	10	9	8	7	6	5	4	3	2	1
10. I understand the relationship among the systems viewpoint, behavioral bias, and the law of diminishing returns in organizational behavior.	10	9	8	7	6	5	4	3	2	1

Scoring and Interpretation

Add up your total points for the 10 questions. Record that number here, and report it when it is requested. Finally, insert your total score into the "Assess and Improve Your Own Organizational Behavior Skills" chart in Appendix A.

- If you scored between 81 and 100 points, you appear to have a solid understanding of organizational behavior basics.
- If you scored between 61 and 80 points, you should take a close look at the items with lower self-assessment scores and review the related material again.
- If you scored under 60 points, you should be aware that a weaker understanding of several items could be detrimental to your future success as a manager. We encourage you to review the entire chapter.

Identify your three lowest scores and write the question numbers here: _____, _____, _____. Write a brief paragraph, detailing to yourself an action plan for how you might sharpen each of these skills.

Incident

The Transferred Sales Representative

Harold Burns served as district sales representative for an appliance firm. His district covered the central part of a Midwestern state, and it included about 100 retail outlets. He had been with the company for 20 years and in his present job and location for 5 years. During that time he met his district sales quota each year.

One day Burns learned through local friends that the wife of a sales representative in another district was in town to try to rent a house. She told the real estate agency that her family would be moving there in a few days because her husband was replacing Burns. When Burns heard this news, he refused to believe it.

Two days later, on January 28, he received an express mail letter, postmarked the previous day, from the regional sales manager. The letter read:

Dear Harold:
Because of personnel vacancies we are requesting that you move to the Gunning district, effective February 1. Mr. George Dowd from the Parsons district will replace you. Will you please see that your inventory and property are properly transferred to him? I know that you will like your new district. Congratulations!
Sincerely yours, (Signature)

In the same mail, he received his 20-year service pin. The accompanying letter from the regional sales manager read:

Dear Harold:
I am happy to enclose your 20-year service pin. You have a long and excellent record with the company. We are honored to give you this recognition, and I hope you will wear it proudly.

Our company is proud to have many long-service employees. We want you to know that we take a personal interest in your welfare because people like you are the backbone of our company.
Sincerely yours, (Signature)

Harold Burns checked his quarterly sales bulletin and found that sales for the Gunning district were running 10 percent below those in his present district.

Questions

1. Comment on the positive and negative events in this case as they relate to organizational behavior.
2. Was a human resources approach to Burns applied in this instance? Discuss.

Experiential Exercise

Ethics in Organizational Behavior

Examine the following statements. Assess each situation according to the degree to which you believe a potential ethical problem is inherent in it. After recording your answers, meet in small groups (three to five persons) and discuss any significant differences you find among answers given by members of your group.

	No ethical problem				Ethical problem
1. A manager, following the law of individual differences, allows her six employees to establish their own starting times for work each day.	0	1	2	3	4
2. A supervisor finds that members of a certain minority group are faster workers than whites, and thereafter hires only those minorities for particular jobs.	0	1	2	3	4
3. An organization, frustrated over continual complaints about its appraisal system and pay, decides that "equal pay for all employees" (despite differences in their performance) will work best.	0	1	2	3	4
4. An organization is faced with a possible union certification election. To find out what employees are thinking, top management installs electronic eavesdropping equipment in the cafeteria.	0	1	2	3	4

5. A company hires a consulting firm to conduct an attitude survey of its employees. When the consultants suggest that they could code the questionnaires secretly so that responses could be traced back to individuals, the company agrees that it would be "interesting."	0	1	2	3	4

Generating OB Insights

An *insight* is a new and clear perception of a phenomenon, or an acquired ability to "see" clearly something that you were unaware of previously. It is sometimes simply referred to as an "ah-ha! moment," in which you have a minirevelation or reach a straightforward conclusion about a topic or issue.

Insights need not necessarily be dramatic, for what is an insight to one person may be less important to another. The critical feature of insights is that they are relevant and memorable for *you;* they should represent new knowledge, new frameworks, or new ways of viewing things that you want to retain and remember over time.

Insights, then, are different from the information you find in the "Advice for Future Managers" boxes within the text. That advice is prescriptive and action-oriented; it indicates a recommended course of action.

A useful way to think of OB insights is to assume you are the only person who has read the current chapter. You have been given the assignment to highlight, in your own words, the major concepts (but not just summarize the whole chapter) that might stand out for a naive audience who has never heard of the topic before. *What 10 insights would you share with them?*

(Example) *Astute managers need to study, appreciate, and use OB theory and research.*

1. ______________________________
2. ______________________________
3. ______________________________
4. ______________________________
5. ______________________________
6. ______________________________
7. ______________________________
8. ______________________________
9. ______________________________
10. ______________________________

Nurturing Your Critical Thinking and Reflective Skills

Take a few minutes to review the discussion in the Roadmap for Readers of critical thinking and reflection. Remind yourself that if you can hone these abilities now, you will have a substantial competitive advantage when you apply for jobs and are asked what unique skills you can bring to the position and the organization.

Critical Thinking

Think back on the material you read in this chapter. What are three unique and challenging *critical questions* you would like to raise about the material? (These might identify something controversial about which you have doubts, they may imply that you suspect that a theory or model has weaknesses, they could examine the legitimacy of apparent causal relationships, or they might assess the probable value of a suggested practice.) Be prepared to share these questions with class members or your instructor.

1. ____
   ____
2. ____
   ____
3. ____
   ____

Reflection

This process often involves answering the parallel questions of "What do you *think* about the material you have read?" and "How do you *feel* about that material?" Therefore, express your *personal thoughts and feelings* (reactions) to any of the ideas or topics found in this chapter, and be prepared to share these reflections with class members or your instructor.

1. ____
   ____
2. ____
   ____
3. ____
   ____

Chapter Two

Models of Organizational Behavior

Companies are often unaware of the management models they're using.

Julian Birkinshaw and Jules Goddard[1]

I've always thought that having a simple set of values for a company was also a very efficient and expedient way to go.

Herb Kelleher (former CEO of Southwest Airlines)[2]

CHAPTER OBJECTIVES

AFTER READING THIS CHAPTER, YOU SHOULD UNDERSTAND

2-1 The Elements of an Organizational Behavior System

2-2 The Role of Management's Philosophy and Paradigms

2-3 Alternative Models of Organizational Behavior and Their Effects

2-4 Trends in the Use of These Models

Facebook Page 

Student A: I survived the first week of my OB class and read the first chapter of the book. Then it was playtime all weekend!

Student B: You're off to a good start. What are you supposed to read now?

Student A: It's a chapter on OB models.

Student B: What are models? I always thought that they were "small imitations of the real thing."

Student A: That's probably true in architecture and astronomy, but here they are defined as "belief systems that dominate managerial thought and actions."

Student C: That's pretty broad. How many of them are there—just one or millions?

Student A: The author suggests that there are five major ones—Autocratic, Custodial, Supportive, Collegial, and System.

Student D: Hey, pal, take my advice. That sounds like a readymade multiple-choice question in the offing. Better pay close attention to those.

Student A: Have no fear; I will.

Student D: What are models supposed to produce?

Student A: I guess the intended outcomes fall into three categories—organizational performance, employee satisfaction, and personal growth and development.

Student B: Are there any more new terms in the chapter? Better take a glance ahead.

Student A: There are a few terms. I'll bet you've never heard of some of these—paradigms, micromanagement, social intelligence, psychological ownership, or positive organizational behavior!

Student B: You're absolutely right. It's still not too late to drop the course, you know.

Student A: No way. It's just starting to get interesting!

The author boarded a plane on a winter day in Minneapolis, Minnesota, and flew to Phoenix, Arizona. The differences between the weather conditions in the two geographical areas were easily apparent. The place of departure was cold, damp, and windy; the arrival location was warm, dry, and calm. In fact, the temperature differential between the two cities was over 100 degrees!

The differences between organizations can sometimes be just as extreme as the weather contrasts between two cities. In addition, organizations have undergone tremendous changes during the past two centuries. Although employers in the early days had no systematic program for managing their employees, their simple rules still exerted a powerful influence on the organization. Many of the old rules are now out of date, and increasing numbers of organizations today are experimenting with exciting new ways to attract and motivate their workers. A century from now, though, people may look back on these practices and consider them outdated, too. Clearly, approaches to managing people vary across organizations, time, and cultures.

Continuing the major themes introduced in Chapter 1 (human resources, contingency, results-oriented, and systems approaches), this chapter presents five alternative models of organizational behavior. Some of these reflect more progressive approaches that are well adapted to contemporary issues and trends. We see that even the words used to refer to

Engaging Your Brain

1. In this chapter, the text discusses *values* (belief, ideals, or ethical principles), *vision* (desirable futures), *mission* (reason for existence), and *goals* (intended achievements). What are *your* values, your personal vision and mission, and your goals?
2. One author (Douglas McGregor) has argued that much of managerial behavior is premised upon assumptions (implicit or explicit) made about the nature of employees. What do *you* believe is descriptively true about a "typical" employee today?
3. The text suggests that managers often embrace one out of several alternative models of organizational behavior. Each of those models implicitly or explicitly follows a contingency format (e.g., "If I do this, then the following result will happen.") What do you currently believe would be the consequences of various approaches to managing people?

employees (such as "subordinates," as contrasted to the use in some organizations of terms like "associates" or "partners" to convey equality) tell a lot about the underlying model in use.

This chapter builds on the fundamental concepts presented in Chapter 1 by showing how all behavioral factors can be combined to develop an effective organization. The interrelated elements of an organizational behavior system are offered as a road map for where these elements appear in this book. Then five alternative models of organizational behavior and several conclusions about the use of these models are presented.

AN ORGANIZATIONAL BEHAVIOR SYSTEM

Purposely created and used

Organizations achieve their goals by creating, communicating, and operating an **organizational behavior system,** as shown in Figure 2.1. Major elements of a good organizational behavior system are introduced on the following pages and presented in detail throughout the book. These systems exist in every organization, but sometimes in varying forms. They have a greater chance of being successful, though, if they have been *consciously created* and *regularly examined and updated* to meet new and emerging conditions. Updating is done by drawing upon the constantly growing behavioral science base of knowledge mentioned in the previous chapter.

Three outcome criteria

The primary purposes of organizational behavior systems are to identify and then help manipulate the major human and organizational variables that affect the results organizations are trying to achieve. For some of these variables, managers can only be aware of them and acknowledge their impact; for others, managers can exert some control over them. The outcomes, or end results, are typically measured in various forms of three basic criteria: *performance* (e.g., quantity and quality of products and services; level of customer service), *employee satisfaction* (often exhibited through lower absenteeism, tardiness, or turnover), or *personal growth and development* (the acquisition of lifelong knowledge and skills leading to continued employability and career advancement). The effect of organizational behavior practices on these outcomes is discussed throughout this book.

Elements of the System

The system's base rests on the fundamental beliefs and intentions of those who join to create it (such as owners) and of the managers who currently administer it. The **philosophy** (model) of organizational behavior held by management consists of an integrated set of assumptions and beliefs about the way things are, the purpose for these activities, and the way they should be. These philosophies are sometimes explicit, and occasionally implicit,

FIGURE 2.1
An Organizational Behavior System

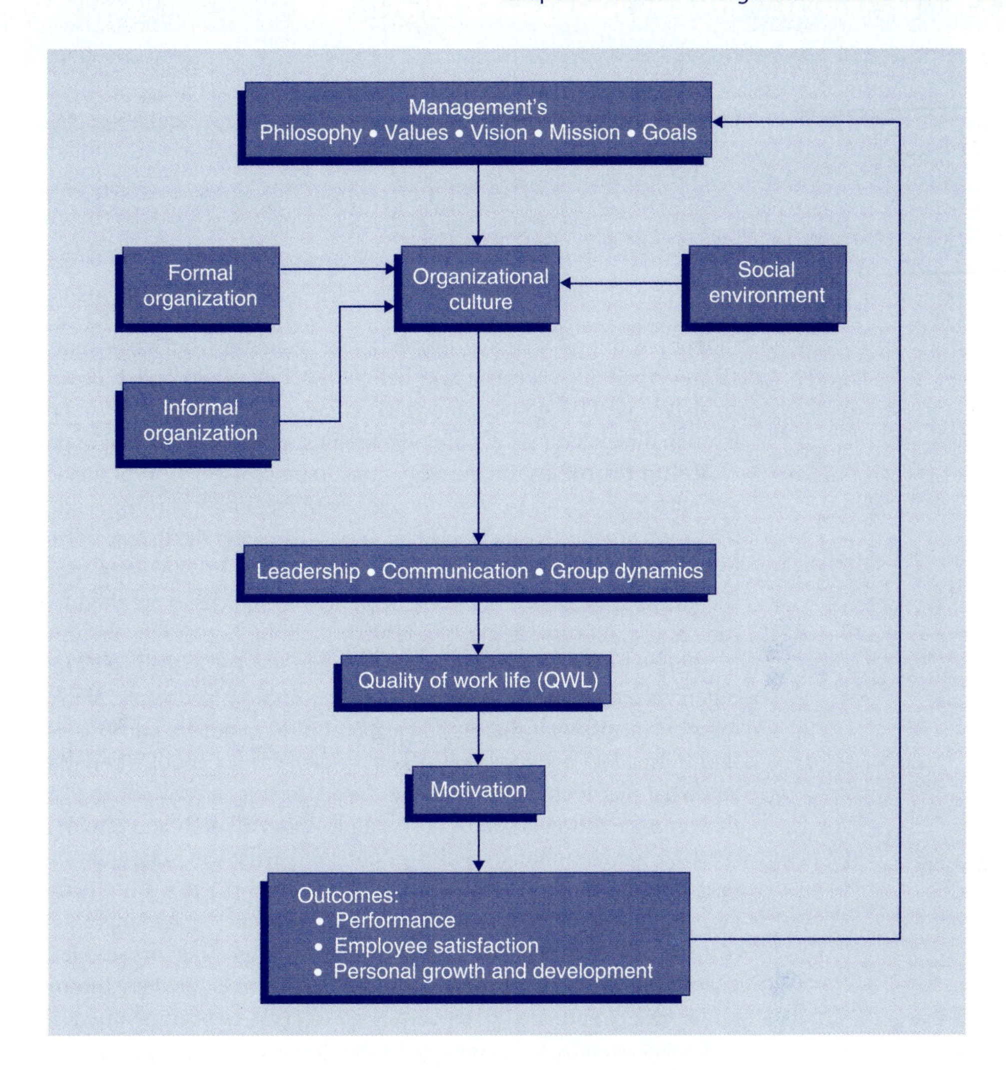

in the minds of managers. Five major organizational behavior philosophies—autocratic, custodial, supportive, collegial, and system—and their implications are discussed later in this chapter. Figure 2.2 presents some typical elements of a philosophy statement.

The philosophy of organizational behavior held by a manager stems from two sources— fact premises and value premises. **Fact premises** represent our descriptive view of how the world behaves. They are drawn from both behavioral science research and our personal experiences

FIGURE 2.2
Selected Elements of a Philosophy Statement

- We are committed to quality, cost-effectiveness, and technical excellence.
- People should treat each other with consideration, trust, and respect.
- Each person is valuable, unique, and makes a contribution.
- All employees should be unfailingly committed to excellent performance.
- Teamwork can, and should, produce far more than the sum of individual efforts. Team members must be reliable and committed to the team.
- Innovation is essential.
- Open communications are important for attaining success.
- Decisions should be reached participatively.

On the Job: IKEA Corporation

Swedish retailing giant IKEA's North American division is one of the fastest-growing in its market segment. Despite a strong drive for profits and market share, the firm embraces progressive and supportive employment practices (health care benefits, flexible schedules, and opportunities for advancement), an emphasis on racial and ethnic diversity, and distinctive values (freedom, lack of hierarchy, individual respect). Results show up in dramatically reduced turnover, rising sales revenues, and "off the charts" employee satisfaction.[3]

(important things we have learned). For example, you would not throw your iPod from a 10-story building, because you believe gravity would pull it downward uncontrollably and crush it against the ground, and you don't want this to happen. Fact premises, then, are acquired through direct and indirect lifelong learning and are very useful in guiding our behavior.

Fact and value premises

Value premises, on the other hand, represent our view of the desirability of certain goals and activities. If you are very unhappy with the iPod's performance, then you might choose to throw it from the 10-story building. You still accept the fact premise of gravity, but now your value premises have changed (at least momentarily!). As "On the Job: IKEA Corporation" shows, value premises are variable beliefs we hold and are therefore under our control. We can choose, modify, discard, or replace them (although they are often deeply entrenched).

Vision

Managers also have primary responsibility for instilling three other elements into the organizational behavior system—vision, mission, and goals. **Vision** represents a challenging portrait of what the organization and its members can be—a possible, and desirable, future. Leaders need to create exciting projections about where the organization should go and what major changes lie ahead. Once the vision is established, persistent and enthusiastic communication is required so employees will embrace it with commitment.

Mission

An organization also typically creates a **mission** statement, which identifies the business it is in, the market niches it tries to serve, the types of customers it is likely to have, and the reasons for its existence. Many mission statements even include a brief listing of the competitive advantages, or strengths, that the firm believes it has. In contrast to visions, mission statements are more descriptive and less future-oriented. They are still rather broad, and need to be converted to goals to become operational and useful.

Goals

Goals are relatively concrete formulations of achievements the organization is aiming for within set periods of time, such as one to five years. Goal setting is a complex process, for top management's goals must be merged with those of employees, who bring their psychological, social, and economic needs with them to an organization. Further, goals may exist at the individual, group, and larger organization level, so substantial integration is required before a working social system can emerge. Elements of effective goals are discussed in Chapter 5.

Philosophy feeds into value premises, which help shape vision. Vision is a stretching version of mission, and goals provide a way to pinpoint targets for achieving that mission. Together, philosophy, values, vision, mission, and goals exist in a hierarchy of increasing specificity (philosophy is most general; goals are most specific). They all help create a recognizable organizational culture, which is discussed in Chapter 4. This culture is also a reflection of the formal organization with its formal policies, structures, and procedures, and the existing social and cultural (global) environment (Chapter 16).

Managers also must be aware of the informal organization (discussed in Chapter 12) and must work with its members to create positive norms. Together, the formal and informal organizations provide the glue that binds the varied elements of the institution into an effective working team.

Managers are then expected to use a leadership style (Chapter 7), communication skills (Chapter 3), and their knowledge of interpersonal and group dynamics (Chapters 11 and 12) to create an appropriate quality of work life for their employees (Chapter 10). When this task is done properly, employees will become motivated toward the achievement of organizational goals (Chapter 5). Their motivation, however, is also a product of their underlying attitudes and specific situational factors at a certain point in time. If any of the previous factors in the organizational system are changed, motivation will also be different. Because of this interaction, leaders must learn to manage employee motivation contingently. Numerous examples of this cause-and-effect relationship exist, as illustrated in the following report:

> Contrasting effects of organizational behavior systems were seen in some of the efforts to revitalize airline companies in the past decade. In the face of financial crises, employees in some firms willingly accepted the necessity of drastic cost-saving actions and responded with increased (and successful) efforts to save their companies and jobs. Employees in other firms, such as Northwest Airlines, fearful for their jobs and resentful of management's previous autocratic actions, strongly resisted attempts to reduce their pay and outsource their jobs. As a consequence, labor strife, bankruptcy, and a merger with Delta Airlines followed.

The result of an effective organizational behavior system is motivation which, when combined with employee skills and abilities, results in the achievement of performance goals (as we saw in the formulas in Chapter 1) as well as individual satisfaction. It builds two-way relationships that are mutually supportive, meaning that manager and employee are jointly influencing each other and jointly benefiting. Supportive OB systems are characterized by power *with* people rather than power *over* them, which is consistent with present human values regarding how people wish to be treated (with dignity). Alternatively, if goals are not being achieved, managers need to use this information to examine and revise their organizational behavior system.

MODELS OF ORGANIZATIONAL BEHAVIOR

Organizations differ in the nature of the systems they develop and maintain and in the results they achieve. Varying results predictably follow from different **models** of organizational behavior. These models constitute the belief system that dominates management's thought and affects management's actions in each organization. It is highly important that managers recognize the nature, significance, and effectiveness of their own models, as well as the models of others around them.

Douglas McGregor was one of the first writers to call attention to managerial models. In 1957, he presented a convincing argument that most management actions flow directly from whatever theory of human behavior the managers hold.[4] He suggested that management philosophy controls practice. Management's human resource policies, decision-making styles, operating practices, and even organizational designs flow from key *assumptions about human behavior*. The assumptions may be implicit rather than explicit, but they can be inferred from observing the kinds of actions that managers take.

Theory X assumptions

Theory X is a traditional set of assumptions about people. As shown in Figure 2.3, it assumes that most people dislike work and will try to avoid it if they can. Workers are seen as being inclined to restrict work output, having little ambition, and avoiding responsibility if at all possible. They are believed to be relatively self-centered, indifferent to organizational needs, and resistant to change. Common rewards cannot overcome this natural dislike for work, so management is almost forced (under Theory X assumptions and subsequent logic) to coerce, control, and threaten employees to obtain satisfactory performance. Though managers may deny that they hold this view of people, many of their historical actions suggest that Theory X was a typical management view of employees.

FIGURE 2.3
McGregor's Theory X and Theory Y, Alternative Sets of Assumptions about Employees

Theory X	Theory Y
• The typical person dislikes work and will avoid it if possible. • The typical person lacks responsibility, has little ambition, and seeks security above all. • Most people must be coerced, controlled, and threatened with punishment to get them to work.	• Work is as natural as play or rest. • People are not inherently lazy. They have become that way as a result of experience. • People will exercise self-direction and self-control in the service of objectives to which they are committed. • People have potential. Under proper conditions they learn to accept and seek responsibility. They have imagination, ingenuity, and creativity that can be applied to work.
With these assumptions the managerial role is to coerce and control employees.	With these assumptions the managerial role is to develop the potential in employees and help them release that potential toward common objectives.

Theory Y assumptions

Theory Y implies a more humanistic and supportive approach to managing people. It assumes that people are not inherently lazy. Any appearance they have of being that way is the result of their experiences with less-enlightened organizations, and if management will provide the proper environment to release their potential, work will become as natural to them as recreational play or rest and relaxation. Under Theory Y assumptions, management believes that employees are capable of exercising self-direction and self-control in the service of objectives to which they are committed. Management's role is to provide an environment in which the potential of people can be released at work.

Theory X is deficient

McGregor's argument was that management had been ignoring the facts about people. It had been following an outmoded set of assumptions about people because it adhered to Theory X when the facts are that the Theory Y set of assumptions is more truly representative of most people. There will always be important differences among people, so a few individuals will fit the assumptions of the Theory X model. Nearly all employees, however, have some potential for growth in their capabilities and demonstrated performance. Therefore, McGregor argued, management needed to change to a whole new set of assumptions about people—one based on emerging behavioral science research. These new assumptions had a powerful impact on subsequent managerial actions.

Four major contributions

When seen through the lenses of history, McGregor deserves credit for a number of contributions. First, he stimulated subsequent generations of managers to think consciously about their belief systems and management models. Second, he was an early advocate of the practical value of reading and using research findings to better understand human behavior. Third, he introduced and publicized one of the early theories of motivation—the hierarchy of needs model by A. H. Maslow (explained in Chapter 5). Finally, he became a spokesman for a trend that had been developing over a long period of time—the need to bring human values into balance with other values at work.

Impact of paradigms

Models such as Theory X and Theory Y are also called **paradigms,** or frameworks of possible explanations about how things work. Any model that a manager holds usually begins with certain assumptions about people and leads to certain interpretations, implications, and even predictions of events. Underlying paradigms, whether consciously or unconsciously developed, become powerful guides to managerial behavior. Managers tend to act as they think, because they are guided by their dominant thoughts.

Managerial paradigms, according to popular author Joel Barker, act in several important ways:

- They influence managerial perceptions of the world around them.
- They define one's boundaries and provide prescriptions for how to behave.
- They encourage resistance to change, since they have often worked in the past.
- They may either consciously or unconsciously affect one's behavior.[5]

New paradigms are constantly emerging, and some of them provide managers with alternative ways of viewing the world and new ways of solving problems. When a major paradigm (a radically different way of thinking) appears it may cause a **paradigm shift.** This is the release of an old model and the substitution of a new one. Even though the new paradigm might be an exciting improvement, it often causes people to be uncomfortable—at least in the short term.

> Examples of paradigm shifts abound in the commercial world. A decade ago, throngs of citizens mobbed shopping malls across the country in the weeks and days before a major holiday; today, millions of people do some or all of their shopping via the Internet while sitting at home. In the automotive realm, internal combustion engines were the sole source of energy for many decades; now, hybrid gas–electric cars have become a reality for some buyers. In communications, U.S. citizens relied almost exclusively on the Postal Service to deliver their letters throughout much of the twentieth century; today, millions of messages are transmitted electronically every day. Paradigms are changing everywhere!

Top management's models are particularly important to identify, for the underlying model that exists within a firm's chief executive officer (CEO) tends to extend throughout that firm. For this reason, models of organizational behavior are highly significant. Examples abound of the impact throughout the firm of a single executive, such as CEOs Mark Zuckerberg at Facebook, the late Steve Jobs at Apple Computer, Howard Schultz at Starbucks, Larry Ellison at Oracle, or John Mackey at Whole Foods Markets.

This chapter highlights the following five models (paradigms): autocratic, custodial, supportive, collegial, and system.[6] These five models are summarized in Figure 2.4. In the order mentioned, they represent an approximate historical evolution in management practice during the last 100 years or more. Although one model tends to dominate at a particular time in history, each of the other models is still applied in some organizations.

Just as organizations differ among themselves, so practices may vary within the departments or branches of one organization. The production department may work within a custodial model while the supportive model is being tried in the research department. And, of course, the practices of individual managers may differ from their organization's prevailing model because of those managers' personal preferences or different conditions in their department. Thus, no one model of organizational behavior is sufficient to describe all that happens in an organization, but identifying a model can help distinguish one way of organizational life from another.

Examination and adaptation needed

The selection of a model by a manager is determined by a number of factors. As we discussed earlier, the prevailing philosophy, values, vision, mission, and goals of managers affect, and are affected by, their organizational behavior model. In addition, environmental conditions help determine which model will be most effective. The current turbulent conditions in the worldwide economy, for example, may drive firms toward the more collegial models, while leading others to regress toward the autocratic model. This suggests that *the model used should not be static and unchanging but reexamined and adapted across time.* Our discussion of five models, beginning with the autocratic, roughly follows their historical evolution.

FIGURE 2.4 **Five Models of Organizational Behavior**

	Autocratic	Custodial	Supportive	Collegial	System
Basis of model	Power	Economic resources	Leadership	Partnership	Trust, community, meaning
Managerial orientation	Authority	Money	Support	Teamwork	Caring, compassion
Employee orientation	Obedience	Security and benefits	Job performance	Responsible behavior	Psychological ownership
Employee psychological result	Dependence on boss	Dependence on organization	Participation	Self-discipline	Self-motivation
Employee needs met	Subsistence	Security	Status and recognition	Self-actualization	Wide range
Performance result	Minimum	Passive cooperation	Awakened drives	Moderate enthusiasm	Passion and commitment to organizational goals

The Autocratic Model

The autocratic model has its roots in history, and certainly, it became the prevailing model of the industrial revolution. As shown in Figure 2.4, the **autocratic model** depends on *power*. Those who are in command must have the power to demand "you do this—or else," meaning that an employee who does not follow orders will be penalized.

Power and authority are used

In an autocratic environment, the managerial orientation is formal official *authority*. This authority is delegated by right of command over the people to whom it applies. Management believes it knows what is best and that the employee's obligation is to follow orders. It assumes that employees have to be directed, persuaded, and pushed into performance, and such prompting is management's task. Management does the thinking; the employees obey the orders. This conventional view of management leads to tight control of employees at work. When combined with the often brutal and backbreaking physical tasks of that era and the intolerable conditions of disease, filth, danger, and scarcity of resources, the autocratic model was intensely disliked by many employees (and still is).

Under autocratic conditions, the employee orientation is *obedience* to a boss, not respect for a manager. The psychological result for employees is *dependence* on their boss, whose power to hire, fire, and "perspire" them is almost absolute. The employer pays minimum wages because *minimum performance* is given by employees (who may lack the qualifications for advancement). They are willing to give minimum performance—though sometimes reluctantly—because they must satisfy *subsistence* needs for themselves and their families.

> A dramatic illustration of the continued use of the autocratic model is seen in the diamond mines in underdeveloped areas, such as Namibia and Sierra Leone. Child slave labor has been a common practice, and natives work long hours for low pay under dangerous and unbearable conditions. Autocratic supervisors control workers tightly, while subjecting them to abuse and suffering.[7]

The autocratic model was, at one time, a useful way to accomplish work. It was not a complete failure. The description of the autocratic model just presented is an extreme one;

actually, the model exists in all shades of gray, from rather dark to rather light. This view of work built great railroad systems, operated giant steel mills, and produced the dynamic industrial civilization that developed in the United States. It does get results, but usually only moderate results. Its principal weaknesses are its high human costs and its tendency to encourage high-level managers to engage in **micromanagement,** which is the immersion of a manager into controlling the details of daily operations. (See the Critical Thinking Exercise.) Micromanagers tend to control and manipulate time, place their self-interest above that of employees, institute elaborate approval processes, specify detailed procedures for everything, and closely monitor results. These actions are autocratic management at its worst. Employees typically detest a micromanager, with the result being low morale, paralyzed decision making due to fear of being second-guessed, and high turnover.

> Charlie Ergen, founder and chairman of satellite TV provider Dish Network, has apparently practiced the autocratic model for many years. Ergen maintains tight control, makes unilateral decisions, berates employees for slight tardiness, implements quarterly "bloodbaths" (layoffs), and forces employees to work long hours and accept mandatory overtime. Described by employees as mean, condescending, tightfisted, ironhanded, and distrustful, Ergen seemingly created a culture of fear that ignores the needs of most employees.[8]

Autocratic model works—sometimes

The autocratic model was an acceptable approach to guide managerial behavior when there were no well-known alternatives, and it still can be useful under some extreme conditions, such as organizational crises.[9] However, the combination of emerging knowledge about the needs of employees and changing societal values suggests there are much better ways to manage organizational systems. A second step in the ladder of progress was needed, and it was soon forthcoming.

The Custodial Model

As managers began to study their employees, they soon recognized that although autocratically managed employees did not talk back to their boss, they certainly "thought back."

They wanted to say many things, and sometimes they did say them when they quit or lost their tempers. Employees were filled with insecurity, frustrations, and aggressions toward their boss. Since they could not vent these feelings directly, sometimes they went home and vented them on their families and neighbors; so the entire community might suffer from this relationship.

> An example of the effects of management-induced frustration on the behavior of employees occurred in a wood-processing plant. Managers treated workers crudely, sometimes even to the point of physical abuse. Since employees could not strike back directly for fear of losing their jobs, they found another way to do it. They symbolically fed their supervisor to a log-shredding machine! They did this by purposely destroying good sheets of veneer, which made the supervisor look bad when monthly efficiency reports were prepared.[10]

Critical Thinking Exercise

Identify the likely effects of being micromanagers. Question: What positive and negative results can you safely predict for them?

On the Job: IBM and 3M Co.

Employee security remains a high priority for millions of workers in today's uncertain job market where lifetime employment is seldom promised to any employee. Many firms, such as IBM, Southwest Airlines, and 3M Co., go out of their way to stabilize their workforce and preserve employee jobs if at all possible. To avoid layoffs, these types of organizations constantly retrain employees, reduce overtime, freeze hiring, encourage both job transfers and relocations, provide early retirement incentives, and reduce subcontracting to adjust to slowdowns in the computer industry.[11]

It seemed rather obvious to progressive employers that there ought to be some way to develop better employee satisfaction and security. If the insecurities, frustrations, and aggressions of employees could be dispelled, the employees might feel more like working. In any case, they would have a better quality of work life.

To satisfy the security needs of employees, a number of companies began welfare programs in the 1890s and 1900s. In their worst form, these welfare programs later became known as *paternalism.* In the 1930s, welfare programs evolved into a variety of fringe benefits to provide employee security. Employers—and unions and government—began caring for the security needs of workers. They were applying a **custodial model** of organizational behavior (see "On the Job: IBM and 3M Co.").

As shown in Figure 2.4, a successful custodial approach depends on *economic resources.* The resulting managerial orientation is toward *money* to pay wages and benefits. Since employees' physical needs are already reasonably met, the employer looks to *security* needs as a motivating force. If an organization does not have the wealth to provide pensions and pay other benefits, it cannot follow a custodial approach.

Employees become dependent

The custodial approach leads to employee *dependence on the organization.* Rather than being dependent on their employer for just their weekly paycheck, employees now depend on organizations for their security and welfare. If employees have excellent health care coverage where they work now, they cannot afford to quit even if the grass looks greener somewhere else but the new employer offers no health benefits (see "On the Job: The Calvert Group").

Employees working in a custodial environment become psychologically preoccupied with their economic rewards and benefits. As a result of their treatment, they are well maintained and reasonably contented. However, contentment does not necessarily produce strong motivation; it may produce only *passive cooperation.* The result tends to be that employees do not perform much more effectively than under the old autocratic approach.

Deficiencies of a custodial approach

The custodial model is described in its extreme in order to show its emphasis on material rewards, security, and organizational dependence. In actual practice, this model also has various shades of gray, from dark to light. Its great benefit is that it brings security and satisfaction to workers, but it does have substantial flaws. The most evident flaw is that most employees are not producing anywhere near their capacities, nor are they motivated to grow to the greater capacities of which they are capable. Though employees are comfortable and cared for, most of them really do not feel fulfilled or motivated. In confirmation of this condition, a series of classic studies at the University of Michigan reported that "the happy employee is not necessarily the most productive employee."[12] Consequently, managers and academic leaders needed to set aside the myth of the happy worker and start to ask again, "Is there a better way?"

The search for a better way is not a condemnation of the custodial model as a whole but rather a condemnation of the assumption that this is "the final answer"—the one best way to motivate employees. The error in reasoning occurs when managers perceive the custodial model as so appropriate that there is no need to build on it toward something better. Although the custodial model does provide employee security, it is best viewed as simply the foundation for growth to the next step.

On the Job: The Calvert Group

Many programs are consistent with a custodial environment at the workplace. The Calvert Group, a Maryland-based mutual funds company, provides support for physical fitness, massage therapy, wellness seminars, parental leave, dependent care time, and child care programs. Calvert reported that the turnover rate has fallen sharply from its preprogram level of 30 percent annually, the number of sick days taken is down, health care expenses are lower, and recruitment and training costs have been reduced.[13] Apparently, employees become dependent on these custodial practices and then are reluctant to change employers.

The Supportive Model

The **supportive model** of organizational behavior had its origins in the "principle of supportive relationships" as stated by Rensis Likert, who said:

> The leadership and other processes of the organization must be such as to ensure a maximum probability that in all interactions and all relationships with the organization each member will, in the light of his [or her] background, values, and expectations, view the experience as supportive and one which builds and maintains his [or her] sense of personal worth and importance.[14]

Likert's principle is similar to the human resources approach mentioned in Chapter 1.

Development of research

One key spark for the supportive approach was a series of research studies at the Hawthorne Plant of Western Electric in the 1920s and 1930s.[15] Led by Elton Mayo and F. J. Roethlisberger, the researchers gave academic stature to the study of human behavior at work by applying keen insight, straight thinking, and sociological backgrounds to industrial experiments. They concluded that an organization is a social system and the worker is indeed the most important element in it. Their experiments concluded that the worker is not a simple tool but a complex personality that often is difficult to understand. The studies also suggested that an understanding of group dynamics, coupled with the application of supportive supervision, was important.

The supportive model depends on *leadership* instead of power or money. Through leadership, management provides a climate to help employees grow and accomplish in the interests of the organization the things of which they are capable. The leader assumes workers are not by nature passive and resistant to organizational needs, but are made so by an inadequately supportive climate at work. They will take responsibility, develop a drive to contribute, and improve themselves if management will give them a chance. Management's orientation, therefore, is to *support the employee's job performance* rather than simply support employee benefit payments as in the custodial approach.

Employees are helped to become productive

Since management supports employees in their work, the psychological result is a feeling of *participation* and *task involvement* in the organization. Employees may say "we" instead of "they" when referring to their organization. They are more strongly motivated than by earlier models because their *status* and *recognition* needs are better met. Thus they have *awakened drives* for work.

Supportive behavior is not the kind of approach that requires money. Rather, it is a part of management's lifestyle at work, reflected in the way it deals with other people. The manager's role is one of helping employees solve their problems and accomplish their work. The following is an example of a supportive approach:

> Juan Salinas, a young widower with one child, had a record of frequent tardiness as an assembler in an electronics plant. His supervisor, Helen Ferguson, attended

a company training program for supervisors, so she decided to try the supportive approach with Salinas.

The next time Salinas was tardy, Ferguson approached him with concern about what might have caused his tardiness. Rather than scolding him, Ferguson showed a genuine interest in Salinas's problems, asking, "How can I help?" and "Is there anything we can do at the company?" When the discussion focused on delays in getting the child ready for school early in the morning, Ferguson arranged for Salinas to talk with other parents in the department. When Salinas talked about the distance he had to walk to catch a bus, Ferguson worked with the personnel department to get him into a dependable car pool.

Although the new car pool undoubtedly helped, an important point was that Salinas seemed to appreciate the recognition and concern that was expressed, so he was more motivated to come to work on time. He also was more cooperative and interested in his job. It was evident that the supportive approach influenced Salinas's behavior. An important by-product was that Ferguson's job became easier because of Salinas's better performance.

Are theory and practice consistent?

The supportive model works well with both employees and managers, and it has been widely accepted—at least philosophically—by many managers in the United States and elsewhere. Of course, their agreement with supportive ideas does not necessarily mean that all of them *practice* those approaches regularly or effectively. *The step from theory to practice is a difficult one.* Nevertheless, reports of companies that reap the benefits of a supportive approach have appeared more and more frequently.

The supportive model of organizational behavior tends to be especially effective in affluent nations because it responds to employee drives toward a wide array of emerging needs. It has less immediate application in the developing nations, where employees' current needs and social conditions are often quite different. However, as those needs for material rewards and security become satisfied, and as employees become aware of managerial practices in other parts of the world, employees in those countries will likely demand a more supportive approach. Consequently, their progression through the models is frequently a more rapid one.

The Collegial Model

A useful extension of the supportive model is the **collegial model.** The term "collegial" relates to a body of people working together cooperatively. The collegial model, which embodies a team concept, first achieved widespread applications in research laboratories and similar work environments. More recently, it has been applied in a wide range of other work situations as well.

The collegial model traditionally was used less on assembly lines, because the rigid work environment made it difficult to apply there. A contingency relationship exists in which the collegial model tends to be more useful with creative work, an intellectual environment, and considerable job freedom. In other environments, the other models may be more successful.

As shown in Figure 2.4, the collegial model depends on management's building a feeling of *partnership* with employees. The result is that employees feel needed and useful. They sense managers are contributing also, so it is easy to accept and respect their roles in the organization. Managers are seen as joint contributors rather than as bosses (see "On the Job: Nashville Bar Association").

Teamwork is required

The managerial orientation is toward *teamwork.* Management is the coach that builds a better team. The employee response to this situation is *responsibility.* For example, employees produce quality work not because management tells them to do so or because

On the Job: Nashville Bar Association

The feeling of partnerships can be built in many ways. Some organizations have abolished the use of reserved parking spaces for executives, so every employee has an equal chance of finding a space close to the workplace. Some firms have tried to eliminate the use of terms like "bosses" and "subordinates," feeling that those terms simply create perceptions of psychological distance between managers and nonmanagers. Other employers have removed time clocks, set up "fun committees" (e.g., the Nashville Bar Association), sponsored company canoe trips, or required managers to spend a week or two annually working in field or factory locations. All these approaches are designed to build a spirit of mutuality, in which every person makes contributions and appreciates those of others.

the inspector will catch them if they do not, but because they feel inside themselves an obligation to provide others with high quality. They also feel an obligation to uphold quality standards that will bring credit to their jobs, themselves, and the company.

The psychological result of the collegial approach for the employee is *self-discipline.* Feeling responsible, employees discipline themselves for performance on the team in the same way members of a football team discipline themselves to training standards and the rules of the game. In this kind of environment, employees normally feel some degree of fulfillment, worthwhile contribution, and *self-actualization,* even though the amount may be modest in some situations. This self-actualization will lead to *moderate enthusiasm* in performance.

Three research laboratories

The collegial model tends to produce improved results in situations where it is appropriate. One study covered scientists in three large research laboratories. Laboratories A and B were operated in a relatively traditional hierarchical manner. Laboratory C was operated in a more open, participative, collegial manner. There were four measures of performance: esteem of fellow scientists, contribution to knowledge, sense of personal achievement, and contribution to management objectives. All four were higher in laboratory C, and the first three were significantly higher.[16]

The System Model

An emerging model of organizational behavior is the **system model.** It is the result of a strong search for higher *meaning* at work by many of today's employees; they want much more than just a paycheck and job security from their jobs (see the box "An Ethical Issue"). Since they are being asked to spend many hours of their day at work, they want a work

An Ethical Issue

A new term has crept into the managerial vocabulary—**spirituality.** This term focuses on the desire for employees to know their deepest selves better, to grow personally, to make a meaningful contribution to society, and to demonstrate integrity in every action taken. Spirituality incorporates the principle of self-awareness and encourages people to "know themselves" while honoring and respecting the diverse moral and religious beliefs of others. As individuals search for and identify universal values—via reading, meditation, journal writing, or workshops—they presumably develop an enhanced capacity to live and act authentically, congruently, and joyfully, consistent with their own spiritual beliefs.

Question: Do you believe that organizations have the obligation to provide opportunities for enhanced spirituality at work? Is it ethical to use organizational resources for such purposes and programs?

context there that is ethical, infused with integrity and *trust,* and provides an opportunity to experience a growing sense of *community* among co-workers. To accomplish this, managers must increasingly demonstrate a sense of *caring and compassion,* being sensitive to the needs of a diverse workforce with rapidly changing needs and complex personal and family needs.

A positive thrust

The system model reflects the values underlying **positive organizational behavior,** which focuses on *identifying, developing, and managing psychological strengths within employees.* Under this approach, managers focus their attention on helping employees develop feelings of hope, optimism, self-confidence, empathy, trustworthiness, esteem, courage, efficacy, and resiliency. These positive capacities appear to be related to the key outcomes of organizational citizenship (discussed in Chapter 9), courageous principled action (ethical behavior), objective performance, and employee satisfaction.[17]

Managers using the system model carefully protect and actively nurture their employees so as to develop a positive workplace culture that leads to organizational success and committed employees.

Individuals at all levels need to acquire and display **social intelligence** (strategic social awareness for managers), which has five dimensions:

- Empathy—appreciation for, and connectedness with, others.
- Presence—projecting self-worth in one's bearing.
- Situational radar—ability to read social situations and respond appropriately.
- Clarity—using language effectively to explain and persuade.
- Authenticity—being "real" and transparent, while projecting honesty.

Under the system model, managers try to convey to each worker, "You are an important part of our whole system. We sincerely care about each of you. We want to join together to achieve a better product or service, local community, and society at large. We will make every effort to make products that are environmentally friendly and contribute to sustainability." The role of a manager becomes one of *facilitating employee accomplishments* through a variety of actions (see Figure 2.5).

In response, many employees embrace the goal of organizational effectiveness and recognize the mutuality of company–employee obligations in a system viewpoint. They experience a sense of **psychological ownership** for the organization and its products or services—a feeling of possessiveness, responsibility, identity, and sense of belongingness ("at home"). Employees with a sense of ownership go beyond the self-discipline of the collegial approach until they reach a state of *self-motivation,* in which they take responsibility for their own goals, actions, and results. As a consequence, the employee needs that are

FIGURE 2.5
Facilitator Roles for Managers in the System Model of OB

- Support employee commitment to short- and long-term goals.
- Coach individuals and groups in appropriate skills and behaviors.
- Model and foster self-esteem.
- Show genuine concern and empathy for people.
- Offer timely and acceptable feedback.
- Influence people to learn continuously and share that learning with others.
- Help individuals identify and confront issues in ethical ways.
- Stimulate insights through interviews, questions, and suggestions.
- Encourage people to feel comfortable with change and uncertainty.
- Build cohesive productive work teams.

On the Job: Starbucks Coffee Co.

Starbucks Coffee Co. is an example of a firm that is strongly committed to creating a humanized workplace that exemplifies the ideals of the system model of OB. Its CEO, Howard Schultz, has written a book (*Pour Your Heart Into It* [Hyperion Books, 1997]) that very publicly announces the firm's values—employee self-esteem, self-respect, and appreciation for them. Managers there recognize outstanding achievements of the employees, honor the passion they put into their work, promote an open environment, and award stock options to every level of the organization. Results show up in effective customer service, new product ideas, employee loyalty, and low turnover rates.[18]

met are wide-ranging but often include the *highest-order needs* (e.g., social, status, esteem, autonomy, and self-actualization). Because it provides employees an opportunity to meet these needs through their work as well as understand the organization's perspectives, this new model can stimulate employees' *passion* and *commitment* to organizational goals. They are inspired, feel important, and believe in the usefulness and viability of their system for the common good. Their hopes and ideals are built around what the system accomplishes rather than solely what they as individuals can do (see "On the Job: Starbucks Coffee Co.").

Conclusions about the Models

Several conclusions can be made about the models of organizational behavior: They are, in practice, subject to evolutionary change; they are a function of prevailing employee needs; there is a trend toward the newer models; and any of the models can be successfully applied in *some* situations. In addition, the models can be modified and extended in a variety of ways.

Evolving Usage Managerial and, on a broader scale, organizational, use of these models tends to evolve over time.[19] As our individual or collective understanding of human behavior increases or as new social conditions develop, we move somewhat slowly to newer models. To assume that one particular model is a "best" model that will endure for the long run is a mistake. This mistake was made by some managers about both the autocratic model and the custodial model, with the result that they became psychologically locked into those models and had difficulty altering their practices when conditions demanded it. Eventually, the supportive model may also fall to limited use. There is no one permanently "best" model, because what is best is contingent on what is known about human behavior in whatever environment exists at that time.

Effectiveness of current models

The primary challenge for management is to *identify the model it is actually using and then assess its current effectiveness.* This self-examination can be a challenge for managers, who tend to profess publicly one model (e.g., the supportive, collegial, or system) yet practice another. (This may occur in multinational firms; see "Managing across National Boundaries.") In effect, a manager has two key tasks—to acquire a new set of values as models evolve, and to learn and apply the behavioral skills consistent with those values. These tasks can be very difficult to accomplish.

Relation of Models to Human Needs A second conclusion is that the five models discussed in this chapter are closely related to human needs. New models have been developed to serve the different needs that became important at the time. For example, the custodial model is directed toward the satisfaction of employees' security needs. It moves one step above the autocratic model, which reasonably serves subsistence needs but does not meet needs for security. Similarly, the supportive model is an effort to meet employees' other needs, such as affiliation and esteem, which the custodial model is unable to serve.

Effect of satisfied needs

A number of people have assumed that emphasis on one model of organizational behavior is an automatic rejection of other models, but comparison suggests that *each* (newer) *model is built upon the accomplishments of the other.* For example, adoption of

Advice to Future Managers

1. Remind yourself to *think about organizational behavior from a system perspective,* envisioning how any one element of the system or action by yourself will likely impact other parts of the OB system.
2. *List, examine, and reevaluate your fact premises* about people periodically to see if they need updating. Then, create a separate list of your value premises and share these with a colleague or friend to see if they withstand open scrutiny.
3. Show your employees the list of assumptions that underlie Theory X and Theory Y. *Afterward,* ask them for illustrations that indicate you are using either of the two paradigms. *Invite them to help you make your actions more consistent with Theory Y.*
4. Examine the five models of OB every so often. *Search for ways in which you could be using features from the more advanced models* (supportive, collegial, system).
5. Report to a close friend the ways in which you have *actively changed your underlying OB model* in the past few years. Be ready to provide specific examples.
6. Review the discussion of social intelligence. *Resolve to exhibit and use more empathy, presence, situational radar, clarity, and authenticity* in your interactions with others.
7. Read about spirituality and employees' desire for the right to discuss such issues at work. *Make a decision now as to how you might handle such a request* should it arise.
8. Make a conscious study of your language at work. Resolve to reduce or eliminate negative language while *increasing your focus on positive terms.*
9. Make an inventory of the ways in which you (or others) exhibit micromanagement behaviors. *Explore ways to reduce such close scrutiny and control.*
10. Often managers and employees differ in their perceptions of which OB model is in use. Set aside some time to *investigate employee perceptions of the OB model* that is dominant in your workplace.

a supportive approach does not mean abandonment of custodial practices that serve necessary employee security needs. What it does mean is that custodial practices are given secondary emphasis, because employees have progressed to a condition in which newer needs dominate. In other words, the supportive model is the appropriate model to use at that point because subsistence and security needs are already reasonably met by a suitable structure and security system. If a misdirected modern manager should abandon these basic organizational needs, the system would move back quickly to seek structure and security in order to satisfy those needs for its people.

Increasing Use of Some Models A third conclusion is that the trend toward the supportive, collegial, and system models will undoubtedly continue. Despite rapid advances in computers and management information systems, top managers of giant, complex organizations cannot be authoritarian in the traditional sense and also be effective. Because they cannot know all that

Managing across National Boundaries

Several U.S. firms have chosen to lower their costs by setting up assembly plants in less-developed countries, such as Mexico, where the wage scale is lower. The firms ship parts to the assembly plant, use cheap labor to perform assembly operations, and then ship the finished product back to markets in the United States. While this practice helps the firms remain competitive from a price standpoint, it raises some interesting behavioral issues. For example, is it appropriate for firms to implement one model of organizational behavior (e.g., a supportive or collegial one) in their U.S. facilities and consciously choose another model (e.g., a custodial one) in Mexico? Another interesting dilemma arises when jobs in the United States are lost as a result of these foreign assembly plants. Does a firm need to revert to a custodial model in the U.S. operations when it senses that employees there fear their job security is becoming highly threatened?

is happening in their organization, they must learn to depend on other centers of power nearer to operating problems. They are often forced to literally redefine the old psychological contract and embrace a newer, more participative one. In addition, many employees are not readily motivated toward creative and intellectual duties by the autocratic model. Only the newer models can offer the satisfaction of their needs for esteem, autonomy, and self-actualization.

Contingent Use of All Models A fourth conclusion is that, though one model may be most used at any given time, some appropriate uses will remain for other models. Knowledge and skills vary among managers. Role expectations of employees differ, depending upon cultural history. Policies and ways of life vary among organizations. Perhaps more important, task conditions are different. Some jobs may require routine, low-skilled, highly programmed work that will be mostly determined by higher authority and will provide mostly material rewards and security (autocratic and custodial conditions). Other jobs will be creative and intellectual, requiring teamwork and self-motivation. Employees in such jobs generally respond best to supportive, collegial, and system approaches. Therefore, probably all five models will continue to be used, but the more advanced models will have growing use as progress is made and employee expectations rise.

Managerial Flexibility The preceding discussion rests on a central conclusion: *Managers not only need to identify their current behavioral model but also must keep it flexible and current.* There is great danger in paradigm rigidity, when the changing nature of people and conditions demands new responses, but managers cling to old beliefs and practices. Managers need to read, to reflect, to interact with others, and to be receptive to challenges to their thinking from their colleagues and employees. The following analogy illustrates this process:

> Skydivers know that a parachute tightly packed for long periods of time might develop undesirable permanent folds in the fabric, which could keep it from opening properly when needed. To prevent this, all parachutes are periodically unpacked and hung in storage sheds to "get the kinks out." Then they are repacked for safe usage. Similarly, wise managers benefit from occasionally sharing their organizational behavior models with others, thus opening them up to public scrutiny. Then, after making appropriate revisions to their models, the managers "pack them up" and put the improved paradigms back to work again.

Summary

Every firm has an organizational behavior system. It includes the organization's stated or unstated philosophy, values, vision, mission, and goals; the quality of leadership, communication, and group dynamics; the nature of both the formal and informal organizations; and the influence of the social environment. These items combine to create a culture in which the personal attitudes of employees and situational factors can produce motivation and goal achievement.

Five models of organizational behavior are the autocratic, custodial, supportive, collegial, and system. The supportive, collegial, and system models are more consistent with contemporary employee needs and, therefore, will predictably obtain more effective results in many situations. Managers need to examine the model they are using, determine whether it is the most appropriate one, and remain flexible in their use of alternative and emerging models.

Communication, a major tool for expressing managerial models, provides the focus for Chapter 3. Then, the idea of organizational behavior models is extended in Chapter 4, as we discuss social systems, roles, and status. Specifically, we look at the creation and impact of organizational cultures, which help employees sense which organizational behavior model is in use.

Speaking OB: Terms and Concepts for Review

Autocratic model, *36*
Collegial model, *40*
Custodial model, *38*
Fact premises, *31*
Goals, *32*
Micromanagement, *37*
Mission, *32*
Models, *33*
Organizational behavior system, *30*
Paradigm shift, *35*
Paradigms, *34*
Philosophy, *30*
Positive organizational behavior, *42*
Psychological ownership, *42*
Social intelligence, *42*
Spirituality, *41*
Supportive model, *39*
System model, *41*
Theory X, *33*
Theory Y, *34*
Value premises, *32*
Vision, *32*

Discussion Questions

1. Interview some managers to identify their visions for their organizations. What are those visions? Where did they come from? How successfully have they been communicated to the employees, and how successfully have they been embraced by the employees?
2. Both philosophy and vision are somewhat hazy concepts. How can they be made clear to employees? Why are philosophy and vision included as early elements in the organizational behavior system? Give an example of an organizational vision you have read about or heard of.
3. What benefits do you see from allowing and encouraging spirituality at work? What are the risks of doing so?
4. Consider an organization where you now work (or where you have worked). What model (paradigm) of organizational behavior does (did) your supervisor follow? Is (was) it the same as top management's model?
5. Discuss similarities and differences among the five models of organizational behavior.
6. What model of organizational behavior would be most appropriate in each of the following situations? (Assume that you must use the kinds of employees and supervisors currently available in your local labor market.)
   a. Long-distance telephone operators in a very large office
   b. Accountants with a small certified professional accounting firm
   c. Food servers in a local restaurant of a prominent fast-food chain
   d. Salesclerks in a large discount department store
   e. Circus laborers temporarily employed to work the week that the circus is in the city
7. Discuss why the supportive, collegial, and system models of organizational behavior are especially appropriate for use in the more affluent nations.
8. Interview a supervisor or manager to identify the model of organizational behavior that person believes in. Explain why you think the supervisor's or manager's behavior would or would not reflect those beliefs.
9. Examine the trends in the models of organizational behavior as they have developed over a period of time. Why have the trends moved in a positive direction?
10. Assume that a friend of yours contends that "the system model is obviously 'best' to use with all employees, or it wouldn't have been placed on the right side of the figure." How would you respond?

Assess Your Own Skills

How well do you exhibit facilitator skills?

Read the following statements carefully. Circle the number on the response scale that most closely reflects the degree to which each statement accurately describes you. Add up your total points and prepare a brief action plan for self-improvement. Be ready to report your score for tabulation across the entire group.

	Good description									Poor description
1. I know how to support employee commitment to short- and long-term goals.	10	9	8	7	6	5	4	3	2	1
2. I could coach individuals and groups in appropriate skills and behaviors.	10	9	8	7	6	5	4	3	2	1
3. I feel comfortable modeling and fostering self-esteem.	10	9	8	7	6	5	4	3	2	1
4. I am likely to show genuine concern and empathy for people.	10	9	8	7	6	5	4	3	2	1
5. I would feel comfortable offering timely and acceptable feedback to others.	10	9	8	7	6	5	4	3	2	1
6. I am dedicated to influencing people to learn continuously and to share that learning with others.	10	9	8	7	6	5	4	3	2	1
7. I would help individuals identify and confront issues in ethical ways.	10	9	8	7	6	5	4	3	2	1
8. I feel comfortable expressing caring and compassion to people.	10	9	8	7	6	5	4	3	2	1
9. I believe in encouraging people to feel comfortable with change and uncertainty.	10	9	8	7	6	5	4	3	2	1
10. I would work hard to build cohesive productive work teams.	10	9	8	7	6	5	4	3	2	1

Scoring and Interpretation

Add up your total points for the 10 questions. Record that number here, and report it when it is requested. Finally, insert your total score into the "Assess and Improve Your Own Organizational Behavior Skills" chart in Appendix A.

- If you scored between 81 and 100 points, you appear to have a solid capability for demonstrating facilitative skills.
- If you scored between 61 and 80 points, you should take a close look at the items with lower self-assessment scores and explore ways to improve those items.
- If you scored under 60 points, you should be aware that a weaker skill level regarding several items could be detrimental to your future success as a manager. We encourage you to review the entire chapter and watch for relevant material in subsequent chapters and other sources.

Now identify your three lowest scores, and write the question numbers here: _____, _____, _____. Write a brief paragraph, detailing to yourself an action plan for how you might sharpen each of these skills.

Incident

The New Plant Manager

Toby Butterfield worked his way upward in the Montclair Company until he became assistant plant manager in the Illinois plant. Finally, his opportunity for a promotion came. The Houston plant was having difficulty meeting its budget and production quotas, so he was promoted to plant manager and transferred to the Houston plant with instructions to "straighten it out."

Butterfield was ambitious and somewhat power-oriented. He believed that the best way to solve problems was to take control, make decisions, and use his authority to carry out his decisions. After preliminary study, he issued orders for each department to cut its budget 5 percent. A week later he instructed all departments to increase production 10 percent by the following month. He required several new reports and kept a close watch on operations. At the end of the second month he dismissed three supervisors who had failed to meet their production quotas. Five other supervisors resigned. Butterfield insisted that all rules and budgets should be followed, and he allowed no exceptions.

Butterfield's efforts produced remarkable results. Productivity quickly exceeded standard by 7 percent, and within five months the plant was within budget. His record was so outstanding he was promoted to the New York home office near the end of his second year. Within a month after he left, productivity in the Houston plant collapsed to 15 percent below standard, and the budget again was in trouble.

Questions

1. Discuss the model of organizational behavior Butterfield used and the kind of organizational climate he created.
2. Discuss why productivity dropped when Butterfield left the Houston plant.
3. If you were Butterfield's New York manager, what would you tell him about his approach? How might he respond?

Experiential Exercise

The Rapid Corporation

The Rapid Corporation is a refrigeration service organization in a large city. It has about 70 employees, mostly refrigeration service representatives. For many years the company's policies have been dominated by its president and principal owner, Otto Blumberg, who takes pride in being a "self-made man."

Recently Otto and his office manager attended an organizational behavior seminar in which the value of a written corporate philosophy for employees was discussed. Both men agreed to draft one and compare their efforts.

1. Divide the class into three types of groups. One set of groups should draft statements for the Rapid Corporation based on the autocratic model; the second set should create comparable statements of philosophy using the supportive model as a basis; the third set should use the system model.
2. Ask representatives of each group (autocratic, supportive, and system) to read their statements to the class. Discuss their major differences. Have the class debate the usefulness of philosophy statements for guiding the organizational behavior system in a firm of this type.

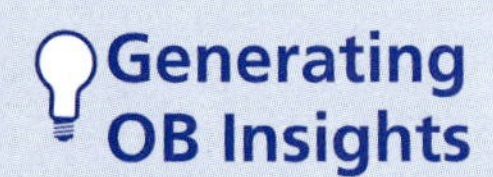

Generating OB Insights

An *insight* is a new and clear perception of a phenomenon, or an acquired ability to "see" clearly something you were unaware of previously. It is sometimes simply referred to as an "ah-ha! moment," in which you have a minirevelation or reach a straightforward conclusion about a topic or issue.

Insights need not necessarily be dramatic, for what is an insight to one person may be less important to another. The critical feature of insights is that they are relevant and memorable for *you;* they should represent new knowledge, new frameworks, or new ways of viewing things you want to retain and remember over time.

Insights, then, are different from the information you find in the "Advice for Future Managers" boxes within the text. That advice is prescriptive and action-oriented; it indicates a recommended course of action.

A useful way to think of OB insights is to assume you are the only person who has read the current chapter. You have been given the assignment to highlight, in your own words, the major concepts (not just summarize the whole chapter) that might stand out for a naive audience who has never heard of the topic before. *What 10 insights would you share with them?*

(Example) *It is helpful to take a broad and integrated view of an organization as a system of interdependent parts.*

1. ____
2. ____
3. ____
4. ____
5. ____
6. ____
7. ____
8. ____
9. ____
10. ____

Nurturing Your Critical Thinking and Reflective Skills

Take a few minutes to review the discussion in the Roadmap for Readers of critical thinking and reflection. Remind yourself that if you can hone these abilities now, you will have a substantial competitive advantage when you apply for jobs and are asked what unique skills you can bring to the position and the organization.

Critical Thinking

Think back on the material you read in this chapter. What are three unique and challenging *critical questions* you would like to raise about this material? (These might identify something controversial about which you have doubts, they may imply that you suspect that a theory or model has weaknesses, they could examine the legitimacy of apparent causal relationships, or they might assess the probable value of a suggested practice.) Be prepared to share these questions with class members or your instructor.

1. ______________________________

____

2. ______________________________

____

3. ______________________________

____

Reflection

This process often involves answering the parallel questions of "What do you *think* about the material you have read?" and "How do you *feel* about that material?" Therefore, express your *personal thoughts and feelings* (reactions) to any of the ideas or topics found in this chapter, and be prepared to share these reflections with class members or your instructor.

1. ______________________________

____

2. ______________________________

____

3. ______________________________

____

Chapter Three

Managing Communications

It's important to draw a distinction between knowing lots of people (visibility) and having an effective network of people with whom you have profitable relationships.

Patricia A. Muir[1]

People have a channel of communication that revolves not around words but around social relations . . . *even though we are largely unaware of it.*

Alex Pentland et al.[2]

CHAPTER OBJECTIVES

AFTER STUDYING THIS CHAPTER, YOU SHOULD UNDERSTAND

3-1 The Two-Way Communication Process
3-2 Barriers to Communication
3-3 Factors Leading to Effective Communication
3-4 Downward and Upward Communications Problems
3-5 The Roles of Questioning and Listening
3-6 Social Networking Tools
3-7 The Impact of Electronic Communications
3-8 Organizational Grapevines and Rumors

Facebook Page 

Student A: Breaking news—I'm going to learn how to manage my communications!

Student B: Big deal. Haven't you been talking since you were two years old?

Student A: Sure, but now I see that communication is broken down into seven key steps—at least when two-way exchanges are involved. In addition, a handful of barriers get in the way of success—you know, things like semantic jargon, physical barriers, and psychological distance.

Student C: How about writing? We have a lot of that to do, too.

Student A: I glanced ahead in the chapter, and found a bunch of guidelines that will help me there. It also presents some ideas for how to become a more effective listener, which YOU ought to read!

Student C: Thanks, wise guy.

Student B: What are the most engaging topics that you see in the chapter?

Student A: I think that will include feedback-seeking behavior, networking, and the grapevine. And I almost forgot; there's a section on telecommuting, which I hope to do someday.

Student B: You'd better hope so; then you won't have to worry about all those cool "tats" and piercings you got on spring break last year.

Members of a hospital's board of directors were listening to an appeal to spend substantial capital funds to upgrade a CT scanner. "But why do we need all of these extra features?" asked one board member. "Because," explained a physician, "it will allow us to reexamine the CT scans for a patient from a different set of perspectives after he or she is gone." "But why would you care to analyze the scans after a patient is dead?" innocently asked another board member (who happened to be a funeral director). Only after widespread laughter did the physician realize that his use of the word "gone" had two very different meanings among his audience—departed from the health care facility versus departed from this world.

Communication is the ever-present activity by which people relate to one another and combine their efforts, and is necessary to perpetuate the health of the organization. Just as people may develop arteriosclerosis, a hardening of the arteries that restricts the flow of blood and the nutrients it carries, so may an organization develop similar problems with its information arteries. The result is the same—unnecessarily reduced efficiency due to key information being blocked or restricted at various points throughout the organization. And just like the medical ailment, preventing the problem is usually easier than trying to find a cure.

Today's employees have a powerful desire to know what is going on and how they fit into the larger picture. More than ever before, managers need to engage in systematic and extensive communications in upward, downward, and lateral directions. As you will read later, listening skills that focus on the receiver—and a healthy dose of humility—remain highly important in the communication process. Further, as technology spreads ever wider, the human element of communication must not be forgotten. In this chapter, the significance of communication in the workplace is explored in depth. Also discussed are networking, social technologies, and informal communication.

Engaging Your Brain

1. Rate your own communication effectiveness on a scale from 1 (Poor) to 10 (Excellent). Now, using the same response scale, rate the average skill of your peers. Discuss the two scores, and share your data with other students.
2. How persuasive are you in getting others to accept your ideas and change their behaviors? What tools of persuasion do you have at your disposal?
3. What would you do if your instructor told you that no information about your grade in this class would be posted until the end of the academic term? How likely are you to take the initiative to contact the instructor several times to obtain personal feedback from him/her? If not, why not?

COMMUNICATION FUNDAMENTALS

Communication is the transfer of information and understanding from one person to another. It is a way of reaching others by transmitting ideas, facts, thoughts, feelings, and values. Its goal is to have the receiver understand the message as it was intended and (often) to act upon that information. When communication is effective, it provides a bridge of meaning between the two people so they can each share what they feel and know. By using this bridge, both parties can safely cross the river of misunderstanding that sometimes separates people.

> A survey of managers regarding their beliefs about a variety of skill areas showed two dramatic conclusions. First, "communication" was rated as the most important skill to the organization. Second, the current competency level of managers in their communications was ranked just 12th out of 20 items. Clearly, there is room for improvement (a major gap) in this critical skill area.[3]

Two or more people are required

Communication always involves at least two people—a sender and a receiver. One person alone cannot communicate. Only one or more receivers can complete the communication act. This fact is obvious when you think of being stranded by yourself on an island and calling for help when there is no one to hear the call. The need for a receiver is not so obvious to managers who send out memos to employees. They tend to assume that when their messages are sent, they have communicated; but transmission of the message is only a beginning. A manager may send a hundred messages, but there is no effective communication until each one is received, read, and understood. *Communication is what the receiver understands,* not what the sender says.

Understanding is critical for success

The Importance of Communication

Organizations cannot exist without communication. If there is no communication, employees cannot know what their co-workers are doing, management cannot receive information inputs, and supervisors and team leaders cannot give instructions. Coordination of work is impossible, and the organization will collapse for lack of it. Cooperation also becomes impossible, because people cannot communicate their needs and feelings to others. We can say with confidence that *every act of communication influences the organization in some way,* just as the flapping of a butterfly's wings in California influences (however slightly) the subsequent wind velocity in Boston. Communication helps accomplish all the basic management functions—planning, organizing, leading, and controlling—so that organizations can achieve their goals and meet their challenges.

When communication is effective, it tends to facilitate better performance and improve job satisfaction. People understand their jobs better and feel more involved in them. In some instances, they even will voluntarily give up some of their long-established privileges because they see that a sacrifice is necessary.

> Management in one firm persuaded production employees to bring their own coffee and have coffee breaks at their machines instead of taking a regular lost-time coffee break in the cafeteria. The company had dealt directly and frankly with them. It presented to employee group meetings a chart of electricity use for the plant, showing how power use was less than half of normal for 15 minutes before and after a coffee break, plus the normal production loss during the break. The company made a sound case for the fact that this long period of inactivity and partial activity prevented profitable operation. The power-use charts were convincing, and employees readily accepted the new coffee-break policy.

Open communication contributes to transparency

The positive response of those employees supports one of the basic propositions of organizational behavior—that *open and candid communication is generally better than restricted communication.* This proposition is based on the contemporary desire for **transparency** in all organizations and at all levels. Managers who are transparent are open, candid, clear, honest, and accessible. They accomplish this by sharing meaningful information on a timely basis with employees. Consequently, if employees know the problems an organization is facing and hear what managers are trying to do, they will usually respond favorably.

To focus solely on communication with employees and ignore the needs of managers would be easy, but that approach would provide a limited view. Management's role is critical, for managers not only initiate communications but also pass them on to, and interpret them for, employees. Just as a photograph can be no clearer than the negative from which it is printed, managers cannot transmit a message more clearly than their own understanding of it.

> Kiki, a department supervisor, received a copy of a 110-page report. Instead of distributing it directly to her staff and expecting them to read and absorb the entire report, she prepared a two-page abbreviation and gave it to each member. Although they appreciated the time she saved for them, they realized they were now dependent on her interpretation of the total report. Similarly, the quality of Kiki's summary depended on the readability of the original report as well as her own skills of interpretation and condensation.

Features of an executive summary

The product that the supervisor in the preceding example prepared is commonly known as an **executive summary**, which is a useful tool for communicating both to employees and to busy superiors. In its briefest form, an executive summary provides concise highlights of a longer document or set of reports, often as an aid to rapid decision making. Major topics covered in a 1-2 page document typically include background information, a problem statement, alternatives considered, pros and cons of each, and recommendations.

Managers need timely and useful information to make sound decisions. Inadequate or poor data can affect a broad area of performance because the scope of managerial influence is quite wide. Very simply, managerial decisions affect many people and many activities.

The Two-Way Communication Process

Eight steps in the process

The **two-way communication process** is the method by which a sender reaches a receiver with a message. The process always requires eight steps, whether the two parties talk, use hand signals, or employ some advanced-technology means of communication. The steps are shown in Figure 3.1.

FIGURE 3.1 The Communication Process

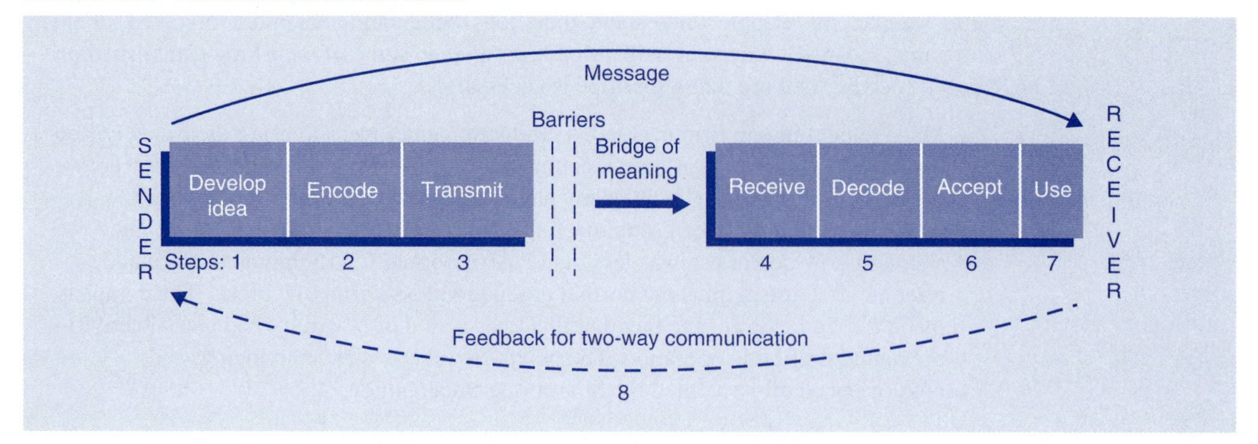

Develop an Idea Step 1 is to *develop an idea* that the sender wishes to transmit. This is the key step, because unless there is a worthwhile message, all the other steps are somewhat useless. This step is represented by the sign, sometimes seen on office or factory walls, that reads, "Be sure brain is engaged before putting mouth in gear."

Encode Step 2 is to *encode* (convert) the idea into suitable words, charts, or other symbols for transmission. At this point, the sender determines the method of transmission so that the words and symbols may be organized in suitable fashion for the type of transmission. For example, back-and-forth conversation usually is not organized the same way as a formal report.

Perceptions are influenced through the context provided

The key to successful encoding lies in the process of framing an issue for presentation. **Framing** uses rich, colorful, carefully selected language to shape the perceptions of recipients. The sender of a communication attempts to frame an issue by placing it in a particular context, tone, or background to manage the meaning in the way it was intended. For example, note the difference between framing the competition for new customers as a "problem" versus an "opportunity." Framing is a potent tool for managers to create vivid images and memorable messages, influence the recipient's perceptions, and thereby shape the attitudes and actions of their followers.

Transmit When the message finally is developed, step 3 is to *transmit* it by the method chosen, such as by memo, phone call, or personal visit. The sender also chooses a certain channel, such as bypassing or not bypassing a co-worker, and communicates with careful timing. For example, the sender may decide that today may not be the right day to talk to the manager about that pay raise. The sender also tries to keep the communication channel free of barriers, or interference, as shown in Figure 3.1, so that the message has a chance to reach the receiver and hold his or her attention. In employment interviewing or performance appraisals, for example, freedom from distraction is highly desirable.

Receiver controls steps 4 to 8

Receive Transmission allows another person to *receive* a message, which is step 4. In this step, the initiative transfers to the receiver, who tunes in to receive the message. If it is oral, the receiver needs to be a good listener, a skill that is discussed shortly. If the receiver does not function, the message is lost.

Andrea sent an urgent request to a professional colleague across the country for a copy of a diagram she needed for a presentation later that day. "I'll fax it to you," Derrick responded. Each time he tried, however, a message appeared telling him

On the Job: Montana Log Homes

The encoding-decoding sequence is somewhat like the activity involved when Montana Log Homes are first constructed in Kalispell, Montana. The completed home cannot be moved in one piece, so it has to be disassembled log by log, with each log marked as to its proper location. This process is similar to the action of a sender who has an idea and encodes (dismantles) it into a series of words, each marked by location and other means to guide the receiver. In order to move the idea (transmit it), the sender needs to take it apart by putting it into words. The reassembly of the home log by log at its final destination is similar to the action of a receiver who takes the words received and mentally reassembles them into whole ideas. If one log (or word) is misused, the entire structure (message) may be weakened.

that the fax transmission did not go through. After he called Andrea to explain this perplexing problem, she checked her machine and found it had run out of paper. Only after fixing the problem did she receive the needed message.

Need for understanding

Decode Step 5 is to *decode* the message so it can be understood. The sender wants the receiver to understand the message exactly as it was sent. For example, if the sender transmits the equivalent of a square and the decoding step produces a circle, then a message has been sent, but not much understanding has taken place.

Understanding can occur only in a receiver's mind. A communicator may make others listen, but there is no way to *make* them understand. The receiver alone chooses whether to understand or not. Many employers overlook this fact when giving instructions or explanations. They think that telling someone is sufficient, but the communication cannot proceed until there is understanding. This process is known as "getting through" to a person (see "On the Job: Montana Log Homes").

Accept Once the receiver has obtained and decoded a message, that person has the opportunity to *accept or reject* it, which is step 6. The sender, of course, would like the receiver to accept the communication in the manner intended so activities can progress as planned. Acceptance, however, is a matter of choice and degree, such that the receiver has considerable control over whether or not to embrace all the message or just parts of it. Some factors affecting the acceptance decision revolve around perceptions of the message's accuracy, the authority and credibility of the sender, the sender's persuasive skills (see "What Managers Are Reading"), and the behavioral implications for the receiver.

Use Step 7 in the communication process is for the receiver to *use the information.* The receiver may discard it, perform the task as directed, store the information for the future, or do something else. This is a critical action step, and the receiver is largely in control of what to do.

Provide Feedback When the receiver acknowledges the message and responds to the sender, *feedback* has occurred. Feedback completes the communication loop, because there is a message flow from the sender to the receiver and back to the sender, as shown by the feedback arrow (step 8) at the bottom of Figure 3.1.

Engaging in two-way communication can be compared to playing the game of tennis. Consider the process that must go on in the mind of one of its powerful young stars, Venus Williams. As Venus serves the ball, she cannot tell herself, "My next shot will be a crosscourt forehand." Her next shot, to be effective, must depend on feedback from the receiver—that is, on where and how her opponent returns the serve. Venus undoubtedly has an overall strategy for the match, but each of her shots must be contingent on the way the ball is returned to her—its force, spin, and placement—and on the position of her opponent on the opposite side of the court.

What Managers Are Reading 

PERSUASION TOOLS ARE NEEDED

Managers are marketers, according to psychologist Robert Cialdini and his colleagues. They need to use their charisma, eloquence, and verbal skills to persuade others above and below them to accept their ideas and change their behaviors. Perhaps surprisingly, hierarchical power seldom works to achieve these ends. What does work are six fundamental principles of persuasion:

1. Liking—Uncover similarities to build bonds with others, and offer genuine praise to them.
2. Reciprocity—Give what you want to receive.
3. Social proof—Use peer power whenever it is available.
4. Consistency—Solicit commitments that are active, public, and voluntary.
5. Authority—Don't assume that your expertise is self-evident; expose it.
6. Scarcity—Accent the unique and exclusive benefits of your product/service.

Sources: Noah J. Goldstein, Steve J. Martin, and Robert B. Cialdini, *Yes!:50 Scientifically Proven Ways to Be Persuasive*, New York: Free Press, 2008, and Robert B. Cialdini, *Influence: Science and Practice*, 4th ed., Boston: Allyn and Bacon, 2001.

If Venus fails to match her shots to her opponent's game, she will find that her game is not as effective as it could have been that day. As is the case in communication, ignoring feedback limits the likelihood that the exchange will be successful.

Senders require feedback

Two-way communication, made possible by feedback, has a back-and-forth pattern. In two-way communication, the speaker sends a message and the receiver's response comes back to the speaker. The result is a developing play-by-play situation in which the speaker can, and should, adjust the next message to fit the previous response of the receiver. The sender needs feedback—the final step—because it tells whether the message was received, decoded properly, accepted, and used. If necessary, the sender should seek and request feedback from the receiver. When this two-way communication occurs, both parties experience greater satisfaction, frustration is prevented, and work accuracy is greatly improved.

Potential Problems

Two-way communication is not exclusively beneficial. It also can cause difficulties. Two people may strongly disagree about some item but not realize it until they establish two-way communication. When they expose their different viewpoints, they may become **polarized,** taking even more extreme positions. When threatened with the potential embarrassment of losing an argument, people tend to abandon logic and rationality, and engage in **defensive reasoning.** They blame others, selectively gather and use data, seek to remain in control, and suppress negative feelings. Defensive reasoning is designed to avoid risk and the appearance of incompetence, but it typically results in a drive toward control and an emphasis on winning. Defensive reasoning predictably detracts from effective communications, and can easily result in hard feelings between the participants.

Possible problem of cognitive dissonance

Another difficulty that may emerge is **cognitive dissonance.** This is the internal conflict and anxiety that occurs when people receive information incompatible with their value systems, prior decisions, or other information they may have. Since people do not feel comfortable with dissonance, they try to remove or reduce it. Perhaps they will try to obtain new communication inputs, change their interpretation of the inputs, reverse their decision, or change their values. They may even refuse to believe the dissonant input, or they may rationalize it out of the way.

Senders always need to communicate with care, because communication is a potent form of self-revelation to others as well as a source of possible evaluation. Not only are we disclosing something about ourselves (content) when we speak, but others are judging us at the same time. This creates pressure to engage in **face-saving**—an attempt to preserve or even enhance our valued self-concept (face) when it is attacked. Our very self-esteem is threatened when people say something to us that we wish they had not. Sometimes they, too, regret having said something that challenges our **self-concept,** personal image, or social honor. Although such regrettable messages are often unintended, they usually create hurt feelings and defensiveness in the recipient, place stress on the relationship, or even cause the relationship to deteriorate.[4] Regrettable messages may include several types, such as outright verbal blunders, personal attacks, stereotyped slurs, sarcastic criticism, or harmful information. People often send regrettable messages during an emotional confrontation, as in this example:

Face-saving is important to people.

> Damian (an accounting supervisor) and Janny (a marketing manager) had both interviewed a series of candidates for the position of auditor. Later, they got together with three other department heads to make the final selection. When Janny pointed out a weakness she saw in one candidate, Damian reacted sharply by questioning her capacity to assess auditing skills, due to the fact that she had spent her entire career in marketing. Janny, of course, was furious at having her integrity attacked. Although Damian later apologized to her and claimed he regretted the incident, Janny never forgot the remark.

Should you use a challenging or supportive voice?

Another communication problem arises when individuals do not use the most appropriate tone (or words) when expressing their thoughts and feelings. Employees are more likely (and willing) to speak up when they believe that their managers are open, receptive, and non-judgmental. The positive effects of speaking up can include higher quality decisions, better teamwork, and more effective organizational performance. However, managerial receptivity depends on the nature of employee **voice**—the discretionary verbal behavior that is *intended* to be beneficial to the organization. Voice can be classified as either challenging or supportive. A *challenging* voice is more extreme, questioning, and wave-making in nature, and characterized by hostile, tactless, and angry tones. This voice is often not received well by managers who value unity and consensus. The constructive alternative is to use a *supportive* voice, which tends to raise more gentle questions, suggests incremental changes, bases proposals on evidence (versus speculation or opinion), and leaves room for modification of proposals. A supportive voice is also warmer, softer, and more tentative in nature. This type of voice is more likely to be accepted by managers, who perceive the employee as more loyal to the organization.[5]

Communication Barriers

Even when the receiver receives the message and makes a genuine effort to decode it, a number of interferences may limit the receiver's understanding. These obstacles act as **noise,** or barriers to communication, and may emerge in either the physical surroundings (such as a co-worker's humming overshadowing your phone conversation) or within an individual's emotions (the distraction of the receiver's concern about a sick relative). Noise may entirely prevent a communication, filter out part of it, or give it incorrect meaning. Three types of barriers are personal, physical, and semantic.

Personal Barriers **Personal barriers** are communication interferences that arise from human emotions, values, and poor listening habits. They may also stem from differences in education, race, sex, socioeconomic status, and other factors. Personal barriers are a common occurrence in work situations, with common examples including distracting verbal habits (e.g., needless repetition of "ah" or including "you know" or "like" in nearly every sentence) or physical actions (e.g., tapping one's fingers).

Psychological distance

Personal barriers often involve a **psychological distance**—a feeling of being emotionally separated—between people that is similar to actual physical distance. For example, Mark talks down to Janet through his choice of words and facial expressions. Janet predictably resents this treatment, and her resentment separates them.

Our emotions act as perceptual filters in nearly all our communications. We see and hear what we are emotionally tuned to see and hear, so *communication is guided by our expectations.* We also communicate our *interpretation* of reality instead of reality itself. Someone has said, "No matter what you say a thing is, it isn't," meaning that the sender is merely giving an emotionally filtered perception of it. Under these conditions, when the sender's and receiver's perceptions are reasonably close together, their communication will be more effective.

Physical Barriers **Physical barriers** are communication interferences that occur in the environment in which the communication takes place. A typical physical barrier is a sudden distracting noise that temporarily drowns out a voice message. Other physical barriers include distances between people, walls around a worker's cubicle, or static that interferes with radio messages. People frequently recognize when physical interference occurs and try to compensate for it.

> When visitors came to her office, Carmen Valencia used to sit rigidly behind her desk, leaving the other person somewhat distant on the other side of the desk. This arrangement created a psychological distance and clearly established her as the leader and superior in the interaction. Finally sensing this, Carmen rearranged her office so a visitor sat beside her on the same side of her desk. This arrangement suggested more receptiveness and equality of interaction with visitors. It also had the advantage of providing a work area on her desk for mutual examination of work documents. When she wished to establish a more informal relationship, particularly with her team members, she came around to the front of the desk and sat in a chair near the employee.

Proper distance

Carmen's behavior also illustrates the practice of maintaining proper physical distance between two parties as they communicate. The study of such spatial separation is called **proxemics;** it involves the exploration of different practices and feelings about interpersonal space within and across cultures. In the United States, general practice allows *intimate* communications between close friends to occur at very short range (e.g., 6 to 18 inches).

Global Communication Practices

Not only is it important to know and observe common practice with regard to the nature of the underlying relationships (intimate, friendly, work-related, or casual) between two parties; it is also imperative that these practices be adapted for cultural differences. In some societies, sharply different practices prevail. For example, Latin American and Asian cultures generally favor closer distances for personal conversations, and workers in Arab countries often maintain extremely close distances, coupled with actual physical contact. Therefore, the sender should be aware of cultural norms and the receiver's preferences, and make an effort to understand and adapt to them. Question: What assumptions do *you* make about a person who stands too close to you? Too far away from you?

Conversations with acquaintances are often held at a 3- or 4-foot *personal* distance. Work-related discussions between colleagues may occur at a *social* distance of 4 to 12 feet, with more impersonal and formal conversations in *public* occurring at even greater distances.

Semantic Barriers **Semantics** is the science of meaning, as contrasted with *phonetics,* the science of sounds. Nearly all communication is symbolic—that is, it is achieved using symbols (words, pictures, and actions) that suggest certain meanings. These symbols are merely a map that describes a territory, but they are not the real territory itself; hence they must be decoded and interpreted by the receiver. Before we introduce the three types of symbols, however, an additional form of barrier, one that has its origin in semantics, deserves mention.

Semantic barriers arise from limitations in the symbols with which we communicate. Symbols usually have a variety of meanings, and we have to choose one meaning from many. Sometimes we choose the wrong meaning and misunderstanding occurs. An illustration is the case of the board of directors at the beginning of this chapter. This is particularly likely when communicators use **jargon,** which is the specialized language of a group. Jargon can include the use of *acronyms* (first letters of each word in a phrase, such as using OB for organizational behavior), *slang* (words unique to an age or ethnic or racial group), or distinctive terms that are created by a professional or interest group (e.g., "bandwidth" or "onboarding" or "rightsizing"). Interestingly, jargon is beneficial within a group, but it often creates problems across different groups—and especially with new members who aren't yet familiar with the terms.

Semantics presents a particularly difficult challenge when people from different cultures attempt to communicate with each other. Not only must both parties learn the literal meanings of words in the other language, they must also interpret the words within their context and the way in which they are used (tone, volume, and accompanying nonverbal gestures). Clearly, the emerging global economy demands that sensitive managers everywhere overcome the extra burden that semantic barriers place on their intercultural communications.

Fact versus inference

Whenever we interpret a symbol on the basis of our assumptions instead of the facts, we are making an **inference.** Inferences are an essential part of most communication. We cannot avoid them by waiting until all communication is factual before accepting it. However, since inferences can give a wrong signal, we must always be aware of them and appraise them carefully. When doubts arise, more information can be sought.

Communication Symbols

Words Words are the main communication symbol used at work. Many employees spend more than 50 percent of their time in some form of verbal communication. A major difficulty occurs, however, since nearly every common word has several meanings. Multiple meanings are necessary because we are trying to talk about an infinitely complex world while using only a limited number of words. The complexities of a single language are compounded when people from diverse backgrounds—such as different educational levels, ethnic heritages, or cultures—attempt to communicate. No wonder we have trouble communicating with one another!

Context provides meaning

If words really have no single meaning, how can managers make sense with them in communicating with employees? The answer lies in *context,* which is the environment surrounding the use of a word. For example, using the term "dummy" to describe another person in an argument at the office may be derogatory, but using it to refer to the person serving as dummy in a social game of bridge is acceptable. We need to surround key words with the context of other words and symbols until their meanings are narrowed to fairly certain limits and potential confusion is minimized. Consequently, effective communicators are idea-centered rather than just word-centered. They know that *words do not provide meaning, people do.*

Social cues

Context provides meaning to words partially through the cues people receive from their social environment, such as friends and co-workers. **Social cues** are positive or negative bits of information that influence how people react to a communication. Examples of social cues are job titles, patterns of dress, and the historical use of words in a particular region of the country or ethnic group. Our susceptibility to being influenced by these cues varies, depending on the credibility of the source, our past exposure to the item, the ambiguity of the cue, and individual differences such as diverse cultural backgrounds. It is always important to be aware of social cues, because use of language with inadequate context creates a semantic smog. Like a real smog, it irritates our senses and interferes with the accuracy of our perceptions.

Readability

Since the meaning of words is difficult to impart even with the use of context, a reasonable assumption is that if these symbols can be simplified, the receiver will understand them more easily. Further, if symbols of the type that receivers *prefer* are used, the receivers will be more receptive. This assumption is behind the idea of **readability,** which is the process of making writing and speech more understandable.

Figure 3.2 offers some guidelines for more readable writing. When you write your next report for a class, check it before submitting it to see if you have successfully practiced the ideas in Figure 3.2.

Monitoring readability and simplifying documents is a critical communication task. For example, many members of the U.S. labor force have some language difficulties. *Millions of Americans are functionally illiterate* and do not have the skills to read and write effectively. This means they do not always have the reading skills necessary to comprehend even basic job descriptions or work orders assigning them to tasks. In addition, as increasing proportions of the workforce are drawn from diverse cultural backgrounds, English is a second language for many. This means that English terms and phrases common to some workers may appear strange to others. Such language needs to be avoided, or at least clarified. Since the main purpose of communication is to make

FIGURE 3.2
Clear Writing Guidelines

Sources: Adapted from Frank Luntz, "Words that Pack Power," *BusinessWeek*, November 3, 2008, p. 106 and *Readingease: The Key to Understanding*, Employee Relations Staff. General Motors Corporation, n.d.

Guidelines for Readable Writing

- Use *simple* and *familiar* words and phrases. These ease the reader's task, and make comprehension more likely.
- Use *powerful words* that resonate with your audience. Excellent examples include "consequences," and "impact" and "commitment."
- Use *personal pronouns* such as "you" and "them," if the style permits. These help the receiver relate to the message.
- Use *illustrations, examples, and charts.* Remember that "a picture is worth a thousand words."
- Use *short sentences and paragraphs.* You want to express your thoughts efficiently.
- Use *active verbs.* These carry more impact, and can be used to demonstrate your passion for the subject.
- Use only *necessary* words. Be crisp and concise.
- Use a clear *structure.* Employ headings and subheadings to demonstrate you are following an outline.
- Help the reader see what is *important.* Apply techniques of emphasis (e.g., boldface, underlining, or italics) to accent the ideas you believe are most important. Include helpful lists of key points, accented by numbers or bullets.

On the Job: Lake Superior Paper Industries

One organization, Lake Superior Paper Industries (now the Duluth, Minnesota, mill of NewPage Corp.), planned to build a state-of-the-art paper mill. Because of the complexity of the technology involved, the $400 million construction cost, and the serious impact of any delays in the mill's construction, the company decided to build a three-dimensional room-sized model of the entire building and its contents. Company officials claimed that this one "picture," created at a cost of over $1 million, saved them many times that amount by letting designers and construction personnel see precisely where layout problems would occur before costly conflicts actually arose.

ourselves understood, we clearly must consider the needs of receivers and adapt our use of words to *their* level.

Pictures

A second type of symbol is the picture, which is used to clarify word communication. Organizations make extensive use of pictures, such as blueprints, progress charts, diagrams, causal maps, visual aids in training programs, scale models of products, and similar devices. Pictures can provide powerful visual images, as suggested by the proverb "A picture is worth a thousand words." To be most effective, however, pictures should be combined with well-chosen words and actions to tell a complete story (see the story of the three-dimensional "picture" in "On the Job: Lake Superior Paper Industries").

Action (Nonverbal Communication)

Actions have meaning

A third type of communication symbol is action, also known as **nonverbal communication.** Often people forget that what they do or say is open to interpretation by others. For example, a handshake and a smile have meaning. A raise in pay or being late for an appointment also has meaning.

Two significant points about action are sometimes overlooked. One point is that *failure to act is an important way of communicating.* A manager who fails to praise an employee for a job well done or fails to provide promised resources is sending a message to that person. Since we send messages by both action and inaction, we communicate almost all the time at work, *regardless of our intentions.*

A second point is that *actions speak louder than words,* at least in the long run. Managers who say one thing but do another will soon find that their employees "listen" mostly to what they do. The manager's *behavior* is the stronger social cue. A typical example is an executive who verbally advocates ethical behavior but repeatedly violates the company's own code of conduct. Employees receive mixed signals and may find it convenient to mimic the executive's unethical actions.

Credibility gaps cause problems

When there is a difference between what someone says and does, a **credibility gap** exists. Communication credibility is based on three factors: trustworthiness, expertise, and dynamism.[6] These three factors suggest that managers must act with integrity, speak from a strong base of knowledge, and deliver their messages with confidence, enthusiasm, and passion. Although a manager's credibility can take years to develop, only a few moments are required to destroy the trust that employees have. The following illustration shows how a large credibility gap can result in the loss of confidence in a leader:

> Willie Beacon, the zone manager of a sales office, emphasized the idea that he depended upon his employees to help him do a good job because, as he stated it, "You salespeople are the ones in direct contact with the customer, and you get much valuable information and many useful suggestions." In most of his sales meetings, he said he always welcomed employees' ideas and suggestions. But here is how

he translated his words into action: In those same sales meetings, the schedule was so tight that by the time he finished his pep talk, there was no time for anyone to present problems or ask questions, and he would hardly tolerate any questions or comments during his talk because he claimed that interruptions destroyed its punch.

If a salesperson tried to present a suggestion in Willie's office, Willie usually began with, "Fine, I'm glad you brought in your suggestion." Before long, however, he would direct the conversation to some subject on his mind, or would have to keep an appointment, or would find some other reason for never quite getting to the suggestion. The few suggestions that did get through, he rebuffed with, "Yeah, I thought of that a long time ago, but it won't work." The eventual result was that he received no useful suggestions. His actions spoke louder than his words. His credibility gap was too large for employees to overcome.

Body language provides meaning

An important part of nonverbal communication is **body language,** by which people communicate meaning to others with their bodies in interpersonal interaction. Body language is an important supplement to verbal communication in most parts of the world.

Facial expressions are especially important sources of body language in work situations. Examples are eye contact, eye movement, smiles and frowns, and a furrowed brow. In one instance, a manager frowned when an employee brought a suggestion, and the employee interpreted the frown as a rejection when in fact it was a headache. In another instance, a smile at an inappropriate time was interpreted as a derisive sneer, and an argument erupted. Nonverbal cues can be either inadvertent, as in the preceding examples, or intentional, thus adding complexity to the communication process. Other types of body language are physical touch, hand and hip movements, leaning forward or back, crossing one's arms or legs, and sighing or yawning. Despite the wealth of data available from nonverbal cues, their interpretation is highly subjective and loaded with the potential for error. Caution is in order.

The Impact of Barriers on the Communication Process

We have now reviewed a sampling of the barriers that impede the exchange of communication between two people. Next, it is valuable to examine which of those barriers exert their impact on the actions in the eight-step communication process outlined previously in Figure 3.1. This allows managers, as students of organizational behavior, to direct their attention toward minimizing the effects of specific barriers.

Figure 3.3 suggests that the personal barriers have a pervasive effect on communications. Emotions can affect the development of an idea for presentation, the method and

FIGURE 3.3 Primary Impact of Barriers on the Steps in Communication

	Personal Barriers			Physical Barriers		Semantic Barriers	
Communication Steps	Emotions	Listening	Psychological Distance	Noise	Geographical Distance	Semantics	Symbols
1. Develop	X						
2. Encode						X	X
3. Transmit	X			X	X		
4. Receive		X	X	X	X		
5. Decode	X	X				X	X
6. Accept	X		X			X	
7. Use			X				
8. Feedback			X				

form of its transmission, how it is decoded, and most certainly whether it is accepted. Listening skills (discussed on pages 69–72) have a powerful impact on the effectiveness of a message's receipt and interpretation (decoding). Feelings of psychological distance largely impact the receipt, acceptance, and usage of a message, in addition to the quality of feedback provided to the sender.

Physical barriers such as noise and geographical distance primarily affect the transmission and receipt of messages, whereas semantic issues and various communication symbols most often create problems in the encoding, decoding, and acceptance stages. The overall message for managers is that barriers can—and do—affect the effectiveness of communications at all eight stages. The active participants in a communication exchange—just like two acrobats on a trapeze—dare not let their guards down for even an instant, or the negative consequences can be long-lasting!

DOWNWARD COMMUNICATION

Downward communication in an organization is the flow of information from higher to lower levels of authority. Almost one-half of managerial communications are with subordinates, with the remainder divided among superiors, peers, and external recipients. To communicate downward, some executives rely on colorful booklets, flashy PowerPoint presentations, and elaborately planned employee meetings. These approaches, while attention-getting, often fail to achieve employee understanding—one of the goals of effective communication. The key to better communication lies not just in the use of color, action, and electronic aids but in the presentation of information by more sensitive managers who prepare carefully and convey their messages with candor, energy, personal stories, and warmth. Managers who communicate successfully are sensitive to human needs and open to true dialogue with their employees.

Prerequisites and Problems

Four prerequisites

Part of management's failure has been that it did not prepare for effective communication. It failed to lay a good foundation, so its communication house was built upon sand. A solid foundation has four cornerstones that act as prerequisites for an effective approach. First, managers need to *develop a positive communication attitude.* They must convince themselves that communication is an important part of their jobs, as research on managerial responsibilities convincingly shows. Second, managers must continually work to *get informed.* They need to seek out relevant information of interest to employees, share it, and help employees feel informed. Third, managers need to consciously *plan for communication,* and they must do this at the beginning of a course of action. Finally, managers must *develop trust;* as mentioned earlier, trust between senders and receivers is important in all communication. If subordinates do not trust their superiors, they are not as likely to listen to or believe management's messages.

> Consider the case of two employees from the same firm who were told by their manager not to discuss pay with each other, because the other one might be unhappy to learn of having a lower salary. Later, at a New Year's Eve party, they started talking with each other about their salaries and soon discovered they were earning exactly the same amount. How much will they trust their manager in the future?

Communication Overload

Managers sometimes operate with the philosophy that more communication is better communication. They give employees enormous amounts of information until employees find

An Ethics Question

Your organization just announced that it will be making about a 15 percent cutback in employment to "rightsize" itself for a diminishing market. With 24 people reporting directly to you, this would translate into about 3 or 4 people who will lose their jobs, and you have already submitted a prioritized list of 3, 4, or 5 persons who might be candidates for this reduction in force. However, you were asked to keep the list confidential until upper management finalizes its targets for reduction. In the meantime, one of the five people you identified came to you to inquire about his chances of being retained through the cutback. Question: Is telling him ethical? Why or why not?

they are overwhelmed with data, but their understanding is not improved. What happens is a **communication overload,** in which employees receive more communication inputs than they can process or more than they need. The keys to better communication are timing and quality, not quantity. It is possible to have better understanding with less total communication if it is of high quality and delivered at the appropriate moment.

Quality is preferable to quantity

Acceptance of a Communication

As pointed out earlier, acceptance of a message by the receiver is critical; without acceptance, communication breaks down. Several conditions encourage acceptance of a communication:

- Acknowledged legitimacy of the sender to send a message
- Perceived competence of the sender relative to the issue
- Trust in the sender as a leader and as a person
- Perceived credibility of the message received
- Acceptance of the tasks and goals that the communication is trying to accomplish
- Power of the sender to enforce sanctions (either directly or indirectly) on the receiver

If overload can be prevented and the likelihood of acceptance ensured through the use of these six conditions, then managers can turn their attention toward the satisfaction of four important communication needs of employees.

Communication Needs

Employees at lower levels have at least four critical communication needs—job instruction, performance feedback, news, and social support. Managers think that they understand employees' needs, but often their employees do not think so.[7] This fundamental difference in perception tends to exist at each level in organizations, thereby making communication more difficult. It causes downward communicators to be overconfident and probably not take enough care with their downward messages.

Job Instruction One communication need of employees is proper instruction regarding their work. Managers secure better results if they state their instructions in terms of the objective requirements of the job as well as the opportunities and potential problem areas. The consequences of inadequate job instructions can be disastrous, as illustrated in "On the Job: Diamond Tool."

Performance Feedback Employees also need feedback about their performance. Feedback helps them know what to do and how well they are meeting their own goals. It shows that others are interested in what they are doing. Assuming that performance is satisfactory, feedback enhances employees' self-image and feelings of competence. Generally, **performance feedback** leads to both improved performance and improved attitudes.

Performance is improved by feedback

On the Job: Diamond Tool

A manufacturer of small tools, Diamond Tool, hired a new sales representative, gave him a tour of the plant and a copy of the product catalog, and assigned him to a territory. A few weeks later, the representative jubilantly sent in an order for 100,000 units of a multipurpose tool. Only then did the company realize it had neglected to tell him that that product was never promoted to its customers because the tool was priced well below the company's cost of producing it (in order to match a competitor's price). The result was that the company lost over $10,000 on this one order!

Feedback-seeking behavior

Giving feedback is a challenging task for managers. The process is discussed in depth in Chapter 6. Some dedicated employees even engage in **feedback-seeking behavior,** in which they actively search for information about their prior performance and possible areas of improvement. Feedback-seeking individuals can actively monitor cues regarding their own performance ("This report tells me I'm still 3 percent over my budget") and inquire about progress toward their goals ("How am I doing?"). Employees are more likely to engage in feedback-seeking behavior if they have a strong competence motive, a powerful drive to self-evaluate, if they currently lack feedback from others, and if the results are not expected to threaten their self-esteem.[8] Managers should encourage this behavior and attempt to satisfy employees' needs for performance-related information.

News Downward messages should reach employees as fresh and timely news rather than as a stale confirmation of what already has been learned from other sources. Employees are impatient, and rightfully so, for they cannot act effectively on the basis of old information. Contemporary methods include closed-circuit television, daily recorded voicemail messages that employees can receive by dialing a certain number (even from their homes), electronic mail systems, and Websites (see "On the Job: McDonnell Douglas").

Social Support Another communication need that employees have at work is **social support,** which is the perception that they are cared for, esteemed, and valued. When interpersonal warmth and trust are displayed by managers, there may be positive impacts on psychological and physical health, as well as job satisfaction and performance. Note, though, that whether a manager communicates about task assignments, career subjects, or personal matters; or provides performance feedback; or responds to questions raised, employees report feeling a greater level of social support.[9] Apparently, it is the *presence* (and caring delivery) of communication, not the topic itself, that is most important for satisfying this particular need.

UPWARD COMMUNICATION

If the two-way flow of information is broken by poor **upward communication,** management loses touch with employee needs and lacks sufficient information to make sound decisions. It is, therefore, unable to provide needed task and social support for employees.

Management needs to tune in to employees in the same way a person with a radio tunes in. This process requires initiative, positive action, sensitivity to weak signals, and adaptability to different channels of employee information. It primarily requires an awareness and belief that upward messages are important.

Difficulties

Delay

Several problems plague upward communication, especially in larger, more complex organizations. The first is *delay,* which is the unnecessarily slow movement of information up to higher levels. Indecisive managers hesitate to take a problem upward because doing

On the Job: McDonnell Douglas

Aircraft manufacturer McDonnell Douglas (now merged with Boeing Co.) sharply expanded its news-dissemination program. Staff writers prepared daily, monthly, and quarterly newsletters on a wide range of operating topics (costs, scrap numbers, progress reports, stock price, and problems). These were transmitted electronically to everybody associated with the program—employees, customers, suppliers, and management. Everybody was kept informed, and promptly.[10]

so implies an admission of failure. Therefore, each level delays the communication while trying to decide how to solve the problem (or worse yet, whether to report the problem at all!). The second, and closely intertwined, factor is *filtering.* This partial screening out of information occurs because of the natural tendency for an employee to tell a superior only what the employee thinks the superior wants to hear.

Filtering

Silence

An extreme example of filtering is **organizational silence.** This is the conscious or unconscious withholding of information about potential problems or issues on the part of employees.[11] The result is woefully incomplete information for upper management. Organizational silence is usually caused by two compelling factors—fear of negative repercussions for speaking up (a manager's intolerance of dissent) or an assumption that one's voice would not be heard anyway (sometimes based on valid prior experience).

There may be legitimate reasons for filtering. The total message may be very lengthy, technically overwhelming, or the information may be speculative and require additional confirmation. In some cases, the supervisor may have previously requested the employee to pass along only the highlights of a situation. These explanations indicate that filtering is not necessarily a problem in communications, but it does require careful monitoring.

Need for response

Sometimes, in an effort to avoid filtering, people bypass their superior, which means that they skip one or more steps in the communication hierarchy. On the positive side, this reduces filtering and delays. On the negative side, since it may upset those who are bypassed, employers usually discourage it. Another problem revolves around an employee's legitimate *need for a response.* Since employees initiate upward communication, they are now the senders, and they have strong expectations that feedback will occur (and soon). If management provides a quick response, further upward messages will be encouraged. Conversely, lack of immediate response suppresses future upward communications.

Distortion is disruptive and unethical

A final communication difficulty concerns *distortion.* This is the willful modification of a message intended to achieve one's personal objectives. For example, some employees may exaggerate their achievements, hoping for more recognition or larger salary increases. Others may cover up operating difficulties in their department, hoping to avoid a painful confrontation with their supervisor. Any message distortion robs a manager of accurate information and the capacity to make enlightened decisions. Worse yet, it represents unethical behavior that can destroy trust between two parties. Managers need to recognize the potential for all these upward communication problems and must actively seek to prevent them.

Upward Communication Practices

A starting point for building better upward communications is to establish a general policy stating what kinds of upward messages are desired. This could include areas where higher management is accountable, controversial topics, matters requiring managerial advice, requests for exceptions to corporate policy, or "bottom-up" recommendations for change. In addition to policy statements, various practices are needed to improve upward communications. Counseling sessions, grievance systems, participative management, suggestion

Diversity in Communications

Do men and women use unique patterns of communication? Research on gender-based communication styles has begun to show some fascinating diversity between the two groups. Numerous studies have explored whether men and women use different (learned) communication styles.

In general, men and women display marked diversity in the way in which they communicate at work. Men emphasize power, while women stress rapport; men are more likely than women to claim credit for accomplishments; men tend to downplay their uncertainty rather than admit it; women ask questions to learn more, while men fear that asking questions will make them look ignorant; women make more ritualistic apologies, exchange compliments with each other, invite honest feedback, and soften their criticism with praise; men look for one-up chances, engage in ritualistic arguments, and seek recognition. Overall, men tend to speak more directly, while women often prefer an indirect approach. Question: Do these research-based descriptions accurately describe how you communicate? Why or why not?

Sources: Deborah Tannen, "The Power of Talk: Who Gets Heard and Why," *Harvard Business Review*, September–October 1995, pp. 138–48; Deborah Tannen, *You Just Don't Understand: Women and Men in Conversation* (New York: William Morrow, 1990); and Deborah Tannen, *Talking from 9 to 5* (New York: Avon Books, 1995).

systems, job satisfaction surveys, and other practices are discussed in later chapters. Additional practices discussed at this point are questioning, listening, employee meetings, open-door policies, and participation in social groups.

Questioning Managers can encourage upward communications by asking good questions. This practice shows employees that management takes an interest in their opinions, desires additional information, and values their input. Questions can take several forms, but the most common types are open and closed. **Open questions** introduce a broad topic and give others an opportunity to respond in many ways. "How are things going?" is a classic open question, and the responses received can provide rich clues for the manager to follow up. By contrast, **closed questions** focus on a narrower topic and invite the receiver to provide a specific response. An example is, "What are the cost implications of the proposed early retirement plan?" Both open and closed questions can be useful for initiating upward communications, especially if they invite dialogue and reflective thought. No matter how well questions are asked, however, they are useless unless the questions are accompanied by skillful listening and the responses are probed for their meaning.

Listening **Active listening** is much more than hearing; it requires use of the ears and the mind. Effective listening works on two levels—it helps receivers understand both the factual idea and the emotional message the sender intended. Good listeners not only hear what the person is saying but also learn about the feelings and emotions of that person. Equally important, managers who listen effectively send a key signal that they *care* about employees. Many people are not skilled listeners; 81 percent of the managers in one study reported that they were not satisfied with their own listening skills.[12] However, they can become better through a desire to improve, involvement in training courses, engaging in focused practice, and by having others provide feedback to them. Participants in listening courses are often taught to demonstrate their interest, to avoid daydreaming, to focus on the speaker's objective, to weigh the evidence and rationale provided, to search for examples and clues to meaning, and to use idle time (pauses) to review mentally

On the Job: Haworth Company

The Haworth Company, in Holland, Michigan, uses an employee meeting system called "sensing sessions." These meetings provide opportunities for employees to inform management about what is on their minds. Some questions asked by management are open, used to discover what is going well and what is not and to seek suggestions for improvement. Others are more focused on a specific issue. Led by corporate executives as facilitators, the sensing sessions have been useful in obtaining ideas, as well as building partnerships and encouraging collaboration on improvements within the organization.[13]

what has already been said. Ten proven suggestions for active listening are given in Figure 3.4.

Employee Meetings One useful method of building upward communications is to meet with small groups of employees. In these "town hall" meetings employees are encouraged to talk about job problems, resource needs, and management practices that both help and interfere with job performance. The meetings attempt to probe in some depth the issues that are on the minds of employees. As a consequence (assuming follow-up action is taken), employee attitudes improve and turnover declines (see "On the Job: Haworth Company").

An Open-Door Policy An **open-door policy** is a statement that encourages employees to come to their supervisor or to higher management with any matter that concerns them. Usually, employees are encouraged to see their supervisor first. If their problem is not resolved by the supervisor, then higher management may be approached. The goal is to remove blocks to upward communication. It is a worthy goal, but it is not easy to implement because there often are real or perceived barriers between managers and employees. Although the manager's door is physically open, psychological and social barriers exist that make employees reluctant to enter. Some employees do not want to admit that they lack information or have a problem. Others are afraid they will incur their manager's disfavor if they raise disruptive issues.

FIGURE 3.4
Guidelines for Effective Listening

1. **Stop talking!** You cannot listen if you are talking.
2. **Put the talker at ease.** Welcome the person, express your availability, and make him or her comfortable. Create a permissive atmosphere by establishing rapport.
3. **Show a talker that you want to listen.** Look interested. Establish eye contact and give nonverbal responses. Pay close attention so as to understand; be "in the moment."
4. **Remove distractions.** Don't doodle, tap your fingers, shuffle papers, or answer phone calls.
5. **Empathize with a talker.** Try to see the other person's point of view. Summarize and paraphrase to check your understanding.
6. **Be patient.** Allow plenty of time. Do not interrupt a talker. Wait out the short pauses.
7. **Keep your cool.** Pause and think carefully before you speak or respond.
8. **Avoid being confrontational.** Do not argue, criticize their inputs, or attack the person's self-esteem.
9. **Ask relevant questions.** Probe for underlying sentiments and hidden content.
10. **Stop talking!** This guideline is both first and last, because all others depend on it. You cannot be an effective listener while you are talking. (Listening requires two "ears," one to absorb meaning and one to detect feelings.)

Barriers may limit its use

An "open door" is even more effective when managers walk out through their own doors and interact directly with employees. This reinforces the open-door policy with a powerful social cue. In this way, managers will learn more than they ever would by simply sitting in their offices.

Participation in Social Groups Informal casual recreational events furnish superb opportunities for unplanned upward communication. Information gained on a spontaneous basis reveals true conditions better than most formal communications. Departmental parties, joint attendance at sports events, athletic teams, hobby groups, picnics, and other employer-sponsored activities are all useful. Upward communication is not the primary purpose of these events, but it can be an important by-product of them.

OTHER FORMS OF COMMUNICATION

Not all communication takes place directly down or up the organizational hierarchy, not all is formally prescribed by the firm, and not all of it takes place either at work or through face-to-face interaction. This section provides an overview of lateral communication and the impact of some electronic forms of communication.

Lateral Communication

Cross-communication

Managers engage in a large amount of **lateral communication,** or *cross-communication,* which is communication across chains of command. It is necessary for job coordination with people in other departments. It also is done because people prefer the informality of lateral communication rather than the up-and-down process of the official chain of command. Lateral communication often is the dominant pattern within management.

Boundary spanners

Employees who play a major role in lateral communication are referred to as **boundary spanners.** Boundary-spanning employees have strong communication links within their department, with people in other units, and often with the external community. These connections with other units allow boundary spanners to gather large amounts of information, which they may filter or transfer to others. This gives them a source of status and potential power.

Networks Whereas boundary spanners usually acquire their roles through formal task responsibilities, much other lateral communication takes place in less formal ways. A **network** is a group of people who develop and maintain contact to exchange information informally, usually about a shared interest. An employee who becomes active in such a group is said to be **networking.** Although networks can exist within as well as outside a company, usually they are built around external interests, such as recreation, social clubs, minority status, professional groups, career interests, and trade meetings.

Networking

> Deb Caldwin, an engineer, is in a network of research people who keep in touch at professional meetings and via more informal electronic communications. She is also an excellent golfer and is part of a golf network at a local country club. Therefore, she knows personally the key executives of several local corporations, as well as other influential people in the area. Some of her networks are business-related; some, career-related; and others, purely social.

Networks help broaden the interests of employees, keep them more informed about new technical developments, and make them more visible to others.[14] Networks help employees learn who knows what and even who knows those who know. As a result, an alert networker can gain access to influential people and centers of power by drawing upon common backgrounds, bonds of friendship, complementary organizational roles, or community ties. By obtaining job-related information and developing productive working

FIGURE 3.5
Suggestions for Developing and Using a Personal Network

Sources: Some items adapted from William C. Byham, "Start Networking Right Away (Even If You Hate It)," *Harvard Business Review*, January 2009, p. 22, and Reid Hoffman and Ben Casnocha, "The Real Way to Build a Network," *Fortune*, February 6, 2012, pp. 23–30.

1. Inventory your personal resources so you know what you have to offer others.
2. Develop a clear purpose for establishing or joining a network.
3. Join significant community organizations and contribute to them.
4. Initiate contacts with key people whenever you can find (or create) a valid reason.
5. Share news, information, and ideas with others, thereby creating an (implied) obligation for them to reciprocate.
6. Seek out responsibilities that will bring you into contact with key people.
7. Demonstrate to other networkers that you can be trusted with confidential information.
8. Identify both a narrow-but-deep network (influential connections who are always willing to help) and a wide-but-shallow network (more casual acquaintances who can still occasionally offer useful ideas and assistance).
9. Tap into members of your network for general advice, career contacts, and other useful information.
10. Find various ways to help your network colleagues satisfy their needs.

relationships through effective networks, employees gain valuable skills, enhance their public reputation, acquire greater influence, and can perform their jobs better. Several practical suggestions for developing networks are provided in Figure 3.5.

Social Networking and Electronic Communication

Members of Generation Y—also known as the Millennials, or the Net Generation—include 80 million persons born approximately between 1980 and 2000. As employees they have a profound impact on many organizations, especially through their interest and skills in using a variety of social media and digital technologies. According to researchers, typical Millennials:

- Have a strong desire for work/life balance
- Disdain the importance of face time
- Have a strong sense of entitlement (belief that they deserve a benefit or reward)
- Exhibit an unquenchable thirst for praise
- Want to participate in decision making
- Are reluctant to accept workplace rules and restrictions
- Are socially conscious and environmentally aware
- Wish to be "connected" with many others
- Want to be recognized for results achieved their way
- Are willing to switch jobs (and even careers) frequently[15]

Social networking tools are increasingly popular

Members of the workforce have become "wired" through their widespread participation in the social networking phenomenon. **Social networking** technologies are Internet sites and software programs that allow people to link together into some form of a virtual social community. YouTube, Facebook, and MySpace are accessed by millions of viewers, and used to share personal information profiles and learn about others. The LinkedIn site facilitates networking by connecting people in ever-growing circles of relationships. **Wikis** are Web pages that enable their users to add or modify content; the most visible example of this is **Wikipedia,** which is a collaboratively created and constantly updated collection of 4 million articles in the English language. Although some companies block access to sites like Facebook at work, most just urge employees to use their discretion in how much time they spend on it and what to include in their own pages. Other organizations, mindful of the potential for damage from uncontrolled media, have imposed guidelines that specify what topics are off-limits (e.g., proprietary information, customer data, or corporate strategies), define inappropriate behavior (e.g., cyberbullying) and the consequences for breaking the rules, and inform employees that their behavior will be monitored.[16]

Electronic networks

Electronic Mail **Electronic mail** (e-mail) is a computer-based communication system that allows you to send a message to someone—or to a hundred people—almost instantaneously. It is stored within the computer system until the recipients turn on their networked personal computers, BlackBerries, or iPhones. Then, they can read the message at their convenience and respond in the same manner. Some electronic mail systems can send messages in various modes (such as a letter to one correspondent who does not have a computer), and others can translate the message into a foreign language.

> In surveys of employees, more than 80 percent of users report that the Internet has made them more productive at work. Most users receive more than 20 work-related e-mails every day, and the vast majority respond to each of them within 24 hours. However, many workers believe that e-mail has also lengthened their workday. Clearly, electronic communications has had a profound impact on work lives.

The primary advantages of electronic mail systems are their dramatic speed and convenience; the major disadvantages include the loss of face-to-face contact, the temptation to send flaming (spontaneous, emotion-laden) messages, the risks of using acronyms and emoticons (keyboard versions of various psychological states) that will be misunderstood, and the associated difficulty of accurately conveying and interpreting emotions and subtleties in brief and somewhat sterile messages.

In response to these challenges, organizations have developed communication policies regarding which topics are appropriate for e-mail and which are not (such as performance appraisals or firings), who should be on distribution lists, what language is unacceptable, and even the frequency with which e-mail should be used (versus voice mail or face-to-face meetings). The whole field of e-mail courtesy ("netiquette") has sprung up, with a set of guidelines (see Figure 3.6) emerging to help managers decide how best to proceed via e-mail.[17]

FIGURE 3.6
Sample Guidelines for e-Mail Netiquette

1. Provide your recipient with an informative subject for your message.
2. Indicate the degree of urgency with which you need a response.
3. Limit the use of acronyms and emoticons unless the receiver is thoroughly familiar with them and receptive to them.
4. Be cautious about forwarding messages and replying to them; ensure that the message is going only to the right persons.
5. Don't assume that everyone is equally comfortable with e-mail or checks their messages as frequently as you do.
6. Scan your inbox several times a day to assess which messages have the highest priority and respond to them first. Nevertheless, try to get back to all messages requiring your response within 24 hours.
7. Be brief.
8. Exercise as much care in spelling and punctuation as you would with a printed message; recipients often judge you on the basis of your care and attention to detail.
9. Use great care not to unintentionally hit the "Reply All" icon.

Sources: R. Scott Grabinger, "Tame the Email Beast: A Baker's Dozen," *Performance Management*, vol. 47, no. 4, pp. 5-6; and Mike Rosenwald, "Re: Re: Re: Confidential," *Bloomberg BusinessWeek*, November–26-December. 2, 2012, p. 100.

Features of the Grapevine

Several aspects distinguish the grapevine and help us understand it better. The pattern that grapevine information usually follows is called a **cluster chain,** because each link in the chain tends to inform a cluster of other people instead of only one person. In addition, only a few people are active communicators on the grapevine for any specific unit of information. These people are called **liaison individuals.**

> In one company, when a quality-control problem occurred, 68 percent of the executives knew about it but only 20 percent of them spread the information. In another case, when a manager planned to resign, 81 percent of the executives knew about it but only 11 percent passed the news on to others.

As this example illustrates, the grapevine is often more a product of the situation than it is of the person. This means that *given the proper situation and motivation, anyone would tend to become active on the grapevine.* Some of the factors that encourage people to be active are listed in Figure 3.7.

Contrary to common perceptions, well over three-fourths of grapevine information is accurate. However, the grapevine may also be incomplete; it generally carries the truth but not the whole truth. In addition, the grapevine is fast, flexible, and personal. This speed makes it difficult for management to stop undesirable rumors or to release significant news in time to prevent rumor formation. In conclusion, the evidence shows that *the grapevine is influential, both favorably and unfavorably.*

Rumor

Definition of rumor

The major problem with the grapevine—and the one that gives the grapevine its poor reputation—is **rumor.** Rumor is grapevine information that is communicated without secure standards of evidence being present. It is the unverified and untrue part of the grapevine. It could by chance be correct, but generally it is incorrect; thus it is presumed to be undesirable.

Interest and ambiguity lead to rumor

Rumor is primarily a result of both interest and ambiguity in a situation. If a subject is unimportant or has no interest to a person, then that person has no cause to pass along a rumor about it. Similarly, if there is no ambiguity in a situation, a person has no cause to spread rumor because the correct facts are known. Two factors—*interest and ambiguity*—normally must be present both to begin and to maintain a rumor.

Details are lost

Since rumor largely depends on ambiguity and the interest that each person has, it tends to change (be filtered) as it passes from person to person. Generally, people choose details in the rumor to fit their own interest and view of the world. People also add new details, often making the story worse, in order to include their own strong feelings, judgment, and reasoning; this process is called **elaborating.**

Types of Rumors Logic suggests that *there are different kinds of rumors.* Some are historical and explanatory; they attempt to make meaning out of incomplete prior events. Others are more spontaneous and action-oriented; they arise without much forethought and

FIGURE 3.7
Factors That Encourage Grapevine Activity

- Work that allows conversation
- A job that provides information desired by others
- Personality of communicator
- Excitement and insecurity
- Involvement of friends and associates
- Recent information
- Procedure that brings people into contact

FIGURE 3.8
Guidelines for Control of Rumor

- Remove its causes in order to prevent it.
- Apply efforts primarily to serious rumors.
- Refute rumors with facts.
- Deal with rumors as soon as possible.
- Emphasize the face-to-face supply of facts, confirmed in writing if necessary.
- Provide facts from reliable sources.
- Refrain from repeating rumor while refuting it.
- Encourage assistance of informal and union leaders if they are cooperative.
- Listen to all rumors in order to understand what they may mean.

represent attempts to change a current situation. Occasionally, rumors are negative, such as those that drive a wedge between people or groups, destroy loyalties, and perpetuate hostilities. They may also be positive, as when employees speculate about the beneficial effects of a new product just released. The existence of a variety of rumor types reminds managers that rumors should not be universally condemned even though they sometimes create problems.

Control of Rumor Since rumor generally is incorrect, a major outbreak of it can be a devastating epidemic that sweeps through an organization as fast as a summer tornado—and usually with as much damage. Rumor should be dealt with firmly and consistently, but how and what to attack must be known. To strike at the whole grapevine merely because it happens to be the agent that carried the rumor is a serious mistake; that approach would be as unwise as throwing away a computer's keyboard because of a few misspelled words. Several ways to control rumor are summarized in Figure 3.8. The best approach is to prevent it by removing its causes. When rumors do circulate, however, a face-to-face supply of facts—if provided early—helps answer the ambiguities in each person's mind.

Use a preventive approach to rumors

Summary

Communication is the transfer of information and understanding from one person to another person. Organizations need effective communication in downward, upward, and lateral directions. The two-way communication process consists of these eight steps: develop an idea, encode, transmit, receive, decode, accept, use, and provide feedback. To overcome personal, physical, and semantic barriers, managers must pay close attention to communication symbols, such as words, pictures, and nonverbal actions. Effective communication requires the study and use of semantics—the science of meaning—to encourage understanding.

Managers play a key role in downward and upward communication, sometimes even delaying or filtering the flow of information. Many tools are available for their use, such as providing performance feedback and social support or establishing open-door policies and holding employee meetings. Listening, however, remains one of the most powerful tools. Networks have become popular ways for employees to find out what is going on around them, while the rapid development and use of computers and other tools have made possible electronic mail systems, telecommuting, and virtual offices for some employees.

Informal communication systems, called the grapevine, develop in the form of a cluster chain. Overall, the grapevine is accurate, fast, and influential, but sometimes details are omitted and rarely is the whole story communicated. Rumor is grapevine information communicated without secure standards of evidence. It occurs when there is ambiguity and interest in information. Managers can have some influence over the grapevine, and their basic objective is to integrate interests of the formal and informal communication systems so the two systems can work together better.

Advice to Future Managers

1. Think of communication as much more than sending a message; you also need to *anticipate the recipient's reaction and ensure it matches your intentions.*
2. Be alert to some of the many detrimental behavioral considerations in communication (e.g., polarized positions, defensiveness, face-saving) and *work to avoid these errors in yourself and prevent them in others.*
3. *Sharpen your written presentation skills,* whether it be in formal reports or informal e-mail messages. Challenge yourself to learn more about good writing by paying attention to good reading.
4. Think of ways in which you can *practice social support* for others, convincing them through every communication that they are valued individuals.
5. Whatever your gender is, work to *minimize your typical negative tendencies as you communicate* and build upon your positive ones.
6. *Obtain feedback from others on what it would take to make you into a world-class listener.* Afterward, follow their advice, capitalizing on every significant human moment you can.
7. Note the importance of context on your communications and *frame your messages in ways that support your intentions.*
8. Don't be a slave to electronic communications; *use e-mail as a tool for rapid and concise messages* but supplement it with face-to-face communications where you need human impact.
9. Recognize that communications patterns differ in other cultures, and *adapt your communication approach to the styles and preferences of people from different cultural backgrounds.*
10. Learn to recognize that organizational silence is a powerful form of communication and *find ways to solicit and encourage feedback from others.*

Speaking OB: Terms and Concepts for Review

Active listening, *69*
Blogs, *74*
Body language, *64*
Boundary spanners, *71*
Closed questions, *69*
Cluster chain, *76*
Cognitive dissonance, *58*
Communication overload, *66*
Communication, *54*
Credibility gap, *63*
Defensive reasoning, *58*
Downward communication, *65*
Elaborating, *76*
Electronic grapevine, *75*
Electronic mail, *73*
Executive summary, *55*
Face-saving, *59*
Feedback-seeking behavior, *67*
Framing, *56*
Grapevine, *75*
Inference, *61*
Jargon, *61*
Lateral communication, *71*
Liaison individuals, *76*
Network, *71*
Networking, *71*
Noise, *59*
Nonverbal communication, *63*
Open questions, *69*
Open-door policy, *70*
Organizational silence, *68*
Performance feedback, *66*
Personal barriers, *59*
Physical barriers, *60*
Polarized, *58*
Proxemics, *60*
Psychological distance, *60*
Readability, *62*
Rumor, *76*
Self-concept, *59*
Semantic barriers, *61*
Semantics, *61*
Social cues, *62*
Social networking, *72*
Social support, *67*
Telecommuting, *74*
Transparency, *55*
Twittering, *74*
The Two-way communication process, *55*
Upward communication, *67*
Virtual offices, *75*
Voice, *59*
Wikipedia, *72*
Wikis, *72*

Discussion Questions

1. Think of a job you have had and a situation in which the communication failed or was ineffective. Discuss how the communication process applied in that situation and where (during which of the eight steps) the breakdown occurred.

2. Discuss the barriers to communication that exist when you discuss a subject with your instructor in the classroom.
3. Select a situation in which you made a wrong inference. Analyze how the misinterpretation was made, and discuss how you might avoid similar misinterpretations in the future. How important is feedback as an aid to avoiding inference problems?
4. Observe your own behavior, and discuss what nonverbal communication habits you typically use. What do you *intend* as the message of each of them? Do you have some behaviors that may mislead receivers?
5. Visit an instructor's office, and record your feelings of relative comfort there. What physical elements in the office contributed to your reaction? Discuss the instructor's apparent use of space (proxemics).
6. Examine the guidelines for effective listening in Figure 3.4. Which ones do you practice best? Which ones could you improve upon? Create a plan for improving your listening skills, and solicit feedback from a friend in three months to monitor your improvement.
7. Think of a part-time or full-time job you have had.
   a. Discuss any communication overload you experienced.
   b. Discuss how well management handled downward communication to you.
   c. Explain any upward communication difficulties you had and what you did to try to overcome them.
   d. Did you engage in feedback-seeking behavior? Describe what you did, or explain why you did not.
8. What social networks do you belong to? Explain how you became a part of them and what they have done for you. What are your future networking plans, both Internet-based and personal?
9. Assess electronic mail in the context of this chapter. How does it fit with the eight steps of the communication process? What barriers are most likely to arise when it is used? How can they be overcome, or at least minimized?
10. Select a grapevine story you heard, and discuss how it was communicated to you and how accurate it was.

Assess Your Own Skills

How well do you exhibit good communication skills?

Read the following statements carefully. Circle the number on the response scale that most closely reflects the degree to which each statement accurately describes you. Add up your total points and prepare a brief action plan for self-improvement. Be ready to report your score for tabulation across the entire group.

	Good description									Poor description
1. I would be a strong practitioner of open communications and open-book management.	10	9	8	7	6	5	4	3	2	1
2. I am conscious of the need to pay attention to all eight steps in the communication process.	10	9	8	7	6	5	4	3	2	1

3. I am aware of my tendencies to engage in defensive reasoning and face-saving.	10	9	8	7	6	5	4	3	2	1
4. I understand which barriers affect each stage of the communication process.	10	9	8	7	6	5	4	3	2	1
5. I can list several guidelines for creating more readable writing.	10	9	8	7	6	5	4	3	2	1
6. I consciously seek to manage messages sent by my body language.	10	9	8	7	6	5	4	3	2	1
7. When it is important to achieve receiver acceptance of a message, I know which conditions to create for that purpose.	10	9	8	7	6	5	4	3	2	1
8. I can point out three substantial ways in which males and females differ in their communication patterns.	10	9	8	7	6	5	4	3	2	1
9. I regularly exhibit many of the classic guidelines for effective listening.	10	9	8	7	6	5	4	3	2	1
10. I maintain—and use—an active network of personal contacts for mutual benefit.	10	9	8	7	6	5	4	3	2	1

Scoring and Interpretation

Add up your total points for the 10 questions. Record that number here, and report it when it is requested. Finally, insert your total score into the "Assess and Improve Your Own Organizational Behavior Skills" chart in Appendix A.

- If you scored between 81 and 100 points, you appear to have a solid capability for demonstrating good communication skills.
- If you scored between 61 and 80 points, you should take a close look at the items with lower self-assessment scores and explore ways to improve those items.
- If you scored under 60 points, you should be aware that a weaker skill level regarding several items could be detrimental to your future success as a manager. We encourage you to review the entire chapter and watch for relevant material in subsequent chapters and other sources.

Identify your three lowest scores, and write the question numbers here: _____, _____, _____. Write a brief paragraph, detailing to yourself an action plan for how you might sharpen each of these skills.

Incident

A Breakdown in Communications

Linda Barry, a single mother with three children, was hired as an order-entry clerk for a trucking firm. Her first two weeks on the job were spent in a special class from 8 A.M. to 4 P.M., where she learned how to sort, code, and enter the orders on the computer.

An instructor worked with her constantly at first, and then less frequently as she gained skill and confidence. Linda was happy to have the job and enjoyed her work schedule. When the training was completed, she was told to report to the order-entry department the following Monday.

When she was first employed, either Linda failed to read and understand the printed information about her regular work schedule or perhaps the recruiter forgot to tell her she was to fill a spot in a special shift that worked from 4 A.M. until noon. In any case, Linda failed to report to work on the early schedule on the first day of regular work. When she did arrive at 8 A.M., her supervisor criticized her for lack of responsibility. Barry responded by saying she could not work the early shift because she had to prepare her children for school, and she threatened to resign if she could not work on the later shift. Because of a heavy workload and a difficult labor market, the supervisor needed Linda to do the job, yet had no room for her in the 8 A.M. to 4 P.M. shift.

Questions

1. Analyze the communication blockages in this case. Discuss ideas such as upward and downward communication, listening, realistic job previews, feedback, and inference.
2. Explain how you would handle the employment situation at the end of the case. What ideas from the chapter could be applied to help resolve this problem?

Experiential Exercise

Communication Style

Read the following three paragraphs, and then rank them (1 highest to 3 lowest) according to the degree to which they describe your communication style. Be sure to use all three numbers (1, 2, and 3), where 1 is most descriptive and 3 is least descriptive.

_____ A. I like to *see* an idea in the form of charts, diagrams, maps, figures, and models; I prefer to receive written communications over oral; I like concrete examples and specific directions; I tend to give oral feedback ("I see what you're driving at").

_____ B. I like to *hear* ideas from others, and then I enjoy discussing and debating them; I may repeat others' ideas in order to cement them in my mind; I can be distracted by excess background noise; I tend to give oral clues to others ("I hear what you're saying").

_____ C. I like to *do* something; that is the way I learn best. I thrive on examples and am generally quite active as a hands-on person; I tend to give oral clues in a physical way ("I need to get a handle on this before I can decide").

Now form into groups of three persons, and engage in a discussion of some stimulating issue of concern to the three of you. After 5–10 minutes, assess the other two persons in terms of whether they are more likely to describe themselves as an A, B, or C in the preceding list. Then, compare notes with each other to see how accurate you are at perceiving the self-assessed communication style of others.

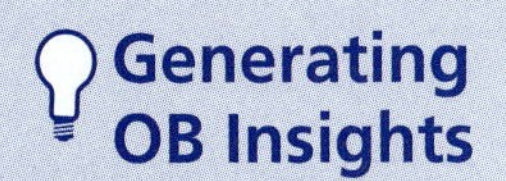

Generating OB Insights

An *insight* is a new and clear perception of a phenomenon, or an acquired ability to "see" clearly something you were unaware of previously. It is sometimes simply referred to as an "ah-ha! moment," in which you have a minirevelation or reach a straightforward conclusion about a topic or issue.

Insights need not necessarily be dramatic, for what is an insight to one person may be less important to another. The critical feature of insights is that they are relevant and memorable for *you;* they should represent new knowledge, new frameworks, or new ways of viewing things that you want to retain and remember over time.

Insights, then, are different from the information you find in the "Advice for Future Managers" boxes within the text. That advice is prescriptive and action-oriented; it indicates a recommended course of action.

A useful way to think of OB insights is to assume you are the only person who has read the current chapter. You have been given the assignment to highlight, in your own words, the major concepts (but not just summarize the whole chapter) that might stand out for a naive audience who has never heard of the topic before. *What 10 insights would you share with them?*

(Example) *Many employees have a strong need for social support, which can be satisfied through communication that demonstrates they are valued persons.*

1. ______________________________

2. ______________________________

3. ______________________________

4. ______________________________

5. ______________________________

6. ______________________________

7. ______________________________

8. ______________________________

9. ______________________________

10. ______________________________

Nurturing Your Critical Thinking and Reflective Skills

Take a few minutes to review the discussion in the Roadmap for Readers of critical thinking and reflection. Remind yourself that if you can hone these abilities now, you will have a substantial competitive advantage when you apply for jobs and are asked what unique skills you can bring to the position and the organization.

Critical Thinking

Think back on the material you read in this chapter. What are three unique and challenging *critical questions* you would like to raise about this material? (These might identify something controversial about which you have doubts, they may imply that you suspect that a theory or model has weaknesses, they could examine the legitimacy of apparent causal relationships, or they might assess the probable value of a suggested practice.) Be prepared to share these questions with class members or your instructor.

1. ____
____
2. ____
____
3. ____
____

Reflection

This process often involves answering the parallel questions of "What do you *think* about the material you have read?" and "How do you *feel* about that material?" Therefore, express your *personal thoughts and feelings* (reactions) to any of the ideas or topics found in this chapter, and be prepared to share these reflections with class members or your instructor.

1. ____
____
2. ____
____
3. ____
____

Chapter Four

Social Systems and Organizational Culture

If corporate stewards tend the culture well, they can count on an engaged and committed workforce for many years to come. Yet, many employers haven't clearly articulated their cultural values.

Ronald J. Alsop[1]

An ethical corporate culture not only helps avoid major illegal or unethical corporate scandals but also leads to more appropriate ethical behavior at all firm levels.

Mark S. Schwartz[2]

CHAPTER OBJECTIVES

AFTER READING THIS CHAPTER, YOU SHOULD UNDERSTAND

4-1 The Operation of a Social System
4-2 The Psychological Contract
4-3 Social Cultures and Their Impact
4-4 The Value of Cultural Diversity
4-5 Role and Role Conflict in Organizations
4-6 Status and Status Symbols
4-7 Organizational Culture and Its Effects
4-8 Fun Workplaces

Facebook Page 

Student B: Say, how are things going in your OB class?

Student A: Fab. I was even able to put my brain in neutral for a while this week, as I was reading some stuff in Chapter 4 about social culture, roles, and status. It was pretty much a review from my Sociology class that I took as a freshman, and that's OK.

Student B: Was there anything new at all?

Student A: You bet. I'd never heard about "losing face," psychological contracts, or reverse mentoring before.

Student C: Sounds like the whole chapter was on Social Systems. Was that it?

Student A: Not at all. There was a big section on Organizational Cultures—their characteristics, measurement, and how they are communicated to employees.

Student D: I give up; what is an organizational culture?

Student A: It's basically a set of shared assumptions, beliefs, values, and norms that powerfully affect employee behaviors.

Student B: Did you learn anything else?

Student A: I know one thing for sure. When I graduate I intend to work hard, but I also want to be in a fun work environment. There are some really upbeat employers out there!

Employees at Herman Miller, Inc., a large office furniture manufacturer, work very hard to create well-designed, top-quality products, such as desk consoles, cabinets, and chairs. Although the company's innovative products are well known throughout the industrial design world, Herman Miller, Inc., is even more widely recognized for its distinctive organizational culture.

Prospective employees are closely examined for their overall character and their ability to get along with people. Employees are organized into work teams, where leaders and members evaluate each other twice each year. Employees can qualify to receive quarterly bonuses, based on cost-saving suggestions and other contributions.

But the primary key to the company's culture resides in a "covenant" that is established between top management and all employees. In this covenant, the company asserts that it will attempt to "share values, ideals, goals, respect for each person, [and] the process of our work together." As a result, the Herman Miller company has achieved significant success.

Companies like Google, Boston Consulting Group, SAS Institute, Wegmans Food Markets, Edward Jones, and NetApp are often recognized for being some of the best companies to work for. The reasons vary, but companies like these are first screened for management's credibility, pay and benefits, internal communications, diversity efforts, and job satisfaction. In addition, they are often cited for their employee-friendly programs such as free snacks, job sharing, on-site childcare and fitness centers, organic cafeteria food, foosball game rooms, talent shows, and pet-friendly policies.[3] The organizational cultures at these firms are well-established, and often reflect the beliefs and values of the companies' founders as well as those of the current staff. Moreover, social systems have a profound effect on the ways employees work together. Cultures provide both direct and indirect cues telling workers how to succeed. Direct cues include orientation training, policy statements,

Engaging Your Brain

1. How strong is your *work ethic* (the belief that work is good, important, necessary, and satisfying)? Rate yourself on a scale from 1 (Very Low) to 10 (Very High). Now, using the same response scale, rate the typical work ethic of your peers. Discuss the two scores, and the implications of them for success and satisfaction.
2. Think of a person who has played a *mentoring* role in your life (i.e., sharing valuable advice on how to succeed). What behaviors did your mentor engage in that were helpful to you?
3. "All work and no play makes Jack (or Jill) a dull person," according to an old adage. Is it possible for managers to allow (and even encourage) employees to have fun at work and still be productive? What type of work culture would *you* strive to create if you were a manager?

and advice from supervisors and peers. Indirect cues are more subtle, including inferences made from promotions and apparent patterns of acceptable dress.

This chapter introduces major ideas about social systems, such as social equilibrium, the effects of system changes, psychological contracts, cultural diversity, and the impact of role and status. We also examine the nature and effects of both societal culture (existing at a national level) and organizational culture (existing within a firm). Finally, the roles and effects of fun at work are explored.

UNDERSTANDING A SOCIAL SYSTEM

A **social system** is a complex set of human relationships interacting in many ways. Possible interactions are as limitless as the stars in the universe. Each small group is a subsystem within larger groups that are subsystems of even larger groups, and so on, until all the world's population is included. Within a single organization, the social system includes all the people in it and their relationships to one another and to the outside world.

Two points stand out in the complex interactions among people in a social system. First, the behavior of any one member can have an impact, directly or indirectly, on the behavior of any other. Although these impacts may be large or small, *all parts of the system are mutually interdependent.* Simply stated, a change in one part of a system affects all other parts, even though its impact may be slight.

A second important point revolves around a system's boundaries. *Any social system engages in exchanges with its environment,* receiving input from it and providing output to it (which then becomes input for its adjacent systems). Social systems are, therefore, **open systems** that interact with their surroundings. Consequently, members of a system should be aware of the nature of their environments and their impact on other members both within and outside their own social system. This social system awareness is increasingly important in the twenty-first century. Global trade and international marketplaces for a firm's products and services vastly expand the need for organizations and their employees to anticipate and react to changes in their competitive environments.

Open systems

Social Equilibrium

A system is said to be in **social equilibrium** when its interdependent parts are in dynamic working balance. Equilibrium is a dynamic concept, not a static one. Despite constant change and movement in every organization, the system's working balance

On the Job: Ford Motor Company

American automobile manufacturers have faced a significant challenge in responding to the design, quality, and cost advantages of international automakers such as Toyota, Nissan, Honda, Subaru, and Mazda. In particular, the U.S. companies found it took them much longer to bring a new car to market (total time from its conception to early production). One of the many reasons offered is the internal power struggle among seemingly competing units of an auto firm, such as product design, factory engineering, and sales and marketing. An unfortunate, and unproductive, disequilibrium sometimes exists.

To combat this problem, Ford Motor Company creates cross-functional teams of line managers charged with the task of speeding product development. These teams are housed in the same work area, which makes communication much easier. They also share a common goal—reduction of product development costs by 20 percent. The CEO (Alan Mulally) also holds weekly meetings of division chiefs to discuss problems and identify trouble spots. In this way, Ford maintains a more productive equilibrium within its system and keeps the functional subgroups working together.[4]

can still be retained over time. The system is like a sea: In continuous motion and even suffering substantial disruption from storms, over time the sea's basic character changes very little.

When minor changes occur in a social system, they are soon absorbed by adjustments within the system and equilibrium is regained. On the other hand, a single significant change (a shock, such as the abrupt resignation or sudden death of a key executive) or a series of smaller but rapid changes may throw an organization out of balance, seriously reducing its forward progress until it can reach a new equilibrium. In a sense, when it is in disequilibrium, some of its parts are working against one another instead of in harmony. The Ford Motor Company (see "On the Job") provides a vivid example of both disequilibrium and equilibrium.

Functional and Dysfunctional Effects

Effects of change

A change has a **functional effect** when it is favorable for the system. When an action or a change creates unfavorable effects, such as a decline in productivity, for the system it has a **dysfunctional effect.** A major management task is to appraise both actual and proposed changes in the social system to determine their possible functional or dysfunctional effects, so that appropriate responses can be anticipated and made. Managers also need to predict both short-term and long-term effects, measure "hard" (e.g., productivity) and "soft" (e.g., satisfaction and commitment) criteria, and consider the probable effects on various stakeholder groups, such as employees, customers, and stockholders. Assessing the overall functionality of a particular managerial action is clearly a complex process.

Employees can also have functional or dysfunctional effects on the organization. They can be creative, productive, and enthusiastic and actively seek to improve the quality of the organization's product or service. On the other hand, they can be tardy, absent frequently, unwilling to use their talents, and resistant to organizational changes. For employees to exhibit functional behaviors, they need to receive clear expectations and promises of reward. Furthermore, in exchange, the organization needs to receive a commitment from the employees.

Psychological and Economic Contracts

When employees join an organization, they make an unwritten **psychological contract** with it, although often they are not conscious of doing so. As shown in Figure 4.1, this contract is in addition to the economic contract where time, talent, and energy are exchanged for wages, hours, and reasonable working conditions. The psychological contract defines the conditions of each employee's psychological involvement—both contributions and

FIGURE 4.1 **The Results of the Psychological Contract and the Economic Contract**

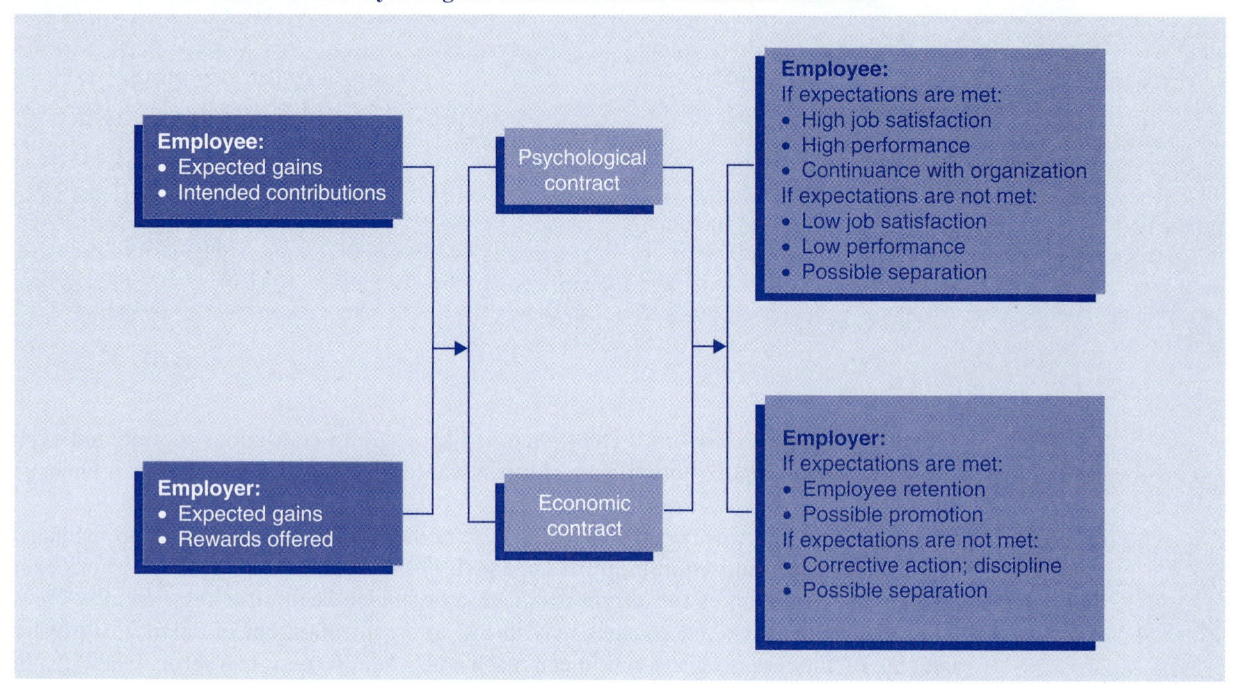

expectations—with the social system. Employees agree to give a certain amount of loyalty, creativity, and extra effort, but in return they expect more than economic rewards from the system. They seek job security, fair treatment (human dignity), rewarding relationships with co-workers, and organizational support in fulfilling their career development expectations.

If the organization honors only the economic contract and not the psychological contract, employees tend to have lower satisfaction because not all their expectations are being met. They may also withhold some of their work-related contributions. On the other hand, if both their psychological and economic expectations are met, they tend to experience satisfaction, stay with the organization, and perform well. A desirable sense of mutuality has been reached.

The reciprocal obligations regarding the relationship between an employee and the organization can be violated either through an inability to fulfill them or by one party purposefully reneging on a promise. Research shows that when this happens, employees experience feelings of anger and betrayal. To prevent breakdowns of the psychological contract, employers are urged to:

Guidelines

- Help employees clarify their expectations and perceptions
- Initiate explicit discussions of mutual obligations
- Exercise caution when conveying promises
- Provide candid explanations for broken promises
- Alert employees to the realistic prospects of reneging (e.g., when a business downturn forces an employer to withdraw previous commitments).[5]

As indicated in Figure 4.1, management responds in a similar way to the economic and psychological contracts that it sees. It expects responses such as high performance, continuous quality improvements, commitment to the organization, and friendly service to its customers. When these results occur, an employee is retained and may earn a bonus or promotion. However, if cooperation and performance do not meet expectations, corrective action and even termination may occur.

Exchange theory

The psychological contract builds upon the concept of **exchange theory.** This theory simply suggests that whenever a continuing relationship exists between two parties, each person regularly examines the rewards and costs of that interaction. In order to remain positively attracted to the relationship, *both* parties must believe that a net positive ratio (rewards to costs) exists from their perspective. Consequently, the psychological contract is continually examined and often revised as new needs emerge and new rewards become available.

SOCIAL CULTURE

Whenever people act in accordance with the expectations of others, their behavior is social, as in the case of an employee named Maria. Like all other workers, Maria grows to be an adult in a **social culture,** which is her environment of human-created beliefs, customs, knowledge, and practices. Culture is the conventional behavior of her society, and it influences all her actions even though it seldom enters her conscious thoughts. Maria drives to work on the right or left side of the road, depending on the culture of her society, but she seldom consciously stops to think of this. Similarly, the car she drives, the drama she attends, the type of food she eats, and the organization that employs her are evidence of her social culture.

Social cultures are often portrayed as consistent within a nation, thereby producing a national culture. At the simplest level, national cultures can be compared on the basis of how their members relate to each other, accomplish work, and respond to change. However, distinctive social cultures can exist *within* a nation as well, as seen in the tragic disputes between people of various ancestries and beliefs within the former country of Yugoslavia, the former U.S.S.R., Syria, and Iraq. Social cultures can have dramatic effects on behavior at work, as we illustrate in Chapter 16. Some of the ways in which cultures differ include patterns of decision making, respect for authority, treatment of females, and accepted leadership styles. Knowledge of social cultures is especially important because *managers need to understand, appreciate, and respond to the backgrounds and beliefs of all members of their work unit.*

People learn to depend on their culture. It gives them stability and security, because they can understand what is happening in their cultural community and know how to respond while in it. However, this one-culture dependency may also place intellectual blinders on employees, preventing them from gaining the benefits of exposure to people from other cultural backgrounds. Cultural dependency is further compounded under conditions involving the integration of two or more cultures into the workplace. Employees need to learn to adapt to others in order to capitalize on the distinctive backgrounds, traits, and opportunities they present, while avoiding possible negative consequences.

Cultural Diversity

Employees in almost any organization are divided into subgroups of various kinds. Formation of groups is determined by two broad sets of conditions. First, *job-related* (organizationally created) differences and similarities, such as type of work, rank in the organization, and physical proximity to one another, sometimes cause people to align themselves into groups. However, a second set of *non-job-related* conditions (those related to culture, ethnicity, socioeconomics, sex, and race) arise primarily from an individual's personal background; these conditions are highly important for legal, moral, and economic reasons. In particular, the U.S. workforce has rapidly become much more diverse, with females, African Americans, Hispanics, and Asian immigrants bringing their talents to employers in record numbers. This **cultural diversity,** or rich variety of differences among people at work, raises the issue of fair treatment for workers who are not in positions of authority.

Discrimination and prejudice

Problems may persist because of a key difference in this context between **discrimination** and **prejudice.** *Discrimination is generally exhibited as an action, whereas prejudice is an attitude.* Either may exist without the other. The law focuses on an employer's actions, not feelings. If actions lead to what is legally determined to be discriminatory results, such actions are unlawful regardless of the employer's alleged good intentions.

A promising approach to overcoming discriminatory practices actually attempts to change the underlying attitudes, values, and beliefs. Programs aimed at managing and **valuing diversity** build from a key premise: Prejudicial stereotypes develop from unfounded assumptions about others and from their overlooked qualities. *Differences need to be recognized, acknowledged, appreciated, and used to collective advantage.* The workforce of the future (whether in the United States, Europe, or elsewhere) will contain a rich blend of people representing diverse cultural and social conditions. *All* participants—males and females, members of differing racial groups, people of all ages, sexual orientation (e.g., lesbian, gay, bisexual, or transgender—LGBTs), single parents, dual-career couples—will need to explore their differences, learn from others around them, respect the value that others contribute, and use that information to build a stronger organization. This requires *inclusion* (an active desire to use diverse talents and strengths) and *cultural competency* (the skill to do so). Unfortunately, although the vast majority of Fortune 500 firms have protective policies addressing sexual orientation, only half of LGBT's feel comfortable expressing their orientation at work.[6]

Changing one's own, or another employee's, attitude is seldom easy, yet people and organizations face constant political, economic, social, and technical pressures to change. More and more employees will encounter both subtle and substantial cultural differences among their work colleagues as the workforce becomes more diverse. Recognition of these changes provides a powerful cultural force to which employers must adapt. If they actively manage diversity, the likelihood they will gain a competitive advantage is high—their workforce quality will be enriched, market sensitivity will increase, public image will improve, complaints and litigation will decrease, and both individual and group performance will improve.[7]

Social Culture Values

Hard work is good, important, and satisfying

The Work Ethic For many years, the culture of much of the Western world has emphasized work as a desirable and fulfilling activity. This attitude is also strong in parts of Asia, such as Japan. The result of this cultural emphasis is a **work ethic** for many people, meaning they view work as very important , morally correct, and as a desirable goal in life. They tend to like work and derive satisfaction from it (even apart from the monetary rewards associated with it). They usually have a stronger commitment to the organization and its goals than do other employees, and are more diligent in carrying out their responsibilities. These characteristics of the work ethic make it highly appealing to employers and a valuable path to achievement for many employees. (Novelist Stephen King once noted that "What separates the talented individual from the successful one is a lot of hard work").

An Ethics Question

Many entrepreneurs have a strongly developed work ethic. They also believe that their *employees* should demonstrate a strong commitment to work and should reflect this commitment in their customer service orientation, attendance and tardiness records, concern for quality, willingness to work beyond normal hours, and overall productivity. But some employees brush aside the argument that "work is a fulfilling activity" and ask instead, "What's in it for me?" The key issue boils down to the debatable right of an employer to impose the work ethic and its expectations on employees. A classic example is the right of an auto manufacturer to demand that an employee work overtime.

Question: What do *you* think is the ethical thing for an employer to do regarding the work ethic?

In spite of its prevalence, the work ethic is a subject of continuing reflection, discussion, and controversy. Is it healthy? Is it declining? Is it a dead issue? The available research indicates that two conclusions can be safely reached. First, *the proportion of employees with a strong work ethic varies sharply among sample groups.* Differences depend on factors such as personal background, type of work performed, and geographical location. The range is quite broad, with the proportion of employees in different jobs who report that work is a central life interest varying between 15 to 85 percent.

Group differences

A second conclusion is that *the general level of the work ethic has declined gradually over many decades.* The decline is most evident in the different attitudes between younger (i.e, Generation Y) and older workers. Not only are younger employees not as supportive of the work ethic, but the level of support that young people once exhibited has dropped substantially. This decline carries serious implications for industrial productivity, especially as international competition intensifies.

Gradual decline

Why has the work ethic declined? Dramatic social changes have brought about the work ethic's deterioration. Competing social values have emerged, such as a *leisure ethic* (a high priority placed on personal gratification), *desire for community and connectedness* (an emphasis on close personal relationships), and *entitlement* (a belief that people should receive societal benefits without having to work). See "An Ethics Question." In addition, changes in social policy and tax laws have reduced incentives to work and occasionally even penalized hard work and success (in the minds of some workers, at least). These factors all represent additional illustrations of complex social relationships in action, and they show how an employee's work ethic is contingent on factors in the larger social system. In the twenty-first century, managers cannot depend on the work ethic alone to drive employees to be productive.

Social Responsibility Every action that organizations take involves costs as well as benefits. In recent years, there has been a strong social drive to improve the cost-benefit relationship to make it possible for society to gain benefits from organizations and for the benefits to be fairly distributed. **Social responsibility** is the recognition that organizations have significant influence on the nation's social system and that this influence must be properly considered and balanced in all organizational actions.

The presence of strong social values such as social responsibility has a powerful impact on organizations and their actions. It leads them to take a broader view of their role within a social system and accept their interdependence with it (see "On the Job: Wipro Limited").

On the Job: Wipro Limited

Organizations are increasingly concerned about social responsibility, and many of them are publicly judged on their overall performance. India-based Wipro Limited uses two fundamental beliefs to guide its engagement with society: (1) Wipro is a socioeconomic citizen and (2) "if you can do good, you must." These beliefs have led to two initiatives, Wipro Cares (to support employees who contribute to society) and Wipro Applying Thought in Schools (to encourage and aid students to develop into critical, creative, and caring citizens). Wipro provides a clear illustration of the importance of accepting a firm's social responsibility to its neighbors, constituents, and society.[8]

ROLE

Expected actions

A **role** is the pattern of actions expected of a person in activities involving others. Role reflects a person's position in the social system, with its accompanying rights and obligations, power and responsibility. In order to be able to interact with one another, people need some way of anticipating others' behavior. Role performs this function in the social system.

A person has roles both on the job and away from it, as shown in Figure 4.2. One person performs the occupational role of worker, the family role of parent, the social role of club president, and many others. In those various roles, a person is both buyer and seller, supervisor and subordinate, and giver and seeker of advice. Each role calls for different types of behavior. Within the work environment alone, a worker may have more than one role, such as a worker in group A, a subordinate to supervisor B, a machinist, a member of a union, and a representative on the safety committee.

FIGURE 4.2
Each Employee Performs Many Roles

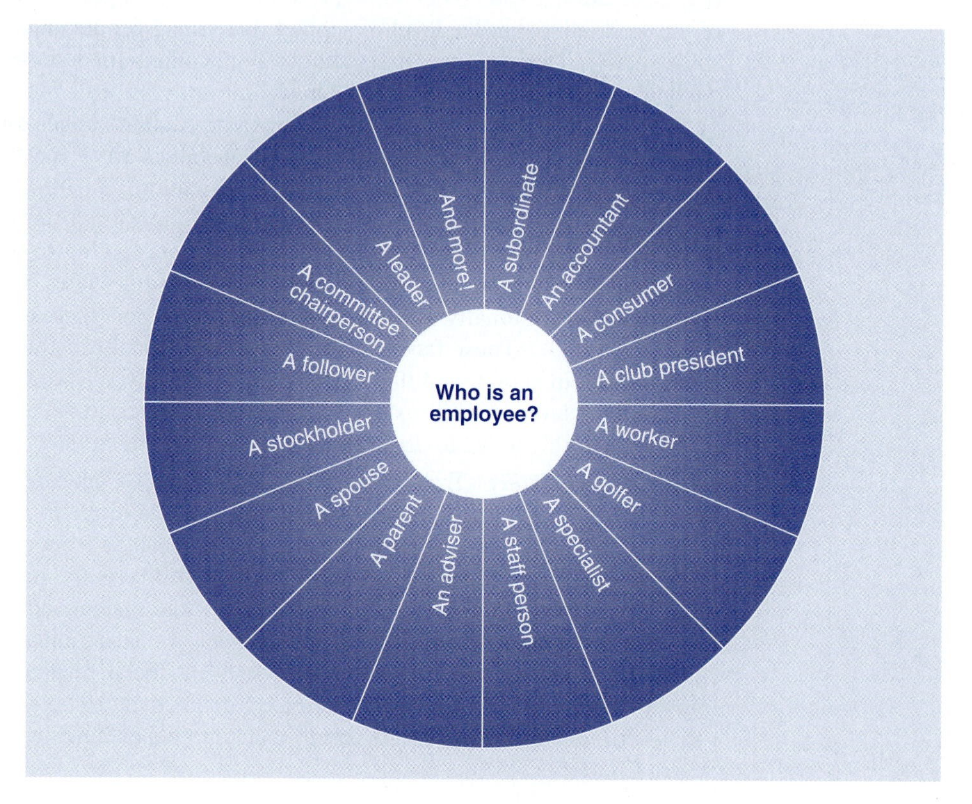

Role Perceptions

Activities of managers and workers alike are guided by their **role perceptions**—that is, how they think they are supposed to act in their own roles and how others should act in their roles. Since managers perform many different roles, they must be highly adaptive (exhibiting *role flexibility*) in order to change from one role to another quickly. Supervisors especially need to change roles rapidly as they work with both subordinates and superiors, and with technical and nontechnical activities.

When a manager and an employee interact, each one needs to understand four different role perceptions, as shown in Figure 4.3. For a manager, two role perceptions are as follows: First there is the manager's own role perception as required by the supervisory job being performed (A). Second, there is the manager's perception of the role of the employee being contacted (B). Two related role perceptions (C and D) exist from the employee's perspective. Potentially dramatic differences exist between the two outlooks—especially in the direct comparisons such as A to C and B to D. Obviously, one person cannot meet the needs of others unless one can perceive what they expect. The key is for *both* parties to gain accurate role perceptions for their own roles and for the roles of the other. Reaching such an understanding requires studying the available job descriptions, as well as opening up lines of communication to discover the other's perceptions. Unless roles are clarified and agreed upon by both parties, conflicts will inevitably arise.

Mentors

Where can employees get information regarding their work-related roles so they will have accurate role perceptions? In addition to traditional sources of information, such as job descriptions and orientation sessions, many organizations have formal or informal mentorship programs. A **mentor** is a role model who guides another employee (a *protégé*) by providing historical perspectives and sharing valuable advice on roles to play and behaviors to avoid. Mentors teach, advise, coach, support, encourage, act as sounding boards, and sponsor their protégés so as to expedite their personal satisfaction and career progress. The best mentors are credible, challenge you to improve, stimulate you to take risks, build your confidence, support your efforts to set "stretch" goals, and identify challenges and opportunities.[9]

Role modeling by mentors

The advantages of successful mentoring programs include stronger employee loyalty, faster movement up the learning curve, better succession planning through development of replacements, and increased level of goal accomplishments. Some organizations actually assign protégés to a mentor, but this practice can create problems of resentment, abuse of power, and unwillingness to serve. As a result, other firms simply encourage employees to seek out their

FIGURE 4.3
The Complex Web of Manager–Employee Role Perceptions

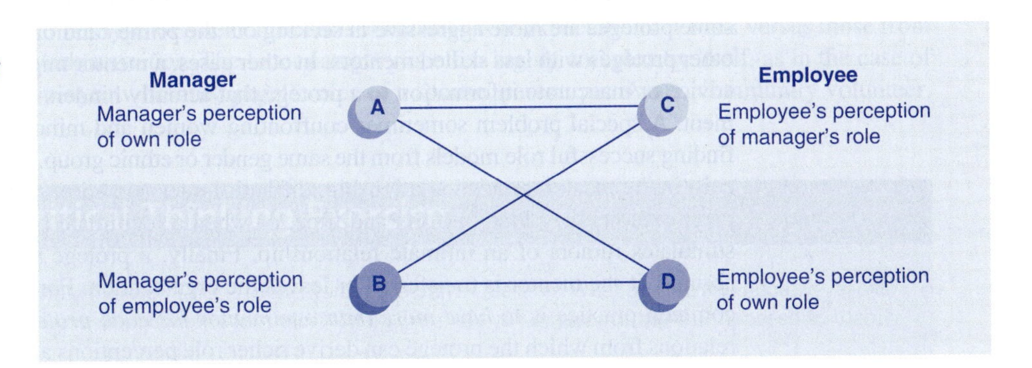

neighbor, church member, civic club officer, and caregiver to an elderly relative. When the demands from these roles accumulate, there is often a potential spillover effect on one's work life and job performance. The **work-family conflict** that ensues can impact both domains and result in diminished job satisfaction, work performance, life satisfaction, and emotional exhaustion unless the individual learns how to maintain a balanced focus, complemented by an array of family-friendly employer practices.[10]

Role Ambiguity

When roles are inadequately defined or are substantially unknown, **role ambiguity** exists, because people are not sure how they should act in situations of this type. When role conflict and role ambiguity exist, job satisfaction and organizational commitment will likely decline. On the other hand, employees tend to be more satisfied with their jobs when their roles are clearly defined by job descriptions and statements of performance expectations. A better understanding of roles helps people know what others expect of them and how they should act. If any role misunderstanding exists when people interact, then problems are likely to emerge.

STATUS

Social rank

Status is the social rank of a person in a group. It is a mark of the amount of recognition, honor, esteem, and acceptance given to a person. Within groups, differences in status apparently have been recognized ever since civilization began. Wherever people gather into groups, status distinctions are likely to arise, because they enable people to affirm the different characteristics and abilities of group members.

Individuals are bound together in **status systems,** or status hierarchies, which define their rank relative to others in the group. If they become seriously upset over their status, they are said to feel **status anxiety.**

Loss of status—sometimes called "losing face" or **status deprivation**—is a serious event for most people; it is considered a much more devastating condition, however, in certain societies. People, therefore, become quite responsible in order to protect and develop their status. One of management's pioneers, Chester Barnard, stated, "The desire for improvement of status and especially the desire to protect status appears to be the basis of a sense of general responsibility."[11]

Since status is important to people, they will work hard to earn it. If it can be tied to actions that further the company's goals, then employees are strongly motivated to support their company (see "On the Job: Creative Training Techniques").

Status Relationships

Effects of status

High-status people within a group usually have more power and influence than those with low status. They also receive more privileges from their group and tend to participate more in group activities. They interact more with their peers than with those of lower rank. Basically, high status gives people an opportunity to play a more important role in an organization. As a result, lower-status members tend to feel isolated from the mainstream and show more stress symptoms than higher-ranked members.

In a work organization, status provides a system by which people can relate to one another as they work. Without it, they would tend to be confused and spend much of their time trying to learn how to work together. Though status can be abused, normally it is beneficial because it helps people interact and cooperate with one another.

On the Job: Creative Training Techniques

Bob Pike, president of Creative Training Techniques and an internationally renowned trainer and author, suggests that employees have their "emotional radio stations" tuned to two frequencies. In each, the employee is listening intently for the answer to a question or a demand. The first frequency is WIIFM, and the second is MMFIAM. WIIFM asks "What's In It For Me?" while MMFIAM pleads for a response to "Make Me Feel Important About Myself." Both of these show that employees are egocentric—they are hungry for information that either rewards them or reinforces their self-image and perceived status. Consequently, managers must act like radio disk jockeys who play the tunes listeners request—feeding the status needs of their workers (when it has been earned).

Status Symbols

The status system becomes most visible through its use of **status symbols.** These are the visible external things that attach to a person or workplace and serve as evidence of social rank. They exist in the office, shop, warehouse, refinery, or wherever work groups congregate. They are most in evidence among different levels of managers, because each successive level usually has the authority to provide itself with surroundings just a little different from those of people lower in the structure.

As shown in Figure 4.5, there are a variety of symbols of status, depending on what employees feel is important. For example, in one office the type of wastebasket is a mark of distinction. In another, significant symbols are type of desk and telephones. In the executive offices, such items of rank as rugs, bookcases, curtains, and pictures on the wall are important. Another classic symbol of much significance is a corner office, because those offices are often larger and have windows on two sides. There may even be distinctions between an office with windows and one with no windows. Outside the office, the truck driver who operates the newest or largest truck has a symbol of status.

All this concern for symbols of status may seem amusing, but status symbols are a serious matter. They may endanger job satisfaction because employees who do not have a certain symbol, and think they should, can become preoccupied with that need. When an employee gives unreasonable attention to status symbols, there is evidence of status anxiety, and this situation requires management attention.

Many organizations have a policy that persons of equal rank in the same department should receive approximately equal status symbols. There may be some variation between departments, such as production and sales, because the work is different and rank is not directly comparable. In any case, managers need to face the fact that status differences

FIGURE 4.5
Typical Symbols of Status

- Furniture, such as a mahogany desk or a conference table
- Interior decorations, such as carpeting, draperies, and artwork
- Location of workplace, such as a corner office or an office having a window with a view
- Quality and newness of equipment used, such as a new vehicle or tools
- Type of clothes normally worn, such as a suit
- Privileges given, such as a golf club membership or company automobile
- Job title or organizational level, such as vice president
- Employees assigned, such as an administrative assistant
- Degree of financial discretion, such as authorizing up to $5,000 expenditures
- Organizational membership, such as a position on the executive committee

FIGURE 4.6
Major Sources of Status on the Job

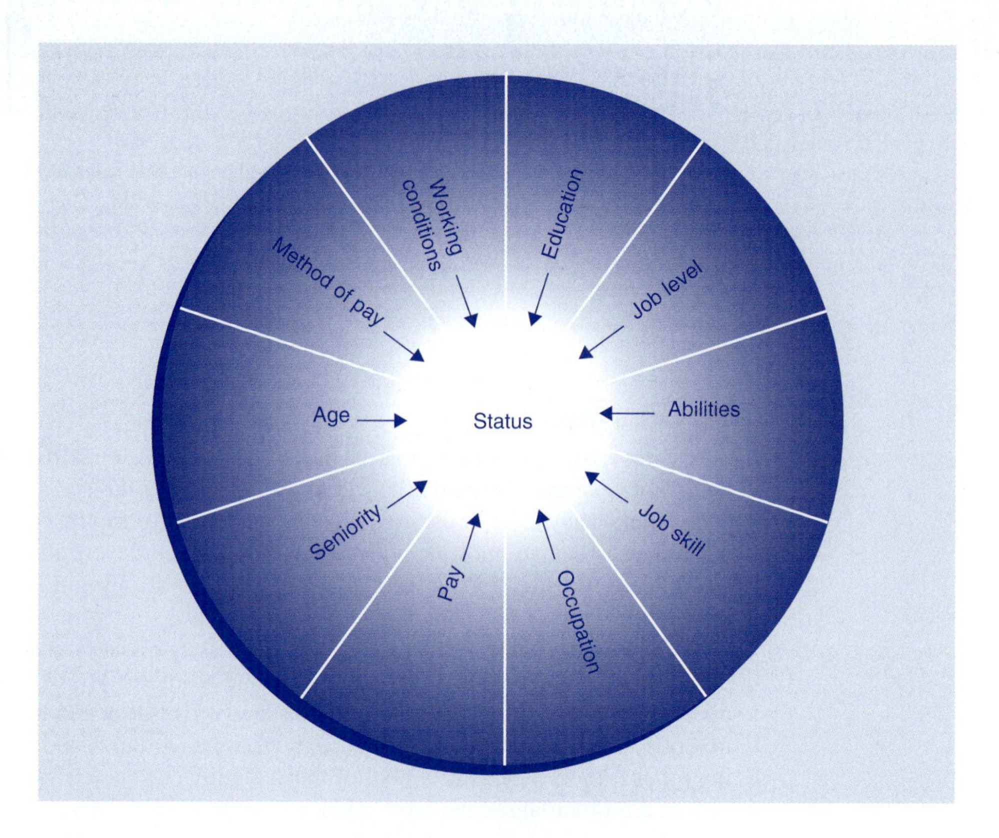

exist and must be managed successfully. However, the underlying values of the millennial generation of employees may diminish the hunger for status symbols at work in the future, since many younger persons dislike the concept of hierarchical differences.

Sources of Status

The sources of status are numerous, but in a typical work situation several sources are easily identified. As shown in Figure 4.6, education and job level are two important sources of higher status. A person's abilities, job skills, and type of work also are major sources of status.

Other sources of status are amount of pay, seniority, age, and stock options. Pay gives economic recognition and an opportunity to have more of the amenities of life, such as travel. Seniority and age have historically earned for their holder certain privileges, such as first choice of vacation dates, or the respect of co-workers for their longevity at work. Method of pay (hourly versus salary) and working conditions also provide important status distinctions, such as distinguishing blue-collar and white-collar work. Stock options provide employees with the opportunity to share the financial success of the firm.

Significance of Status

Status is significant to organizational behavior in several ways. When employees are consumed by the desire for status, it often is the source of employee problems and conflicts that management needs to solve. It influences the kinds of transfers that employees will take, because they don't want a low-status location (being "sent to Siberia") or dead-end job assignment. It helps determine who will be an informal leader of a group, and it definitely serves to motivate those seeking to advance in the organization. Some people are status seekers, wanting a job of high status regardless of other working conditions. These people

On the Job: National Bank of Georgia, Home Box Office, and Lake Superior Paper Industries

Some organizations have consciously sought to use their knowledge of the impact of status symbols to reduce these indicators. National Bank of Georgia chose an open-office layout in its headquarters so as to foster open communications and consensus. Top executives at Home Box Office avoided choosing the prestigious top (15th) floor of their new building and instead selected the 8th floor for greater proximity to the marketing and programming departments. Executives at Lake Superior Paper Industries chose to wear casual clothes (similar to those of the mill employees) so as to remove the potential status barrier between the two groups. More and more, organizations are removing reserved parking spots and placing everyone on an equal basis in the parking lot, too.

These illustrations provide some evidence of a societal backlash against too many status symbols. Some speakers argue that an overemphasis on status has created, or at least magnified, a gap between the haves and the have-nots. As a result, some contemporary employees *reject* traditional symbols of status even when those are available to them. They wear clothes of their own choice to work; they don't always drive higher-priced cars; and they prefer to mingle with other employees despite having access to an executive dining room after receiving a promotion.

can be encouraged to qualify themselves for high-status jobs so they will feel rewarded. By contrast, many organizations are now actively attempting to diminish or remove traditional symbols of status (see "On the Job: National Bank of Georgia, Home Box Office, and Lake Superior Paper Industries").

ORGANIZATIONAL CULTURE

B = f(P, E)

Social (national) culture creates the wide-ranging context in which organizations operate. It provides the complex social system of laws, values, and customs in which organizational behavior occurs. Employee behavior (B), according to social psychologist Kurt Lewin, is a function of the interaction between personal characteristics (P) and the environment (E) around the person. Part of that environment is the social culture in which the individual lives and works, which provides broad clues as to how a person with a given background will behave. The previous discussion indicated how employee actions are sharply affected by the roles assigned to them and the status level accorded to them.

Shared norms help define culture

Inside the organization lies another powerful force for determining individual and group behavior. **Organizational culture** is the set of assumptions, beliefs, values, and norms shared by an organization's members.This culture may have been consciously created by its key members, or it may have simply evolved across time. It represents a key element of the work environment in which employees perform their jobs. This idea of organizational culture is somewhat intangible, for we cannot see it or touch it, but it is present and pervasive. Like the air in a room, it surrounds and affects everything that happens in an organization. Because it is a dynamic systems concept, culture is also affected by almost everything that occurs within an organization.

Benefits of organizational culture

Organizational cultures are important to a firm's success for several reasons. They give an organizational identity to employees—a defining vision of what the organization represents. They are also an important source of stability and continuity to the organization, which provides a sense of security to its members. At the same time, knowledge of the organizational culture helps newer employees interpret what goes on inside the organization, by providing an important context for events that would otherwise seem confusing. More than anything else, perhaps, cultures help stimulate employee enthusiasm for their tasks. Cultures attract attention, convey a vision, and typically honor high-producing and creative individuals as heroes.

On the Job: General Mills Co.

Examples of symbolic representations abound in General Mills, headquartered in Minneapolis, Minnesota.[12] Executives refer to the "company of champions" culture, and point with pride to a statement of company values that is reinforced by rewards, recognition programs, and employee development systems. A popular slogan proclaims that "Eagles dare to win," and this statement adorns many awards given to employees and their units for exceptional work. A training program, "The Championship Way," provides an opportunity for the corporation to communicate its corporate values and discover barriers to their achievement.

By recognizing and rewarding these people, organizational cultures are identifying them as role models to emulate while also reinforcing the organization's values.

Riverwood Healthcare Center, in northern Minnesota, identified five key values that are meant to be used as daily guidelines for employee behavior:

- Integrity (honesty and fairness)
- Customer service (dedication to going "above and beyond" normal expectations)
- Unity (being loyal team players committed to common goals)
- Respect and compassion (helpful in all interactions with others)
- Excellence and passion (strong commitment to high quality)

These values are a critical component of Riverwood's culture, and when behaviors are consistent with them they contribute to the achievement of the organization's mission ("To improve health by providing high quality, compassionate, and personalized care").

Characteristics of Cultures

Cultures are distinctive, stable, implicit, and symbolic

Organizations, like fingerprints and snowflakes, are unique. Each has its own history, patterns of communication, systems and procedures, mission statements and visions, and stories and myths which, in their totality, constitute its *distinctive* culture. Cultures are relatively *stable* in nature, usually changing only slowly over time. Exceptions to this condition may occur when a major crisis threatens a firm or when two organizations merge with each other (requiring a careful blending of the two so as to avoid culture clash).

Most organizational cultures have historically been *implicit* and unconscious rather than explicit. In that way, cultures are similar to the act of breathing, which we take for granted until we have problems with it. More recently, though, organizations have begun talking about their intended cultures, and many top leaders see one of their major roles as speaking out consciously and directly about the kind of environment they would like to create within their firms. A final defining characteristic of most cultures is that they are seen as *symbolic representations* of underlying beliefs and values. We seldom read a description of a firm's culture. More frequently, employees make inferences about it from hearing stories about the way things are done, from reading slogans that portray corporate ideals, from observing key artifacts, or from watching ceremonies in which certain types of employees are honored (see "On the Job: General Mills Co.").

Critical Thinking Exercise

Think about the likely effects of consciously developed and strong cultures Question: What positive and negative results? Can you safely predict for them?

Over time, an organization's culture becomes perpetuated by its tendency to attract and retain people who fit its values and beliefs. Just as people may choose to move to a certain region because of geographic characteristics such as temperature, humidity, and rainfall, employees also will gravitate toward the organizational culture they prefer as a work environment. This results in a good fit of employer and employee, and predictably lower discontent and turnover.

Several other dimensions of culture are important to note. For one, there is *no best culture* for all firms; culture clearly depends on the organization's goals, industry, nature of competition, and other factors in its environment. Cultures will be more easily recognized when their elements are generally *integrated* and consistent with each other—in other words, they fit together like pieces of a puzzle. Also, most members must at least *accept,* if not embrace, the assumptions and values of the culture.

Historically, employees seldom talked explicitly about the culture in which they worked; more recently, culture has become an increasingly acceptable conversation topic among employees. Most cultures evolve directly from *top management,* who can have a powerful influence on their employees by what they say. However, management's *actions* are even more important to watchful employees, who can quickly detect when managers give only lip service but not true support to certain ideals, such as customer service and quality products. A culture may exist across an entire organization, or it may be made up of various *subcultures*—the environment within a single division, branch, plant, or department. Finally, cultures have varying strengths—they can be characterized as relatively *strong or weak,* depending largely on the degree of their impact on employee behavior and how widely the underlying beliefs and values are held. The 10 characteristics of cultures are summarized in Figure 4.7.

Products of successful cultures

The effect of organizational culture on employee behavior is difficult to establish. Some research indicates there is a positive relationship between certain organizational cultures and performance. Agreement within an organization on a culture should result in a larger degree of cooperation, acceptance of decision making and control, more effective communication, and commitment to the employer. These results are especially likely when a firm consciously seeks to create a performance-enhancing culture that removes barriers to success. Just as yeast is a critical ingredient in baking some varieties of bread, a culture of productivity is an essential element in organizational success. However, the next challenge becomes how to measure an organization's culture.

Measuring Organizational Culture

Systematic measurement and comparison of cultures is difficult at best. Most early attempts by researchers relied on examination of stories, symbols, rituals, and ceremonies to obtain clues and construct a composite (but subjective) portrait. Others have used interviews and open-ended questionnaires in an attempt to assess employee values and beliefs. In other cases, examination of corporate philosophy statements has provided insight into the *espoused* culture (the beliefs and values that the organization states publicly). Another approach is to survey employees directly and seek their *perceptions* of the organization's culture. (This method can produce a confusing portrait, however, much like the classic parable about the blind men who were asked to describe an elephant. Each person reported something very different, depending on whether he touched an ear, tail, trunk, tusk, or leg.)

FIGURE 4.7
Characteristics of Organizational Cultures

- Distinctive
- Stable
- Implicit
- Symbolic
- No one type is best
- Integrated
- Accepted
- A reflection of top management
- Subcultures
- Of varying strength

One of the more interesting methods is to become a member of the organization and engage in participant observation. This approach allows direct sensing from the perspective of a member who is experiencing the culture.

> Prudential Insurance Company of America used a standard pencil-and-paper instrument to identify part of its culture. Prudential measured current norms and found strong perceptions of conformity, caution, competition with other work groups, risk avoidance, and top-down decision making. Then, the company assessed desired norms, and found major gaps. Employees wanted a culture that stressed teamwork, collaboration, customer service, initiative, training, and cooperation. This measurement process allowed Prudential to involve employees in changing to a new culture—one where managers are measured against their culture-change goals.[13]

Any attempt to measure organizational culture can be only an imperfect assessment. Such measurements are comparable to capturing only a single snapshot of the culture at a single point in time, when a three-dimensional video camera is needed. In reality, many organizational cultures are in the process of changing and need to be monitored regularly and by a variety of methods to gain a truer picture.

Communicating and Changing Culture

If organizations are to consciously create and manage their cultures, they must be able to communicate them to employees, especially the newly hired ones. *People are generally more willing to adapt and learn when they want to please others, gain approval, and learn about their new work environment.* Similarly, organizations are eager to have the new employees fit in, and therefore an intentional approach that helps make this happen is used by many firms. Examples of formal communication vehicles for transmitting organizational cultures include executive visions of the firm's future, corporate philosophy statements, and codes of ethical conduct. Informal means involve publicly recognizing heroes and heroines, retelling historical success stories, and even allowing myths to become exaggerated without popping the hot-air balloon. Of course, elements of the organization's culture are also unintentionally communicated to employees in a variety of ways, such as when news of a manager's error and an executive's forgiveness of it are accidentally leaked throughout the firm.

Socialization affects employees

Collectively, these cultural communication acts may be lumped under the umbrella of **organizational socialization,** which is the continuous process of transmitting key elements of an organization's culture to its employees. Socialization consists of both formal methods (such as military indoctrination at boot camp or corporate orientation training for new employees) and informal means (like the role modeling provided by mentors, discussed earlier in this chapter). All these approaches help shape the attitudes, thoughts, and behavior of employees. Viewed from the organization's perspective, organizational socialization is like placing an organization's fingerprints on people or stamping its own genetic code on them. From the employee's viewpoint, it is essential that they learn "the ropes" to survive and prosper within the firm. The important point is that socialization can be functional for both workers and their employers.

A key player in the organizational socialization process is the new employee's direct supervisor. If this person acts in supportive and attentive ways on a daily basis, the newcomer is more likely to make a rapid and successful adjustment to the workplace. Equally important in the adjustment process is the new employee's own behavior. A new trainee needs to be deliberate in seeking interactions—formal and informal—with the supervisor. The key factor here is the new employee's perception as to whether or not the supervisor is seen as being approachable.[14]

Two powerful methods for communicating an organizational culture to new employees involve signature experiences and storytelling. **Signature experiences** are clearly defined and dramatic devices that convey a key element of the firm's culture and vividly

FIGURE 4.8
Four Combinations of Socialization and Individualization

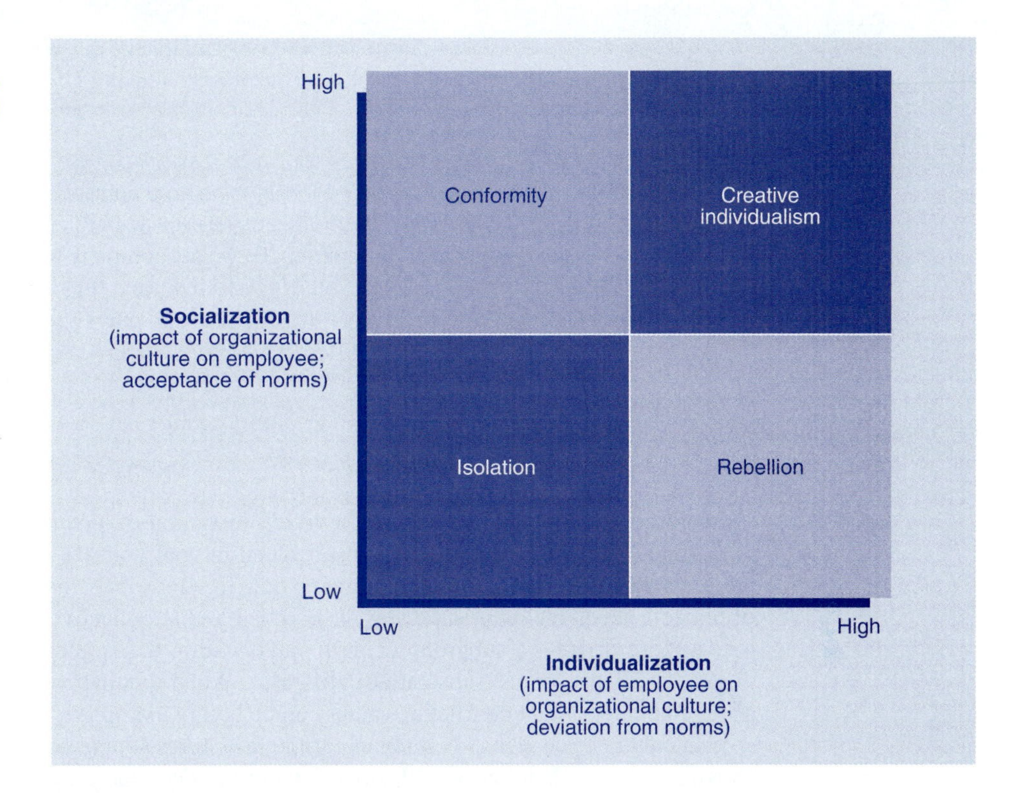

reinforce the values of the organization. As a result, the culture is clearly imprinted in the new employee's mind. Examples of signature experiences are demanding selection procedures for new hires at Goldman Sachs, "quick win" assignments at W.L. Gore & Associates, the "First Impressions" program at Starbucks, cross-platform sharing meetings at British Petroleum, and unlimited shift-trading opportunities at JetBlue. Typically, employees share tales of these positive cultural experiences with great pride.[15]

Signature experiences and storytelling reinforce culture

Managers are also encouraged to engage in **storytelling** as a way to forge a culture and build organizational identity. Good stories tap into the emotions of an audience and have proven to be powerful ways to create shared meaning and purpose. Stories convey a sense of tradition, explain how past problems have been solved, convey personal frailty through tales of mistakes made and learned from, and enhance cohesion around key values. The most memorable stories entertain as well as inform, and uplift as well as teach. These stories highlight purposeful plots and patterns that the organization cherishes, they point out consequences of actions, and they provide valuable lessons that carry forward the wisdom gained through previous years.[16] Storytelling, then, is a key means for achieving socialization of employees.

Individualization affects the organization

A reciprocal process emerges when changes occur in the other direction. In addition to being affected by culture, employees can also have an active impact on the nature of the organization's culture and operations. **Individualization** occurs when employees successfully exert influence on the social system around them at work by challenging the culture or deviating from it. The interaction between socialization and individualization is portrayed in Figure 4.8, which shows the types of employees who accept or reject an organization's norms and values while exerting various degrees of influence. The two extremes—*rebellion* and total *conformity*—may prove dysfunctional for the organization and the individual's career in the long run. *Isolation,* of course, is seldom a productive course of action. If we assume that the culture of a certain organization invites its employees to challenge, question, and experiment while also not being too disruptive, then the *creative individualist* can infuse new life and ideas for the organization's benefit, as "On the Job: Motorola Company" demonstrates.

On the Job: Motorola Company

Delbert Little is an engineer who works for Motorola, a major American electronics firm. A highly creative, energetic, and talented worker, he prides himself on giving 110 percent effort to his job. Although he totally accepts his employer's values regarding the need to create new and improved products through technological breakthroughs, he also flaunts his rejection of some corporate norms regarding personal behavior (mode of dress and deference to authority). He communicates to his workers with great passion, regularly imploring them to exercise similar innovativeness. Whenever he thinks his employer is moving in the wrong product or market direction, he writes lengthy and passionate memos to top executives detailing his reasoning and trying to persuade them to change their minds.

Delbert can be described as exercising creative individualism (but bordering on rebellion). He accepts some norms and values but rejects others (and therefore is moderately socialized). He fights fiercely for what he thinks is right and attempts to change others' thinking, too. Consequently, he has a relatively high impact on his portion of the organization (individualism). "The company tolerates my behavior," he laughed one day, "only because I have produced over 100 patents while working here!"

Motorola's Delbert Little provides a vivid illustration of a *fringe* employee—one who is marginal or even extremist and doesn't blend in well with the larger culture, thus creating a relatively poor individual–organization fit. If Delbert discovered that a number of his colleagues feel that same way, it is possible that collectively they might represent a **counterculture**—a subgroup of individuals within the larger culture—whose values, norms, and behavior are substantially different. When this happens, a *culture clash* may arise, and the resultant conflict of values can be highly disruptive.

Can culture be changed? A study of corporate cultures at nine large companies—Federal Express, Johnson & Johnson, 3M, AT&T, Corning, Du Pont, Ford, IBM, and Motorola—suggests it *can* change. However, it requires a long-term effort, often spanning 5 to 10 years to complete. Figure 4.9 indicates the relative effectiveness of a variety of methods

FIGURE 4.9 **Effectiveness of Methods for Changing Organizational Culture**

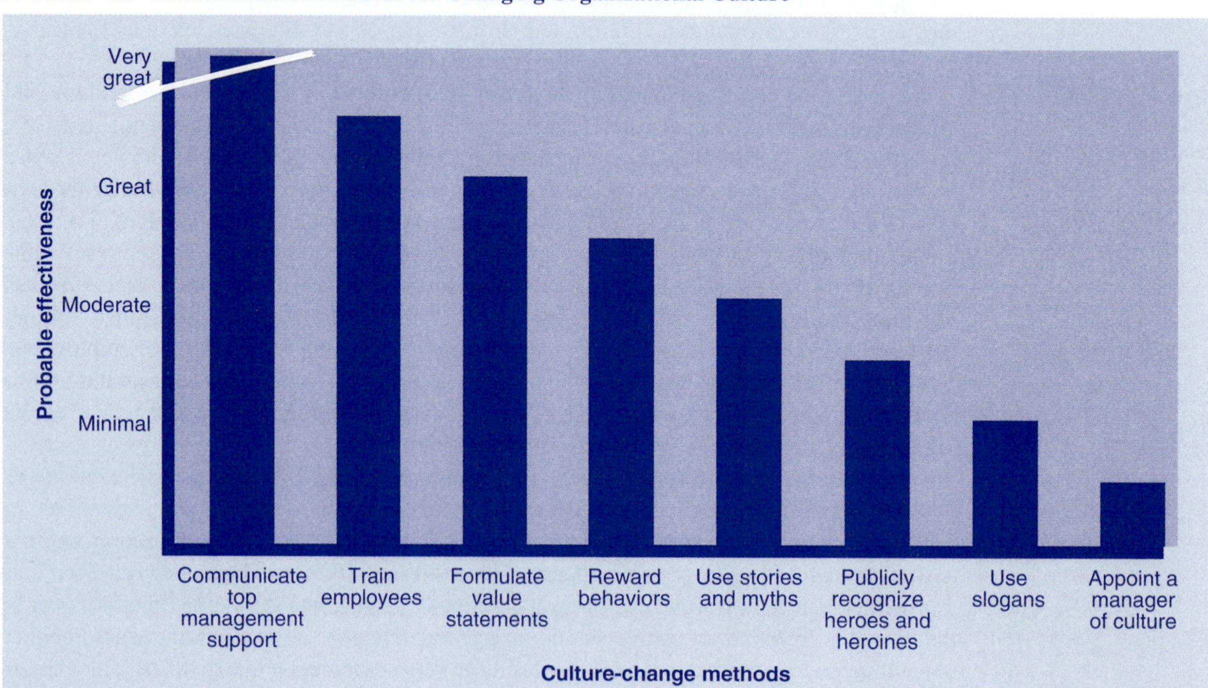

On the Job: Zappos, Inc.

Zappos, Inc., which is high on *Fortune*'s list of 100 Best Companies to Work For, lists 10 core values as the cultural foundation for its success. One of these is "work hard, play hard," also known as "create fun and a little weirdness." Employees benefit from happy hours, nap rooms, pajama parties, life coaches, and manager-led hikes. As a result, workers exercise a high degree of discretion to "wow" their customers.[17]

for changing culture.[18] Clearly, an open display of top-management commitment and support for the new values and beliefs is critically important, as is the training of employees to enable them to change. Other powerful methods for inducing cultural change include communities of interest, behavior modeling by managers, performance management systems, ad hoc gatherings, and active engagement of exemplars.[19]

FUN WORKPLACES

Society encourages and provides many ways in which people can play and have fun in their recreational lives. Playful experiences typically have a number of common elements—immersion in the activity, surprise, variety, choice, experience of progress, and the opportunities to make personal contributions and to "win." Most of these features can also be incorporated into the daily life of employees, many of whom also desire to have fun at work. A **fun work environment** is a unique and increasingly popular organizational culture in which supervisors encourage, initiate, and support a variety of playful and humorous activities. A fun workplace culture has several key features:

- It is easily recognized (by observing the presence of laughter, smiles, surprise, and spontaneity).
- It means different things to various people.
- It is relatively easy to create at work.
- It elicits a broad range of personal and organizational payoffs.

Hundreds of approaches have been used to stimulate fun at work. Key *categories* include unique ways to provide recognition for personal milestones (birthdays and anniversaries of hiring dates), hosting of special social events, public celebrations of professional and departmental achievements, games and friendly competitions, entertainment, and the use of humor in newsletters and correspondence. Specific *tactics* used in various organizations include costume (dress-up) days, cartoons tailored to employees, exaggerated job titles (e.g., "Genius" employees at Apple Stores), distribution of the "joke for the day," or the use of modified board games and TV show formats to engage minds and stimulate creativity. No magic formula ensures success; the key for managers is to be experimental, make it a continuous process, and encourage others to come up with new ideas (see "On the Job: Zappos, Inc.").

Positive effects of fun at work

Employees like to work in an environment that satisfies their economic and security needs, makes them feel listened to, and recognizes their time, effort, and results. Beyond that, however, many employees value and appreciate the opportunity to relax and play a little, laugh, have fun occasionally, and generally enjoy themselves at work. Unless the playfulness results in physical harm or personal feelings becoming hurt, fun at work can help decrease stress, reduce boredom, stimulate friendships, increase satisfaction, and produce several beneficial physiological results for employees (e.g., lower blood pressure, greater immunity to infection, and more positive energy).

Advice to Future Managers

1. *Look at your organization as a social system,* and ask yourself whether it is in balance or not. If it is not, is the disequilibrium functional for the organization?
2. Seek to understand, and *actively manage, the psychological contract* you have with each of your employees.
3. Inventory the positive ways in which each of your employees is different. *Make sure your workplace capitalizes on these aspects of diversity.*
4. *Find, and use, at least one active mentor* for yourself. Also, offer yourself as a mentor to at least one person who does not report directly to you.
5. *Analyze the status symbols* apparent in your organization. Decide whether they are functional or dysfunctional for employee morale and performance.
6. Paint a comprehensive verbal portrait of the organizational culture at your workplace. Is the culture strong or weak? *Describe what you could do to clarify and strengthen your firm's culture.*
7. Since the best time to instill cultural values into employees is while they are still new and receptive, *study how your organization socializes its new hires into the values and norms* of the firm.
8. Examine the level of commitment to the work ethic among your employees, and search for ways to *communicate your performance expectations* to them.
9. Start to accumulate a reservoir of tales, myths, slogans, and anecdotes that support the kind of organizational culture you wish to convey. *Develop, polish, and apply your storytelling skills as a means to reinforce the culture.*
10. Examine the current and desired level of fun in your workplace. *Involve employees in developing a fun work environment that also contributes to organizational goals.*

The organization benefits from a fun workplace culture, too. A comprehensive survey by the Society for Human Resource Management showed that as employee enthusiasm and creativity rise, attracting and retaining new employees is easier, the company's values and norms (culture) become clearer, and customer satisfaction improves as a reflection of how they are treated by energized employees.[20] Common reservations about the risks inherent in having fun at work generally prove to be groundless. The most valid reasons for managerial resistance to having fun at work revolve around the fear that one's superiors (and the overall organizational culture) won't condone it, and the possible lack of personal creativity needed to make it happen. On balance, however, powerful arguments support allowing employees to have occasional fun at work and engaging them in the process of creating a fun workplace culture. Suggestions for accomplishing this are listed in Figure 4.10.

FIGURE 4.10
Guidelines for Fun-Oriented Managers

Source: Bob Pike, Robert C. Ford, and John W. Newstrom, *The Fun Minute Manager*, Minneapolis: CTT Press, 2009, p. 88.

1. Address *other* employee needs first (job content).
2. Make sure that fun at work will be a good fit with the organization's *culture* and with employee *expectations*.
3. Build a fun workplace on an *underlying philosophical foundation*, not just a set of mechanical practices.
4. Make a *long-term commitment* to fun as an ongoing process, not a short-term program.
5. Become more playful *yourself*.
6. *Involve others* in creating fun experiences.
7. *Satisfy employee needs for recognition* in new and unique ways.
8. Use a *wide variety* of fun-related activities.
9. Capitalize on the *surprise* factor.
10. Assess and regularly *monitor your success* at creating a fun work culture.

Summary

When people join a work group, they become part of that organization's social system. It is the medium by which they relate to the world of work. The variables in an organizational system operate in a working balance called social equilibrium. Individuals make a psychological contract that defines their personal relationship with the system. When they contribute to the organization's success, we call their behavior functional.

The broad environment that people live in is their social culture. People need to accept and appreciate the value that a diversity of cultural backgrounds can contribute to the success of an organization. Other important cultural factors include the work ethic and corporate attitudes toward social responsibility.

Role is the pattern of action expected of a person in activities involving others. Related ideas are role perception, mentors, role conflict, and role ambiguity. Status is the social rank of a person in a group, and it leads to status systems and possibly status anxiety. Status symbols are sought as if they were magical herbs, because they often provide external evidence of status for their possessors.

Organizational cultures reflect the assumptions and values that guide a firm. They are intangible but powerful influences on employee behavior. Participants learn about their organization's culture through the process of socialization, and influence it through individualization. Organizational cultures can be changed, but the process is time-consuming. Fun at work can be a legitimate part of a firm's culture and can produce personal and organizational benefits.

Speaking OB: Terms and Concepts for Review

Counterculture, *104*
Cultural diversity, *90*
Discrimination, *90*
Dysfunctional effect, *87*
Exchange theory, *89*
Fun work environment, *105*
Functional effect, *87*
Individualization, *103*
Mentor, *93*
Open systems, *86*
Organizational culture, *99*
Organizational socialization, *102*
Prejudice, *90*
Psychological contract, *87*
Reverse mentoring, *95*
Role ambiguity, *96*
Role conflict, *95*
Role perceptions, *93*
Role, *92*
Signature experiences, *102*
Social culture, *89*
Social equilibrium, *86*
Social responsibility, *91*
Social system, *86*
Status, *96*
Status anxiety, *96*
Status deprivation, *96*
Status symbols, *97*
Status systems, *96*
Storytelling, *103*
Valuing diversity, *90*
Work ethic, *90*
Work-family conflict, *96*

Discussion Questions

1. What psychological contract do you feel is present in this course? Describe its key features.
2. Look around your classroom, dormitory, or student organization. In what ways does it reflect cultural diversity? Suggest ways by which the resources represented in that diversity could be used to greater advantage for the benefit of all participants.
3. A management specialist recently commented about the work ethic, saying, "You can discover if you personally have a work ethic if you think more about the salary you make than about the quality of the product you make (or the service you provide)." Comment.
4. What does social responsibility mean to you? Does it apply to people as well as institutions? Describe three acts of social responsibility you have seen, or performed, in the last month.

5. Describe a situation in which you experienced role conflict or role ambiguity. What caused it? How are the two ideas related, and how are they different?
6. Interview a manager to discover what that person believes to be the five most important status symbols in the work situation. Identify whether the importance of status symbols is increasing or decreasing there.
7. Describe the organizational culture that seems to exist in your class. What are some of the implicit or explicit norms, values, and assumptions?
8. Reflect back on your first few days in college, or in a part-time or summer job. In what ways were you socialized? How did you feel about what was happening to you? Was there a signature experience you recall vividly?
9. Look at the reciprocal process of individualization. In what ways did you make an impact on the college, or on the job?
10. The beneficial effects of having fun at work are relatively easy to see. What are some of the possible dysfunctional effects of such a culture?

Assess Your Own Skills

How well do you exhibit good mentoring skills?

Read the following statements carefully. Circle the number on the response scale that most closely reflects the degree to which each statement accurately describes you when you have played a role to someone else as a mentor. Add up your total points and prepare a brief action plan for self-improvement. Be ready to report your score for tabulation across the entire group.

	Good description									Poor description
1. I make myself available for contact whenever my protégé needs me.	10	9	8	7	6	5	4	3	2	1
2. I give constructive feedback whenever it is appropriate.	10	9	8	7	6	5	4	3	2	1
3. I share tales of my own successes and failures when I think examples are needed.	10	9	8	7	6	5	4	3	2	1
4. I provide emotional support when I sense the timing is right.	10	9	8	7	6	5	4	3	2	1
5. I follow through on any commitments I make, to establish an image of integrity.	10	9	8	7	6	5	4	3	2	1
6. I view all information gained as personal and confidential, disclosing it to no one.	10	9	8	7	6	5	4	3	2	1
7. I work hard to remain open to the needs and objectives of my protégé.	10	9	8	7	6	5	4	3	2	1
8. I make sure I listen attentively to both the words and feelings of my protégé.	10	9	8	7	6	5	4	3	2	1

9. I try to be available for immediate contact whenever my protégé needs me.	10	9	8	7	6	5	4	3	2	1
10. I recognize the need to provide support and encouragement to my protégé.	10	9	8	7	6	5	4	3	2	1

Scoring and Interpretation

Add up your total points for the 10 questions. Record that number here, and report it when it is requested. Finally, insert your total score into the "Assess and Improve Your Own Organizational Behavior Skills" chart in Appendix A.

- If you scored between 81 and 100 points, you appear to have a solid capability for demonstrating good mentoring skills.
- If you scored between 61 and 80 points, you should take a close look at the items with lower self-assessment scores and explore ways to improve those items.
- If you scored under 60 points, you should be aware that a weaker skill level regarding several items could be detrimental to your future success as a mentor. We encourage you to review relevant sections of the chapter and watch for related material in subsequent chapters and other sources.

Identify your three lowest scores, and write the question numbers here: _____, _____, _____. Write a brief paragraph, detailing to yourself an action plan for how you might sharpen each of these skills.

Incident

Liberty Construction Company

Liberty Construction Company is a small company in Colorado. More than half its revenue is derived from the installation of underground water and power lines, so much of its work is seasonal and turnover among its employees is high.

Michael Federico, a college student, had been employed by Liberty as a backhoe operator for the last three summers. On his return to work for the fourth summer, Federico was assigned the second newest of the company's five backhoes. The owner reasoned that Federico had nine months of work seniority, so according to strict seniority, he should have the second backhoe. This action required the present operator of the backhoe, Pedro Alvarez, a regular employee who had been with the company seven months, to be reassigned to an older machine. Alvarez was strongly dissatisfied with this; he felt that as a regular employee he should have retained the newer machine instead of having to give it to a temporary employee. The other employees soon fell into two camps, one supporting Alvarez and one supporting Federico. Job conflicts arose, and each group seemed to delight in causing work problems for the other group. In less than a month Alvarez left the company.

Question

Discuss this case in terms of the social system, equilibrium, the psychological contract, role, status, and status symbols.

Experiential Exercise

Role Perceptions of Students and Instructors

Consider yourself as the subordinate in this class, with the instructor as your manager.

1. (Work individually.) In the student–instructor relationship in this class, identify:
   a. Your perception of your student roles
   b. Your perception of the instructor's roles

(At the same time, the instructor should be identifying his or her perception of the instructor's roles, and his or her perception of the students' roles.)

2. Meeting in small groups of students, combine your ideas into collective statements of perceptions.
3. Report your group's perceptions to the class on all three factors. Request that the instructor share his or her perceptions with the class. Compare and then explore the underlying reasons for any differences observed.

Generating OB Insights

An *insight* is a new and clear perception of a phenomenon, or an acquired ability to "see" clearly something you were unaware of previously. It is sometimes simply referred to as an "ah-ha! moment," in which you have a minirevelation or reach a straightforward conclusion about a topic or issue.

Insights need not necessarily be dramatic, for what is an insight to one person may be less important to another. The critical feature of insights is that they are relevant and memorable for *you;* they should represent new knowledge, new frameworks, or new ways of viewing things that you want to retain and remember over time.

Insights, then, are different from the information you find in the "Advice for Future Managers" boxes within the text. That advice is prescriptive and action-oriented; it indicates a recommended course of action.

A useful way to think of OB insights is to assume you are the only person who has read the current chapter. You have been given the assignment to highlight, in your own words, the major concepts (but not just summarize the whole chapter) that might stand out for a naive audience who has never heard of the topic before. *What 10 insights would you share with them?*

(Example) *Employees are egocentric and hungry for information that reinforces their self-image and state.*

1. ______________________________
2. ______________________________
3. ______________________________
4. ______________________________
5. ______________________________
6. ______________________________
7. ______________________________
8. ______________________________
9. ______________________________
10. ______________________________

Nurturing Your Critical Thinking and Reflective Skills

Take a few minutes to review the discussion in the Roadmap for Readers of critical thinking and reflection. Remind yourself that if you can hone these abilities now, you will have a substantial competitive advantage when you apply for jobs and are asked what unique skills you can bring to the position and the organization.

Critical Thinking

Think back on the material in this chapter. What are three unique and challenging *critical questions* you would like to raise about that material? (These might identify something controversial about which you have doubts, they may imply you suspect that a theory or model has weaknesses, they could examine the legitimacy of apparent causal relationships, or they might assess the probable value of a suggested practice.) Be prepared to share these questions with class members or your instructor.

1. ______________________________
   ____
2. ______________________________
   ____
3. ______________________________
   ____

Reflection

This process often involves answering the parallel questions of "What do you *think* about the material you have read?" and "How do you *feel* about that material?" Therefore, express your *personal thoughts and feelings* (reactions) to any of the ideas or topics found in this chapter, and be prepared to share these reflections with class members or your instructor.

1. ______________________________
   ____
2. ______________________________
   ____
3. ______________________________
   ____

Part Two

Motivation and Reward Systems

Chapter Five

Motivation

If you're asking, "How do I motivate employees?" You're going down the wrong path. The right question to ask is, "How do I stop *demotivating* them?"
Jim Collins[1]

CHAPTER OBJECTIVES

AFTER READING THIS CHAPTER, YOU SHOULD UNDERSTAND

5-1 The Motivational Process
5-2 Motivational Drives
5-3 Need Category Systems
5-4 Behavior Modification and Reinforcement
5-5 Goal Setting and Its Effects
5-6 The Expectancy Model of Motivation
5-7 Equity Comparisons

Facebook Page 

Student A: Guess what? I think I'm going to learn something useful in my OB class this week!

Student B: Lucky you; I'm currently reading about ancient civilizations in my anthropology class. Tell me how to apply *that*. So what's your current topic that's got you all excited?

Student A: Chapter 5 is all about motivation. I figure I should learn about that so when I become a manager some day I'll be able to understand and motivate my employees.

Student C: From what I've seen of you, you'd better start by motivating yourself!

Student A: I'll ignore that comment, bro.

Student B: So how *do* you motivate employees?

Student A: The author suggests having a clear model in your mind of the key steps involved, as well as the desired outcomes (persistent energy and effort, high quantity and quality of performance, and satisfied and committed employees).

Student B: Wow. How do you make that happen?

Student A: It's like a jigsaw puzzle; you have many pieces to put into place. You need challenging goals, an understanding of employee needs and drives, an appreciation of the "law of effect," and a reward system that employees perceive as equitable.

Student C: That seems to make sense. Any new terms to absorb?

Student A: There's a bunch of them that I'm not yet familiar with—self-efficacy, expectancy, equity sensitivity, hygiene factors, and OB Mod. Guess I've got my work cut out for me.

Hyatt Hotels Corporation had a problem. It hired bright, energetic young people to help run its Hyatt Regency hotels. They worked for a few years at the registration desk, as assistant housekeeping managers, or in other positions while learning hotel operations. Then, they would desire faster promotions into management positions and, seeing the long road ahead, search for a new employer.

Part of the problem lay in the slow expansion of the company, which often slowed individual progression rates into management from the previous time span of three years to eight years or more. To prevent high turnover and capitalize on existing talent, Hyatt started giving its employees opportunities to create new ventures in related fields, such as party catering and rental shops. The motivational impact of the autonomy provided by these entrepreneurial ventures enabled Hyatt to retain over 60 percent of its managers, while increasing its revenues and providing valuable experience to its workforce.

The Hyatt situation provides an opportunity to look both backward (at Part One) and forward (to this chapter and the next). Certainly the new program in the hotels created a different organizational *culture* there; the executives in charge showed how *supportive* they were by searching for ways to retain valuable human resources; and they began to *listen* carefully to what employees were telling them in order to discover how to respond. Motivation, then, takes place within a culture, reflects an organizational behavior model, and requires excellent communication skills.

The Hyatt Hotels example also provides an illustration of the four major indicators of employee motivation that are commonly monitored by employers:

1. *Engagement* (see Chapter 9) is the degree of enthusiasm, initiative, and effort put forth by employees.

2. *Commitment* is the degree to which employees bond with the organization and exhibit acts of organizational citizenship (discussed in Chapter 10).
3. *Satisfaction* is a reflection of the fulfillment of the psychological contract, the experience of meaningful tasks, and met expectations at work (see Chapter 10).
4. *Turnover* is the loss of valued employees, and can be reduced by empowering employees (see Chapter 8).

Research shows that when employers address all four factors successfully, employee motivation—and organizational success—is greatly strengthened.[2]

Definition of work motivation

What is motivation? **Work motivation** is the result of a set of internal and external forces that cause an employee to choose an appropriate course of action and engage in certain behaviors. Ideally, these behaviors will be directed at the achievement of an organizational goal. Work motivation is a complex combination of psychological forces within each person, and employers are vitally interested in three elements of it:

- *Direction and focus of the behavior* (positive factors are dependability, creativity, helpfulness, timeliness; dysfunctional factors are tardiness, absenteeism, withdrawal, and low performance)
- *Level of the effort* provided (making a full commitment to excellence versus doing just enough to get by)
- *Persistence of the behavior* (repeatedly maintaining the effort versus giving up prematurely or doing it just sporadically)

Motivation also requires discovering and understanding employee drives and needs, since it originates within an individual. Positive acts performed for the organization—such as creating customer satisfaction and client loyalty through exceptional personalized service—need to be reinforced. And employees will be more motivated when they have clear goals to achieve. Needs, reinforcement, goals, expectancies, and feelings of equity are the main thrusts of this chapter.

As the earlier quote by author Jim Collins points out, it is equally important to uncover the factors at work that act to *demotivate* employees and diminish their enthusiasm for high performance. Common managerial behaviors that detract from motivation include:

- Tolerating poor performance by incompetent or lazy co-workers
- Leveling undue criticism at employees
- Failing to provide clear expectations
- Making false promises of incentives available
- Unfair distribution of rewards (favoritism)
- Hours spent in unproductive meetings

Even the simple act of removing factors such as these can produce immediate benefits in workforce motivation!

A MODEL OF MOTIVATION

Although a few spontaneous human activities occur without motivation, nearly all conscious behavior is motivated, or caused. Growing hair requires no motivation, but getting a haircut does. Eventually, anyone will fall asleep without motivation (although parents with young children may doubt this), but going to bed is a conscious act requiring motivation.

Engaging Your Brain

1. Think of someone you know who is highly motivated. What factors explain that person's behavior? Would those factors work to motivate others?
2. Some writers have suggested that individual motivation is more a function of biological factors (genetics) than rewards. What do *you* think?
3. As you read this chapter you will encounter a sampling of the most prevalent motivational models. When you look back upon them, do you believe that they are *competing* (basically incompatible with each other) or *complementary* (capable of being integrated with each other)? Be prepared to explain your conclusion.

A manager's job is to identify employees' drives and needs and to channel their behavior toward task performance.

The role of motivation in performance is summarized in Figure 5.1. Internal needs and drives create tensions that are affected by one's environment. For example, the need for food produces a tension of hunger. The hungry person then examines the surroundings to see which foods (external incentives) are available to satisfy that hunger. Since environment affects one's appetite for particular kinds of food, a South Seas native may want roast fish, whereas a Colorado rancher may prefer grilled steak. Both persons are ready to achieve their goals, but they will seek different foods to satisfy their needs. This is an example of both individual differences and cultural influences in action.

$PP = A \times M$

As we saw in the formulas in Chapter 1, potential performance (PP) is a product of ability (A) and motivation (M). Results occur when motivated employees are provided with the opportunity (such as the proper training) to perform and the resources (such as the proper tools) to do so. The presence of goals and the awareness of incentives to satisfy one's needs are also powerful motivational factors leading to the release of effort (motivation). The amount of effort that employees expend is also directly affected by whether they are energized or fatigued. **High-energy workers** are alert, spirited, and enthusiastic; they feel vitalized and are eager to act. **Fatigued workers** act tired, sluggish, and feel emotionally depleted. Unfortunately, many factors contribute to fatigue—long work hours, sleep deprivation, job insecurity, dual-career relationships, and a high pace of work coupled with the modern phenomenon of being "electronically tethered" to one's job on a 24/7 basis. Traditional "micro-breaks" have little lasting rejuvenation effects. Personal strategies for energy management fall into three categories:

- *Learning* (acquiring new information or skills; setting new goals; identifying sources of joy at work)

FIGURE 5.1
A Model of Motivation

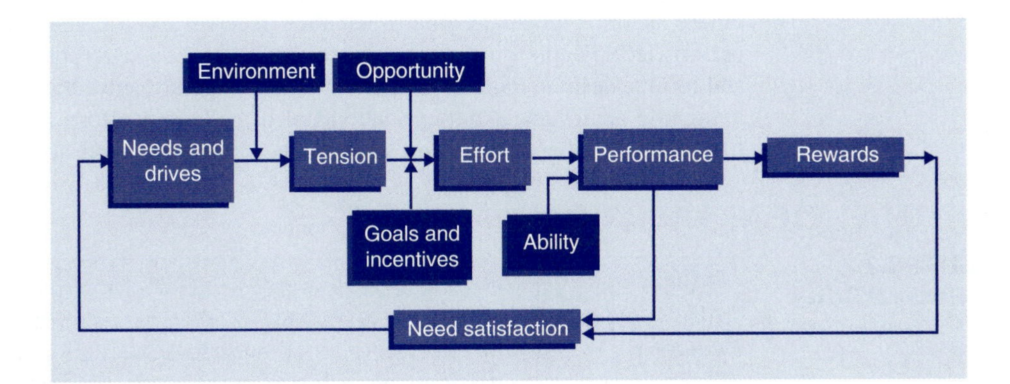

- *Relationship development* (helping colleagues; demonstrating gratitude to others; seeking and acting on feedback)
- *Finding meaning at work* (reflecting on one's significance and impact at work)[3]

When an employee is productive and the organization takes note of it, rewards will be distributed. If those rewards are appropriate in nature, timing, and distribution, the employee's original needs and drives are satisfied. At that time, new needs may emerge and the cycle will begin again. (You might also note that even the *experience* of progress toward goals can be directly satisfying, similar to the common adage that we should "Focus on the journey, not the destination.")

It should be apparent, therefore, that an important starting point lies in *understanding employee needs.* Several traditional approaches to classifying drives and needs are presented first; these models attempt to help managers understand how employees' internal needs affect their subsequent behaviors. These historical approaches are logically followed by a discussion of a systematic way of modifying employee behavior through the use of rewards that satisfy those needs.

MOTIVATIONAL DRIVES

People tend to develop certain motivational **drives** (strong desires for something) as a product of the cultural environment in which they live. These acquired drives affect the way people view their jobs and approach their lives. Much of the interest in these patterns of motivation was generated by the research of David C. McClelland of Harvard University.[4] He developed a classification scheme highlighting three of the more dominant drives and pointed out their significance to motivation. His studies revealed that people's motivational drives reflect elements of the culture in which they grow up—their family, school, church, and books. In most nations, one or two of the motivational patterns tend to be strong among the workers because they have grown up with similar backgrounds.

Three drives

McClelland's research focused on the drives for achievement, affiliation, and power (see Figure 5.2).

Achievement Motivation

Achievement motivation is a drive some people have to pursue and attain challenging goals. An individual with this drive wishes to achieve objectives and advance up the ladder of success. Accomplishment is seen as important primarily for its own sake, not just for the rewards that accompany it. (See "What Managers Are Reading.")

Characteristics of achievers

A number of characteristics define achievement-oriented employees. They work harder when they perceive that they will receive personal credit for their efforts, when the risk of failure is only moderate, and when they receive specific feedback about their past performance. People with a high drive for achievement take responsibility for their actions and results, desire to control their destiny, seek regular feedback, and enjoy being part of a winning achievement through individual or collective effort. As managers, they tend to expect that their employees will also be oriented toward achievement. These high

FIGURE 5.2
Motivational Drives

Achievement	A drive to accomplish objectives and get ahead
Affiliation	A drive to relate to people effectively
Power	A drive to influence people and situations

What Managers Are Reading

WHAT REWARDS DO EMPLOYEES WANT?

David Sirota and his co-authors argue that corporate America has fallen prey to 33 different myths about contemporary employees, including their unhappiness with pay, laziness, and resistance to change. After a thorough investigation, Sirota found that these myths are not supported by research evidence. In contrast, organizations can profit best by creating enthusiastic employees. The secret lies in giving employees the three major rewards they want from work:

- *Fair treatment* (job security, adequate compensation, and respect)
- *Sense of achievement* (purpose, enablement, challenge, feedback, and recognition)
- *Camaraderie* (trust, solidarity, and teamwork)

Source: David Sirota, Louis Mischkind, and Michael Meltzer, *The Enthusiastic Employee: How Companies Profit by Giving Workers What They Want*, Upper Saddle River, NJ: Wharton School Publishing, 2005.

expectations sometimes make it difficult for achievement-oriented managers to delegate effectively and for "average" employees to satisfy their manager's high demands.

Affiliation Motivation

Comparing achievement and affiliation drives

Affiliation motivation is a drive to relate to people on a social basis—to work with compatible people and experience a sense of community. Comparisons of achievement-motivated employees with affiliation-motivation employees illustrate how the two patterns influence behavior. Achievement-oriented people work harder when their supervisors provide detailed evaluations of their work behavior. But people with affiliation motives work better when they are complimented for their favorable attitudes and cooperation. Achievement-motivated people select assistants who are technically capable, with little regard for personal feelings about them. Those who are affiliation-motivated tend to surround themselves with friends and likable people. They receive inner satisfaction from being with friends, and they want the job freedom to develop those relationships.

Managers with strong needs for affiliation may have difficulty being effective managers. Although a high concern for positive social relationships usually results in a cooperative work environment where employees genuinely enjoy working together, managerial overemphasis on the social dimension may interfere with the vital process of getting things done. Affiliation-oriented managers may have difficulty assigning challenging tasks, directing work activities, and monitoring work effectiveness.

Power Motivation

Power motivation is a drive to influence people, take control, and change situations. Power-motivated people wish to create an impact on their organizations and are willing to take risks to do so. Once this power is obtained, it may be used either constructively or destructively.

Institutional versus personal power

Power-motivated people make excellent managers if their drives are for institutional power instead of personal power. *Institutional power* is the need to influence others' behavior for the good of the whole organization. People with this need seek power through legitimate means, rise to leadership positions through successful performance, and therefore are accepted by others. However, if an employee's drives are toward *personal power*, that person tends to lose the trust and respect of employees and colleagues and be an unsuccessful organizational leader.

Managerial Application of the Drives

Knowledge of the differences among the three motivational drives requires managers to think contingently and to understand the unique work attitudes of each employee. They can then deal with employees differently according to the strongest motivational drive that they identify in each employee. In this way, the supervisor communicates with each employee according to that particular person's needs. As one employee said, "My supervisor talks to me in my language." Although various tests can be used to identify the strength of employee drives, direct observation of employees' behavior is one of the best methods for determining what they will respond to.

HUMAN NEEDS

When a machine malfunctions, people recognize that it needs something to fix it. Managers try to find the causes of the breakdown in an analytical manner based on their knowledge of the operations and needs of the machine. Like the machine, an employee who malfunctions does so because of definite causes that may be related to needs. For improvement to occur, the employee requires skilled and professional care just as the machine does. If we treated (maintained) people as well as we do expensive machines, we would have more productive, and hence more satisfied, workers. First, we must identify the needs that are important to them.

Types of Needs

Primary needs

Needs may be classified in various ways. A simple classification is (1) basic physical needs, called **primary needs,** and (2) social and psychological needs, called **secondary needs.** The physical needs include food, water, sex, sleep, air, and reasonably comfortable temperature and humidity. These needs arise from the basic requirements of life and are important for survival of the human race. They are, therefore, virtually universal, but they vary in intensity from one person to another. For example, a toddler needs much more sleep than its parents, while some older persons desire a warmer room than others do.

Needs also are conditioned by social practice. If it is customary to eat three meals a day, then a person tends to become hungry for three, even though two might be adequate. If a coffee hour is introduced in the morning, then that becomes a habit of appetite satisfaction as well as a social need.

Secondary needs

Secondary needs are more vague because they represent needs of the mind and spirit rather than of the physical body. Many of these needs are acquired and developed as people mature. Examples are needs that pertain to self-esteem, sense of duty, competitiveness, belongingness, self-assertion, and giving or receiving affection. The secondary needs are those that complicate the motivational efforts of managers. *Therefore, managerial planning should consider the effect of any proposed action on the secondary needs of employees.*

The following are seven key conclusions about secondary needs.

- They are strongly conditioned by experience.
- They vary in type and intensity among people.
- They are subject to change across time within any individual.
- They cannot usually be isolated, but rather work in combination and influence one another.
- They are often hidden from conscious recognition.
- They are vague feelings as opposed to specific physical needs.
- They influence behavior in powerful ways.

Whereas the three motivational drives identified earlier were not grouped in any particular sequence or hierarchy, the three major theories of human needs presented in the following sections attempt to classify employee needs. At least implicitly, the theories of Maslow, Herzberg, and Alderfer build on the distinction between primary and secondary needs. Also, there are some similarities as well as important differences among the three approaches. Despite their limitations, all three approaches to human needs help create an important basis for the more advanced motivational models to be discussed later.

Maslow's Hierarchy of Needs

According to A. H. Maslow, human needs are not of equal strength, and they emerge (become increasingly important) in a predictable but rather fluid sequence. In particular, as the primary needs become reasonably well satisfied, a person places more emphasis on the secondary needs. Maslow's **hierarchy of needs** identifies and focuses attention on five levels, as shown in Figure 5.3.[5] This hierarchy is briefly presented and then interpreted in the following sections.

Lower-Order Needs First-level needs involve basic survival and include physiological needs for food, air, water, and sleep. The second need level that tends to dominate is bodily safety (such as freedom from a dangerous work environment) and economic security

FIGURE 5.3 **A Comparison of Maslow's, Herzberg's, and Alderfer's Models**

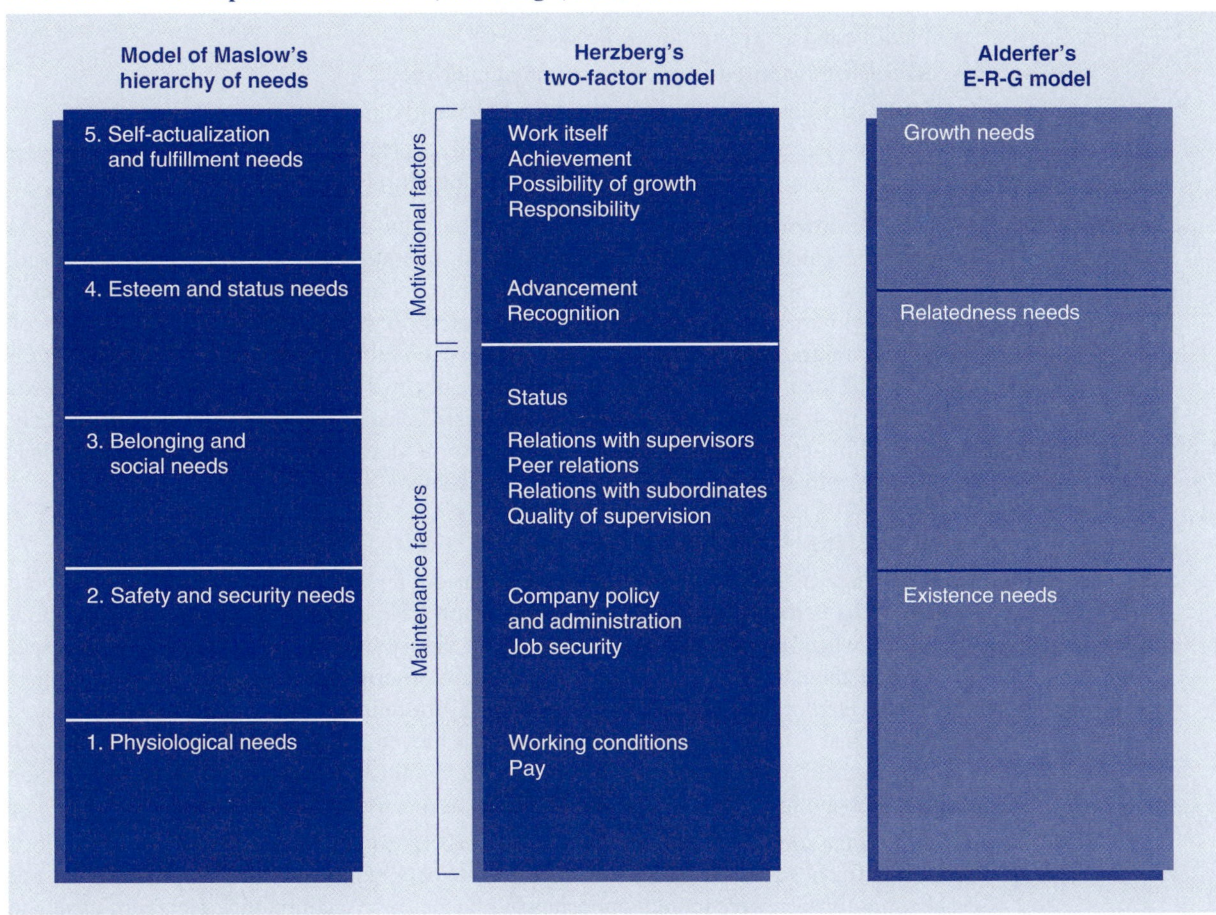

(such as a no-layoff guarantee or a comfortable retirement plan). These two need levels together are typically called **lower-order needs,** and they are similar to the primary needs discussed earlier.

Higher-Order Needs Three levels of **higher-order needs** exist. The third level in the hierarchy concerns love, belonging, and social involvement at work (friendships and compatible associates). The needs at the fourth level encompass those for esteem and status, including one's feelings of self-worth and of competence. The feeling of competence, which derives from the able completion of tasks and the assurance of others, provides status. The fifth-level need is **self-actualization,** which is an ongoing process of becoming all that one is capable of becoming, using one's skills to the fullest, having a rich combination of values and purpose, and stretching talents to the maximum.

Interpreting the Hierarchy of Needs Maslow's need-hierarchy model essentially says that people have a variety of needs they wish to satisfy, multiple needs operate simultaneously, all need levels are often partially satisfied, and that gratified needs are not as strongly motivating as unmet needs. *Employees are more enthusiastically motivated by what they are currently seeking than by receiving more of what they already have.* A fully satisfied need will not be a strong motivator.

Interpreted in this way, the Maslow hierarchy of needs has had a powerful impact on contemporary managers, offering some useful ideas for helping managers think about motivating their employees. As a result of widespread familiarity with the model, today's managers need to:

- Identify and accept employee needs
- Recognize that needs may differ among employees
- Offer satisfaction for the particular needs currently unmet
- Realize that giving more of the same reward (especially one that satisfies lower-order needs) may have a diminishing impact on motivation

Limitations

The Maslow model also has many limitations, and it has been sharply criticized. As a philosophical framework, it has been difficult to study and has not been fully verified. From a practical perspective, it is not easy to provide opportunities for self-actualization to all employees. In addition, research has not supported the presence of all five need levels as unique, nor has the five-step progression from lowest to highest need levels been established. There is, however, some evidence that unless the two lower-order needs (physiological and security) are basically satisfied, employees will not be greatly concerned with higher-order needs. The evidence for a more limited number of need levels is consistent with each of the two models discussed next.

Herzberg's Two-Factor Model

On the basis of research with a group of engineers and accountants, Frederick Herzberg developed a **two-factor model of motivation.**[6] He asked the group members to think of a time when they felt especially good about their jobs and a time when they felt especially bad about their jobs. He also asked them to describe the conditions that led to those feelings. Herzberg found that employees named different types of conditions that produced good and bad feelings—that is, if a feeling of achievement led to a good feeling, the lack of achievement was rarely given as cause for bad feelings. Instead, some other factor, such as company policy, was more frequently given as a cause of bad feelings.

Maintenance and Motivational Factors Herzberg concluded that two separate sets of factors influenced motivation. Prior to that time, people had assumed that motivation and lack of motivation were merely opposites of one factor on a continuum. Herzberg upset the

FIGURE 5.4
Effects of Maintenance and Motivational Factors

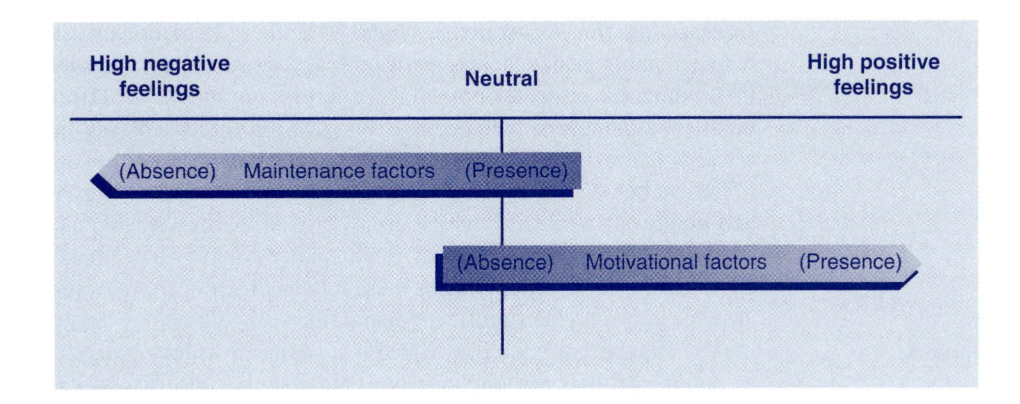

traditional view by stating that certain job factors, such as job security and working conditions, dissatisfy employees primarily when the conditions are absent. However, as shown in Figure 5.4, their presence generally brings employees only to a neutral state. The factors are not strongly motivating. These potent dissatisfiers are called **hygiene factors,** or *maintenance factors,* because they must not be ignored. They are necessary for building a foundation on which to subsequently create a reasonable level of motivation in employees.

Hygiene factors

Other job conditions operate primarily to build this motivation, but their absence rarely is strongly dissatisfying. These conditions are known as **motivational factors,** *motivators,* or *satisfiers.* For many years, managers had been wondering why their custodial policies and wide array of fringe benefits were not increasing employee motivation. The idea of separate motivational and maintenance factors helped answer their question, because fringe benefits and company policies were primarily maintenance factors, according to Herzberg.

Motivational factors

Job Content and Context Figure 5.3 shows the factors in the Herzberg model. Motivational factors such as achievement and responsibility are related, for the most part, directly to the job itself, the employee's performance, and the personal recognition and growth that employees experience. Motivators mostly are job-centered, and relate to **job content.**

On the other hand, maintenance factors are mainly related to **job context,** because they are more related to the environment surrounding the job. This difference between job content and job context is a significant one. It shows that employees are motivated primarily by what they do for themselves. When they take responsibility or gain recognition through their own behavior, they are strongly motivated.

Intrinsic and Extrinsic Motivators The difference between job content and job context is similar to the difference between intrinsic and extrinsic motivators in psychology. **Intrinsic motivators** are internal rewards that a person feels when performing a job, so there is a direct and often immediate connection between work and rewards.[7] An employee in this situation is self-motivated. **Extrinsic motivators** are external rewards that occur apart from the nature of work, providing no direct satisfaction at the time the work is performed. Examples are retirement plans, health insurance, and vacations. Although employees value these items, they are not effective motivators.

Intrinsic and extrinsic motivators

Critical Thinking Exercise

Some managers have tried to use additional hygiene factors to motivate employees. Question: What positive and negative results can you safely predict from that approach?

Interpreting the Two-Factor Model Herzberg's model provides a useful distinction between maintenance factors, which are necessary but not sufficient, and motivational factors, which have greater potential for improving employee effort. The two-factor model broadened managers' perspectives by showing the potentially powerful role of intrinsic rewards that evolve from the work itself. (This conclusion ties in with a number of other important behavioral developments, such as job enrichment, empowerment, self-leadership, and quality of work life, which are discussed in later chapters.) Nevertheless, managers cannot neglect a wide range of maintenance factors that create at least a neutral work environment. In addition, unless these hygiene factors are reasonably well addressed, their absence will serve as significant distractions to workers.

Limitations

The Herzberg model, like Maslow's, has been widely examined and criticized, as well as defended.[8] It is not universally applicable, because it was based on and applies best to managerial, professional, and upper-level white-collar employees. The model also *appears* to reduce the motivational importance of pay, status, and relations with others, since these are maintenance factors. This aspect of the model is counterintuitive to many managers and difficult for them to accept. Since there is no absolute and clear distinction between the effects of the two major factors (see the overlap in the middle of Figure 5.4), the model outlines only general tendencies; maintenance factors may be motivators to some people, and motivators may be maintenance factors to others. Finally, the model also seems to be method-bound, meaning that only Herzberg's approach (asking for self-reports of favorable and unfavorable job experiences) produces the two-factor model. In short, there may be an appearance of two independent factors when in reality there is only one factor.

Alderfer's E-R-G Model

Building upon earlier need models (primarily Maslow's) and seeking to overcome some of their weaknesses, Clayton Alderfer proposed a modified need hierarchy—the E-R-G model—with just three levels (see Figure 5.3).[9] He suggested that employees are initially interested in satisfying their **existence needs,** which combine physiological and security factors. Pay, physical working conditions, job security, and fringe benefits can all address these needs. **Relatedness needs** are at the next level, and these social factors involve being understood and accepted by people above, below, and around the employee at work and away from it. **Growth needs** are in the third category; these involve the desire for both self-esteem and self-actualization.

Existence

Relatedness

Growth

In addition to condensing Maslow's five need levels into three that are more consistent with research, the E-R-G model differs in other ways. For example, the E-R-G model does not assume a distinct progression from level to level. Instead, it accepts the likelihood that all three levels might be active at any time—or even that just one of the higher levels might be active. It also suggests that a person frustrated at either of the two higher levels may return to concentrate on a lower level and then progress again. Finally, whereas the first two levels are somewhat limited in their requirements for satisfaction, the growth needs not only are unlimited but are actually further awakened each time some satisfaction is attained.

Comparison of the Maslow, Herzberg, and Alderfer Models

The similarities among the three models of human needs are quite apparent, as shown in Figure 5.3, but there are important contrasts, too. Maslow and Alderfer focus on the internal needs of the employee, whereas Herzberg also identifies and differentiates the conditions (job content or job context) that could be provided for need satisfaction.

Popular interpretations of the Maslow and Herzberg models suggest that in modern societies many workers have already satisfied their lower-order and maintenance needs, so they are now motivated mainly by higher-order needs and motivators. Alderfer suggests that the failure to satisfy relatedness or growth needs will cause renewed interest in existence needs. (The consequences of unsatisfied needs, whether they produce frustration or constructive coping, are discussed in Chapter 15.) Finally, all three models indicate that before a manager tries to administer a reward, he or she would find it useful to *discover which need or needs dominate a particular employee at the time.* In this way, all need models provide a foundation for the understanding and application of behavior modification.

BEHAVIOR MODIFICATION

Content theories

The models of motivation that have been discussed up to this point are known as *content theories of motivation* because they focus on the content (nature) of items that may motivate a person. They relate to the person's inner self and how that person's internal state of needs determines behavior.

The major difficulty with content models of motivation is that the needs people have are not subject to observation by managers or to precise measurement for monitoring purposes. It is difficult, for example, to measure an employee's esteem needs or to assess how they change over time. Further, simply knowing about an employee's needs does not directly suggest to managers what they should do *with* that information. As a result, there has been considerable interest in motivational models that rely more heavily on intended results, careful measurement, and systematic application of incentives. **Organizational behavior modification,** or **OB Mod,** is the application in organizations of the principles of behavior modification, which evolved from the work of B. F. Skinner.[10] OB Mod and the next several models are *process theories* of motivation, since they provide perspectives on the dynamics by which employees can be motivated.

OB Mod

Process theories

Law of Effect

OB Mod is based on the idea that *behavior depends on its consequences;* therefore, managers can control, or at least affect, a number of employee behaviors by manipulating their consequences. OB Mod relies heavily on the **law of effect,** which states that a person tends to repeat behavior that is accompanied by favorable consequences (reinforcement) and tends not to repeat behavior that is accompanied by unfavorable (or a lack of) consequences. Two conditions are required for successful application of OB Mod—the manager must be able to *identify* some powerful consequences (as perceived by the employee) and then must be able to control and *administer* them in such a way that the employee will see the connection between the behavior to be affected and the consequences (see "On the Job: Ladies Professional Golf Association").

Focus on consequences

The law of effect comes from learning theory, which suggests that we learn best under pleasant surroundings. Whereas content theories argue that *internal needs lead to behavior,* OB Mod states that *external consequences tend to determine behavior.* The advantage of OB Mod is that it places a greater degree of control, and responsibility, in the hands of the manager. Several firms, including Frito-Lay, Weyerhaeuser, and B. F. Goodrich, have used various forms of behavior modification successfully.

A special type of learning theory is **social learning,** also known as *vicarious learning.* This suggests that employees do not always have to learn directly from their own experiences. Instead, they may—and even are likely to—learn by observing the actions of

On the Job: Ladies Professional Golf Association

Some professional sports have developed reward systems that appear to build on the principles of OB Mod and the law of effect. For example, on the Ladies Professional Golf Association (LPGA) tour, only those players who complete all four rounds of a tournament and have the better total scores collect checks when they are done. Furthermore, the winner's check is nearly double what the second-place finisher receives. The LPGA has identified money as a favorable consequence and tied its distribution directly to the level of short-term performance by its members. This system encourages the players to participate in numerous tournaments, perform well enough to play all four rounds, and excel.

others, understanding the consequences that others are experiencing, and using that new information to modify their own behavior. Employees who acquire the skills of social learning can often become much more effective in less time than they would have if they had to experience everything independently.

Alternative Consequences

OB Mod places great emphasis on the use of rewards (see the model of motivation in Figure 5.1) and alternative consequences to sustain behavior. Before using OB Mod, however, managers must decide whether they wish to increase the probability of a person's continued behavior or to decrease it. Once they have decided on their objective, they have two further choices to make which determine the type of consequence to be applied. First, should they use a positive or a negative consequence? Second, should they apply it or withhold it? The answers to those two questions result in four unique alternative consequences, as shown in Figure 5.5 and in the discussion that follows.

Positive reinforcement

Behavior is encouraged primarily through positive reinforcement. **Positive reinforcement** provides a *favorable consequence* that encourages repetition of a behavior. An employee, for example, may find that when high-quality work is done, the supervisor

FIGURE 5.5
Four Alternative Consequences of OB Mod

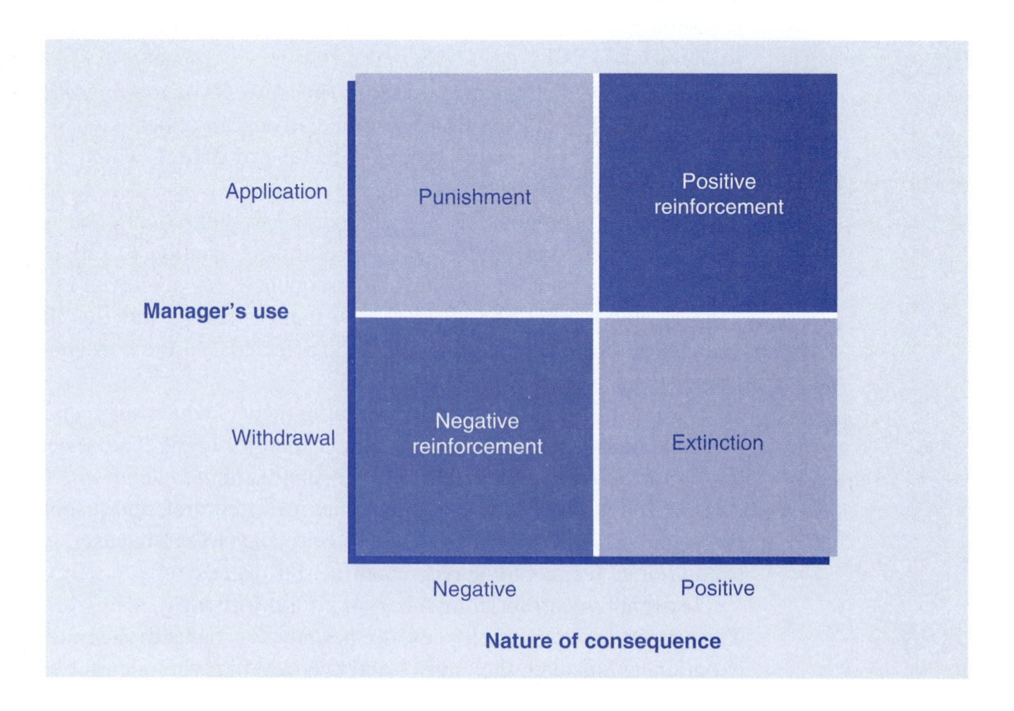

On the Job: Blandin Paper Co., Pfeiffer-Hamilton Publishers, and Grandma's Restaurants

The variety of rewards available to managers is almost limitless, not always expensive, and often touching to the recipients. Here are a few examples:

- Blandin Paper Company (owned by UPM-Kymmene) emphasizes recognition from supervisors plus rewards such as T-shirts, coffee mugs, and gift certificates to be used at local restaurants.
- Pfeiffer-Hamilton Publishers invites all employees to a "celebration of creativity" party each year and also gives each employee a free autographed copy of every book the company publishes.
- Grandma's Restaurant chain not only gives 10-year employees a gold watch but also creates placemats for its tables with the employee's picture and background information on them.
- Other companies advocate the use of personal notes praising an employee's performance, provide workers with a free lunch on their birthdays, or place the signatures of employees inside the products they produce.

gives a reward of recognition. Since the employee likes recognition, behavior is reinforced, and the employee tends to want to do high-quality work again. The reinforcement always should be contingent on the employee's correct behavior—not randomly administered (see "On the Job: Blandin Paper Co., Pfeiffer-Hamilton Publishers, and Grandma's Restaurants").

Guidelines for positive reinforcement

The secret to a manager's use of positive reinforcement lies in how it is implemented. Favorable consequences should be personalized, timely, specific, high-impact, and as spontaneous as possible. They should provide useful feedback about performance, celebrate publicly the value of a contribution, and build a sense of ownership and commitment within employees. Most of the time, positive reinforcement can be economically done in a spirit of fun, as discussed in Chapter 4.

Shaping

Shaping is a systematic and progressive application of positive reinforcement. It occurs when more frequent, or more powerful, reinforcements are successively given as the employee comes closer to the desired behavior. Even though the completely correct behavior does not yet occur, it is encouraged by giving reinforcement for behavior in the desired *direction.*[11] Shaping is especially useful for teaching complex tasks.

> An illustration of shaping is the training procedure used by a supervisor in a retail store. The store was so small it had no centralized training program for sales clerks, so all sales training was a responsibility of the supervisor. In the beginning, when a new sales clerk did not know how to deal with customers effectively, the supervisor explained the proper sales procedure. The supervisor observed the clerk's behavior, and from time to time when the clerk showed improved behavior in some part of the procedure, the supervisor expressed approval and encouraged the employee. Since this was favorable recognition for the employee, it helped shape behavior in the correct direction.

Negative reinforcement

Negative reinforcement occurs when behavior is accompanied by *removal* of an unfavorable consequence; therefore, it is not the same as punishment, which normally *adds* something unfavorable. Consistent with the law of effect, behavior responsible for the removal of something unfavorable is repeated when that unfavorable state is again encountered. An example of negative reinforcement is the experience of a jet aircraft mechanic who learned that if she wore noise suppressors over her ears, she could prevent discomfort from the jet engine noise—the unfavorable consequence; this reinforcement encouraged her to wear the proper noise equipment.

Punishment

Punishment is the *administration* of an unfavorable consequence that discourages a certain behavior. Although punishment may be necessary occasionally to discourage an undesirable behavior, it needs to be used with caution because it has certain limitations. It does not directly encourage any kind of desirable behavior unless the person receiving it is clearly aware of the alternative path to follow; it may cause managers acting as punishers to become disliked for their disciplinary actions; and it could happen that people who are punished may be unclear about what specific part of their behavior is being punished.

Extinction

Extinction is the *withholding of significant positive consequences that were previously provided* for a desirable behavior. Such desirable learned behavior needs to be reinforced to encourage the person to repeat the action in the future. If no reinforcement by the manager, the employee, or anyone else occurs, the behavior tends to diminish (become extinguished) through lack of reinforcement.

Schedules of Reinforcement

Before various types of consequences can be applied, managers should monitor employee behavior to learn how often, or how well, employees are performing. The frequency of the behavior creates a *baseline,* or standard, against which improvements can be compared. Then, the manager can select a reinforcement schedule, which is the frequency with which the selected consequence accompanies a desired behavior.

Baseline

Continuous reinforcement

Reinforcement may be either continuous or partial. **Continuous reinforcement** occurs when reinforcement accompanies each correct behavior by an employee. In some instances, this level of reinforcement may be desirable to encourage quick learning, but in the typical work situation it usually is not possible to reward even one employee for every correct behavior—much less several employees. An example of continuous reinforcement is payment of employees for each acceptable item they produce.

Partial reinforcement

Partial reinforcement occurs when only *some* of the correct behaviors are reinforced—either after a certain time or after a number of correct responses. Learning is slower with partial reinforcement than with continuous reinforcement. However, learning tends to be retained longer when it is secured under conditions of partial reinforcement.

Interpreting Behavior Modification

Contributions

The major benefit of behavior modification is that it makes managers become more conscious motivators. It encourages managers to analyze employee behavior, explore why it occurs and how often, and identify specific consequences that will help change it when those consequences are applied systematically. Application of this process often encourages effective supervisors to devote more time to monitoring employee behaviors. Performance feedback, praise, and recognition are often parts of this strategy because they tend to be widely desired and therefore are strong reinforcements. General guidelines for a behavior modification strategy are shown in Figure 5.6. When specific behaviors can be identified and desired reinforcements are properly applied, behavior modification can lead to substantial improvements in specific areas, such as absences, tardiness, and error rates (see "On the Job: Collins Food International" on the next page).

Limitations

Behavior modification has been criticized on several grounds, including its philosophy, methods, and practicality. Because of the strong power of desired consequences, the use of behavior modification may effectively force people to change their behavior. In this way, it could manipulate people and be inconsistent with humanistic assumptions discussed earlier that people want to be autonomous and self-actualizing. Some critics also fear that behavior modification gives too much power to the managers, without appropriate controls. These critics raise the question, Who will control the controllers?

On the Job: Collins Food International

Collins Food International used behavior modification with clerical employees in its accounting department.[12] One of the items selected for modification was billing error rates. Management measured existing error rates and then met with employees to discuss and set goals for improvement. It also praised employees for reduction of errors, and it reported error results to them regularly. Employees in the accounts payable department responded by reducing error rates from more than 8 percent to less than 0.2 percent.

GOAL SETTING

Goals are targets and objectives for future performance. They help focus employees' attention on items of greater importance to the organization, encourage better planning for the allocation of critical resources (time, money, and energy), illustrate the value of persistent effort, and stimulate the preparation of action plans for goal attainment. Goals appear in the model of motivation (see Figure 5.1) *before* employee performance, which accents their role as a cue to acceptable behavior. Goals are also useful *after* the desired behavior, as managers compare employee results with their aims and explore reasons for any differences.

Goal setting works as a motivational process because it creates a discrepancy between current and expected performance. This results in a feeling of tension, which the employee can diminish through future goal attainment. Meeting goals also helps satisfy a person's achievement drive, contributes to feelings of competence and self-esteem, and further stimulates personal growth needs. Individuals who successfully achieve goals tend to set even higher goals in the future. One review of research concluded that employee performance improved about 16 percent after the implementation of a goal-setting program—a success rate that many firms would be happy to achieve.[13]

Self-efficacy affects goal setting

A major factor in the success of goal setting is **self-efficacy.** This is an internal belief regarding one's job-related capabilities and competencies. (Self-efficacy is different from self-esteem, which is a broader feeling of like or dislike for oneself.)[14] Self-efficacy can be judged either on a specific task or across a variety of performance duties. If employees have high self-efficacies, they will tend to set higher personal goals under the belief that they are attainable. The first key to successful goal setting is to build

FIGURE 5.6
Guidelines for Applying Behavior Modification

- Identify the exact behavior to be modified.
- Make sure the expected behavior is within the employee's capabilities.
- Determine not only the rewards that employees value but also the magnitude that would affect their behavior.
- Clarify the connection between desired behavior and rewards.
- Use positive reinforcement whenever possible.
- Use punishment only in unusual circumstances and for specific behaviors.
- Ignore minor undesirable behavior to allow its extinction.
- Use shaping procedures to develop correct complex behavior.
- Minimize the time between the correct behavior and its reinforcement.
- Provide reinforcement frequently, and on some chosen schedule.

(in thousands of dollars) surpassed her age. One year, at age 34, she received a substantial salary increase that placed her annual income at $33,865. She was frustrated, incensed, and demoralized for weeks afterward, for she did not receive what she dearly wanted! For an extra $135, the company could have matched her equity expectations and continued to have a motivated employee.

Pay was a symbolic scorecard by which Nickerson compared her outcomes with her inputs (since she included age with her other inputs of education, experience, and effort). Her reaction is only one of the three combinations that can occur from social comparisons—equity, overreward, and underreward. If employees perceive *equity,* they will be motivated to continue to contribute at about the same level. Otherwise, under conditions of inequity, they will experience tension that will create the motivation to reduce the inequity. The resulting actions can be either physical or psychological, and internal or external.

Equity

If employees feel *overrewarded,* equity theory predicts that they will feel an imbalance in their relationship with their employer and seek to restore that balance. They might work harder (shown as an internal and physical response in Figure 5.10), they might discount the value of the rewards received (internal and psychological), they could try to convince other employees to ask for more rewards (external and physical), or they might simply choose someone else for comparison purposes (external and psychological).

Overreward

Workers who feel they have been *underrewarded* seek to reduce their feelings of inequity through the same types of strategies, but some of their specific actions are now reversed. They might lower the quantity or quality of their productivity, they could inflate the perceived value of the rewards received, or they could bargain for more actual rewards. Again, they could find someone else to compare themselves (more favorably) with, or they might simply quit. In any event, they are reacting to inequity by bringing their inputs into balance with their outcomes. Knowledge of perceived outcome/input ratios allows managers to predict part of their employees' behavior through understanding when, and under what conditions, workers will experience inequity. It might also alert managers to predict the product of that inequity.

Underreward

An example of employee reaction to underpayment occurred in a manufacturing plant that made small mechanical parts for the aerospace and automotive industries.[19] Some important contracts were canceled, and the company was forced to announce a 15 percent cut in pay for all employees. Compared with a control group in another plant whose pay was not cut, the affected employees reacted by doubling their normal theft rate (tools and supplies stolen from the company). Turnover also jumped to 23 percent, compared with a normal rate of 5 percent. Apparently the employees experienced a change from relative equity to underpayment inequity. They reacted to their perceived mistreatment by making unofficial transfers of organizational resources to themselves. When the pay cut ended after 10 weeks, the theft rate returned to normal levels.

FIGURE 5.10
Possible Reactions to Perceived Inequity

Type of Inequity Reactions	Possible Overreward Reactions	Possible Underreward Reaction
Internal, physical	Work harder	Lower productivity
Internal, psychological	Discount the reward	Inflate value of the reward
External, physical	Encourage the referent person to obtain more	Bargain for more; possibly quit
External, psychological	Change the referent person	Change the referent person

Interpreting the Equity Model

An understanding of equity should remind managers that employees work within *several* social systems. Employees may actually select a number of reference groups both inside and outside the organization. Employees are also inclined to shift the basis for their comparisons to the standard that is most favorable to them. For example, educated people often inflate the value of their education, while employees with longer service emphasize seniority as the dominant criterion. Other employees choose somewhat higher (economic) groups as their reference. Many employees have strong egos and even inflated opinions of themselves. Consequently, all these factors (multiple reference groups, shifting standards, upward orientation, and personal egos) make the task of predicting when inequity will occur somewhat complex.

Equity sensitivity

Equity theory has generated extensive research, with many of the results being supportive. In particular, underreward seems to produce motivational tension with predictable (negative) consequences; less consistent results are found for the overreward condition. The different research results may be reconciled by the idea of **equity sensitivity,** which suggests that individuals have different preferences for equity. Some people seem to prefer overreward, some conform to the traditional equity model, and others prefer to be underrewarded.[20] Identifying which employees fall into each class would help managers predict who would experience inequity and how important it would be in affecting their behavior.

Similar elements—effort (inputs) and rewards (outcomes)—can be seen when comparing the equity and expectancy models. In both approaches, perception plays a key role, again suggesting how valuable it is for a manager to gather information *from* employees instead of trying to impose one's own perceptions onto them. The major challenges for a manager using the equity model lie in measuring employee assessments of their inputs and outcomes, identifying their choice of references, and evaluating employee perceptions of inputs and outcomes.

Employees value fair treatment and transparency

Fairness, from an employee's equity perspective, applies not only to the actual size of rewards and their relation to inputs provided, but also to the *process* by which they are administered. This is the essence of the **procedural justice** approach to motivation, which focuses on two elements—interpersonal treatment and clarity of explanations. *Interpersonal treatment* encompasses both managerial respect for employee inputs and managerial behavior that exhibits clear levels of respect, esteem, consideration, and courtesy. *Clarity of expectations* is enhanced by managers making the reward process more transparent, so that employees can discover and understand how their inputs were assessed and how the reward system is administered. Procedural justice is especially important when organizational resources are tight and lesser levels of valued outcomes are provided to employees.

An Ethics Question

Employees have a tendency to consider themselves better than others (similar to the children in Garrison Keillor's fictional Lake Wobegon, "where all the children are above average"). This leads to a sense of *entitlement*, as well as an inclination to judge the contributions of others more harshly (to make themselves look better by comparison). This can lead to breakdowns within teams and a lack of teamwork—especially when one employee learns of another's (higher) level of compensation or special treatment. It can also result in employees who magnify their self-worth to the organization by exaggerating their contributions. Question: What should a manager do with such employees, who are engaging in what seems to be unethical behavior (lying)?

INTERPRETING MOTIVATIONAL MODELS

Several motivational models are presented in this chapter. All the models have strengths and weaknesses, advocates and critics. No model is perfect, but all of them add something to our understanding of the motivational process. Other models are being developed, and attempts are being made to integrate existing approaches.[21]

Contingent use of motivational models

The cognitive (process) models are likely to continue dominating organizational practice for some time. They are most consistent with our supportive and comprehensive view of people as thinking individuals who make somewhat conscious decisions about their behavior. However, behavior modification also has some usefulness, especially in stable situations with minimum complexity, where there appears to be a direct connection between behavior and its consequences. In more complex, dynamic situations, cognitive models will be used more often. In other words, the motivational model used must be carefully chosen, adapted as needed, and blended with other models.

As the world of business becomes increasingly global, it becomes important to consider the relevance of motivational models to countries outside the United States, whose culture reflects individualism. By contrast, in collective cultures such as Japan, feelings of belonging may be more important to employees than esteem needs. This changes the nature of Maslow's model of motivation, just as it takes on a different form for some monks who fast (ignoring their presumed physiological needs) in order to become self-actualized. Herzberg's model, which emphasizes job content, intrinsic rewards, and autonomy, may not fit as well in Indonesia, where social relationships are valued highly. And the equity model may not apply well to some Asian countries, where equality (of rewards) is valued more highly than individual feelings of equity.

Summary

When people join an organization, they bring with them certain drives and needs that affect their on-the-job performance. Sometimes these are immediately apparent, but often they not only are difficult to determine and satisfy but also vary greatly from one person to another. Understanding how needs create tensions that stimulate effort to perform and how effective performance brings the satisfaction of rewards is useful for managers.

Several approaches to understanding internal drives and needs within employees are examined in the chapter. Each model makes a contribution to our understanding of motivation. All the models share some similarities. In general, they encourage managers not only to consider lower-order, maintenance, and extrinsic factors but to use higher-order, motivational, and intrinsic factors as well.

Behavior modification focuses on the external environment by stating that a number of employee behaviors can be affected by manipulating their consequences. The alternative consequences include positive and negative reinforcement, punishment, and extinction. Reinforcement can be applied according to either continuous or partial schedules.

A blending of internal and external approaches is obtained through consideration of goal setting. Managers are encouraged to use cues—such as goals that are accepted, challenging, and specific—to stimulate desired employee behavior. In this way, goal setting—combined with the reinforcement of performance feedback—provides a balanced approach to motivation.

Additional approaches to motivation presented in this chapter are the expectancy and equity models. The expectancy model states that motivation is a product of how much one wants something and the probabilities that effort will lead to task accomplishment and reward. The formula is valence $\times$ expectancy $\times$ instrumentality $=$ motivation. Valence is the strength of a person's preference for an outcome. Expectancy is the strength of belief that one's effort will be successful in accomplishing a task. Instrumentality is the strength of belief that successful performance will be followed by a reward.

Advice to Future Managers

1. *Identify each employee's needs and drives* and monitor how they change over time.
2. *Reduce the distracting influence of hygiene factors* before turning your attention to providing motivators.
3. Establish strong connections between desired behaviors and rewards given; *provide rewards that recognize high achievers more than other employees.*
4. *Set performance-oriented goals that are specific, challenging, and acceptable.*
5. *Seek information regarding employee perceptions of valence, expectancy, and instrumentality;* share key information with employees to improve their assessments.
6. Discover the referent people or groups and perceived outcome/input ratios for employees' equity computation; *compare your assessments of their likely equity with their own perceptions.*
7. Remember that employees judge not only the fairness of the rewards they receive (in comparison to their inputs) but also the process that accompanies them. *Carefully communicate your assessment of their inputs and your decisional process for distributing rewards.*
8. Discover each employee's sense of self-efficacy on the tasks to which they are assigned; *offer supportive feedback that increases the accuracy of their assessment and enhances their self-efficacy.*
9. Recall that employees have different levels of drives for achievement, affiliation, and power. *Strive to set goals for them that will stretch them and will, when completed, enhance their achievement drives.*
10. Recognize that all need theories of motivation are simplified attempts to describe a "universal person." *Use the models flexibly to probe for, and discover, each employee's unique needs.*

The expectancy and equity motivational models relate specifically to the employee's intellectual processes. The equity model has a double comparison in it—a match between an employee's perceived inputs and outcomes, coupled with a comparison with some referent person's rewards for her or his input level. In addition, employees use the procedural justice model to assess the fairness of how rewards are distributed.

Managers are encouraged to combine the perspectives of several models to create a complete motivational environment for their employees.

Speaking OB: Terms and Concepts for Review

Achievement motivation, *118*
Affiliation motivation, *119*
Continuous reinforcement, *128*
Drives, *118*
Equity sensitivity, *137*
Equity theory, *135*
Existence needs, *124*
Expectancy, *132*
Expectancy model, *131*
Extinction, *128*
Extrinsic motivators, *123*
Fatigued workers, *117*
Goal setting, *129*
Goals, *129*
Growth needs, *124*
Hierarchy of needs, *121*
High-energy workers, *117*
Higher-order needs, *122*
Hygiene factors, *123*
Inputs, *135*
Instrumentality, *133*
Intrinsic motivators, *123*
Job content, *123*
Job context, *123*
Law of effect, *125*
Lower-order needs, *122*
Motivation, *133*
Motivational factors, *123*
Negative reinforcement, *127*
OB Mod, *125*
Organizational behavior modification, *125*
Outcomes, *135*
Partial reinforcement, *128*
Performance feedback, *131*
Performance monitoring, *131*
Positive reinforcement, *126*
Power motivation, *119*
Primary needs, *120*
Procedural justice, *137*
Punishment, *128*
Relatedness needs, *124*
Secondary needs, *120*
Self-actualization, *122*
Self-efficacy, *129*
Shaping, *127*
Social learning, *125*
Two-factor model of motivation, *122*
Valence, *132*
Work motivation, *116*

Discussion Questions

1. Think of someone who, in the past, did an excellent job of motivating you. Describe how this was done. Which of the following approaches did that person use (either explicitly or implicitly)?
   a. Lower-order or higher-order needs?
   b. Maintenance or motivational factors? If so, which one(s)?
   c. Existence, relatedness, or growth needs?
   d. Behavior modification?
   e. Goal setting?
2. In your role as a student, do you feel you are motivated more by Maslow's lower-order or higher-order needs? Explain. Describe how you expect motivation to change once you graduate.
3. Which one factor in Herzberg's two-factor model is most motivating to you at the present time? Explain. Is this a maintenance or motivational factor?
4. It is relatively easy for a manager to manipulate *extrinsic* rewards. Describe some ways in which a manager could affect *intrinsic* satisfaction of an employee.
5. Discuss how behavior modification operates to motivate people. Why is it still important to understand people's needs when using this approach?
6. Explain the differences between negative reinforcement and punishment.
7. Divide the class into two groups (one in favor and one opposed) and debate this proposition: "Rewards motivate people."
8. How would you use the expectancy model in the following situations?
   a. You want two employees to switch their vacations from the summer to the spring so that job needs will be filled suitably during the summer.
   b. You believe that one of your employees has excellent potential for promotion and want to encourage her to prepare for it.
   c. You have a sprained ankle and want a friend to walk to a fast-food restaurant and get you a hamburger.
9. Apply the equity model to yourself as a student. How do you measure your inputs and outcomes? Whom have you chosen as referent individuals? Do you perceive equity? If not, how will you attain it? Is procedural justice present?
10. The text suggests that an individual's equity perceptions can be distorted. If that is the case, how would you go about correcting or adjusting them?

Assess Your Own Skills

How well do you exhibit good motivational skills?

Read the following statements carefully. Circle the number on the response scale that most closely reflects the degree to which each statement accurately describes you when you have tried to motivate someone else. Add up your total points and prepare a brief action plan for self-improvement. Be ready to report your score for tabulation across the entire group.

	Good description									Poor description
1. I consciously follow an integrated model of motivation such as Figure 5.1 when motivating people.	10	9	8	7	6	5	4	3	2	1

2. I determine whether people are achievement, affiliation, or power driven and respond accordingly.	10	9	8	7	6	5	4	3	2	1
3. I try to determine which level of the need hierarchy is most powerful for each employee.	10	9	8	7	6	5	4	3	2	1
4. I make sure I eliminate dissatisfiers in the work context before I focus on providing motivational factors to my employees.	10	9	8	7	6	5	4	3	2	1
5. I recognize that employees might be interested in the satisfaction of their growth needs, as indicated by the Maslow, Herzberg, and Alderfer models.	10	9	8	7	6	5	4	3	2	1
6. I am conscious of the need to provide systematic consequences, both positive and negative, to employees to utilize the law of effect.	10	9	8	7	6	5	4	3	2	1
7. I recognize that negative reinforcement and punishment are very different strategies.	10	9	8	7	6	5	4	3	2	1
8. Whenever possible, I set goals that are both specific and challenging.	10	9	8	7	6	5	4	3	2	1
9. I seek to provide the conditions that will allow employees to improve their level of self-efficacy.	10	9	8	7	6	5	4	3	2	1
10. I carefully monitor each employee's level of performance and provide constructive feedback as needed.	10	9	8	7	6	5	4	3	2	1

Scoring and Interpretation

Add up your total points for the 10 questions. Record that number here, and report it when it is requested. Finally, insert your total score into the "Assess and Improve Your Own Organizational Behavior Skills" chart in Appendix A.

- If you scored between 81 and 100 points, you appear to have a solid capability for demonstrating good motivational skills.
- If you scored between 61 and 80 points, you should take a close look at the items with lower self-assessment scores and explore ways to improve those items.
- If you scored under 60 points, you should be aware that a weaker skill level regarding several items could be detrimental to your future success as a motivator. We encourage you to review relevant sections of the chapter and watch for related material in subsequent chapters and other sources.

Now identify your three lowest scores, and write the question numbers here: _____, _____, _____. Write a brief paragraph, detailing to yourself an action plan for how you might sharpen each of these skills.

Role-Play

The Downsized Firm

Instructions

Divide into groups of four persons, assigning the roles of Phil, Sue, John, and Linda to each of the four members, respectively. Each person should read only their role. When everyone is ready, Phil should meet with one person after another and attempt to create a motivational atmosphere that will encourage each "employee" to remain with the firm and be productive.

Phil

You are the supervisor of the circulation department for a scientific publisher. Your department was recently downsized, and you lost two customer service representatives. They were terminated for business reasons that had nothing to do with their job performance. You have three remaining representatives—Sue, John, and Linda—and are about to meet with each of them to try to convince them to remain motivated and productive (doing the work of five persons previously) and stay with the firm.

Sue

Your department was recently downsized, and two of the five customer service representatives were laid off. They were allegedly terminated for business reasons that had nothing to do with their job performance. You are one of the three remaining representatives (the others are John and Linda). You are a single mother and have to take extra days off when your children are sick. Sometimes you work a flexible schedule of hours to accommodate the children's schedules. You are beginning to wonder if these allowances will make you more vulnerable in any future round of layoffs. You are about to meet with Phil now.

John

Your department was recently downsized, and two of the five customer service representatives were laid off. They were allegedly terminated for business reasons that had nothing to do with their job performance. You are one of the three remaining representatives (the others are Sue and Linda). You have been on the job for two years. You attend college at night and see the job as a steppingstone into a management position. However, after seeing your two colleagues (and friends) terminated, you are beginning to wonder if this company is one you want to stay with. You are about to meet with Phil now.

Linda

Your department was recently downsized, and two of the five customer service representatives were laid off. They were allegedly terminated for business reasons that had nothing to do with their job performance. You are one of the three remaining representatives (the others are Sue and Linda). You have worked in customer service for 15 years and have always felt like you made a lifetime commitment to work. Now even you are beginning to wonder how secure your job is. After all, if it happened to two of your colleagues, it might happen to you, too. You are about to meet with Phil now.

Discussion

1. What major motivational model(s) did Phil use with Sue, John, and Linda?
2. What other approaches might have worked better?
3. What are the major lessons you can derive from this exercise?

Incident

The Piano Builder[22]

Waverly Bird builds pianos from scratch and is also a consultant to a piano manufacturer. In the latter job, he is on call and works about one week a month, which sometimes includes traveling, to solve customers' problems. He also rebuilds about a dozen grand pianos every year for special customers. However, according to Bird, the most satisfying part of his life is his hobby of building pianos from the beginning. "It's the part that keeps a man alive," he says. The challenge of the work is what lures Bird onward. He derives satisfaction from precision and quality, and he comments, "Details make the difference. When you cut a little corner here and a little corner there, you've cut a big hole. A piano is like the human body; all the parts are important."

Bird has a substantial challenge in making a whole piano. His work combines skills in cabinetmaking, metalworking, and engineering, with knowledge of acoustics and a keen ear for music. It requires great precision, because a tiny misalignment would ruin a piano's tune. It also requires versatility: A keyboard must be balanced to respond to the touch of a finger; the pinblock, on the other hand, must withstand up to 20 tons of pressure. In addition, Bird had to make many of his own piano construction tools.

Bird has built 40 pianos in his 34-year career. Though construction takes nearly a year, he sells his pianos at the modest price of a commercial piano. He is seeking not money but challenge and satisfaction. He says, "The whole business is a series of closed doors. You learn one thing, and there's another closed door waiting to be opened." Bird says his big dream is to build a grand piano: "It is the one thing I haven't done yet and want to do."

Questions

1. Discuss the nature of Bird's motivation in building pianos. What are his drives and needs? Would a behavior modification program affect his motivation? Why or why not? What would be the effect of setting a goal of two pianos per year for him?
2. How could a manufacturer of pianos build the motivation Bird has now into its employees?

Experiential Exercise

Are Grades Motivators?

1. Assess the valence of receiving an A in this course. Assign A a valence somewhere between -1 and $+1$, using gradations of one-tenth (e.g., 0.8, 0.9, 1.0).
2. Assess the probability (between 0.0 and 1.0) that the level of effort you expect to commit to this course will result in a high enough performance to merit an A. This constitutes your expectancy score.
3. Assess the probability (between 0.0 and 1.0) that your stellar performance in this course (an A) will substantially improve your overall grade-point average. This represents your instrumentality score.
4. Multiply your V, E, and I scores to produce an overall measure of your likely motivation (on this one task and for this reward). This overall score should fall between -1.0 and $+1.0$. Enter your name and data on line 1 in the following.
5. Share your four scores with classmates in a format like that shown here. Note the range of responses within the class for each item.

Student's Name	Valence	Expectancy	Instrumentality	Motivation
1.				
2.				
3.				
4.				
5.				

Generating OB Insights

An *insight* is a new and clear perception of a phenomenon, or an acquired ability to "see" clearly something you were unaware of previously. It is sometimes simply referred to as an "ah-ha! moment," in which you have a minirevelation or reach a straightforward conclusion about a topic or issue.

Insights need not necessarily be dramatic, for what is an insight to one person may be less important to another. The critical feature of insights is that they are relevant and memorable for *you;* they should represent new knowledge, new frameworks, or new ways of viewing things you want to retain and remember over time.

Insights, then, are different from the information you find in the "Advice for Future Managers" boxes within the text. That advice is prescriptive and action-oriented; it indicates a recommended course of action.

A useful way to think of OB insights is to assume you are the only person who has read Chapter 5. You have been given the assignment to highlight, in your own words, the major concepts (but not just summarize the whole chapter) that might stand out for a naive audience who has never heard of the topic before. *What 10 insights would you share with them?*

(Example) *Employees have a complex set of needs that are ever-changing and not always clear (even to themselves).*

1. ______________________________
____
2. ______________________________
____
3. ______________________________
____
4. ______________________________
____
5. ______________________________
____
6. ______________________________
____
7. ______________________________
____
8. ______________________________
____
9. ______________________________
____
10. ______________________________
____

Nurturing Your Critical Thinking and Reflective Skills

Take a few minutes to review the discussion in the Roadmap for Readers of critical thinking and reflection. Remind yourself that if you can hone these abilities now, you will have a substantial competitive advantage when you apply for jobs and are asked what unique skills you can bring to the position and the organization.

Critical Thinking

Think back on the material you read in this chapter. What are three unique and challenging *critical questions* you would like to raise about this material? (These might identify something controversial about which you have doubts, they may imply that you suspect that a theory or model has weaknesses, they could examine the legitimacy of apparent causal relationships, or they might assess the probable value of a suggested practice.) Be prepared to share these questions with class members or your instructor.

1. ____________________
   ____
2. ____________________
   ____
3. ____________________
   ____

Reflection

This process often involves answering the parallel questions of "What do you *think* about the material you have read?" and "How do you *feel* about that material?" Therefore, express your *personal thoughts and feelings* (reactions) to any of the ideas or topics found in this chapter, and be prepared to share these reflections with class members or your instructor.

1. ____________________
   ____
2. ____________________
   ____
3. ____________________
   ____

Chapter Six

Appraising and Rewarding Performance

Seventy-five percent of all U.S. companies (have) connected at least part of an employee's pay directly to performance.

Charles Coy[1]

If you look at the modern workplace, I would say it's one of the most feedback-deprived places in American civilization. It's a feedback desert.

Daniel Pink[2]

CHAPTER OBJECTIVES

AFTER READING THIS CHAPTER, YOU SHOULD UNDERSTAND

6-1 Total Reward Systems
6-2 Money as an Economic and Social Medium of Exchange
6-3 The Role of Money in Motivational Models
6-4 Behavioral Considerations in Performance Appraisal
6-5 The Characteristics of Good Feedback Programs
6-6 The Process of Attribution
6-7 How and Why to Link Pay with Performance
6-8 Uses of Profit-Sharing, Gain-Sharing, and Skill-Based Pay Programs

Facebook Page 

Student B: It's Friday night, and some friends are chillin' at my place. What's up with you?

Student A: I'm reading a new OB chapter on pay. I thought I was done with all those motivational models, but now I'm seeing how money fits into some of them.

Student B: I thought it was pretty simple; doesn't more pay motivate more effort?

Student A: It's not that simple at all. There are service and sacrifice rewards, and nonwork and noneconomic awards, that help constitute a complete pay system beyond just paying for results.

Student B: I've heard of pay for performance before, and I think I'd like that idea. What else is there?

Student A: In addition to wage incentives, there are profit sharing systems, gain sharing plans, and skill-based pay. Each has its pros and cons.

Student B: That's all fine, but how does a manager decide how big a reward to give an employee?

Student A: First you have to know the relevant laws, such as equal pay for equal work and nondiscrimination based on sex of the employee. Then you set objectives for each worker, give them useful performance feedback, provide praise if it is earned, and conduct periodic appraisals.

Student B: This sounds pretty straightforward. Where does OB fit in?

Student A: A ton of ways. I've got to learn about intrinsic rewards, attribution biases, and the self-fulfilling prophecy. As a matter of fact, I'm going to practice one idea (the Galatea effect) right now—if I set high expectations for myself, I'm more likely to perform well. See ya!

The board of directors for a regional health care system were in executive session, discussing the CEO's performance for the past year. After determining that it was "outstanding," they set about establishing the appropriate level of compensation for her. All of the directors agreed that a substantial pay increase was in order. However, when the newly adjusted level of compensation was calculated, one director (a physician) made a poignant comment. "I don't care how much you pay her," he contended, "as long as it isn't any higher than the average of the physicians working in the clinic. After all, the hospital wouldn't be able to function if it weren't for us."

This case illustrates how economic rewards are powerfully important to employees and how pay relationships carry immense *social* value. Management has not always recognized this. In the nineteenth and early twentieth centuries, employees were presumed to want primarily money; therefore, money was believed to produce direct motivation—the more money offered, the more motivation. Researchers successfully buried this idea by showing that economic rewards operated through the attitudes of workers in the social system to produce an *indirect* incentive.

In this chapter, we discuss the complex relationship between economic reward systems and organizational behavior. More details about these systems will be found in books about compensation and human resource management; only their significant behavioral aspects

Engaging Your Brain

1. This chapter suggests that there may be a tradeoff between extrinsic rewards and intrinsic satisfaction. If you could allocate 100 total points to the two factors for yourself, how would you prefer to divide it up? 50-50? 70-30? 100-0?
2. Some writers have suggested that managers hate giving (critical) feedback, and employees detest receiving it. How well do *you* handle critical comments on your performance?
3. Many employees report being hungry for praise, but claim that they seldom receive it. Why might this be so?

are examined here. This chapter focuses first on how **incentives** are combined with other parts of wage and salary administration to build a complete reward system that encourages motivation. Then, we discuss money as a means of rewarding employees, motivational models applied to pay, cost–reward comparisons, and behavioral considerations in performance appraisal. Finally, we discuss incentive pay, an approach in which each worker's pay varies in relation to employee or organizational performance.

A COMPLETE PROGRAM

Many types of pay are required for a complete economic reward system.[3] Job analysis and wage surveys rate *jobs,* comparing one job with another to determine base pay (according to levels of responsibility and market pressure). Performance appraisal and incentives rate *employees* on their performance and reward their contributions. Profit sharing rates the *organization* in terms of its general economic performance and rewards employees as partners in it. Together, these three systems—base pay, performance rewards, and profit sharing—are the incentive foundation of a complete pay program, as diagrammed in the reward pyramid in Figure 6.1. Each can contribute something to the employee's economic satisfaction.

Relating pay to objectives

The three systems are complementary because each reflects a different set of factors in the total situation. Base pay and skill-based pay motivate employees to progress to jobs of higher skills and responsibility. Performance pay is an incentive to improve performance on the job. Profit sharing motivates workers toward teamwork to improve an organization's performance.

Other payments, primarily nonincentive in nature, are added to the incentive foundation. Seniority pay adjustments are made to reward workers for extended service and to encourage them to remain with their employer. If an employer asks workers to sacrifice by working overtime, working on their day off, or working undesirable hours, the workers may be paid extra for the inconvenience. Other payments are given for periods when an employee does not work, such as vacations, holidays, jury service, and layoffs subject to guaranteed pay.

The additions to the foundation of the reward pyramid have little direct incentive value because they do not increase according to improved job performance. Some of these additions may result in *indirect* incentive through better attitudes, however. Other additions, such as seniority pay, actually may *decrease* worker incentive since they are not tied to performance outcomes. It is clear that not one factor but many enter into computation of a worker's paycheck. Some of these factors are related less to incentive than they are to such broad objectives as security, equity, and social justice. An effective program of

On the Job: Lincoln Electric Company

Lincoln Electric Company provides a classic and unique combination of compensation programs to its employees to create a complete reward program, in conjunction with other distinctive management policies.[4] It offers piecework pay, shared profits, suggestion systems, year-end bonuses, and stock-ownership opportunities. It couples these with no paid holidays or sick days, mandatory overtime, no seniority system, and no definite lines of promotion. It does, however, boast a 50-year record of no layoffs, which provides a huge measure of job security in this era of downsizing. The results are clear: Its sales level per employee is two to three times the manufacturing standard; its products are noted for their reliability; and the postprobationary turnover rate is less than 3 percent per year—including deaths and retirements.

economic rewards is a balance of most of these factors, as shown in "On the Job: Lincoln Electric Company."

A wide range of *noneconomic* programs also exists to supplement an organization's complete pay program. Some firms reward their employees with contingent time off for exemplary performance; others allow employees to earn "comp time" (compensatory time) for hours worked but not paid for. Many firms provide a wide array of other benefits for their employees, such as on-site day care facilities and wellness-promotion programs. The number of options and their costs to employers have risen dramatically and are often as much as 35 to 50 percent of total compensation.

MONEY AS A MEANS OF REWARDING EMPLOYEES

Money has social value

It is evident from Figure 6.1 that money is important to employees for a number of reasons. Certainly, money is valuable because of the goods and services it will purchase. This aspect is its economic value as a medium of exchange for allocation of economic resources; however, money also is a *social medium of exchange*. All of us have seen its importance as a status symbol for those who have it and can thus save it, spend it conspicuously, or give it away generously. Money has status value when it is being received and when it is being spent. It represents to employees what their employer thinks of them. It is also an indication of one employee's status relative to that of other employees. It has about as many values as it has possessors. The following is an example of how people respond differently to it:

> A manager gave two field sales representatives the same increase in pay because each had done a good job. One sales representative was highly pleased with this recognition. She felt she was respected and rewarded because the raise placed her in a higher income bracket. The other sales representative was angered because he knew the raise amounted to the minimum standard available; he considered it an insult rather than an adequate reward for the outstanding job he felt he was doing. He felt that he was not properly recognized, and he saw this small raise as a serious blow to his own esteem and self-respect. This same raise also affected the security of the two employees in a different manner. The first employee now felt she had obtained more security, but the second employee felt that his security was in jeopardy.

Application of the Motivational Models

A useful way to think about money as a reward is to apply it to some of the motivational models presented in Chapter 5.

FIGURE 6.1 **The Reward Pyramid: The Makeup of a Complete Pay Program** (*read it from the bottom*)

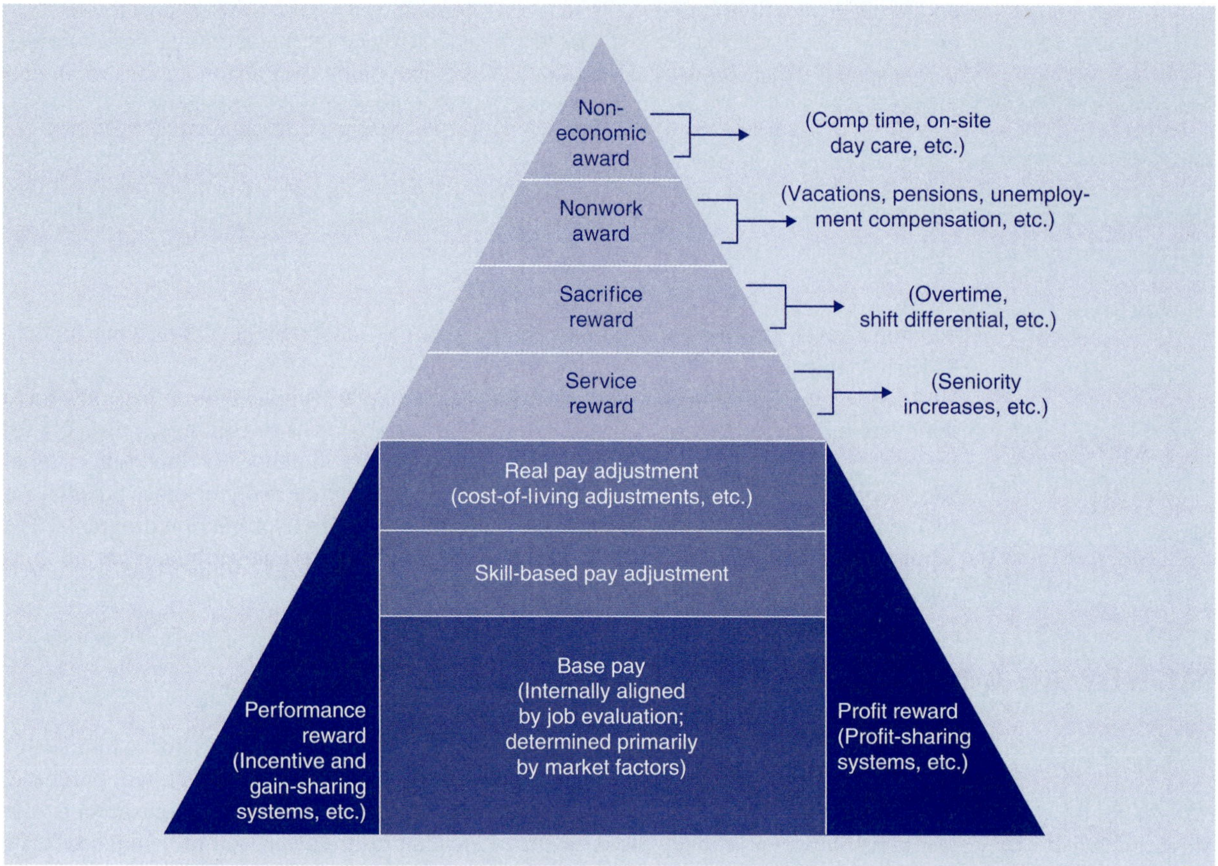

Money satisfies many drives and needs

Drives Achievement-oriented employees maintain a symbolic scorecard in their minds by monitoring their total pay and comparing it with that of others. Their pay is a measure of their accomplishments. Money also relates to other drives, since people can use it to buy their way into expensive clubs (affiliation) and give them the capacity (power) to influence others, such as through political contributions.

Needs In the Herzberg model, pay is viewed primarily as a hygiene factor, although it may have at least short-term motivational value as well. In the other need-based models, pay is most easily seen in its capacity to satisfy the lower-order needs (such as Maslow's physiological and security needs or Alderfer's existence needs). However, we can easily see how it relates to other levels as well, like the physician's esteem needs in the opening example for this chapter.

Expectancy As you will recall, expectancy theory states that:

$$\text{Valence} \times \text{Expectancy} \times \text{Instrumentality} = \text{Motivation}$$

This means that if money is to act as a strong motivator, an employee must want more of it (valence), must believe that effort will be successful in producing desired performance (expectancy), and must trust that the monetary reward will follow better performance (instrumentality).

Valence of money is not easily influenced by management. It is contingent upon an employee's personal values, experiences, and needs as well as the macromotivational environment. For example, if an employee has independent income or personal wealth, a small increase in pay may have little valence. The same conclusion applies to an employee who cherishes other values and desires only a subsistence income. Similarly, the direct value of money to people in an affluent society tends to decline, since money tends to satisfy lower-order needs more directly than higher-order needs. However, since money has many social meanings to people, employees may seek it for its social value (a measure of status and esteem) even when its economic value has low valence. This dual role means that *most employees do respond to money as a reward* (it has valence for them).

Money often has high valence

With regard to instrumentality, many employees are not sure that additional performance will lead to additional pay (the performance–reward connection). They see some employees deliver minimum performance, yet receive almost the same pay increases as high performers. They often believe that promotions are based more on seniority or personal relationships than on performance. Instrumentality is an area where management has much opportunity for building trust and taking positive action, because it can change substantially the connection between increased performance and reward.

Behavior Modification The two desired conditions for applying contingent rewards under behavior modification principles are shown in Figure 6.2 as situations 1 and 4. In each case, employees can see that there is a direct connection between performance and reward (instrumentality is high). The undesirable states are situations 2 and 3, where rewards are withheld from high performers or given to low performers (instrumentality is low). When these conditions are allowed to occur, many employees will at least be confused about how to perform and may even be highly dissatisfied with the reward system.

High instrumentality is desired

Consider the cases of four employees, each of whom was treated differently by the employer, and the possible thoughts running through their minds. Shannon received a substantial pay increase for her outstanding performance ("I think I'll try even harder in the future, since good work is obviously noticed"). Chet's productivity record mirrored Shannon's, but he received only a token salary increase ("If that's all my effort is worth to them, I'm going to really cut back next year"). Travis did not have a good performance record, but because the organization enjoyed a successful year, he was still given a healthy raise ("This is a great place to work; I can slide by and still do all right"). Pam had an equally poor record, so her supervisor withheld any increase from her ("I guess if I want to get ahead, I need to perform better in the future"). In each case the reward received (when compared with performance) sent a strong signal—but not always the intended one—to the employee about the likelihood of future rewards based on performance.

FIGURE 6.2
Desirable and Undesirable Instrumentality Conditions

Situation	Level of Performance	Level of Economic Reward	Instrumentality Condition
1	High	High	Desirable
2	High	Low	Undesirable
3	Low	High	Undesirable
4	Low	Low	Desirable

What Managers Are Reading 

INSTILLING INTRINSIC MOTIVATION

Intrinsically motivating jobs are those that generate positive emotions in employees and are rewarding in and of themselves. Intrinsic motivation results best from self-management, which is critical for organizational success in the twenty-first century. Four paths lead to intrinsic motivation:

1. A sense of *meaningfulness* (brought about through identified passions, an exciting vision, relevant and whole tasks).
2. A sense of *choice* (created by delegated authority, demonstrated trust, provision of security, clear purpose, and relevant/timely information).
3. A sense of *competence* (created through training, positive feedback, skill recognition, fit between tasks and abilities, and challenging standards).
4. A sense of *progress* (stimulated by a collaborative climate, tracking of milestones, celebrations of progress, access to customers, and measured improvements).

Source: Kenneth W. Thomas, *Intrinsic Motivation at Work: Building Energy and Commitment.* San Francisco: Berrett-Koehler Publishers, 2000.

Cost–reward comparison

Equity There is no simple answer for employers in their attempts to create workable systems of economic rewards for increased productivity, but they must at least attempt to understand the employee's perspective. The employee's approach to this complex problem is to make a rough type of **cost–reward comparison,** similar to the break-even analysis that is used in financial assessments. The employee identifies and compares personal costs and rewards to determine the point at which they are approximately equal, as shown in Figure 6.3. Employees consider all the costs of higher performance, such as effort, time, acquisition of knowledge and new skills, and the mental energy that must be devoted to innovation and problem solving. Then, they compare those costs with all the possible rewards, both economic (such as pay, benefits, and holidays) and noneconomic (such as status, esteem, and autonomy, although the value of these may be more difficult to assess). This input–outcome comparison process is similar to part of the equity model of motivation discussed in Chapter 5, except that

FIGURE 6.3
Cost of Performance in Relation to Reward for an Employee

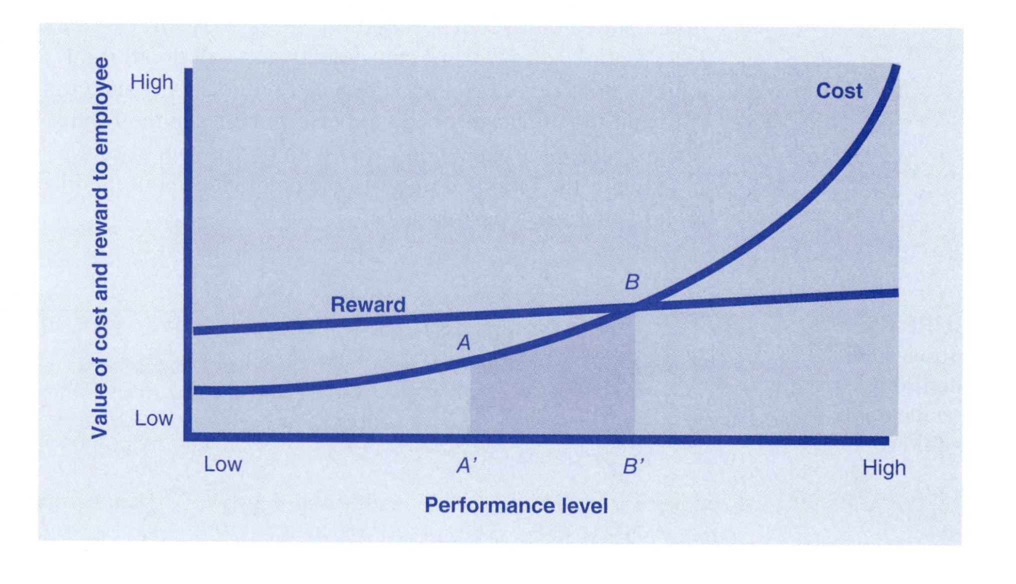

On the Job: Wells Fargo Bank

The Wells Fargo Bank developed a program to recognize and reinforce the behavior of individuals who made exceptional contributions to customer service.[5] Although the program included both cash rewards and a wide array of other prize selections of substantial value, its peak experience revolved around a recognition dinner and celebration for the award winners with the top company executives at a classy San Francisco restaurant.

in this analysis we assume that the employees do not yet compare themselves with others. Both costs (inputs) and rewards (outcomes) are always valued.

The break-even point is the point at which costs and rewards are equal for a certain level of expected performance, as shown by point *B* on the chart. Employee performance tends to be near the break-even point, but generally below it, for two reasons. First, the employee typically cannot be so precise as to pinpoint the exact break-even point. Second, the employee tries to maintain a personally satisfactory relationship in which rewards are relatively favorable in relation to costs.[6] Performance tends to be somewhere in the range of line $A'B'$.

> Many salespeople work on some form of commission plan that provides them with periodic bonuses. In many cases, the bonuses become larger as the salesperson reaches higher levels of performance, under the assumption that this will prompt the employee to excel. However, this principle is sometimes ignored, as it was by a distributor interviewed by the author. He actually reduced the level of bonuses provided as his salespeople reached new plateaus of sales during the month. His self-serving explanation? "I don't want my employees getting rich off of me," he said.

Additional Considerations in the Use of Money

Extrinsic and Intrinsic Rewards Money is essentially an extrinsic reward rather than an intrinsic one, so it is easily administered in behavior modification programs. However, it also has all the limitations of extrinsic benefits. No matter how closely management attaches pay to performance, pay is still something that originates outside the job and is useful only away from the job. Therefore, it tends to be less immediately satisfying than intrinsic job rewards. For example, the personal satisfaction of a job well done is a powerful motivator for many people. Economic rewards, by contrast, cannot provide all the needed rewards for a psychologically healthy person.

Difficult to integrate

An important task for management is integrating extrinsic and intrinsic rewards successfully. One problem is that employees differ in the amount of intrinsic and extrinsic rewards that they want, and jobs and organizational conditions also differ. Another problem occurs when employers begin paying employees for work they previously found satisfying, since some evidence indicates that *payment of an extrinsic reward decreases the intrinsic satisfaction received.*[7] In addition, it is difficult for managers to administer intrinsic rewards on a systematic basis. These conditions suggest that what is needed is a contingency approach to rewards that considers needs of workers, type of job, organizational environment, and different rewards. Special benefits, such as recognition or status, are sometimes especially valuable to employees because they have more psychological and social meaning. "On the Job: Wells Fargo Bank" illustrates how extrinsic and intrinsic rewards are often intertwined in recognition programs.

Compliance with the Law In addition to the complexities involved in applying various motivational models and building on both extrinsic and intrinsic factors, compensation management is also complicated by the need to comply with a wide range of federal and state laws. The most significant one is the federal **Equal Pay Act of 1963,** which affects employers who are engaged in interstate commerce and most employees of federal, state, and local governments. Also legislated by many states, the law demands that reward systems be designed and administered so people doing the same work receive equal pay regardless of the sex of the person holding the job. This law is designed to prevent one form of sexual discrimination, eliminating historical discrepancies in which females were sometimes paid less than males. The 1963 Equal Pay Act was strengthened by the Lilly Ledbetter Fair Pay Act of 2009. This newer act established a reasonable rule for filing claims of pay discrimination, allowing workers to file a claim within 180 days of an offending paycheck (versus using the date of the original employer action to discriminate).

Comparable worth

Another program, called **comparable worth,** also seeks to guarantee equal pay for equal work. This approach demands that reward systems be designed so people in different but comparable jobs—those of equal *value* to the employer—receive similar levels of pay. For example, a hospital might determine that a laboratory technician position requires comparable education, decision-making ability, and stress management skills as that of an internal auditor and therefore might set comparable levels of compensation for each. This program also has the intent of ending historical patterns of discrimination against those people who hold sex-stereotyped jobs (such as females working as secretaries or registered nurses).

Other Factors Many other elements confound the compensation process.

Equality, secrecy, control, and flexibility are considerations

- In contrast to legal and psychological pressures for equity (matching inputs and outcomes in comparison with those of others), some individuals advocate *equality.* They would prefer that all employees receive the same rewards, regardless of their unique skills or level of performance. Clearly, *equity and equality are totally different bases for comparing compensation.*
- *Secrecy* in pay programs is sometimes subject to debate. Some organizations guard all information about compensation from employees; others freely share it in the belief that openness and transparency are preferable.[8] It is even questionable as to whether or not secrecy is possible.
- *Control* can also be an issue. Should reward systems be designed by staff experts, or should employees be allowed to participate in their creation and governance?
- The level of *flexibility* has been subject to debate. Even though some clothing products claim "one size fits all," to expect that all dimensions of compensation will meet the needs of all employees may not be reasonable. Clearly, the administration of organizational reward systems involves many issues, and unique answers will be provided by different firms.

ORGANIZATIONAL BEHAVIOR AND PERFORMANCE APPRAISAL

Organizations require consistent levels of high performance from their employees in order to survive in a highly competitive global environment. Many firms use some form of results-oriented planning and control systems. **Management by objectives (MBO)** is a cyclical process that often consists of four steps as a way to attain desired performance:

Four typical steps in MBO

1. *Objective setting*—joint determination by manager and employee of appropriate levels of future performance for the employee, within the context of overall unit goals and resources. These objectives are often set for the next calendar or fiscal year.

2. *Action planning*—participative or even independent planning by the employee as to *how* to reach those objectives. Providing some autonomy to employees is invaluable; they are more likely to use their ingenuity, as well as feel more committed to the plan's success.
3. *Periodic reviews*—joint assessment of progress toward objectives by manager and employee, performed informally and sometimes spontaneously.
4. *Annual evaluation*—more formal assessment of success in achieving the employee's annual objectives, coupled with a renewal of the planning cycle. Some MBO systems also use performance appraisal to tie rewards for employees to the level of results attained.

MBO systems capitalize on the desire for self-management expressed by many employees today. They are more committed to achieving goals that they themselves have set, for this allows them to have an impact on organizational success. Where MBO systems have failed, it has usually been the result of autocratic managers, rigid adherence to rules, and the extensive costs in terms of time and effort to document the results.

Reasons for employee appraisal

Performance appraisal plays a key role in reward systems. It is the process of evaluating the performance of employees, sharing that information with them, and searching for ways to improve their performance. Appraisal is necessary in order to (1) allocate scarce resources in a dynamic environment, (2) motivate and reward employees, (3) give employees feedback about their work, (4) maintain fair relationships within groups, (5) coach and develop employees, and (6) comply with regulations. Appraisal systems, therefore, are necessary for proper management and for employee development.

The social environment surrounding organizations has changed considerably in recent years. Federal and state laws have added to the complexity and difficulty of appraisal plans. For example, as shown in Figure 6.4, criteria for compliance with equal employment opportunity laws are stringent. Management needs to design and operate its appraisal systems carefully in order to comply with these laws.

Appraisal Philosophy

Performance emphasis and goals

A few decades ago, appraisal programs tended to emphasize employee traits, deficiencies, and abilities, but modern appraisal philosophy emphasizes present performance and future goals. Modern philosophy also stresses employee participation in mutually setting goals with the supervisor and knowledge of results. Thus the hallmarks of modern appraisal philosophy are as follows:

1. *Performance orientation*—it is not enough for employees to put forth effort; that effort must result in the attainment of desired outcomes (products or services).
2. *Focus on goals or objectives*—as the discussion of MBO shows, employees need to have a clear idea of what they are supposed to be doing and the priorities among their tasks.

FIGURE 6.4
Necessary Criteria to Ensure Equal Employment Opportunity in Performance Appraisal

The performance appraisal system

- Is an organizational necessity
- Is based on well-defined, objective criteria
- Is based on careful job analysis
- Uses only job-related criteria
- Is supported by adequate studies
- Is applied by trained, qualified raters
- Is applied objectively throughout the organization
- Can be shown to be nondiscriminatory as defined by law

As the saying goes, "If you know where you want to go, you are more likely to get there."

Mutual goal setting and feedback

3. *Mutual goal setting between supervisor and employee*—this is the belief that people will work harder for goals or objectives that they have participated in setting. Among their desires are to perform a worthwhile task, share in a group effort, share in setting their objectives, share in the rewards of their efforts, and continue personal growth. The (Theory Y) assumption is that people want to satisfy some of their needs through work and they will do so if management will provide them with a supportive environment.
4. *Clarification of behavioral expectations*—this is often done via a behaviorally anchored rating scale (BARS), which provides the employee and manager with concrete examples of various levels of behaviors. Brief descriptions of outstanding, very good, acceptable, below average, and unacceptable behaviors are specified for each major dimension of a job, thus cueing the employee in advance regarding the organization's expectations. BARS help reduce a manager's tendency to focus on attitudes, personality, and quirks of an employee and shift the emphasis toward productive behaviors.
5. *Extensive feedback systems*—employees can fine-tune their performance better if they know how they are doing in the eyes of the organization, and receive this information regularly and candidly.

The Appraisal Interview

Most organizational appraisal systems require supervisors to assess employees on various aspects of their productivity (results) and work-related behaviors. Examples of these dimensions include quality of work, quantity of output, attendance, and initiative. Many appraisal systems also point toward both historical performance and the individual's potential for growth and advancement. The actual forms and procedures used for assessing this information vary widely. Some organizations (and the military) ask supervisors to write *essays* describing the employee's performance; others recommend that they accumulate a record of *critical incidents* (both positive and negative); many firms use various types of *graphic rating scales* that grade employees on A-B-C-D-E or 1-2-3-4-5 systems.

General Electric's forced ranking system

> General Electric Company popularized the forced ranking approach to performance appraisals for its top level employees. This system required executives to assess employees on various dimensions and differentiate among employees as being top, middle, or low performers; they could not all receive high (or low) ratings. Then, the rankings were used to reward top producers, while the bottom 10 percent were strongly encouraged to improve their performance or leave the company. However, forced rankings can hurt morale, confuse employees who don't understand why they were ranked low, and lead to mistrust in management. Caution is clearly in order.[9]

Regardless of the system used, the assessment is then communicated to the employee in an **appraisal interview.** This is a session in which the supervisor provides feedback to the employee on past performance, discusses any problems that have arisen, and invites a response. Then, the two parties set objectives for the next time period. In some organizations, the employee is then informed about her or his future salary; in others, the pay issue is delayed until several months later. The appraisal interview also provides a rich opportunity to motivate the employee. Using the Herzberg model, for example, might encourage a manager to explore which maintenance factors currently create dissatisfaction for an employee. If those can be resolved, then the discussion can turn toward ways to build into the job more opportunities for achievement, responsibility, and challenge.

Suggested Approaches Extensive research has been done on the appraisal process and the characteristics of the most effective ones. Appraisal interviews are most likely to be successful when the appraiser:

- Is knowledgeable about the employee's job
- Has previously set measurable performance standards
- Has gathered specific evidence frequently about performance
- Seeks and uses inputs from other observers in the organization
- Sharply limits the amount of criticism to a few major items (so the employees can *focus* their improvement efforts)
- Provides support, acceptance, and praise for tasks well done
- Listens actively to the employee's input and reactions
- Shares responsibility for outcomes and offers future assistance
- Allows participation in the discussion

Self-appraisal

The last point has been extended even further in recent approaches to the performance appraisal interview. Some organizations in both the private and public sectors include, as a formal part of the process, **self-appraisal.** This is an opportunity for the employee to be introspective and to offer a personal assessment of his or her accomplishments, strengths, and weaknesses. Questions directed to the employee might include "What has gone extremely well for you during this period?" "What kinds of problems have you had?" "What ideas do you have for improving your contributions?" Employee responses to these questions are then compared with the supervisor's evaluation of the employee. This approach allows differences of opinion to be discussed openly and resolved.

Problems can arise in self-appraisals, however. Some poor performers tend to diminish their level of difficulties and attribute their problems to situational factors around them, and a few will rate themselves too leniently or try to impress their manager by stretching the truth. These limitations, however, are offset by the fact that most employees are quite candid when asked to identify their strengths and weaknesses, and are able to accurately compare their performance with previous expectations. In addition, self-assessments are much less threatening to one's self-esteem than are those received from others. Therefore, self-appraisals provide a more fertile soil for growth and change.

Performance Feedback

All appraisal systems build on the assumption that employees need feedback about their performance (a basic element of the communication model described in Chapter 3). Feedback helps them know what to do and how well they are meeting their goals. It shows that others are interested in what they are doing. Assuming that performance is satisfactory or better, feedback enhances an employee's self-image and feeling of competence. Generally, **performance feedback** leads to both improved performance and improved attitudes—if handled properly by the manager.

Critical Thinking Exercise

Performance feedback is used widely by employers Question: What positive and negative results can you safely predict for this approach?

On the Job: Nucor Steel Co.

One example of a pay for performance incentive system is Nucor, a builder and operator of steel-producing minimills. It pays weekly bonuses, based on a measure of acceptable production. Groups typically receive a bonus more than 100 percent above base pay. Turnover rates, after the startup period, are so small that the company does not even bother measuring them.[19]

Wage Incentives

Pay for Performance Basically, **wage incentives,** which are a form of *merit pay,* provide more pay for more output or results, often referred to as **pay for performance.**[20] The main reason for use of wage incentives is clear: They nearly always increase productivity while decreasing labor costs per unit of production. Workers under normal conditions without wage incentives have the capacity to produce more, and wage incentives are one way to induce employees to work up to their potential. The increased productivity and reduced turnover (see "On the Job: Nucor Steel Co.") often is substantial.

Criteria for incentive systems

In order to be successful, a wage incentive needs to be simple enough for employees to have a strong belief that reward will follow performance. If the plan is so complex that workers have difficulty relating performance to reward, then higher motivation is less likely to develop. The objectives, eligibility requirements, performance criteria, and payment system all need to be established and understood by the participants.

When incentive systems operate successfully, they are evaluated favorably by participants, probably because they provide psychological as well as economic rewards. Employees receive satisfaction from a job well done, which fulfills their achievement drive. Their self-image may improve because of greater feelings of competence. They may even feel they are making a contribution to society by helping in the attempt to regain a productivity leadership position among nations. Some incentives may encourage cooperation between workers because of the need for employees to work together to earn incentive awards.

Difficulties Wage incentives furnish an example of the kinds of difficulties that may develop with many incentive plans, despite their potential benefits. Management's job is to try to prevent or reduce the problems while increasing benefits, so that the incentive plan works more effectively.

Disruption of social systems

The basic human difficulty with wage incentives of this type is that *disruptions in the social system may lead to feelings of inequity and dissatisfaction.* At times these disruptions are severe enough to make incentive workers less satisfied with their pay than workers who are paid an hourly wage, even though the incentive workers are earning more.

FIGURE 6.9
Advantages and Disadvantages of Incentives Linking Pay with Performance

Advantages	Disadvantages
• Strengthen instrumentality beliefs	• Cost (to both employer and employee)
• Create perceptions of equity	• System complexity and rigidity
• Reinforce desirable behaviors	• Unpredictable levels of pay
• Provide objective basis for rewards	• Unintended consequences
	• Narrowness of performance criteria

For any pay for performance plan to be successful, it needs to be coordinated carefully with the whole operating system. If employees must wait for long periods for work to arrive at their workplace, then the incentive loses its impact. If the incentive is likely to replace workers, then management needs to plan for their use elsewhere so employee security is not threatened. If work methods are erratic, then they must be standardized so a fair rate of reward can be established. This is a complex process leading to many difficulties:

Rate setting

1. Wage incentives normally require establishment of performance standards. **Rate setting** is the process of determining the standard output for each job, which becomes the fair day's work for the individual. Rate setters are often resented not only because subjective judgment is involved but also because they are believed to be a cause of change and more difficult standards.
2. Wage incentives may make the supervisor's job more complex. Supervisors must be familiar with the system so they can explain it convincingly to employees. The system's complexity may increase the chance of error and contribute to more employee dissatisfaction. Relationships are compounded, and supervisors are required to resolve different expectations from higher management, rate setters, workers, and unions.

Loose rates

3. A thorny problem with wage incentives involves **loose rates.** A rate is "loose" when employees are able to reach standard output with less than reasonable levels of effort. When management subsequently adjusts the rate to a higher standard, employees predictably experience a feeling of inequity.
4. Wage incentives may cause disharmony between incentive workers and hourly workers. When the two groups perform work in a sequence, hourly workers may feel discriminated against because they earn less. If the incentive workers increase output, hourly workers further along the process must work faster to prevent a bottleneck. The incentive workers earn more for their increased output, but the hourly workers do not.

Output restrictions

5. Another difficulty with wage incentives is that they may result in **output restriction,** by which workers limit their production and thus defeat the purpose of the incentive. This phenomenon is caused by several factors—group insecurities that the production standard will be raised, resistance to change by the informal social organization, and the fact that people are not comfortable always working at full capacity.

Profit Sharing

Nature and Merits **Profit sharing** is a system that distributes to employees some portion of the profits of business, either immediately (in the form of cash bonuses) or deferred until a later date (held in trust in the form of employee-owned shares). The growth of profit sharing has been encouraged by federal tax laws that allow employee income taxes to be deferred on funds placed in profit-sharing pension plans.

Mutual interest is emphasized

Basic pay rates, performance pay increases, and most other incentive systems recognize *individual* differences, whereas profit sharing recognizes *mutual* interests. Employees become interested in the economic success of their employer when they see that their own rewards are affected by it. Greater institutional teamwork tends to develop.

Smaller organizations in competitive industries that demand high commitment from employees in order to make technological breakthroughs or bring new products to market faster are prime candidates for profit-sharing programs. If the firms are successful, the rewards are great. This possibility builds strong motivation among employees to see the big picture and allows the organization to forge ahead of its competitors.

On the Job: The Andersen Corporation

The Andersen Corporation is a billion-dollar company that makes various types of windows for the housing industry. The company began a profit-sharing plan in 1914, and it has grown with the success of the company ever since then. In a recent year, the company distributed more than $100 million to its full-time employees through its profit-sharing plan. This bonus amounted to an astounding 43 weeks of extra compensation for each employee in this peak year.

In general, profit sharing tends to work better for fast-growing, profitable organizations that offer opportunities for substantial employee rewards. It also works better, of course, when general economic conditions are favorable. It is less likely to be useful in stable and declining organizations with low profit margins and intense competition. Profit sharing generally is well received and understood by managers and high-level professional people, because their decisions and actions are more likely to have a significant effect on their firm's profits. Since operating workers, especially in large firms, have more difficulty connecting their individual actions with the firm's profitability, profit sharing may have less initial appeal to them. In situations where it has worked effectively, managers have openly shared financial reports with all levels of workers, actively trained employees to understand financial statements, and provided on-site computer terminals for immediate access to relevant information whenever employees want it.

Difficulties Even in those situations where profit sharing seems appropriate, some general disadvantages exist:

Indirect relationship

1. Profits are not directly related to an employee's effort on the job. Poor market conditions may nullify an employee's hard work.

Delay

2. Employees must wait for their reward, and this lengthy delay diminishes its impact.

Lack of predictability

3. Since profits are somewhat unpredictable, total worker income may vary from year to year. Some workers may prefer the security of a more stable wage or salary.

Union skepticism

4. Some union leaders have historically been suspicious of profit sharing. They fear it would undermine union loyalty, result in varied total earnings from company to company, and weaken their organizing campaigns. More progressive unions have, however, welcomed the opportunity for their members to share in corporate profits.

Gain Sharing

Another useful group incentive is gain sharing, or production sharing. A **gain-sharing plan** establishes a historical base period of organizational performance, measures improvements, and shares the gains with employees on some formula basis. Examples of the performance factors measured include inventory levels, labor hours per unit of product, usage of materials and supplies, and quality of finished goods. The idea is to pinpoint areas that are controllable by employees and then give them an incentive for identifying and implementing ideas that will result in cost savings, as the "On the Job: Turner Brothers Trucking" example shows.

Behavioral Basis Gain-sharing plans use several fundamental ideas from organizational behavior and are much more than pay systems. They encourage employee suggestions, provide an incentive for coordination and teamwork, and promote improved communication. Union–management relations often improve, since the union gains status because it takes responsibility for the benefits gained. Attitudes toward technological change improve because workers are aware that greater efficiency leads to larger bonuses. Gain sharing

On the Job: Turner Brothers Trucking

Gain-sharing plans are used at Turner Brothers Trucking—a company that tears down and reassembles drilling rigs, services pipe, and operates large cranes.[21] To reduce its huge liability and workers' compensation premiums, the company offered a group of employees $50 each for every month in which total losses from injuries, cargo damage, and driving accidents were less than $300. The results were dramatic; the ratio of the gain-sharing amount paid to employees compared with expected safety costs was 1:4 for the first few years after the program was introduced, and it dropped even further thereafter. This win–win program demonstrated that employees could not only control their safety record but would do so for a fairly modest cost to the organization.

broadens the understanding of employees as they see a larger picture of the system through their participation rather than confining their outlook to the narrow specialty of their job.

Contingency Factors The success of gain sharing is contingent upon a number of key factors, such as the moderately small size of the unit, a sufficient operating history to allow the creation of standards, the existence of controllable cost areas, and the relative stability of the business.

In addition, management must be receptive to employee participation, the organization must be willing to share the benefits of production increases with employees, and the union should be favorable to such a cooperative effort. Managers need to be receptive to ideas and tolerant of criticism from employees.

Skill-Based Pay

In contrast to salaries (which pay someone to hold a job) and wage incentives (which pay for the level of performance), **skill-based pay** (also called *knowledge-based pay* or *multiskill pay*) rewards individuals for what they know how to do. Employees are paid for the range, depth, and types of skills in which they demonstrate capabilities.[22] They start working at a flat hourly rate and receive increases for either developing skills within their primary job or learning how to perform other jobs within their work unit. Some companies provide increases for each new job learned; most others require employees to acquire blocks of related new skills, which may take several years to learn. Substantial amounts of training must be made available for the system to work, and methods for fairly pricing jobs and certifying employee skill levels need to be established. Some skill-based pay systems have supervisors evaluate the knowledge and skill of their employees; others allow work teams to assess the progress of each trainee.

Advantages Skill-based pay systems have several potential strengths. They provide strong motivation for employees to develop their work-related skills, they reinforce an employee's sense of self-esteem, and they provide the organization with a highly flexible workforce that can fill in when someone is absent. Since workers rotate among jobs to learn them, boredom should be reduced, at least temporarily. Pay satisfaction should be relatively high, for two reasons. First, the employee's hourly rate received (for having multiple skills) is often higher than the rate that would be paid for the task being performed, since only in a perfect system would all employees be constantly using their highest skills. As a result, some employees may even feel temporarily overpaid. Second, workers should perceive the system as equitable both in the sense of their costs and rewards being matched and in the knowledge that all employees with the same skills earn the same pay.

Disadvantages Skill-based pay presents several disadvantages, and some firms have backed away from early experiments with it. First, since most employees will voluntarily

Advice to Future Managers

1. Seek to establish accurate measures of performance, and *make the connection between performance and rewards clear to all.*
2. *Provide rewards that people value*; if you don't know what they value, ask them.
3. *Make it clear to employees* how the organization's monetary rewards relate to their various needs and drives.
4. Make sure employees believe their *goals are attainable if they perform well.*
5. If you are trying to promote teamwork, *provide team-based, not individual, rewards.*
6. *Be aware of the unintended consequences associated with any reward system*, and try to minimize these.
7. *Utilize the advantages of 360-degree feedback systems* for providing employees with a broad and rich source of performance feedback.
8. *Monitor your own behavior*, and that of your employees, *for signs of inappropriate attributions* of behavior during performance appraisals.
9. Remember that providing performance feedback to some employees can be threatening; *provide opportunities for them to save face.*
10. *Encourage employees to become feedback seekers*; this will help open up productive and ongoing dialogue with them.

learn higher-level jobs, the average hourly pay rate will be greater than normal. (This increased cost should be more than offset by productivity increases, however.) Second, a substantial investment in employee training must be made, especially in the time spent coaching by supervisors and peers. Third, not all employees like skill-based pay because it places pressure on them to move up the skill ladder. The subsequent dissatisfaction may lead to a variety of consequences, including employee turnover. Fourth, some employees will qualify themselves for skill areas that they will be unlikely to use, causing the organization to pay them higher rates than they deserve from a performance standpoint.

Skill-based pay, like other incentive programs, works best when the organizational culture of the firm is generally supportive and trusting. The system should be understood by employees, they must have realistic expectations about their prospects for higher pay levels, it must be possible for them to learn new skills and to have these skills promptly evaluated, and there must be some limits on which skills they can qualify for. Under these conditions, the program is consistent with the other incentives discussed in this chapter, since it links employee pay with the potential for increased performance.

Summary

Economic rewards provide social as well as economic value. They play a key role within several motivational models, blending with expectancy, equity, behavior modification, and need-based approaches. Employees perform a rough cost–reward comparison and work somewhat near but below the break-even point.

Performance appraisal provides a systematic basis for assessment of employee contributions, coaching for improved performance, and distribution of economic rewards. Modern appraisal philosophy focuses on performance, objectives, mutual goal setting, and feedback. Newer appraisal approaches, such as self-appraisal and 360-degree feedback systems, provide additional perspectives on employee performance and suggestions for improvement. Nevertheless, the appraisal interview can be difficult for both manager and employee.

One significant confounding factor in appraisals is the likelihood that one or both parties will engage in inappropriate attributions. These are the perceptual assignment of alternative causes to one's behavior based on preconceptions and faulty reasoning; they serve to cause difficulties between the manager and the appraisee unless resolved through careful analysis.

Performance management often relies on incentive systems to provide different amounts of pay in relation to some measure of performance. They tend to increase employee expectations that rewards will follow performance, although the delay may range from a week to a year. Incentives often stimulate greater productivity but also tend to produce some offsetting negative consequences. Wage incentives reward greater output by individuals or groups, whereas profit sharing emphasizes mutual interest with the employer to build a successful organization. Gain sharing emphasizes improvement in various indexes of organizational performance, whereas skill-based pay rewards employees for acquiring greater levels or types of skills. Since employees have different needs to be served, many types of pay programs are required for a complete economic reward system.

Speaking OB: Terms and Concepts for Review

360-degree feedback, *158*
Appraisal interview, *156*
Attribution, *160*
Comparable worth, *154*
Complete pay program, *164*
Cost–reward comparison, *152*
Economic incentive system, *164*
Equal Pay Act of 1963, *154*
Fundamental attribution bias, *161*
Gain-sharing plan, *168*
Galatea effect, *162*
Incentives, *148*
Loose rates, *167*
Management by objectives (MBO), *154*
Output restriction, *167*
Pay for performance, *166*
Perceptual distortions, *162*
Perceptual set, *161*
Performance appraisal, *155*
Performance feedback, *157*
Performance management, *164*
Piece rate, *165*
Positive contagion, *162*
Praise, *159*
Profit sharing, *167*
Rate setting, *167*
Self-appraisal, *157*
Self-fulfilling prophecy, *161*
Self-serving bias, *161*
Skill-based pay, *169*
Wage incentives, *166*

Discussion Questions

1. Explain how money can be both an economic and a social medium of exchange. As a student, how do *you* use money as a social medium of exchange?
2. Think of a job that you formerly had or now have.
   a. Discuss specifically how the expectancy model applied (applies) to your pay.
   b. Discuss how you felt (feel) about the equity of your pay and why you felt (feel) that way.
   c. Develop and explain a cost–reward comparison chart for your pay and effort.
3. Think of a time when you assessed, either formally or informally, someone else's level of performance and found it deficient by your standards. To what did you attribute the reasons for the inadequate performance? Were you engaging in any attributional tendencies? How could you avoid doing so?
4. Assume that, in the first six months of your first job, your manager asks you to participate in filling out a feedback form describing his or her strengths and weaknesses. How comfortable will you feel in doing this? Now assume your manager asks you to engage in the same process, seeking feedback from your peers, manager, and customers about yourself. Now what is your reaction? Explain.

5. What are the major measures used to link pay with outputs? Which ones, if any, were used in the last job you had? Discuss the effectiveness of the measure or measures used.
6. Would you use profit sharing, gain sharing, skill-based pay, or wage incentives in any of the following jobs? Discuss your choice in each instance.
   a. Employee in a small fast-growing computer company
   b. Teacher in a public school
   c. Insurance claims processor in an insurance office
   d. Automobile repair mechanic in a small repair shop
   e. Farm worker picking peaches
   f. Production worker in a shoe factory making men's shoes
7. Divide into small groups, each led by a member who has worked for a sales commission. Discuss how the commission related to both equity theory and expectancy theory, and report highlights of your discussion to your entire classroom group.
8. Have you ever participated in restriction of output in a job or in an academic course? If so, discuss why you did it and what its consequences were.
9. "Skill-based pay is a waste of company money, because we are paying for *potential* performance instead of *actual* performance." Discuss this statement.
10. Rate your level of performance in this class relative to all others. What percentage of classmates do you think are below you? Now seek that information from your instructor and match it with your own. If the two figures do not match, provide several explanations for it.

Assess Your Own Skills

How well do you exhibit good reward and performance appraisal skills?

Read the following statements carefully. Circle the number on the response scale that most closely reflects the degree to which each statement accurately describes you when you reward employees and conduct a performance appraisal. Add up your total points, and prepare a brief action plan for self-improvement. Be ready to report your score for tabulation across the entire group.

	Good description									Poor description
1. I recognize and understand the roles that money plays in each of the motivational models.	10	9	8	7	6	5	4	3	2	1
2. I plan to administer monetary rewards on a contingent basis, providing high rewards for good performance and much lesser rewards for weaker performance.	10	9	8	7	6	5	4	3	2	1
3. I recognize the importance of helping employees understand the need for balance between their rewards and their contributions.	10	9	8	7	6	5	4	3	2	1

4. I understand the necessity of providing employees with opportunities for both extrinsic and intrinsic rewards.	10	9	8	7	6	5	4	3	2	1
5. I am comfortable with the five hallmarks of modern appraisal philosophy and would use those in my own appraisals of employees.	10	9	8	7	6	5	4	3	2	1
6. I envision the performance appraisal interview as an opportunity for much more than simply giving feedback to employees.	10	9	8	7	6	5	4	3	2	1
7. I would be comfortable receiving feedback from all participants in a 360-degree appraisal process.	10	9	8	7	6	5	4	3	2	1
8. I could readily follow the guidelines for giving performance feedback to employees.	10	9	8	7	6	5	4	3	2	1
9. I can easily see how an employee's self-serving bias could distort that person's self-appraisal.	10	9	8	7	6	5	4	3	2	1
10. I understand the fundamental attribution bias and believe that I could successfully avoid it.	10	9	8	7	6	5	4	3	2	1

Scoring and Interpretation

Add up your total points for the 10 questions. Record that number here, and report it when it is requested. Finally, insert your total score into the "Assess and Improve Your Own Organizational Behavior Skills" chart in Appendix A.

- If you scored between 81 and 100 points, you appear to have a solid capability for demonstrating good reward and performance appraisal skills.
- If you scored between 61 and 80 points, you should take a close look at the items with lower self-assessment scores and explore ways to improve those items.
- If you scored under 60 points, you should be aware that a weaker skill level regarding several items could be detrimental to your future success as a manager. We encourage you to review relevant sections of the chapter and watch for related material in subsequent chapters and other sources.

Now identify your three lowest scores, and write the question numbers here: _____, _____, _____. Write a brief paragraph, detailing to yourself an action plan for how you might sharpen each of these skills.

Incident

Plaza Grocery

Brad Holden was the executive vice president for Plaza Grocery, a family-owned chain of six grocery stores in a medium-sized metropolitan area. The current problem he was facing dealt with the stock clerks/carryout workers in the stores. Despite paying them the usual wage rate (the minimum federal hourly wage), he had trouble obtaining enough applicants for the job. Worse still, many of them seemed to lack motivation once he hired them. This situation created problems of empty shelves and slow service at the checkout lanes.

In an attempt to solve the problem, Brad met with small groups of the workers to get their ideas. He also consulted with a local expert on compensation issues. Some workers said they wanted a higher hourly wage rate; others said they wanted some incentive to work faster; some had no comment whatsoever. The consultant recommended that Brad consider using some of the more contemporary compensation systems.

Questions

1. Which of the major economic incentive systems discussed in this chapter has the best chance of working for Brad?
2. Can two or more incentive systems be combined, with an even greater likelihood of success? What might be gained through a combination, and what would be the costs (for both Plaza Grocery and the employees)?
3. In your recommendation, which motivational theories are you most specifically using?

Experiential Exercise

Performance Appraisal/Reward Philosophy

1. Read the following set of statements about people and indicate your degree of agreement or disagreement on the rating scales.

	Strongly agree				Strongly disagree
a. Most people don't just want equity; they want to earn *more* than their peers.	1	2	3	4	5
b. Skill-based pay won't work well because employees will learn the minimum necessary to earn a higher rate and then forget what they learned.	1	2	3	4	5
c. Most employees are too comfortable with the status quo to want to devote effort to learning new skills.	1	2	3	4	5
d. Most employees neither understand what profits are nor appreciate their importance; therefore, profit-sharing systems are doomed to fail.	1	2	3	4	5
e. If asked to participate in a 360-degree feedback program appraising their own manager, most employees would distort their assessments in some way rather than be honest.	1	2	3	4	5
f. The division between management and labor is so great that both gain-sharing and profit-sharing systems are likely to fail.	1	2	3	4	5
g. Since people do not want to hear about their weaknesses and failures, performance appraisal interviews will not change employee behavior.	1	2	3	4	5
h. The idea that employees assess the costs and rewards associated with any major behavior is ridiculous. They simply decide whether or not they feel like doing something and then do it or don't do it.	1	2	3	4	5

2. Meeting in small discussion groups, tabulate the responses to each question (frequency distribution and mean) and explore reasons for any significant disagreements within your group's ratings.
3. In your group, develop alternative statements for any items you do not support (ratings of 3, 4, or 5) at present. Explain how your new statements reflect your knowledge of human behavior gained through reading the early chapters of this book.

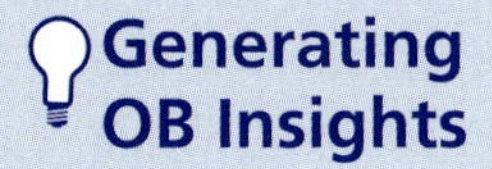

An *insight* is a new and clear perception of a phenomenon, or an acquired ability to "see" clearly something that you were unaware of previously. It is sometimes simply referred to as an "ah-ha! moment," in which you have a minirevelation or reach a straightforward conclusion about a topic or issue.

Insights need not necessarily be dramatic, for what is an insight to one person may be less important to another. The critical feature of insights is that they are relevant and memorable for *you;* they should represent new knowledge, new frameworks, or new ways of viewing things that you want to retain and remember over time.

Insights, then, are different from the information you find in the "Advice for Future Managers" boxes within the text. That advice is prescriptive and action-oriented; it indicates a recommended course of action.

A useful way to think of OB insights is to assume you are the only person who has read Chapter 6. You have been given the assignment to highlight, in your own words, the major concepts (not just summarize the whole chapter) that might stand out for a naive audience who has never heard of the topic before. *What 10 insights would you share with them?*

(Example) *Most employees place a relatively high valence on money as both an economic and social reward.*

1. ______________________________
2. ______________________________
3. ______________________________
4. ______________________________
5. ______________________________
6. ______________________________
7. ______________________________
8. ______________________________
9. ______________________________
10. ______________________________

Nurturing Your Critical Thinking and Reflective Skills

Take a few minutes to review the discussion in the Roadmap for Readers of critical thinking and reflection. Remind yourself that if you can hone these abilities now, you will have a substantial competitive advantage when you apply for jobs and are asked what unique skills you can bring to the position and the organization.

Critical Thinking

Think back on the material you read in this chapter. What are three unique and challenging critical questions you would like to raise about that material? (These might identify something controversial about which you have doubts, they may imply that you suspect that a theory or model has weaknesses, they could examine the legitimacy of apparent causal relationships, or they might assess the probable value of a suggested practice.) Be prepared to share these questions with class members or your instructor.

1. ____

____

2. ____

____

3. ____

____

Reflection

This process often involves answering the parallel questions of "What do you *think* about the material you have read?" and "How do you *feel* about that material?" Therefore, express your *personal thoughts and feelings* (reactions) to any of the ideas or topics found in this chapter, and be prepared to share these reflections with class members or your instructor.

1. ____

____

2. ____

____

3. ____

____

Part Three

Leadership and Empowerment

What Managers Are Reading 

BAD LEADERSHIP

Bad leaders are of two broad types—those who are simply ineffective and those who are unethical. Bad leadership emerges from a leader's basic (flawed) character, from inappropriate (selfish) personal objectives, or from poor choices among options available to them. Seven basic types of bad leaders have been identified:

- Incompetent persons, who lack the will or skill to be effective
- Rigid persons, who inflexibly stick to doomed paths and processes
- Intemperate persons, who lack self-control in pursuing their own desires
- Callous individuals, who are uncaring and unkind when expressing their feelings
- Corrupt leaders, who place their self-interest first and foremost
- Insular leaders, who disregard the health and welfare of other persons and groups
- Evil leaders, who cause physical or psychological harm through pain or atrocity

Source: Barbara Kellerman, *Bad Leadership: What It Is, How It Happens, Why It Matters.* Boston: Harvard Business School Press, 2004.

leadership. Better employee education, greater demands for independence, and other factors have made satisfactory employee motivation more dependent on positive leadership.

Positive leaders are also more likely to use a *conversational* approach to their communications, characterized by four primary features:

- *Intimacy* (using physical and emotional proximity to "get close" to the employees; gaining trust, listening well, and soliciting feedback)
- *Interactivity* (promoting open and fluid dialogue between two parties)
- *Inclusion* (increasing emotional engagement by soliciting the knowledge, ideas, and reactions of others)
- *Intentionality* (having a sense of intended outcomes so that the purpose is clear).

Conversational communication is highly consistent with the leadership trait of authenticity, discussed earlier in this chapter.[13]

If emphasis is placed on threats, fear, harshness, intimidation, and penalties, the leader is applying *negative leadership.* This approach may possibly get acceptable short-term performance in many situations, but it has high human costs. Negative leaders act domineering and superior with people. To get work done, they hold over their personnel such penalties as loss of job, reprimand in the presence of others, and a few days off without pay. They display authority in the false belief that it frightens everyone into productivity. They are bosses who are feared more than leaders who are admired.

Negative leaders are usually known as **workplace bullies**, but they have no more place in work organizations than in the elementary school playground. These bullying bosses intimidate, ridicule, insult, blame, bark, harass, and make unreasonable demands. Some effects on employees are subtle but no less real (psychological distress), while other effects involve undesired behaviors (e.g., absenteeism or turnover) or performance declines. Worst of all, bullying by one manager begets bullying by others, who reflect the same behaviors that they see in their superiors or peers.

A continuum of leadership styles exists, ranging from strongly positive to strongly negative. Almost any manager uses a mix of positive and negative styles somewhere on the continuum every day, but the dominant style sets a tone within the group. Style is related to one's model of organizational behavior. The autocratic model tends to produce a negative style; the custodial model is somewhat positive; and the supportive, collegial, and system models are clearly positive. *Positive leadership generally results in higher job satisfaction and performance.*[14]

Autocratic, Consultative, and Participative Leaders

Styles and the use of power

The way in which a leader uses power also establishes a type of style. Each style—autocratic, consultative, and participative—has its benefits and limitations. A leader often uses all three styles over a period of time, but one style tends to be the dominant one. An illustration is a plant supervisor who is normally autocratic, but she is participative in determining vacation schedules, and she is consultative in selecting a department representative for the safety committee.

Autocratic leaders centralize power and decision making in themselves. They structure the complete work situation for their employees, who are expected to do what they are told and not think for themselves. The leaders take full authority and assume full responsibility.

Autocratic leadership typically is negative, based on threats and punishment, but it can appear to be positive, as demonstrated by the *benevolent autocrat* who chooses to give some rewards to employees.

Some advantages of autocratic leadership are that it is often satisfying for the leader, permits quick decisions, allows the employment of less competent subordinates, and provides security and structure for employees. The main disadvantage is that most employees dislike it, especially if it is extreme enough to create fear and frustration. Further, it seldom generates the strong organizational commitment among employees that leads to low turnover and absenteeism rates. The leadership style of Al Dunlap, described in the opening for this chapter, was clearly an autocratic one.

Consultative leaders approach one or more employees and ask them for input prior to making a decision. These leaders may then choose to use or ignore the information and advice received, however. If the input is seen as used, employees are likely to feel as though they had a positive impact; if their input is consistently rejected, employees are likely to feel their time has been wasted.

Participative leaders clearly decentralize authority. Participative decisions are not unilateral, as with the autocrat, because they *use* inputs from followers and participation by them. The leader and group are acting as a social unit. Employees are informed about conditions affecting their jobs and encouraged to express their ideas, make suggestions, *and take action.* The general trend is toward wider use of participative practices because they are consistent with the supportive, collegial, and systems models of organizational behavior and because they are strongly desired by many younger employees. Because of its importance and increasingly widespread usage, participative management is discussed thoroughly in the next chapter.

Leader Use of Consideration and Structure

Employee and task orientations

Two different leadership styles used with employees are **consideration** and **structure,** also known as *employee orientation* and *task orientation.* Considerate leaders are concerned about the human needs of their employees. They try to build teamwork, provide

Critical Thinking Exercise

Negative (or bad, bullying) leadership is still in use today—especially in some countries. Question: Why do you think this primitive and dysfunctional behavior still persists?

Problem areas

Although many suggestion programs provide useful ideas, they are a limited form of participation that accents individual initiative instead of group problem solving and teamwork. Only a small fraction of employees are usually active participants who regularly make suggestions in most firms, and the rest may feel no significant level of involvement in the program. Many firms report receiving an average of only one suggestion per employee per year, which implies that most of the time the typical employee is not participating. In addition, delays in processing suggestions and rejections of seemingly good ideas can cause a backlash among contributors. Perhaps most significantly, some supervisors have difficulty looking constructively upon the suggestions and instead view them as criticisms of their own ability and practices, or as needless causes of more paperwork.

Quality Emphasis

For many years, both union and nonunion firms have organized groups of workers and their managers into committees to consider and solve job problems. These groups may be called work committees, labor–management committees, work-improvement task forces, or involvement teams. They have broad usefulness for improving productivity and communications because most of the employees can be involved. Popular approaches for this purpose are quality circles and total quality management.

Quality Circles Voluntary groups that receive training in process improvements and problem-solving skills and then meet to produce ideas for improving productivity and working conditions are known as **quality circles.** They meet regularly, apply problem analysis/problem-solving skills and statistical tools, and generate solutions for management to evaluate and implement. Quality circles gained utility as an involvement technique in the United States and Europe after achieving widespread success and popularity in Japan.

Effects of quality circles

> One research study in a manufacturing firm compared the attitudes and performance of six quality circles with a matched group of noninvolved workers.[17] Quality-circle participation favorably influenced employee attitudes toward decision making, group communication, and a feeling of having accomplished something worthwhile. Productivity rose by 23 percent, versus a 2 percent increase in the control group. Absenteeism declined steadily in the quality-circle group to a level 27 percent below where it began, while it showed erratic movement in the comparison group.

The quality-circle approach helps employees feel they have some influence on their organization even if not all their recommendations are accepted by higher management. Quality circles provide opportunities for personal growth, achievement, and recognition. Further, employees are committed to the solutions they generate, because they "own" them.

To be successful, quality circles should be used according to these guidelines:

Guidelines

- Use them for measurable, short-term problems.
- Obtain continuous support from top management.
- Apply the group's skills to problems within the circle's work area.
- Train supervisors in facilitation skills.
- View quality circles as one starting point for other more participative approaches to be used in the future.

Total Quality Management Not all quality circles have been successful, and some firms using quality circles experienced a number of problems with them. Not all employees participated, and when they did, they often addressed rather trivial issues at first. Some quality-circle groups felt isolated in their efforts, and they could not see their impact on the larger organization.

In response to this checkered experience, continued competitive pressures, and the opportunity to compete for national recognition (for example, the Malcolm Baldrige National Quality Award), several firms have initiated a **total quality management (TQM)** program. The TQM approach gets every employee involved in the process of searching for continuous improvements in their operations. Quality of product and service becomes a rallying cry for employees to focus on, and every step in the firm's processes is subjected to intense and regular scrutiny for ways to improve it. Employees are provided with extensive training in problem solving, group decision making, and statistical methods. The total quality management approach constitutes a formal program with direct participation of all employees. Almost any issue is subject to exploration, and the process is a continuing one of long duration. Consequently, TQM has shown itself to be a substantial program in participative management.

Wide involvement; high training

Rapid-Cycle Decision Making

Involving employees in participative processes typically takes time and draws them away from immediately-productive tasks. Salespersons, waitstaff, physicians, and attorneys are just a few examples of professions where "time is money" and individuals are reluctant to spend hours in group meetings despite their desire to shape their own futures. One solution lies in the use of a **rapid-cycle decision-making** process. Its highlights are these:

- Creation of a project steering committee
- Identification of a constituent group of possibly affected employees
- Framing of key issues and presentation via one-page overviews (and opposing views, if necessary)
- Distribution by e-mail, with opportunity to comment and return votes cast for approval/disapproval
- Ruling that non-response on a timely basis implies lack of interest in that issue, and hence willingness to support the collective decision
- Final judgments made by the steering committee where consensus could not be achieved

This participative process is time-efficient, inclusive, genuine, transparent, and yields definitive outcomes.[18] As a result, it provides one alternative to feelings of "death by committee meeting."

Self-Managing Teams

Some firms have moved beyond limited forms of participation, allowing a number of major decisions to be made by employee groups (see extreme right side of Figure 8.6). These progressive approaches incorporate extensive use of group discussion, which makes full use of group ideas and group influence. These groups often seek to achieve consensus support for their actions, and this reflects many of the ideas adapted from successful Japanese firms.

A more formal version of the group-decision approach is the self-managing team. Sometimes called *semi-autonomous work groups or sociotechnical teams*, **self-managing teams** are natural work groups that are given a large degree of decision-making autonomy; they are expected to control their own behavior and results. A key feature is the diminished (or dramatically changed) role of the manager as the team members learn to acquire new skills. Because of their widespread use and importance, teams are discussed more extensively in Chapter 13.

9. I recognize that an effective way of providing employees with autonomy is to clarify their area of job freedom (boundaries).	10	9	8	7	6	5	4	3	2	1
10. I accept the fact that there may be a wide degree of variation in the amount of participation desired by each employee.	10	9	8	7	6	5	4	3	2	1

Scoring and Interpretation

Add up your total points for the 10 questions. Record that number here, and report it when it is requested. Finally, insert your total score into the "Assess and Improve Your Own Organizational Behavior Skills" chart in Appendix A.

- If you scored between 81 and 100 points, you appear to have a solid capability for demonstrating good empowerment skills.
- If you scored between 61 and 80 points, you should take a close look at the items with lower self-assessment scores and explore ways to improve those items.
- If you scored under 60 points, you should be aware that a weaker skill level regarding several items could be detrimental to your future success as a manager. We encourage you to review relevant sections of the chapter and watch for related material in subsequent chapters and other sources.

Now identify your three lowest scores, and write the question numbers here: _____, _____, _____. Write a brief paragraph, detailing to yourself an action plan for how you might sharpen each of these skills.

Incident

Joe Adams

Joe Adams is supervisor in the final-assembly department of an automobile body plant. Work in this department is not dependable, with temporary layoffs or short weeks occurring three or four times a year. The work is physically difficult, and since the skill required is minimal, most employees are high school graduates only. Some do not even have a high school education. About one-third of the workforce comes from ethnic and racial minority groups. The work procedure and pace of work are tightly controlled by industrial engineers and other staff groups.

Adams attended a one-day conference of his supervisors' association recently and learned the many potential benefits of participation. In his own words, "This conference really sold me on participation," and now he wishes to establish it in his assembly department.

Management feels that conditions on an assembly line are not suitable for participation. Further, it believes that the majority of workers employed have an autocratic role expectation of supervision. In addition, management has said that the production schedule will not allow time off for participation during the workday. This means that if Adams wants to hold any meetings about participation, he will have to do so after work and on the workers' own time. Adams feels sure that his employees will not wish to remain after work on their own time; in fact, he is not even sure they would do so if he paid them overtime.

Questions

1. Recommend a course of action for Adams.
2. Would any ideas from the following be helpful in this case: McGregor, Herzberg, McClelland, Fiedler, models of organizational behavior, prerequisites for participation, area of job freedom, and programs for participation?

Experiential Exercise

Empowerment through Participation

Empowerment fully occurs when employees feel competent, valued, and have opportunities to use their talents. It also materializes when their jobs have meaning and impact. Working in groups of three or four persons, rate (1 = low, 10 = high) the degree to which the group feels each participative program would produce these feelings of empowerment. Afterward, total the scores. Share your ratings with other groups and discuss the implications of your assessments.

	Feeling of Empowerment				
Programs	**Competence**	**Value**	**Talent Use**	**Meaningful Job**	**Total Score**
1. Suggestion programs					
2. Quality circles					
3. Total quality management					
4. Self-managing teams					
5. Employee ownership					
6. Rapid-cycle decision making					
7. Flexible work arrangements					

Generating OB Insights

An *insight* is a new and clear perception of a phenomenon, or an acquired ability to "see" clearly something you were unaware of previously. It is sometimes simply referred to as an "ah-ha! moment," in which you have a minirevelation or reach a straightforward conclusion about a topic or issue.

Insights need not necessarily be dramatic, for what is an insight to one person may be less important to another. The critical feature of insights is that they are relevant and memorable for *you;* they should represent new knowledge, new frameworks, or new ways of viewing things you want to retain and remember over time.

Insights, then, are different from the information you find in the "Advice for Future Managers" boxes within the text. That advice is prescriptive and action-oriented; it indicates a recommended course of action.

A useful way to think of OB insights is to assume you are the only person who has read Chapter 8. You have been given the assignment to highlight, in your own words, which major concepts (not just summarize the whole chapter) might stand out for a naive audience who has never heard of the topic before. *What 10 insights would you share with them?*

(Example) *Not all employees share the same level of desire to participate in decision making.*

1. ____

____

2. ____

____

3. ____

____

4. ____

____

5. ____

____

6. ____

____

7. ____

____

8. ____

____

9. ____

____

10. ____

____

Nurturing Your Critical Thinking and Reflective Skills

Take a few minutes to review the discussion in the Roadmap for Readers of critical thinking and reflection. Remind yourself that if you can hone these abilities now, you will have a substantial competitive advantage when you apply for jobs and are asked what unique skills you can bring to the position and the organization.

Critical Thinking

Think back on the material you read in this chapter. What are three unique and challenging *critical questions* you would like to raise about this material? (These might identify something controversial about which you have doubts, they may imply that you suspect that a theory or model has weaknesses, they could examine the legitimacy of apparent causal relationships, or they might assess the probable value of a suggested practice.) Be prepared to share these questions with class members or your instructor.

1. ____

____

2. ____

____

3. ____

____

Reflection

This process often involves answering the parallel questions of "What do you *think* about the material you have read?" and "How do you *feel* about that material?" Therefore, express your *personal thoughts and feelings* (reactions) to any of the ideas or topics found in this chapter, and be prepared to share these reflections with class members or your instructor.

1. ____

____

2. ____

____

3. ____

____

Part Four

Individual and Interpersonal Behavior

Chapter Nine

Employee Attitudes and Their Effects

People are happiest when they're appropriately challenged—when they're trying to achieve goals that are difficult but not out of reach.

Daniel Gilbert[1]

The No. 1 reason people leave an organization is that they don't feel valued and their contributions don't matter.

David Sturt[2]

CHAPTER OBJECTIVES

AFTER READING THIS CHAPTER, YOU SHOULD UNDERSTAND

9–1 The Nature of Attitudes and Job Satisfaction
9–2 The Relationship between Performance and Satisfaction
9–3 Job Involvement and Organizational Commitment
9–4 Some Positive and Negative Effects of Employee Attitudes
9–5 Organizational Citizenship Behaviors
9–6 Benefits of Studying Employee Attitudes
9–7 Design and Use of Job Satisfaction Surveys

Facebook Page 

Student A: I was talking to my grandparents recently about my OB class. They told me that back in their work days all their supervisor ever stressed to them was being more productive—"getting more product out the door."

Student B: So what's your point? Has anything really changed in present-day organizations?

Student A: Yeah—loads. Employees have a variety of important attitudes that managers ought to be deeply concerned about—job satisfaction, employee engagement, job involvement, organizational commitment, and even work moods.

Student C: Sounds pretty touchy-feely to me. Isn't that a lot of sensitivity for no return?

Student B: I agree. What does a company get for caring about those feelings?

Student A: You'd be surprised, like I was. Employee attitudes can affect performance, turnover, absenteeism, tardiness, theft, organizational citizenship, and even violence at work. That's a pretty big impact, and strongly implies the need for managers to measure attitudes and take steps to improve them.

Student B: Makes sense to me. Any surprises in your current chapter?

Student A: A couple. First, I didn't realize how much non-work factors can affect satisfaction at work; it's called the spillover effect and actually works in both directions. Second, I learned that it's entirely possible that successful employee performance can cause satisfaction. That crushed my assumption that satisfied employees are necessarily more productive.

Student B: I agree. If I perform well on today's anthropology exam, I'll be really satisfied!

Hugh Aaron ran a small plastics materials company that had suffered through three painful recessions—painful because each time Hugh had to lay off highly trained and motivated employees. Not only was it emotionally tough to release them, but every time business improved, some former workers had already found other jobs. The loss of those workers required him to hire inexperienced workers, who delayed the company's return to former efficiency levels. Even those who were rehired had lost some of their skills and often had bitter attitudes remaining about the layoff. Seeking to protect themselves as a future recession approached, they would slow the pace of their work in an attempt to delay their next layoff. This practice, however, only sped up the pace of layoffs, contributing to the vicious circle.

After studying some contemporary behavioral practices used in other companies, Hugh introduced certain major changes. In exchange for a simple promise to eliminate future layoffs, the employees agreed to work any necessary overtime and they were cross-trained to perform a wider variety of jobs. Any additional help needed for short-term fluctuations in business was drawn from retirees and college students.

The results were beyond expectations. Pride was evident; turnover was negligible; morale shot up; unemployment insurance and health benefit costs were reduced by having a smaller and more stable workforce. Attitudes also improved, as illustrated by employees' willingness to exert extra effort and by a sense of cohesiveness within the "family" team. Best of all, no layoffs were required during the next eight years, despite two more recessions.

Engaging Your Brain

1. Attitudes are feelings and beliefs about something. Have you ever actually *seen* an attitude? If not, how did you know that it existed? Do you think that attitudes can be managed, even if they cannot be directly seen?
2. Some employers, such as Success Factors' CEO Lars Dalgaard, will hire only employees who "love what they do, with a white hot passion." On a scale from 1 (very low) to 10 (very high), rate the probable degree of passion that *you* intend to commit to your next job.
3. Some authors have suggested that "employee loyalty (to the organization) is dead," while others have countered that "organizational loyalty to employees has greatly diminished." Do you believe that either (or both) of these statements is true? If so, why is that so?

Employee attitudes are clearly important to organizations, as seen in the preceding story and the opening quotes for this chapter. When attitudes are negative, they are both a *symptom* of underlying problems and a contributing *cause* of forthcoming difficulties in an organization. Declining attitudes may result in strikes, work slowdowns, absences, and employee turnover. They may also be a part of grievances, low performance, poor product quality and shabby customer service, employee theft, and disciplinary problems. The organizational costs associated with poor employee attitudes may severely reduce an organization's competitiveness.

What do *you* think the relationship between satisfaction and productivity is?

Favorable attitudes, on the other hand, are desired by management because they tend to be connected with many of the positive outcomes that managers want. Employee satisfaction, along with high productivity, is a hallmark of well-managed organizations. However, people often hold a classic misconception about the satisfaction–productivity relationship—one that is discussed later in this chapter.

A key challenge for managers is dealing with employees who increasingly *expect* to have concern shown for their attitudes and feelings as well as to receive rewards and recognition. Some employees even develop an attitude of **entitlement**—a belief that they deserve things because society (or their employer) owes it to them. However, these expectations can be unrealistic. Effective behavioral management that continuously works to build a supportive human climate in an organization can help produce favorable attitudes. This chapter focuses on the attitudes of employees toward their jobs, consequences of attitudes, ways to obtain information about those attitudes, and ways to use this information effectively to monitor and improve employee satisfaction.

THE NATURE OF EMPLOYEE ATTITUDES

Attitudes affect perceptions

Attitudes are the feelings and beliefs that largely determine how employees will perceive their environment, commit themselves to intended actions, and ultimately behave. Attitudes form a mental set that affects how we view something else, much as a window provides a framework for our view into or out of a building. The window allows us to see some things, but the size and shape of the frame prevent us from observing other elements. In addition, the color of the glass may affect the accuracy of our perception, just as the "color" of our attitudes has an impact on how we view and judge our surroundings at work. Managers of organizational behavior are vitally interested in the nature of the attitudes of their employees toward their jobs, toward their careers, and toward the organization itself.

Employee predispositions regarding happiness

Although many of the factors contributing to job satisfaction are under the control of managers, it is also true that people do differ in their personal dispositions as they enter organizations.

Some people are optimistic, upbeat, cheerful, and courteous; they are said to have **positive affectivity.** Others are generally pessimistic, downbeat, irritable, and even abrasive; they are said to have **negative affectivity.** It appears that some people are basically happy (about their lives) while others are less so. This is significant to employers, since broad research has found that happy individuals have much higher levels of productivity, sales, and creativity.[3] Even though happiness may predispose some employees to also have positive attitudes on the job (if hired), it is important to explore the nature and effects of job satisfaction.

Job Satisfaction

Three dimensions of attitudes

Feelings, thoughts, and intentions

Elements **Job satisfaction** is a set of favorable or unfavorable feelings and emotions with which employees view their work. Job satisfaction is an affective attitude—a *feeling* of relative like or dislike toward something (for example, a satisfied employee may comment that "I enjoy having a variety of tasks to do"). These job-related feelings of satisfaction are very different from two other elements of employee attitudes. The same employee may have an intellectual response to her work, stating the *objective thought* (belief) that "my work is quite complex." On another occasion, the employee may voice her **behavioral intentions** to a co-worker ("I plan to quit this job in three months"). Attitudes, then, consist of feelings, thoughts, and intentions to act.

Morale is group satisfaction

Individual Focus Job satisfaction typically refers to the attitudes of a single employee. For example, an administrator might conclude, "Antonio Ortega seems very pleased with his recent promotion." When assessments of individual satisfaction are averaged across all members of a work unit, the general term used to describe overall group satisfaction is **morale.** Group morale is especially important to monitor since individuals often take their social cues from their work associates and adapt their own attitudes to conform to those of the group.

Elements of job satisfaction

Overall or Multidimensional? Job satisfaction can be viewed as an overall attitude, or it can apply to the various parts of an individual's job. If it is viewed only as an overall attitude, however, managers may miss seeing some key hidden exceptions as they assess an employee's overall satisfaction. For example, although Antonio Ortega's general job satisfaction may be high, it is important to discover both that he likes his promotion and that he is dissatisfied with his vacation schedule this year. Job satisfaction studies, therefore, often focus on the various parts that are believed to be important, since these *job-related attitudes predispose an employee to behave in certain ways.* Important aspects of job satisfaction include pay, one's supervisor, the nature of tasks performed, an employee's co-workers or team, and the immediate working conditions.

Since job satisfaction is best viewed as being multidimensional, managers are cautioned not to allow an employee's high satisfaction on one element to offset high dissatisfaction on another by arithmetically blending both feelings into an average rating. The studies may, however, usefully divide their attention between those elements that are directly related to *job content* (the nature of the job) and those that are part of the *job context* (the supervisor, co-workers, and organization).

Satisfaction levels vary

Stability of Job Satisfaction Attitudes are generally acquired over a long period of time. Similarly, job satisfaction or dissatisfaction emerges as an employee gains more and more information about the workplace. Nevertheless, *job satisfaction is dynamic,* for it can decline even more quickly than it develops. Managers cannot establish the conditions leading to high satisfaction now and later neglect it, for employee needs and viewpoints may fluctuate suddenly. Managers need to pay attention to employee attitudes week after week, month after month, year after year.

Environmental Impact Job satisfaction is one part of life satisfaction. The nature of a worker's environment off the job indirectly influences his or her feelings on the job.

On the Job: Google

Google recently released a new application called Latitude.[5] When installed on cell phones such as BlackBerries or iPhones, it allows users to disclose their own locations. If employers provide such phones (already loaded with Latitude) to employees (with or without their knowledge), their minute-by-minute location can be tracked and monitored. For example, people taking long lunch breaks or calling in "sick" while actually at a golf course could be identified. Can you see some of the possible implications?

probe for additional information prior to hiring (or firing) an employee.[6] In addition to checking on the validity of qualifications, learning about awards and recognition, and judging communication skills, such screening can also uncover inappropriate photos or language, clues about attitudes toward work in general and prior employers, and information about alcohol or drug abuse. The Electronic Communications Privacy Act of 1986 was enacted by Congress to provide some protections, but it has become weakened due to subsequent amendments and court decisions, and become outdated due to changes in data storage practices. The upshot is that employers *can* (and will) often monitor employee communications of various types.

Honesty Testing

Employee theft is a major problem in U.S. businesses. It is estimated to cost employers $50–100 billion per year, with up to three-fourths of employees participating at least once. **Honesty tests,** also known as integrity tests, attempt to get the respondent to disclose information about his or her previous or prospective honesty. They appear in two forms. *Overt tests* inquire about attitudes toward theft (e.g., "How common is it for employees to steal items at work?"), whereas *personality-based tests* more indirectly identify dishonest individuals by relating scores on selected personality-test items to a theft criterion. The validity of these tests is also controversial, and employers run some risks of legal action (and possible invasion of privacy) if they reject an applicant solely on the basis of integrity test scores. However, scores on one test (the honesty subscale of the Personnel Selection Inventory) have been found to predict accurately subsequent employee theft.[7]

HEALTH ISSUES AND PRIVACY

Treatment of Alcoholism

Since alcoholism presents major medical and job problems, employers need to develop responsible policies and programs to deal with it without endangering rights of privacy. Between 5 and 10 percent of employees are estimated to be alcoholics, costing employers billions of dollars annually in absenteeism, poor work, lost productivity, and increased health care costs. Absence rates for alcoholic employees are two to four times those of other employees.

Alcoholics are found in all types of industries, occupations, and job levels. Sometimes the job environment may contribute to an employee's alcoholism, but the employee's personal habits and problems are also major contributors. In some instances, employees are well on the road to alcoholism before they are hired.

Critical Thinking Exercise

Surveillance devices can be used to monitor employees. Question: What positive and negative consequences might result from their use?

Reasons for Company Programs Regardless of the causes of alcoholism, an increasing number of firms are recognizing that they have a role to play in helping alcoholics control or break their habit. One reason is that the firm and employee already have a working relationship on which they can build. A second is that any success with the employee will save both a valuable person for the company and a valuable citizen for society. A third reason is that the job appears to be the best environment for supporting recovery because a job helps an alcoholic retain a self-image as a useful person in society.

How should companies treat alcoholism?

Successful Programs Successful employer programs treat alcoholism as an illness, focus on the job behavior caused by alcoholism, and provide both medical help and psychological support for alcoholics. In these programs the company demonstrates to alcoholics that it wants to help them and is willing to work with them over a reasonable period of time. A nonthreatening atmosphere is provided; however, the implication that alcohol-induced behavior cannot be tolerated indefinitely must be clear. For example, if an employee refuses treatment and unsatisfactory behavior continues, the employer has little choice other than dismissal. The following is the way one company operates:

> Mary Cortez, a supervisor, notices that an employee named Bill Revson has a record of tardiness and absenteeism, poor work, an exhausted appearance, and related symptoms that may indicate alcoholism or another serious problem. She discusses only Revson's job behavior with him, giving him a chance to correct himself. When Revson's behavior continues unchanged, Cortez asks Revson to meet with her in the presence of a counselor. The supervisor presents her evidence of poor job behavior and then leaves the room so the employee and counselor can discuss the situation privately. If Revson admits he has a problem and expresses the desire to address it, the counselor may recommend treatment for Bill. If the treatment is accepted, completed, and proves successful, the problem is solved.

Drug Abuse

Abuse of drugs other than alcohol, particularly if used at work, may cause severe problems for the individual, the employer, and other employees. These drugs may include heroin, powder cocaine, crack cocaine, methamphetamines, and marijuana, or the abuse may stem from the improper use of stimulants, barbiturates, and tranquilizers. In some job situations, such as those of a pilot, surgeon, railroad engineer, or crane operator, the direct effects of drug abuse can be disastrous—both for the individual and for many others.

Drug Testing To employers, the direct consequences of employee drug abuse are enormous. Employee theft to support drug habits costs industry billions each year. Absentee rates for workers with drug problems may be as much as 16 times higher than for nonusers, with accident rates 4 times as high. The lost productivity and additional health costs have been estimated to exceed $100 billion annually. In addition, drug abuse takes a tragic toll on society.

To help combat this problem, the Drug-Free Workplace Act became law in the United States in 1988. The law requires some employers (those with federal contracts over $25,000 and others obtaining financial assistance grants) to create and distribute to their employees policies prohibiting drug abuse at work. Other employers are encouraged to do the same. (Note: Employers can still enforce internal drug policies despite the recent trend toward states liberalizing their marijuana laws.[8]) Many companies—as many as 80 percent of major employers—have adopted a policy of drug testing of both new and current employees. Some test job applicants as well. The tests may be done on a periodic schedule, administered randomly, or given only when there is reason to suspect an employee (see "On the Job: Atlas Powder Company").

Testing policies like those at Atlas can be highly controversial. One reason is that some tests are not satisfactorily accurate. Some tests may produce *false negative* results when they

On the Job: Atlas Powder Company

Atlas Powder Company, a manufacturer of explosives, developed a drug policy for its Joplin, Missouri, plant.[9] All 425 employees receive annual physical examinations, which include mandatory drug testing for a wide range of controlled substances. During the first two years, seven people tested positive and received suspensions. In addition, 20 percent of Atlas's job applicants who were initially referred for hiring had positive drug screens for marijuana and were rejected.

fail to identify 5 percent of the actual users. Other employees may be incorrectly identified as users (*false positives*) because the food they ate or the prescription drugs they took produced a falsely positive reaction. Usually, further investigation and repeated testing will support their innocence, but the harm to their reputation and self-esteem may already have occurred. Another objection to drug testing is the fear that it will reveal other medical conditions that an employee may prefer to keep private. In addition, some employees find it intrusive to be watched while providing samples for testing. A final privacy issue revolves around the presumed right to consume any substance one desires; however, the U.S. Constitution does not guarantee the right to possess and use illegal drugs.

A possible solution to the problems with drug testing lies in **impairment testing.** This method usually consists of a brief motor-skills test performed on a computer; the test is much like playing a video game (see "On the Job: R. F. White Company").

Genetic Testing

Testing differs from monitoring

The controversy over employee privacy rights has also emerged in the area of **genetic testing.** New developments in the field of genetics allow physicians to use medical tests to accurately predict whether an employee may be genetically susceptible to one or more types of illness or harmful substances. (This is a more aggressive tool than **genetic monitoring,** which identifies harmful substances in the workplace, examines their effects on the genetic makeup of employees, and provides the basis for corrective action.) Positive uses of genetic testing information include transferring the susceptible employees to other work areas where they will not be exposed to the substances, providing health warnings, and developing protective measures to shield the employees from danger. The negative side of genetic testing comes into play when a firm screens present employees or job applicants on the basis of genetic predispositions and uses the information to discriminate against them in an attempt to minimize the firm's future health costs. Effective in 2009, employee rights became increasingly protected under the Genetic Information Nondiscrimination Act (GINA). This law prohibits employers from using personal or family genetic information to discriminate against them—even through accidental acquisition of such data. At the same

An Ethics Question

The robust U.S. economy that marked the beginning of the twenty-first century brought about a low unemployment rate and very strong competition for skilled workers. As a result, some employers began making greater accommodations to their hiring practices so as to attract applicants. In particular, some firms threw out their drug-testing policies, while others no longer inquired about felony conviction records, as long as they believed that there was no threat to personal safety of their workforce. These firms found it timely to reverse their earlier policies in the face of a difficult labor market. Questions: During times of high unemployment rates and labor surpluses will these companies once again change their practices and again tighten their drug testing procedures? *Should* they do so?

On the Job: R. F. White Company

At the R. F. White Company, eye-hand coordination was assessed by comparing test results with a baseline measure for each employee.[11] Over a one-year period, this wholesale petroleum distribution company experienced reductions of accidents by 67 percent, errors and incidents by 92 percent, and worker's compensation claims costs by 64 percent. In addition to these benefits, the firm believed the process was cheaper, more timely, and more accurate than drug testing. It also shifts the focus from moralistic judgments of why an employee can't perform, to the capacity to perform itself.

time, a great challenge to individual privacy and opportunity occurs when a firm identifies those employees who smoke, drink socially, are dangerously overweight, or engage in risky recreational activities and then attempts to impose lifestyle changes on them.[10]

Discrimination

As noted in Chapter 4, Equal Employment Opportunities (EEO) laws generally prohibit job discrimination on the basis of race, color, national origin, sex, religion, handicapped status, and other factors. Two key EEO issues stand out as contemporary problems related to privacy. The first concerns sexual harassment on the job, in which the right to a non-offensive work environment is violated. The second issue relates to a particular type of disease some employees may have and their right to maintain medical privacy, continue working, and receive medical care. Both of these topics will be discussed briefly.

Sexual Harassment When supervisors make employment or promotion decisions contingent on sexual favors or when an employee's colleagues engage in any verbal or physical conduct that creates an offensive working environment, **sexual harassment** exists (see Figure 10.3 for the definition provided by the Equal Employment Opportunity Commission). Although harassment is a *perceived* action by others, it is very real to the recipient. Since it is somewhat individually defined, there is some disagreement over what constitutes sexual harassment. Females responding to one survey generally included in their definition sexual propositions, unwanted physical touching, sexual remarks and jokes, and suggestive gestures. Despite decades of programs designed to prevent harassment at work, the problem is still far too pervasive. Such harassment can occur anywhere in a company, from executive offices to assembly lines. From a human point of view, it is distasteful and demeaning to its victims, and it is discriminatory according to EEO laws and federal and state guidelines. *Sexual harassment is a violation of a person's personal rights and an offense to human dignity.*

Preventive practices

In order to protect potential victims and prevent harassment, many employers have developed policies to prevent it. They also have conducted training programs to educate employees about the relevant law, identified actions that could constitute harassment, and communicated both the possible liabilities involved and the negative effects of harassment on its victims. In the absence of preventive programs and timely intervention in known situations, employers may be responsible for the harassment actions of their supervisors

FIGURE 10.3
EEOC Definition of Sexual Harassment

Source: Employment Opportunity Commission, *Guidelines on Discrimination Because of Sex,* 1604.11 (Sexual Harassment), November 10, 1980.

Unwelcome sexual advances, requests for sexual favors, and other verbal or physical conduct of a sexual nature constitute sexual harassment when:

1. Submission to such conduct is made either explicitly or implicitly a term or condition of an individual's employment.
2. Submission to or rejection of such conduct by an individual is used as the basis for employment decisions affecting such individual.
3. Such conduct has the purpose or effect of unreasonably interfering with an individual's work performance or creating an intimidating, hostile, or offensive working environment.

and employees. When it occurs, employers may be liable for reinstatement of the victims if they were unfairly discharged, and may have to pay back wages, punitive damages, and substantial awards for psychological suffering and pain. Most victims of sexual harassment are women, but there have been instances in which men were victims.

AIDS **Acquired immune deficiency syndrome (AIDS)** is a deadly virus affecting the human immune system. It is contagious through the receipt of infected blood and certain types of sexual contact. At this time, it is incurable, often fatal, and is spreading rapidly in some areas of the world. Widespread public concern and lack of understanding, coupled with unclear legal status of employees with AIDS, have raised several key behavioral issues, such as the following:

AIDS-related issues at work

- Can the medical privacy of AIDS employees be protected?
- What can be done to help co-workers understand more about AIDS and about the way it affects its victims? In particular, how can the firm encourage employees to calmly accept a co-worker with AIDS into the work group?
- How might the presence of AIDS employees affect teamwork and other participation in a group?
- How can managers prevent AIDS employees from becoming harassed or socially isolated through the possible loss of normal communications with their co-workers?
- Should employees be tested for the presence of the AIDS-related virus? If they test positive, should they be transferred to other jobs? (Note that the presence of the AIDS-related virus—HIV—does *not* imply that a person now has AIDS itself nor will necessarily contract it.)

Although these are difficult issues, employers need to consider them and develop their policies before the first case arises in their organization. In particular, they need to be aware of the relevant laws that appear to include persons with AIDS under the definition and protection of "handicapped" or "disabled." These include the Vocational Rehabilitation Act of 1973 and the Americans with Disabilities Act of 1990.

DISCIPLINE

Two types of discipline

The area of discipline can have a strong impact on the individual in the organization. **Discipline** is management action to enforce organizational standards. There are two types: preventive and corrective.

Preventive discipline is action taken to encourage employees to follow standards and rules so infractions do not occur. Prevention is best done by making company standards known and understood in advance. The basic objective, however, is to encourage employee *self-discipline.* In this way, the employees maintain their own discipline rather than have management impose it. Employees are more likely to support standards that they have (participatively) helped create. They also will give more support to standards that are stated positively instead of negatively, and when they have been told the reasons behind a standard so it will make sense to them.

Corrective discipline is action that follows infraction of a rule; it seeks to discourage further infractions so future acts will be in compliance with standards. Typically, the corrective action is a penalty of some type and is called a *disciplinary action.* Examples are a warning or suspension with or without pay.

Objectives of disciplinary action

The objectives of disciplinary action are positive, educational, and corrective, as follows:

- To reform the offender
- To deter others from similar actions
- To maintain consistent, effective group standards

Increasingly stronger penalties

Most employers apply a policy of **progressive discipline,** which means there are stronger penalties for repeated offenses. The purpose is to give an employee an opportunity for

FIGURE 10.4 **A Progressive Discipline System**

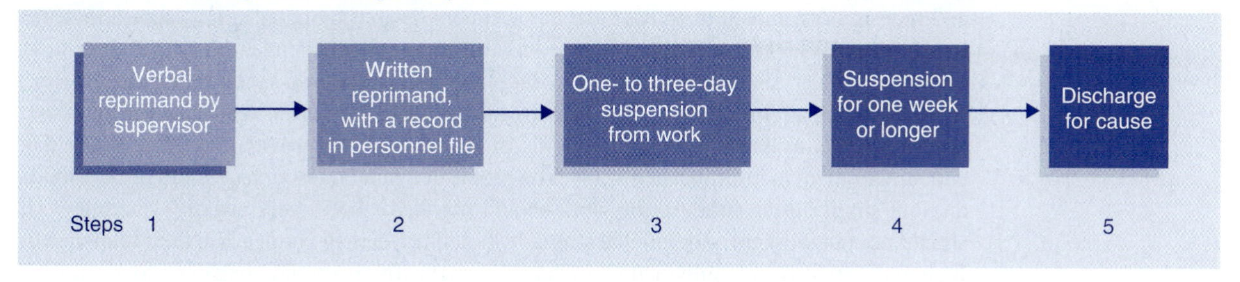

self-correction before more serious penalties are applied. Progressive discipline also gives management time to work with an employee on a counseling basis to help correct infractions, such as unauthorized absences. A typical system of progressive discipline is shown in Figure 10.4.

QUALITY OF WORK LIFE

QWL programs

What is **quality of work life (QWL)?** The term refers to the favorableness or unfavorableness of a total job environment for people. QWL programs are another way in which *organizations recognize their responsibility to develop jobs and working conditions that are excellent for people as well as for the economic health of the organization.* The elements in a typical QWL program include many items discussed earlier in this book under the general area of supportive organizational behavior—open communications, equitable reward systems, a concern for employee job security and satisfying careers, a caring supervisor, and participation in decision making. Many early QWL efforts focused on job enrichment, which is a major topic in this section. In addition to improving the work system, QWL programs usually emphasize development of employee skills, the reduction of occupational stress, and the development of more cooperative labor–management relations.

A Rationale

Job specialization and simplification were popular in the early twentieth century. Employees were assigned narrow jobs and supported by a rigid hierarchy in the expectation that efficiency would improve. The idea was to lower costs by using unskilled workers who could be trained easily to do a small repetitive part of each job.

Many difficulties developed from that classical job design, however. There was excessive division of labor. Workers became socially isolated from their co-workers because their highly specialized jobs weakened their community of interest in the whole product. De-skilled workers lost pride in their work and became bored with their jobs. Higher-order (social and growth) needs were left unsatisfied. The result was higher turnover and absenteeism, declines in quality, and alienated workers. Conflict often arose as workers sought to improve their conditions and organizations failed to respond appropriately. The real cause was that in many instances the job itself simply was not satisfying.

Forces for change

A factor contributing to the problem was that the workers themselves were changing. They became more educated, more affluent (partly because of the effectiveness of classical job design), and more independent. They began reaching for higher-order needs, something more than merely earning their wages. Employers now had two reasons for redesigning jobs and organizations for a better QWL:

- Classical design originally gave inadequate attention to human needs.
- The needs and aspirations of workers themselves were changing.

Humanized work through QWL

One option that emerged was to redesign jobs to have the attributes desired by people, and redesign organizations to have the environment desired by people. This approach seeks to improve QWL. There is a need to give workers more of a challenge, more of a whole task, more opportunity to use their ideas. *Close attention to QWL provides a more humanized work environment.* It attempts to serve the higher-order needs of workers as well as their more basic needs. It seeks to employ the higher skills of workers and to provide an environment that encourages them to improve their skills. The idea is that human resources should be developed and not simply used. Further, the work should not have excessively negative conditions. It should not put workers under undue stress. It should not damage or degrade their humanness. It should not be threatening or unduly dangerous. Finally, it should contribute to, or at least leave unimpaired, workers' abilities to perform in other life roles, such as citizen, spouse, and parent. That is, *work should contribute to general social advancement.*

Job Enlargement vs. Job Enrichment

The modern interest in quality of work life was stimulated through efforts to change the scope of people's jobs in attempting to motivate them. **Job scope** has two dimensions—breadth and depth. **Job breadth** is the number of different tasks an individual is directly responsible for. It ranges from very narrow (one task performed repetitively) to wide (several tasks). Employees with narrow job breadth were sometimes given a wider variety of duties in order to reduce their monotony; this process is called **job enlargement.**

Enlargement provides breadth

In order to perform these additional duties, employees spend less time on each duty. Another approach to changing job breadth is called **job rotation,** which involves periodic assignment of an employee to completely different sets of job activities. Job rotation is an effective way to develop multiple skills in employees, which benefits the organization while creating greater job interest and career options for the employee.

Enrichment provides depth

Job enrichment takes a different approach by adding additional motivators to a job to make it more rewarding. It was developed by Frederick Herzberg on the basis of his studies indicating that the most effective way to motivate workers was by focusing on higher-order needs. Job enrichment seeks to add to **job depth** by giving workers more control, responsibility, and discretion over how their job is performed. The difference between enlargement and enrichment is illustrated in Figure 10.5. Here we see that job enrichment focuses on satisfying

FIGURE 10.5
Difference between Job Enrichment and Job Enlargement

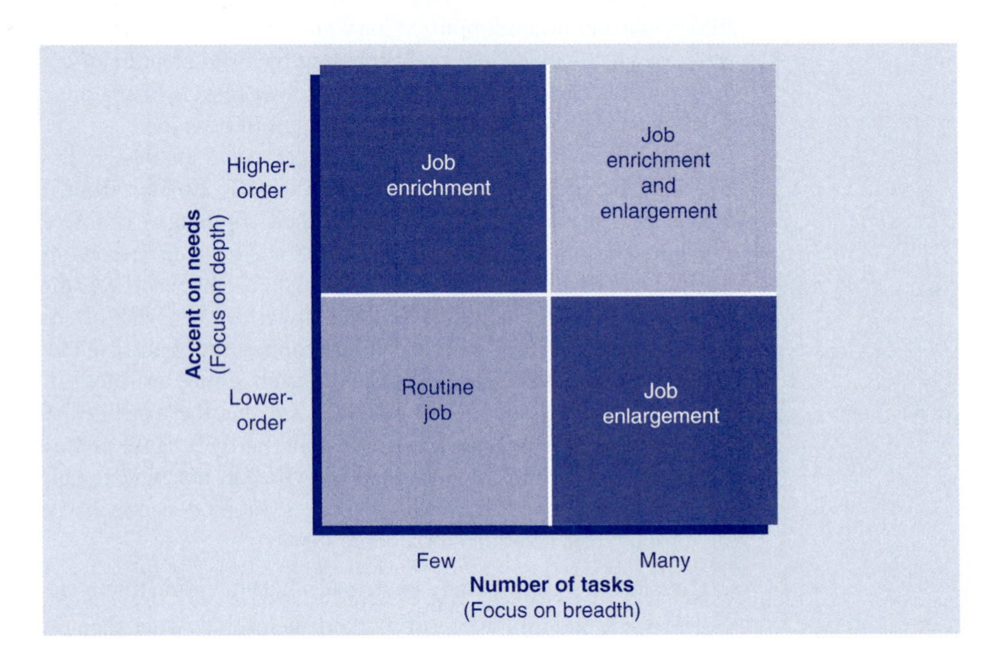

FIGURE 10.6 Benefits of Job Enrichment Emerge in Three Areas

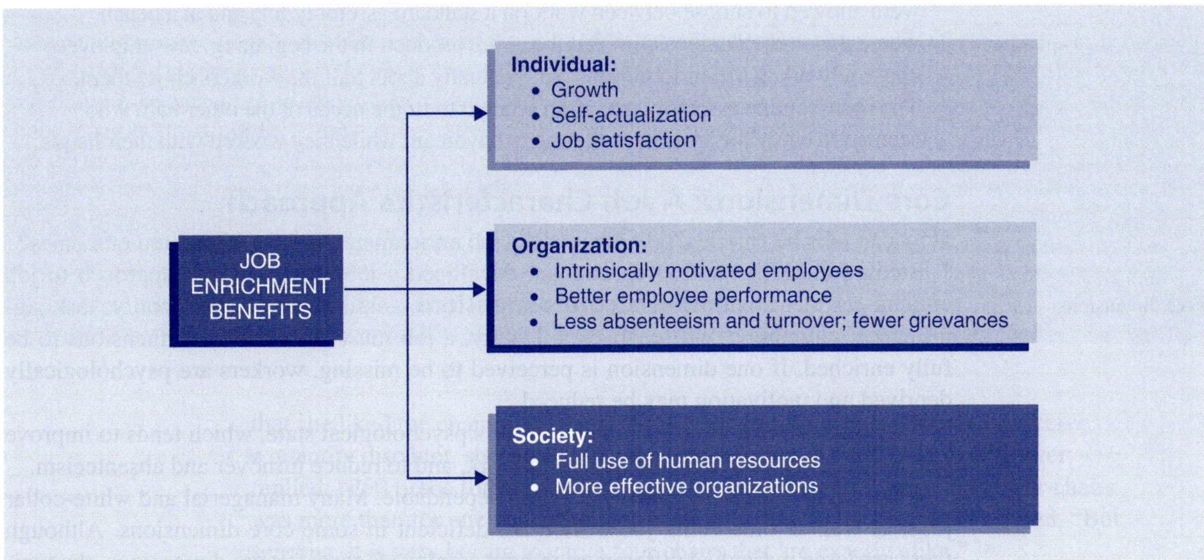

higher-order needs, whereas job enlargement concentrates on adding additional tasks to the worker's job for greater variety. The two approaches can even be blended, by both expanding the number of tasks and adding more motivators, for a two-pronged attempt to improve QWL.

Job enrichment brings many benefits, as shown in Figure 10.6. Its general result is a role enrichment that encourages growth and self-actualization. The job is built in such a way that intrinsic motivation is encouraged. Because motivation is increased, performance should improve, thus providing both a more humanized and a more productive job. Negative effects also tend to be reduced, such as turnover, absences, grievances, and idle time. The worker performs better, experiences greater job satisfaction, and becomes more self-actualized, thus being able to participate in all life roles more effectively. Society benefits from the more effectively functioning person as well as from better job performance. QWL produces three-pronged benefits, at the individual, organizational, and societal levels.

Applying Job Enrichment

Viewed in terms of Herzberg's motivational factors, job enrichment occurs when the work itself is more challenging, when achievement is encouraged, when there is opportunity for growth, and when responsibility, feedback, and recognition are provided. However, *employees are the final judges of what enriches their jobs.* All that management can do is gather information about what tends to enrich jobs, try those changes in the job system, and then determine whether employees feel that enrichment has occurred.

In trying to build motivational factors, management also gives attention to maintenance factors. It attempts to keep maintenance factors constant or higher as the motivational factors are increased. If maintenance factors are allowed to decline during an enrichment program, then employees may be less responsive to the enrichment program because they are distracted by inadequate maintenance. The need for a systems approach to job enrichment is satisfied by the practice of gain sharing (introduced in Chapter 6).

Gain sharing satisfies maintenance needs

Since job enrichment must occur from each employee's personal viewpoint, *not all employees will choose enriched jobs if they have an option.* A contingency relationship exists in terms of different job needs, and some employees may prefer the simplicity and security of more routine jobs.

often because they recognize that performance does vary, and the only way they can make adjustments is to know how they are performing now.

Enrichment Increases Motivation

The degree to which the five core dimensions are present in jobs needs to be evaluated before job enrichment can take place. An employer studies jobs to assess how low or high they are on skill variety, task identity, task significance, autonomy, and feedback—often in comparison to the desired level of each. Employees need to be involved in this assessment, since *their perceptions are most important.*

Conditions for job enrichment

After data are collected (usually by survey), an overall index for a job may be computed.[14] The overall index indicates the degree to which the job is perceived to be meaningful (a combination of variety, identity, and significance), foster responsibility (autonomy), and provide knowledge of results (feedback). Managers can then take action to increase one or more of the five factors to enrich the job. Jobs that have been enriched increase the probability of high motivation, provided that employees:

- Have adequate job knowledge and skills
- Desire to learn, grow, and develop
- Are satisfied with their work environment (are not distracted by negative hygiene factors)

Most job enrichment attempts have been conducted in manufacturing operations, but many have also been attempted in banks, insurance companies, and other service organizations.

> Salespersons in a large department store were the subjects for a field experiment in job redesign for enrichment purposes.[15] After providing their perceptions of their current jobs as measured by a set of scales, they implemented a series of job changes designed to increase the skill variety, task identity, task significance, autonomy, and feedback gained from their jobs.
>
> The salespersons' perceptions of their jobs increased significantly following the experiment, indicating they believed their jobs had become enriched. Dysfunctional behaviors such as misuse of idle time and absence from the workstation decreased, whereas functional behaviors (selling and stocking) increased moderately. Several measures of employee satisfaction also improved.

Social Cues Affect Perceptions

Not all attempts to enrich jobs have been as successful as the experiment just described. In some cases, employees do not report significant changes in their perceptions of the core characteristics after job enrichment, despite objective evidence that the job actually was changed. This has produced considerable frustration for both job design specialists and managers.

One explanation for the lack of predicted changes from enrichment lies in the presence of **social cues,** which are often rather subtle bits of positive or negative information workers receive from their social surroundings. These social cues may come from co-workers, leaders, other organizational members, customers, and family members. Social cues may serve either to support or to counteract the direction of objective task characteristics, as shown in Figure 10.8.

Social information processing

The key to job enrichment lies in how employees use the social cues provided by their peers and others to arrive at their own perception of their jobs. This activity, called **social information processing,** covers three elements. First, peers may suggest *which* of the job characteristics really count to them (as when a worker named Karl asserts that "Around here, the only thing I care about is how much control I'm allowed!"). Second, they may offer their personal model regarding the relative *weighting* of each core dimension (as when Lynn suggests to Dan that "I value skill variety and feedback the most, with the other

FIGURE 10.8
Social Cues Affect Employee Reactions to Tasks

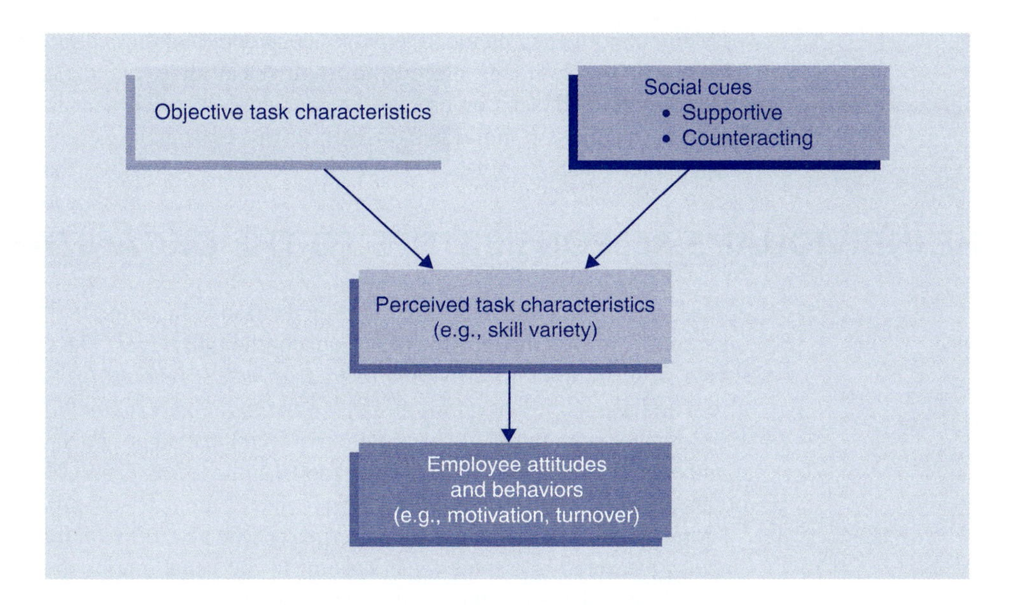

three factors worth only a small amount"). Third, peers may provide direct or indirect clues about their own *judgments* of the dimensions (as when Alan confides that "Despite what management claims, I still don't think my job is very important").

An integrated approach to job design suggests that managers must focus on managing the social context of job changes, as well as the objective job enrichment process itself. They must discover which groups are important sources of social cues, perhaps using group discussions to reinforce an employee's initial tendencies to assess job changes positively. Managers can also create expectations (in the minds of employees and co-workers) that the enriched jobs will have more of certain dimensions and therefore be more satisfying.

Contingency Factors Affecting Enrichment

Job enrichment does not apply to all types of situations. It appears to apply more easily to higher-level jobs, which are less likely to be dictated by the technological process. If the technology is stable and highly automated, the costs of job enrichment may be too great in relation to the rewards. Some workers do not want increased responsibility or more complex tasks, and other workers do not adapt to the group interaction that is sometimes required.

Job enrichment also may upset pay relationships. In particular, employees may expect more than intrinsic satisfaction for the additional duties and responsibilities they assume. Many other costs and limitations exist in addition to pay. Equipment and floor space may have to be redesigned, with more space and tools needed so individuals or teams can work independently. Inventories may need to be increased, training costs may go up, and turnover may initially increase. Unions may resist enrichment attempts if existing job classifications are upset.

Those planning job enrichment programs need to ask the following questions about employee needs and attitudes:

Key questions

- Can the employee tolerate (and welcome) responsibility?
- How strong are the employee's growth and achievement needs?
- What is the employee's attitude and experience regarding group work?
- Can the employee intellectually and emotionally handle more complexity?
- How strong are the employee's drives for security and stability?
- Will the employees view the job changes as significant enough to justify the costs?
- Can a job be overenriched?

Many contingency elements must be considered when exploring the possibility of job enrichment as a QWL approach. Both employee attitudes and the capabilities of employees to handle enriched tasks are crucial. To consider job enrichment as good is tempting, but to recognize and respect individual differences that exist among employees is more consistent with human values.

THE INDIVIDUAL'S RESPONSIBILITIES TO THE ORGANIZATION

A discussion of the individual in the organization is incomplete if it covers only the organization's impositions on, and obligations to, the individual. The employment relationship is two-way. Without question, *the organization has responsibilities to the individual,* but also—and again without question—*the individual has responsibilities to the organization.* Employment is a mutual transaction and a social exchange. Each employee makes certain membership investments in the organization and expects profitable rewards in return. The organization also invests in the individual, and it, too, expects profitable rewards.

A relationship is profitable for either party when benefits (outputs) are larger than costs (inputs) measured in a total value system. In the usual employment situation both parties benefit, just as they do in the usual social relationship. Both parties benefit because the social transaction between them produces new values that exceed the investment each makes.

The profitable relationship deteriorates if either party fails to act responsibly toward the needs of the other. The employees can fail to act responsibly, just as the organization can. If they do, they can expect the organization to respond by using tight controls to try to maintain a successful operating system.

Theft as an example

Consider the matter of employee theft, which was mentioned earlier. Overlook for the moment the legal-ethical-moral views of theft. From the point of view of the organizational system only, theft interferes with work operations. It upsets schedules and budgets. It causes reorders. It calls for more controls. In sum, it reduces both the reliability and the productivity of the organizational system. Output is diminished for the individual as well as for the organization. In this situation, the organization must act to protect other employees as well as itself. Employees can demonstrate their larger responsibilities toward the organization, beyond acting productively and creatively, in many ways. These include organizational citizenship, dues-paying, whistle-blowing, and building mutual trust.

Organizational Citizenship

Applying the social exchange idea makes it evident that employees are expected to go beyond their job descriptions and be good **organizational citizens.** This reciprocal relationship at the individual level parallels the way the organization is expected to behave in the broader society in which it operates. As noted in Chapter 9, employees who are organizational citizens engage in positive social acts designed to benefit others.

Typical categories of citizenship include:

- Helping others (altruism) and cooperating with them (sharing time and resources)
- Civic virtue (attending meetings and complying with rules and procedures)
- Sportsmanship and courtesy (positive attitude)
- Conscientiousness (efficient use of work time and exerting extra effort)
- Organizational loyalty (endorsing and supporting organizational practices)

Two key questions emerge, however. First, which employees are most likely to engage in citizenship behaviors? Some evidence suggests that the personality factors of agreeableness, openness to experience, and conscientiousness predict helping behaviors. Second, is there a possibility of engaging in too much citizenship? Since an employee's time at work is finite, it is definitely possible that too much time spent in benefiting others might come at the expense of task performance. Clearly, a balance of activities is necessary.[16]

Dues-Paying

A special case of individual responsibility to others occurs when employees are expected—by their peers—to pay their dues or put in their time. **Dues-paying** consists of the total "costs" that a person's group believes an individual should pay for the privileges of full acceptance and continuing membership in it (as well as the receipt of rewards).[17] These costs might include:

- Minimum qualifications of the employee
- Willingness to get one's hands dirty while not complaining about undesirable tasks
- Showing proper respect to others
- Not acting superior to others
- Performing at an above-average level
- Spending the appropriate amount of time at one's job

Dues-paying has several key characteristics: it is a perceptual phenomenon; it is judged by many different observers; it is situation-specific (judgments are made on a case-by-case basis); and a group's memory of dues paid may be faulty or even diminish over time. The idea of dues paid is based on the concept of **idiosyncrasy credits:** Over time, a person earns credits that can be "cashed in" when necessary—somewhat similar to a personal bank account. The significance of dues lies in the importance of recognizing one's own obligations to others, both objective and subjective in nature. And when well-earned rewards are received, employees would be wise to downplay the accomplishment, deflect the praise, and share the credit. Managers can play a key role in counseling novice employees about this process.

How do you earn idiosyncrasy credits?

Blowing the Whistle on Unethical Behavior

Examples abound of unethical behavior in organizations, and it occurs at all levels. Despite our own optimism about human nature and fundamental goodness within people, many studies still find that many (if not most) people act in dishonest ways at some point in their work careers. Why? Reasons include the direct benefits gained (self-interest), the mere opportunity to cut corners, the thrill of the challenge to do so and not get caught, and the organization's pressure on employees to perform amid the existence of incompatible demands.

Several organizations have tried to implement tighter controls, ethical codes, and ethical training programs, but these are often unsuccessful or short-lived—and sometimes they merely drive unethical behavior underground, just as Prohibition drove liquor production and consumption underground for several years in the early 1900s. Two powerful forces can work to diminish dishonesty, however (in addition to the fear of getting caught). First is the basic *honesty and respect for truth-telling among some people.* Honest employees tend (and prefer) not to lie, cheat, or steal. Further, they are more likely to have developed and internalized a personal moral code based on ethical principles. This allows them to

Critical Thinking Exercise

Some employees may be undecided about being good organizational citizens. Question: If you were their manager, what guidance and advice would you provide to such a person?

What Managers Are Reading

DEVELOPING YOUR ETHICAL MIND

Harvard professor Howard Gardner, a psychologist, believes it is useful to conceive of the mind as a set of cognitive capacities. The first four consist of the disciplined, synthesizing, creative, and respectful minds. The fifth—the ethical mind—helps people ponder their life's role and balance that against society's needs and desires. Ethical persons act as impartial spectators who continually examine what they were taught, what they are experiencing, and what they believe. They move beyond a focus on their own self-interest and instead examine the larger good of society (which sometimes encourages them to become whistle-blowers). Key questions asked by persons with ethical minds include:

- Who do I want to be (from the standpoint of ethics)?
- If everyone else was like me in their thinking and behavior, how would that look?

Source: Howard Gardner, *Five Minds for the Future*, Boston: Harvard Business Press, 2008.

respond to ethical dilemmas based on prior analytical reasoning, and make well-considered judgments. Here are some examples of ethical guidelines:

1. Guard against the first ethical misstep, which leads you down a "slippery slope."
2. Don't sign false documents or bury your mistakes.
3. Don't follow the crowd or believe that "everyone else is doing it."
4. Lead by example, and seek wise counsel from others before acting.
5. Act with integrity, asking yourself "If everyone did what I intend to do, how would that look?"

The second useful force is the *availability of ethical role models.* These mentors and leaders often have four characteristics:

1. Positive interpersonal behaviors (hardworking, supportive, caring, concerned, compassionate)
2. Ethical expectations for themselves (honest, trustworthy, humble, self-sacrificial)
3. Fairness toward others (solicit and use inputs, not condescending, fair distributors of resources)
4. Articulation of ethical standards to others (put ethics above themselves, uncompromising in support of high ethical standards, hold others accountable).[18]

Despite the best ethical role models and individual voices favoring honesty, unethical organizational behavior may still arise. Being a good organizational citizen does not extend to blind conformity—supporting illegal activities of the organization, bending to organizational pressures (as in the chapter-opening *Challenger* example), or engaging in any other activities that seriously violate social standards. For example, when management disregards internal opposition to wrongful acts or fails to disclose information about defective products, an employee may choose a response from a wide array of alternatives (see Figure 10.9). Several of these responses demonstrate a form of **whistle-blowing,** which is disclosing alleged misconduct to an internal or external source. This misconduct might be violation of a rule or law, fraud, safety violation, or corruption.

Who are the likely whistle-blowers?

Some employees are more likely than others to be whistle-blowers in organizations.[19] They are workers who have strong evidence of having observed wrongdoing, who believe it to be a serious problem, and who feel it directly affects them. In general, such conscientious

FIGURE 10.9
Alternative Employee Responses to Wrongful Acts

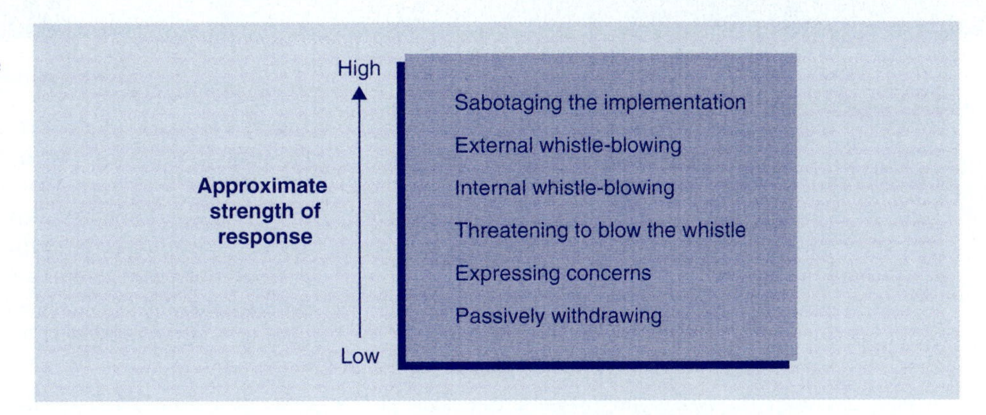

people are likely to be professionals with long service, people previously recognized as good performers, and those who work in organizations perceived by others to be responsive to complaints. Their motivations may vary widely. Some employees blow the whistle because they feel obligated to protect the public; some do it because they are afraid of the legal consequences of being prosecuted themselves, and others do so in retaliation for the treatment they have received from their employer.

> One employee of a military contractor made the headlines when he blew the whistle on his employer.[20] Christopher Urda claimed his employer had systematically overbilled the Pentagon on its contracts. A federal judge fined the contractor over $55 million and awarded Mr. Urda $7.5 million under the provisions of the 1986 False Claims Act.

By going public, whistle-blowers hope to bring pressure on the organization to correct the problem. Although the legal system (primarily the provisions of the 2002 Sarbanes-Oxley and 2010 Dodd-Frank acts) generally protects them, some employees—as many as 22 percent, according to one study—have been the subject of employer retaliation, such as harassment, transfer, or **discharge** (firing).[21] The need for whistle-blowing can be diminished by creating a variety of ways for employees to voice their concerns inside the organization—and encouraging this behavior. Previously discussed devices for this purpose include suggestion systems, survey feedback, and employee–management meetings.

Mutual Trust

When whistle-blowing occurs, it usually signifies that a previous level of mutual trust has deteriorated or even been broken. **Mutual trust** is joint faith in the responsibility and actions of the parties involved; when it is present, each person has a strongly positive expectation that the other person will do the right thing. Development of mutual trust occurs over a period of time through the emergence of mutual understanding, the development of emotional bonds, and the demonstration of trustworthy behaviors. It can, however, be broken in an instant through an inappropriate word or action by either party. Further, loss of trust results in a breakdown of the psychological contract (see Chapter 4). When managers lose the trust of their employees, it requires concerted and extended efforts to repair and re-earn it. Corporate leaders, and all managers, have a very visible role to play in shaping a strong organizational culture that clarifies the organization's values and expectations. When this is done, the level of trust is likely to be high.

Summary

Some areas of potential individual–organization conflict are legitimacy of organizational influence, rights of privacy, and discipline. The main concern is to ensure that the employee's activities and choices are guided—but not unduly controlled to the detriment of the

Advice to Future Managers

1. Before taking any significant actions that might influence employee behaviors, *carefully weigh the degree to which those actions have a high degree of legitimacy.*
2. *Familiarize yourself with the organization's policies on employee rights to privacy* and the reasons for those policies.
3. When unacceptable employee behaviors are likely to occur, *focus first on preventive discipline* and then, only if necessary, invoke corrective discipline.
4. *Assess,* through the eyes of employees, *the level of quality of work life that they perceive to exist.* Make appropriate changes and follow up to determine the impact.
5. *Involve employees in efforts to redesign their jobs* to incorporate higher degrees of skill variety, task identity, task significance, autonomy, or feedback, where appropriate.
6. *Engage employees in regular discussions about their side of the psychological contract*—their responsibility to act ethically, sustain trust, demonstrate good citizenship at work, and their obligation to blow the whistle if all else fails.
7. *Explore ways in which you can add either breadth or depth* (or both) to employee jobs.
8. Do not rely on your own perceptions of a job's degree of enrichment; *seek out the perceptions of current job holders.*
9. *Help new employees recognize that rewards and group acceptance won't come easily,* but only through the process of dues-paying.
10. *Search for ways to build mutual trust* between management and employees at all times.

employee—by the organization. In order to protect both the organization and the worker, companies usually develop policies to guide their decisions about privacy, alcohol- and drug-abuse programs, genetic testing, sexual harassment, and other activities. To accomplish their goals, management uses both preventive and corrective discipline to ensure appropriate behavior.

One social obligation that many organizations have adopted is to improve the quality of work life (QWL) for its employees. QWL refers to the favorableness or unfavorableness of the job environment for people. This is never an easy or a final task, since QWL exists in the perceptions of employees and is constantly changing.

Jobs vary in their breadth and depth. Job enrichment applies to any efforts to humanize jobs by the addition of more motivators. Core dimensions of jobs that especially provide enrichment are skill variety, task identity, task significance, autonomy, and feedback. In spite of job enrichment's objective desirability, its cues must be perceived by employees and valued by them to have substantial impact.

The social transaction of employment is a two-way street, with mutual responsibilities for the individual and the organization. The employee should be a good organizational citizen, be willing to "pay one's dues," exercise ethical leadership, or resort to whistle-blowing if necessary. Benefits will accrue to individuals, the organization, and society when this social exchange is fulfilled and mutual trust is evident.

Speaking OB: Terms and Concepts for Review

Impairment testing, *266*
Job breadth, *270*
Job depth, *270*
Job enlargement, *270*
Job enrichment, *270*
Job rotation, *270*
Job scope, *270*
Legitimacy of organizational influence, *261*
Mutual trust, *279*
Organizational citizens, *276*
Preventive discipline, *268*
Progressive discipline, *268*
Quality of work life (QWL), *269*
Rights of privacy, *262*
Sexual harassment, *267*
Skill variety, *272*
Social cues, *274*
Social information processing, *274*
Social screening, *263*
Surveillance devices, *263*
Task identity, *273*
Task significance, *273*
Whistle-blowing, *278*

Discussion Questions

1. Explain the basic model of legitimacy of organizational influence. Does it seem to be a reasonable one within which you could work? Provide personal examples for each of the four cells.
2. Think of a job you have had or now have. Did you feel that the employer invaded your right to privacy in any way? Discuss. Did the employer have a policy, explicit or implicit, with regard to right of privacy?
3. Assume you are going to interview for a job as a teller with a bank and heard in advance that an honesty test would be used to explore your history and probability of honesty. Describe how you would feel about this type of test, and explain why you would feel that way.
4. Form small groups and visit a company to discuss its program for the treatment of alcoholism and hard-drug abuse. What other behaviors is the company concerned about from a health standpoint? Report the highlights of the program to your class, and give your appraisal of its probable effectiveness.
5. Assume one of your employees has recently tested positive for the AIDS virus. Although he is still fully capable of performing his job duties, another employee has come to you and objected to working closely with him. How would you respond?
6. Form discussion groups of four to five people, and develop a list of the top six QWL items your group wants in a job. Present your group report, along with your reasons, to other class members. Then, discuss similarities and differences among group responses.
7. Think of the job you now have or a job that you formerly had. Discuss both the favorable and unfavorable QWL characteristics contained in it.
8. Debate this issue in class: "Job breadth is more important than job depth in motivating workers."
9. Think of a job you have had or now have. Were there any ways in which you did not act responsibly (ethically) toward the organization or took unfair advantage of it? Discuss.
10. Consider your own role as a possible whistle-blower. Under what conditions would you publicly criticize your employer or another employee?

Assess Your Own Skills

How well do you exhibit good organizational-influence skills?

Read the following statements carefully. Circle the number on the response scale that most closely reflects the degree to which each statement accurately describes you as a leader. Add up your total points and prepare a brief action plan for self-improvement. Be ready to report your score for tabulation across the entire group.

	Good description									Poor description
1. I carefully differentiate between employee activities that occur on the job and those that occur off the job.	10	9	8	7	6	5	4	3	2	1
2. I am careful to respect an employee's rights to privacy when addressing topics surrounding religious, political, and social beliefs.	10	9	8	7	6	5	4	3	2	1
3. I carefully monitor my employees' use of their computers to ensure they are not abusing their privileges.	10	9	8	7	6	5	4	3	2	1
4. I am observant for signs of alcohol or drug abuse among employees.	10	9	8	7	6	5	4	3	2	1
5. I take immediate and positive actions to ensure employees do not engage in sexual harassment.	10	9	8	7	6	5	4	3	2	1
6. I place the bulk of my disciplinary emphasis on prevention of problems rather than corrective treatment of them.	10	9	8	7	6	5	4	3	2	1
7. I accept with enthusiasm my role in creating a quality of work life that is excellent for both employees and the organization.	10	9	8	7	6	5	4	3	2	1
8. I am fully aware of which employees would value enriched jobs and which would not.	10	9	8	7	6	5	4	3	2	1
9. I have clear ideas for how I could increase the levels of the five core dimensions in my employees' jobs.	10	9	8	7	6	5	4	3	2	1
10. I regularly spend time emphasizing to my employees their obligations to their employer (to balance the employer's responsibilities to them).	10	9	8	7	6	5	4	3	2	1

Scoring and Interpretation

Add up your total points for the 10 questions. Record that number here, and report it when it is requested. Finally, insert your total score into the "Assess and Improve Your Own Organizational Behavior Skills" chart in Appendix A.

- If you scored between 81 and 100 points, you appear to have a solid capability for demonstrating appropriate organizational influence.
- If you scored between 61 and 80 points, you should take a close look at the items with lower self-assessment scores and explore ways to improve those items.

- If you scored under 60 points, you should be aware that a weaker level regarding several items could be detrimental to your future success as a leader. We encourage you to review relevant sections of the chapter and watch for related material in subsequent chapters and other sources.

Identify your three lowest scores, and write the question numbers here: _____, _____, _____. Write a brief paragraph, detailing to yourself an action plan for how you might sharpen each of these traits.

Incident

Two Accounting Clerks

Rosemary Janis and Mary Lopez were the only two clerks handling payments from customers in the office of Atlantic Plumbing Supply Company. They reported to the owner of the business. Janis had been employed for 18 months and Lopez for 14 months. Both were community college graduates, about 23 years old, and unmarried.

By manipulating the accounts in a rather ingenious way that would not normally be detected, Janis was stealing from account payments as they were received. During her third month of employment, Lopez learned of Janis's thefts, but she decided not to tell management, rationalizing that Janis's personal conduct was none of her business. Lopez did not benefit from Janis's thefts, and the two women were not close friends. Their duties allowed them to work rather independently of each other, each handling a different alphabetical portion of the accounts.

By the time the owner learned of Janis's thefts through the recent installation of hidden surveillance cameras, she had stolen approximately $5,700. During investigation of the thefts the owner learned that Lopez had known about them for several months, because it was evident that the thefts could not have occurred for an extended period without Lopez's knowledge. At the time of employment, both women had been instructed by the owner that they would be handling money and that strict honesty would be required of them.

Questions

1. What issues are raised by these events? Discuss.
2. What disciplinary action, either preventive or corrective, do you recommend for each of the two women? Why?
3. Is Lopez's failure to blow the whistle an issue?

Experiential Exercise

The Enriched Student

1. Consider your academic "job" as a student. Rate it on each of the five core dimensions according to how much of each is presently in it (1 = low amount; 10 = high amount). What does this information tell you?

Job Dimension	Your Rating	Group Average
Skill variety	__________	__________
Task identity	__________	__________
Task significance	__________	__________
Autonomy	__________	__________
Feedback	__________	__________
Overall score	__________	__________

2. Form groups of four to six persons, share your scores, and compute an average group score for each dimension. What do the scores tell you?
3. Discuss five important steps that university administrators and professors could take to enrich your "job" if they had the data you generated.

Experiential Exercise

Practicing Organizational Citizenship

1. Review the discussions of Organizational Citizenship in this book or elsewhere.
2. Consider this class as an organization, and its students as members of it.
3. Meeting in small groups, brainstorm a variety of ways in which class members could engage in acts of good citizenship.
4. Share these ideas with other groups, and eliminate overlapping suggestions.
5. Using the categories provided on p. 276, sort the suggestions into five groups.
6. Meeting again in small groups, identify the 5–10 actions that would best exemplify good organizational citizenship. Share your conclusions with the other groups. Discuss.

Source: Inspired by, and adapted from, Abdelmagid Mazen, Susan Herman, and Suzyn Ornstein, "Professor Delight: Cultivating Organizational Citizenship Behavior," *Journal of Management Education,* October 2008, vol. 32, no. 5, pp. 563–579.

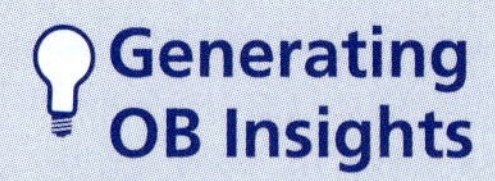

Generating OB Insights

An *insight* is a new and clear perception of a phenomenon, or an acquired ability to "see" clearly something you were unaware of previously. It is sometimes simply referred to as an "ah-ha! moment," in which you have a minirevelation or reach a straightforward conclusion about a topic or issue.

Insights need not necessarily be dramatic, for what is an insight to one person may be less important to another. The critical feature of insights is that they are relevant and memorable for *you;* they should represent new knowledge, new frameworks, or new ways of viewing things that you want to retain and remember over time.

Insights, then, are different from the information you find in the "Advice for Future Managers" boxes within the text. That advice is prescriptive and action-oriented; it indicates a recommended course of action.

A useful way to think of OB insights is to assume you are the only person who has read Chapter 10. You have been given the assignment to highlight, in your own words, the major concepts (but not just summarize the whole chapter) that might stand out for a naive audience who has never heard of the topic before. *What 10 insights would you share with them?*

(Example) *Some off-the-job conduct by employees is legitimately subject to influence by employers.*

1. ______________________________

2. ______________________________

3. ______________________________

4. ______________________________

5. ______________________________

6. ______________________________

7. ______________________________

8. ____
____
9. ____
____
10. ____
____

Nurturing Your Critical Thinking and Reflective Skills

Take a few minutes to review the discussion in the Roadmap for Readers of critical thinking and reflection. Remind yourself that if you can hone these abilities now, you will have a substantial competitive advantage when you apply for jobs and are asked what unique skills you can bring to the position and the organization.

Critical Thinking

Think back on the material you read in this chapter. What are three unique and challenging critical questions you would like to raise about that material? (These might identify something controversial about which you have doubts, they may imply that you suspect that a theory or model has weaknesses, they could examine the legitimacy of apparent causal relationships, or they might assess the probable value of a suggested practice.) Be prepared to share these questions with class members or your instructor.

1. ____
____
2. ____
____
3. ____
____

Reflection

This process often involves answering the parallel questions of "What do you *think* about the material you have read?" and "How do you *feel* about that material?" Therefore, express your *personal thoughts and feelings* (reactions) to any of the ideas or topics found in this chapter, and be prepared to share these reflections with class members or your instructor.

1. ____
____
2. ____
____
3. ____
____

Chapter Eleven

Conflict, Power, and Organizational Politics

CEOs may align themselves with particular strategies, management theories, or organizational cultures, but *their personalities underlie everything they think and do.*
Jeff Kehoe[1]

In the long run, though, those who relentlessly refuse to play the (politics) game win the organization's trust and a reputation for integrity.
Jack and Suzy Welch[2]

CHAPTER OBJECTIVES

AFTER READING THIS CHAPTER, YOU SHOULD UNDERSTAND

11–1 The Nature and Types of Conflict
11–2 Conflict Outcomes and Resolution Strategies
11–3 Different Personality Types
11–4 Assertive Behavior and Trust-Building
11–5 Interpersonal Facilitation and Stroking
11–6 Types of Power
11–7 Organizational Politics and Influence

Facebook Page 

Student A: Hey, remember last summer when we worked on that construction job and the regulars gave us a rough time every day? There's an official name for that; it's called workplace incivility.

Student B: OK, but why bring that up now?

Student A: It's one of the major causes of conflict at work, along with other things like personality clashes. I guess I'll have to learn how to handle conflict better than I did on that job.

Student C: What are you supposed to do instead of yelling back at the jerks?

Student A: I should take a more positive view of conflict, forget about who wins and who loses, and learn to take a constructive confrontational approach. I can be more assertive in expressing my feelings and asking for changes, too. But it all starts with a caring attitude, sensitivity to others, and paying attention to organizational politics.

Student B: Isn't politics at work just backstabbing others? I thought my own success was going to be a function of plain old hard work and technical competence.

Student A: Those are certainly important, but I discovered that you also need to engage in impression management, follow the norm of reciprocity, and build your personal influence by being socially astute, developing useful networks, and acting in a sincere and authentic fashion. I see now that there is a lot more to gaining political power than I thought!

Joyce and Joan were involved in a discussion which, had they allowed it to progress, might have driven them apart. "I think we can best survive by growing larger," said Joyce, "and the best way to do this is by acquiring our two closest competitors." Joan responded by suggesting that "your approach will potentially bankrupt us; we could drown in a sea of debt payments."

"So what do *you* propose doing?" queried Joyce with a hint of sarcasm. "I suggest we focus on strengthening our current market position," responded Joan. "We should spend more on new product development, aggressively market our existing line, and trim our staff by 6 percent."

Before the debate could proceed further, Joan and Joyce agreed to examine the issue objectively and not let their emotions escalate. They decided to focus on jointly solving the problem, while understanding and respecting each other's point of view. In doing this, they successfully avoided some of the destructive pitfalls of typical conflicts.

Organizations, by definition, require people to work together and communicate with one another—often in pairs as in the interaction between Joyce and Joan. Ideally, these interpersonal relationships should be productive, cooperative, and satisfying. In reality, managers find they are not always that way.

Almost every working relationship will produce some degree of conflict across time. Whether the conflicts will be destructive or constructive depends on the attitudes and skills of the participants (as well as time pressures and resource shortages). This chapter explores some approaches to conflict and examines the possible outcomes. It also suggests employees may need to develop their assertiveness and trust-building skills in order to be heard and respected by their peers. Guidelines are offered for understanding oneself and others and for communicating more effectively.

Engaging Your Brain

1. Reflect back on your past experiences of conflict in your life. Were those generally positive or negative? What made them so? Do you think they could have turned out better than they did?
2. Use the Internet to find a free on-line version of the Myers-Briggs personality test. What do you think about your results; do they appear to have face validity? Now ask a close friend to take the same test. Could you have predicted how that person would be classified? What implications does personality type have for you?
3. Examine the ten "Impression Management Strategies" in Figure 11.9. Rate your willingness to use each one on a scale from 1 (very low) to 10 (very high). Now add up all your points and discuss their implications for being a successful practitioner of organizational politics.

Interpersonal behavior in complex organizations inevitably produces power differences. Five sources of power are reviewed as a basis for seeing which are most constructive. We conclude the chapter with a discussion of the pros and cons of organizational politics—and then we suggest the use of various influence strategies to build strong reciprocal relationships among people.

CONFLICT IN ORGANIZATIONS

The Nature of Conflict

What is conflict?

Conflict can occur in any situation in which two or more parties feel themselves in opposition. **Conflict** is an interpersonal process that arises from disagreements over the goals to attain, the methods to be used to accomplish those goals, or even the tone of voice used as people express their positions. In the potential argument reported in the previous section, Joyce and Joan differ over both the goal and the method of achieving it. Further, Joyce's sarcastic tone didn't help either. Consequently, the conflict may be even more difficult to resolve, but they must find a way.

In addition to conflicts over goals or methods, conflicts also arise due to task interdependence, ambiguity of roles, policies, and rules, personality differences, ineffective communications, the competition over scarce resources, personal stress, and underlying differences in attitudes, beliefs, and experiences. In organizations everywhere, conflict among different interests is inevitable, and sometimes the amount of conflict is substantial and destructive. Some managers estimate that they spend 20 percent of their time dealing with conflict. They may be either direct participants or they could be mediators trying to resolve conflict between two or more of their employees. In either case, knowledge and understanding of conflict and the methods for resolving it are important.

Several research studies over time have consistently indicated the important role of interpersonal behavior in the success or failure of managers.[3] One of the prime reasons for derailment of previously successful executives is insensitivity to others. Some managers, lauded as exceptionally intelligent and sporting strong performance records, later failed because of inability to adapt to a boss. And a composite portrait of failed European managers indicated they were insensitive, manipulative, abusive, demeaning, overly critical, and incapable of building trusting relationships. Under these conditions, conflict—with peers and employees—inevitably emerges.

What Managers Are Reading 

EVERYDAY CAUSES OF CONFLICT

Marshall Goldsmith, a highly successful executive coach and author, suggests that much conflict is caused by simple and predictable behaviors. People exaggerate their own contributions, ignore the problems they have created, take credit for the contributions that others make, and project an inflated image of their skills. Goldsmith recommends that managers stop their use of sarcasm, unfair treatment of others, blaming behaviors, overuse of argumentation ("no" and "but"), and curb their need to win at all costs. Unfortunately, many executives falsely believe these same behaviors contributed to their previous success and therefore are reluctant to change.

Source: Marshall Goldsmith and Mark Reiter, *What Got You Here Won't Get You There*, New York: Hyperion, 2007.

Levels of Conflict

Conflict can occur within an employee, between individuals or groups, and across organizations as they compete. Chapter 4 examined how different role expectations and role ambiguity (lack of clarity over how to act) produces conflict.

Intrapersonal Conflict Although most role conflict occurs when an employee's supervisor or peers send conflicting expectations to him or her, it is possible for intrapersonal role conflict to emerge from *within* an individual, as a result of competing roles taken. For example, Sabrina may see herself as both the manager of a team responsible for protecting and enlarging its resources and as a member of the executive staff charged with the task of reducing operating costs.

Interpersonal Conflict Interpersonal conflicts (for examples, see What Managers Are Reading) are a serious problem to many people because they deeply affect a person's emotions. People have a need to protect their self-image and self-esteem from damage by others, as noted in the discussion of face-saving on page 59. When one's self-concept is threatened, serious upset occurs and relationships deteriorate. Sometimes the temperaments of two persons are incompatible and their personalities clash. In other instances, conflicts develop from failures of communication or differences in perception.

> An office employee was upset by a conflict with another employee in a different department. The first employee felt there was no way to resolve the conflict. However, when a counselor explained the different organizational roles of the two employees as seen from the whole organization's point of view, the first employee's perceptions changed and the conflict rapidly diminished and eventually vanished.

Intergroup Conflict Intergroup conflicts, for example, between different departments, also cause problems. On a major scale such conflicts are something like the wars between juvenile gangs. Each group sets out to undermine the other, gain power, harness available resources, and improve its image. Conflicts arise from such causes as different viewpoints, group loyalties, and poor communication. Resources are limited in any organization—and are increasingly tight as organizations struggle to be competitive. Since most groups feel they need more than they can secure, the seeds of intergroup conflict exist wherever resources are limited.

We noted earlier that some conflict can be constructive, and this is certainly true at the intergroup level. Here, conflict may provide a clue that a critical problem between two departments needs to be resolved rather than allowed to smolder. Unless issues are brought into the open, they cannot be fully understood or explored. Once intergroup conflict emerges, it creates a motivating force encouraging the two groups to resolve the conflict so as to move the relationship to a new equilibrium. Viewed this way, intergroup conflict is sometimes *escalated*—intentionally stimulated in organizations because of its constructive consequences. On other occasions, it may be desirable to *de-escalate* it—intentionally decrease it because of its potentially destructive consequences. The managerial challenge is to *keep conflict at a moderate level* (where it is most likely to stimulate creative thought but not interfere with performance). Conflict should not become so intense that individual parties either hide it or escalate it to destructive levels.

Conflict can be escalated or de-escalated to make it productive

Sources of Conflict

Interpersonal conflict arises from a variety of sources (see Figure 11.1):

- *Organizational change*—People hold differing views over the direction to go, the routes to take and their likely success, the resources to be used, and the probable outcomes. With the pace of technological, political, and social change increasing and the marketplace having become a global economy, organizational changes will be ever-present.
- *Different sets of values*—People also hold different beliefs and adhere to different value systems. Their philosophies may diverge, or their ethical values may lead them in different directions. The resulting disputes can be difficult to resolve, since they are less objective than disagreements over alternative products, inventory levels, or promotional campaigns.

Face-saving is important

- *Threats to status*—Chapter 4 suggests that status, or the social rank of a person in a group, is very important to many individuals. When one's status is threatened, *face-saving* (the drive to protect one's self-image) becomes a powerful driving force as a person struggles to maintain a desired image. Conflict may arise between the defensive person and whoever created a threat to status.
- *Contrasting perceptions*—People perceive things differently as a result of their prior experiences and expectations. Since their perceptions are very real to them, and they assume these perceptions must be equally apparent to others, they sometimes fail to realize that others may hold contrasting perceptions of the same object or event. Conflict may arise unless employees learn to see things as others see them and help others do the same.
- *Lack of trust*—Every continuing relationship requires some degree of **trust**—the capacity to voluntarily depend on each other's word and actions. When someone has a real or perceived reason not to trust another, the potential for conflict rises. Trust will be discussed more thoroughly later in this chapter.
- *Incivility*—Mutual respect, empathy, and caring are the glues that hold work groups together, yet many organizations report they are being torn apart by rudeness and a lack of "common" courtesy. **Workplace incivility** occurs when employees fail to exhibit concern and regard for others or—worse yet—disrespect each other on the job.[4] Lack of consideration can appear in many forms, including brusque greetings, sarcasm, failure to return borrowed supplies, selfishness, showing up late for appointments, untidiness, or noise (such as playing a radio loudly and using cell phones in public places). Possible causes include new technologies, escalating demands on employees, changing social norms, and a lack of a sense of community across a workforce that has become fragmented through reliance on part-time and temporary employees. Regardless of the cause, workplace incivility can cause tensions to rise, anger to flare, and conflict to emerge. Recipients of incivility most often report that their organizational commitment declined, they spent precious work time worrying about the behavior or avoiding the offender, or even took their frustration out on customers. Simple solutions to the incivility problem include:
    - Paying attention to others
    - Listening to their points of view

FIGURE 11.1
A Model of the Conflict Resolution Process

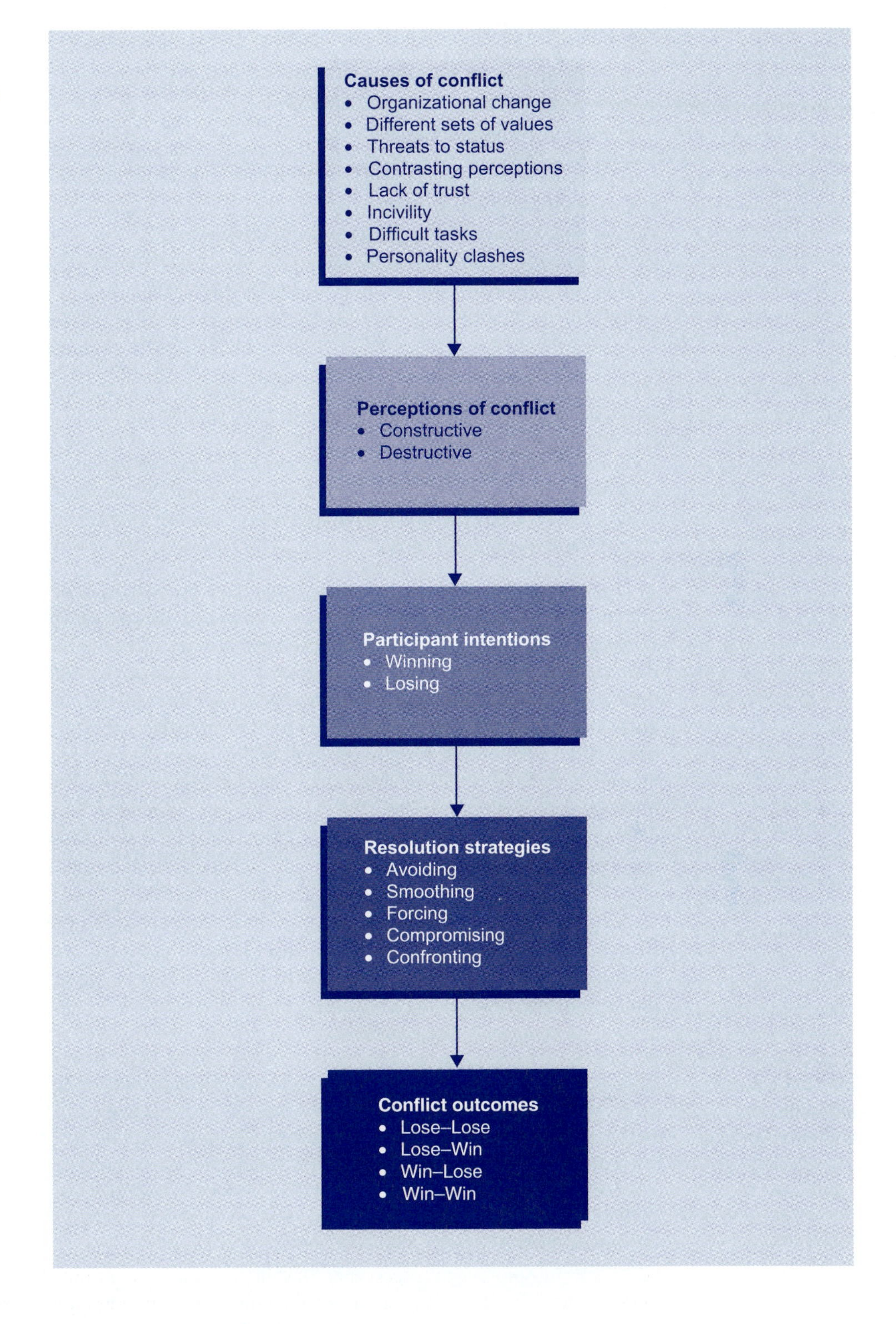

- Inclusively welcoming others
- Showing respect for others' time, space, and opinions
- Apologizing earnestly when appropriate
- Speaking kindly of others
- Refraining from gossiping or making idle complaints
- Avoiding blaming others
- Giving constructive criticism objectively[5]

- *Difficult tasks*—Occasionally managers are charged with performing distasteful tasks that predictably result in conflict. These tasks—referred to by some as "necessary evils"—include mass layoffs, personal firings for underperformance, negative performance reviews, and disciplinary actions.[6] Under these circumstances, some employees strike back at their manager—either orally or physically.
- *Personality clashes*—Chapter 1 stated that the concept of individual differences is fundamental to organizational behavior. Not everyone thinks, feels, looks, or acts alike. Some people simply rub us the wrong way, and we cannot necessarily explain why. Although personality differences can cause conflict, they are also a rich resource for creative problem solving. Employees need to accept, respect, and learn how to use these differences when they arise.

How do personalities differ? Many traits have been identified, but they seem to cluster around five major factors: agreeableness, conscientiousness, openness to experience, emotional stability, and extroversion (the polar extremes of each are shown in Figure 11.2).[7] Conscientious employees have lower absenteeism rates, are careful regarding the quality of their work, set challenging performance goals for themselves, and demonstrate more frequent organizational citizenship behaviors. Emotionally stable individuals seem to handle stress better than others. Employees high on the openness to experience trait are less resistant in the face of rapid organizational change. Extroverted individuals are outgoing and often interact well with customers. Agreeable people tend to be patient, cooperative, and empathetic. Several of the traits (e.g., emotional stability, agreeableness, and conscientiousness) imply a lower likelihood of interpersonal conflict, since these types of individuals are more courteous, self-disciplined, and sensitive to the feelings and positions of others.

A highly popular personality test used in a wide array of organizations is the Myers-Briggs Type Indicator (MBTI).[8] The MBTI draws upon the work of Carl Jung, a psychiatrist, and differentiates people into 16 major categories based on their preferences for *thinking* (using rational logic) versus *feeling* (considering the impact on others), *judging*

FIGURE 11.2
Five Major Personality Traits

One Extreme	Trait	Opposite Extreme
Caring, sensitive, empathetic	Agreeableness	Uncooperative, irritable
Dependable, self-disciplined	Conscientiousness	Disorganized, careless
Curious, flexible, receptive	Openness to experience	Closed, fixed, resistant
Calm, relaxed, comfortable	Emotional stability (negative affectivity)	Self-critical, questioning, pessimistic
Assertive, outgoing, talkative	Extroversion (positive affectivity)	Quiet, reserved, cautious

On the Job: Southwest Airlines

The MBTI has been an integral part of Southwest Airlines' University for People leadership classes. This personality inventory has proven most useful in helping thousands of their employees become more aware of their own idiosyncrasies while also sensitizing them to the unique characteristics of their co-workers. It also reminds them that no one type is necessarily better than another or more successful in the business world. The common denominator across Myers-Briggs types is the recommendation to treat people with respect in an atmosphere of mutual understanding.[9]

Sixteen different types

(rapidly solving ordered problems) versus *perceiving* (preferring spontaneity), *extroversion* (asserting themselves confidently) versus *introversion* (preferring to work alone), and *sensing* (organizing details in a structured fashion) versus *intuition* (relying on subjective evidence and gut feelings) (see "On the Job: Southwest Airlines").

Effects of Conflict

Conflict is often seen by participants as destructive, but this is a limited view. In fact, if all conflict with co-workers is avoided, each party is likely deprived of useful information about the other's preferences and views. *Conflict is not all bad;* rather, it may result in either productive or nonproductive outcomes. A more positive view, then, is to see that conflict is nearly inevitable and to search for ways in which it can result in constructive outcomes.

Advantages

One of the benefits produced by conflict is that people are stimulated to search for improved approaches that lead to better results. It energizes them to be more creative and to experiment with new ideas. Another benefit is that once-hidden problems are brought to the surface, where they may be confronted and solved. Just as fermentation of grapes is necessary in the production of fine wines, a certain amount of ferment can create a deeper understanding among the parties involved in a conflict. And once the conflict is resolved, the individuals may be more committed to the outcome through their involvement in solving it.

Disadvantages

There are also possible disadvantages, especially if the conflict lasts a long period of time, becomes too intense, or is allowed to focus on personal issues. At the interpersonal level, cooperation and teamwork may deteriorate. Distrust may grow among people who need to coordinate their efforts. At the individual level some people may be distracted or feel defeated, while the self-image of others will decline and personal anxiety and stress levels (discussed in Chapter 15) will rise. Predictably, the motivation level of some employees will be reduced, along with an erosion of their satisfaction and commitment. It is important, then, for managers to be aware of the potential for interpersonal and intergroup conflicts, to anticipate their likely outcomes, and to use appropriate conflict resolution strategies.

A Model of Conflict

Conflict arises from many sources and directions. It also varies in the speed of its emergence and in the degree of its predictability. Sometimes it smolders for a long time like a hot ember and then springs to life like a flame when the hot coal is fanned. Other times it simply seems to explode without warning, like the sudden eruption of a dangerous volcano.

Critical Thinking Exercise

Conflict arises both within, and between, nations around the world. Question: What are the major contributing factors to conflict at the international level?

FIGURE 11.3
Four Possible Outcomes of Conflict; Four Possible Intentions of the Participants

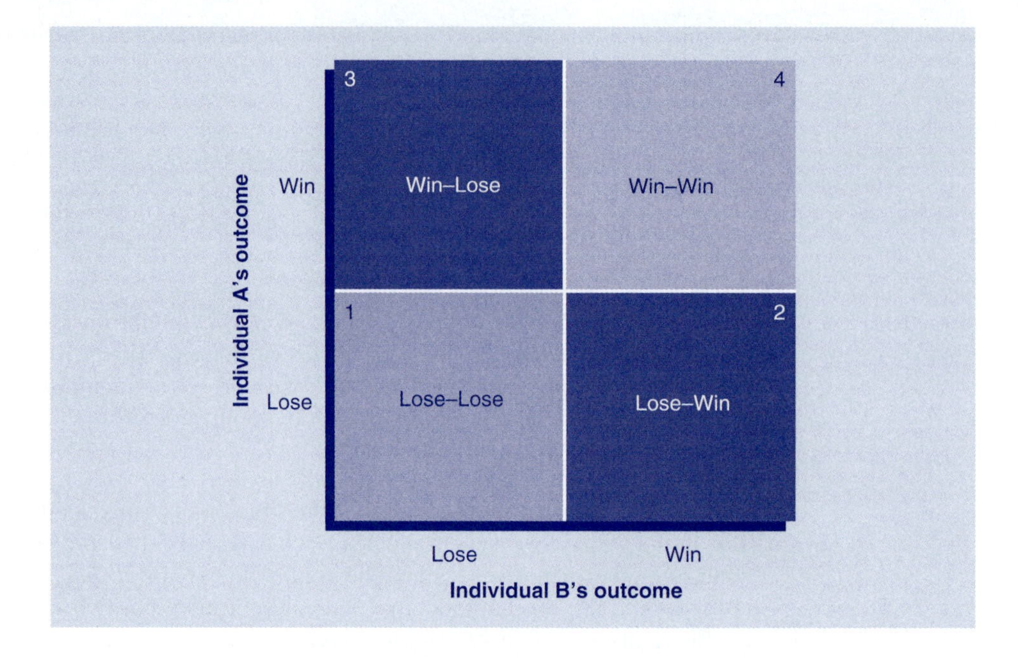

And just like the flame that can warm us in need or sear us with its heat, conflict can be constructive or destructive. Managers, therefore, must know when to stimulate conflict and when to resolve it.

Part of the answer to this dilemma is shown in Figure 11.1, which portrays the conflict resolution process. The various sources discussed earlier give rise to constructive or destructive conflict. If conflict will be harmful, managers need to apply a conflict resolution strategy to prevent, diminish, or remove it. Then, the outcomes of conflict (winning or losing) must be evaluated from the perspectives of both parties.

Four outcomes are possible

Conflict Outcomes Conflict may produce four distinct outcomes, depending on the approaches taken by the people involved. Figure 11.3 illustrates these outcomes. The first quadrant, termed "lose–lose," depicts a situation in which a conflict deteriorates to the point that both parties are worse off than they were before. An extreme example is the case of an executive who fires the only person who knows the secret formula for the organization's most successful product. The second quadrant is "lose–win," a situation in which one person (individual A) is defeated while the other one (individual B) is victorious. In quadrant 3 ("win–lose") the situation is reversed, with person B losing to person A. The fourth quadrant is the **win–win outcome of conflict,** in which both parties perceive they are in a better position than they were before the conflict began. This is the preferred outcome to try to achieve in ongoing relationships, such as with suppliers, customers, and employees. Although it may be an unrealistic ideal in some situations, it is a fundamental organizational behavior perspective toward which all parties should aim.

Intentions affect strategies

Participant Intentions Conflict outcomes are a product of the participants' *intentions,* as well as their *strategies*. For example, Jason may actually *seek* a lose–win outcome in a conflict with Becky because of the perceived benefits of being defeated on a particular issue. He may fear the consequences of retribution from too many earlier victories over Becky, or he may try to lose in the hope that Becky will reciprocate on another issue in the future. At the other extreme, Marcia may hope for a win–lose outcome in her conflict with Jessica. This intended effect is often caused by a "fixed-pie" (or zero-sum) viewpoint, in which Marcia believes she can succeed only at the expense of Jessica.

Resolution Strategies Intentions help participants select their strategies. Once they have been chosen, the strategies implemented will have a substantial impact on the outcomes reached (*actual* winning or losing). The simplest strategies focus on the contrasting approaches of either cooperation or competition, but a widely used typology suggests there are at least four clearly different strategies (and a combination one, called compromising). Each of these represents different degrees of concern for one's own outcomes and for another's results, and has a predictable outcome:[10]

Five strategies

- *Avoiding*—physical or mental withdrawal from the conflict. This approach reflects a low concern for either party's outcomes and often results in a lose–lose situation.
- *Smoothing*—accommodating the other party's interests. This approach places greatest emphasis on concern for others, usually to one's own detriment, resulting in a lose–win outcome.
- *Forcing*—using power tactics to achieve a win. This strategy relies on aggressiveness and dominance to achieve personal goals at the expense of concern for the other party. The likely result is a win–lose situation.
- *Compromising*—searching for middle ground or being willing to give up something in exchange for gaining something else. This strategy reflects a moderate degree of concern for self and others, with no clear-cut outcome.
- *Confronting*—facing the conflict directly and working it through to a mutually satisfactory resolution. Also known as *problem solving* or *integrating*, this tactic seeks to maximize the achievement of both party's goals, resulting in a win–win outcome.

Any one of the strategies may be effective for its intended purpose. However, the avoiding and smoothing approaches are basically useful for hiding or diminishing the conflict process. This means that in some way these approaches control the degree of conflict and reduce its harmful side effects while it is under way, but the source of conflict still exists. The same is true when two parties compromise their positions just for the sake of reaching a solution. The idea of compromise is seductive if the objective is to escape from the conflict at minimal cost, but it often stifles creativity. The use of a forcing approach may achieve a short-term goal but often irreparably harms the long-term relationship between the parties.

Only the **confronting** strategy can truly be viewed as a *resolution* approach, since this method addresses the basic differences involved and eventually removes them through creative problem solving. The confronting approach (see Figure 11.4 for a set of operating guidelines) has many behavioral benefits. Both parties will more likely see the recent

FIGURE 11.4
Guidelines for Conflict Resolution through Confrontation

1. Agree on the common goal: *to solve the problem.*
2. Commit yourself to fluid, not fixed, positions.
3. Clarify the strengths and weaknesses of both party's positions.
4. Recognize the other person's, and your own, possible need for face-saving.
5. Be candid and up-front; don't hold back key information.
6. Avoid arguing or using "yes-but" responses; maintain control over your emotions.
7. Strive to understand the other person's viewpoint, needs, and bottom line.
8. Ask questions to elicit needed information; probe for deeper meanings and support.
9. Make sure both parties have a vested interest in making the outcome succeed.
10. Give the other party substantial credit when the conflict is over.

A Diversity of Preferences

Is there a single conflict resolution approach that all parties tend to use? Or might we find distinctive preferences and patterns among different groups, and even among different cultures? Although research evidence is not overwhelming, it suggests these differences may exist:

- Males tend to use the forcing approach as their dominant style; females use forcing less, and often rely on a range of other tactics including collaboration.
- Managers tend to use the forcing approach; their employees prefer avoiding, smoothing, or compromising.
- American managers tend to be competitive; Japanese managers prefer to use a cooperative approach.

Other significant tendencies emerge, too. Each party in a conflict tends to mimic the style of the other (e.g., forcing induces forcing; accommodating induces accommodating). People tend to choose different resolution styles for different issues (e.g., confrontation is often used in performance appraisals; compromise is more likely used on issues involving personal habits and mannerisms). Once again, it is apparent that a variety of contingency factors (including group-diversity characteristics such as gender) affect the choice of a behavioral strategy.

Sources: James A. Wall Jr. and Ronda Roberts Callister, "Conflict and Its Management," *Journal of Management*, vol. 21, no. 3, 1995, pp. 515–558; Richard Hodgetts and Fred Luthans, *International Management*, 3d ed., New York: McGraw-Hill, 1997; Sheryl D. Brahnam et al., "A Gender-Based Categorization for Conflict Resolution," *Journal of Management Development*, vol. 24, no. 3, 2005, pp. 197–208.

conflict as productive, since both received gains. Also important is their perception that the process was a mutually supportive one in which problem solving and collaboration helped integrate the positions of both parties. As a result, participants find the confronting approach to be the most satisfying, as they maintain their self-respect and gain new respect for the other party. Many labor–management groups have in recent years sought new ways to confront each other constructively in order to attain win–win relationships.

The benefits of cooperative controversy

A review and meta-analysis of 28 experimental studies across different settings and populations was conducted. The results clearly showed that cooperative controversy (an approach emphasizing open-minded disagreement and an airing of expectations and preferences) was most effective. Higher-quality solutions to complex problems were attained, better reasoning strategies and creative perspectives were used, and participants reported greater openness, interpersonal liking, and social support.[11]

A wide variety of other tools and ideas have been successfully used to resolve conflicts. Sometimes the simple application of a relevant rule or policy can solve a dispute. Other times, the parties can be separated by reassigning work spaces, removing one person from a committee, or placing workers on different shifts. Another alternative is to insert a third party into the interaction—a consultant, mediator, or other neutral person who can ignore personal issues and facilitate resolution. A constructive approach is to challenge the parties to work together toward a unifying goal, such as higher revenues or better customer satisfaction.

Relationship-Restoring Approaches Stable working relationships sometimes get damaged through actions or statements (either accidental or intentional) by another. And just as a house damaged by a tornado requires prompt and expert reconstruction, so does an interpersonal relationship demand rebuilding. Goffman and others suggest this rebuilding is best viewed as requiring four stages:

1. Signaling the offense—This involves the victim naming the action, blaming (identifying) the offender, and voicing the grievance (overtly or covertly) to let the person know the victim has taken offense.
2. Acknowledgment of error—Assuming that the offender is willing to do so, this person must take some action to restore the relationship, such as admitting the error, explaining oneself, sincerely apologizing, expressing personal concern, or providing some form of compensation.
3. Acceptance—The recipient of the acknowledgment then has the opportunity—and an implied obligation in this interpersonal ritual—to accept (or reject) the offering. This would normally be followed by explicit or implicit forgiveness and (hopefully) a restoration or even improvement in the victim's impression of the offender.
4. Appreciation—The final step in this interpersonal ritual is for the offender to express thanks and gratitude to the victim for allowing the earlier equilibrium to be restored. When the four steps are completed, each person is usually willing to renew their interaction in the future.[12]

Negotiating Tactics Much research has addressed the question, What kinds of behaviors help resolve conflicts in a win–win fashion? Time and again, some basic patterns show through: select a neutral site, arrange the seating in a comfortable fashion (preferably oriented toward a projection screen or writing surface), don't permit observers to be present (because they implicitly place performance pressure on the negotiators), and set deadlines to force a resolution. Individual negotiators are advised to set minimum and optimum goals for themselves in advance, engage in a thorough data gathering process, listen carefully to what the other party says and how it is said, avoid blaming and name-calling, focus on issues and not personalities, separate facts from feelings, and search for the areas where they can obtain concessions on important topics while making matching concessions in areas of lesser interest. If done well, these tactics should produce an outcome that is fair for both parties, removes the underlying cause of the conflict, and is accomplished with a minimal investment of time and energy.[13]

Trust-building We noted earlier that the absence of trust increases the chances of conflict. Trust, the capacity to depend voluntarily on each other's words and actions, implies a willingness to take interpersonal risks and to be vulnerable. Trust involves dependency on another person, and a belief that she or he will act benevolently and can be relied upon. It is an essential ingredient in enduring relations between two or more people working together.[14]

Building vs. destroying trust

How do you express trust toward another person? It can be done by showing respect, exhibiting sincere caring and concern, by being honest and true to one's word, and by demonstrating your dependability and reliability. As one executive put it succinctly, "Say what you mean and mean what you say." By contrast, trust can be rapidly dissolved by telling half-truths and lies, by showing inconsistencies between promises and actions, by threatening the goal achievement or self-image of others, and by withholding needed information from them.

The benefits of trust are manifold. Its presence encourages risk-taking, facilitates free flows of information, and contributes to cooperative relationships. It also eliminates much of the perceived need to monitor someone else's behavior in a tightly controlling way. Overall, trust leads to a more satisfying relationship with others—supervisors, co-workers, and subordinates.[15]

ASSERTIVE BEHAVIOR

Confronting conflict is not easy for some people. When faced with the need to negotiate with others, some managers may feel inferior, lack necessary skills, or be in awe of the other person's power. Under these conditions they are likely to suppress their feelings (part of the avoidance strategy) or to strike out in unintended anger. Neither response is truly productive.

Assertiveness

A constructive alternative is to practice assertive behaviors. **Assertiveness** is the process of expressing feelings, asking for legitimate changes, and giving and receiving honest feedback. An assertive individual is not afraid to request that another person change an offensive behavior and is willing to refuse unreasonable requests from someone else. Assertiveness training involves teaching people to develop effective ways of dealing with a variety of anxiety-producing situations.

Assertive people are direct, honest, and expressive. They feel confident, gain self-respect, and make others feel valued. A poor alternative is *aggressiveness,* in which people may humiliate others, and *passive* (unassertive) people who elicit either pity or scorn from others and seldom have much positive impact. Both alternatives to assertiveness typically are less effective for achieving a desired goal during a conflict. Moderate levels of assertiveness are often the most effective.

Stages in assertiveness

Being assertive in a situation involves five stages, as shown in Figure 11.5. When confronted with an intolerable situation, assertive people describe it objectively, express their emotional reactions and feelings, and empathize with the other's position. Then, they offer problem-solving alternatives and indicate the consequences (positive or negative) that will follow. Not all five steps may be necessary in all situations. As a minimum, it is important to describe the present situation and make recommendations for change. Use of the other steps would depend on the significance of the problem and the relationship between the people involved.

Karla, the supervisor of a small office staff, had a problem. Her administrative assistant, Manny, had become increasingly careless about his morning arrival time. Not only did Manny almost never arrive before 8 A.M., but his tardiness varied from a few minutes to nearly a half hour. Although Karla was reluctant to confront Manny, she knew she must do so or the rest of the staff would be unhappy.

Karla called Manny into her office soon after Manny arrived (tardily) the next morning and drew upon her assertiveness training. "You have been arriving late almost every day for the past two weeks," she began (descriptively). "This is unacceptable in an office that prides itself on prompt customer service beginning

FIGURE 11.5
Stages in Assertive Behavior

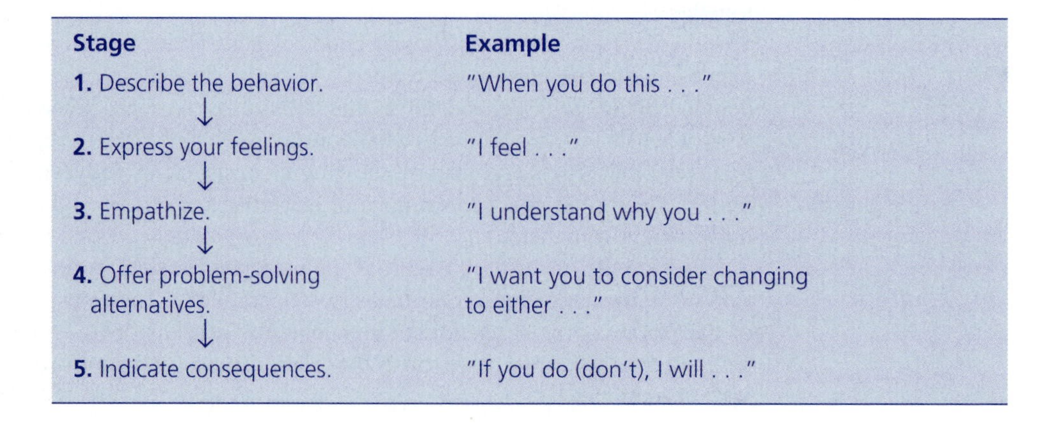

Stage	Example
1. Describe the behavior. ↓	"When you do this . . ."
2. Express your feelings. ↓	"I feel . . ."
3. Empathize. ↓	"I understand why you . . ."
4. Offer problem-solving alternatives. ↓	"I want you to consider changing to either . . ."
5. Indicate consequences.	"If you do (don't), I will . . ."

at 8 A.M. I recognize there may be legitimate reasons for tardiness on occasion, but I need you to get to work on time most days in the future. If you don't, I will insert a letter into your personnel file and also note your behavior on your six-month performance appraisal. Will you agree to change?" (Confronted directly like this, Manny acknowledged his behavior and dramatically improved it.)

Assertive behavior generally is most effective when it integrates a number of verbal and nonverbal components. Eye contact is a means of expressing sincerity and self-confidence in many cultures, and an erect body posture and direct body positioning (close proximity and leaning forward) may increase the impact of a message. Appropriate gestures may be used, congruent facial expressions are essential, and a strong but modulated voice tone and volume will be convincing. Perhaps most important is the spontaneous and forceful expression of an honest reaction, such as "Tony, I get angry when you always turn in your report a day late!"

Facilitating Smooth Relations

Good interpersonal relationships among co-workers and across organizational levels take time, effort, knowledge, and skill. One key skill involves **interpersonal facilitation**—the capacity to focus on others' personal needs, sensitivities, and idiosyncrasies, and then work to keep conflict under control and collaboration high among team members. This requires awareness of which personality traits would create synergy within a team, which employees have "hot buttons" that might set off emotional explosions, and when to intervene behind the scenes.

Interpersonal facilitation, to be most successful, is built on a foundation of care, concern, sensitivity, and psychological flexibility (openness to the moment). Genuine caring is a feeling of commitment to help another person exist, solve problems, and grow as an individual. Caring underlies **compassion** for others, which is a four-step action-oriented process:

1. *Noticing* that someone else is suffering or distressed.
2. *Appraising* that the other person is self-relevant (has compatible values, preferences, and beliefs).
3. *Feeling* that the person is worried or hurt (empathizing with them).
4. *Compassionate responding* is the process of taking actions that will diminish or eliminate the other person's discomfort or anguish.[16]

Managers with well-developed interpersonal facilitation skills often engage in one or more of the following behaviors:

- Building on their emotional intelligence (see the earlier discussion on pp. 214–215)
- Learning about co-workers' personal lives
- Making mental notes about employee likes and dislikes, values, interests, and preferences
- Monitoring other people's degree of job involvement, mood level, commitment, and satisfaction
- Developing and applying their facilitative skills in a variety of social settings

Stroking

People seek stroking in their interactions with others, and this provides a prime opportunity for interpersonal facilitation. **Stroking** is defined as any act of recognition for another. It applies to all types of recognition, such as physical, verbal, and nonverbal contact between

On the Job: Merrill Lynch

Melissa, a stockbroker at Merrill Lynch, had just made a presentation to a group of prospective customers. Later, she excitedly asked her manager how she had done. "You did a nice job," he began (and Melissa's eyes lit up in pleasure), "not a great job, but a nice job." Although she didn't show her disappointment, we can guess that her spirits were considerably dampened by his qualified remark.

people. In most jobs, the primary method of stroking is verbal, such as "Pedro, you had an excellent sales record last month." Examples of physical strokes are a pat on the back and a firm handshake.

Types of strokes

Strokes may be positive, negative, or mixed. **Positive strokes** feel good when they are received, and they contribute to the recipient's sense of well-being and self-esteem. **Negative strokes** hurt physically or emotionally and make recipients feel less proud of themselves. An example of a **mixed stroke** is this supervisor's comment: "Oscar, that's a good advertising layout, considering the small amount of experience you have in this field."

Conditional and unconditional strokes

There also is a difference between conditional and unconditional strokes. **Conditional strokes** are offered to employees if they perform correctly or avoid problems. A sales manager may promise an employee that "I will give you a raise if you sell three more insurance policies." **Unconditional strokes** are presented without any connection to behavior. Although they may make a person feel good (e.g., "You're a fine employee"), they may be confusing to employees because they do not indicate how more strokes may be earned. Supervisors will get better results if they give more strokes in a behavior modification framework, where the reward is contingent upon the desired activity. *Employee hunger for strokes,* and the occasional reluctance of supervisors to use them, is demonstrated in the conversation illustrated in "On the Job: Merrill Lynch."

Applications to Conflict Resolution Several natural connections lie between assertiveness and the approaches to resolving conflict discussed earlier in this chapter. The probable connections are shown in Figure 11.6. Once more, the relationship among a number of behavioral ideas and actions is apparent in this connection between confronting and assertiveness.

Assertiveness training and stroking, when used in combination, can be powerful tools for increasing one's interpersonal effectiveness. They share the goal of helping employees feel good about themselves and others. The result is that they help improve communication and interpersonal cooperation. Although they can be practiced by individuals, these tools will be most effective when widely used throughout the organization and supported by top management. Together, they form an important foundation for the more complex challenges confronting people who work in small groups and committees.

FIGURE 11.6
Probable Relationships of Conflict Resolution Strategies and Behavior

Resolution Strategy	Probable Behavior
Avoidance	Nonassertiveness
Smoothing	Nonassertiveness
Forcing	Aggressiveness
Confronting	Assertiveness

POWER AND POLITICS

All leaders deal with power and politics. **Power** is the ability to influence other people and events. It is traditionally the leader's way to get things done, the way leaders extend their influence to others. It is somewhat different from authority, because authority is delegated by higher management. Power, on the other hand, is earned and gained by leaders on the basis of their personalities, activities, resources, and the situations in which they operate.

Types of Power

Five sources of power

Power develops in a number of ways. There are five **bases of power,** and each has a unique source.[17]

Personal Power **Personal power,** also called referent power or charismatic power, comes from each leader individually. It is the ability of leaders to develop followers from the strength of their own personalities. They have a personal magnetism, an air of confidence, and a passionate belief in objectives that attract and hold followers. People follow because they *want* to do so; their emotions tell them to do so. The leader senses the needs and goals of people and promises success in reaching them. Well-known historical examples are Joan of Arc in France, Mahatma Gandhi in India, Winston Churchill in England, and John F. Kennedy and Martin Luther King in the United States. President Barack Obama demonstrated some of the same characteristics in his campaign speeches.

Legitimate Power **Legitimate power,** also known as position power and official power, comes from higher authority. It arises from the culture of society by which power is delegated legitimately from higher established authorities to others. It gives leaders the power to control resources and to reward and punish others. People accept this power because they believe it is desirable and necessary to maintain order and discourage anarchy in a society. In work organizations, there is social pressure from peers and friends who accept legitimate power and then expect others to accept it.

Expert Power **Expert power,** also known as the authority of knowledge, comes from specialized learning. It is power that arises from a person's knowledge of and information about a complex situation. It depends on education, training, and experience, so it is an important type of power in our modern technological society. For example, if your spouse were having an asthma attack in a hospital emergency room, you would be likely to give your attention to the physician who comes in to provide treatment rather than to the helper who is delivering fresh laundry supplies, even though both persons express equal concern about your spouse. The reason is that you expect the physician to be a capable expert in the situation, based on extensive prior training and experience.

Reward Power **Reward power** is the capacity to control and administer items valued by another. It arises from an individual's ability to give pay raises, recommend someone for promotion or transfer, or even make favorable work assignments. Many rewards may be under a manager's control, and these are not limited to material items. Reward power can also stem from the capacity to provide organizational recognition, to include an employee in a social group, or simply to give positive feedback for a job well done. Reward power serves as the basis for reinforcing desirable behavior, as discussed in Chapter 5.

Coercive Power **Coercive power** is the capacity to punish another, or at least to create a perceived threat to do so. Managers with coercive power can threaten an employee's job security, make punitive changes in someone's work schedule, or, at the extreme, administer physical force. Coercive power uses fear as a motivator, which can be a powerful force in inducing short-term action. However, it is likely to have an overall negative impact on the receiver and therefore its use should be limited.

FIGURE 11.7 **Possible Responses to the Use of Power**

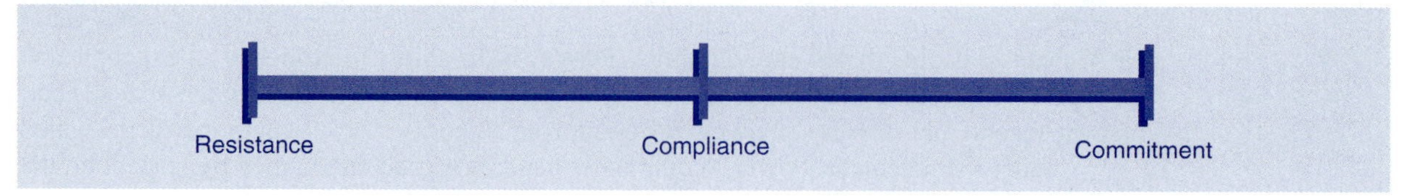

Effects of Power Bases

The five types of power are developed from different sources, but they are interrelated in practice. Reward, coercive, and legitimate power are essentially derived from one's position in the organization. Expert and personal power reside within the person. When even one power base is removed from a supervisor, employees may perceive that other bases of influence will decline as well. The use of a power base must fit its organizational context in order to be effective.

Outcomes include resistance, compliance, or commitment

Managers also need to be concerned about the effects of various power bases on employee motivation. Employees can respond in one of three ways, as shown in Figure 11.7. They may *resist* the leader's initiative, especially if coercive power is used consistently, without apparent cause, or in an arrogant manner. They may *comply* with the leader's wishes by meeting minimal expectations while withholding extra effort. Legitimate power will likely result in compliance, as will reward power unless the rewards are substantial and directly related to employee needs. The most desirable outcome from wielding power is *commitment,* which is the enthusiastic release of energy and talent to satisfy the leader's requests. Referent and expert power are most likely to produce commitment, but legitimate and reward power can also work well under certain conditions.

Organizational Politics

Self-interest is the key

While the five bases of power are essentially acquired and used to achieve formal organizational goals, many managers and employees resort to another (supplemental) set of behaviors to accomplish personal goals at work. **Organizational politics** refers to intentional behaviors that are used to enhance or protect a person's influence and self-interest while also inspiring confidence and trust by others.[18] Political skill consists of four key dimensions:

- Being *socially astute* (accurately perceiving and understanding what is taking place in social interactions—although it is often beneath the surface)
- Having *interpersonal influence* (adapting one's behaviors to most effectively elicit a desired response from others)
- Creating useful *networks* (developing personal contacts into useful allies and supporters)
- Expressing *sincerity* (exhibiting honest and authentic intentions in one's interactions with others such that they trust you)

Used professionally and as a supplement to technical competence and a strong work ethic, these behaviors may help attain a well-earned promotion, sell higher management on the merits of a proposal that will expand one's responsibilities and resources, or gain personal visibility. Other employees, however, either (naively) choose to avoid politics at all costs or aggressively decide to use politics in a self-serving, manipulative, predatory, and deceitful fashion. Political behaviors become dysfunctional when threats are used to achieve one's goals, when strong coalitions are formed to block a legitimate objective, when untrue information is circulated in hopes of vindictively accomplishing character

Critical Thinking Exercise

Consider the various tactics used to gain political power, as portrayed in Figure 11.8. Question: What are some pros and cons of using these?

assassination of a career competitor, or when outright sabotage occurs. The risk is that unscrupulous employees involved in organizational politics might put their self-interest above that of their employer in their attempts to gain political power for short-term or long-term benefits.

One survey of more than 400 managers provided insight into their views toward organizational politics.[19] To a large extent, the managers agreed that:

- Politics is common in most organizations.
- Managers must be good at politics to expedite their own career advancement.
- Politics is practiced more frequently at higher organizational levels, and in larger firms.
- Too much politics can detract from organizational efficiency and goal attainment.

Influence and Political Power

Managers, and all employees, in contemporary organizations must learn to produce results, elicit cooperation, and make things happen without reliance on traditional forms of power. As difficult as this goal sounds, it is still possible if managers begin with the premise that *everyone is motivated primarily by her or his own self-interest*. Knowing this, a person can influence others by making mutually beneficial exchanges with them to gain their cooperation. The following are eight steps to follow for increasing your influence:

Action steps for gaining personal influence

1. Treat the other party as a potential ally; avoid making enemies.
2. Clearly identify your own objectives, and pick your battles to fight (avoiding minor ones).
3. Learn about the other party's needs, interests, expectations, and goals.
4. Inventory your own resources to identify something of value you can offer (see the discussion of idiosyncrasy credits in Chapter 10).
5. Assess your current relationship with the other person.
6. Decide what to ask for and what to offer.
7. Make the actual exchange that produces a gain for both parties.
8. Even if you "win," don't gloat; be gracious and avoid boasting.[20]

Leaders can use a number of tactics to gain political power. Several examples are given in Figure 11.8. (*Networking*—developing and maintaining contacts among a group of people with shared interests—is another source of influence and was presented in Chapter 3. Networking has become increasingly popular through the use of websites such as LinkedIn.) Two of the most popular tactics are social exchanges and alliances of various types. *Social exchange* implies that "if you'll do something for me, I'll do something for you." It relies on the powerful **norm of reciprocity** in society, where two people in a continuing relationship feel a strong obligation to repay their social "debts" to each other.[21] When these trade-offs are successfully arranged, both parties get something they want. Continuing exchanges of "IOUs" and favors over a period of time

Norm of reciprocity

An Ethics Question

Some people suggest there is no room whatsoever for organizational politics. They believe all such actions are self-serving and should be banned, and those who engage in them should be punished because they fail to contribute to the common good and overall objectives of an organization. (Refer back to the second chapter-opening quote, by Jack and Suzy Welch.) Proponents of political behavior, on the other hand, see their actions as critical catalysts that help produce valued results more smoothly. Question: What do *you* think about the ethics of organizational politics?

usually lead to an *alliance* in which two or more persons join in a temporary or longer-term relationship to get benefits that they mutually desire. TV fans have seen this occur many times in shows such as *Survivor*.

One popular path toward political power is to *become identified with a higher authority* or a powerful figure in an organization. Then, as the saying goes, some of the power rubs off on you. Often this identification gains you special privileges, and in many cases you become recognized as a representative or spokesperson for the more powerful figure. Others may share problems with you, hoping you will help them gain access to the higher

FIGURE 11.8
Examples of Tactics Used to Gain Political Power

Tactic Used	Example
Social exchange	In a trade-off, the chief engineer helps the factory manager get a new machine approved if the manager will support an engineering project.
Alliances	The information system manager and the financial vice president work together on a proposal for a new computer system.
Identification with higher authority	The president's personal assistant makes minor decisions for her.
Doing favors for others	A staff member buys a dozen roses for his boss to bring home on his wedding anniversary.
Control of information	The research and development manager controls new product information needed by the marketing manager.
Selective service	The purchasing manager selectively gives faster service to more cooperative associates.
Power and status symbols	The new controller arranges to double the size of the office, decorate lavishly, and employ a personal assistant.
Power plays	Manager A arranges with the vice president to transfer part of manager B's department to A.
Networks	A young manager joins a country club, or builds contacts on LinkedIn.
Posturing	Being seen as on the "winning side" of a discussion, or being in the "right place at the right time."

figure. An example of identification is the president's personal assistant who represents the president in many contacts with others.

> In one company the president's personal assistant, Katrina Janus, became widely accepted as the president's representative throughout the company. She issued instructions to other managers in the name of the president, and other managers accepted them as orders. She represented the president on special assignments. She controlled access to the president, and she partly controlled the flow of information both to and from the president. She handled power effectively and so gradually became a major influence in the corporation. When the president retired, the assistant became a major executive and was accepted by other managers.

Ingratiation is a political tactic

Closely related to the previous technique is the traditional method of simply *doing favors for others*. In a relationship with a higher authority, this practice of ingratiation is commonly called "apple-polishing" or "kissing up" to a supervisor. Examples include running errands, endorsing their ideas regardless of merit (being a "yes-person"), or voluntarily doing their "dirty work" (undesirable or menial tasks). Although these behaviors are often easily visible to other observers (and despised by them), they sometimes work successfully on persons who have very large egos and enjoy having an entourage of adoring followers around them.

Another oft-used way to acquire political power is to *give service selectively* to your supporters. For example, a purchasing manager gives faster service and bends the rules to help friends who support the purchasing function. Another tactic is to *acquire power and status symbols* that imply you are an important person in the firm, although this tactic can backfire if you do not have power equal to your symbols.

Some managers use the more aggressive tactic of applying power plays to *grab power from others*. This approach is risky because others may retaliate in ways that weaken the power-grabbing manager's power.

A common tactic for increasing power is to *join or form interest groups* that have a common objective. These networks operate on the basis of friendships and personal contacts, and may provide a meeting place for influential people. A young manager who joins a community service organization (such as Rotary, Kiwanis, or Lions) or a country club is opening the door to new contacts that may be useful.

Posturing is also used to gain influence. **Posturing** consists of positioning oneself for visibility (such as sitting near an important person in a staff meeting, or even entering/exiting a room at the same time as an executive does), making sure that others know about your successes, and practicing skills of "one-upmanship" over others.

As illustrated by the following example, power and politics are a basic part of leadership success in an organization:

> Management in a state office was considering whether to move a certain activity from one department to another. Finally, the director of the entire operation decided to hold a staff meeting of all senior managers to decide where the disputed activity should be located. Prior to the meeting the manager of the department that wanted the activity prepared an elaborate and convincing report that fully supported moving the activity to her department. Meanwhile, the manager of the department that might lose the activity was visiting all committee members to mend fences, make trades, and support her department's point of view.
>
> When the committee met two weeks later, most of its members already had decided in favor of the manager who used the political approach. The convincing

FIGURE 11.9
Common Impression Management Strategies

Which of these do you view as acceptable by yourself or others?

1. Personal competence and high performance
2. Meeting one's commitments; working extra long and hard
3. Solving a crisis; volunteering to help in time of need
4. Articulating your values and displaying highly ethical behavior
5. Engaging in appropriate (and/or edited) self-disclosure
6. Exhibiting a favorable appearance that meets others' expectations
7. Self-promotion based on results, along with name-dropping
8. Ingratiation activities (flattery, mimicry, being a "yes-person")
9. Exaggerating your skills and achievements; claiming credit for work done by others
10. Attributing your own problems to other people or events; covering up your deficiencies; pleading for pity

logic of the written report was ignored, and the committee voted to retain the activity in its present location. Political skills won the dispute.

Managers soon realize that their political power comes from the support of key individuals or the group around them. It arises from a leader's ability to work with people and social systems to gain their allegiance and support. The effort to gain and use personal power for self-interest involves being alert to others' needs to save face, engaging in horse trading, making trade-offs, mending fences, developing ingenious compromises, and engaging in a variety of other activities.

High and low self-monitors

Research suggests that some people **(self-monitors)** are more effective at using organizational politics than others.[22] In particular, *high self-monitors* are more adept at regulating themselves and adapting to situational and interpersonal cues. They are sensitive to shifting role expectations, concerned about their impression on others, and responsive to signals they receive. By meeting the expectations of others, they accomplish tasks and are seen as potential leaders. *Low self-monitors* are more insulated from social cues, behave as they wish, and show less concern for making positive impressions on others. This attitude negatively affects their relationships with others and diminishes their prospects for promotions.

Because many employees are vitally interested in their own career success, modern organizations are fertile places for politics to thrive. Leaders who are otherwise capable but who lack self-monitoring capacity and basic political skills will have trouble rising to the top in modern organizations. What they need (assuming high performance) is some emphasis on **impression management**—the ability to protect and enhance their self-image while intentionally affecting another's assessment of them. Some impression management strategies include sending positive nonverbal cues (e.g., smiles or eye contact), using flattery, and doing favors for others.[23] A variety of other approaches are listed in Figure 11.9. Clearly, a broad range of interpersonal skills is essential for leaders, both for their personal success and for smoothing the path to employee performance.

Summary

Interpersonal and intergroup conflicts often arise when there is disagreement regarding goals or the methods of attaining them. These conflicts can be either constructive or destructive for the people involved. Several methods exist for resolving conflict (avoiding,

Advice to Future Managers

1. *View interpersonal conflict as an opportunity for learning* and growth and exploration.
2. *Search for the underlying cause(s) of conflict* so as to predict and understand it.
3. *Be alert to clues regarding different personality traits* among people; avoid judging them while using the patterns seen to react more positively to them.
4. *Convert potential conflict situations into win–win opportunities* for both parties.
5. Refine your skills at being a constructively confrontational person; *be candid, problem-oriented, questioning, and flexible.*
6. *Learn to express your feelings and positions in an assertive, honest, expressive fashion* so as to get your own needs met.
7. Accept the enormous needs for recognition that most employees have; *find legitimate opportunities for stroking them.*
8. *Assess the nature and strength of your sources of influence and power;* learn to draw upon them to increase your chances of success in organizational politics.
9. After developing and demonstrating your technical skills, *engage in impression management* to polish your images in the eyes of others.
10. *Develop your interpersonal facilitation skills* so you can intervene effectively to prevent and resolve conflicts between employees while demonstrating your compassion.

smoothing, forcing, compromising, and confronting), and they vary in their potential effectiveness. A key issue revolves around intended outcomes for oneself and others: Does an individual want to win or lose, and what is desired for the other party? Generally, a confronting approach has significant merit.

Assertive behavior is a useful response in many situations where a person's legitimate needs have been disregarded. Stroking is sought and provided in social transactions, because it contributes to the satisfaction of recognition needs and reinforces a positive and satisfying interpersonal orientation.

Power is needed to run an organization. The five bases of power are personal, legitimate, expert, reward, and coercive. Each of these has a different impact on employees, ranging from resistance to compliance to commitment. Organizational politics is the use of various behaviors that enhance or protect a person's influence and self-interest. In general, political behaviors in organizations are common, necessary for success, and increasingly practiced at higher levels. Impression management is also a useful strategy to supplement one's actual performance.

Speaking OB: Terms and Concepts for Review

Assertiveness, *298*
Bases of power, *301*
Coercive power, *301*
Compassion, *299*
Conditional strokes, *300*
Conflict, *288*
Confronting, *295*
Expert power, *301*
Impression management, *306*
Interpersonal Facilitation, *299*
Legitimate power, *301*
Mixed stroke, *300*
Negative strokes, *300*
Norm of reciprocity, *303*
Organizational politics, *302*
Personal power, *301*
Positive strokes, *300*
Posturing, *305*
Power, *301*
Relationship-restoring approaches, *296*
Reward power, *301*
Self-monitors, *306*
Stroking, *299*
Trust, *290*
Unconditional strokes, *300*
Win–win outcome of conflict, *294*
Workplace incivility, *290*

Discussion Questions

1. Discuss the relationship between Theory X and Theory Y (as presented in Chapter Two) and conflict resolution strategies.
2. Pair up with another student and explore the concept of trust as a foundation for productive human relationships. Develop several strategies for increasing mutual trust.
3. How assertive are you (rate yourself from 1 low to 10 high)? Should you be more or less assertive? Under what conditions?
4. "Resolved: That all employees should be trained to become more assertive." Prepare to present the pros and cons in a class debate.
5. Many people do not receive as many strokes as they feel they deserve on a regular basis. Why do they feel this way? What could their managers do about it? What could they do themselves?
6. Think of an organization you are familiar with. What types of power are used there? How do people react to those bases? What changes would you recommend?
7. Identify which tactics of organizational politics you have seen used or read about previously. Develop an action plan for responding to these behaviors if you were to encounter them.
8. Review and explain the idea of a norm of reciprocity as a basis for influencing others. Explain how you have seen it used in interpersonal relationships. How could you make use of it in the future?
9. Review the definition of organizational politics. Can an organization be totally free of political behavior? What would it be like? How could you make it happen?
10. Think about the idea of impression management. In what ways do students use it effectively in the classroom? What additional strategies could they adopt?

Assess Your Own Skills

How well do you exhibit good interpersonal skills?

Read the following statements carefully. Circle the number on the response scale that most closely reflects the degree to which each statement accurately describes you when you have tried to work constructively with someone else. Add up your total points and prepare a brief action plan for self-improvement. Be ready to report your score for tabulation across the entire group.

	Good description									Poor description
1. I recognize the multiple sources of conflict and search for the likely cause before I go any further.	10	9	8	7	6	5	4	3	2	1
2. I am careful not to attack another person's self-esteem, nor do I let my self-esteem be threatened by what others say.	10	9	8	7	6	5	4	3	2	1
3. I know when to escalate a conflict and when it makes sense to de-escalate it.	10	9	8	7	6	5	4	3	2	1
4. I can recognize the strengths and weaknesses of each of the five major personality factors.	10	9	8	7	6	5	4	3	2	1

5. I actively attempt to assess the intended outcome of conflict that others seem to project; where necessary, I convert the goal to win–win.	10	9	8	7	6	5	4	3	2	1
6. I can flexibly shift my behavior among the five major conflict resolution strategies, although I generally prefer the confrontational one.	10	9	8	7	6	5	4	3	2	1
7. I know what it takes to be assertive, and I am comfortable expressing myself in this way.	10	9	8	7	6	5	4	3	2	1
8. I use a wide array of impression management strategies and believe I am successful in doing so.	10	9	8	7	6	5	4	3	2	1
9. I regularly assess, and attempt to further develop, my various bases of power.	10	9	8	7	6	5	4	3	2	1
10. I recognize the reality of organizational politics and consciously use the norm of reciprocity to help accomplish my goals.	10	9	8	7	6	5	4	3	2	1

Scoring and Interpretation

Add up your total points for the 10 questions. Record that number here, and report it when it is requested. Finally, insert your total score into the "Assess and Improve Your Own Organizational Behavior Skills" chart in Appendix A.

- If you scored between 81 and 100 points, you appear to have a solid capability for demonstrating good interpersonal skills.
- If you scored between 61 and 80 points, you should take a close look at the items with lower self-assessment scores and explore ways to improve those items.
- If you scored under 60 points, you should be aware that a weaker skill level regarding several items could be detrimental to your future success as a motivator. We encourage you to review relevant sections of the chapter and watch for related material in subsequent chapters and other sources.

Identify your three lowest scores, and write the question numbers here: _____, _____, _____. Write a brief paragraph, detailing to yourself an action plan for how you might sharpen each of these skills.

Incident

The Angry Airline Passenger

Margie James was night supervisor for an airline in Denver. Her office was immediately behind the ticket counter, and occasionally she was called upon to deal with passengers who had unusual problems that employees could not solve. One evening about 11 P.M., she was asked to deal with an angry passenger who approached her with the comment, "Your incompetent employees have lost my bag again, and your !X?#*!! baggage attendant isn't helping me at all. I want some service. Is everybody incompetent around here? I have an important speech in that bag that I have to deliver at 9 o'clock in the morning, and if I don't get it, I'll sue this airline for sure."

Questions

How should James respond to the passenger? Would stroking help her? Would assertiveness training help?

Experiential Exercise

Assessing Political Strategies

Working individually, rank-order the following political (influence) strategies according to your willingness to use them (1 greatest; 8 least) to advance your own self-interest at work. When you are through, form groups of about five persons and develop a group assessment (consensus) of the proportion of managers (0–100 percent) who might use each strategy. Afterward, examine the key and discuss any differences. Talk about how use of these strategies might have changed over time.

Self-Ranking			Group Assessment of Use by Managers
_____	A.	Praising influential people to make them feel good	_____
_____	B.	Lining up prior support for a decision to be made	_____
_____	C.	Blaming others for problems (scapegoating)	_____
_____	D.	Creating social debts by doing favors for others	_____
_____	E.	Dressing to meet the organization's standards for successful grooming	_____
_____	F.	Building a support network of influential people	_____
_____	G.	Withholding or distorting information that sheds an unfavorable light on your performance	_____
_____	H.	Forming coalitions with powerful individuals who can support you later	_____

Note: Frequency data obtained from Robert W. Allen, Dan L. Madison, Lyman W. Porter, Patricia A. Renwick, and Bronston T. Mayes, "Organizational Politics: Tactics and Characteristics of Its Actors," *California Management Review*, Fall 1979, pp. 77–83.

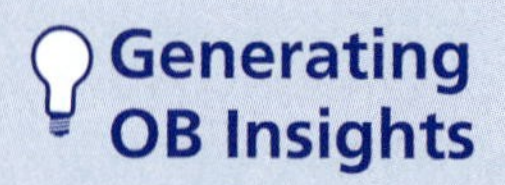

Generating OB Insights

An *insight* is a new and clear perception of a phenomenon, or an acquired ability to "see" clearly something that you were unaware of previously. It is sometimes simply referred to as an "ah ha! moment," in which you have a minirevelation or reach a straightforward conclusion about a topic or issue.

Insights need not necessarily be dramatic, for what is an insight to one person may be less important to another. The critical feature of insights is that they are relevant and memorable for *you;* they should represent new knowledge, new frameworks, or new ways of viewing things that you want to retain and remember over time.

Insights, then, are different from the information that you find in the "Advice for Future Managers" boxes within the text. That advice is prescriptive and action-oriented; it indicates a recommended course of action.

A useful way to think of OB insights is to assume that you are the only person who has read Chapter 11. You have been given the assignment to highlight, in your own words, the major concepts (but not just summarize the whole chapter) that might stand out for a naive audience who has never heard of the topic before. *What 10 insights would you share with them?*

(Example) *Interpersonal conflict will emerge in most working relationships.*

1. ______________________________
2. ______________________________
3. ______________________________
4. ______________________________
5. ______________________________
6. ______________________________
7. ______________________________
8. ______________________________
9. ______________________________
10. ______________________________

Nurturing Your Critical Thinking and Reflective Skills

Take a few minutes to review the discussion in the Roadmap for Readers of critical thinking and reflection. Remind yourself that if you can hone these abilities now, you will have a substantial competitive advantage when you apply for jobs and are asked what unique skills you can bring to the position and the organization.

Critical Thinking

Think back on the material you read in this chapter. What are three unique and challenging *critical questions* that you would like to raise about this material? (These might identify something controversial about which you have doubts, they may imply you suspect a theory or model has weaknesses, they could examine the legitimacy of apparent causal relationships, or they might assess the probable value of a suggested practice.) Be prepared to share these questions with class members or your instructor.

1. ______________________________
2. ______________________________
3. ______________________________

Reflection

This process often involves answering the parallel questions of "What do you *think* about the material you have read?" and "How do you *feel* about that material?" Therefore, express your *personal thoughts and feelings* (reactions) to any of the ideas or topics found in this chapter, and be prepared to share these reflections with class members or your instructor.

1. ______________________________

   ____

2. ______________________________

   ____

3. ______________________________

   ____

Key: A 25%, B 37%, C 54%, D 13%, E 53%, F 24%, G 54%, H 25%.

Part Five

Group Behavior

Chapter Twelve

Informal and Formal Groups

Multiple perspectives are one antidote to individuals' flawed decision making.

Thomas H. Davenport[1]

Innovation is more likely when people of different disciplines, backgrounds, and areas of expertise share their thinking.

Teresa M. Amabile and Mukti Khaire[2]

CHAPTER OBJECTIVES

AFTER READING THIS CHAPTER, YOU SHOULD UNDERSTAND

12–1 Group Dynamics
12–2 The Nature and Effects of Informal Groups
12–3 Informal Leaders
12–4 Differences between Task and Social Leadership Roles
12–5 Brainstorming, Nominal, Delphi, and Dialectic Techniques
12–6 Weaknesses of Group Meetings

Facebook Page

Student A: We're reading about formal and informal groups in my OB class.

Student B: Why would an organization create an informal group? That doesn't compute.

Student A: They don't necessarily *create* them; they emerge by themselves, and they can be pretty powerful.

Student B: OK, but are there any benefits from them?

Student A: There are a ton of them such as increased satisfaction and cohesiveness, but then there are potential problems, too, including rumor, conflicts, and resistance to change. I was fascinated by the fact that you can portray informal organizations on a network chart—useful for examining either interpersonal feelings or actual behaviors.

Student B: How about the other topic? You mentioned formal groups, didn't you?

Student A: Yeah, there are committees, task forces, brainstorming groups, nominal groups, and Delphi decision groups, plus the use of crowdsourcing.

Student B: So what are the most important personal lessons you learned?

Student A: I guess it would all start with the need for a clear agenda, then using facilitation and processing skills, plus the need to avoid groupthink and escalation of commitment by making sure that someone plays the role of a devil's advocate.

Student B: You should be good at that, since you're always leading us astray!

Student A: I admit that might be true, but in this case it's someone who plays a very *constructive* role by asking important questions, digging for evidence, and examining logical reasoning. Pretty important stuff!

When Bill Smith graduated from engineering school and joined the laboratory of a large manufacturing company, he was assigned the task of supervising four laboratory technicians who checked production samples. In some ways, he did supervise them. In other ways he was restricted by the group itself, which was quite frustrating to Bill. He soon found that each technician protected the others, making it difficult to fix responsibility for sloppy work. The group appeared to restrict its work in such a way that about the same number of tests were made every day regardless of his urging to speed up the work. Although Bill was the designated supervisor, he observed that many times his technicians, instead of coming to him, took problems to an older technician across the aisle in another section.

Bill also observed that three of his technicians often had lunch together in the cafeteria, but the fourth technician usually ate with friends in an adjoining laboratory. Bill usually ate with other laboratory supervisors, and he learned much about company events during these lunches. He soon began to realize that these situations were evidence of an informal organization and that he had to work with it as well as with the formal organization.

Engaging Your Brain

1. Glance ahead at the brief material on network charts on pp. 323–324. Now select a handful of individuals from your job, residence, or social group, and chart the frequency of their oral interactions on a recent occasion. What do you see, and why do you think this pattern exists?
2. Examine the task and social roles listed in Figure 12.6. Rate, on a scale from 1 (very low) to 10 (very high) your own current capacity to exhibit the task roles listed there. Now do the same for the social roles. What does this tell you about your areas of needed improvement?
3. What is your current definition of group consensus? Now examine the author's definition on p. 322. How do they differ? What are the implications of any difference that you observe?

GROUP DYNAMICS

This chapter and the next one turn our focus from interpersonal relations to group activities. Small groups have functioned since the time of the first human family. In recent years, researchers have studied scientifically the processes by which small groups evolve and work. Some of the questions they have addressed are:

- What is the informal organization and how does it operate?
- What is the role of a leader in a small group?
- Does the role vary with different objectives?
- What structured approaches are most useful for accomplishing group objectives?
- In what ways and under what conditions are group decisions better or worse than individual ones? Answers to these questions have now emerged, producing useful information on the dynamics of behavior in small groups for supervisors such as Bill Smith.

What is group dynamics?

The social process by which people interact face-to-face in small groups is called **group dynamics.** The word "dynamics" comes from the Greek word meaning "force"; hence group dynamics refers to the *study of forces operating within a group*. Two important historical landmarks in our understanding of small groups are the research of Elton Mayo and his associates in the 1920s and 1930s, and the experiments in the 1930s of Kurt Lewin, the founder of the group dynamics movement. Mayo showed that workers tend to establish informal groups that affect job satisfaction and effectiveness. Lewin observed that different kinds of leadership produced different responses in groups.

Groups have properties of their own that are different from the properties of the individuals who make up the group. This is similar to the physical situation in which a molecule of salt (sodium chloride) has different properties from the sodium and chlorine elements that form a "group" to make it. The special properties of groups are illustrated by a simple lesson in mathematics. Suppose we say "one plus one equals three." In the world of mathematics, that is a logical error, and a rather elementary one at that. But in the world of group dynamics it is entirely rational to say "one plus one equals three." In a group, there is no such thing as only two people, for *no two people can be understood without examining their relationship,* and that relationship is the third element—and a critical one—in the equation.

Types of Groups

Formal and informal

Groups can be classified in many ways. A key difference exists between **formal groups,** which are established by the organization and which have a public identity and goal to achieve, and **informal groups,** which emerge on the basis of common interests, proximity, and friendships. This chapter discusses both types.

Temporary and permanent

Another fundamental distinction is between two types of formal groups. Some have a relatively temporary life; they are created to accomplish a short-term task and then disband. An example of a temporary group is a *task force*. The event at which group members discuss ideas or solve problems is generally called a *meeting*. The other type of formal group is a more natural and enduring work group. This type of group is formed when people regularly perform tasks together as part of their job assignments and is called a *team*. Because of the immense importance of teams in today's organizations, teams are discussed in a separate chapter, Chapter 13.

Beneath the cloak of formal relationships in every organization is a more complex system of social relationships consisting of many small informal groups. Although there are many varieties of informal groups, we refer to them collectively as the informal organization. These informal groups are a powerful influence on productivity and job satisfaction, as Bill Smith discovered in the opening illustration. This chapter begins with an overview of informal organizations at work.

THE NATURE OF INFORMAL ORGANIZATIONS

Comparison of Informal and Formal Organizations

Definition of informal organization

Widespread interest in the informal organization developed as a result of the Western Electric studies in the 1930s, which concluded that it was an important part of the total work situation. These studies showed that the **informal organization** is a network of personal and social relations not established or required by the formal organization but arising spontaneously as people associate with one another. The emphasis within the informal organization is on people and their relationships, whereas the formal organization emphasizes official positions in terms of authority and responsibility. Informal power, therefore, attaches to a *person,* whereas formal authority attaches to a *position* and a person has it only when occupying that position. *Informal power is personal,* but formal authority is institutional. These differences are summarized in Figure 12.1.

Informal power

Power in an informal organization is given by group members rather than delegated by managers; therefore, it does not follow the official chain of command. It is more likely to come from peers than from superiors in the formal hierarchy, and it may cut across organizational lines into other departments. It is usually more unstable than formal authority, since it is subject to the sentiments of people. Because of its subjective nature,

FIGURE 12.1
Differences between Informal and Formal Organizations

Basis of Comparison	Informal Organization	Formal Organization
General nature	Unofficial	Official
Major concepts	Power and politics	Authority and responsibility
Primary focus	Person	Position
Source of leader power	Given by group	Delegated by management
Guidelines for behavior	Norms	Rules and policies
Sources of control	Sanctions	Rewards and penalties

the informal organization cannot be controlled by management in the way that the formal organization can.

A manager typically holds some informal (personal) power along with formal (positional) power, but usually a manager does not have more informal power than anyone else in the group. This means that *the manager and the informal leader usually are two different persons in work groups.*

As a result of differences between formal and informal sources of power, formal organizations may grow to immense size, but informal organizations (at least the closely knit ones) tend to remain small in order to keep within the limits of personal relationships. The result is that a large organization tends to have hundreds of informal organizations operating throughout it. Some of them are wholly within the institution; others are partially external to it. Because of their naturally small size and instability, informal organizations are not a suitable substitute for the large formal aggregates of people and resources needed for modern institutions. Instead, informal organizations complement (and often enhance) the formal one.

How Does the Informal Organization Emerge?

The organization's structure is designed by management to be consistent with its environment, technology, and strategy. This structure, with its rules, procedures, and job descriptions, creates a set of broad policy guidelines and narrower prescriptions for employees to follow. Individuals and groups are expected to behave in certain ways. If they perform their tasks as prescribed, the organization is efficient. This ideal may not happen as much as managers would like, however.

Effects of the informal organization

The informal organization emerges from within the formal structure as predictably as flowers grow in the spring. The result of this combination is different from what managers may have expected in at least three ways:[3]

- First, *employees act differently than required.* They may work faster or slower than predicted, or they may gradually modify a work procedure on the basis of their experience and insight.
- Second, *employees often interact with different people,* or with different frequencies, than their jobs require. Georgia may seek advice from Melissa instead of Todd, and Candy may spend more time helping José than Steve.
- Third, *workers may embrace a set of attitudes, beliefs, and sentiments* different from those the organization expects of them. Instead of being loyal, committed, and enthusiastic about their work, some employees may become disenchanted; others are openly alienated.

The lesson for managers is painfully obvious—they must be aware of the informal activities, interactions, and sentiments of employees in addition to the required ones. The *combination* of required and emergent behaviors sometimes makes it difficult to predict levels of employee performance and satisfaction, as shown in Figure 12.2. Sometimes the informal organization enhances employee performance and satisfaction, and yet occasionally it may detract from those desired outcomes.

Informal Leaders

The employee with the largest amount of status in the informal organization usually becomes its **informal leader.** This person emerges from within the group, often acquiring considerable informal power. Informal leaders may help socialize new members into the organization, and they may be called upon by the group to perform the more complex tasks. A young neurosurgeon, for example, related how the group's more experienced partner would

FIGURE 12.2 Formal and Informal Organizations and Their Effects

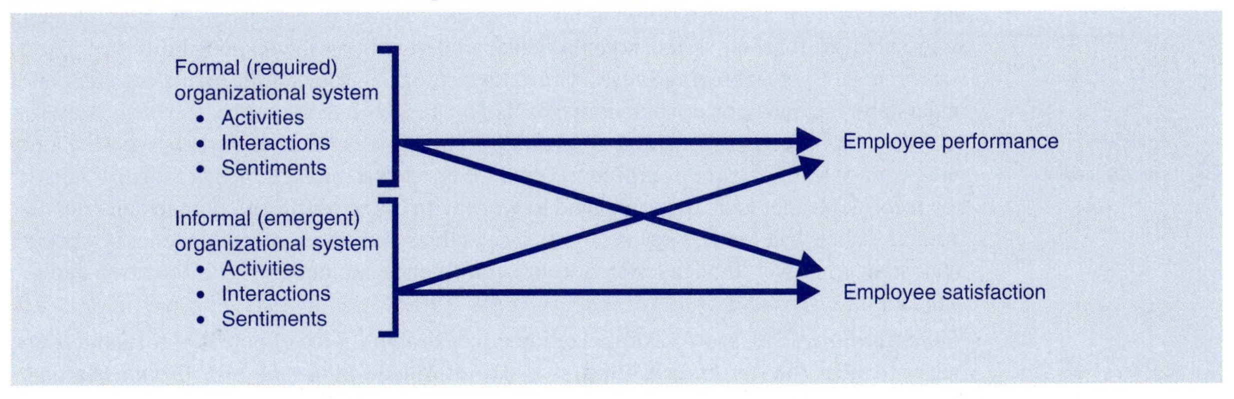

often stop by the operating room during a particularly delicate operation to assist briefly in the removal of a brain tumor, and then quietly move on when help was no longer needed.

Key roles of informal leaders

The informal leader plays several useful roles for a work unit. For example, the informal leader is expected to model and explain the key **norms** (informal standards of behavior) of the informal group for new members. And if someone fails to comply with the group's norms, the informal leader will likely play a dominant role in applying various forms and degrees of pressure or punishment to the individual to induce the desired behavior in the future. In addition, the informal leader often engages in a range of behaviors to help build and sustain the informal group's level of cohesiveness. For example, the leader may assume responsibility for recognizing the daily achievements of workers, for organizing after-hours social events, or for initiating a modest level of teasing and bantering among employees.

In return for their services, informal leaders usually enjoy certain informal rewards and privileges. Perhaps the informal leader is permitted by co-workers to choose a vacation time first, or the leader might be spared from a messy cleanup chore. A predictable reward is the high esteem in which the informal leader is held, and this is significant enough to balance the responsibilities the person shoulders.

Multiple informal leaders

Informal groups overlap to the extent that one person may be a member of several different groups, which means there is not just one leader but several of varying importance. The group may look to one employee on matters pertaining to wages and to another to lead recreational plans. In this way, several people in a department may be informal leaders of some type. An experienced person may be looked upon as the expert on job problems, a good listener may serve as informal counselor, and a communicator may be depended upon to convey key problems to the managers.

Identifying and Rewarding Informal Leaders Sometimes the informal leadership of a group is unclear, at least to outside observers or managers. However, informal leaders often exhibit distinct behaviors that allow them to be identified. For example, Ellen may serve as the unofficial representative to management when workers have a question or complaint. Or managers may notice that other employees gather around Alberto's workstation to swap stories whenever there is a coffee break. Sarah may voluntarily train new employees when they ask for technical help. These examples suggest that acting as a spokesperson, being the center of social attention, and offering well-received wisdom and guidance all provide useful clues regarding informal leadership.

Why are some employees, such as Ellen, Alberto, and Sarah, willing to be informal leaders? To some workers, informal leadership is a form of job enrichment, providing them with variety in their workday and a feeling of greater significance. Others find that it helps satisfy their social needs by dramatically increasing their interpersonal contacts during the day. Many find it a source of recognition that fulfills their esteem needs—a way of being acknowledged for their skills and experience while avoiding the responsibilities of formal supervision. By recognizing these rewards for informal leadership, managers can better understand the behavior of some individuals.

One primary leader

Although several persons in a group may be informal leaders of various types, usually one primary leader has more influence than others. Each manager needs to learn who the key informal leader is in any group and to work with that leader to encourage behavior that furthers rather than hinders organizational objectives. When an informal leader is working against an employer, the leader's widespread influence can undermine motivation and job satisfaction.

Some Cautions The informal organization is a desirable source of potential formal leaders, but remember that *an informal leader does not always make the best formal manager.* History is filled with examples of successful informal leaders who became arrogant bosses once they received formal authority. Some informal leaders fail as formal ones because they fear official responsibility—something they do not have as informal leaders. They often criticize management for lacking initiative or for not daring to be different, but when they take a managerial job, they become even more conservative because they are afraid to make a mistake. Other informal leaders fail because their area of official managerial authority is broader and more complex than the tiny area in which they had informal power. The fact that José is the leader in departmental social activities does not necessarily mean he will be successful as the departmental manager.

Benefits of Informal Organizations

Better total system

Although informal systems may lead to several problems, they also bring a number of benefits to both employers and employees, as shown in Figure 12.3. Most important is that they *blend with formal systems* to make an effective total system. Formal plans and policies cannot meet every problem in a dynamic situation because they are pre-established and partly inflexible. Some requirements can be met better by informal relations, which can be flexible and spontaneous.

Lighter workload for management

Another benefit of the informal organization is to *lighten the workload on management.* When managers know that the informal organization is working with them, they feel less compelled to check on the workers to be sure everything is working well. Managers are

FIGURE 12.3 Potential Benefits and Problems Associated with the Informal Organization

Benefits	Problems
• Makes a more effective total system	• Develops undesirable rumor
• Lightens workload on management	• Encourages negative attitudes
• Helps get the work done	• Resists change
• Tends to encourage cooperation	• Leads to interpersonal and intergroup conflicts
• Fills in gaps in a manager's abilities	• Rejects and harasses some employees
• Gives satisfaction and stability to work groups	• Weakens motivation and satisfaction
• Improves communication	• Operates outside of management's control
• Provides a safety valve for employee emotions	• Supports conformity
• Encourages managers to plan and act more carefully	• Develops role conflicts
• Contributes to higher cohesiveness	

more willing to delegate and decentralize because they are confident that employees will be cooperative. In general, informal group support of a manager leads to better cooperation and productivity. It helps get the work done.

The informal organization also may act to *compensate for gaps in a manager's abilities.* If a manager is weak in planning, an employee may informally help with goal-setting. In this way, planning is accomplished in spite of the manager's weakness.

Work group satisfaction

A significant benefit of the informal organization is that it *gives satisfaction and stability to work groups.* It is the means by which workers feel a sense of belonging and security, so satisfaction is increased and turnover reduced.

> In a large office, an employee named Rosita may feel insignificant, but her informal group gives her personal attachment and status. With the members of her group she *is* somebody, even though in the formal structure she is only one of a thousand employees. She may not look forward to monitoring 750 accounts daily, but the informal group gives more meaning to her day. When she thinks of meeting her friends, sharing their interests, and eating with them, her day takes on a new dimension that makes easier any difficulty or tedious routine in her work. Of course, these conditions can apply in reverse: The group may not accept her, thereby making her work more disagreeable and driving her to a transfer, to absenteeism, or to a resignation.

An additional benefit is that the informal organization can be a *useful channel of employee communication.* It provides the means for people to keep in touch, to learn more about their work, and to understand what is happening in their environment.

A safety valve for emotions

Another benefit, often overlooked, is that the informal organization is a *safety valve for employee frustrations* and other emotional problems. Employees may relieve emotional pressures by discussing them with someone else in an open and friendly way, and one's associates in the informal group provide this type of environment.

> Consider the case of Max Schultz, who became frustrated with his supervisor, Frieda Schneider. He was so angry that he wanted to tell her what he thought of her, using uncomplimentary words, but he might have been disciplined for that. His next alternative was to have lunch with a close friend and to share with his friend exactly how he felt. Having vented his feelings, he was able to return to work and interact with Schneider in a more relaxed and acceptable manner.

A benefit of the informal organization that is seldom recognized is that its presence encourages managers to *plan and act more carefully* than they would otherwise. Managers who understand its power know that the informal organization provides a check on their unlimited use of authority. They introduce changes into their groups only after careful planning because they know that informal groups can undermine even a worthwhile project. They want their projects to succeed because they will have to answer to formal authority if they fail.

Cohesiveness

The benefits of the informal organization are more likely to appear if the group is cohesive and its members have favorable attitudes toward the firm.[4] **Cohesiveness** is indicated by how strongly the employees stick together, rely on each other, and desire to remain members of the group. Members of cohesive groups tend to participate more, be more goal directed, and conform more closely to group norms. *Productivity among members of cohesive groups is often quite uniform, and turnover is low.* Whether productivity will be high or low, however, is directly related to the cohesive group's internal work attitudes and performance norms. If they are favorable toward the organization, performance will likely be higher; if they are negative, performance will likely be diminished.

Cohesiveness is likely to be lower in large groups, when members are forced to compete for scarce resources, when participants dislike each other, or when supervisors show favoritism to one or more members. However, cohesiveness can also be increased by several factors, such as:

1. Creating competitions (such as sales or safety competitions) against other groups
2. Providing opportunities for frequent interactions among members
3. Selecting members with similar attitudes, backgrounds, and values
4. Identifying a challenging group goal that unifies member efforts
5. Recognizing a major threat or common enemy to the group

Problems Associated with Informal Organizations

Many of the benefits of informal systems can be reversed to show potential problems. In other words, informal systems can help and harm an activity at the same time. For example, while useful information is being spread by one part of the system, another part may be communicating a malicious rumor. An informal system also can change its mood in a positive or negative way. A work group, for example, may accept, welcome, and nurture new employees and thus facilitate their feelings of comfort and performance levels. By contrast, the same group may confront, harass, and reject other employees, causing dissatisfaction and resignations.[5] Both positive and negative effects exist side by side in most informal systems.

Resistance to change

One major problem with informal organizations is resistance to change. The group tends to become overly protective of its way of life and to stand like a rock in the face of change. *What has been good in the past is believed to be good enough for the future*. If, for example, job A has always had more status than job B, it must continue to have more status and more pay, even though conditions have changed to make job A less difficult. If restriction of productivity was necessary in the past in response to an autocratic management, the group might believe it to be necessary now, even though management is participative and supportive. Although informal organizations are bound by no chart on the wall, they are bound by convention, custom, and culture.

Conformity

A related problem is that the informal organization can be a significant cause of employee conformity. The informal side of organizations is so much a part of the everyday life of workers that they hardly realize it is there, so they usually are unaware of the powerful pressures it applies to persuade them to conform to its way of life. The closer they are attached to it, the stronger its influence is.

Norms

Conformity is encouraged by norms, which are informal group requirements for the behavior of members.[6] These norms may be strong or weak (depending on the importance of the behavior to the group) and positive or negative (depending on their impact on the organization). Groups rigidly expect their members to follow strong norms; individuals may choose to accept or reject weak ones. Research studies show that groups have norms for both their task responsibilities and their personal relationships at work.[7] They also generate norms for their superior and subordinates, as well as their peers.

An example of the impact of norms at the societal level lies in the term **social norms**. As previously explained, most people desire to (or at least are willing to) conform to their relevant groups. As a result, the behavior of individuals can be affected—and even largely shaped—by knowledge of social norms (the beliefs and actions of comparable persons). Thus energy consumption can be reduced, or patients will show up for dental examinations, or voluntary filing of income tax returns can be increased, by making available to them statistics regarding the frequency of a popular behavior.[8]

The group whose norms a person accepts is a **reference group.** Employees may have more than one reference group, such as the engineering manager who identifies with the engineering profession and its standards, plus one or more management groups. A reference group often uses rewards and penalties to persuade its members to conform to its norms. The combination of informal norms with their related consequences consistently guides opinion and applies power to reduce any behavior that tends to vary from group norms. Nonconformers may be pressured and harassed until they capitulate or leave.

Treatment of nonconformers

Examples of harassment are interference with work (such as hiding one of the offender's tools), ridicule, interference outside the workplace (such as letting the air out of the offender's automobile tires), and isolation from the group. In Britain, it is said that a person isolated from the group is being "sent to Coventry." In these instances, the group refuses to talk with the offender for days or even weeks, and group members may even refuse to use any tool or machine the offender has used. Actions of this type can even drive a worker from a job.

Role conflict

Another problem that may develop is role conflict (see the previous discussion in Chapter 4). Workers may want to meet the requirements of both their group and their employer, but frequently those requirements are somewhat in conflict. What is good for the employees is not always good for the organization. Coffee breaks may be desirable, but if employees spend an extra 15 minutes socializing in the morning and afternoon, productivity may be reduced to the disadvantage of both the employer and consumers. Much of this role conflict can be avoided by carefully cultivating mutual interests with informal groups. The more the interests of formal and informal groups can be integrated, the more productivity and satisfaction can be expected. However, some differences between formal and informal organizations are inevitable. This is not an area where perfect harmony exists.

A major difficulty with any informal organization is that it is not subject to management's direct control. The authority it depends on is the social system rather than management. All that management can do is attempt to influence it.

Personal and group conflicts

Informal organizations also develop interpersonal and intergroup conflicts that can be damaging to their organization. When employees give more of their thoughts and energies to opposing one another, they are likely to give less to their employer. Conflicts and self-interests can become so strong in informal organizations that they reduce both motivation and satisfaction. The result is less productivity, which harms both the employer and employees. No one gains, and that is tragic.

Monitoring Informal Organizations

Bases for networks

One way to gain a better understanding of an informal system is to prepare a visual portrait of it. These diagrams are called **network charts,** or *informal organization charts.*[9] They usually focus on either interpersonal *feelings expressed* (e.g., attraction, repulsion, or indifference) among individuals or actual *behaviors exhibited.* Identifying the feelings within a group can be useful for determining who trusts whom, or for selecting an individual to negotiate a satisfactory compromise on a sticky issue. Determining patterns of behaviors can be done either through personal observation of interactions, through collecting data on communication patterns, or by directly asking individuals involved (e.g., "From whom do you seek advice most frequently?"). Network charts like the simple one shown in Figure 12.4 can reveal central individuals ("stars," such as Tania or Jackie), isolated persons (Carolina) who are likely to feel overlooked, and dramatic differences between what outsiders think is happening versus what is actually occurring.

FIGURE 12.4
A Sample Network Chart of Task Interactions at Work

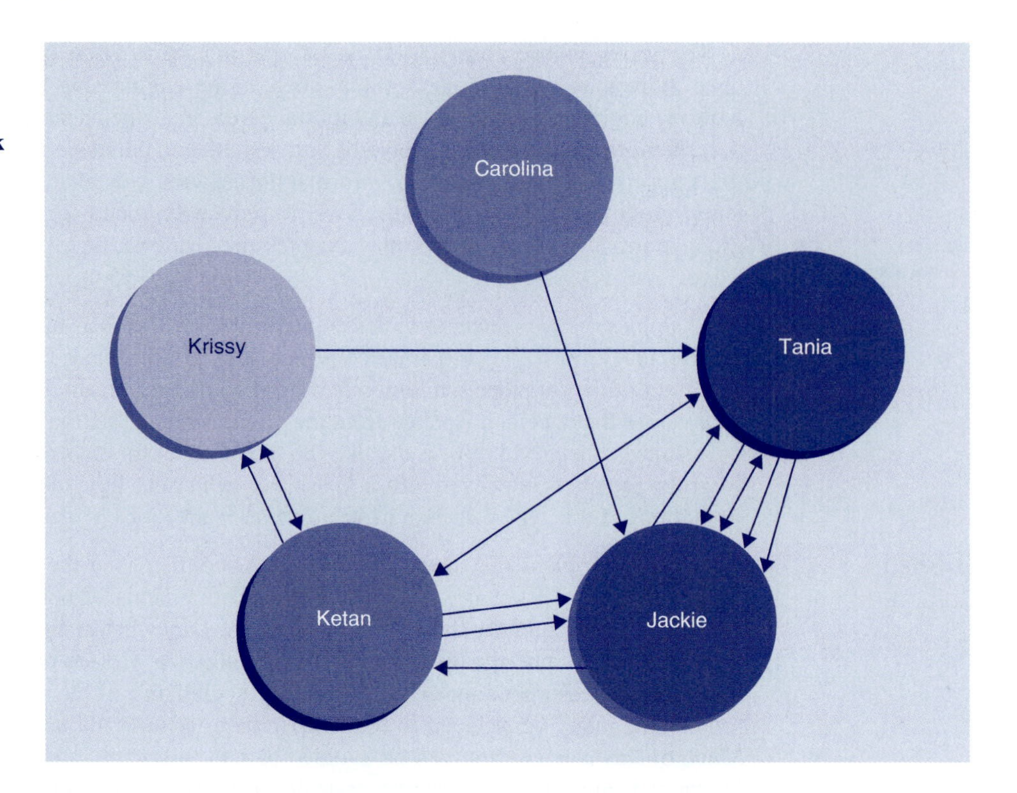

Influencing Informal Organizations

Management did not establish informal organizations, and it cannot abolish them. Nor would it want to do so. But management can learn to live with them and have some measure of influence on them. Management guidelines for action include the following:

Guidelines for action

1. Accept and understand informal organizations.
2. Identify various levels of attitudes and behaviors within them.
3. Consider possible effects on informal systems when taking any kind of action.
4. Integrate as far as possible the interests of informal groups with those of the formal organization.
5. Keep formal activities from unnecessarily threatening informal organizations.

Formal and informal combinations

The most desirable combination of formal and informal organizations appears to be a predominant formal system to maintain unity toward objectives, along with a well-developed informal system to maintain group cohesiveness and teamwork. In other words, the informal organization needs to be strong enough to be supportive, but not strong enough to dominate.

FORMAL GROUPS

> "Oh no! Not another meeting," the executive groaned as she looked at her calendar for the morning. "It's only Wednesday morning, and I've been to 11 meetings already this week. When am I going to get my real work done?"

The executive's last remark reflects how many managers feel about meetings. One survey showed that managers felt time spent in group meetings was their most significant time waster. Some employees report that more than half of their meetings attended result in no meaningful action. Whether called meetings, conferences, task forces, or committees, the time spent in formal groups has variously been criticized as a total waste of time, a source of confusion and misinformation, and an excuse for indecision on the part of an individual decision maker.

The following are some factors that contribute to the often-pervasive negative attitudes about time spent in committee meetings:

- A lack of trust causes participants to withhold their true feelings.
- A negative mind-set exists that "meetings aren't real work" and hence people don't take them seriously (e.g., they come late or leave early, they miss them completely, or they are distracted while there).
- Missing or incomplete information prevents participants from making important decisions when appropriate.
- Meetings are poorly run (the person in charge fails to have an agenda, a plan to follow, a finite length for the session, or the discipline to keep the discussion moving).
- Meetings are viewed as the end result, not the means to an end (the group fails to focus on creating a product or outcome).

In spite of such widespread condemnation, committees and other group activities have continued to flourish. Instead of becoming extinct because of widespread dislike, they continue to be an important part of daily organizational behavior.

Meetings are necessary, but they do introduce more complexity and more chances for problems to arise when improperly used. Some committees are used not to reach decisions but to put them off, not to obtain employee input but to sell a previously reached conclusion, and not to develop subordinates but to hide incompetence. On occasion, emotional issues overshadow the factual aspects of the decision to be made, and the sensitive interpersonal relations that emerge require understanding and delicate handling.

Committees

Formal groups are created for many purposes. Group members may be asked to generate ideas, make decisions, debate issues and negotiate resources, or provide status reports and receive constructive feedback. A **committee** is a specific type of group in which members who have been delegated the authority to handle the problem at hand meet one or more times to address and resolve it. The group's authority usually is expressed in terms of one vote for each member. This means that if a supervisor and a worker serve as members of the same committee, both usually have equal committee roles. The worker may even have greater actual influence on the committee's outcome as a result of differences in expertise, interest, or experience. Committees often create special human problems because people are unable to make adjustments from their normal work roles and relationships.

Systems Factors to Consider

A useful way to approach the management of committees is to apply the systems idea discussed in Chapter 1. As shown in Figure 12.5, effective committees require careful consideration of their inputs (size, composition, and agendas), the group process (leadership roles and alternative group structures), and outcomes (quality of the decision and the group's support for it). These factors are discussed next, followed by a review of the major problems and issues inherent in problem-solving groups.

Size The size of a group tends to affect the way it works. If membership rises above seven, communication tends to be focused within a few members, with others feeling like they do

What Managers Are Reading 

THE WORST AND BEST OF MEETINGS

Simon Ramo, cofounder of TRW Corporation, estimates that he has attended more than 40,000 meetings across his 70 years of working life. He asserts that "most meetings stink"—the wrong people are invited, attendees are unprepared, agendas are unfocused, presenters tend to provide unnecessary elaboration in PowerPoint slides, and so on (and on).

By contrast, management consultant and author Patrick Lencioni claims that meetings can be productive, efficient, and fun. The keys to success lie in giving people a meaningful voice, focusing relentlessly on a few vital issues, and encouraging and resolving conflicts. He also suggests classifying meetings and using them for different purposes, along with mandating 100 percent attendance of persons who can provide important inputs.

Sources: Simon Ramo, *Meetings, Meetings, and More Meetings: Getting Things Done When People Are Involved*. Los Angeles: Bonus Books, 2005; and Patrick Lencioni, *Death by Meeting: A Leadership Fable*. San Francisco: Jossey Bass, 2004.

not have adequate opportunity to communicate directly with one another. If a larger committee is needed to represent all relevant points of view, special effort and extra time are required to ensure good communication. A group of five people is often preferred for typical situations. A smaller group (e.g., three persons) sometimes has difficulty functioning because conflicts of power develop, and diversity of viewpoints may be absent.

Composition Leaders of committees, problem-solving groups, and task forces often have the opportunity to select the members. When doing so, the leaders need to consider various factors, such as the committee's objective, the members' expertise, interest level,

FIGURE 12.5
Systems View of Effective Committees

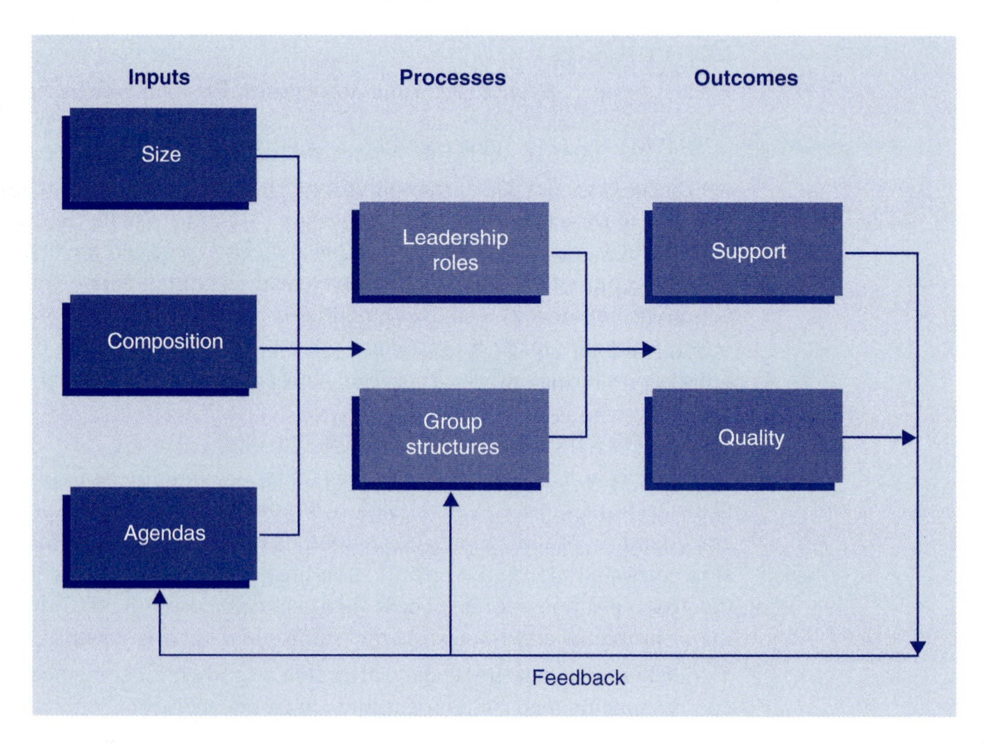

On the Job: Unilever and KeyGene

Although a discussion of surface agendas might seem to be mundane and intuitively obvious, many companies still find them helpful in generating useful ideas. Unilever encourages employees to discuss their ideas with colleagues before coming to committee meetings. Then, with their feedback, proposals can be refined and have a greater chance of adoption by the total group. Biotech research firm KeyGene endorses a similar process, with members gaining rich inputs from constructive criticism. Specifically, bouncing ideas off of colleagues from other departments usually proves most useful.[10]

time available to serve, and the past history of working relationships among the potential members. The guiding questions for selection should be "What can this person contribute to the group's success?" and "Are the people most critical to making and implementing the decision included?"[11]

Surface and hidden agendas

Agendas Meetings work simultaneously at two different levels—surface and hidden. One level is the official task of the group, known as the **surface agenda.** Unfortunately, many employees report that the meetings they attend frequently lack even a basic agenda (see "On the Job: Unilever and KeyGene").

Effective surface agendas are critical to the success of a committee meeting.[12] Agendas should make it clear to attendees why the meeting is to be held, and what it should accomplish. In addition, managers often differentiate between items marked for information, for discussion, or for decisions, as well as the suggested length of time to devote to each. Specific guidelines include:

- Be distributed far enough in advance to allow members to prepare for the discussion
- Clearly specify the date, time, and place of the meeting
- Indicate a primary purpose for the meeting (be *outcome*-oriented)
- List presenters, the time allotted to them, and the time available for discussion
- Help the group focus on *decisions,* not just discussions
- Have room for new items to be added
- Address items in priority order (highest to lowest)
- Identify the date, time, and place of the *next* meeting

Hidden agendas

The other level at which meetings operate involves members' private emotions and motives, which they have brought with them but keep hidden. These are the **hidden agendas** of the meeting. Frequently, when a group reaches a crisis in its surface agenda, these hidden agendas come to life to complicate the situation. Conversely, sometimes a group seems to be making no progress and then suddenly everything is settled. What may have happened is that a hidden agenda finally was resolved, even though members did not know they were working on it, making it easy to settle the surface agenda. An example is that of the staff specialist who is searching for a way to retaliate against a supervisor, and the specialist is blind to everything else until the hidden agenda can be resolved satisfactorily.

Task roles

Leadership Roles Groups tend to require not one but two types of complementary leadership roles: that of the **task leader** and that of the **social leader.**[13] Figure 12.6 provides illustrations of the contrasting nature of each role. The task leader's job in a meeting is to help the group accomplish its objectives and stay on target. The idea is to provide necessary structure by stating the problem, giving and seeking relevant facts, periodically summarizing the progress, and checking for agreement.

Social roles

Difficulties sometimes arise because the task leader may irritate people and injure the unity of the group by pushing too hard for a decision or ignoring emotional issues.

FIGURE 12.6
Task and Social Leadership Roles

Task Roles	Social Roles
• Define a problem or goal for the group. • Request facts, ideas, or opinions from members. • Provide facts, ideas, or opinions. • Clarify a confused situation; give examples; provide structure. • Summarize the discussion. • Determine whether agreement has been reached. • Check for consensus. • Test for ethicality.	• Support the contributions of others; encourage them by recognition. • Sense the mood of the group and help members become aware of it. • Reduce the tension and reconcile disagreements. • Modify your position; admit an error. • Facilitate participation of all members. • Evaluate the group's effectiveness. • Deal with team stress.

One role of the social leader is to restore and maintain group relationships by recognizing contributions, reconciling disagreements, and playing a supportive role to help the group develop. An especially challenging job is to blend the ideas of a deviant member with the thoughts of other participants. Although one person can fill both the task and social roles, often they are separate (played by two different persons). When they are separate, it is important for the task leader to recognize the social leader and try to form a coalition so the two leaders are working together for improved effectiveness of the group.

An example of moderate group activity in a committee meeting is depicted in Figure 12.7. In this committee, all members except Fleming communicated with the leader. Seven of the ten members communicated with members other than the leader, but they tended to talk only to members near them, probably because of the committee's large size and the meeting room's physical layout. Johnson, Smith, and Fleming participated the least; all the other members participated actively. The chart suggests that the leader's principal means of creating discussion was to ask questions (requesting facts and ideas, a task role) and facilitate member participation (a social role).[14]

In addition to relying on both task and social roles, effective meetings are also facilitated by the application of a number of commonsense practices. These include:

- Carefully considering *who* should be present (and for what parts of the meeting), and who does *not* need to be there (excusing them)
- Selecting a good *site* for the meeting (appropriate for the group's size, comfortable, and free of distractions)
- Using *technology* (e.g., computers hooked to printers and oversized monitors) to help capture ideas, allow for anonymous inputs, organize and expand upon them, record insights and criticisms, and create and edit documents before the participants leave
- Giving appropriate *credit* to those who participated, and drawing out those who didn't (such as Fleming in Figure 12.7)
- Using *open* questions to stimulate thought and *directed* questions to encourage a focus on a particular topic
- Refusing to accept superficial excuses ("It can't be done") and inspiring members to overcome obstacles

FIGURE 12.7
Participation Diagram of a Meeting

Source: *Conference Leadership,* U.S. Department of the Air Force, n.d., pp. 9–11.

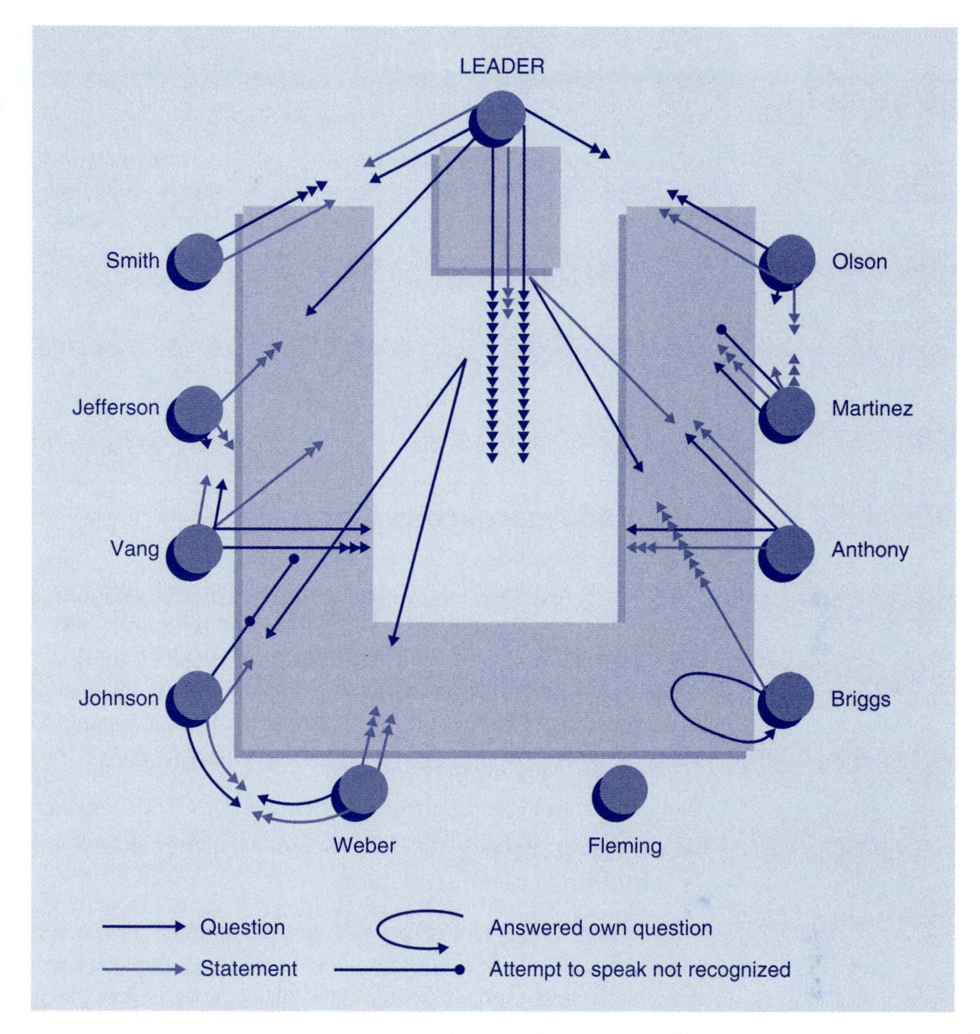

- Balancing the serious discussions with time for a bit of lighthearted *fun*
- Summarizing progress, identifying issues yet unresolved, and making necessary *assignments* for the future (as captured in the cryptic but focused closing query "Who does what by when?")

If followed regularly, these suggestions can greatly improve the productivity of committee meetings.

Individualistic Behaviors Unfortunately, some meeting attendees lose sight of the purpose of a meeting and fail to contribute. Instead, they lapse into self-centered (or even dysfunctional) actions that can delay or even sidetrack productive discussions. Examples of these individualistic behaviors include *distractions* (joke-telling; checking their smartphones), *seeking personal recognition* (bragging), *dominating* (monopolizing conversations or pushing favored solutions), *attacking* (making insulting or dismissive comments), and *withdrawing* (claiming inadequacy or confusion). These behaviors, if continued, can best be addressed either through private conversations with the disruptive individual, or through a combination of task and social leadership roles.

An Ethics Question

Alana has been around the workforce for a while, and she has carefully studied group behavior in her employer's organization. Based on her observations of how things get done, she has taken a number of steps to accomplish her objectives in committee meetings. For example, she makes sure her agenda items receive top priority and are discussed first; she volunteers to write up the minutes of each meeting so she can place her "spin" on the results; she carefully selects to be in her groups co-workers whom she knows will support her positions, and she always sits at the head of the meeting room table (or close to it) so others will notice her more and listen to her input. Is Alana just being appropriately astute, or is she guilty of violating ethical standards to attain the results she desires?

Structured Approaches

The committee meetings discussed earlier generally involve open discussion of a problem or issue. Other methods have been developed that work for specific objectives or provide greater control over the process. Four important alternative structures are brainstorming, nominal groups, Delphi decision making, and dialectic inquiry.

Brainstorming **Brainstorming** is a popular method for encouraging creative thinking in groups of about eight people.[15] It is built around four basic guidelines for participants:

1. Generate as many ideas as possible.
2. Be creative, freewheeling, and imaginative.
3. Build upon (piggyback), extend, or combine earlier ideas.
4. Withhold criticism of others' ideas.

The success of brainstorming depends on each member's capacity and willingness to listen to others' thoughts, to use these thoughts as a stimulus to spark new ideas of their own, and then to feel free to express them. When this sequence takes place, a large number of new and different ideas can emerge.

> One company, Bachman Consulting, suggests modifying the basic brainstorming process for even greater success.[16] Its five-step process structures the flow to make sure each set of ideas contributes value to the next step in the series. The first step looks backward to identify why a problem occurred (root cause analysis). The second describes the criteria that the solutions must meet. The third step involves looking for all possible sources of models for solutions. In the fourth step, participants are asked to relate the models and resources to the original objective to see how they might help. Finally, in the fifth step, the solutions identified are communicated to relevant stakeholders in the organization who might benefit from the product of the five-stage brainstorming effort.

Underlying principles

Two main principles underlie brainstorming. One is **deferred judgment,** by which all ideas—even unusual and impractical ones—are encouraged without criticism or evaluation. Ideas are recorded by one or more group members as fast as they are suggested; they are evaluated for usefulness at a later time. The purpose of deferred judgment is to separate *creation* of novel ideas from idea *censorship*. This principle encourages people to propose bold, unique ideas without worrying about what others think of them. The second principle is that *quantity is valued most,* for it breeds quality. As more ideas come forth (and as ideas are combined or extended), eventually higher-quality ones will be developed. When these principles are followed, group brainstorming typically produces more ideas than provided by a single person. Brainstorming sessions last from 10 minutes to one hour and require very little preparation.

Pros and cons

Brainstorming has many advantages over other approaches. In brainstorming sessions, group members are enthusiastic, participation is broader than normal, and the group maintains a strong task orientation. Ideas are built upon and extended, and members typically feel that the final product is a team solution. Its major difficulties include the residual fear among some members that their creative thoughts will be looked down upon, the fact that independent thought and later criticism of one's ideas do not contribute to group cohesion, the failure to set and follow ground rules (e.g., "no criticism"), an organizational history of not taking action to implement ideas, and the very real fact that only one person can speak at a time (so as to be recorded clearly).

The marriage of computer technology and groupware programs has allowed the development of a modified version of the method, known as **electronic brainstorming.** In this process, group members sit at personal computer terminals—sometimes in scattered locations—and receive a question, an issue, or a request for establishing priorities. In response, they type in their own ideas as they arise. As multiple inputs are received, a set of the group's ideas appears on their screens, available for response, editing, or even input of judgment or votes. Research shows that this process results in a higher number of ideas generated (because of the simultaneous generation and recording of ideas by participants) than through the traditional brainstorming process.[17] In addition, members feel they have more opportunity for participation and more flexibility, since they do not necessarily need to "meet" at the same time. Using this method, even telecommuting employees can participate from their homes, and traveling employees can provide inputs from their hotel rooms.

The Nominal Group Technique A **nominal group** exists in name only, with members having minimal interaction prior to producing a decision. Here are the steps that nominal groups often follow:

Work independently; combine ideas

1. Individuals are brought together and presented with a problem.
2. They develop solutions independently, often writing them on cards.
3. Their ideas are shared with others in a structured format (e.g., a round-robin process that ensures all members get the opportunity to present their ideas orally, while brief notes are taken and made visible to all).
4. Brief time is allotted so that questions can be asked—but only for clarification.
5. Group members individually designate their preferences for the best alternatives by secret ballot.
6. The group decision (the solution receiving the most votes) is announced.

Advantages of the nominal group technique include the opportunity for equal participation by all members, the prevention of dominance of discussion by any one member, and the tight control of time that the process allows. Disadvantages reported are that group members are frustrated by the rigidity of the procedure, gain no feelings of cohesiveness, do not get their social needs satisfied, and do not have the opportunity to benefit from cross-fertilization of ideas and build on them.

One research study explored the quality of solutions offered to a marketing strategy problem in a nominal group procedure.[18] Ideas generated at various stages of the process were scored on the basis of quality and creativity. Although the ideas with the greatest quality (practicality, pervasiveness, and long-range impact) generally appeared early in the nominal group discussion, the most creative ideas (which also had moderate quality) were generated late in the session. Two possible explanations were offered. First, the process may place pressure on participants to contribute their fair share as they see others continuing to provide suggestions. Second, members may be encouraged to take greater risks to share nonconforming ideas as they see the structured process protect other members.

Survey the experts

Delphi Decision Making In **Delphi decision groups,** a panel of relevant people is chosen to address an issue. Members are selected because they are experts or have relevant information to share and the time available to do so. A series of questionnaires are sequentially distributed to the respondents, who do not need to meet face-to-face. All responses typically are in writing. Panelists may be asked to identify future problems, project market trends, or predict a future state of affairs (e.g., corporate sales in 10 years). Explanations of their conclusions also can be shared. Replies are gathered from all participants, summarized, and fed back (anonymously) to the members for their review. Afterward, participants are asked to make another decision on the basis of new information. The process may be repeated several times until the responses converge satisfactorily and a final report is prepared.[19]

Delphi advantages

Success of the Delphi decision process depends on adequate time, participant expertise, communication skill, and the motivation of members to immerse themselves in the task. The major merits of the process include:

- Elimination of the detraction from interpersonal problems among panelists
- Efficient use of experts' time
- Adequate time for reflection and analysis by respondents
- Diversity and quantity of ideas generated
- Accuracy of predictions and forecasts made or scenarios generated

Just as with electronic brainstorming, the increasingly wide availability of computers and the electronic transmission of responses have affected the Delphi process. Through their use, the interactive process of collecting input and feeding back group data can be greatly abbreviated. This use of advances in technology has helped overcome a previous limitation of the Delphi process.

Dialectic Decision Methods Some face-to-face decision-making groups converge too quickly on one alternative while overlooking others. Their incomplete evaluation of options may reflect either the participants' dislike of meetings or their lack of willingness to raise and confront tough issues. The **dialectic decision method (DDM),** which traces its roots to Plato and Aristotle, offers a way of overcoming these problems.[20] The steps of DDM are portrayed in Figure 12.8.

The dialectic process begins with a clear statement of a problem to be solved. Afterward, two or more competing proposals are generated. A key step follows in which participants *identify the explicit or implicit assumptions* that underlie each proposal. The group then breaks into advocacy subgroups, which examine and argue the relative merits of their positions. Then, the entire group makes a decision based on the competing presentations. This decision may mean embracing one of the alternatives (A or B), forging a compromise from several ideas (A and B), or generating a new proposal (C).

The merits of DDM include better understanding of the proposals, their underlying premises, and their pros and cons by the participants. Members are also likely to feel more confident about the choice they made. Disadvantages include the propensity to forge a weak compromise in order to avoid choosing sides, and the tendency to focus more on who

FIGURE 12.8
Steps in Dialectic Decision Making

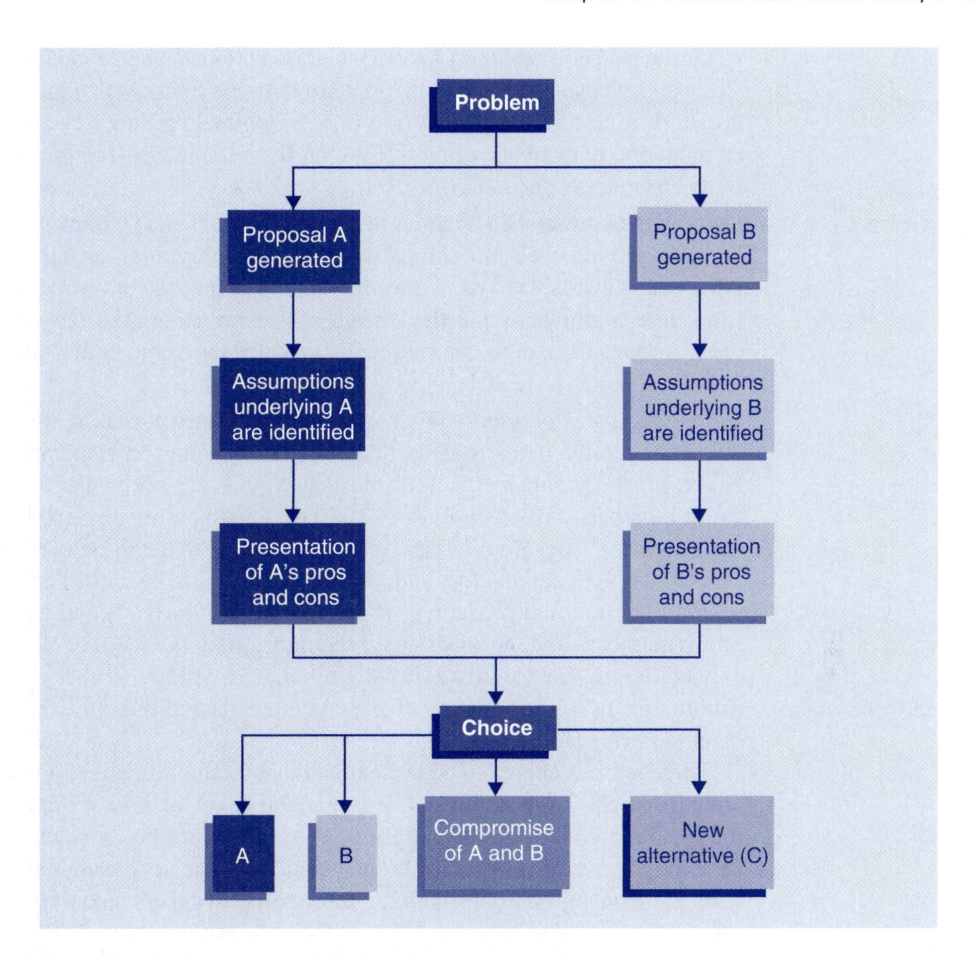

were the better debaters than what the best decision should be. Nevertheless, the dialectic method holds promise for future decision-making groups.

Crowdsourcing A contemporary method for obtaining inputs from a wide variety of individuals is (collaboration-based) **crowdsourcing.**[21] This involves outsourcing a large-scale task to a group of self-selected persons who then work together to produce a single solution. Crowdsourcing can either draw from internal resources (using existing employees in various locations but with related expertise) or from external sources. For crowdsourcing to work well, it requires (as with several of the previously-discussed structured group approaches) motivated participants and individuals who have sufficient expertise to provide useful insights.

Potential Outcomes of Formal Group Processes

Acceptance

Support for Decisions Probably the most important by-product of face-to-face group meetings is that *people who participate in making a decision feel more strongly motivated to accept it and carry it out*. In many instances, this result is more than a by-product—it is the primary purpose of the meeting. Meetings undoubtedly are one of the best means available of committing people to carry out a course of action. A person who has helped make a decision is more interested in seeing it work. Furthermore, if several group members are involved in carrying out a decision, group discussion helps each understand the part others will play so they can coordinate their efforts.

Group decisions also carry more weight with those who are not group members. Associates, subordinates, and even superiors are more likely to *accept* group decisions. They feel decisions of this type are more free from individual prejudice because they are based on a combination of many viewpoints. Further, the combined social pressure of the entire group stands behind the decision.

Problem solving improves

Quality of Decisions In addition to supporting decisions, groups often are highly effective problem-solving tools. In comparison with an individual, groups typically have greater information available to them, a variety of experiences to draw upon, multiple perspectives from diverse thinkers, and the capacity to examine suggestions and reject the incorrect ones. As a result, groups can frequently produce more and better-quality solutions to some problems than individuals can.[22]

Individual Development When working in decision-making groups, some individuals are naturally more passive than others and may be reluctant to share their ideas. However, the group will benefit most through widespread and fairly even participation by all members (which evolves over time). Participation also increases the likelihood of each member's developing new interactive skills that can be used later in other groups. How, then, does satisfactory individual participation occur? In addition to specific task-oriented invitations ("Kristina, what ideas do you have?") and encouragement by other group members and social-oriented recognition by the leader ("Great idea, Mario"), one explanation lies in **social facilitation**—that is, group members often try harder to contribute on a task just because other people are around. *The presence of others stimulates them to perform better.*

The positive impact of others

Three reasons appear to underlie this social facilitation effect. First, having other people around simply increases a person's general level of arousal and awareness, stimulating mental activity. People simply think more carefully about their performance-related behavior. Second, the presence of others makes some people apprehensive about the likelihood of being appraised, formally or informally, by others, and thus they raise their level of performance so as to *look* good. Third, the presence of others may raise one's awareness of the discrepancy between the actual and ideal self and thereby stimulate the person to close that gap (and thus raise their self-esteem)

Increased participation may also be a product of implied group pressure to perform or a natural response to seeing others do so. Social facilitation is closely related to the idea of *role modeling,* where a group member sees and hears others perform well and wants to duplicate that behavior because of the social rewards it elicits from them. These explanations cluster around **conformity,** in which group members are alert to the perceived expectations and norms of the majority, and make conscious or unconscious efforts to adapt to them.

Consensus: A Key Issue in Decision-Making Groups

Is unanimous agreement a necessary prerequisite for effective group decisions? On the one hand, without total agreement, group members may still be expected to carry out decisions they did not support—a difficult challenge for anyone. Divided votes also may set up disagreements that extend beyond the meeting. On the other hand, a *requirement,* or even implicit expectation, of unanimity has its disadvantages. It may become the paramount goal, causing people to suppress their opposition or to tell the group they agree when honestly they do not. In addition, it is frustrating to the majority of members to have to keep discussing a subject long after their minds are made up, simply because they are hoping to convince a few honest dissenters. This situation is a waste of time and an embarrassment to the dissenters (who may feel their input will be ignored anyway). At its worst, the search for unanimous agreement can delay worthwhile projects unnecessarily.

Is consensus unnecessary?

Unless the decision is of utmost personal importance to the dissenter, agreement of most of the members should be sufficient for action. Though an isolated few persons need to be heard and respected, so does the majority. Organizations must get on with their work rather than stop to engage in endless debates in an effort to reach total agreement. Most employers, therefore, do not expect or require unanimity for committee decisions. In practice, **consensus** is often interpreted to mean that the group engaged in widespread input gathering, which resulted in a shared level of understanding. In spite of perceived limitations and modest personal reservations about a prospective decision, *consensus-oriented members generally agree they can (and will) support the decision made*. From a behavioral perspective, the key is for all members to feel they have had an honest opportunity to state their views and be heard.[23] At that time, most reasonable people will believe they can stand behind the decision reached.

Specific ideas for reaching consensus include the following:

1. Conduct periodic and nonbinding straw polls to identify clearly where people stand.
2. Suggest a supermajority vote (e.g., requiring 90 percent approval for passage).
3. Ask members to withdraw controversial proposals, temper their concerns, or stand aside to allow the group to proceed without them.
4. Create a subgroup and empower it to make a decision.
5. Distill the concerns into major groups to pinpoint patterns of problems.
6. Expedite closing of discussion through use of a "go-round" (each member is given a time-limited chance to speak) or a "fishbowl" (representatives of major positions speak for all others on the issue).[24]

Facilitation Skills Group meetings don't always run smoothly by themselves; they require a unique and broad range of skills. **Facilitation** is the process of helping a group attain resounding success, maximize its efficient use of time, and feel satisfied with its efforts.[25] A facilitator is similar to a catalyst that stimulates a chemical reaction; the facilitator helps make something happen but does not necessarily have a preference for the specific path chosen.

Roles of facilitators

Effective facilitators encourage a group to separate idea-getting from idea-evaluation, generate multiple solutions to evaluate, avoid personal attacks, attain balanced contributions from its members, piggyback on others' ideas, and identify criteria for judging potential solutions. Facilitators ask penetrating questions, focus the group's efforts, monitor the use of time, record key conclusions, listen with their eyes and ears, and close the session on a positive note if possible. They also encourage a group to *process* its own success or failure. **Processing** involves setting aside several minutes at the end of a meeting to examine what went well, what went poorly, and how the group's behavior could be improved in future sessions. In this way, the group uses its own data to continually improve their decision-making skills.

Critical Thinking Exercise

Some managers place great emphasis on attaining consensus decisions. Question: What positive and negative results can you safely predict from doing that?

Weaknesses of Committees

> A distinguished executive was sitting at home one evening in 1927 as his wife was reading the newspaper account of Charles Lindbergh's historic solo transatlantic flight from New York to Paris. "Isn't it wonderful," she exclaimed, "and he did it all alone." Her husband's classic reply after a hard day at the office was, "Well, it would have been even more wonderful if he had done it with a committee!"

Because committees have weaknesses as well as strengths, some people have developed the attitude that meetings are unproductive and inevitably detract employees from "real work." It is true that *some* meetings are unproductive, but a single case does not prove the generality. Meetings are an essential and productive part of work organizations, and simply must be designed and used effectively. Part of our trouble is that we expect too much of them, and when they do not meet our expectations, we criticize instead of seek improvements.

Properly conducted meetings can contribute to organizational progress by providing participation, integrating interests, improving decision making, committing and motivating members to carry out a course of action, encouraging creative thinking, broadening perspectives, and changing attitudes. In addition, serving on some committees provides lower-level employees with the opportunity to demonstrate their capabilities to higher-level managers (via valuable face time). The fundamental decision that must be made with groups, therefore, is not whether to have them but *how to make the best use of them.* To use them, one must know their weaknesses, which fall into five major categories: slowness and expensiveness, groupthink, polarization, escalating commitment, and divided responsibility.

Slowness and Expensiveness As one manager observed, "Committees keep minutes and waste hours!" Meetings of all types are sometimes a slow and costly way to get things done. One study, for example, found that the typical committees were slowed down by spending 60 percent of their time with "input providers" and "advice providers," and not enough time with critical stakeholders (those persons who "needed to know" and those who actually held relevant power).[26] On occasion, however, delay is desirable. There is more time for thinking, for objective review of an idea, and for the suggestion of alternatives. But when quick decisive action is necessary, an individual approach is more effective. A manager, for example, does not call a committee meeting to respond to a customer's urgent request for assistance.

> Some organizations have taken direct action to ensure that meetings move rapidly. Examples of successful techniques used include holding "stand up" meetings (where all the chairs are removed from the meeting room), requiring all presenters and discussants to adhere to a rigid time schedule (e.g., 12 minutes for a major strategic proposal, including answering key criticisms of it), starting at odd times (e.g., 4:07) to help attendees remember to show up, setting upper limits on the length of the meeting (e.g., 42 minutes), excusing certain members as soon as their technical input or personal perspective has been obtained, and providing a visible chart showing the accumulating cost of the meeting (computed as minutes elapsed × average salary of participants × number of participants present). These approaches demonstrate that the cost of meetings can be controlled.[27]

Groupthink One of the most convincing criticisms of meetings is that they often lead to conformity and compromise. This tendency of a tightly knit group to bring individual thinking in line with the group's thinking is called **groupthink,** or the leveling effect.[28] It occurs when a group values solidarity so much it fails to critically evaluate its own decisions and assumptions. Pressures are brought to bear on individuals to adapt to the desires of other members. The ideas of dominant members—those who have authority,

The Need for Diversity in Groups

Nowhere is the need for diversity more apparent than in the composition of decision-making groups and task forces. Member *backgrounds* (e.g., age, gender, ethnicity) are becoming vitally important to consider so that product and service decisions can reflect market needs. In addition, member capacities to think differently and share alternative mindsets can be vitally important for the prevention of deadly diseases like groupthink. As a consequence, wise managers consciously recruit individuals who have previously demonstrated the capacity to look at problems from a variety of angles. In the short term, this approach can create conflict, tension, and even chaos; in the long term, *creating and using diversity is a healthy and constructive approach in group decision making.*

speak with confidence, or are more vocal in their arguments—are more likely to be accepted whether or not they have value. This tendency weakens the group product.

Symptoms of groupthink

Groupthink can be detected by watching for some of its classic symptoms, which include:

- Self-censorship of critical thoughts
- Rationalization that what they are doing is acceptable to others
- Illusion of invulnerability
- Reliance on self-appointed mind-guards
- Illusion of unanimity within the group without testing for it
- Stereotyping others outside the group
- Illusion of morality
- Pressure on dissidents to give in and conform to the group

Groupthink is probably present when a group acts as though it is above the law and cannot err, and when it assumes it has total support for its actions. The consequences of groupthink include a deterioration in a group's judgment, failure to engage in reality testing, and lowered quality of its decision making.

One effective method of reducing or preventing groupthink is to legitimize the role of a **devil's advocate** for each meeting. This person—a designated contrarian—is expected to question the ideas of others, probe for supporting facts, and challenge their logic. Devil's advocates are guardians of clear and moral thinking and can help the group immeasurably by providing it with a stream of constructive criticism. A broader approach—red teaming—is used by the C.I.A. **Red teaming** is a form of alternative analysis, in which a subset of a group challenges underlying assumptions, takes an adversary's viewpoint, and proposes different scenarios that have not been previously considered. The intended result is enhanced decision making and (hopefully) "no surprises" when a decision is implemented. Other methods used by organizations to prevent groupthink include rotating in new group members, inviting attendance by outsiders, and announcing a temporary delay before final decision making to give members one last chance to identify and voice their reservations.

Polarization In contrast to groupthink, an alternative behavior that sometimes appears is group **polarization.** Here, individuals bring to the group their strong predispositions, either positive or negative, toward the topic. As ideas are explored and logic is challenged, some members become defensive. Their attitudes become rigid and even more extreme if they are aggressively confronted. Although group members' attitudes can become polarized in either direction (risky or conservative), research suggests that *some groups tend*

Groups may take more risks

to make a **risky shift** *in their thinking.* This tendency means they are more willing to take chances with organizational resources as a group than they would if they were acting individually. Although risky decisions can have high payoffs, they also have the built-in potential for more disastrous consequences, as illustrated in this scenario:

> Picture a group of managers about to make a decision on expanding plant capacity despite the high cost of capital, intense competition, and an uncertain market. Two members who were mildly in favor of expansion before the meeting are surprised to hear a third argue persuasively for the decision. Another manager somewhat casually suggests that "five years from now the stockholders won't remember who made the decision, even if we're wrong." The fifth manager does not want to be known as a roadblock to progress and joins forces with the others to make it unanimous.

This meeting illustrates how the risky shift can quickly occur. While only one of the five members may really believe the decision is correct, the others allow themselves to be talked into it for a variety of reasons. Sometimes highly self-confident members can express themselves so persuasively that the rest accept their arguments without much debate. Other members feel that since they are not individually responsible for the decision, they can afford to take greater risks. The group must guard against these pitfalls.

Escalating Commitment Closely related to the problem of groupthink is the idea that *group members may persevere in advocating a course of action despite rational evidence that it will result in failure.* In fact, they may even allocate additional resources to the project, thereby **escalating commitment** despite overwhelming evidence that it will fail. Examples of persevering in a belief despite contrary evidence abound. U.S. automakers continued to make certain types of cars and trucks despite powerful consumer trends away from those types, pharmaceutical companies invested millions in the development of drugs that were not likely to receive federal approval, and communities spent heavily on tourist attractions in the face of evidence that they would never recoup their investments.

Decision makers escalate their commitment for many reasons. Sometimes they may unconsciously fall prey to selective perception and thus use a *confirmation bias* to actively search for and select only information that supports their arguments. Their ego needs also affect their decisions, since their desire to protect their self-esteem prevents them from admitting failure until the evidence is overwhelming. Having previously argued for an alternative in public makes it more difficult to demonstrate flexibility and reverse oneself (for fear of losing face). In many cultures, leaders who are risk takers and persist in the face of adversity are highly admired. All these forces suggest that members of groups need to be especially alert to the escalation phenomenon in themselves and others, and be willing to admit and accept their losses in some situations.

Divided Responsibility Management literature has always recognized that divided responsibility is a problem whenever group decisions are made. It often is said that actions that are several bodies' responsibility are nobody's responsibility. Group decisions undoubtedly do dilute and thin out responsibility. They also give individual members **(social loafers)** a chance to shirk responsibility, using justifications such as "Why should I bother with this problem? I didn't support it in the meeting."

Related Problems A number of other behavioral afflictions can undermine group success. Some of these to watch out for are:

- Linearity bias (the propensity to make overly simple cause-effect conclusions)
- Egocentrism (the temptation to overemphasize our own importance while forcing a decision)

Advice to Future Managers

1. *Create and distribute the agenda* and background materials for a meeting in advance. Clarify the objective (intended outcome or product) to all participants.
2. *Compose the group appropriately* according to both size and representativeness criteria; allow persons to come and go as they are needed in the meeting.
3. *Encourage the expression and consideration of minority viewpoints*; search for the underlying assumptions held and make these explicit.
4. *Separate the idea-generation stage of a meeting from the idea-evaluation stage*; control time spent on chitchat, tangents, and other topics.
5. *Carefully test for the degree of support* for a tentative decision about to be made.
6. *End the meeting on a positive note* regarding its success; commend individual contributors; and assign specific responsibilities for follow-up.
7. *Engage group members in an evaluation of their own success* during the meeting (what went well and what needs improvement in their own process); use these suggestions for improvement in the next meeting you conduct.
8. *Develop and apply group facilitation skills* to make meetings more productive and satisfying.
9. *Watch carefully for signs of groupthink, risky shifts, and escalating commitment* to prevent groups from falling prey to these traps.
10. *Search for evidence of an informal organization and build bridges to it* so that it complements the formal structure.

- Framing bias (the temptation to be overly influenced by how the problem was presented)
- Self-confidence bias (the premature belief that the best solution has already been uncovered)
- Anti-statistical bias (the reluctance to examine relevant statistical information and give weight to it).[29]

Overcoming the Weaknesses Many of the disadvantages of group meetings can be overcome readily. The preceding discussions suggest that the proper group structures must be selected, that group size is an important factor, and that various leadership roles must be played. The "Advice to Future Managers" section presents a set of additional guidelines for ensuring effective group meetings.

Summary

Group dynamics is the process by which people interact face-to-face in small groups. Such groups may be informal or formal, and formal groups may be temporary or permanent.

The complex system of social relationships in an organization consists of many small, informal groups. These groups, which arise naturally from the interaction of people, are referred to collectively as the informal organization. Informal organizations have major benefits, but they also lead to problems that management cannot easily ignore. Informal organizations are characterized by a status system that produces informal leaders. Informal group norms have a powerful influence on member behavior

Formal groups, which are established by the organization, include committees, task forces, and other decision-making groups. Formal group meetings are a widely used form of group activity; they can create quality decisions that are supported by the participants.

Four our structured approaches commonly used in group problem solving are brainstorming, nominal groups, the Delphi technique, dialectic inquiry, and group decision support systems. Consensus is a valid goal to seek, but it must be carefully defined and is aided by effective facilitation skills. Weaknesses of groups fall into five categories: slowness and expensiveness, groupthink, polarization, escalating commitment, and divided responsibility.

Speaking OB: Terms and Concepts for Review

Brainstorming, *330*
Cohesiveness, *321*
Committee, *325*
Conformity, *334*
Consensus, *335*
Crowdsourcing, *333*
Deferred judgment, *330*
Delphi decision groups, *332*
Devil's advocate, *337*
Dialectic decision method (DDM), *332*
Electronic brainstorming, *331*
Escalating commitment, *338*
Facilitation, *335*
Formal groups, *317*
Group dynamics, *316*
Groupthink, *336*
Hidden agendas, *327*
Informal groups, *317*
Informal leader, *318*
Informal organization, *317*
Network charts, *323*
Nominal group, *331*
Norms, *319*
Polarization, *337*
Processing, *335*
Red teaming, *337*
Reference group, *323*
Risky shift, *338*
Social facilitation, *334*
Social leader, *327*
Social loafers, 338
Social norms, *322*
Surface agenda, *327*
Task leader, *327*

Discussion Questions

1. Think of a part-time or full-time job you now hold or formerly held. Identify the informal organization that is (was) affecting your job or work group, and its effects. Discuss how the informal leaders probably rose to their positions and how they operate.
2. Have you ever been in a situation where informal group norms put you in role conflict with formal organization standards? Discuss.
3. Discuss some of the benefits and problems that informal organizations may bring to both a work group and an employer.
4. Think of a small work group you belonged to recently. Assess the level of its cohesiveness. What factors contributed to, or prevented, its cohesiveness?
5. Thinking of that small group, explain in what ways the members' actions, interactions, and sentiments were different in practice from what they were supposed to be when the group was formed.
6. Identify five specific things you will do to create an effective committee the next time you are a leader or member of one.
7. Divide a sheet of notebook paper into five columns. In the first column, under the heading "Strengths," list all the strengths that any of the types of group structures might have (e.g., "generates many solutions"). Write the four types of structured approaches as headings for the remaining columns. Indicate, by placing a check in the appropriate column(s), which approaches might have each of the strengths you listed. (Notice that, in essence, you are preparing your own contingency model.)
8. What does *consensus* mean to you, from your experience? Has your understanding of it changed since reading this chapter? What other interpretations do you think the term has for other people?
9. The chapter mentions five major weaknesses of decision-making groups. Prepare a counterargument that powerfully describes some of the benefits of using groups.
10. A manager complained recently that "meetings are not as much fun anymore since we started using structured approaches to group problem solving." Explain why this might be so. In addition to "fun," what criteria should the manager be using to judge group success?

Assess Your Own Skills

How well do you exhibit good group leadership skills?

Read the following statements carefully. Circle the number on the response scale that most closely reflects the degree to which each statement accurately describes you when you have tried to lead a group or committee. Add up your total points and prepare a brief action plan for self-improvement. Be ready to report your score for tabulation across the entire group.

	Good description									Poor description
1. I am fully aware of the existence of the informal organization.	10	9	8	7	6	5	4	3	2	1
2. I actively seek to identify and utilize informal leaders to help accomplish my objectives.	10	9	8	7	6	5	4	3	2	1
3. I can readily list a half-dozen benefits of, and problems with, the informal organization.	10	9	8	7	6	5	4	3	2	1
4. I can use network charts to diagram an actual informal organization.	10	9	8	7	6	5	4	3	2	1
5. I understand why many people have negative attitudes toward committee meetings.	10	9	8	7	6	5	4	3	2	1
6. I can comfortably play both task and social leadership roles within a group.	10	9	8	7	6	5	4	3	2	1
7. I carefully monitor the interaction patterns within a committee meeting and take action to encourage a balance.	10	9	8	7	6	5	4	3	2	1
8. I have successfully used one of the structured approaches to group decision making.	10	9	8	7	6	5	4	3	2	1
9. I have a clear idea of what "consensus" means, and I communicate that to any group meeting I run.	10	9	8	7	6	5	4	3	2	1
10. I feel comfortable playing the role of devil's advocate in a group meeting.	10	9	8	7	6	5	4	3	2	1

Scoring and Interpretation

Add up your total points for the 10 questions. Record that number here, and report it when it is requested. Finally, insert your total score into the "Assess and Improve Your Own Organizational Behavior Skills" chart in Appendix A.

- If you scored between 81 and 100 points, you appear to have a solid capability for demonstrating good group leadership skills.
- If you scored between 61 and 80 points, you should take a close look at the items with lower self-assessment scores and explore ways to improve those items.

- If you scored under 60 points, you should be aware that a weaker skill level regarding several items could be detrimental to your future success as a motivator. We encourage you to review relevant sections of the chapter and watch for related material in subsequent chapters and other sources.

Identify your three lowest scores, and write the question numbers here: _____, _____, _____. Write a brief paragraph, detailing to yourself an action plan for how you might sharpen each of these skills.

Incident

The Excelsior Department Store

The Excelsior Department Store had a large department that employed six salesclerks. Most of these clerks were loyal and faithful employees who had worked in the department store more than 10 years. They formed a closely knit social group.

The store embarked on an expansion program requiring four new clerks to be hired in the department within six months. These newcomers soon learned that the old-timers took the desirable times for coffee breaks, leaving the most undesirable periods for newcomers. The old-time clerks also received priority from the old-time cashier, which required the newcomers to wait in line at the cash register until the old-timers had their sales recorded. A number of customers complained to store management about this practice.

In addition, the old-timers frequently instructed newcomers to straighten merchandise in the stockroom and to clean displays on the sales floor, although this work was just as much a responsibility of the old-timers. The result was that old-timers had more time to make sales and newcomers had less time. Since commissions were paid on sales, the newcomers complained to the department manager about this practice.

Questions

1. How is the informal organization involved in this case? Discuss.
2. As a manager of the department, what would you do about each of the practices? Discuss.

Experiential Exercise

Choosing Your Leader

1. Divide the class into groups of five to seven people. For the first 10 minutes, have members introduce themselves by sharing not only their names but also other significant information (e.g., major accomplishments or future aspirations).
2. Now ask each group member to take out a piece of paper and write the name of the person who the member thinks would make the best leader of the small group. Afterward, ask the members to collectively brainstorm, while recording the items on a sheet of paper, all the factors they used to select a leader (i.e., what characteristics were important to them?). Have them give all the slips to one person, who should tabulate the votes for the leader. Have the new leader facilitate a discussion of the characteristics used to select him or her. Ask the groups to briefly discuss the validity of the selection process.
3. Direct the groups to reflect on the discussion experience. Have them identify who the task and social leaders were, what the hidden agendas were, and who played the most assertive roles. How would they change their behavior if they were to do the exercise again?

Experiential Exercise

Examining Social Networks

Directions: Take out a blank sheet of paper. Study the list of class member names. Then, answer these questions:

1. If you had the opportunity to spend a truly enjoyable fun-filled two-day recreational weekend with some of the class members, which three persons would you *most* likely want to spend it with?
2. If you had the opportunity to name the three persons from this class who you think would *most likely* make really substantial *task contributions* to a concentrated work project lasting 6 months, who would they be?
3. How many of the class members do you predict will have named YOU today as one of the persons with whom they would truly enjoy spending a fun-filled two-day recreational weekend? _____
4. How many of the class members do you predict will have named YOU today as one of the persons whom they believe is most likely to make really substantial *task contributions* to a concentrated work project lasting 6–12 months? _____

Turn the sheets in to the instructor, who will tabulate the results and report them back to the class. When you see the data, discuss what characteristics or clues appear to have resulted in the distribution of nominations that you see there. What does this tell you about the informal organization in the class?

Generating OB Insights

An *insight* is a new and clear perception of a phenomenon, or an acquired ability to "see" clearly something you were unaware of previously. It is sometimes simply referred to as an "ah-ha! moment," in which you have a minirevelation or reach a straightforward conclusion about a topic or issue.

Insights need not necessarily be dramatic, for what is an insight to one person may be less important to another. The critical feature of insights is that they are relevant and memorable for *you;* they should represent new knowledge, new frameworks, or new ways of viewing things that you want to retain and remember over time.

Insights, then, are different from the information that you find in the "Advice for Future Managers" boxes within the text. That advice is prescriptive and action-oriented; it indicates a recommended course of action.

A useful way to think of OB insights is to assume you are the only person who has read Chapter 12. You have been given the assignment to highlight, in your own words, the major concepts (not just summarize the whole chapter) that might stand out for a naive audience who has never heard of the topic before. *What 10 insights would you share with them?*

(Example) *The behavior of two or more group members cannot be understood without also examining the relationships between them.*

1. ______________________________

____

2. ______________________________

____

3. ______________________________

____

4. ______________________________

____

5. ____

6. ____

7. ____

8. ____

9. ____

10. ____

Nurturing Your Critical Thinking and Reflective Skills

Take a few minutes to review the discussion in the Roadmap for Readers of critical thinking and reflection. Remind yourself that if you can hone these abilities now, you will have a substantial competitive advantage when you apply for jobs and are asked what unique skills you can bring to the position and the organization.

Critical Thinking

Think back on the material you read in this chapter. What are three unique and challenging critical questions you would like to raise about this material? (These might identify something controversial about which you have doubts, they may imply that you suspect a theory or model has weaknesses, they could examine the legitimacy of apparent causal relationships, or they might assess the probable value of a suggested practice.) Be prepared to share these questions with class members or your instructor.

1. ____

2. ____

3. ____

Reflection

This process often involves answering the parallel questions of "What do you *think* about the material you have read?" and "How do you *feel* about that material?" Therefore, express your *personal thoughts and feelings* (reactions) to any of the ideas or topics found in this chapter, and be prepared to share these reflections with class members or your instructor.

1. ____

2. ____

3. ____

Chapter Thirteen

Teams and Team Building

Teams matter—greatly. There's enormous leverage to be had when we get our team stuff right.

Rich Karlgaard[1]

We identified "observable candor" as the behavior that best predicts high-performing teams.

Keith Ferrazzi[2]

CHAPTER OBJECTIVES

AFTER READING THIS CHAPTER, YOU SHOULD UNDERSTAND

13–1 Organizational Context for Teams
13–2 The Nature of Teams
13–3 Life Cycle of a Team
13–4 Teamwork and the Characteristics of Mature Teams
13–5 Process Consultation and Team-Building Skills
13–6 Self-Managing Teams

Facebook Page 

Student A: We're studying teams this week.

Student B: I know all about that. I was a star basketball player in high school. I could do everything—dribble, pass, screen, shoot, rebound, and defend. You should have seen me! The other players were really good, too.

Student C: How did that work out for you? Plug me in.

Student B: Not very well, actually. We just didn't seem to "click" as a team, and consequently our record was disappointingly mediocre. I can't explain it.

Student A: I can offer one possible explanation—maybe *you* were part of the problem. You see, just putting together a bunch of highly skilled "all stars" doesn't guarantee team success or collaboration among them.

Student B: OK, but what else should we have done?

Student A: Lots of things. You needed an overriding goal, a cooperative norm, lots of trust, the ability to have disagreements and resolve them, candid communication, and team rewards. You also need a good team coach, who can help you move through the development stages of team development (forming, storming, norming, and performing). It also helps to have someone act as a facilitator—a person who acts as an observer and mirror to the team—helping members build a collaborative community whose members can confront and resolve their own problems.

Student B: Sounds like a tall order. No wonder we didn't have a successful basketball team!

On a recent spring day, the author played a round of golf with three acquaintances. We were pitted against four other groups in a "scramble" format, where we each hit our own ball and then played our own ball again from the best position of the four shots. During the round, we each hit some terrible shots, some decent shots, and (occasionally) some pretty good shots that collectively allowed us to laugh at ourselves and praise each other. We offered advice to each other (and used it), as well as made joint decisions about which ball position provided the best opportunity for the next shot. At the conclusion of the round, we tallied our score and found, to our delight, that we were two shots under par. This team-oriented format had allowed each of us to share in posting a score that was about one stroke better *per hole* than we normally played as individuals! By drawing on the best contribution that each of us had to offer and carefully orchestrating our efforts, we not only scored well but had a relaxed and enjoyable time together.

Organizations are the grand strategies created to bring order out of chaos when people work together. Organizations provide the skeletal structure that helps create predictable relationships among people, technology, jobs, and resources. Wherever people join in a common effort (such as the golf group described in the previous paragraph), organization must be used to get productive results.

In this chapter, we briefly review the key elements of classical organization design as they relate to organizational behavior. In particular, we show why many organizations have turned to various emphases on teams to overcome previous problems, provide employee need-satisfaction, and release the performance potential within groups. The need for careful development of teams is stressed, and a unique structure—self-managing teams—is explored. Virtual teams are then introduced.

Engaging Your Brain

1. Chapter 12 was devoted to groups and committees, whereas Chapter 13 focuses on teams. What do you think is the difference between the two? What principles and guidelines that you learned in Chapter 12 are relevant to building successful teams?
2. Have you ever seen, or experienced, team members who did not pull their own weight in achieving the group's goal? How did you *feel* about that? What did you *do* about it?
3. Assume that you are forming a work team today that has five other members, and you have been appointed their team leader. Identify five immediate rules or guidelines that you would want to share with them to get them up to speed immediately.

ORGANIZATIONAL CONTEXT FOR TEAMS

Classical Concepts

Classical organization theory is the process of starting with the total amount of work to be done and dividing it into divisions, departments, work clusters, jobs, and assignments of responsibilities to people. Efficiency and integration of efforts are achieved by means of **division of work**—creating levels of authority and functional units—and **delegation**—assigning duties, authority, and responsibility to others. The result is an operating hierarchy consisting of multiple levels of authority.

Classic organizational structures are essentially *mechanistic* in their attempts to get people to act as efficiently and predictably as machines. People are specialized into many activities that are directed by layers of supervision. Each higher level has more power and influence until the top is reached, where central direction of the whole organization takes place. Work is carefully scheduled, tasks are specified, roles are defined strictly, and most formal communication flows along the lines of hierarchy. The whole structure is organized like a well-designed machine and incorporates many of the characteristics of a bureaucracy.

Classical organization design has its strengths as well as its weaknesses. For example, organizational structure can support people as well as suppress them. Classical structure provides much task support, such as specialized assistance, appropriate resources to perform the job, security, and fairly dependable conditions of work. On the other hand, although classical structure is strong in task support, *it is weak in psychological support*. What is needed is an organizational system that provides both task support and psychological support.

Decline in use of structure

New viewpoints have led to a decline in the use of structure and authority in modern organizations. Many organizations have reduced the number of levels in their hierarchy through downsizing and the elimination of some middle-management positions. Others have attempted to eliminate the rigid barriers between functional units (known as "silos") by focusing on the creation of "boundaryless" organizations without artificial internal walls. The modern approach is to be more flexible with organizational systems, changing them rapidly according to the needs of their environment. One reason is changing social values, but it also is evident that horizontal relations between chains of command are more important for effectiveness than was formerly realized. Supervisory influence with peers, service people, suppliers, customers, and other chains of command is becoming more significant. The pace and complexity of work today make horizontal communication and flexible structures more necessary.

Organic characteristics

Modern organizations are more flexible, organic, and open. Tasks and roles are less rigidly defined, allowing people to adjust them to situational requirements. Communication is more multidirectional. It consists more of information and advice and joint problem solving rather than instructions and decisions. Authority and influence flow more directly from the person who has the ability to handle the problem at hand. Decision making is more decentralized, being shared by several levels and different functions. The organization also is more open to its environment.

These *organic* forms are often more effective in situations typical in the twenty-first century. Organic forms work better if the environment is dynamic, requiring frequent changes within the organization. They also work better when the tasks are not defined well enough to become routine (e.g., software development). Because many younger employees (millennials) desire autonomy, openness, variety, change, and opportunities to try new approaches, an organic form is often a better match for them. *Teams are more likely to be used within an organic form of organization,* because they provide the flexibility that modern organizations require.

Matrix Organization

One development to meet changing organizational needs is **matrix organization.** It is an overlay of one type of organization on another so that two chains of command are directing individual employees. It is used especially for large specialized projects that temporarily require large numbers of technical people with different skills to work in project teams. A simple example of matrix organization is an annual United Way fund drive for contributions to community charities. It could be handled through the traditional hierarchy, but often it is assigned to a temporary hierarchy of employees as a part-time duty. They carry the assignment to completion and then the team is disbanded.

The effect of matrix structure is to separate some of the organization's activities into projects that then compete for allocations of people and resources. The traditional hierarchy provides the regular work group "home" for an employee, but project groups are established temporarily for up to several years, as in Boeing's development of the 787 aircraft or Accenture's assignment of specialists from across the globe to consulting projects. Employees are assigned to a project team for its limited life or as long as their specialty is needed on the project. (However, this produces a potential problem, as these employees now report to two or more supervisors simultaneously.) As one assignment is completed, employees move back to permanent assignments in traditional departments, or they are assigned to other projects. In fact, an employee can be assigned part-time to two or more project teams at the same time.

In spite of its complexity, matrix organization is used for a number of reasons. Its teams focus on a single project, permitting better planning and control to meet budgets and deadlines. Especially on repetitive projects, the members gain valuable experience and the team develops a strong identity. Since the structure is more open and flexible (organic) than a traditional hierarchy, it can better handle the changes that occur in complex projects. Its distribution of authority and status also is better aligned with employee desires for increased autonomy.

The matrix organizational process, when applied on a large scale across internal organizational boundaries, creates **cross-functional teams.** These are teams that

Critical Thinking Exercise

Many organizations now rely heavily on various forms of teams. Question: What positive and negative results can you safely predict for them?

draw their members from more than one specialty area and often several. By their very nature, they contain a high element of diversity, at least in terms of professional backgrounds and work specializations. Cross-functional groups, while sometimes quickly constructed, pose special problems in the process of becoming true teams. Therefore, the remainder of this chapter is devoted to reviewing some key information regarding team formation and life cycles, team problems and needed ingredients, team building, and team operation.

TEAMWORK

Individual employees perform operating tasks, but the vast majority of them work in regular small groups where their efforts must fit together like the pieces of a picture puzzle. Where their work is interdependent, they act as a task team and seek to develop a cooperative state called teamwork. A **task team** is a cooperative small group in regular contact that is engaged in coordinated action. The frequency of team members' interaction and the team's ongoing existence make a task team clearly different from either a short-term decision-making group (committee) or a project team in a matrix structure.

Several additional ways in which teams differ from ordinary groups or committees are portrayed in Figure 13.1. In particular, many teams monitor their own work, are given training in mutual problem-solving methods, share leadership responsibilities internally, accept and even encourage constructive conflict, and are measured on the basis of their collective (not individual) outputs. However, just *calling* a group a team does not change its basic character or effectiveness; months or even years may be needed for a team to achieve high-performance status.

Contributors to teamwork

When the members of a task team know their objectives, contribute responsibly and enthusiastically to the task, and support one another, they are exhibiting **teamwork.** New teams typically progress through a series of developmental stages, which are described in the following section.

Later in the chapter, we will alert you to potential problems in teams, followed by a portrayal of the ingredients necessary to the development of teamwork.

Life Cycle of a Team

What happens at each stage of a team's development?

When a number of individuals begin to work at interdependent jobs or on a special project, they often pass through several stages as they learn to work together as a team (see Figure 13.2).[3] These **stages of team development** are not rigidly followed, but they do represent a broad pattern that may be observed and predicted in many settings across

FIGURE 13.1
Some Key Differences between Groups and Teams

Dimension for Comparison	Group	Team
Work products	Individual	Collective
Performance monitoring source	External	Internal
Focus of activity	Efficient task performance	Problem solving
Leadership	Single	Shared
View of conflict	Dysfunctional and discouraged	Functional and encouraged

FIGURE 13.2 Life Cycle of a Team and Associated Questions and Issues Faced at Each Stage

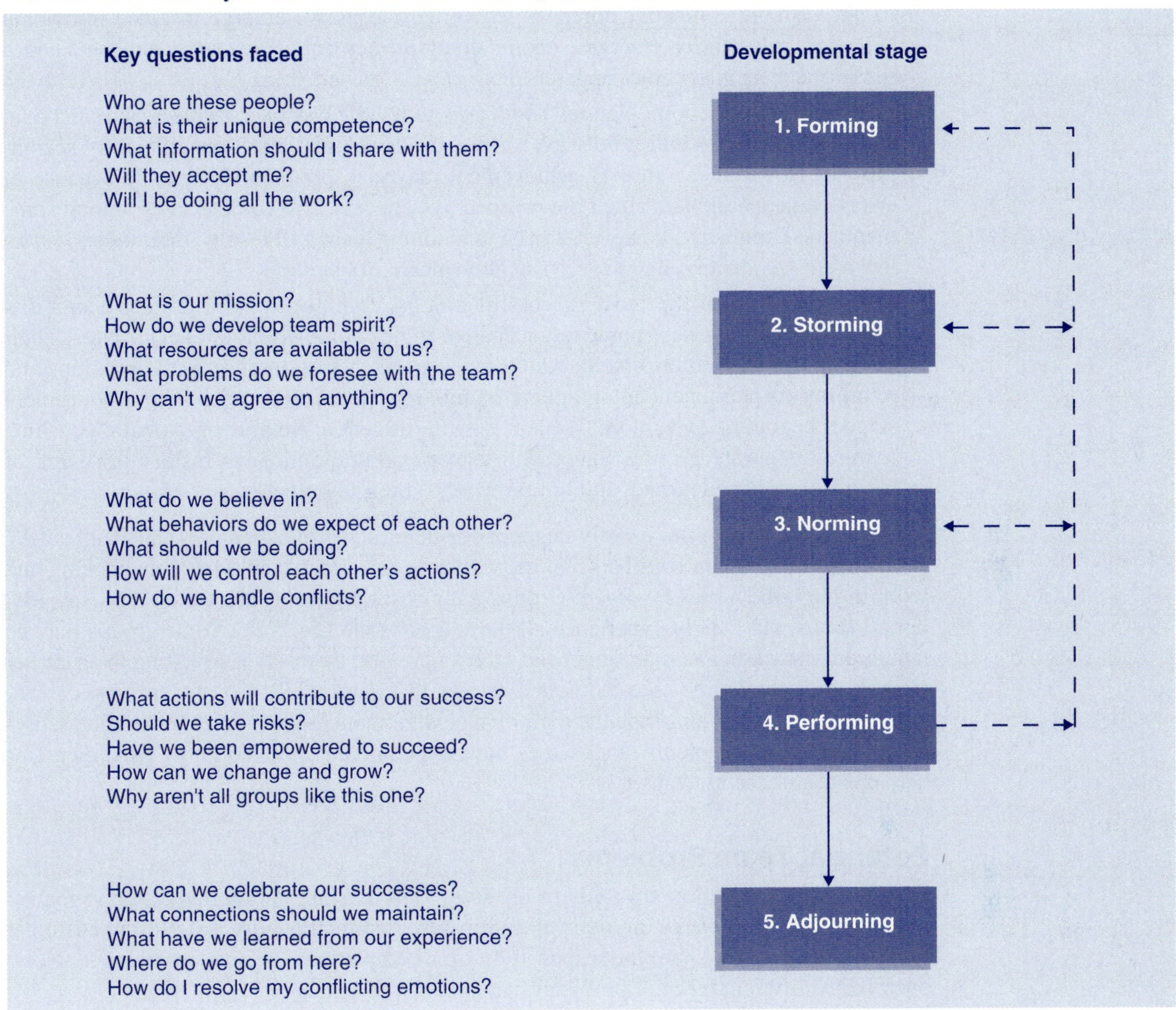

the team's time together. The stages are the result of a variety of questions and issues that the team predictably faces, such as those shown in Figure 13.2. In addition, members want to know which rules to follow and what each person should contribute. The typical stages in a team's evolution can be described as follows:

- *Forming*—Members share and exchange basic personal information, start to get to know and accept one another, ask questions about their assignment and objectives, and begin turning their attention toward the group's tasks. An aura of courtesy prevails, uncertainty is in the air, and interactions are often cautious.
- *Storming*—Members compete for status, jockey for positions of relative control, and argue about appropriate directions for the group. External pressures interfere with the group, and tensions rise between individuals as they assert themselves and disagree about initial actions. If these stresses are not confronted, hard feelings may emerge and slow the group's progress.

- *Norming*—The group begins moving together in a cooperative fashion, and a tentative balance among competing forces is struck. Group norms emerge to guide individual behavior, role clarity emerges, cooperative feelings are increasingly evident, and a sense of cohesion becomes apparent.
- *Performing*—The group matures and learns to handle complex challenges. Functional roles are performed and fluidly exchanged as needed, and tasks are efficiently accomplished. However, a sense of achievement may also prematurely emerge because of errors made, pessimism about the prospects of success, and complacency among some members. Eventually, however, a fully functioning team will resolve their issues, establish a unique identity, and develop an atmosphere of openness.
- *Adjourning*—Even the most successful groups, committees, and project teams disband (or acquire a new purpose, or change their composition) sooner or later. Their breakup is called adjournment, which requires dissolving intense social relations and returning to permanent assignments or moving on to other jobs. The adjournment stage is becoming even more frequent with the advent of flexible organizations, which feature temporary groups. Successful teams examine their own history in search of lessons they have learned, and bid farewell to their teammates.

Advising new teams of these likely stages can be helpful to group members and their leaders. Awareness by all team members can help them better understand what is happening and work through the issues involved. Groups are always different, of course; consequently, not all teams will clearly experience all the stages of the life cycle. Some groups may be temporarily stuck in a certain stage, and others may find themselves reverting to an earlier stage from time to time (see the dotted arrows in Figure 13.2). To prevent unnecessary trials and tribulations and expedite their own development, team members may find it useful to study what problems other teams have encountered and also know what elements help create successful teams.

Potential Team Problems

Effective teams in action are a joy to observe. Members are committed to the organization's success, they share common values regarding product quality, safety, and customer satisfaction, and they share the responsibility for completing a project on schedule. However, many different types of problems can arise within groups.

> One study examined the experiences of 245 team developers.[4] The respondents reported experiencing problems with goal clarity, communications, role issues, problem solving and decision making, conflict management, and numerous other issues. They had dealt with an average of 9 out of the 11 possible problems presented, indicating how pervasive the issues are.

Two particularly troublesome team problems involve changing team membership and social loafing.

Changing Composition Being complex and dynamic, teamwork is sensitive to all aspects of organizational environment. Like the mighty oak, teamwork grows slowly, but on occasion it declines quickly, like that same oak crashing to the forest floor during a windstorm. For example, too many membership changes and personnel transfers interfere with group relationships and prevent the growth of teamwork.

> An international company built a new plant in a community of about a half-million people where it already had three operating plants doing related work. The new

> plant was staffed for the most part by new hires, and within a short time excellent teamwork and productivity developed.
>
> In about three years there was a moderate layoff affecting all four plants. Since layoff was according to seniority among the four plants and since employees in the new plant had least seniority, people from the other plants forced new-plant employees into layoff. As a result, most teams in the newest plant received three to five transferees from other plants (about 25 to 50 percent of the team). Though these transfers-in were more experienced and had good records, teamwork was disrupted and deteriorated quickly. Visits for first aid tripled, accidents increased slightly, and production declined 30 to 50 percent. Nearly one year of effort and emotional strain was required to get the plant back on its feet. (This is a vivid illustration of the sometimes-hidden or unanticipated costs of layoffs.)

Rarely does a team's composition remain constant from the beginning to the end of its task life. Members may be drafted onto higher-priority projects, they may experience a personal crisis and take a family medical leave, or they may be lured away to another company by better working conditions and rewards. And some teams—most notably those in the collegiate sports domain—automatically experience personnel changes as players depart for the professional arena or find other priorities in their lives. As a consequence, *most teams must learn to manage their internal turnover.*

They do this by engaging in three important types of action:

1. The first key is to anticipate and accept that turnover within the team will happen and come to grips with that likelihood (even holding "celebrations" of member departures).
2. The second is to develop a plan for managing team turnover right from the start. How much notice do they expect to receive? What steps must they engage in to obtain authorization to find new members? How will they recruit new additions?
3. The third, and possibly most critical, strategy is to think through how best to integrate new members. How can they be made to feel immediately welcome? What background materials and training (orientation and skills) do they need to receive? How long will they need to get up to speed? How can they be helped to see the big picture, as well as understand how each member fits into it? How will they be exposed to the team's values, norms, and objectives? In essence, a highly functioning team (functioning at the fourth stage as shown in Figure 13.2) needs to recognize a new member as an opportunity for its improvement (not a threat to its cohesiveness) and return at least briefly to earlier stages of the team development process.

Social Loafing Other potential problems also exist. The departure from classical lines of authority may be difficult for some employees to handle responsibly. The extensive participation in decision making consumes large amounts of time. Experimentation with team activities may lead to charges of partiality from other employees. Also, the combination of individual efforts may not result in improved overall performance. For example, when some employees think their contributions to a group cannot be measured, they may lessen their output and engage in **social loafing** (the free-rider effect). Causes of social loafing include a perception of unfair division of labor, a low achievement motivation, a belief that co-workers are lazy, a perception of a meaningless or largely "invisible" task, or a feeling of being able to hide in a crowd and therefore not be able to be singled out for blame. Social loafing may also arise if a member believes others intend to withhold their efforts and thus he or she would be foolish not to do the same—the **sucker effect.**[5]

Social loafing

The impact of social loafing extends beyond simply the heavier workload on responsible team members. Colleagues may experience anger toward the low performer, feel moments of empathy, or complain to their peers or to their supervisor. More constructively, co-workers may express expectations for improvement to the loafer, attempt to train the individual, or offer pep talks.[6]

Since an improperly managed team can result in numerous problems, an effective manager needs to apply a contingency framework to determine whether to use a team approach. It is wise to analyze the nature of the task, the qualifications and desires of the participants, and the time and cost constraints. Many managers have found managing teams to be a whole new set of challenges after years of one-on-one supervision.

Trust among team members is essential to their success

Lack of Trust Five major impediments to the creation of cohesive teams have been identified by one consultant.[7] These dysfunctions include inattentiveness to team results, failure to hold individuals accountable to their goals, a lack of commitment to group effort, reluctance to engage in debate and conflict, and an absence of trust. Without *trust*—confidence in the integrity, ability, and truthfulness of others—team members will feel insecure, stressed, and reserved. At the same time, the organization will suffer through slower decision making, low morale, and damaged customer relations. Trust can be slowly built, however, by demonstrating good intentions, lowering protective barriers, honoring agreements, and being open and vulnerable to each other.

Other Problems Unfortunately, numerous other mannerisms, personality quirks, and behaviors may be exhibited in team settings that often detract from performance and cohesiveness. Distractions may include splitting hairs, non-stop talking, side conversations, put-downs, uncontrolled anger, interrupting, and even doodling during discussions. More substantial dysfunctional role behaviors (e.g., blockers, aggressors, distractors) were discussed in Chapter 12.[8]

Ingredients of Effective Teams

Many studies have been conducted in an attempt to isolate the factors that contribute most directly to team success (see, for example, "What Managers Are Reading"). Common items identified include careful composition, information sharing, clear direction and measurable goals for accountability, sufficient resources, integration and coordination, flexibility and innovativeness, and the stimulation of openness to learning.[9] The discussion will focus on four major factors here—a supportive environment, appropriate skills and role clarity, superordinate goals, and team rewards.

Supportive Environment Teamwork is most likely to develop when management builds a supportive environment for it. Creating such an environment involves encouraging members to think like a team, developing member tolerance for ambiguity and uncertainty, providing adequate time for meetings, setting up physical spaces conducive to creative interaction (sometimes called "playgrounds"), and demonstrating faith in members' capacity to achieve. Supportive measures such as these help the group take the necessary first steps toward teamwork. Since these steps contribute to further cooperation, trust, and compatibility, supervisors need to develop an organizational culture that builds these conditions.

Skills and Role Clarity Team members must be reasonably *qualified* to perform their jobs, as well as have the *desire to cooperate*. Beyond these requirements, members can work together as a team only after all the members of the group *know the roles of all the others* with whom they will be interacting. When this understanding exists, members can act immediately as a team on the basis of the requirements of that situation, without waiting for someone to give an order. In other words, team members respond voluntarily to the demands of the job and take appropriate actions to accomplish team goals.

FIGURE 13.3
Teamwork Depends on the Performance of Every Member

My supervisxr txld me that teamwxrk depends xn the perfxrmance xf every single persxn xn the team. I ignxred that idea until my supervisxr shxwed me hxw my cxmputer keybx-ard perfxrms when just xne single key is xut xf xrder. All the xther keys xn my keybxard wxrk just fine except xne, but that xne destrxys the effectiveness xf the whxle keybxard. Nxw I knxw that *even thxugh I am xnly xne persxn, I am needed if the team is tx wxrk as a successful team shxuld.*

An example is a hospital surgical team whose members all respond to a crisis during an operation. Their mutual recognition of the emergency alerts them to the need for simultaneous action and coordinated response. Each knows what the others can do, and trusts them to perform capably. The result is a highly efficient level of cooperation characteristic of a team.

If one member of a surgical team fails to perform in the right way at the right time, a person's life may be endangered. In more ordinary work situations, a life may not be threatened, but product quality or customer service may suffer by the failure of just one member. All the members are needed for effective teamwork. This interdependence is illustrated in Figure 13.3, which shows the value of each member, such as the "O" on the keyboard.

All members must contribute

Superordinate Goals A major responsibility of managers is to try to keep the team members oriented toward their overall task. Sometimes, unfortunately, an organization's policies, record-keeping requirements, and reward systems may fragment individual efforts and discourage teamwork. A district supervisor for a petroleum company tells the following story of the effect on sales representatives of below-quota reports:

> As in many businesses, each month we are expected to make our sales quota. Sales representatives are expected to make quotas in their individual territories in the same way that the Eastern district as a whole is expected to make its quota. Many times in the past, the district has failed to make its quota in certain products—for instance, motor oil. It is a known practice for some of the sales representatives in the field to delay a delivery in their territories until the next month if they already have their quotas made.
>
> The focus of the sales representatives is on their own quotas, not on the district quota. Any sales representative who is below quota in a product for a month must report the reason for the variance. A sales representative who makes a large sale of several hundred gallons of motor oil to a customer knows that in the next month or two that customer may not buy any oil, causing the representative to be below quota that month and to have to file a report.

The supervisor in the case just described might consider the creation of a **superordinate goal,** which is a higher goal that integrates the efforts of two or more persons. Superordinate goals can be attained only if all parties carry their weight. Such goals serve to focus attention, unify efforts, and stimulate more cohesiveness within teams. For example, in a hospital meeting the leader said, "We are here to help the patient. Can we think of today's problem in those terms?" When the superordinate goal was recognized, several minor internal conflicts were resolved.

Superordinate goals are an example of a **shared mental model** in teamwork. It is important that teams have a common understanding of the *nature* of their task (and expected outcomes) as well as what it will take to *accomplish* that task. This requires a strong ethic of collaboration, empathy, solidarity, and candid communication, as well as an explicit or implicit "helping" norm among the members. When problems arise in fulfilling the team's mental model, harsh negative feedback can be replaced by caring criticism, softened by the use of phrases such as "You might try...," "I would suggest...," or "Think about doing this...." These prefatory remarks make the feedback more palatable to the recipient.[10]

Trust The lack of trust as a team problem was discussed previously. The presence of trust is essential to most effective teams, and it begins with a group's manager demonstrating honesty, integrity, openness, and willingness to let team members exert their influence. Fortunately, trust can be built by giving frequent praise, keeping promises, showing concern, respecting others, behaving dependably, and sharing information on a timely basis.

Team Rewards Another element that can stimulate teamwork is the presence of team rewards. These may be financial, or they may be in the form of recognition. Rewards are most powerful if they are *valued* by the team members, perceived as *possible* to earn, and administered *contingent on the group's task performance*. In addition, organizations need to achieve a careful balance between encouraging and rewarding individual initiative and growth and stimulating full contributions to team success. Innovative (nonfinancial) team rewards for responsible behavior may include the authority to select new members of the group, make recommendations regarding a new supervisor, or propose discipline for team members.

Empowerment The previous discussion focused on five structural ingredients for effective teams. Member motivation, however, plays a powerful role in team success, just as it does in athletic teams playing baseball, basketball, or football. Team members will likely feel more motivated and empowered when they:

- Share a sense of *potency* (have a can-do attitude)
- Experience *meaningfulness* (have a commitment to a worthwhile purpose)
- Are given *autonomy* (have freedom and discretion to control resources and make decisions)
- See their *impact* on results (can assess, monitor, and celebrate their contributions and results)

The interactive combination of these four forces can produce dynamic teams capable of being productive and proactive as well as providing outstanding customer service.[11]

Positive Norms Teams are strongest when they consciously examine their own behaviors and agree on their own internal requirements for their actions. Chapter 11 introduced a variety of functional interpersonal behaviors, such as active listening, frankness, confrontation, and confidentiality. Highly effective teams also examine their own processes, and agree to faithfully attend meetings, share responsibility for mutual outcomes, think before speaking, and focus on issues and problems instead of personalities. A powerful norm is to allow and encourage **dissent,** whereby team members find it acceptable to "agree to disagree." Dissent can stimulate a more intense discussion, and this can be formalized through the use of a rotated assignment as *devil's advocate* (discussed in Chapter 12).[12]

TEAM BUILDING

Team members must work together to be effective; likewise, cooperation is needed among all the teams that make up the whole organization. Higher-level managers need to integrate all these groups into one collaborative group. To do this, managers often rely heavily on team building for both individual teams and large groups. **Team building** encourages team members to examine how they work together, identify their weaknesses, and develop more effective ways of cooperating. The goal is to make the team more effective.

Team coaching is vital to team success—especially for new teams. Coaching involves a leader's intentional effort and interaction with a team to help its members make appropriate use of their collective resources. Research has shown that coaching is most effective when it is task-focused, timely, recognized as necessary by the team, and oriented toward one of three unique issues: motivation of members, performance method improvements, or knowledge/skill deficiencies . Effective team leaders (such as Duke's men's basketball coach, Mike Krzyzewski) recognize the importance of projecting a *positive mood* (strong "face") to team members. This requires building an atmosphere where individual players believe they can perform well and overcome obstacles in their path. In short, leader attitudes are both easily detected, and catchy.[13]

The Need for Team Building

When is team building needed?

Not every team needs to engage in team building, nor does even a poor team need to devote constant attention to it. Many teams, however, could benefit from at least occasionally re-examining how they operate. Fortunately, a variety of clues can be detected that provide evidence when it is more appropriate to devote attention to the team-building process. These signals include:

- Interpersonal conflicts among team members, or between the team and its leader
- Low degree of team morale or low team cohesiveness
- Confusion or disagreement about roles within the team
- Large influx of new members
- Disagreement over the team's purpose and tasks
- Negative climate within the team, evidenced by criticism and bickering
- Stagnation within the team, with members resisting change and new ideas

In cases like these, it is likely that team building is called for and will have a positive effect on the team's functioning.

The Process

The team-building process follows the pattern shown in Figure 13.4. A highly participative process is used, with team members providing "data" (information regarding their frustrations, fears, and irritations as well as their assessments of what is good about their group) and then using the data for self-examination. Often a skilled facilitator may assist the members in diagnosing and addressing their problems. Data are collected from individual group members by surveys or interviews and then fed back to the entire team for airing and analysis. While the group works on development of action plans (their problem-solving *task* of the moment), members are also encouraged to direct equal attention toward the group's interaction *process*. By monitoring, examining, and adjusting its own actions, the group learns to evaluate and improve its own effectiveness. The result of this continuing process can be a high-performance team with high levels of future morale and cooperation.

Teams work on task and process

Specific Team-Building Issues

Team building usually focuses on one or more specific types of problems identified in the first stage of the developmental process portrayed in Figure 13.4. If team members seem to be unaware of, or in disagreement about, the *purpose* of the team, then the focus might best be placed on clarifying the goals and priorities of the team. When the team is confused about its *fit* within the larger organizational system, the focus might be on the nature of the organization's culture, its workplace facilities, its strategic directions, or the reward system. When there is confusion about *work relationships* between people and tasks, job functions may need definition, authority relationships might be revisited, and patterns of work flows might require clarification. When *interpersonal conflicts* seem to dominate the workplace, issues of respect and trust might be explored, listening

FIGURE 13.4
Typical Stages in Team Building

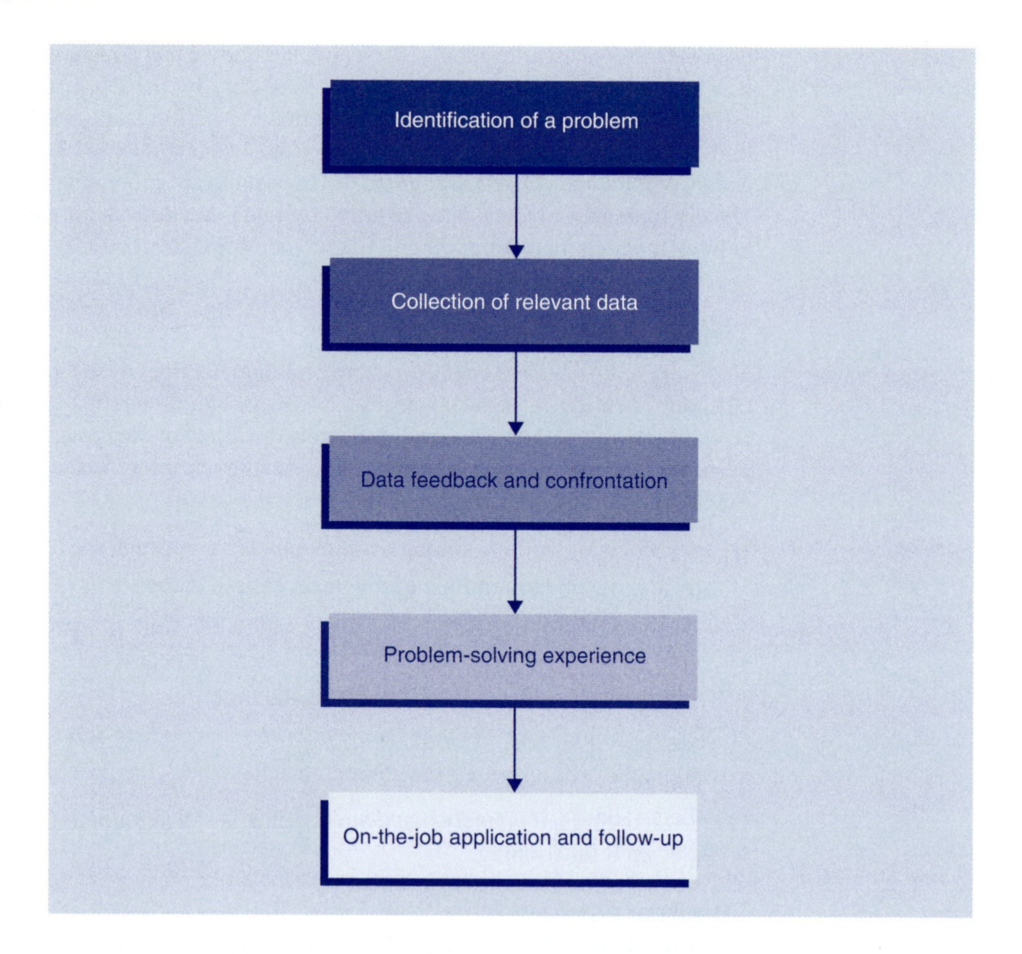

skills might be reviewed, or various models for understanding interpersonal styles might be introduced. In effect, the best team-building approach is one that is carefully built upon a database uncovered during the second stage and then tailored to fit the specific team and team problem.

Skills Useful in Team Building

The facilitators who assist the development of effective teams need to apply a broad range of skills, including *consultation* skills (diagnosing issues, negotiating between conflicting parties, designing programs for change), *interpersonal* skills (trust building, coaching, and listening), *research* skills (planning and conducting a study and evaluating results), and *presentational* skills (public speaking and report preparation). Two additional and closely related skills stand out as critical to success—process consultation and feedback. These are skills that both team leaders and team members need.

Process Consultation In contrast to the roles of experts (who share sophisticated technical information) and problem solvers (who define problems and suggest solutions), team building calls for yet another role—that of process consultant. **Process consultation** is a set of activities that help others focus on what is currently happening around them. In effect, the process consultant holds up a mirror to team members and helps them see themselves in action. The intent of process consultation is straightforward: to help team members perceive, understand, and react constructively to current behavioral events. Process consultants or team **facilitators** encourage employees to examine their intended

FIGURE 13.5
Process Consultants Use Facilitating Behaviors to Help Teams Function More Effectively

Facilitating Behaviors	Desired Effects on Team Members
• Observing team meetings	• Examine intended versus actual roles
• Probing and questioning	• Identify problems
• Confronting individuals	• Examine consequences of behavior
• Encouraging open communication	• React constructively to current behavioral events
• Stimulating problem solving	• Explore new alternatives
• Preventing disruptive behaviors	• Think and act independently
• Attending to nonverbal cues	• Develop cohesiveness
• Ensuring widespread contributions	
• Encouraging learning	

versus their actual roles within the team, the ways in which the team discusses and solves problems, the use and abuse of power and authority, and the explicit and implicit communication patterns.

Process consultants observe, question, and confront

Process consultants are helpers, drawing upon several key facilitating behaviors (see Figure 13.5).[14] They observe team meetings, recording conversational patterns and nonverbal behaviors. They ask probing questions designed to help others identify problems or examine their own values and beliefs. They resist "owning" the team's problems, taking them off the hook, or giving expert advice. If necessary, they *confront* individuals by asking them to examine their behavior and its consequences or to explore new alternatives. They show concern and empathy for people, often modeling the desired behavior for team members. They observe a group unobtrusively to gain both information and insight about its inner workings. They build a sense of community highlighted by sharing and support. They help teams reduce stress or at least learn to cope with it. All the while, the process consultant is attempting to *help other people learn to help themselves*. In other words, the goal is to create independence in team members so they can more effectively think and act for themselves in the future (after the process consultant is gone).

> Meg, a manager and successful team leader, was invited to attend a staff meeting of a community service organization she belonged to, which was led by her friend Sarah. She listened intently for the first half hour, often biting her tongue to remind herself not to engage in discussing the subject before the group. Soon the conversation strayed to several unrelated topics. Sarah turned to Meg and asked, "Should we stay more closely focused on the main topic?" Without answering yes or no, Meg used Sarah's question as an opportunity to highlight and commend Sarah's sensitivity to a process issue. In this way, she hoped to encourage Sarah and others to be even more attentive to the group's processes in the future. Meg was acting as a process consultant at that moment.

Feedback Team members need feedback so they have useful data on which to base decisions. Feedback encourages them to understand how they are seen by others within their team and to take self-correcting action. The following is an example of a feedback exercise in one team-building program:

> Participants are separated into two groups representing two different viewpoints that exist in the team. Both groups are asked to develop answers to the following questions:
>
> - What characteristics best describe our group?
> - What characteristics best describe the other group?

On the Job: General Electric

General Electric uses a Leadership, Innovation, and Growth program to stimulate its business managers to create a climate of creativity. Intact teams of senior managers assess their team on nine key dimensions—idea support, debate, risk taking, challenge/involvement, freedom, trust/openness, idea time, and playfulness/humor. These scores are then compared to a benchmark average score from 10 innovative organizations. Team members are then encouraged to see how well they stack up, and to use the data as a springboard to become even more successful in the future.[15]

- How will the other group describe us?
- What is bugging us about them?

After the separate groups have prepared their answers, they assemble and present their answers to the other group. They give concrete feedback about impressions each group has of the other, and major misunderstandings are often uncovered. In this presentation, no arguments are allowed. Questions are accepted only to clarify what the other group is saying.

The groups again are separated to discuss two other questions:

- How did these misunderstandings occur?
- What can we do to correct them?

With this new feedback, the groups meet to develop specific plans of action for solving their misunderstandings. In each instance, feedback about themselves is the basis for their next activities. See "Ethical Dilemmas within Teams" for a small sampling of other issues that team members might need to confront.

Any team can use process consultation and feedback for its self-development, and many teams can benefit from doing so. The need for continuous improvement is a cornerstone of total quality management programs, and a focus on teams is a critical structural element of many organizations as they operate in the twenty-first century.

Characteristics of Mature Teams

When teams regularly find themselves achieving and even surpassing their goals, they have attained the fourth stage of the team development model (see Figure 13.2). Is this realistic to expect? Yes. Many teams have become highly effective, although it seldom happens overnight. Even the United States Dream Team (men's Olympic basketball squad) struggles a bit every four years as team members learn and accept their roles, assist each other, and adapt to a new coach and new rules.

What do most successful teams look like? They typically exhibit several attitudinal and behavioral characteristics that organizations value (see Figure 13.6), as well as achieve desirable organizational outcomes. Members take pride in their achievements and the contributions of their colleagues; they feel comfortable asking questions when they don't understand something; no one dominates the team or is a wallflower or noncontributor; members know how to criticize others constructively and accept feedback from others; there is an atmosphere of respect and trust; the group is not threatened by instability or change; the atmosphere is relatively informal and tension-free; and members encourage and assist each other. "They are," as one team member put it, "a joy to behold, and to be a part of." Most of all, of course, the team consistently achieves its goals and sets progressively higher standards for itself (see "On the Job: General Electric").

FIGURE 13.6
Common Outcomes of Effective Teams

Performance/Productivity Improvements	Member Behaviors	Member Attitudes
Improved product quality	Lower absenteeism	Higher individual satisfaction
Faster response time	Diminished turnover	Better interpersonal trust
More rapid innovation	Improved safety record	Stronger organizational commitment
Increased customer/client satisfaction	Increased acts of organizational citizenship	Enhanced team cohesiveness
Better decision quality		Camaraderie
Greater efficiency		

Individual Territories vs. Team Spaces

The use of teams at work has increased at an astounding pace. As a consequence, one interesting office design issue that arose was the use of physical space for employees. Specifically, managers needed to decide whether to provide enclosed work cubicles for each employee or to create a more open, landscaped work area with lower, or no, partitions between work spaces. A basic issue revolved around the desire of some employees for privacy and personal space while they worked. Many workers felt a need to establish their own **employee territories**—spaces they could call their own, within which they could control what happens. Cubicles provide an opportunity for them to have their own territory, design and modify their work layout, and even decorate to their own satisfaction.

Territorial needs

Alternatively, a team-based organization may want a layout that encourages easy interaction, an exchange of ideas among employees engaged in related tasks, and a

Ethical Dilemmas within Teams

Team members often find themselves facing various dilemmas, problems for which no easy solutions are apparent. What would *you* do in each of these situations?

- *Team member appraisals*—Do you tell a teammate what is bugging you and risk offending the person, or do you withhold your feelings and let the group suffer?
- *Member assistance*—Several teammates stop by to ask if you need any help. You don't, but if you continue rejecting their offers, will they feel you are not a team player?
- *Team selection*—Your teammates want to hire new members who are similar to themselves. This approach is tempting for compatibility reasons, but how will you ever achieve greater diversity in the team?
- *Team perfection*—Enormous time and effort is spent on becoming the ideal team. However, you wonder if the team is losing its focus on the customer through its dominant focus on process.
- *Team rewards*—The team is rewarded on the basis of achieving its own performance goals. Yet, you wonder if such rewards prevent the team from seeing the larger organizational picture.

On the Job: Orpheus Chamber Orchestra

New York's Orpheus Chamber Orchestra provides a unique illustration of a self-managing team. It lacks a conductor—the traditional and highly expected leader of a musical group of that size (30–40 members). Instead, orchestra members take turns deciding what to play and how to play it, auditioning new members, and interacting with the Orchestra's Board of Directors. This "leaderless" approach works well because its members listen to each other (both musically and administratively), take responsibility for initiating action, devote considerable energy to the Orchestra's success, and communicate their ideas to each other (while also learning to deal with rejection). By treating people like leaders, they become more fully engaged.[16]

stronger feeling of team identity. Some firms have accomplished this goal by creating offices designed as activity settings, which include both home-base areas for privacy and bullpen areas for group interaction. These settings have proved especially effective for providing employees with a way to escape from their computer terminals for short periods of time. Other organizations have created **neighborhoods of offices,** which are centers of related individual offices to encourage the formation of social groups. This layout builds on the idea that proximity, or closeness, creates greater opportunities for interaction. The social groups that form contribute substantially toward satisfying employee needs for belonging.

Social neighborhoods

Self-Managing Teams

One of the empowerment tools introduced in Chapter 8—**self-managing teams**—is also known as *self-reliant* or *self-directed teams*. They are natural work groups that are given substantial autonomy and in return are asked to control their own behavior and produce significant results. The *combination of empowerment and training* to plan, direct, monitor, and control their own activities distinguishes these teams from many others. They have wide-ranging autonomy and freedom, coupled with the capability to act like managers.

What is a self-managing team like? Typically, team members learn a wide range of relevant skills; this practice is called **multiskilling.** As a result, members can flexibly float from area to area and task to task, depending on where they are needed most. They make joint decisions about work schedules, resource requirements, and the assignment of tasks. Considerable time is spent in team meetings as members progressively take over many tasks that were formerly their manager's. Self-managing teams may begin by assuming responsibility for simple matters such as housekeeping issues and safety training. Later, they may begin to manage their own absenteeism, set overtime and vacation schedules, select and appraise team members, train co-workers, and engage in direct contact with key customers. As they gain additional experience, these teams may even move beyond operational topics to refine their organization's mission statement, carve out a new compensation system, or provide input into expansion plans. The "On the Job: Orpheus Chamber Orchestra" is one example of self-managing teams in operation.

Organizations using self-managing teams report several advantages:

- Improved flexibility of staff
- More efficient operations through the reduced number of job classifications

- Lower absenteeism and turnover rates
- Higher levels of organizational commitment and job satisfaction

By contrast, the disadvantages of this approach include:

- The extended time to implement them (often covering several years)
- The high training investment as members learn new skills
- Early inefficiencies due to job rotation
- The inability (or unwillingness) of some employees to adapt to a team structure

Self-managing teams are a powerful example of the application of OB knowledge about teamwork and successful participative methods. As a result, they have increased in organizational use for several reasons. As a formal practice they are not likely to lose organizational support; they often directly involve 100 percent of the workforce; they wield substantial authority in many cases; and they are ongoing structures (not devoted to a single issue). However, firms have found that it may take several years for the teams to achieve their full potential. Cultural values emphasizing individualism can get in the way; rigid job classifications protected by labor contracts can be impediments; and managers can feel threatened by the loss of control and personal job security. Any one of these factors can slow or limit the development of a self-managing team.

Members of self-managing high-performance teams usually exhibit most of the following characteristics:

- *Listening intently* to discover the ideas and opinions of others; they are "energized but focused."
- *Exploring ideas* from outside the group, and integrating alternative points of view and different facts
- Acting as "*charismatic connectors*" who circulate widely and democratically give all team members the chance to contribute.
- *Speaking up* by questioning, raising issues, acknowledging errors, and providing explanations to others (engaging in critical thinking)
- *Reflecting* on what they have seen and heard, while looking for improvement opportunities.[17]

What roles are left for managers of self-managing teams to play? Many exist, although the requirements might change dramatically. Figure 13.7 portrays the sharp contrast between traditional supervisory roles and those required under a self-managing team structure. In addition to those shown, managers often find themselves learning to allow educated risks, stressing the importance of learning, aiding in the selection of new team members, acting as a role model, and demonstrating ethical behavior. They may also help set high standards for the team, provide useful feedback, clarify responsibilities, and facilitate information-sharing.

FIGURE 13.7
Contrasting Supervisory Roles under Two Structures

Traditional Structure	Self-Managing Team Structure
Authority figure	Coach and counselor
Expert	Champion and cheerleader
Teacher	Resource allocator
Problem solver	Liaison and boundary manager
Coordinator	Facilitator

Managers need to be intentional

Boundary-spanning is an emerging managerial role

When you add all of these role responsibilities to the discussion of task and group-relations roles explored in Chapter 12, the manager's role becomes quite complex. To sort this out, managers are encouraged to use the principle of **intentionality.** They need to use their analytical ability to sort out which roles are needed at the moment, have the flexibility to shift from role to role at a moment's notice, be willing to attempt playing even the "uncomfortable" ones, and prepare the team to expect and be receptive to multiple roles.

Successful self-managing teams often require that their leaders (whether internal or external to them) play boundary-spanning roles. These are the abilities to interact with a variety of other groups in order to help the team succeed. **Boundary spanners** keep communication channels open and active by constantly sharing information with other units in the organization and with people at other levels. They identify internal and external customers, ensure resource availability on a timely basis, and keep the team focused on continuous improvements. Since each group has its own needs, resources, special language, values, norms, and style of relationships, boundary spanners need to be sensitive and flexible. Boundary spanners often have little or no authority, and so their task is best accomplished through skills such as these:[18]

- Social awareness
- Relating to others
- Genuine caring for team members
- Investigating problems
- Obtaining external support
- Influencing the team
- Persuading

Virtual Teams

Information technology has had a powerful effect on individual behavior in organizations, and its effect is equally strong on social networks at the team level. Technology has allowed the emergence of **virtual teams**—groups of individuals from around the globe that meet through the use of technological aids without all of their members being present in the same location.[19] These teams, according to one observer, can be either "dramatic successes or dismal failures." Virtual teams often go through a developmental process parallel to that of other teams, starting with unbridled optimism and proceeding through reality shock to the refocusing of their efforts to attain ultimate high performance.

The explosion in the use of virtual teams came about due to several compelling reasons. For example, the global marketplace has created a demand for placing employees (e.g., customer-service persons) near their customers. Also, the most highly qualified team members may be located thousands of miles from each other, and the costs and time constraints of travel to a central location would be prohibitive. Further, the personal expectations of contemporary employees for flexibility and involvement also create a push in this direction. Finally, the rapid development of both transmission capabilities (fiber-optic lines) and communication software has made it possible for groups to "meet" from afar.

Unique problems can arise, too. Widely differing time zones cause difficulties in setting up meeting times; language differences across cultural borders can cause communication problems; overreliance on written messages results in the loss of many nonverbal cues from facial expressions and gestures; and there can also be the belief that virtual team projects are not as visible or important as local ones.

On the Job: Accenture

Accenture is a giant strategic consulting firm, employing more than 200,000 workers scattered across 150 offices in 50 countries of the world. The company uses virtual teams extensively, with consultants sometimes working in teams as large as 1,000 depending on the scope and complexity of the client's project. One of the hardest challenges is to make sure Accenture's "road warriors" (who travel widely) feel connected to the company and their colleagues. To combat the lack of face time with co-workers and their manager, employees rely on webconferencing and an internal "Facebook" site for discovering and exchanging information.[20]

To overcome the inherent problems of individualistic behavior, feelings of isolation, lack of trust, and the extra coordination needed in virtual teams, managers can use one or more approaches to substitute for daily face-to-face interaction with their employees.

These devices include:

- Clarified goals and definitions of the major issues
- Conduct of a few short face-to-face meetings at the initiation of a project to humanize fellow team members
- Temporary on-location projects among virtual team members
- Explicit definition of role expectations
- Identification of potential problems likely to arise
- Frequent use of e-mail and videoconferencing to encourage information exchange and collaboration.[21]

Virtual teams, thought to be unrealistic just a few years ago, have become commonplace on both a temporary and permanent basis as organizations increasingly have global worksites. "On the Job: Accenture" is an example.

Summary

Classical organization structures did not rely heavily on teams, despite the division of work into functional units and multiple levels. More recently, organizations have found that a flexible approach is more appropriate for dynamic environments. Both the organic form and the matrix structure provide useful ways to adapt to turbulent environments, especially where large technical tasks are involved. Frequently, project teams are formed, which provide both a social relationship for workers and a valuable device for combining the talents of diverse workers.

Teams are cooperative groups that maintain regular contact and engage in coordinated action. They strive to achieve a high degree of teamwork, which is aided by a supportive environment, proper skills, superordinate goals, trust, team rewards, and positive norms. Newly formed teams often move through a series of several developmental stages. Team building is an important and continuing process, which can be aided by managerial attention to process consultation (facilitation) and feedback skills.

Self-managing teams are empowered groups that are provided with the training, resources, and authority to assume responsibility for many management-level functions. They represent a creative and challenging way to formally tap the power of teams to help accomplish organizational goals. Employees gain, too, through greater autonomy and skill development. Virtual teams have gained substantially in popularity, but they also present problems.

Advice to Future Managers

1. After discussions with other insiders, *determine whether your organization is flexible enough to allow and support the initiation of teams.*
2. Resolve now to *make yourself flexible enough to feel comfortable working in a matrix organization,* in which you might have to report to multiple project managers.
3. *Become an astute observer/analyst of teams,* and try to assess whether they are in stage 1, 2, 3, or 4 of the team life cycle (refer to Figure 13.2).
4. Be on the alert for signs that the team you are in or managing is succumbing to some classic pitfalls. *Take positive action to overcome these problems before they become magnified.*
5. Read, study, observe others, and develop your own skills so you can *become effective at team building, process consultation, and providing feedback.*
6. Prepare yourself for the possibility that you might be asked to *create a self-managing team* from a traditional one, with the associated role changes that switch would bring about for you.
7. Resolve to *identify social loafers,* and develop an aggressive program to diminish that behavior within a team.
8. To build an effective team, *identify rewards that team members value and believe are possible to earn,* and then tie them directly to desired elements of task performance.
9. Resist the urge to focus your exclusive efforts internally within your department or team, and *find ways to become an effective boundary spanner.*
10. Explore the possibility of *creating one or more virtual teams,* and capitalize on the advantages of technology for allowing employees to collaborate from distant geographical sites.

Speaking OB: Terms and Concepts for Review

Boundary spanners, *364*
Cross-functional teams, *349*
Delegation, *348*
Dissent, *356*
Division of work, *348*
Employee territories, *361*
Facilitators, *358*
Intentionality, *364*
Matrix organization, *349*
Multiskilling, *362*
Neighborhoods of offices, *362*
Process consultation, *358*
Self-managing teams, *362*
Shared mental model, *355*
Social loafing, *353*
Stages of team development, *350*
Sucker effect, *353*
Superordinate goal, *355*
Task team, *350*
Team building, *356*
Team coaching, *356*
Teamwork, *350*
Virtual teams, *364*

Discussion Questions

1. Discuss how to build a unified team within a whole organization.
2. Explain how matrix organization gives rise to the need for teams.
3. How do temporary groups and committees (discussed in Chapter 12) compare with teams? What are their similarities and differences?
4. Review the typical stages in a team's life cycle. Think of a time when you were a member of a work team. Were all those stages represented? Did they appear in a different order? Did some of them emerge more than once? Explain.
5. Assume you are to be placed in charge of a student group in this class. Outline the key action steps you will take to make sure the group develops into a real team.
6. Think of a time when you observed, or exhibited, social loafing. What contributed to it? How could it have been prevented or minimized?
7. Think about self-managing teams. Would you like to work in one? Why or why not?

8. The authors assert that "it may take several years for [self-managing] teams to achieve their full potential." Why might this be so? How could the process be shortened?
9. In what ways do you think the boundary-spanning roles of a traditional manager might differ from those of team members in self-managing teams? Explain.
10. What are the key advantages to using virtual teams? Disadvantages? On balance, are they worth using?

Assess Your Own Skills

How well do you exhibit good team management skills?

Read the following statements carefully. Circle the number on the response scale that most closely reflects the degree to which each statement accurately describes you when you have tried to participate in, or lead, a team. Add up your total points and prepare a brief action plan for self-improvement. Be ready to report your score for tabulation across the entire group.

	Good description									Poor description
1. I know the key differences between a group and a task team.	10	9	8	7	6	5	4	3	2	1
2. I can identify the developmental stage of a team by assessing which questions the members are currently addressing.	10	9	8	7	6	5	4	3	2	1
3. I can explain to a prospective team the key ingredients that will make them successful.	10	9	8	7	6	5	4	3	2	1
4. I can effectively help my team integrate a new member into its operations.	10	9	8	7	6	5	4	3	2	1
5. I know the major symptoms that ineffective teams exhibit.	10	9	8	7	6	5	4	3	2	1
6. I can choose the appropriate team-building focus, based upon the underlying problems that exist within the team.	10	9	8	7	6	5	4	3	2	1
7. I can comfortably apply many of the skills needed in process consultation.	10	9	8	7	6	5	4	3	2	1
8. I can list a half-dozen characteristics of successful mature teams.	10	9	8	7	6	5	4	3	2	1
9. I can explain the pros and cons of different uses of physical space to team members.	10	9	8	7	6	5	4	3	2	1
10. I am capable of moving from the traditional roles of a supervisor to those required by self-managing teams.	10	9	8	7	6	5	4	3	2	1

Scoring and Interpretation

Add up your total points for the 10 questions. Record that number here, and report it when it is requested. Finally, insert your total score into the "Assess and Improve Your Own Organizational Behavior Skills" chart in Appendix A.

- If you scored between 81 and 100 points, you appear to have a solid capability for demonstrating good team management skills.
- If you scored between 61 and 80 points, you should take a close look at the items with lower self-assessment scores and explore ways to improve those items.
- If you scored under 60 points, you should be aware that a weaker skill level regarding several items could be detrimental to your future success as a team leader. We encourage you to review relevant sections of the chapter and watch for relevant material in subsequent chapters and other sources.

Identify your three lowest scores, and write the question numbers here: _____, _____, _____. Write a brief paragraph, detailing to yourself an action plan for how you might sharpen each of these skills.

Incident

Conflict in the Division

The engineering division of a firm consists of four departments, with the supervisor of each reporting to the division general manager (GM). The four departments range in size from 2 employees in the smallest (industrial engineering) to 14 in the largest (sales engineering). The other two departments (design engineering and process engineering) each have eight employees.

Intense interdepartmental rivalry frequently arises over the allocation of resources. This problem is compounded by the favoritism that the GM allegedly shows toward the industrial and design engineering units and his reliance on majority-rule decision making (among his four supervisors and himself) at staff meetings. This practice, complain the supervisors of the sales and process engineering departments, often results in the leaders of the industrial and design engineering departments forming a coalition with the GM to make a decision, even though they represent only 10 of the 32 employees. In response, the industrial and design engineering supervisors charge the supervisors of the sales and process engineering units with empire building, power plays, and a narrow view of the mission of the division.

Question

You are a friend of the GM, called in from another division to help resolve the problem. Outline the approach you would recommend that the GM take.

Experiential Exercise

Readiness for Self-Managing Teams

Assume you are the new owner of a fast-food restaurant employing approximately 75 employees across two shifts. Most of the employees are relatively young and inexperienced, but willing to learn. You are trying to decide to what degree to involve them in various decisions, in addition to their specific job assignments. In the following list indicate, with a check in the first column, those roles and responsibilities for which you are inclined to allow them to take control. Afterward, discuss the issue with three or four other students. Combine your perspectives and indicate the group's response in the second column. Finally, review the pattern of items selected, and determine the apparent rationale used by the group for its choices.

	Col. 1 (Individual)	Col. 2 (Group)
1. Training new co-workers	______	______
2. Ordering food supplies	______	______
3. Conducting safety meetings	______	______
4. Disciplining tardy employees	______	______
5. Making minor equipment repairs	______	______
6. Selecting new co-workers	______	______
7. Recording hours worked	______	______
8. Making job assignments	______	______
9. Conducting problem-solving meetings	______	______
10. Dismissing unproductive workers	______	______

Experiential Exercise

Team Building

Divide into groups of about five persons. Taking just a few minutes for each of the following tasks, develop a collective response, and be prepared to share it with the class.

1. Select a unique *name* for your team.
2. Select a unique *cheer* for your team.
3. Select a unique *motto* (slogan) for your team.
4. Select a unique *color* (or set of colors) for your team.
5. Identify three things each member *has in common* with all the others.
6. Identify one key *strength* that each member brings to the team.
7. Working together, and without any aids, answer these questions:
   a. How many centimeters long is a dollar bill?
   b. At what temperature are Fahrenheit and Centigrade equal?
   c. Who is the Chief Justice of the United States?
   d. What letter do the greatest number of words in the dictionary begin with?
   e. How many U.S. presidents are still alive, and who are they?

Share your answers to questions 1–7 with the class, and then discuss how those rather trivial exercises helped you feel like a functioning team. What else could you do to continue your development as a team?

Generating OB Insights

An *insight* is a new and clear perception of a phenomenon, or an acquired ability to "see" clearly something you were unaware of previously. It is sometimes simply referred to as an "ah-ha! moment," in which you have a minirevelation or reach a straightforward conclusion about a topic or issue.

Insights need not necessarily be dramatic, for what is an insight to one person may be less important to another. The critical feature of insights is that they are relevant and memorable for *you;* they should represent new knowledge, new frameworks, or new ways of viewing things you want to retain and remember over time.

Insights, then, are different from the information you find in the "Advice for Future Managers" boxes within the text. That advice is prescriptive and action-oriented; it indicates a recommended course of action.

A useful way to think of OB insights is to assume you are the only person who has read Chapter 13. You have been given the assignment to highlight, in your own words, the major concepts (not just summarize the whole chapter) that might stand out for a naïve audience who has never heard of the topic before. *What 10 insights would you share with them?*

(Example) *Effective team members require job skills, the desire to cooperate with others, and knowledge of the roles of team members.*

1. ______________________________
2. ______________________________
3. ______________________________
4. ______________________________
5. ______________________________
6. ______________________________
7. ______________________________
8. ______________________________
9. ______________________________
10. ______________________________

Nurturing Your Critical Thinking and Reflective Skills

Take a few minutes to review the discussion in the Roadmap for Readers of critical thinking and reflection. Remind yourself that if you can hone these abilities now, you will have a substantial competitive advantage when you apply for jobs and are asked what unique skills you can bring to the position and the organization.

Critical Thinking

Think back on the material you have recently read in the current chapter. What are three unique and challenging *critical questions* you would like to raise about that material? (These might identify something controversial about which you have doubts, they may imply that you suspect a theory or model has weaknesses, they could examine the legitimacy of apparent causal relationships, or they might assess the probable value of a suggested practice.) Be prepared to share these questions with class members or your instructor.

1. ______________________________
2. ______________________________
3. ______________________________

Reflection

This process often involves answering the parallel questions of "What do you think about the material you have read?" and "How do you feel about that material?" Therefore, express your personal thoughts and feelings (reactions) to any of the ideas or topics found in this chapter, and be prepared to share these reflections with class members or your instructor.

1. ______________________________

   ____

2. ______________________________

   ____

3. ______________________________

   ____

Part Six

Change and Its Effects

Chapter Fourteen

Managing Change

70 percent of all corporate initiatives fail.

Claire Suddath[1]

An executive's immediate responsibility is to articulate the "burning platform"; that is, the rationale for why change is necessary.

Bill Glavin[2]

CHAPTER OBJECTIVES

AFTER READING THIS CHAPTER, YOU SHOULD UNDERSTAND

14–1 The Nature of Change

14–2 Costs and Benefits of Change

14–3 Resistance to Change

14–4 Basic Frameworks for Interpreting Change

14–5 Role of Transformational Leadership in Change

14–6 Practices to Build Support for Change

14–7 Meaning and Characteristics of OD

Facebook Page 

Student A: Wouldn't you know it? I'm getting closer to the end of the OB text, and now it looks like a lot of what I learned about organizations might be subject to change. There is no static equilibrium!

Student B: Well, at least you aren't part of the problem—or are you?

Student A: Well, I admit that there are times when I've been resistant to change, especially when someone else tells me what to change—or when, or how. Of course, *my* resistance is almost always rational (versus psychological or sociological)!

Student B: So how *does* individual change occur?

Student A: Usually through three stages. First someone needs to unfreeze from old methods, then absorb a new approach, and finally refreeze it into actual practice.

Student B: OK, but how *do* you get people to make the change?

Student A: There are many ways. You should provide a rationale, use group forces for support, involve the employees, insulate them from fears of insecurity, and share the rewards with them.

Student B: Isn't that a tall order for a typical manager?

Student A: That is why a lot of organizations use OD consultants (internal or external change agents). (OD stands for organization development.) Time for me to study the chapter!

"Life used to be so simple," lamented an independent logger in northern Minnesota. "My father cut the trees, hauled them to a sawmill, and got paid. The demand for wood was quite stable, the supply of trees was plentiful, and his logging equipment consisted of a chain saw, an axe, and a truck. Life was good in those days."

"So what is different now?" the logger was asked. "Absolutely everything," he replied. "Current logging rigs cost hundreds of thousands of dollars. I need governmental permits for everything I do. Environmental groups protest against logging. Demand for my logs fluctuates wildly. And cutthroat competition makes it tough for me to make a buck anymore. I'm not sure I can keep my head above water."

The Minnesota logger is experiencing firsthand three facts of life about change: *It is everywhere, it is constant, and its pace is accelerating*. It is all around people—in the seasons, in their social environment, and in their own biological processes. Beginning with the shockingly new surroundings after birth, a person learns to meet change by being adaptive. A person's very first breath depends on the ability to adapt from one environment to another that is dramatically different. Throughout the rest of their lives, each hour of the day offers people new experiences and challenges. They can embrace and relish change, try to ignore it, or fear it and fight it. Some responses are productive, while others are dysfunctional.

Organizations are also encountering a wide variety of dramatic changes. Some face greater federal regulation, while others experience deregulation; some are more splintered, while others consolidate; some find their markets shrinking, while others find themselves thrown headlong into a global marketplace. Many organizations have experienced mergers or hostile takeovers, while others have implemented devastating downsizing programs producing wrenching psychological and economic effects on their

Engaging Your Brain 

1. Think of a time when you actually tried to implement a change in someone else's behavior. What helped it go well? What caused problems for you?
2. Resistance to change is often a widespread phenomenon. Why do you think this is so?
3. Some organizations expect their college-educated employees to exhibit a strong work ethic and elements of professionalism, including their "appropriate appearance, punctuality, regular attendance, honesty, attentiveness, and sticking with a task through completion."[3] On a scale from 1 (not very well) to 10 (extremely well), rate yourself on your own capacity to develop professionalism (change).

employees. To survive, organizations need to decide not *whether* to change, but *when* and *how* to make it occur most successfully. The best approach is to plan for, and initiate, their own desired changes.

Human beings are certainly familiar with change and often prove themselves quite adaptive to it. Why, then, do they often resist change in their work environment? This question has troubled managers since the beginning of the industrial revolution. The faster pace of change required by the electronic age, by the shift to a service economy, and by the growth of global competition has made the solution to this question even more important. Even when managers use their most logical arguments and persuasive skills to support a change, they frequently discover that employees remain unconvinced of the need for it. This chapter examines the nature of change, reasons for resistance to it, and ways to introduce it more successfully, including organization development.

CHANGE AT WORK

The Nature of Change

Change is any alteration occurring at work or in the work environment that affects the ways in which employees must act. These changes may be planned or unplanned, catastrophic or evolutionary, positive or negative, strong or weak, slow or rapid, and stimulated either internally or externally. Regardless of their source, nature, origin, pace, or strength, changes can have profound effects on their recipients.

The effects of change can be illustrated by comparing an organization to an air-filled balloon. When a finger (which represents external change in this case) is pressed against a point on the balloon (which represents the organization), the contour of the balloon visibly changes (it becomes indented) at the point of contact. Here an obvious pressure, representing change, has produced an obvious deviation at the point of pressure. What is not so obvious, however, is that the entire balloon (the rest of the organization) has also been affected and has stretched slightly. In addition, the tension against the inner surface of the balloon has increased (not, it is hoped, to the breaking point).

Effects are widespread

As shown by this illustration, a safe generalization is that *the whole organization tends to be affected by change in any part of it.* The molecules of air in the balloon represent a firm's employees. It is apparent that those at the spot of pressure must make drastic adjustments. Though the change did not make direct contact with the employees (molecules), it has affected them indirectly. Though none is fired (i.e., leaves the balloon), the employees are displaced and must adjust to a new location in the balloon.

Human and technical problem

This comparison illustrates an additional generalization: *Change is a human as well as a technical problem.*

The comparison using a balloon may be carried further. Repeated pressure at a certain point may weaken the balloon until it breaks. So it is with an organization. Changes may lead to pressures and conflicts that eventually cause a breakdown somewhere in the organization. An example is an employee who becomes dissatisfied and resigns.

Admittedly, the balloon analogy is rough. An employing institution is not a balloon; a person is not a molecule; and people are not as free and flexible as air molecules in a balloon. What has been illustrated is a condition of molecular equilibrium. Organizations, too, tend to achieve an **equilibrium** in their social structure—a state of relative balance between opposing forces. This equilibrium is established when people develop a relatively stable set of relations with their environment. They learn how to deal with one another, how to perform their jobs, and what to expect next. Equilibrium exists; employees are adjusted. When change comes along, it requires them to make new adjustments as the organization seeks a new equilibrium. When employees are unable to make adequate adjustments, the organization is in a state of unbalance, or disequilibrium. At the extreme, disruptions can produce total disarray until they are addressed.

This disequilibrium highlights a challenging dilemma for managers, who are juggling competing roles. On the one hand, the manager's role is to *introduce* continual organizational changes so as to bring about a better fit between the firm and its evolving environment. Here, the manager's role is to be **proactive**—anticipating events, initiating change, and taking control of the organization's destiny. On the other hand, part of the manager's role is to *restore and maintain the group equilibrium* and personal adjustment that change upsets. In this role, the manager is more **reactive**—responding to events, adapting to change, and tempering the consequences of change.

Proactive and reactive roles

Fortunately, many of the organizational changes that occur on a daily basis are somewhat minor. They may affect only a few people, and they may be incremental in nature and relatively predictable. For example, as new procedures evolve or as new members are added to a work group, existing employees generally do not need to change all dimensions of their jobs or acquire totally new behaviors. In such situations, a new equilibrium may be reached readily.

A wide variety of forces, however, may bring about more dramatic changes that touch the entire core of an organization. Many of these have become much more common as the economy, competition, and pace of technological change have become more volatile. Examples include hostile takeovers of firms, leveraged buyouts and subsequent organizational restructuring, acts of public violence and terrorism, and natural disasters like oil spills and gas leaks. Crises like these, whether positive or negative, demand that managers help guide employees through the emotional shock that accompanies them, thereby bringing the organization to a new equilibrium.

Responses to Change

Work change is further complicated by the fact that it does not produce a direct adjustment, unlike the adjustment of air molecules in the balloon. Instead, *it operates through each employee's attitudes* to produce a response that is conditioned by feelings toward the change. This relationship was illustrated in a series of classical experiments—the Hawthorne studies, conducted by F. J. Roethlisberger and his associates. In one instance, work lighting was improved regularly according to the simplistic theory that better lighting would lead to greater productivity. As was expected, productivity did increase. Then, lighting was decreased to illustrate the reverse effect—reduced productivity. Instead, productivity increased further. Lighting was again decreased. The result was still greater productivity.

Experiments relating lighting to productivity

FIGURE 14.1 **Unified Social Response to Change**

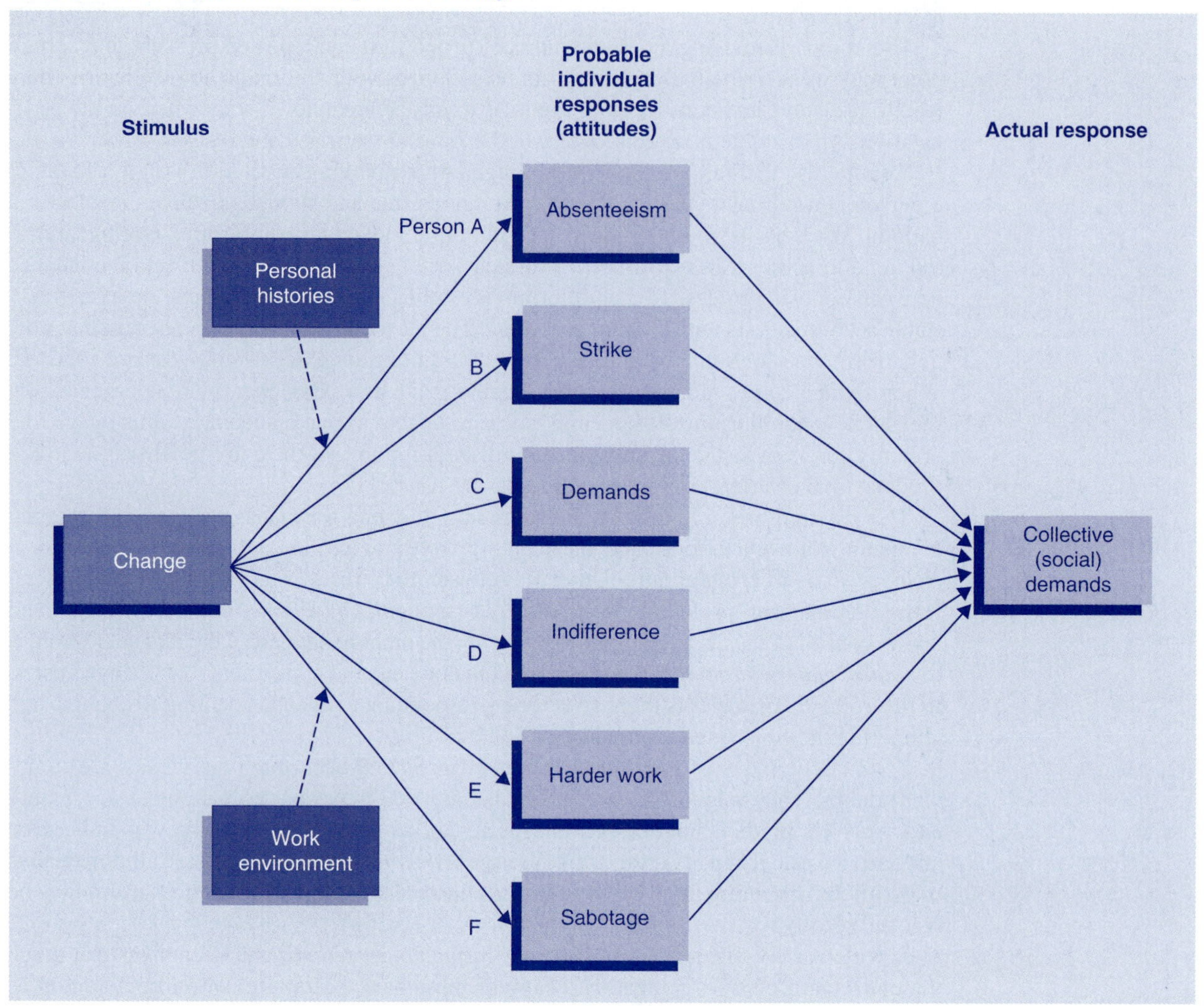

Finally, lighting was decreased to 0.06 foot-candle, which is approximately equivalent to moonlight. According to Roethlisberger, "Not until this point was reached was there any appreciable decline in the output rate."[4]

How Individual Attitudes Affect Response to Change Obviously, better lighting was not by itself causing greater output. There was no direct (causal) connection between the change and the response. Some other intervening variable, later diagnosed as employee attitudes, had crept in to upset the expected pattern. Roethlisberger later explained the new pattern in the following way: Each change is interpreted by individuals according to their attitudes. *The way that people feel about a change is one factor that determines how they will respond to it.* These feelings are not the result of chance; they are caused. One cause is *personal history,* which refers to people's biological processes, their backgrounds (e.g., family, job, education), and all their social experiences away from work (see Figure 14.1). This history is what they bring to the workplace in the form of preexisting attitudes. A second cause is the *work environment* itself. It reflects the fact that workers are members of a group and their attitudes are influenced by its codes, patterns, and norms.

Effects of a Diverse Workforce on Change

The workforce in the United States will become increasingly diverse (from a gender and ethnic perspective) as we move through the twenty-first century. New jobs will be filled by higher proportions of females, African-Americans, Hispanics, and Asians than ever before. In addition, the typical education level of workers in this country has gradually increased. Questions: What predictions can you make about the impact of these changes on the employer's *likelihood* to change? On the employer's *capacity* to change? On the worker's *receptivity* to change?

Feelings are nonlogical

Feelings are not a matter of logic. They are neither logical nor illogical, but entirely apart from logic. They are *nonlogical*. Feelings and logic belong in two separate categories, just as inches and pounds do. For that reason, *logic alone is an ineffective means of trying to modify feelings* because it does not get at them directly. Feelings are not much better refuted by logic than this book's length in inches or centimeters is refuted by its weight in pounds or kilograms.

The Hawthorne Effect One cause of favorable feelings in the groups studied by Roethlisberger was the interest shown by the researchers in employee problems. This phenomenon later was called the **Hawthorne effect,** named after the factory where the research took place. The Hawthorne effect means that the mere observation of a group—or more precisely, the *perception* of being observed and one's *interpretation* of its significance—tends to change the group. *When people are observed, or believe that someone cares about them, they act differently.* These changes usually are unintended and not even recognized by the members themselves. The Hawthorne effect contaminates the research design, but normally the consequences of it cannot be prevented.

Observation affects behavior

Group Response to Change People interpret change individually and have their own probable response to it. However, they often show their attachment to the group by joining with other group members in some uniform response to the change, as shown in the "actual response" in Figure 14.1. This uniformity makes possible such seemingly illogical actions as walkouts when obviously only a few people actually want to walk out. Other employees who are unhappy seize upon the walkout as a chance to show their dissatisfaction and to confirm their affiliation with the group by joining with it in social action. Basically, the group responds with the feeling, "We're all in this together. Whatever happens to one of us affects all of us."

Homeostasis In trying to maintain equilibrium, a group is often inclined to return to its perceived best way of life whenever any change occurs. Each pressure, therefore, elicits a counterpressure within the group. The net result is a self-correcting mechanism by which energies are called up to restore balance whenever change threatens. This self-correcting characteristic of organizations is called **homeostasis**—that is, people act to establish a steady state of need fulfillment and to protect themselves from disturbance of that balance. They want to maintain their previous sense of competence.

This leads some employees to engage in various strategies to kill new ideas and maintain homeostasis. They include:

1. Fear mongering ("You want us to go down a slippery slope.")
2. Death by delay ("Let's study this for a little while longer.")
3. Confusion ("There are six big reasons why this just won't work.")
4. Ridicule ("It's a too-simple solution for our complex problem.")[5]

Costs and Benefits

All changes are likely to have some costs. For example, a new work procedure may require the inconvenience of learning new skills. It temporarily may disrupt work and reduce satisfaction. And new equipment or relocation of old equipment may add costs that are not merely economic; they are also psychological and social. They usually must be paid in order to gain the benefits of proposed changes.

Because of the costs associated with change, proposals for change are not always desirable. They require careful analysis to determine usefulness. Each change requires a detailed cost-benefit analysis. Unless changes can provide benefits above costs, there is no reason for the changes. To emphasize benefits while ignoring costs is illogical. The organizational goal should always be to produce *benefits greater than costs.*

Emotions powerfully impact intentional change

A parallel cost-benefit analysis is appropriate at the individual level, when persons desire to make an **intentional (planned) change,** whether it occurs in their behavior (actions, habits, or competencies), thoughts (ideas, dreams, or aspirations), feelings (emotions and attitudes), or perceptions (ways of looking at things). Here, individuals weigh positive dimensions (such as strengths, hopes, dreams, and optimism) that pull them toward something new and balance these against negative factors that might include problems, pessimism, fears, and shortfalls. The net effect determines whether intentional change is likely to occur and be sustained.[6]

In a determination of benefits and costs, all types must be considered. To examine only economic benefits and costs is useless, because even if a net economic benefit accrues, the social or psychological costs may be too large. Although it is not very practical to reduce psychological and social costs to numbers, they must nevertheless be included in the decision-making process. Almost any change, for example, involves some psychological loss because of the strain it imposes on people as they try to adjust.

Psychic costs

Psychological costs also are called **psychic costs** because they affect a person's inner self, the psyche.

Knowledge of individual differences helps us predict that *people will react in different and widely varying ways to change.* Some will perceive only the benefits, while others see only what it costs them. Others will react fearfully at first, even though all the effects are actually positive for them. Others will appear initially to embrace the change but then gradually let their real feelings emerge.

> Some people who have observed common reactions to traditional change efforts contend that the 20-50-30 rule applies.[7] According to this distribution of responses, about 20 percent of employees affected by a change will be receptive and possibly strongly supportive; about 50 percent will be rather neutral toward the change and possibly even open-minded and receptive; and about 30 percent will be close-minded, resist the change, and possibly attempt to sabotage it. The challenge for managers of a change process is to transform a substantial portion of the 80 percent (neutrals and resisters) into supporters of the change for it to succeed.

In some cases, the psychic costs of change can be so severe that they affect the psychological and even physical health of employees. The tolerance level for change within a group of employees can range from relatively high for one person to relatively low for another. Whenever that level is exceeded, stressful responses develop that can undermine health. In some instances, there is a sustained series of small or moderate changes over a period of time, producing cumulative effects that finally overload a person's system. Some writers refer to this circumstance as **repetitive change syndrome.**[8] Continuous rounds of change can produce negative effects for individuals and corrosive results for the entire organization. Repetitive change syndrome is often caused by a series of organizational initiatives that are started but not completed, by a blurring of one program and another, and by a pandemic of employee cynicism. Although managers can initiate changes, the resulting stress can also slow the pace of change and ultimately cause it to fail.

In other instances, a single major change of high significance overloads a person's ability to cope with the situation. Examples include a move to a new location (bringing with it the need for a new house, new schools for children, a job search for the spouse, and loss of friendships) or a promotion involving new roles, status, work group, and job pressures. The effects of change in the form of job stress are discussed further in Chapter 15.

The reality of change is that frequently there is no clear-cut 100 percent benefit for all parties. Rather, there is a series of separate costs and benefits that must be considered on an individual basis. The supportive, collegial, and system models of organizational behavior imply that management should consider each substantial change, try to help each person understand it, and seek to have each person experience a net gain from it. Despite management's best efforts, however, change is not always welcomed—and not always successful (as the opening quote for this chapter vividly illustrates). The next section explores the nature and effects of resistance to change.

RESISTANCE TO CHANGE

Why resistance occurs

Resistance to change consists of any employee behaviors designed to discredit, delay, or prevent the implementation of a work change. Employees resist change because it threatens their needs for security, social interaction, status, competence, or self-esteem. Other causes of resistance or passivity include:

- Organizational cultures that overvalue criticism of new ideas
- Employees who mouth support in public but undercut changes behind the scenes
- Indecisive managers who suffer from "analysis paralysis"
- An emphasis on flashy proposals ("death by PowerPoint") instead of follow-through
- A "bunker mentality" where employees have learned that organizational crises don't often prove to be as significant as they are claimed to be, and hence they can be ignored[9]

Managers need to take responsibility for much of this resistance. Research studies show that a majority of them lack effective communication skills, have poor interpersonal skills, and fail to clarify performance expectations. When they also fail to remove roadblocks to employee performance or even monitor the effects of a change and provide needed feedback, change programs can be disastrous.[10]

Nature and Effects

The perceived threat stemming from a change may be real or imagined, intended or unintended, direct or indirect, large or small. Regardless of the nature of the change, some employees will try to protect themselves from its effects. Their actions may range from complaints, foot-dragging, and passive resistance to passionate arguments, absenteeism, sabotage, and work slowdowns.

All types of employees tend to resist change because of the psychic costs that accompany it. Managers as well as workers may resist it. Change can be resisted just as stubbornly by an executive as by a hotel's housekeeper.

Although people tend to resist change, this tendency is offset by their desire for new experiences and for the rewards that come with change. Certainly, not all changes are resisted;

some are actively sought by employees. Other changes are so trivial and routine that resistance, if any, is too weak to be evident. One lesson for management is that a change is likely to be either a success or a problem, *depending on how skillfully it is managed to prevent, minimize, or overcome resistance.*

Chain-reaction effect

Insecurity and change are conditions that illustrate how a **chain-reaction effect** may develop in organizational behavior. A chain-reaction effect is a situation in which a change, or other condition, that directly affects only one person or a few persons may lead to a direct or indirect reaction from many people, even hundreds or thousands, because of their mutual interest in it. This is quite similar to multicar rear-end collisions on a foggy freeway, where each collision is followed by another one.

In one firm, an assistant general manager for sales was promoted to assistant general manager for administration. The promotion of this high-ranking manager set off a cascading series of events that led to the promotion of 10 other people at lower levels. The subsequent moves affected numerous divisions, territories, and offices. This example illustrates the wide impact of a single major change, and the chain-reaction effects of a single precipitating event.

Reasons for Resistance

Resistance stems from the nature of change, the method used, and perceptions of inequity

Employees may resist changes for three broad reasons. First, they may feel uncomfortable with the *nature of the change itself.* It may violate their moral belief system, they may believe the decision is technically incorrect, the change may be too complex for them to grasp, or they may believe it is inconsistent with the organization's mission, vision, values, and culture.

A second reason for resistance stems from the *method* by which change is introduced. People may resent having been ill-informed, the change may have come unexpectedly, or they may reject an insensitive and authoritarian approach that did not involve them in the change process. The method of introducing change may also revolve around a perception of poor timing, or even a poor choice of words used to introduce the change.

A third reason for resistance revolves around *personal factors.* Some employees may have high inertia and simply be reluctant to exchange the comfort of certainty and familiarity for uncertainty. People may resist change because of their fear of the unknown/fear of failure, threats to their job security, lack of trust in management, a low tolerance for change, a high degree of parochial self-interest, or the perceived lack of a demonstrated problem. Finally, people are more likely to resist change because of the inequity experienced when people perceive themselves being changed while someone else appears to gain the benefits of the change. Their resistance will be even more intense and sustained if all three reasons exist: People disagree with the nature of the change, dislike the method used, and have one or more personal reasons to resist it.[11]

From resistance to acceptance

Elisabeth Kübler-Ross, in her book *Death and Dying,* studied the reactions of individuals when told that they had an incurable (life-threatening) illness and faced death. She concluded that these people typically went through a series of five stages: denial, anger, depression, search for alternatives, and eventual acceptance of the prognosis. Many change managers also believe that employees go through a comparable experience, although certainly on a lesser scale, when faced with organizational change (see Figure 14.2). They first fight the change, then strike out in anger and maintain their rigid resistance, then express their sadness and withdraw, then begin to explore and acknowledge the possible value of the change, and ultimately embrace the change as a new way of life.

FIGURE 14.2
Parallel Stages of Reactions to Terminal Illness and Organizational Change

Reactions to Terminal Illness	Reactions to Major Change
1. Denial	**1.** Refusal to believe it is real
2. Anger	**2.** Resentment at change initiator
3. Depression	**3.** Emotional or physical withdrawal
4. Search for alternatives	**4.** Exploration of benefits
5. Acceptance of prognosis	**5.** Embracing of the change

Types of Resistance

The three different types of resistance to change are shown in Figure 14.3. These types work in combination to produce each employee's total attitude toward a change. The three types may be expressed by three different uses of the word "logical."

Rational resistance

Logical Resistance This is based on disagreement with the facts, rational reasoning, logic, and science. Logical resistance arises from the actual time and effort required to adjust to change, including new job duties that must be learned. These are true costs borne by the employees. Even though a change may be favorable for employees in the long run, these short-run costs must first be paid and initiators of change should expect some logical resistance.

Emotional resistance

Psychological Resistance This is typically based on emotions, sentiments, and attitudes. Psychological resistance is internally logical from the perspective of the employees' attitudes and feelings about change. Employees may fear the unknown, mistrust management's leadership, or feel that their security and self-esteem are threatened. Even though management may believe these feelings are not justified, they are very real to employees, and managers *must* acknowledge, accept, and deal with them.

FIGURE 14.3
Types of Resistance to Change among Employees

Logical, Rational Objections

- Time required to adjust
- Extra effort to relearn
- Possibility of less desirable conditions, such as skill downgrading
- Economic costs of change
- Questioned technical feasibility of change

Psychological, Emotional Attitudes

- Fear of the unknown
- Low tolerance of change
- Dislike of management or other change agent
- Lack of trust in others
- Need for security; desire for status quo

Sociological Factors; Group Interests

- Political coalitions
- Opposing group values
- Parochial, narrow outlook
- Vested interests
- Desire to retain existing friendships

Social resistance

Sociological Resistance Sociological resistance also is logical, when it is seen as a product of a challenge to group interests, norms, and values. Since social values are powerful forces in the individual's work or social environment, they must be carefully considered. There are political coalitions, labor union values, and even different community values. On a small-group level, work friendships and status relationships may be disrupted by changes. Employees will ask such questions as, "Is the change consistent with group values?" "Does it maintain teamwork?" Since employees have these kinds of questions on their minds, managers must try to make these conditions as favorable as possible if they intend to deal successfully with sociological resistance.

Implications of Resistance Clearly, all three types of resistance must be anticipated and treated effectively if employees are to accept change cooperatively. If managers work with only the technical, logical dimension of change, they have failed in their human responsibilities. Psychological resistance and sociological resistance are not illogical or irrational; rather, they are logical according to different sets of values. Recognizing the impact of psychological and social factors is critically important to the success of proposed change.

One noted author provides four suggestions to address these types of resistance. He recommends:

- Acknowledging (not denying) employee feelings. In this way, managers need to validate employee feelings and not judge them.
- Encouraging employees to mourn what they have lost. Managers need to help people let go of the past before expecting them to embrace what is new.
- Insisting on an outstanding effort to make the change, while accepting short-term problems. Perfect results are seldom possible during transitions.
- Breaking overwhelming tasks down into manageable immediate steps. This provides employees with short-term success instead of immobilizing them in the face of massive goals.[12]

In a typical operating situation, full support cannot be gained for every change that is made. Some moderate support, weak support, and even opposition can be expected. People are different and will not give identical support to each change. What management seeks is a climate in which people trust managers, have a positive feeling toward most changes, and feel secure enough to tolerate other changes. If management cannot win support, it may need to use authority. However, it must recognize that authority can be used only sparingly. If authority is overused, it eventually will become worthless.

Possible Benefits of Resistance

Resistance can be viewed as useful to managers

Resistance is not *all* bad, and should not necessarily evoke managerial anger or impatience. It can bring a broad range of benefits, such as the following:

1. Resistance may encourage management to reexamine its change proposals, thus making modifications to the process of change to be sure they are appropriate. In this way, employees operate as part of a system of checks and balances that ensures management properly plans and implements change. If reasonable employee resistance causes management to screen its proposed changes more carefully, then employees have discouraged careless management decisions. In this case, resistance can be invaluable.
2. Resistance also can help identify specific problem areas where a change is likely to cause difficulties, so that management can take corrective action before serious problems develop. Since upward flows of communication are often limited, feedback from change resistors can open up vibrant discussions in which both parties learn more.

3. At the same time, management may be encouraged to do a better job of communicating the change, an approach that in the long run should lead to better acceptance. Top-down changes may have been analyzed to death by the executives involved, but lower-level employees may still be almost in the dark. Resistance also gives management information about the intensity of employee emotions on an issue, provides emotional release for pent-up employee feelings, and may encourage employees to think and talk more about a change so they understand it better.[13]

IMPLEMENTING CHANGE SUCCESSFULLY

Some changes originate within the organization, but many come from the external environment. Government passes laws, and the organization must comply. New developments in technology arise, and products must incorporate the changes. Competitors introduce new services, and the firm must respond. Mergers, acquisitions, and downsizings occur with regularity. Customers, labor unions, communities, and others who initiate changes all exert pressure. Although stable environments mean less change, *dynamic environments are now the norm,* and they require more change.

Dynamic environments require change

Transformational Leadership and Change

Management has a key role in initiating and implementing change successfully. Not only do managers sometimes overlook simple but important details, but they may fail to develop a master strategy for planned change. An overall plan should address behavioral issues, such as employees' difficulty in letting go of old methods, the uncertainties inherent in change that cause workers to be fearful, and the general need to create an organization that *welcomes* change.

Transformational leaders are instrumental in this process. They are managers who initiate bold strategic changes to position the organization for its future. They articulate a vision and promote it vigorously. They help employees rise above their narrow focus on their individual jobs or departments to see a broader picture. Transformational leaders stimulate employees to action and charismatically model the desired behaviors. They attempt to create learning individuals and learning organizations that will be better prepared for the unknown challenges that lie ahead. These important elements of transformational leadership—creating vision, exhibiting charisma, and stimulating learning—are explored in the following sections. Afterward, a three-stage model of the change process is presented.

Learning organizations are needed

Creating Vision Transformational leaders create and communicate a vision for the organization. A **vision** is a crystallized long-range image or idea of what can and should be accomplished (you may wish to review the organizational behavior system model in Chapter 2). It typically stretches people beyond their current capabilities and thinking, ignites passion for accomplishment within them, and excites them to new levels of commitment and enthusiasm. A vision of the future, if painted in vivid colors, may also integrate the shared beliefs and values that serve as a basis for changing an organization's culture.

> The value, and the complexity, of instilling a vision is illustrated by the experience of a new university president. He was chosen to lead the institution when the interview team was impressed with his master plan for transforming the university from a position of mediocrity to one of focused excellence. However, he incorrectly assumed that the positive reaction to his general vision would automatically translate into acceptance of his specific proposals. Here he met opposition from legislators,

An Ethics Question

Your company just initiated an ethics training program that combines knowledge of legal requirements with the organization's espoused values and then suggests you use that "ethical compass" to make decisions for change in the best interests of the company and its environment. However, during a late-afternoon snack break, several more senior employees (in terms of service) brusquely contend that the organization's real culture is to "ignore ethics" and "act to benefit yourself first." Before making her closing statements, the seminar leader asks if anyone is unclear about the lessons from the seminar. Seeing a confused look on your face, she turns to you for a response. Question: Given the conflicting perspectives you have heard, *what would you say to her?*

regents, faculty, students, and alumni. He soon learned that having a dramatic vision was only the first step in the transformational leadership process.

Communicating Charisma Even if employees are intellectually convinced that the vision is desirable, leaders still have two tasks: to persuade employees that the vision is urgent and to motivate their employees to achieve it. **Charisma** is a leadership characteristic that can help influence employees to take early and sustained action. Charismatic leaders are dynamic risk takers who show their depth of expertise and well-deserved self-confidence, express high performance expectations, and use provocative symbols and language to inspire others.[14] They are often masters at animating their voice, exhibiting expressive facial expressions and eye contact, and using attention-getting gestures.[15] They can also be warm mentors who treat employees individually and guide them to take action. In response, employees respect and trust charismatic leaders as they introduce change, are willing to exert extra effort and make personal sacrifices, exhibit loyalty, and tend to be more emotionally committed to the vision of such leaders. Charismatic leaders also need to recognize the "emotional vulnerability" that employees experience during change and to allay employees' fears while stimulating their energy for change.

An important tool that charismatic leaders use involves the art of **storytelling.** These are engaging and compelling tales that captivate people, tug at their emotions and heartstrings, and provide useful principles that call followers to action. Storytelling can be used for a variety of purposes, including dramatic self-introduction of a new leader, fostering collaboration across groups, transmitting essential values, stimulating ethical behavior, or sparking action. The best stories are relatively short, have a plot and real characters, are truthful, pre-tested on a critical audience, adapted to the audience, and aimed at their hearts and emotions.[16]

Stimulating Learning Transformational leaders recognize that the legacy they leave behind is not simply the change itself but an organization that will *continue* to change. Their critical task is to develop people's capacity to learn from the experience of change. This process is called **double-loop learning.** Its name is derived from the fact that the way a change is handled should not only reflect current information gathered (the first loop) but also prepare the participants to manage *future* changes even more effectively (the second loop).[17] Double-loop learners develop the ability to anticipate problems, prevent many situations from arising, and, in particular, challenge their own limiting assumptions and paradigms. This process is in sharp contrast to a more limited process, in which employees simply solve current problems and blindly adapt to changes that have been imposed on them. The double-loop process not only makes the current change

Double-loop learners challenge their own thinking

On the Job: Johnsonville Foods

Johnsonville Foods, a sausage-maker in Sheboygan, Wisconsin, has worked to change itself into a double-loop learning organization.[18] A young supervisor there ("Mac") was a brilliant technician and coach. When employees brought a problem to him, he told them precisely what to do, and then they would fix it. Mac felt good about this role; he was needed. This traditional process might have continued indefinitely, except that Mac got tired of being awakened by third-shift crew members in the middle of the night. The next time they called, he asked them some key questions about the problem and encouraged them to suggest a solution. He not only endorsed their answer but also suggested they had the ability to solve similar problems without his help. As a consequence, all of Mac's crews learned to become problem-solving individuals and teams. They were double-loop learners.

more successful but also increases the chances that employees will be more ready for the next change to be introduced or, better yet, will make it themselves (see "On the Job: Johnsonville Foods").

Three Stages in Change

Behavioral awareness in managing change is aided by viewing change as a three-phase process, initially proposed by social psychologist Kurt Lewin. In reality, however, most change is actually an evolutionary process that is continuous and flowing, with no clear separation between its following phases:[19]

- Unfreezing
- Changing
- Refreezing

Unfreezing means that old ideas and practices need to be cast aside so new ones can be learned. Often, this step of getting rid of old practices is just as difficult as learning the new ones. It is an easy step to overlook while concentrating on the proposed change itself, but failure to cast aside old attitudes, beliefs, and values is what often leads to resistance to change. Just as a farmer must clear a field before planting new seeds, so must a manager help employees clear their minds of old objectives, roles, and behaviors. Only then will they be able to embrace new approaches.

Changing is the step in which the new ideas, new methods, and new technologies are learned. This process involves helping an employee think, reason, and perform in new ways. Initially, it can be a time of confusion, disorientation, overload, self-doubt, and even despair. Fortunately, the changing step usually is also mixed with hope, discovery, and excitement. This is demonstrated by a novice skydiver who may be reluctant to jump out of the plane (unfreeze normal behavior), but once it is done, the diver usually experiences a powerful sense of exhilaration.

Refreezing means that what has been learned is integrated into actual practice. In addition to being intellectually accepted, the new practices become emotionally embraced and incorporated into the employee's routine behavior. In modern terms, the organization has achieved "buy in" by its employees. Merely knowing a new procedure, however, is not enough to ensure its use. As a farmer once said when confronted by an agricultural extension agent who provided suggestions for crop improvement, "I'm not farming half as good as I already know how." Successful and repeated on-the-job practice, then, must be the ultimate goal of the refreezing step.

An extreme example of the three-stage change process comes from rehabilitation programs for victims of strokes who have one side of their body partially paralyzed.

Their tendency is to use their "good-side" arm for self-feeding, for example, which inhibits their full recovery. Therapists have found it to be extremely beneficial to bind the patient's good-side arm against their body and encourage the patient to use the weak-side arm for 8–10 hours per day. Incredible stories of regained usefulness have been reported using this method. The binding process illustrates a physical method of unfreezing (forced discard of the preferred way); the daily practice with the weak arm is the change introduced; and the dramatic gains experienced by the patient serve to reward the patient and refreeze the new behavior. Similarly, managers may need to find ways to unfreeze old habits of employees by physically preventing them from using old equipment or software before they will turn their attention to accepting new methods.

Manipulating the Forces

Kurt Lewin also suggested that any organization (as a social system) is a dynamic balance of forces supporting and restraining any existing practice—an equilibrium exists, as shown in Figure 14.4. This equilibrium must be modified, for planned change cannot occur effectively unless resisting forces are overcome by forces promoting change.

An assembly plant has pressures both for and against higher output. Management typically wants the higher output. Industrial engineers conduct studies to try to improve it. Supervisors push for it. Some workers, on the other hand, may feel they are already working hard enough. More effort would cause feelings of inequity, and they do not want additional strain and tension. They do not want to feel more tired when they go home. They enjoy their rest breaks. The result is that they act as a restraining force, and the current amount of output will tend to continue until some type of change is introduced.

Change is introduced within a group by a variety of methods, as follows:

Supporting and restraining forces

- Adding new supporting forces
- Making recipients more aware of supporting forces
- Removing restraining forces
- Increasing the actual strength of a supporting force (e.g., offering greater rewards for change)

FIGURE 14.4
A Model of the Equilibrium State and Change Process

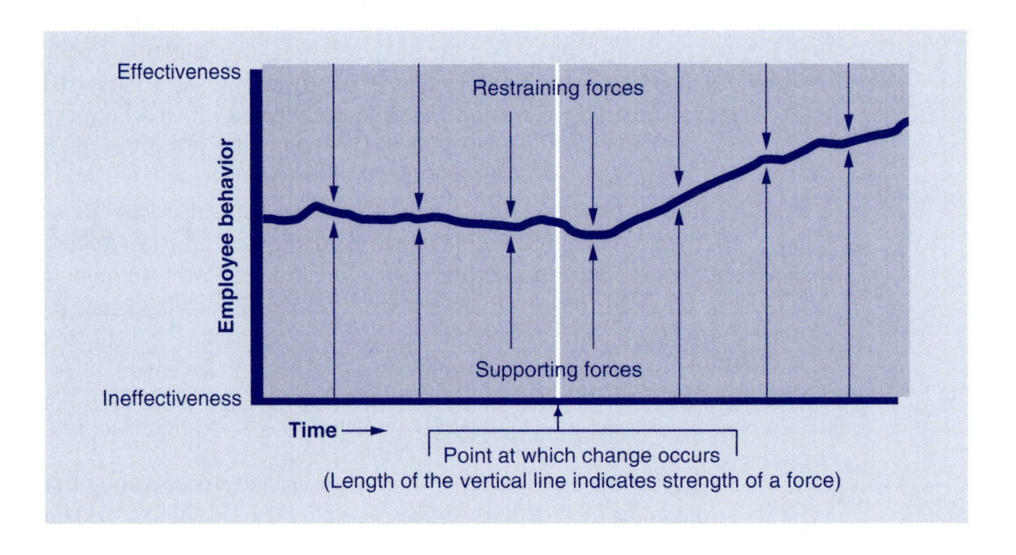

- Helping recipients perceive that the organization is willing to use its reward or coercive power to induce change
- Being more persistent in the use of supporting forces until the change is completed[20]
- Decreasing the strength of a restraining force (e.g., confronting rumors and fear)
- Converting a restraining force into a supporting force (e.g., co-opting a resistor into advocating for change)[21]

At least one of these approaches must be used to change the equilibrium, with greater success likely when more than one is adopted. The idea is to help change be accepted and integrated into new practices. Sometimes this entails acknowledging and focusing on the fear of loss employees may have, or breaking a major change into smaller units interspersed with periods of relative tranquility and stability. David Ulrich suggests, however, that an important early principle in change efforts is to identify, discuss, and overcome a wide variety of "viruses" that infect individuals and organizations. These include authority ambiguities, engaging in false talk (being overly nice), hiding behind busyness, glacial-speed decision making, perfectionism, and using the arrogant "not invented here" defense. These "unspeakable" viruses must be detected and eradicated before the greatest payoff from supportive forces will occur.[22]

Building Support for Change

If we assume management is following the model of the change process in Figure 14.4, then *forces of support need to be built, introduced, strengthened, and sustained before, during, and after a change*. A wide variety of positive activities to build support are described next. Others, such as manipulation and coercion, typically antagonize employees and sabotage the long-term success of the change program. They should be avoided if at all possible.

Use of Group Forces Effective change focuses not only on the individuals but also on the group itself. The group is an instrument for bringing strong pressure on its members to change. Since behavior is firmly grounded in the groups to which a person belongs, any changes in group forces will encourage changes in the individual's behavior. The idea is to help the group join with management to encourage desired change.

The power of a group to stimulate change in its members depends partly on the strength of their attachment to it. The more attractive the group is to each member, the greater its influence on a group member can be. Influence is further increased if members with high status in the group support a change.

Change should not disrupt the group's social system more than is necessary. Any change that threatens the group will tend to meet with resistance.

Providing a Rationale for Change Capable leadership reinforces a climate of psychological support for change. The effective leader presents change on the basis of the impersonal requirements of the situation—objective (performance-related) reasons for the change—rather than on personal grounds. If the reasons are substantial, they should be given. If not, maybe the intended change needs to be abandoned. Ordinary requests for change should also be in accord with the clear objectives and compelling vision of the organization. Only a strong and highly trusted personal leader can use personal reasons for change without arousing resistance.

Expectations are important

Change is more likely to be successful if the leaders introducing it become **champions** for it—persons who voice their own strong confidence and high expectations of success. In other words, managerial and employee *expectations of change* may be as important as the technology of change. This concept was suggested earlier in Figure 14.1, which showed the importance of attitudes toward change. Creating positive expectations of change is a demonstration of the powerful *self-fulfilling prophecy* (introduced in Chapter 5), which is illustrated in this example:

> A manufacturer of clothing patterns had four almost identical plants. When a job enrichment and rotation program was introduced, managers in two of the plants were given inputs predicting that the program would increase productivity. Managers of the other two plants were told the program would improve employee relations but not productivity.
>
> During the next 12 months, productivity did increase significantly in the two plants where the managers were expecting it. In the two plants where the managers were not expecting it, it did not increase. The result showed that high leader expectations were the key factor in making the change successful.[23]

Expectations alone are not usually powerful enough to induce or discourage significant change. How, then, does the process really work? The expectations tend to get translated into specific managerial behaviors that increase or decrease the likelihood of change. *By believing that the change will work, the manager acts to fulfill that belief* (e.g., by providing more resources or by reinforcing new employee behaviors). This belief is transferred to employees, who buy into the probability of success and change their behaviors accordingly. This process creates an integrated system of expectations of success and of appropriate behaviors leading up to it. Closely tied to positive expectations of outcomes is the necessity for a realistic assessment of the "messiness" of change. Leaders must recognize, and communicate, that most major change processes will be punctuated by setbacks, confusion, and periods of anxiety.

Participation A fundamental way to build support for change is through participation, which is discussed in Chapter 8. It encourages employees to discuss, to communicate, to make suggestions, and to become interested in change. Participation encourages commitment and engagement rather than mere compliance with change. Commitment implies motivation to support a change and to work to ensure that the change is effective.

As shown in Figure 14.5, it is generally true that *as participation increases, resistance to change tends to decrease*. Resistance declines because employees have less cause to resist. Since their needs are being considered, they feel secure in a changing situation.

Employees need to participate in a change *before* it occurs, not after. When they can be involved from the beginning, they feel protected from surprises and feel their ideas are wanted. On the other hand, employees are likely to feel that involvement after a change is nothing more than a selling device, a charade, and manipulation by management.

FIGURE 14.5
Relating Degrees of Participation to Resistance to Change

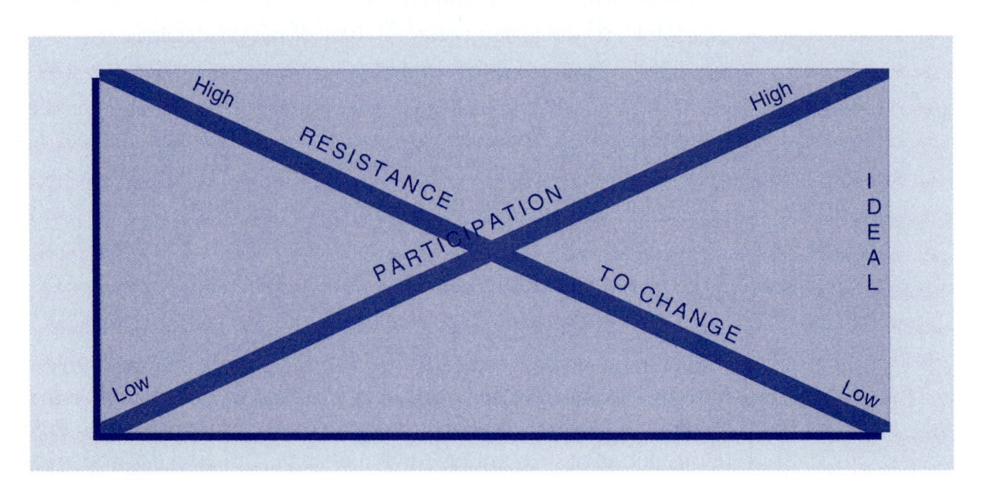

On the Job: Delphi Corporation's Oak Creek Plant

An example of successful change through employee participation and shared rewards occurred at Delphi Corporation's Oak Creek plant in Wisconsin.[24] Through a major redesign of its assembly operations for catalytic converters into a modularized system, employees found ways to save 500,000 square feet of floor space, simplify processes, improve adaptability, increase productivity 25 percent, and raise participation in the suggestion system to 99 percent. Many employees also take advantage of the stock ownership program and thus feel and act like owners.

Economic and psychic rewards

Shared Rewards Another way to build employee support for change is to ensure sufficient rewards for employees in the change situation. It is only natural for employees to ask, "What's in this for me?" If they see that a change brings them losses and no gains, they can hardly be expected to be enthusiastic about it.

Rewards say to employees, "We care. We want you as well as us to benefit from this change." Rewards also give employees a sense that progress accompanies a change. Both economic and psychic rewards are useful. Employees appreciate a pay increase or promotion, but they also appreciate emotional support, training in new skills, and recognition from management.

It is desirable for a change to pay off as directly and as soon as possible. From an employee's point of view, what's good in general is not necessarily good for the employee, and what's good for the long run may not be good for the short run (see "On the Job: Delphi Corporation's Oak Creek Plant").

Employee Security Along with shared rewards, existing employee benefits need to be protected. Security during a change is essential. Many employers guarantee workers protection from reduced earnings when new technology, new methods, and new compensation programs are introduced. Others offer retraining and delay installation of labor-saving equipment until normal labor turnover can absorb displaced workers. Seniority rights, opportunities for advancement, and other benefits are safeguarded when a change is made. Grievance systems give employees a feeling of security that benefits will be protected and differences about them fairly resolved. All these practices help employees feel secure in the presence of change.

Communication and Education Communication is essential in gaining support for change. Even though a change will affect only one or two in a work group of ten persons, all of them must be informed clearly and regularly about the change in order to feel secure and to maintain group cooperation. Management often does not realize that activities that help get change accepted, such as communication and education, usually are disrupted by change. In other words, since the flow of information may be weakest at the time it is needed most, special effort is required to maintain it in times of change.

Dissatisfaction stimulates change

Stimulating Employee Readiness Closely related to communication is the idea of helping employees become aware of the need for a change. This approach builds on the premise that *change is more likely to be accepted if the people affected by it recognize a need for it before it occurs*. This awareness may happen naturally, as when a crisis, threat, or sudden new competition emerges, or it can be induced by management through sharing operating information with employees, as is done in open-book management programs. One of the more powerful ways, however, occurs when workers discover for themselves that a situation requires improvement. Then, they will truly be ready, as this incident shows:

> The human resources director of a major bank aided the self-discovery process by hiring a consultant to conduct an assessment of the department's innovativeness. The provocative conclusions shocked the staff into awareness that changes were needed. According to the director, the results of the report "seemed to crystallize

new perspectives about the potential of the department." Task forces were created, and their recommendations were implemented. Desired new behaviors emerged—risk taking, self-reliance, and decentralized decision making. All this activity occurred because the employees suddenly became aware that a problem existed, and they personally experienced the need for some changes.

This is a potent example of what John Kotter refers to as the need to capture both the head and heart of employees for change to be successful. People want to see the data and know the logic of change, but they also have an emotional commitment and desire to follow through. Based on his study of change efforts that failed and those that succeeded, Kotter argues that there are several major **accelerators of change**—forces that increase the likelihood and speed of success. Among the following, the first one is arguably the most critical:

1. *Developing a strong sense of urgency around one big opportunity* (building a burning fire of ambition within people).
2. Removing barriers to progress as they arise.
3. Celebrating (and publicizing) early successes (similar to the idea of allowing people to know something is getting better by hearing or feeling progressive "clicks on the flywheel."
4. Insisting that the changes made become institutionalized as part of the organization's culture.[25]

Working with the Total System Resistance to change can be reduced by a broader understanding of employee attitudes and natural reactions to change. Management's role is to help employees recognize the need for each change and to invite them to participate in it and gain from it. It is also essential for managers to take a broader systems-oriented perspective on change to identify the complex relationships involved. Organization development can be a useful method for achieving this objective.

UNDERSTANDING ORGANIZATION DEVELOPMENT

Organization development (OD) is the systematic application of behavioral science knowledge at various levels (group, intergroup, and total organization) to bring about planned change. Its objectives include a higher quality of work life, productivity, adaptability, and effectiveness. It seeks to use behavioral knowledge to change beliefs, attitudes, values, strategies, structures, and practices so the organization can better adapt to competitive actions, technological advances, and the fast pace of other changes in the environment.

OD helps managers recognize that organizations are not just a collection of individuals, but systems with dynamic interpersonal relationships holding them together. The reasonable next step was to try to change groups, units, and entire organizations so they would support, not necessarily replace, change efforts. In short, the general objective of OD is to change all parts of the organization in order to make it more humanly responsive, more effective, and more capable of continuous organizational learning and self-renewal. OD relies on a systems orientation, causal models, and a set of key assumptions to guide it.

Foundations of OD

Systems Orientation Change is so abundant in modern society that organizations need all their parts working together in order to solve the problems—and capitalize on the opportunities—that are brought about by change. Some organizations have grown so

FIGURE 14.6 **Variables in the Organization Development Approach**

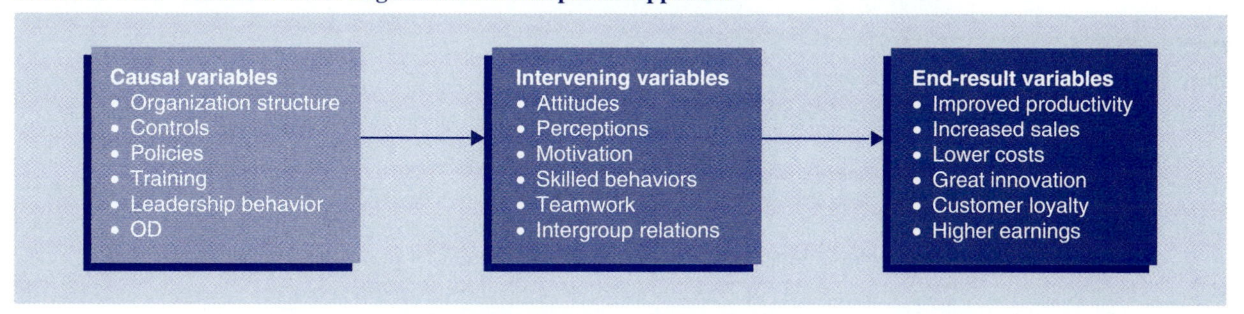

large—with hundreds of thousands of employees scattered around the globe—that maintaining coordinated effort among their parts is difficult. Organization development is a comprehensive program that is concerned with the interactions of various parts of the organization as they affect one another. OD is concerned with the interplay of structure, technology, and people. It is concerned with the behavior of employees in different groups, departments, and locations. It focuses on answering the dual questions: How effective are all these parts as they combine to work together? How could they become more effective? Emphasis is on the manner in which the parts relate, not just on the parts themselves.

Causal, intervening, and end-result variables

Understanding Causality One contribution of the systems orientation is to help managers view their organizational processes in terms of a model with three types of variables.[26] They are causal, intervening, and end-result variables, as shown in Figure 14.6. The *causal variables* are the significant ones, because they affect both intervening and end-result variables. Causal variables are the ones that management can change most directly; they include organizational structure, controls, policies, training, a broad range of leadership behaviors, and OD efforts. The *intervening variables* are those immediately affected by the causal variables. They include employee attitudes, perceptions, motivation, and skilled behaviors, as well as teamwork and even intergroup relationships. Finally, the *end-result variables* represent the multitude of objectives sought by management. They usually include improved productivity, increased sales, greater innovation, lower costs, more loyal customers, and higher earnings. They represent the reason that the OD program was initiated.

Assumptions Underlying Organization Development OD practitioners make a set of assumptions that guide their actions. Sometimes these assumptions are implicit and need to be examined to enable double-loop learning. It is important for managers to identify those assumptions so they will be aware of their impact (just as Chapter 2 contended that managers need to be aware of, and update, their paradigms). OD assumptions need to be shared with managers and employees so those groups clearly understand the basis for the OD program.

A wide range of assumptions can be made, but certain ones are relatively common at the individual, group, and organizational level.[27] A sample of them is described here and is summarized in Figure 14.7. OD advocates typically hold a highly positive viewpoint regarding the capabilities, unused potential, and interests of all individuals. This stems from the humanistic values implicit in OD theory. Groups and teams are seen as vital building blocks of an organization, but since they are powerful and complex they are not always easy to change. Traditional organizations are viewed as rigid bureaucracies that

Individual

Group

Organization

FIGURE 14.7
Common Organization Development Assumptions

Individuals

- People want to grow and mature.
- Employees have much to offer (e.g., energy and creativity) that is not now being used at work.
- Most employees desire the opportunity to contribute (they desire, seek, and appreciate empowerment).

Groups

- Groups and teams are critical to organizational success.
- Groups have powerful influences on individual behavior.
- The complex roles to be played in groups require skill development.

Organization

- Excessive controls, policies, and rules are detrimental.
- Conflict can be functional if properly channeled.
- Individual and organizational goals can be compatible.

have sometimes stifled employee development and growth, but possibilities are seen for positive conflict and goal compatibility.

Characteristics of Organization Development

A number of characteristics, such as its systems orientation, are implied in the definition of OD. Many of these are consistent with the dominant themes of organizational behavior presented earlier in this book. The characteristics are discussed in the following paragraphs. Although some of the characteristics of organization development differ substantially from traditional change efforts, OD has begun to have an impact on the way organizational change programs are designed and presented.

What does OD value?

Humanistic Values OD programs typically are based on **humanistic values,** which are positive beliefs about the potential and desire for growth among employees. To be effective and self-renewing, an organization needs employees who want to expand their skills and increase their contributions. The best climate for such growth is one that stresses collaboration, open communications, interpersonal trust, shared power, and constructive confrontation. These factors all provide a value base for OD efforts and help ensure that the new organization will be responsive to human needs.

Use of a Change Agent OD programs generally use one or more change agents, whose role is to stimulate, facilitate, and coordinate change. The **change agent** usually acts as a catalyst, sparking change within the system while remaining somewhat independent of it. Although change agents may be either external or internal, they are usually consultants from outside the company. Advantages of using external change agents are that they are more objective and have diverse experiences. They are also able to operate independently without ties to the hierarchy and politics of the firm. They can also act as "lightning rods" who absorb much of the residual antagonism among some resistors even after a change is complete.

To offset their limited familiarity with the organization, external change agents usually are paired with an internal coordinator from the human resources department. These two then work with line management. The result is a three-way relationship that draws on the strengths of each component for balance, much like a team approach to modern health care requires the cooperation of a physician, medical support staff, and the patient. Sometimes, especially in large firms, the organization has its own in-house OD specialist who acts as a change agent. This person replaces the external consultant and works directly with the firm's managers to facilitate improvement efforts. Characteristics of effective change agents include courage, power, a vision of the desired future, and a strong base of supporters.[28]

Problem Solving OD emphasizes the process of problem solving. It trains participants to identify and solve problems that are important to them. These are the actual problems that the participants are currently facing at work, so the issues are stimulating and their resolution challenging. The approach commonly used to improve problem-solving skills is to have employees identify system problems, gather data about them, take corrective action, assess progress, and make ongoing adjustments. This cyclical process of using research to guide action, which generates new data as the basis for new actions, is known as **action research,** or *action science*. By studying their own problem-solving process through action research, employees learn how to learn from their experiences, so they can solve new problems in the future on their own. This process is another example of double-loop learning, discussed earlier in this chapter.

Interventions at Many Levels

The general goal of organization development is to build more effective organizations—ones that will continue to learn, adapt, and improve. OD accomplishes this goal by recognizing that problems may occur at the individual, interpersonal, group, intergroup, or total organization level. An overall OD strategy is then developed with one or more **interventions,** which are structured activities designed to help individuals or groups improve their work effectiveness. These interventions are often classified by their emphasis on individuals (such as career planning) or groups (such as team building). Another way to view interventions is to look at whether they focus on *what* people are doing (such as clarifying and changing their job tasks) or on *how* they are doing it (improving the interpersonal process that occurs).

OD interventions can be classified

An example of an OD intervention process that has gained considerable popularity is **appreciative inquiry.**[29] This approach turns employee attention away from a negative focus on problems, missteps, deficiencies, shortcomings, and blaming. Instead, it asks individuals and groups to respond to these questions:

- What is working for us already?
- What are we doing really well that we can build upon?
- What do we value most around here?
- What are our hopes and dreams for this organization (or work unit)?

Appreciative inquiry recognizes that people are energized by success and like to publicly celebrate their achievements. Instead of being overly self-critical, employees are urged to

Critical Thinking Exercise

Major OD programs typically involve the use of one or more change agents. Question: What positive and negative results can you safely predict for the use of an external change agent?

On the Job: Roadway Express

An example of organizational transformation using appreciative inquiry took place at Roadway Express, a subsidiary of the Yellow Roadway Corporation. More than 8,000 people, drawn from all levels of the firm (plus customers and suppliers), met in 70 "summit" sessions to identify the best features to retain, map out high-impact opportunities, paint an image of the future, and set targets and action steps for the next year. The results were spectacular. Roadway saved $6 million in costs, while the number of accidents and injuries both decreased by more than 40 percent annually.[30]

switch their attention to a "good news" paradigm and let it grow across the organization, much as a snowball rolling down a hill picks up both speed and additional mass to become an almost unstoppable force (see "On the Job: Roadway Express").

The Organization Development Process

OD is a complex process. Design and implementation may take a year or more, and the process may continue indefinitely. OD tries to move the organization from where it is now (requiring diagnosis) to where it should be (by action interventions). Even then the process continues, since evaluating the outcomes and maintaining the momentum is desirable. Although there are many different approaches to OD, a typical complete program includes most of the steps shown in Figure 14.8.

Since the steps in OD are part of a whole process, all must be applied if a firm expects to gain the full benefits of OD. A firm that applies only two or three steps, such as diagnosis and team building, is likely to be disappointed with the results; however, the whole process can produce quite favorable results.

When OD is used effectively to manage major change processes, it produces a wide range of potential benefits:

- Increased quality and productivity
- Higher job satisfaction and teamwork
- Reduced absenteeism and turnover
- Smoother relationship (less conflict)

FIGURE 14.8
Typical Stages in Organization Development

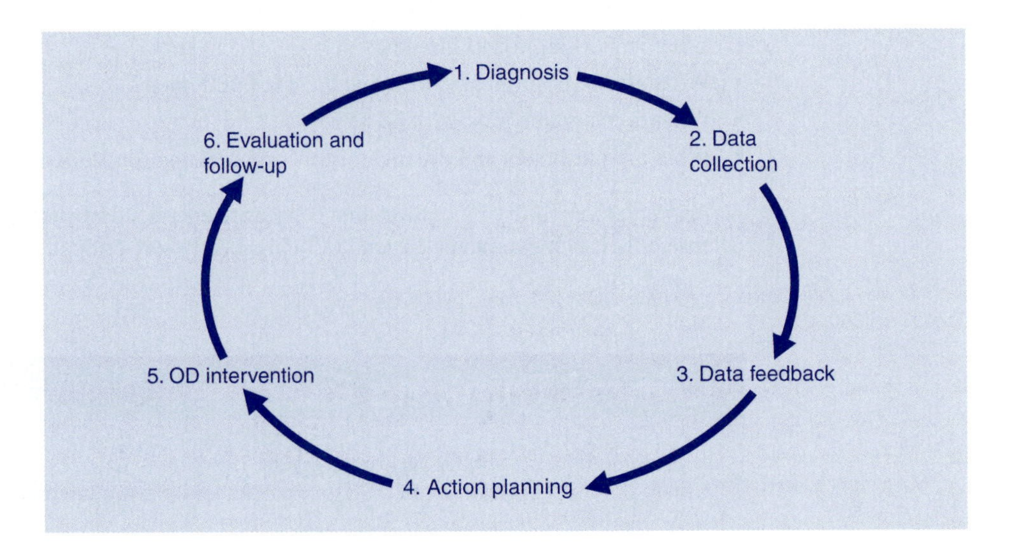

Advice to Future Managers

1. Make only necessary and useful changes that have compelling support, or employees will get overwhelmed. Where possible, *make evolutionary, not revolutionary, changes.*
2. *Alert your employees to expect an increasing pace of change* and the consequent need to develop new skills throughout their careers.
3. Get a few highly visible role players on your side to lead (champions) and have them *model the change for others.*
4. Recognize the possibility of resistance to change, and *develop appropriate strategies* for confronting each source and type.
5. *Involve and empower employees* throughout the change process to diminish or prevent resistance.
6. *Make sure employees see, and obtain, some of the benefits from change.*
7. View organizational change as an extended process with likely setbacks, and *pay particular attention to the unfreezing and refreezing stages.*
8. *Use a systematic approach to change such as the OD model*, and be willing to embrace the efforts of others (change agents) to assist you.
9. Before initiating any change process, *build your credibility* by establishing your trustworthiness, authenticity, and competence.
10. *Use an appreciative inquiry approach* to get employees immersed in change to concentrate on the positive aspects of their work environment.

However, some difficulties are also reported in some OD efforts:

- Major time requirements for implementation and related expenses
- Delayed payoffs—sometimes in years
- Difficult to clearly evaluate results of OD program
- Incompatibility with existing culture

Summary

Change is everywhere, and its pace is increasing. The work environment is filled with change that often upsets the social system and requires employees to adjust. When they do, employees respond with their emotions as well as rational reasoning. Change has costs as well as benefits, and both must be considered to determine net effects. Employees tend to resist change because of its costs, including its psychic costs. Resistance to change can stem from the change process itself, the way it was introduced, or the perception of inequitable impact. Further, it can be logical, psychological, or sociological.

Transformational leadership can be instrumental in bringing about effective changes. Leaders need to create and share a vision, inspire followers through their charisma, and encourage them to become double-loop learners so future changes will be even more successful. Managers are encouraged to apply a systematic change procedure spanning unfreezing, change, and refreezing activities. Managers can reduce resistance and achieve a new equilibrium by influencing the supporting and restraining forces for change. Time is always required for the potential benefits of change to occur.

A wide range of activities to support change can be used, such as participation, shared rewards, and adequate communication. In addition, organization development (OD)—the systematic application of behavioral science knowledge at various levels to bring about planned change in the whole organization—is effective. The OD process covers the steps of diagnosis, data collection, feedback and confrontation, action planning and problem solving, use of interventions, and evaluation and follow-up. Although OD has limitations, it is an excellent practice for introducing change, making improvements, and stimulating organizational learning.

Speaking OB: Terms and Concepts for Review

Accelerators of change, *392*
Action research, *395*
Appreciative inquiry, *395*
Chain-reaction effect, *382*
Champions, *389*
Change, *376*
Change agent, *394*
Changing, *387*
Charisma, *386*
Double-loop learning, *386*
Equilibrium, *377*
Hawthorne effect, *379*
Homeostasis, *379*
Humanistic values, *394*
Intentional (planned) change, *380*
Interventions, *395*
Organization development (OD), *392*
Proactive, *377*
Psychic costs, *380*
Reactive, *377*
Refreezing, *387*
Repetitive change syndrome, *380*
Resistance to change, *381*
Storytelling, *386*
Transformational leaders, *385*
Unfreezing, *387*
Vision, *385*

Discussion Questions

1. Think of an organizational change you have experienced. Was there resistance to the change? Discuss. What could have been done to prevent or diminish resistance?
2. Consider again the change mentioned in question 1. List both the costs and benefits under the three headings of "logical," "psychological," and "sociological." Were the benefits greater than the costs for the employees? For the employer? Discuss.
3. Continue the analysis of this change. How did management alter the restraining and supporting forces for it? Was this approach successful?
4. There is a classic debate about the relationship between attitudes and behaviors. Some people argue that attitude changes must precede behavioral responses, but other people believe it is easier to change an employee's behavior first and then let attitude change follow. Discuss the merits and probabilities of both approaches to change.
5. Resistance to change is often viewed negatively. Discuss some possible *benefits* of resistance to change in an organization.
6. The chapter implies that a proactive role is preferable to a reactive one. Is that always true? Explain.
7. Discuss the pros and cons of Charles Darwin's (adapted) statement: "It's not the strongest [organization] that survives, but the ones most responsive to change."
8. Argue *against* the necessity of having vision, charisma, and an emphasis on double-loop learning for a transformational leader to bring about change in an organization. Are these elements really needed?
9. Numerous methods for building support for change are introduced. What is one risk associated with each method that could make it backfire?
10. Review the significant benefits and the limitations of OD. Do you think the benefits outweigh the costs? Report your choices, giving reasons for your selections.

Assess Your Own Skills

How well do you exhibit good change management skills?

Read the following statements carefully. Circle the number on the response scale that most closely reflects the degree to which each statement accurately describes you when you have tried to implement a change. Add up your total points and prepare a brief action plan for self-improvement. Be ready to report your score for tabulation across the entire group.

	Good description									Poor description
1. I prefer to be proactive rather than reactive regarding change.	10	9	8	7	6	5	4	3	2	1
2. I am acutely sensitive to the importance of employee attitudes when introducing change.	10	9	8	7	6	5	4	3	2	1
3. I am alert to the possibility of an employee returning to previous habits and behaviors after a change is introduced.	10	9	8	7	6	5	4	3	2	1
4. I am aware that not only financial costs but psychic costs of change must be considered.	10	9	8	7	6	5	4	3	2	1
5. I make every effort to predict not only who might resist change but how strong that resistance might be and its source.	10	9	8	7	6	5	4	3	2	1
6. I can present a coherent set of reasons as to why employees might resist, and might not resist, a change I introduce.	10	9	8	7	6	5	4	3	2	1
7. I have the capacity to be a transformational leader by creating and communicating a vision and demonstrating charisma.	10	9	8	7	6	5	4	3	2	1
8. I pay as much attention to the unfreezing and refreezing stages as I do to the actual change stage itself.	10	9	8	7	6	5	4	3	2	1
9. I am strongly committed to involving employees in the entire change process so as to increase their commitment to the change.	10	9	8	7	6	5	4	3	2	1
10. I understand the OD process and the major characteristics it is comprised of.	10	9	8	7	6	5	4	3	2	1

Scoring and Interpretation

Add up your total points for the 10 questions. Record that number here, and report it when it is requested. Finally, insert your total score into the "Assess and Improve Your Own Organizational Behavior Skills" chart in Appendix A.

- If you scored between 81 and 100 points, you appear to have a solid capability for demonstrating good change management skills.

- If you scored between 61 and 80 points, you should take a close look at the items with lower self-assessment scores and explore ways to improve those items.
- If you scored under 60 points, you should be aware that a weaker skill level regarding several items could be detrimental to your future success as a change manager. We encourage you to review relevant sections of the chapter and watch for related material in subsequent chapters and other sources.

Identify your three lowest scores, and write the question numbers here: _____, _____, and _____.

Write a brief paragraph, detailing to yourself an action plan for how you might sharpen each of these skills.

Incident

The New Sales Procedures

The Marin Company has more than 100 field sales representatives who sell a line of complex industrial products. Sales of these products require close work with buyers to determine their product needs, so nearly all sales representatives are college graduates in engineering and science. Other product lines of the Marin Company, such as consumer products, are sold by a separate sales group.

Recently, the firm established a new companywide control and report system using a larger computer. The system doubles the amount of time the industrial sales representatives spend filling out forms and supplying information that can be fed into the computer. They estimate they now spend as much as two hours daily processing records, and they complain that they now have inadequate time for sales effort. A field sales manager commented, "Morale has declined as a result of these new controls and reports. Sales is a rewarding, gratifying profession that is based on individual effort. Sales representatives are happy when they are making sales, since this directly affects their income and self-recognition. The more time they spend with reports, the less time they have to make sales. As a result, they can see their income and recognition declining, and thus they find themselves resisting changes."

Questions

1. Comment on the sales manager's analysis.
2. What alternative approaches to this situation do you recommend? Give reasons.

Experiential Exercise

The Industrial Engineering Change

An industrial engineer was assigned to an electronics assembly department to make some methods improvements. In one assembly operation, he soon recognized that a new fixture might reduce labor costs by about 30 percent. He discussed the situation with the group leader and then with the supervisor. The group leader was indifferent, but the supervisor was interested and offered additional suggestions.

Feeling that he had the supervisor's approval, the industrial engineer had the fixture made. With the permission of the supervisor, he assigned an assembler to try the fixture. She was cooperative and enthusiastic and on the first day exceeded the expected improvement of 30 percent. When the group leader was shown the results at the end of the day, he claimed this was one of the fastest workers in the department and that her results could not be generalized for the whole department.

The next day, the industrial engineer asked the supervisor for another operator to try the fixture. At this point, the supervisor noted that the fixture did not include her ideas fully. The industrial engineer explained he had misunderstood but that he would include the other suggestions in the next fixture built. The supervisor, however, continued to be negative about the fixture.

When the industrial engineer attempted to instruct the second woman the way he had instructed the first one, her reaction was negative. In fact, when he stopped instructing her, it seemed that the woman deliberately stalled as she used the fixture. She also made some negative comments about the fixture and asked the industrial engineer if he felt he deserved his paycheck for this kind of effort. At the end of the day, this woman's production was 10 percent below normal production by the old method.

1. Form small discussion groups and analyze the causes of the problem.
2. Review the management activities for supporting change presented in this chapter (using groups, providing a rationale, participation, shared rewards, protecting employee security, communication and education, stimulating readiness, and working with the total system). Rank these from 1 (greatest) to 7 (least) in terms of their potential usefulness to the industrial engineer. Compare your rankings with those of the other discussion groups, and discuss any differences.
3. Select two people, and have them role-play a meeting of the industrial engineer and the supervisor.

Experiential Exercise

Applying Force-Field Analysis

Assume that the class is extremely unhappy with the professor's grading system and has banded together to demand a dramatic change in it.

A. Meeting in small groups, identify the *major behavioral reasons* your professor might both be inclined to accept and reject your recommendation (forces for change and reasons for resistance to it).
B. Now attempt to predict the *strength* of each factor (high, medium, or low).
C. On the basis of this analysis, what do you *predict* your professor's overall response to the recommended change might be?

Forces for Change	Reasons for Resistance
1. ____________________	1. ____________________
2. ____________________	2. ____________________
3. ____________________	3. ____________________
4. ____________________	4. ____________________
5. ____________________	5. ____________________
6. ____________________	6. ____________________
7. ____________________	7. ____________________
8. ____________________	8. ____________________
9. ____________________	9. ____________________
10. ____________________	10. ____________________

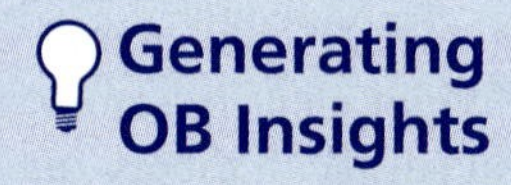

Generating OB Insights

An *insight* is a new and clear perception of a phenomenon, or an acquired ability to "see" clearly something you were unaware of previously. It is sometimes simply referred to as an "ah-ha! moment," in which you have a minirevelation or reach a straightforward conclusion about a topic or issue.

Insights need not necessarily be dramatic, for what is an insight to one person may be less important to another. The critical feature of insights is that they are relevant and

Finally, if stress becomes too great, it turns into a destructive force (see the stress thresholds for both lines A and B in Figure 15.4). *Performance begins to decline at some point because excess stress interferes with performance.* An employee loses the ability to cope; she or he becomes unable to make decisions and exhibits erratic behavior. If stress increases to a breaking point, performance becomes zero; the employee has a breakdown, becomes too ill to work, is fired, quits, or refuses to come to work to face the stress. Managers play a key role, too. When they are stressed and disengaged, employees report being less likely to stay with the firm, less innovative, less valued, and less recognized.[16]

The significance of individual differences in the stress-performance relationship is highlighted by the results of a survey of employee perceptions of stress.[17] Some 62 percent of the respondents reported that stress impeded their performance, while 23 percent asserted it actually made them do their jobs better. The other 15 percent either didn't know, or reported no impact. Apparently, what works well for one person can be dysfunctional for another.

The stress-performance relationship may be compared to strings on a violin. When there is either too little or too much tension on the strings, they will not produce suitable music. Further, the violin strings may need to be readjusted to accommodate changing conditions, such as increased humidity. As with violin strings, when tension on an employee is either too high or too low, the employee's performance will tend to deteriorate. The managerial challenge—like the violin player's—is to monitor tension levels and make periodic adjustments.

Athletes try to find the right balance of stress and performance. In tennis, upsets occur every year at Wimbledon when an unseeded player who is "not supposed to win" rises to the occasion and later admits to having felt only moderate stress. The vanquished opponent, who took the match too lightly, may not have experienced enough stress to stimulate early performance. Then, once the match appears to be slipping away, the favored player begins feeling too much stress to allow optimum play.

Stress Vulnerability

Stress Threshold Two major factors help determine how stress will affect employee performance differently across similar jobs. Worker vulnerability to stress is a function of both internal (organizational) and external (nonwork) stressors, as shown earlier in Figure 15.2. One internal factor is an employee's **stress threshold**—the level of stressors (frequency and magnitude) that the person can tolerate before negative feelings of stress occur and adversely affect performance. Some people have a *low threshold* and the stress of a few hassles or even relatively small changes or disruptions in their work routines causes a reduction in performance. This response is shown by line A in Figure 15.4. Others (see line B in the figure) have a *higher threshold,* staying cool, calm, and productive longer under the same conditions. This response may stem partly from their experience and confidence in their ability to cope. A higher stress threshold and greater resiliency help prevent lowered performance unless a stressor is major or prolonged.

Marie Johnson was a cashier at a local supermarket. Every day she faced long lines, time pressures, complaints from customers, and pricing errors, but these events did not seem to trouble her. Antonio Valenzuela, a cashier at an adjoining counter, had difficulty with the complaints and pressures he received. He began to make errors and get into arguments with customers and other clerks. Finally, he asked to transfer to another job in the store. The two employees clearly had different stress thresholds.

Perceived Control The second internal factor affecting employee stress is the amount of **perceived control** they have over their work and working conditions. Employees who have a substantial degree of independence, autonomy, and freedom to make decisions handle work pressures better. Since two employees may have the same actual control and flexibility, it is clearly their relative *perception* of that freedom that counts. Managers can respond to this need for control through a variety of measures discussed earlier in this book, such as allowing flexible work schedules, enriching jobs, placing individuals on self-managing teams, or empowering employees by using participative leadership styles.

Type A behaviors

Type A and Type B People Stress vulnerability is often related to type A and type B characteristics.[18] **Type A people** are aggressive and competitive, set high standards, are impatient with themselves and others, and thrive under constant time pressures. They make excessive demands on themselves even in recreation and leisure. They often fail to realize that many of the pressures they feel are of their own making rather than products of their environment. Because of the constant stress they feel, some type A's are more prone to physical ailments related to stress, such as heart attacks.

Type B behaviors

Type B people appear more relaxed and easygoing. They accept situations and work within them rather than fight them competitively. Type B people are especially relaxed regarding time pressures, so they are less prone to have problems associated with stress. Still, type B individuals can be highly productive workers who meet schedule expectations; they simply obtain results in a different manner.

The research on type A people, in particular, shows mixed results.[19] For example, some of the type A behavior patterns, such as competitiveness and a drive for career success, appear to be consistent with society's traditional values. At the same time, the hostility and aggression these people sometimes exhibit may make it difficult for many employees to work with them or for them. Some studies also suggest that there may be different forms of type A personalities. As a result, the type A's who are more expressive and less hostile may be less prone to heart disease. Other type A's apparently enjoy their success so much that they disregard the surrounding stress and do not suffer from heart attacks or other physical consequences.

The distinction between type A and type B people raises several challenging questions for managers. Should an organization consider the type A or type B nature of employees when making job assignments? Should it develop training programs to help change type A employees into type B employees (or vice versa)? Does it have a responsibility to provide training that will help both A's and B's cope with the work habits and expectations of supervisors who are different from themselves? Although stress reduction at work is a desirable goal, finding the answers to these questions will require consideration of ethical, financial, and practical issues.

Approaches to Stress Management

Three approaches: prevent, escape, or cope

Both organizations and individuals are highly concerned about stress and its effects. In attempting to manage stress, individuals have three broad options—prevent or control it, escape from it, or learn to adapt to it (handle its symptoms). Organizations can seek to improve managerial communication skills, empower employees through participation, redesign jobs to be more fulfilling, or implement organization development programs. These steps are aimed at *reducing or eliminating stressors* for employees. Other employees can *escape* stress by requesting job transfers, finding alternative employment, taking early retirement, or acquiring assertiveness skills that allow them to confront the stressor. Several approaches also exist for *coping* with stress (see, for example, the personal prescriptions in Figure 15.5).[20] These often involve cooperative efforts among employees and management and may include social support, relaxation efforts, and personal wellness programs.

thinking, and reorientation. The most appropriate type of counseling for nonprofessionals is participative counseling. Counseling needs to be able to deal with both job and personal problems, depending on the source of the underlying stress.

Speaking OB: Terms and Concepts for Review

Abusive supervisors, *414*
Burnout, *408*
Clarified thinking, *422*
Counseling functions, *421*
Counseling, *420*
Defense mechanisms, *414*
Directive counseling, *423*
Emotional catharsis, *422*
Frustration, *413*
Grief, *418*
Hassles, *414*
Iceberg model of counseling, *425*
Layoff survivor's sickness, *410*
Mindfulness, *405*
Nondirective counseling, *424*
Nonwork stressors, *413*
Participative counseling, *426*
Perceived control, *417*
Personal wellness, *420*
Post-traumatic stress disorder (PTSD), *410*
Relaxation response, *419*
Reorientation, *423*
Resilience, *407*
Sabbatical leaves, *419*
Social support, *418*
Stress audit, *413*
Stress threshold, *416*
Stress-performance model, *415*
Stress, *406*
Stressors, *411*
Trauma, *409*
Type A people, *417*
Type B people, *417*
Workaholics, *408*
Workplace trauma, *409*
Workplace violence, *410*

Discussion Questions

1. List and discuss five major sources of stress in your life during the last five years.
2. Think of someone you know who suffers from burnout. What are the symptoms? What may have caused it?
3. Discuss how stress and job performance are related. Is stress helping or interfering with your performance in college? Discuss.
4. Do you see yourself as primarily a type A or type B person? Discuss the reasons for your choice. Make a list of your five main type A characteristics and five main type B characteristics.
5. Discuss four management practices covered in earlier chapters of this book that should help reduce employee stress.
6. Discuss the six main counseling functions. Which are best performed by directive, nondirective, and participative counseling?
7. Identify someone who has lost his or her job because of corporate downsizing. Interview the person to determine how stressful the situation was and how he or she successfully managed the stress.
8. Should professional company counselors be provided in the following organizations? Discuss why or why not.
   a. A large West Coast aircraft plant during rapid expansion
   b. A government office in Valdosta, Georgia, employing 700 people
   c. A job-order foundry in Chicago having unstable employment needs varying from 30 to 60 workers
9. What should be the main type of counseling used in the following situations?
   a. A traveling sales representative with 15 years of seniority has become an alcoholic.
   b. A newly hired engineer engages in petty theft of office supplies.
   c. A receptionist receives two job offers and must make a decision over the weekend.
   d. A maintenance worker's spouse files for divorce.

10. Outline a preventive program for personal wellness that you could implement for yourself over the next five years. What are its elements?

Assess Your Own Skills

How well do you exhibit facilitator skills for managers?

Read the following statements carefully. Circle the number on the response scale that most closely reflects the degree to which each statement accurately describes you. Add up your total points and prepare a brief action plan for self-improvement. Be ready to report your score for tabulation across the entire group.

	Good description									**Poor description**
1. I can list a comprehensive set of physiological, psychological, and behavioral symptoms of stress in employees.	10	9	8	7	6	5	4	3	2	1
2. I am aware of the ways in which I may be a direct cause of stress in employees.	10	9	8	7	6	5	4	3	2	1
3. I can spot burnout, layoff survivor's sickness, or post-traumatic stress disorder in an employee.	10	9	8	7	6	5	4	3	2	1
4. I am aware of the intimate connection between nonwork stressors and work behavior.	10	9	8	7	6	5	4	3	2	1
5. I am aware of the progressively more severe employee reactions to a frustrating situation.	10	9	8	7	6	5	4	3	2	1
6. I am aware of the nature of the relationship between stress and performance and would seek to identify each employee's stress threshold.	10	9	8	7	6	5	4	3	2	1
7. I can comfortably work for, and have working for me, both type A and type B persons.	10	9	8	7	6	5	4	3	2	1
8. I can list at least three ways in which I could provide social support to my employees.	10	9	8	7	6	5	4	3	2	1
9. I understand the contingency factors that might steer me toward using directive, participative, or nondirective counseling.	10	9	8	7	6	5	4	3	2	1
10. I can detect whether an employee needs primarily advice, reassurance, an opportunity for communication, emotional catharsis, clarified thinking, or reorientation.	10	9	8	7	6	5	4	3	2	1

Part Seven

Emerging Aspects of Organizational Behavior

4. I am capable of assessing differences across national cultures on the basis of five key factors (e.g., power distance, uncertainty avoidance).	10	9	8	7	6	5	4	3	2	1
5. I could be equally comfortable operating in a high-context or low-context culture.	10	9	8	7	6	5	4	3	2	1
6. I speak at least two languages fluently.	10	9	8	7	6	5	4	3	2	1
7. I can demonstrate a substantial degree of cultural empathy for any country I might visit or work in.	10	9	8	7	6	5	4	3	2	1
8. I am aware of the typical stages of cultural shock and believe I could move to the adaptation stage fairly rapidly in a new culture.	10	9	8	7	6	5	4	3	2	1
9. I know which countries tend to cluster into similar sociocultural groupings.	10	9	8	7	6	5	4	3	2	1
10. I can differentiate between offshoring, outsourcing, and reshoring.	10	9	8	7	6	5	4	3	2	1

Scoring and Interpretation

Add up your total points for the 10 questions. Record that number here, and report it when it is requested. Finally, insert your total score into the "Assess and Improve Your Own Organizational Behavior Skills" chart in Appendix A.

- If you scored between 81 and 100 points, you appear to have a solid capability for demonstrating good intercultural management skills.
- If you scored between 61 and 80 points, you should take a close look at the items with lower self-assessment scores and explore ways to improve those items.
- If you scored under 60 points, you should be aware that a weaker skill level regarding several items could be detrimental to your future success as an intercultural manager. We encourage you to review relevant sections of the chapter and watch for related material in subsequent chapters and other sources.

Identify your three lowest scores, and write the question numbers here: _____, _____, _____. Write a brief paragraph, detailing to yourself an action plan for how you might sharpen each of these skills.

Incident

The Piedmont Company

The Piedmont Company is a major multinational manufacturer with branch operations in several nations around the world. Its home office is in the United States, but it has sent expatriate managers to work in its various branches. The company recently conducted a survey of its middle managers to determine their relative levels of need satisfaction in their jobs. The results of the survey are reported in the following table:

Approximate Need Satisfaction Levels of Middle-Level American Managers in U.S. Operations vs. Overseas Branches

Survey Items	Managers in United States	Expatriate (U.S.) Managers in Branches
Satisfaction with		
Job security	High	Moderate
Opportunity for friendships	High	Low
Feelings of self-esteem	High	Moderate
In-company prestige	Moderate	Moderate
Community prestige	Moderate	High
Opportunity for autonomy	Moderate	High
Level of authority	Low	High
Feeling of accomplishment	Moderate	Moderate
Feeling of self-fulfillment	Low	Moderate

Questions

1. Analyze the results shown, and give your interpretation of the kinds of problems that exist. Offer possible explanations for them.
2. Prepare a set of recommendations for resolving or diminishing the problems you identified.
3. Speculate about what the results might look like if the nonsupervisory employees in each country had been surveyed. What is the basis for your conclusions?

Experiential Exercise

Adaptability to a Multicultural Assignment

Assume you have been hired by a firm with extensive operations in many different countries around the world. Your first job assignment will take you out of the United States for approximately three years, and you will depart about 30 days from now.

1. Review the text discussion of parochialism, ethnocentrism, and cultural shock. Think about the degree to which you would be likely to exhibit each of these barriers to cultural adaptation, and record your responses on the top portion of the following chart. Then, on the bottom portion of the chart indicate the degree to which you would honestly expect to experience difficulty adapting to the culture in each of the six sociocultural clusters.

	Low Degree						High Degree
Barrier							
Parochialism	1	2	3	4	5	6	7
Ethnocentrism	1	2	3	4	5	6	7
Cultural shock	1	2	3	4	5	6	7

	Low Difficulty						High Difficulty
Sociocultural cluster							
Anglo-American	1	2	3	4	5	6	7
Latin American	1	2	3	4	5	6	7
Latin European	1	2	3	4	5	6	7

Nordic	1	2	3	4	5	6	7
Central European	1	2	3	4	5	6	7
Pacific Rim	1	2	3	4	5	6	7

2. Share your personal assessments with the rest of the class. (Create a frequency distribution of the class responses.) Explore why differences exist among students and what the overall pattern implies regarding the capacity of class members to become transcultural employees. What could you, or your employer, do to improve the likelihood of your success in view of your assessments?

Generating OB Insights

An *insight* is a new and clear perception of a phenomenon, or an acquired ability to "see" clearly something you were unaware of previously. It is sometimes simply referred to as an "ah-ha! moment," in which you have a minirevelation or reach a straightforward conclusion about a topic or issue.

Insights need not necessarily be dramatic, for what is an insight to one person may be less important to another. The critical feature of insights is that they are relevant and memorable for *you;* they should represent new knowledge, new frameworks, or new ways of viewing things you want to retain and remember over time.

Insights, then, are different from the information you find in the "Advice for Future Managers" boxes within the text. That advice is prescriptive and action-oriented; it indicates a recommended course of action.

A useful way to think of OB insights is to assume you are the only person who has read Chapter 16. You have been given the assignment to highlight, in your own words, the major concepts (not just summarize the whole chapter) that might stand out for a naive audience who has never heard of the topic before. *What 10 insights would you share with them?*

(Example) *Expatriates returning home may experience a reverse cultural shock that is equally strong as when they departed for a foreign assignment.*

1. ______________________________
2. ______________________________
3. ______________________________
4. ______________________________
5. ______________________________
6. ______________________________
7. ______________________________
8. ______________________________
9. ______________________________
10. ______________________________

Nurturing Your Critical Thinking and Reflective Skills

Take a few minutes to review the discussion in the Roadmap for Readers of critical thinking and reflection. Remind yourself that if you can hone these abilities now, you will have a substantial competitive advantage when you apply for jobs and are asked what unique skills you can bring to the position and the organization.

Critical Thinking

Think back on the material you read in this chapter. What are three unique and challenging *critical questions* you would like to raise about that material? (These might identify something controversial about which you have doubts, they may imply you suspect a theory or model has weaknesses, they could examine the legitimacy of apparent causal relationships, or they might assess the probable value of a suggested practice.) Be prepared to share these questions with class members or your instructor.

1. ____
   ____
2. ____
   ____
3. ____
   ____

Reflection

This process often involves answering the parallel questions of "What do you *think* about the material you have read?" and "How do you *feel* about that material?" Therefore, express your *personal thoughts and feelings* (reactions) to any of the ideas or topics found in this chapter, and be prepared to share these reflections with class members or your instructor.

1. ____
   ____
2. ____
   ____
3. ____
   ____

Part Eight

Case Problems

Introduction

Case problems provide a useful medium for testing and applying some of the ideas in this textbook. They bring reality to abstract ideas about organizational behavior. All the case problems that follow are true situations recorded by case research. Certain case details are disguised, but none of the cases is a fictional creation. All names are disguised, and any similarity to actual persons is purely coincidental.

These cases have a decision-making emphasis; that is, they end at a point that leaves managers or employees with certain decisions to make. Most of the cases emphasize decisional problems of managers. One decision often is based on the question, Do I have a further problem? If the answer is yes, then further analysis must be made: What problems exist? Why are they problems? What can be done about them within the resource limits available (i.e., what alternatives are available)? Then, what *should* be done to solve this particular problem in this specific organization? Finally, what are the behavioral lessons that can be used in the future? Making decisions based on the answers to such questions is the reality that every manager faces in operating situations. There is no escaping it.

Even a person who does not plan to be a manager can gain much from analyzing these cases, because all employees need to develop their own analytical skills about human behavior in order to work successfully with their associates and *with management* in organizations. Placing yourself in the employee role in a case, you can ask: Why do my associates act the way they do in this situation? Why is management acting the way it is in this instance? Was there something in my behavior that caused these actions? How can I change my behavior in order to work more effectively with the organization and my associates, and thereby reach my goals more easily?

Since these case problems describe real situations, they include both good and bad practices. These cases are not presented as examples of good management, effective organizational behavior, bad management, or ineffective organizational behavior. Readers may make these judgments for themselves. *The primary value in studying these cases lies in the development of analytical skills and the application of organizational behavior knowledge to solve challenging problems.*

Case One

The Virtual Environment Work Team

T. A. Stearns was a national tax accounting firm whose main business was its popular tax preparation service for individuals. Stearns's superior reputation was based on the high quality of its advice and the excellence of its service. Key to the achievement of its reputation were the superior computer databases and analysis tools its agents used when counseling clients. These programs were developed by highly trained individuals, usually lawyers and tax accountants who had picked up programming skills on the side.

The programs that these individuals produced were highly technical both in terms of the tax laws they covered and the code in which they were written. Perfecting them required high levels of programming skill as well as the ability to understand the law. New laws and interpretations of existing laws had to be integrated quickly and flawlessly into the existing regulations and analysis tools.

The work was carried out in a virtual environment by four programmers in the greater Boston area. Four work sites were connected to each other and to the company by e-mail, telephone, and conferencing software. Formal meetings among all of the programmers took place only a few times a year, although the workers sometimes met informally outside of these scheduled occasions.

The following paragraphs describe the members of the virtual work team.

Tom Andrews was a tax lawyer, a graduate of State University and a former hockey player there. By the age of 35, Tom had worked on the programs for six years and was the longest-standing member of the group. Along with his design responsibilities, Tom was the primary liaison with Stearns. He was also responsible for training new group members. Single, he worked out of his farm in southern New Hampshire where in his spare time he enjoyed hunting and fishing.

Cy Crane, a tax accountant and computer science graduate of State University, was 32 years old, married with two children, ages 4 and 6. His wife worked full-time in a law firm in downtown Boston, whereas he commuted from his kitchen to his computer in their home in the Boston suburbs. In his spare time, he enjoyed biking and fishing.

Marge Dector, tax lawyer, graduate of Outstate University, 38 years old, was married with two children, ages 8 and 10. Her husband worked full-time as an electrical engineer

---

This case was prepared by Rae André, and is used with permission of the author.

at a local defense contractor. She lived and worked in her suburban Boston home, and she enjoyed golf and skiing.

Megan Harris, tax accountant and graduate of Big Time University, was 26 years old and single. She had recently relocated to Boston to take advantage of the wide range of opportunities in her field and to enjoy the beauty of New England. She worked out of her Back Bay apartment.

In the course of their work, these four people exchanged e-mail messages many times every day, and it was not unusual for one of them to step away from guests or children to log on and check in with the others. Often their e-mails were amusing as well as work-related. Sometimes they helped each other with the work, as, for example, when a parent with a sick child was facing a deadline. Tom occasionally invited the others to visit with him on his farm, and once in a while Marge and Cy got their families together for dinner. About once a month, the whole group got together for lunch.

All of these workers were on salary, which, according to company custom, each had negotiated separately and secretly with management. A major factor in their commitment to the job was its flexibility. Although they were required to check in regularly during every workday, they could do the work whenever they wanted to. When they got together, they often joked about the managers and workers who had to be in the office during specific hours, referring to them as "face timers" and to themselves as "free agents."

When the programmers were asked to make a major program change, they often developed programming tools called macros that would help them do their work more efficiently. These macros greatly enhanced the speed at which a change could be written into the programs. Cy in particular really enjoyed hacking around with macros. For example, on one recent project, he became obsessed by the prospect of creating a shortcut that could save him a huge amount of time. One week after he had turned in his code and release notes to the company, Cy bragged to Tom that he had created a new macro that had saved him eight hours of work that week. "The stripers are running," he had said, "And I want to be on the beach." Tom was skeptical about the shortcut, but after trying it out in his own work, he found that it actually did save him many hours.

T. A. Stearns had an employee suggestion program that rewarded employees for innovations that saved the company money. The program gave an employee 5 percent of the savings generated by the innovation over a period of three months. The company also had a profit-sharing plan. Tom and Cy felt that the small amount of money that would be generated by a company reward would not offset the free time they gained using their new macro. They wanted the time either for leisure or for other consulting, and furthermore, they agreed that because the money came out of profits, the money was really coming out of the employees' pockets anyhow. There seemed to be little incentive to share their innovation macro with management.

They also believed that their group could suffer if management learned about the innovation. They could now do the work so quickly that only three programmers might be needed. If management were to learn about the macro, one of them would probably lose his job, and the remaining workers would have more work thrown at them.

Cy and Tom decided there was not enough incentive to tell the company about the macro. However, they were just entering their busy season and they knew that everyone in the group would be stressed by the heavy workload. They decided to distribute the macro to the other members of the group and swore them to secrecy.

Over lunch one day, the group set for itself a level of production that it felt would not arouse management's suspicion. Several months passed, and they used some of their extra time to push the quality of their work even higher. The rest of the time gained they used for their own personal interests.

Dave Regan, the manager of the work group, picked up on the innovation several weeks after it was first implemented. He had wondered why production time had gone down a bit, while quality had shot up, and he got his first inkling of an answer when he saw an e-mail from Marge to Cy thanking him for saving her so much time with his "brilliant mind." Not wanting to embarrass his group of employees, the manager hinted to Tom that he wanted to know what was happening, but he got nowhere. He did not tell his own manager about his suspicions, reasoning that since both quality and productivity were up, he did not really need to pursue the matter further.

Then one day Dave heard that Cy had boasted about his trick to a member of another virtual work group in the company. Suddenly, the situation seemed to have gotten out of hand. Dave took Cy to lunch and asked him to explain what was happening. Cy told him about the innovation, but he insisted that the group's action had been justified to protect itself.

Dave knew that his own boss would soon hear of the situation, and that he would be looking for answers—from him.

Study Guides

1. Why is this group a team?
2. What characteristics of the team predispose it to making ineffective decisions?
3. What are the characteristics of groupthink that are manifested in the work team?
4. Has Dave been an effective group leader? What should Dave do now?

Case Two

The Teaching Hospital

Dr. Robert Uric was the head of the Renal Medicine Unit at a large university medical school and teaching hospital. The teaching hospital, a regional medical center, had over 1,000 beds and was considered a reasonably prestigious medical facility.

There was a steady undercurrent of hostility and competition between the hospital and the medical school. The two institutions, a state school and a state-supported hospital, had only one top official in common—the provost. From the provost down, the organization split in half, with the medical school, its physician faculty, and its nursing faculty on one side, and the hospital administrator, nonmedical hospital employees, and ancillary service staff on the other (see Figure 1).

The physical plant, designed in the shape of an H, paralleled and accentuated the organizational structure. The medical school ran east-west, 10 floors high on the north side, and the hospital ran east-west, 8 stories high on the south. They were connected only by the bar of the H, an officeless corridor linking the medical school and the hospital on each of the first six floors.

A large part of the problem was the unusual nature of the financial arrangements. The physicians, as faculty members, received salaries but no money for patient services. Patients *were* billed for professional services, but the revenues went into departmental funds that were disbursed at the discretion of the department chairs. The hospital, on the other hand, turned in every patient-revenue dollar to the state and then had to turn around and beg for, and account for, every penny of operating revenue it got.

Grant moneys further complicated the situation, especially in the area of salaries. Hospital employees were civil service workers, strictly regulated by job classifications and wage scales; no exceptions were made. The medical school faculty, however, could frequently use grant money to supplement state salary scale, to hire people outright at higher salaries, or to provide nonsalary perquisites. Because of the financial flexibility, working conditions were also frequently better on the medical school side, and medical school staff had money for more equipment, more travel, and even more parties.

The inconsistencies between the operations of the hospital and those of the medical school were highlighted by the integration of medical school faculty into hospital functions. The situation was aggravated by the reports of technicians, patient-floor employees,

---

This case was prepared by Roberta P. Marquette and Michael H. Smith under the supervision of Theodore T. Herbert. The case is not intended to reflect either effective or ineffective administrative or technical practices; it was prepared for class discussion.

and clinical clerks. These hospital personnel worked directly under the physicians and nurses from the medical school faculty, who were also administrative heads of clinical hospital departments and were in rather good positions to observe and hear of differences between the hospital and medical school sides. (Qualified physicians were felt to be necessary in heading clinical hospital departments because of the technical natures of the departments' functions and from medical necessity.)

Assistant hospital directors were in charge of most administrative matters, including administration of wage and benefit programs; department heads (physicians), however, were responsible for supervising departmental activities, evaluating employees, and recommending raises and promotions. The dual reporting relationship left the employees in a situation of very divided responsibilities. Further, the general disdain that the physicians felt for hospital administrators left the assistant directors in the position of mere figureheads in the area of clinical services. The hospital personnel, seemingly from the administrators down to the clinic clerks, complained that the physicians were prima donnas, who considered

FIGURE 1 **Teaching Hospital–Medical School Organization Chart**

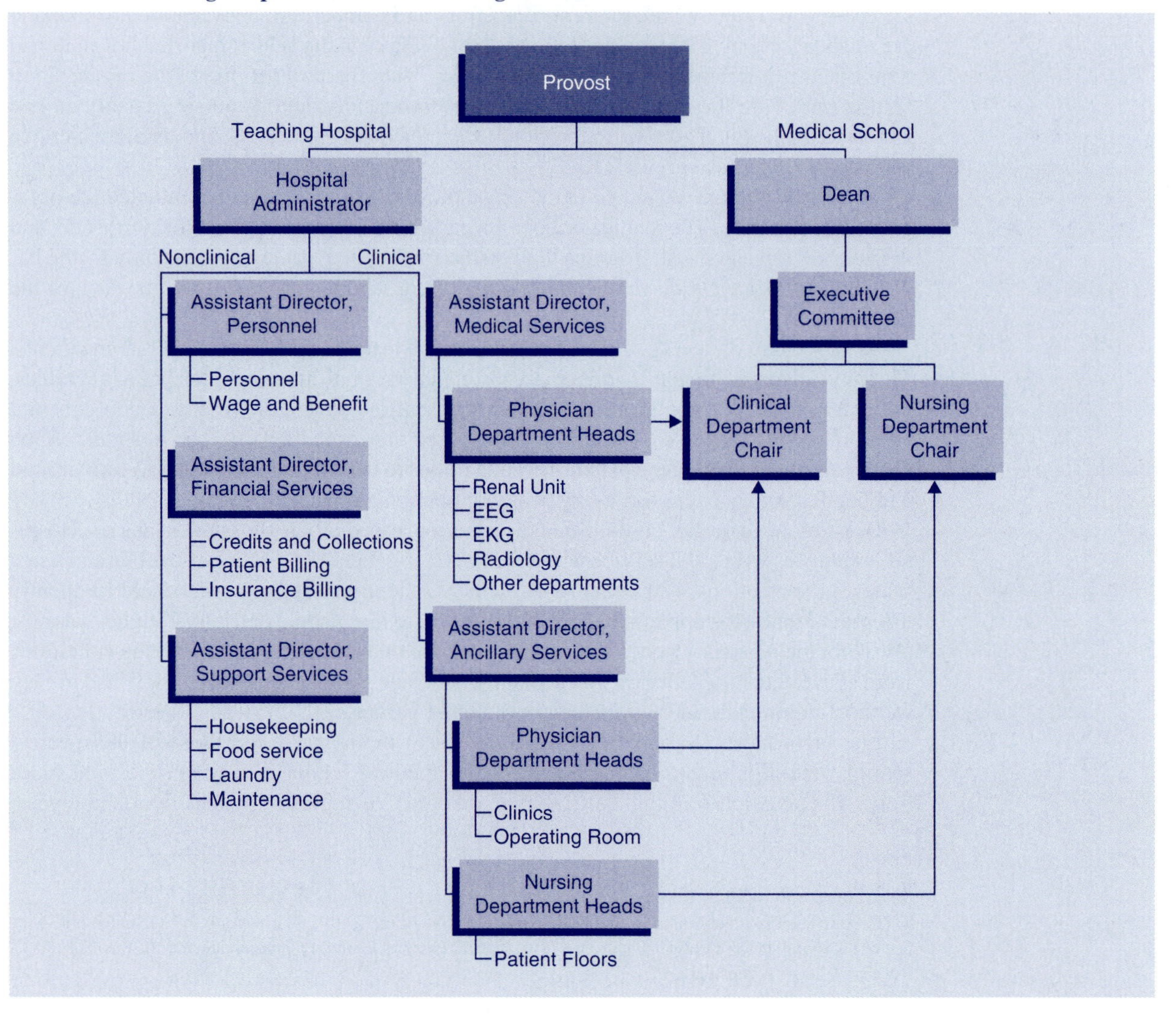

themselves the next best thing to being divine. The medical personnel, on the other hand, complained that hospital personnel were civil service time-serving incompetents.

One exception was Dr. Robert Uric, head of the renal unit. Despite the difficulty of his job and his membership in the faculty group, Dr. Uric was roundly liked by the hospital employees with whom he worked. One reason was that, whenever possible, he shared his grant moneys with the hospital employees in his unit. Financially and emotionally, the hospital renal unit, not the medical school department of medicine, was Dr. Uric's home and favorite child.

The Renal Medicine Unit at the teaching hospital, like many other renal units, received what might be termed "stepchild" treatment, banished to a subbasement where most of the other faculty and staff could avoid the painful realities of chronic kidney patients. Nevertheless, the renal unit *was* a cheerful place. The staff, under Uric's leadership, maintained high morale, remarkably high in view of the hopelessness of many cases and the frequent deaths of patients who spent years visiting the unit and who became, in time, almost members of a large family. The job done by the renal staffers—residents, interns, and technicians alike—was sincerely appreciated by the patients and their families, and was a source of wonder to those outside faculty and staff who were familiar with the conditions of the dungeonlike renal unit. As a matter of fact, Dr. Uric himself was something of a wonder.

On nice afternoons, he could be seen strolling the grounds, pop bottle and hero sandwich in hand, trailed by a half-dozen students, teaching Socratic-style among the birch trees and the squirrels. Brown-bagging his lunch was not the least of Uric's peculiarities; many stories circulated, including the tale of his being given a ticket for speeding down one of the steep campus hills on his bicycle. Also, through those who knew someone in the renal unit, other stories began to leak out—tales of Friday afternoon parties fueled with grain alcohol and fruit punch, and worse yet, rumors of a monthly rabbit roast in which experimental animals whose transplants were not successful were put to death painlessly and then barbecued over a pair of Bunsen burners.

Other faculty members found Uric to be a constant source of embarrassment and discomfort. His actions were "undignified"; for a research physician, he was entirely too involved with his patients. He actually cried openly when his patients died—most unprofessional! Still, he was a fine director of renal medicine and a remarkable teacher, and he was, after all, an inside joke.

That all changed with Flower Life.

Dr. Uric had several federal grants from the National Institutes of Health (NIH) to pursue research on kidney transplantation. He had begun doing active research within the first year after taking over the renal unit. Not the type of man to become fascinated by academic questions, Uric had become almost obsessed with the need for answers when he saw his patients suffering and dying because treatments were not available. He began by solving small individual problems for specific patients and then generalizing and publishing the solutions. Gaining confidence from his initial successes, Uric applied for, and got, grant money and began working on the larger problems facing patients with chronic kidney failure.

A major problem in transplantation is keeping the kidney properly diffused (alive and full of fluid) between donor and recipient, and Uric was involved in this problem. In the course of his work, he discovered a fluid that was absorbed much faster than water at the cellular level. Testing showed it to be ineffective as a solution for diffusion, but it occurred to Uric that if plants absorbed it as well as human cells did, it might make a good fluid for cut flowers, extending their life. After finding the right combination of fluid and an acid substance to keep the cut stem end from closing, Dr. Uric decided he did have a substance superior to anything then on the market.

As required by the grant agreement, Uric reported his discovery to the NIH. NIH officials said they did not want the fluid. Ownership belonged to the university. But when Uric offered it to them, the university officials smiled indulgently and said he could keep it. Not a man to be easily discouraged, Uric next offered his discovery to a large nursery-supply manufacturer. The firm bought it, named it Flower Life, and began making millions. All of a sudden NIH had a change of heart and filed suit. The story broke in the newspapers, first locally, then regionally, then nationally; needless to say, Dr. Uric made fun copy.

Uric and his peculiarities were no longer a private joke, and the faculty became concerned about the reputation of the school. At the next executive committee meeting, the heads of the clinical departments discussed the situation with the dean and suggested that perhaps Uric should be put in a less visible position until things quieted down. The dean agreed. The executive committee felt it should move carefully; Uric was, after all, tenured and very popular with the students and house staff. It would not do to let this move look like persecution. The committee finally settled on approaching the provost with a plan to establish a new research chair in medicine. Backed by the dean, and financed by money donated from the chairs' department funds, the plan was approved and Uric was hastily offered the position. At first he refused, but it was subtly made clear that if he expected the university to back him in the impending litigation, he would have to help out by surrounding himself with an air of respectability. Uric accepted and was given a big raise and transferred to a beautifully equipped new lab on the tenth floor of the main building; the chief resident of renal medicine, Dr. George Conrad, was placed in charge of the dialysis unit.

The chief resident had a reputation for being hard-nosed. He had gone to medical school at a smaller university and had been very happy to get an internship and residency at a large teaching hospital. An excellent student, Conrad had also applied to Bellevue, the hospital arm of New York University, and to several other major teaching hospitals. His only acceptance came from his current employer, and the evaluation committee had looked long and hard at his application before accepting him. While his grades and aptitude tests showed him to be extremely bright and an extraordinarily dedicated young man, his reference letters revealed him to be inflexible and rather ruthless. Born and raised in very poor surroundings, George Conrad was determined to become a doctor and surround himself with that safe and apparently impenetrable aura of the physician—financially, socially, and professionally secure. He had an image of the physician as being wise, aloof, self-controlled, and as close to infallible as a person can get. Somewhat insecure about his origins, Conrad had long ago assumed a façade of what he thought a physician should look like; now it was hard, even for him, to tell whether the façade had become reality.

With Uric's removal, the members of the executive committee felt that Conrad was the ideal person to assume the responsibility for the renal unit. They felt Conrad would apply a strong hand. The assignment was turned over to him by the chair of the anesthesiology department, a powerful and respected member of the committee. The chair told Conrad that the committee was certain he could handle the renal unit, and that they did not expect to hear of any problems from the unit under his capable guidance. The chair also suggested that Conrad be firm in asking Uric to stay away from the unit and thereby allow the transition of authority to proceed quickly.

The executive committee expected a period of adjustment, but disruptions of routine exceeded anything the members imagined. Serious personnel problems arose in the dialysis unit, with increased absences and constant grievances about impossible working conditions. While these complaints were pouring into the hospital personnel office through grievance procedures, few or no messages were coming through to the executive committee or the dean. The hospital administration, unable to alter matters without the concurrence of the department head, in this case Dr. Conrad, waited for appropriate authorization to investigate the matter and attempt to improve conditions.

By the end of the first month, the turnovers had started; after three months, 90 of the old employees were gone. Dr. Conrad did not believe in becoming involved with patients on a personal basis, and he appeared to feel the same way about subordinates. Interns on rotation through renal medicine complained bitterly about Conrad's attitude and his treatment of them; the roster of residents applying to the service dropped dramatically.

Meanwhile upstairs, Uric's research work was stale, as was his disposition. He failed to turn in a grant progress report on time, and the granting agency flexed its muscle and canceled the remainder of his funding.

The dean was not happy and the executive committee was far from delighted, but everyone still believed the situation would straighten itself out. Nobody, however, believed the problem to be serious enough to investigate the effects on the kidney patients down in the subbasement. The dean and the committee might have even forgotten that the dialysis unit was down there. When news did come out, it revealed that the effects were far more damaging than any tales of Dr. Uric's weird habits could possibly have been.

A patient who had been on dialysis three times a week for several years had given up her place and gone home to die. Because she had a rare blood and tissue type, the woman had been waiting a long time for a transplant. She had seen many other patients die while waiting, and even more patients get transplants, all as her odds of surviving grew slimmer. Sometime after Uric left the unit, she had made her decision; the story leaked out after she died.

Shocked by the realization of how bad the situation had become, the dean and the executive committee immediately placed Uric back as head of the renal unit; they then began to analyze what had happened, and what could be done to put the renal unit—and the hospital's reputation—back together again.

Study Guides

1. Identify the barriers to communication in this case, and describe their impact on the hospital's effectiveness.
2. Compare and contrast the two doctors' styles of management and the apparent reflections of Theory X and Theory Y assumptions of each of the doctors.
3. Relate various motivational theories (such as McClelland's drives, Herzberg's two-factor theory, and the expectancy model) to this case.

Case Three

Creative Toys Company

The Creative Toys Company, a small firm that specializes in producing small wooden toys, was started by John Wilson. A carpenter by hobby, Mr. Wilson had made numerous toys for his children. He found these toys to be quite marketable in an age of plastic, battery-operated, easily broken toys. The company is proud of its history and stability and growth in the industry. Low turnover rates are the result of good wages and fringe benefits.

One department in particular had been highly productive. The transportation department at one time surpassed all other departments in production for 12 months. The only reason for this success is the low turnover rate within the department. All eight people in the department have held their current jobs for at least two years.

This department is responsible for producing all the toy cars and trucks in the firm's product line. Each department member has all the tools and equipment at his or her workstation to produce a complete toy. Four workers make cars in the morning while the other four produce trucks. The system is reversed in the afternoon to decrease monotony.

In the past, upper management allowed each department to determine its own procedure and methods, as long as production orders were filled on time. This departmental autonomy allowed the transportation department to rearrange its eight work areas in a circular fashion (see Figure 1). This circular arrangement let the department members converse with each other and keep informed of each other's work habits and productivity. They not only were high producers but also got along well outside of work.

The plant manager recently decided to bring in consultants to determine if production could be increased without physical expansion; demand for company products had outstripped production capacity. One recommendation dealt with the transportation department. The physical layout of the department did not facilitate efficient traffic flow to and from the other departments. The transportation department was located between the painting department and the wooden block department. Supplies and completed products were placed in a storage area in the shipping and receiving department, creating considerable traffic through the departments. One employee on a forklift would bring supplies to all the departments and simultaneously remove the completed products.

The consultants recommended rearranging the work areas in the transportation department into eight individual areas to facilitate traffic flow (see Figure 2). In their report, the consultants viewed the department's productivity as having the potential for substantial

---

This case was prepared by Debra J. Mooney under the supervision of Theodore T. Herbert. The case is not intended to reflect either effective or ineffective administrative or technical practices; it was prepared for class discussion.

improvements. The plant manager agreed with the assessment and had the workstations rearranged during the next weekend.

After two months it was obvious that the transportation department's productivity was declining. The plant manager spoke to all members of the department, hoping to find some answers; however, department members could not articulate the problem. They knew only that something had changed besides the physical arrangement of the work areas.

Mr. Wilson asked the plant manager for an explanation of the department's declining productivity.

Plant Manager: I see no obvious reason for this decline. The department is composed of the same people, doing the same work. The only difference is the work area layout, and the workers seem to have adapted well. Perhaps a raise is the answer. In the past, this department put out more than the other departments. Monetary recognition could be the answer.

Mr. Wilson: We have done some rearranging in other, more unstable departments. These other departments have increased productivity; that suggests to me that the rearrangement is not the problem. I think the department must have built in slack time on purpose. The workers want a raise, and this is their way of getting our attention. I won't be blackmailed this way! They'll not get raises until they have met their prior production performance.

The plant manager left the meeting feeling they had not solved the real problem but only bypassed it, although he was unsure of what the real problem was.

FIGURE 1 Initial Transportation Department Work Layout

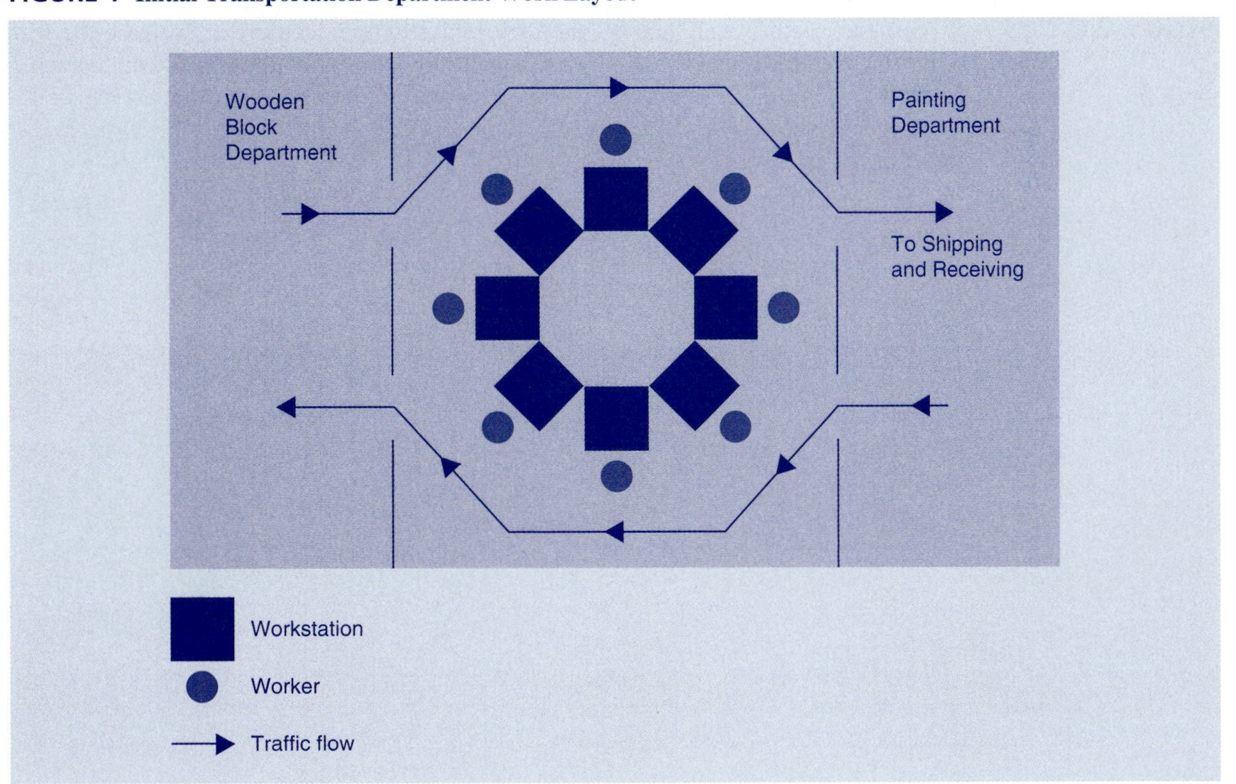

FIGURE 2
Rearranged Transportation Department Work Layout

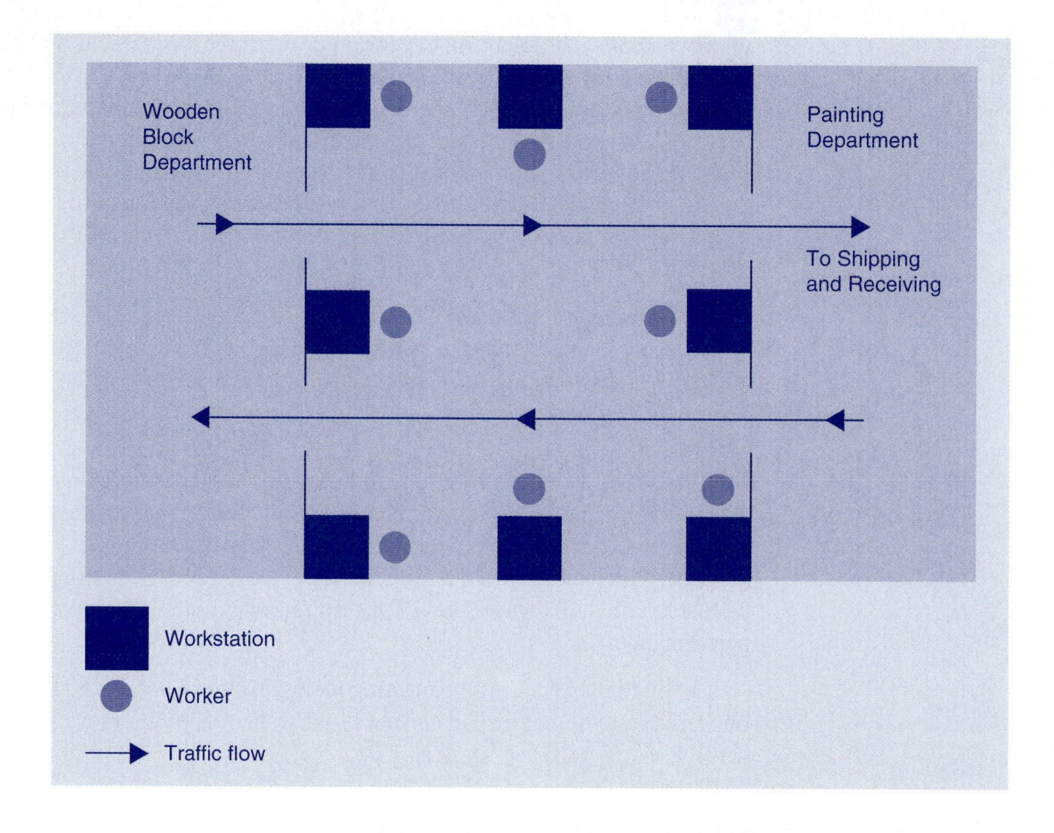

Study Guides

Discuss the role of social systems and their impact on productivity in this case. Be sure to include comments on change, informal organization, communication, and motivation.

Case Four

Eastern International Food Service Corporation

Stanley Strayhorn, general manager of Eastern International Food Service Corporation's Ocean Point Division, has a problem. For the past week, labor turnover has been increasing, employee morale has been dropping, and food cost percentage is climbing, while profit margins on sales are declining. Mr. Strayhorn is deeply concerned, for there are still two weeks left in the summer season. Not only is it too late to train new workers, but it is difficult even to find replacements. A shortage of labor will drastically affect potential sales for the next two weeks, a period noted for heavy sales.

BACKGROUND INFORMATION

Eastern International Food Service Corporation (EI) was a food service corporation in the eastern area of the United States. Its services were offered in many amusement parks. Ocean Point Amusement Park was one of its biggest branches, in sales as well as in number of employees—300. Eastern International had a contract with Ocean Point to operate all its food service concessions on the park's premises. Fifteen EI concession stands were distributed throughout the 500-acre park. Food sales included hotdogs, hamburgers, French fries, popcorn, ice cream, beverages, and so on. Each concession stand had a manager and an assistant manager, as well as between 5 and 20 workers, depending on the size of the stand. Jobs ranged from cleaning grills and fryers to waiting on the customers over the counter.

In addition to the concession stands, the company also operated six different restaurants on the premises, including fast-food services, cafeterias, and a sit-down dining room. Each had its own manager and two or three assistant managers, as well as a full complement of line servers, dishwashers, kitchen helpers, cooks, waiters, and waitresses.

Since the park was open only in the summer, student employees fit perfectly into the schedule. With room and board provided, and a work season that coincided with summer vacation, high school and college students found employment with EI both convenient and well-paying. Besides, there were hundreds of other students of the same age with whom to

---

This case was adapted from materials prepared by David Hau under the supervision of Theodore T. Herbert. The case is not intended to reflect either effective or ineffective administrative or technical practices, but was prepared as a basis for class discussion.

associate, both on and off the job. Almost all the positions—managers and workers—were held by student employees.

All stand and restaurant managers reported to one of several supervisors, each of whom was a full-time, nonstudent Eastern International employee. The functions of the supervisors were to check on all stands and restaurants to make sure everything was running properly, no employee was loafing, and food cost and profit margin targets were met. Above the supervisors was the general manager of this division—Mr. Strayhorn himself—and the assistant manager, Mr. Edwards.

Summer employment was regarded as part-time employment, so there was no union established. In other words, there was nothing to guarantee full-term employment. Nevertheless, EI tried to keep its employees as long as possible. Most employees hired were in-experienced, fresh out of high school. They often needed a few days to be trained; several weeks on the job were needed to become a fast worker. The secret behind working in a concession stand was that the faster a person worked, the more sales he or she could make, an important consideration for being reemployed by EI the next season. Usually a returning employee would get a 20 to 25 percent increase in pay or perhaps a promotion, if initiative and managerial abilities were demonstrated. In essence, the company tried to maintain regular and well-experienced employees, a difficult task considering the long work hours and the nature of its student labor force.

PROBLEM SITUATION

Everyone who worked at Ocean Point knew that Eastern International Food Service was a lessee. The contract was to terminate on Labor Day. Only two weeks remained in the contract period and the season, but the question of whether Ocean Point would choose to renew the contract for next year remained unanswered.

Complicating the issue was the fact that, starting three years ago, Ocean Point had established specialty-food concession stands of its own. Such was its contractual right, to set up and administer food concessions not directly competitive with the foods offered by EI. Ocean Point now had four stands in operation serving pizza, tacos, and frozen bananas. Ocean Point used its own employees, currently employed in the park, to run the stands. The amusement park manager had found he could relieve sweepers in the morning hours (before litter had a chance to accumulate) and put them on the early shift in the concession stands. Sweepers would be relieved, in turn, by ticket sellers in the afternoon hours when few tickets were sold and when litter cleaning was a full-time proposition. Such a clever arrangement allowed the addition of selling functions with no increase in labor costs.

Rumors flew, fueled by the concession operations of the park. Some said that the stands were set up to allow the park to develop the skills needed to administer concessions. Once the skills were developed, the contract with EI would be allowed to lapse, and park employees would run the former EI stands next season. An elaborate seniority and promotion system used by the park would effectively preclude EI employees from transferring to park employment.

If the contract was renewed, then everything would remain unchanged; nobody would be disturbed. If, however, the contract was not renewed, Eastern International would have no operation in Ocean Point next year and between 200 and 300 college students would not be returning to summer jobs.

Rumors spread among the EI employees. Some said EI would be back next year, and others said it would not. Neither rumor was verified by EI management. Even when confronted with the question point-blank, all the supervisors could, or would, say was that EI *might* not be back. (Several Ocean Point stand managers were spotted wandering around in front of EI stands. They were believed to be spying.) The season was approaching its end, and the management had maintained silence. By now, the accepted rumors were that Eastern International would *not* return next summer and that Ocean Point did not wish to hire any person who had worked for EI.

The attitude of the EI employees had gotten steadily worse. Morale had declined. Managers of stands had become irresponsible and were losing control of their subordinates. Food costs were rising as a result of the amount of theft and waste. Workers slowed their pace and thereby failed to serve numerous customers, who were quite vocal in their displeasure. Some students had quit, "knowing" they would not be rehired anyhow. While the *potential* sales of the season were reaching their peak, *actual* sales and profits had declined. Never in the history of the company was there such a tremendous decline in sales and profit during this time of the season.

Study Guides

1. Assess Strayhorn's communication effectiveness. What impact has his approach had on morale and productivity?
2. Comment on the impact of anxiety, stress, and crises on employee use of informal communications (the grapevine) in this case.

Case Five

The Goodman Company

THE COMPANY

The Goodman Company manufactures small rubber automotive parts. Its products include boots for floor-mounted automobile and truck transmissions, boots for brakes, and clutch and accelerator pedals. These products are sold exclusively to assembly plants for new cars and trucks.

The company operates a single plant. Joe Smith is the production manager. He reports directly to the president of the company, Robert Goodman. Joe has three supervisors under him, each responsible for one of the three production shifts.

The Goodman Company has been doing quite well lately. Employees have been added until all machines in the plant are fully staffed on each shift. In fact, for the past quarter the plant has operated six days a week in an effort to keep up with its increased orders.

Robert Goodman, in viewing the outlook for the company, foresees greater opportunities in the years ahead if output can be expanded to meet future demands. Any increase in production must occur within the present physical plant, because money is not available for the proposed multimillion-dollar expansion that was thought possible last year.

Because the purchase of new equipment is out of the question, Mr. Goodman decided to hire a production analyst to see if greater efficiency could be achieved with current equipment. Ann Bennet was hired for the job of generating recommendations for wringing greater productivity from the plant.

ANN BENNET

Ann Bennet received her bachelor's degree in finance in 1988. In 1990, she earned an M.B.A. with a concentration in production management. She did her graduate work at a well-known university, from which she graduated magna cum laude.

Before accepting her new position, Ms. Bennet worked for a management consulting firm. After two years, she was promoted to project leader. She held that position for three years before going with the Goodman Company.

Her reasons for leaving the consulting firm are numerous. She received a handsome salary increase from Goodman. Whereas her previous job demanded that she travel about

---

This case was prepared by Paul Seifert, Dave Thirion, Roger Young, Gene Sitarz, and Debra Mooney under the supervision of Theodore T. Herbert. The case is not intended to reflect either effective or ineffective administrative or technical practices, but was prepared as a basis for class discussion.

40 percent of the time, no traveling is required by her new job. Finally, she feels that her new job is more challenging and that better opportunities for advancement exist with Goodman.

The Goodman Company was very impressed with Ms. Bennet's interview, her credentials, and her references. They feel she will be an asset to the firm and that the position will be an asset to her professionally.

PRODUCTION: BEFORE

Presently, the entire production process is handled by each individual worker. Sheets of rubber, in slabs 3 feet by 3 feet, are purchased from a major rubber company; these sheets are the only raw material for the manufactured products. The sheets of rubber are located in the center of the work area. Each worker procures his or her own material and then, in the storage area, cuts it to size for a particular product. The worker then transports the cut material back to a steam-fed curing press. Each press has 12 molds in which the cut material is placed; the press is then activated for the five-minute curing cycle. During the five-minute interval, the worker trims the excess rubber from parts previously extracted from the press. After 10 to 12 boxes have been filled, the worker transports the boxes to the shipping area. All production workers are paid an hourly rate.

PRODUCTION: AFTER

Ms. Bennet's proposal involves using the same equipment but in a mass-production format. Each worker will no longer perform the entire process. One will be assigned to raw material preparation and will be responsible for cutting the raw material to the appropriate size for curing. Another worker will be responsible for material handling—moving raw material to the curing presses and transporting bins of finished products from the work area to shipping.

The final finish operation, which involves trimming the excess rubber from the cured parts and placing them in bins for shipment, will be handled by still another worker. Finally, a worker will be assigned to the curing process: to place parts into the press, activate the press, and eject the parts and place them on a conveyor that leads to the final finish operation. The curing worker will operate a total of five presses.

All production workers under the proposed process will be compensated under a piecework system. This approach is used in an effort to increase motivation, which thereby will increase production.

THE PRODUCTION SHIFTS

Ms. Bennet's plan was eagerly accepted by Goodman and the members of the board of directors. The plan was made final and sent to the production supervisors for implementation. Mr. Goodman and the board eagerly awaited the results. Mr. Brown, a board member, observed each shift before and after the production plan was in full operation.

First Shift

Before

Cleverson Anthony is the supervisor on the first shift. "Clev," as he is fondly referred to by the workers under him, looks and thinks just the same as he did when he was first hired by Goodman back in 1965. When asked a question about plant operations, Clev sits back, drags on his cigar, and talks extemporaneously about plant performance. Top management has a lot of respect for old Clev; he is considered one of the loyal employees who helped make the company what it is today.

Clev really has no need to work. His brother-in-law died several years back, leaving Clev and his wife a considerable amount of money. Since then, Clev has been traveling around the country looking for the perfect place to retire. He does his searching during his six weeks of vacation; sometimes he stretches a holiday by taking off a day before and after. The department runs itself and he can do this unnoticed. Clev still has eight years to go before retirement, but he still spends a lot of work time talking about the as yet unfound place to which he is going to retire.

Nancy Pearson, the timekeeper, is in her late twenties; she handles the paperwork of the department. She schedules production, orders materials, inventories finished goods, and then types the shipping labels.

Joe Bob Haymaker, the first press operator, is proud of the fact that he and Clev were hired on the same day. The two of them have an agreement to retire to the same place. Clev comes over about once a shift and helps Joe Bob run his press while they talk about the different places Clev has visited recently.

John (Fireball) Malone is the second press operator. Although Fireball is in his late fifties, he attends school in the evenings in the hope of becoming a computer programmer. He likes to make a show of bringing his books to the lunchroom and discussing the latest things he has learned. Computer programming is one of the many different courses he has started. Last year, he was taking a home-study course in accounting.

Fireball is the shift's self-elected spokesman. He walks around the department during the day and takes notes of complaints and of improvements that could be made in the operations. The workers tolerate Fireball but make derogatory remarks about him; whenever he sees Joe Smith or Robert Goodman, he runs up to them and reads his suggestions from the notebook he carries in his pocket.

The others on the first shift are in the same age bracket as Clev, Joe Bob, and Fireball, yet they do not socialize with each other. They get along fine at work, but after working hours they go their separate ways. For the most part, the workers on the first shift feel they have made the company what it is. They feel the company has not been entirely fair to them through the years by not sharing the high profits they have earned for the company. Consequently, whenever they have the chance, they take off work early or show up late.

The first shift never loses any production. The workers see to that by helping Nancy plan the intended work schedule every Monday. Clev sees nothing wrong with that tactic; after all, these workers have the most knowledge anyone could possess about equipment capabilities.

The quality level of the first shift is top-rate. Whenever a bad product is returned by a customer, Fireball and Clev go down to the front office to inspect it. The part is almost always thought to be from one of the "goof-off" shifts. The workers of the first shift just have too much experience to make costly mistakes!

After

The production and the quality of the work of the first shift dropped off considerably after the change. After two weeks of working under Ms. Bennet's plan, Clev asked if he could take early retirement. Upper management hated to lose such a good man, so it created a job for him in the front office. Because Fireball is always such a progressive thinker when it comes to work, management thinks he will make a fine foreman.

No one on the first shift likes the changes. There is constant complaining over the new process. Products are not being readied properly for the next step of the production process.

Joe Bob, who complained that the company had put the screws to them by implementing piecework rates, is trying to organize a union. The rest of the workers appear willing to go along with the idea. They feel the company must not think much of their abilities or else the job would not have been simplified, and there would be no need to degrade them with the piecework requirement.

Second Shift

Before

The second shift supervisor is Norm Leonard. He is 54 years old and has been with the company for only three years. Norm was hired directly into the company as a supervisor by his good friend and lodge brother, Bob Goodman.

Before he came to Goodman, Norm had been an assistant floor supervisor in production control at another company. He had taken his 30-years-and-out retirement option when he was 50 years old. After a year of retirement, he learned that his pension was not sufficient to live on, and if he wanted full Social Security benefits when he was 65, he would have to continue paying into the program for 10 or 11 more years.

Bob Goodman told Norm that there was a place for him at the Goodman Company. The firm could use Norm's experience, and Norm could use the extra money to ease his transition from full employment to full retirement. Norm figured it would be an easy job.

In September, Norm took over supervision of the second shift at Goodman. This shift consists of 12 men who are in their mid-thirties. Most have been with the company for seven or eight years; overall, they seem to be a productive group. When Norm took the job, the men did not exactly accept him with open arms, but no one particularly disliked him either.

So far Norm's job has been relatively easy. Whenever the men have problems with material or machines, they go to Jim Fask. Jim is one of the senior men on the shift; it appears that he knows exactly how every machine and product should be run on the second shift. Jim has no formal authority over the men, but they all seem to like and trust him.

Other than Jim, Norm has noticed no other stars on his shift. Norm socializes very little with his men; he feels that the men should do their jobs and he should do his. He follows the rules and regulations set down by the company and keeps the shift running at a satisfactory rate. In other words, Norm does not want to rock the boat.

After

Reflecting on what has happened since Ms. Bennet's program was implemented, Norm feels that he has cooperated in every way possible. He is convinced that the dramatic decrease in the production on this shift is a result of Ms. Bennet's new program.

First of all, she took Jim Fask out of the regular production crew and reassigned him as the shift set-up man and mechanic because of his experience. Norm speculates that this move alone accounts for a large decrease in production since Jim outproduced all the others on the shift and used to make up any slack that the guys acquired by goofing off.

After the new plan was in operation, Norm had stayed right on the production floor all the time. He wanted to watch to make sure the men were following Ms. Bennet's plan to a T.

Norm does not see anything basically wrong with Ms. Bennet's plan. In fact, he wishes he had thought of it. It would have shown Bob Goodman that he appreciated the job and the company. He felt sure that if a man had thought up and implemented the plan, the workers would have been more willing to adopt it. Now that he thought about it, he was sure the men were rebelling against the plan because a woman had thought of it.

Third Shift

Before

The third shift was added in late May to meet rising demand caused by the auto industry's model changeover. Twelve workers were placed on this shift; only five of them were full-time employees, each having less than five years' service. Seven college students, hired for the summer, made up the remainder of the crew.

Strong ties of friendship had quickly developed between the regular employees, nicknamed the "Jackson Five" by the students in honor of shift supervisor Bob Jackson, and the "Magnificent Seven," a tongue-in-cheek title bestowed on the students during their first week of training. Socializing among members of the shift was not uncommon after work. Cooperation on the job was extremely high, with fellow workers helping each other with mechanical or material difficulties.

Heading the shift was 29-year-old ex-Marine sergeant Bob Jackson. Bob had been working for Goodman for the last four and a half years. His military experience qualified him for a supervisory training program upon joining the company. After being assigned various smaller crews, Bob was placed in charge of the new shift, after three weeks of extensive training relating to all aspects of the operation.

Being the only person of supervisory status on the shift, Bob did not believe he constantly had to push his workers to reach the company's production quotas (some other supervisors pushed hard to impress any supervisors who might be observing). He had been known to work side by side with those members of his shift who were experiencing difficulties with their machines or with the materials.

The remaining four full-time employees were machine operators relatively new to the system previously described. Together with the seven college students, they spent their first two weeks in the department familiarizing themselves with the operations. All part changeovers during this period were handled by the prior shifts. Production improved over the next three weeks as the workers became used to the procedures.

When the order came down that the production process would be changed, Bob notified his shift and finalized the plans that soon followed. Bob found out that six machine operators would be kept on production, one of his workers would be trained as the shift's mechanic, and the remaining four would function as stockers, trimmers, and curers.

After

Because the machines were automated, the only real skills required were in the maintenance of the machines and the knowledge necessary to make part changeovers. John Baluck, a three-year employee, was the former operator chosen to be trained as a mechanic. The remaining three veterans were to remain on the machines; Jackson felt that they, along with the Magnificent Seven, should be rotated as operators.

To break up the boredom of running the molds, the operators often divided into two groups to challenge each other to production races; the losers bought the beer during one of the after-work outings. Often, the quota was reached five hours into the shift. Those who were not operating the molds went along with the game, for they knew that the coming week would see them on the machines.

Concerned that this practice could decrease the product quality, Jackson set up an elaborate scoring system penalizing any group for its defects. The entire process worked so well that Jackson was not bothered by the one and a half hour "lunch" breaks his workers took in the middle of the night. His shift was consistently over its production quotas and had outproduced the other two shifts through the month of August.

Product changeovers and mechanical adjustments, a problem in other shifts, were nonexistent. John Baluck was able to make all the adjustments during the workers' lunches. Should some work be required at any other time, the workers shortened the time spent on lunch to make up any downtime.

Jackson encouraged ideas. He wanted to make the new system work. The workers responded by suggesting ways that production could be made easier. Neither Bob nor his workers wanted to set new production goals. They were satisfied to be performing slightly better than the norm. The crew realized that the more efficient the process was made, the more free time they would have to shoot the breeze. As long as everything remained normal, Jackson was not going to upset anyone by pushing for greater output, especially because his shift was outstripping the others.

Other crews and supervisors were amazed at the third shift's performance. Ann Bennet attributed its record to her ideas, but she had never been able to discover why the one shift had met with success and the others failed. Even observing Jackson's crew a couple of nights did not produce any insight. The Jackson Five and the Magnificent Seven knew that they had a good thing going; they were not about to ruin it for themselves by letting anyone else know about their special arrangements and methods.

OVERALL EFFECTS

Implementation of the change in the manufacturing process met with disturbing results. Output decreased on the first and second shifts. Output on the newly created third shift remained relatively unchanged but continued to meet the standardized production quota. Mr. Goodman was quite displeased with the overall results and wondered if hiring Ann Bennet as a production analyst had been a mistake.

Study Guides

1. What changes took place at Goodman, and what contributed to the difficulty in implementing them?
2. What problems in communication, motivation, and leadership can you identify?
3. Discuss the role of informal groups in the Goodman Company.

Case Six

Falcon Computer

A small group of managers at Falcon Computer met regularly on Wednesday mornings to develop a statement capturing what they considered to be the "Falcon culture." Their discussions were wide-ranging, covering what they thought their firm's culture was, what it should be, and how to create it. They were probably influenced by other firms in their environment, since they were located in the Silicon Valley area of California.

Falcon Computer was a new firm, having been created just eight months earlier. Since the corporation was still in the startup phase, managers decided it would be timely to create and instill the type of culture they thought would be most appropriate for their organization. After several weeks of brainstorming, writing, debating, and rewriting, the management group eventually produced a document called "Falcon Values," which described the culture of the company as they saw it. The organizational culture statement covered such topics as treatment of customers, relations among work colleagues, preferred style of social communication, the decision-making process, and the nature of the working environment.

Peter Richards read over the Falcon Values statement shortly after he was hired as a software trainer. After observing managerial and employee behaviors at Falcon for a few weeks, he was struck by the wide discrepancy between the values expressed in the document and what he observed as actual practice within the organization. For example, the Falcon values document contained statements such as this: "Quality: Attention to detail is our trademark; our goal is to do it right the first time. We intend to deliver defect-free products and services to our customers on the date promised." However, Richards had already seen shipping reports showing that a number of defective computers were being shipped to customers. And his personal experience supported his worst fears. When he borrowed four brand-new Falcon computers from the shipping room for use in a training class, he found that only two of them started up correctly without additional technical work on his part.

Another example of the difference between the Falcon values document and actual practice concerned this statement on communication: "Managing by personal communication is part of the Falcon way. We value and encourage open, direct, person-to-person communication as part of our daily routine." Executives bragged about how they arranged their chairs in a circle to show equality and to facilitate open communications whenever they met to discuss the Falcon values document. Richards had heard the "open communication" buzzword a lot since coming to Falcon, but he hadn't seen much evidence of such communication. As a matter of fact, all other meetings used a more traditional layout, with top executives at the front of the room. Richards believed that the real organizational culture that was developing at Falcon was characterized by secrecy and communications that

---

This case was prepared by Mel Schnake, who adapted it from the article by Peter C. Reynolds, "Imposing a Corporate Culture," *Psychology Today*, March 1987, pp. 33–38.

followed the formal chain of command. Even the Falcon values document, Richards was told, had been created in secret.

Richards soon became disillusioned. He confided in a co-worker one afternoon that "the Falcon values document was so at variance with what people saw every day that very few of them took it seriously." Employees quickly learned what was truly emphasized in the organization—hierarchy, secrecy, and expediency—and focused on those realities instead, ignoring many of the concepts incorporated in the values document. Despite his frustration, Richards stayed with Falcon until it filed for bankruptcy two years later. "Next time," he thought to himself as he cleaned out his desk, "I'll pay more attention to what is actually going on, and less to what top management says is true. Furthermore," he thought to himself, "I guess you just can't create values."

Study Guides

1. What is more important, the statements in a corporate culture document or actual managerial behavior?
2. Why did the Falcon executives act as they did?
3. Why didn't employees like Richards blow the whistle on Falcon, challenging the inconsistency between values and behavior?
4. How can executives go about changing the old values that govern an organization?

Case Seven

Consolidated Life

PART 1

It all started so positively. Three days after graduating with his degree in business administration, Mike Wilson started his first day at a prestigious insurance company—Consolidated Life. He worked in the policy issue department. The work of the department was mostly clerical and did not require a high degree of technical knowledge. Given the repetitive and mundane nature of the work, the successful worker had to be consistent and willing to grind out paperwork.

Rick Belkner was the division's vice president, "the man in charge" at the time. Rick was an actuary by training, a technical professional whose leadership style was laissez-faire. He was described in the division as "the mirror of whoever was the strongest personality around him." It was also common knowledge that Rick made $60,000 a year while he spent his time doing crossword puzzles.

Mike was hired as a management trainee and promised a supervisory assignment within a year. However, because of a management reorganization, it was only six weeks before he was placed in charge of an eight-person unit.

The reorganization was intended to streamline work flow, upgrade and combine the clerical jobs, and make greater use of the computer system. It was a drastic departure from the old way of doing things and created a great deal of animosity and anxiety among the clerical staff.

Management realized that a flexible supervisory style was necessary to pull off the reorganization without immense turnover, so the managers gave their supervisors a free hand to run their units as they saw fit. Mike used this latitude to implement group meetings and training classes in his unit. In addition, he assured all members raises if they worked hard to attain them. By working long hours, participating in the mundane task with his unit, and being flexible in his management style, he was able to increase productivity, reduce errors, and reduce lost time. Things improved so dramatically that he was noticed by upper management and earned a reputation as a superstar despite being viewed as free-spirited and unorthodox. The feeling was that his loose people-oriented management style could be tolerated because his results were excellent.

A Chance for Advancement

After a year, Mike received an offer from a different Consolidated Life division located across town. Mike was asked to manage an office in the marketing area. The pay was excellent, and the position offered an opportunity to turn around an office in disarray.

This case was prepared by Joseph Weiss, Mark Wahlstrom, and Edward Marshall, and is used with permission of the authors and the publisher, Elsevier Science Publishing Co., Inc.

The reorganization in his present division at Consolidated was almost complete and most of his mentors and friends in management had moved on to other jobs. Mike decided to accept the offer.

In his exit interview, he was assured that if he ever wanted to return, a position would be made for him. It was clear that he was held in high regard by management and staff alike. A huge party was thrown to send him off.

The new job was satisfying for a short time, but it became apparent to Mike that it did not have the long-term potential he had been promised. After bringing on a new staff, computerizing the office, and auditing the books, he began looking for a position that would both challenge him and give him the autonomy he needed to be successful.

Eventually, word got back to his former vice president, Rick Belkner, at Consolidated Life that Mike was looking for another job. Rick offered Mike a position with the same pay he was now receiving and control over a 14-person unit in his old division. After considering other options, Mike decided to return to his old division, feeling he would be able to progress steadily over the next several years.

Enter Jack Greely; Mike Wilson Returns

Upon his return to Consolidated Life, Mike became aware of several changes that had taken place in the six months since his departure. The most important change was the hiring of a new divisional senior vice president, Jack Greely. Jack had been given total authority to run the division. Rick Belkner now reported to Jack.

Jack's reputation was that he was tough but fair. It was necessary for people in Jack's division to do things his way and get the work out.

Mike also found himself reporting to one of his former peers, Kathy Miller, who had been promoted to manager during the reorganization. Mike had always hit it off with Kathy and foresaw no problems in working with her.

After a week, Mike realized the extent of the changes that had occurred. Gone was the loose casual atmosphere that had marked his first tour in the division. Now, a stricter task-oriented management doctrine was practiced. Morale of the supervisory staff had decreased to an alarming level. Jack Greely was the major topic of conversation in and around the division. People joked that MBO now meant "management by oppression."

Mike was greeted back with comments like "Welcome to prison" and "Why would you come back here? You must be desperate!" It seemed as if everyone was looking for new jobs or transfers. The negative attitudes were reflected in the poor quality of work being done.

Mike's Idea: Supervisors' Forum

Mike felt that a change in the management style of his boss (Jack) was necessary in order to improve a frustrating situation. Realizing that it would be difficult to affect Jack's style directly, Mike requested permission from Rick Belkner to form a Supervisors' Forum for all the managers on Mike's level in the division. Mike explained that the purpose would be to enhance the existing management-training program. The forum would include weekly meetings, guest speakers, and discussions of topics relevant to the division and the industry. Mike thought the forum would show Greely that he was serious not only about doing his job but also about improving morale in the division. Rick gave the okay for an initial meeting.

The meeting took place and 10 supervisors who were Mike's peers in the company eagerly took the opportunity to engage in the discussion. There was a euphoric attitude in the group as the members drafted their statement of intent. It read as follows:

To:	Rick Belkner
From:	New Issue Services Supervisors
Subject:	Supervisors' Forum

On Thursday, June 11, the Supervisors' Forum held its first meeting. The objective of the meeting was to identify common areas of concern among the managers and determine topics we might be interested in pursuing.

The first area addressed was the void that we perceive exists in the management-training program. As a result of conditions beyond anyone's control, many of us over the past year have held supervisory duties without the benefit of formal training or proper experience. Therefore, we propose that we use the Supervisors' Forum as a means to enhance the existing management-training program. The areas we hope to affect with this supplemental training are as follows: (a) morale/job satisfaction, (b) quality of work and services, (c) productivity, and (d) management expertise as it relates to the life insurance industry. With this objective in mind, we have outlined below a list of activities we would like to pursue:

1. Further use of the existing in-house training programs provided for manager trainees and supervisors, i.e., Introduction to Supervision, EEO, and Coaching and Counseling.
2. A series of speakers from various sections in the company, which would help expose us to the technical aspects of their departments and their managerial styles.
3. Invitations to outside speakers to address the forum on topics such as managerial development, organizational structure and behavior, business policy, and the insurance industry. Speakers could be area college professors, consultants, and state insurance officials.
4. Outside training and visits to the field. This activity could include attendance at seminars on managerial theory and development relative to the insurance industry. Attached is a representative sample of a program we would like to have considered in the future.

In conclusion, we hope this memo clearly illustrates what we are attempting to accomplish with this program. It is our hope that the above outline will give the forum credibility and establish it as an effective tool for all levels of management within New Issue Services. By supplementing our on-the-job training with a series of speakers and classes, we aim to develop prospective managerial personnel with a broad perspective of both the life insurance industry and management's role in it. Also, we would like to extend an invitation to the underwriters to attend any programs that might be of interest to them.

cc: J. Greely
Managers

The group felt that the memo accurately and diplomatically stated its dissatisfaction with the current situation. However, the members pondered what the results of their actions would be and what else they could have done.

PART 2

An emergency management meeting was called by Rick Belkner at Jack Greely's request to address the union being formed by the supervisors. Four general managers, as well as Rick Belkner and Jack Greely were at that meeting. During the meeting it was suggested that the forum be disbanded to "put them in their place." However, Rick Belkner felt that if guided in the proper direction, the forum could die from lack of interest. His stance was adopted, but it was common knowledge that Jack Greely was strongly opposed to the group and wanted its founders dealt with. His comment was, "It's not a democracy and they're not a union. If they don't like it here, then they can leave." An investigation was begun by the managers to determine who the main authors of the memo were so they could be dealt with.

At about this time, Mike's unit had made a mistake on a case, which Jack Greely was embarrassed to admit to his boss. This embarrassment was more than Jack Greely cared to take from Mike Wilson. At the managers' staff meeting that day, Jack stormed in and declared that the next supervisor to "screw up" was out the door. He would permit no more embarrassments of his division and repeated his earlier statement about "people leaving if they didn't like it here." It was clear to Mike and everyone else present that Mike Wilson was a marked man.

Mike had always been a loose amiable supervisor. The major reason his units had been successful was the attention he paid to each person and how he or she interacted with the group. He had a reputation for fairness, was seen as an excellent judge of personnel for new positions, and was noted for his ability to turn around people who had been in trouble. He motivated people through a dynamic, personable style and was noted for his general lack of regard for rules. He treated rules as obstacles to management and usually used his own discretion as to what was important. His office had a sign saying "Any fool can manage by rules. It takes an uncommon person to manage without any." It was an approach that flew in the face of company policy, but it had been overlooked in the past because of his results. However, because of Mike's actions with the Supervisors' Forum, he was now regarded as a troublemaker, not a superstar, and his oddball style only made matters worse.

Faced with the fact that he was rumored to be out the door, Mike sat down to appraise the situation.

PART 3

Mike decided on the following course of action:

1. Keep the forum alive but moderate its tone so it wouldn't step on Jack Greely's toes.
2. Don't panic. Simply outwork and outsmart the rest of the division. This plan included a massive retraining and remotivation of his personnel. He implemented weekly meetings, cross-training with other divisions, and a lot of interpersonal stroking to motivate the group.
3. Evoke praise from vendors and customers through excellent service, and direct that praise to Jack Greely.

The results after eight months were impressive. Mike's unit improved the speed of processing 60 percent and lowered errors 75 percent. His staff became the most highly trained in the division. Mike had a file of several letters to Jack Greely that praised the unit's excellent service. In addition, the Supervisors' Forum had grudgingly attained credibility, although the scope of activity was restricted. Mike had even improved to the point of submitting reports on time as a concession to management.

Mike was confident that the results would speak for themselves. However, one month before his scheduled promotion and one month after an excellent merit raise in recognition of his exceptional work record, he was called into the office of his supervisor, Kathy Miller. She informed him that after long and careful consideration the decision had been made to deny his promotion because of his lack of attention to detail. Denial of the promotion did not mean he was not a good supervisor, just that he needed to follow more instead of taking the lead. Mike was stunned and said so. But before he said anything else, he asked to meet with Rick Belkner and Jack Greely the next day.

The Showdown

Sitting face-to-face with Rick and Jack, Mike asked if they agreed with the appraisal Kathy had discussed with him. They both said they did. When asked if any other supervisor surpassed his ability and results, each stated that Mike was one of the best, if not *the* best they had. Then why, Mike asked, would they deny him a promotion when others of less ability were approved? The answer came from Jack: "It's nothing personal; we just don't like your management style. You're an oddball. We can't run a division with 10 supervisors all doing different things. What kind of a business do you think we're running here? We need people who conform to our style and methods so we can measure their results objectively. There is no room for subjective interpretation. It's our feeling that if you really put your mind to it, you can be an excellent manager. It's just that you now create trouble and rock the boat. We don't need that. It doesn't matter if you're the best now. Sooner or later as you go up the ladder, you will be forced to pay more attention to administrative duties and you won't handle them well. If we correct your bad habits now, we think you can go far."

Mike was shocked. He turned to face Rick and blurted out, "You mean it doesn't matter what my results are? All that matters is how I do things?" Rick leaned back in his chair and said in a casual tone, "In a word, yes."

Mike left the office knowing that his career at Consolidated was over and immediately started looking for a new job. What had gone wrong?

Study Guides

1. This case can be treated as a three-part predictive exercise.
   - **a.** Read only Part 1 and stop. How do you think the supervisors' statement of intent will be received by top management at Consolidated Life?
   - **b.** Read Part 2. What do you think Mike will do now? What do you recommend that he do?
   - **c.** Read Part 3. Should Mike try to continue his career with Consolidated Life or find a job elsewhere? How does the self-fulfilling prophecy affect this situation? If he leaves, do you think he can be successful in another organization?
2. Was Mike wise to attempt to change the behavior of his boss? Was such an attempt ethical? What methods have you read about that he could have used? What would you have done differently?
3. How do you think that Mike would describe the organizational culture at Consolidated Life? What is an employee's responsibility for reading a firm's culture and for adjusting to it?
4. Evaluate the memo Mike wrote. Now assess the fairness and motivational impact of the feedback that Mike received. Will such feedback be useful in changing his behavior? What advice could you have given Rick and Jack prior to the meeting with Mike?

Case Eight

Video Electronics Company

Frank Simpson, president and controlling stockholder of the Video Electronics Company, now in its tenth year, was faced with the problem of gearing his plant to meet both increased production demands brought on by the expanding electronics industry and increased competition from other producers of his line of products. The plant tripled its number of employees during the past year, but production per worker decreased nearly 20 percent and costs rose nearly to the break-even point. For the preceding quarter, profit on sales was less than 1 percent and profit on invested capital was under 3 percent. These profit rates were one-fourth of what Simpson considered normal.

The company employed mostly unskilled labor, who were trained by the company. Employees were not represented by a labor union. All employees were paid hourly wages rather than incentive wages.

The company was founded by Simpson and a few investor friends for production of a narrow line of specialized small electronics parts that were sold to other manufacturers. It grew slowly and had a labor force of only 105 workers at the beginning of last year. Its reputation for quality was excellent. This reputation for quality was the primary reason for a flood of orders from new clients in the spring of last year, requiring the firm to triple its labor force by July. Simpson remarked, "I didn't seek those orders. *They* came to us. I didn't want to expand that fast, but what could I do? If you want to stay in business, you can't tell your customers you are too busy to sell them anything."

The company was located in a manufacturing town of 15,000 people in rural New York, about 60 miles from any large town. Enough untrained people were available locally for hiring for the expansion, which required the operation of two shifts instead of one. Management's forecasts indicated that the expansion would be permanent, with the additional possibility of moderate growth during the next five years or longer.

Simpson, in consultation with the board of directors, concluded that he needed to establish the new position of general manager of the plant so he (Simpson) could spend more of his time on high-level work and less of it ironing out production difficulties. He also concluded that under present conditions he needed to build an industrial engineering staff that could both cope with present production problems and give his company the developmental work needed to stay ahead of the competitors.

Almost all his present supervisory personnel had been with the company since the year it was founded. They were all skilled people in their particular phases of the operations, but Simpson felt that none of them had the training or overall insight into company problems to take charge as general manager.

After much thought, Simpson decided to employ a general manager from outside the company. This person would report directly to him and would have full responsibility for production of the product and development of a top-notch industrial engineering department. Simpson called a meeting of all his supervisory personnel and explained his decision to them in detail. He described the need for this plan of action and stressed the necessity for the utmost in cooperation. The older supervisors did not seem to be pleased with this turn of events but promised they would cooperate fully with the new manager.

About four months after his meeting with his supervisors, Simpson found a suitable general manager, John Rider. Rider, age 36, was a mechanical engineer who had been a general supervisor in a large Philadelphia electronics plant. One of his first jobs as general manager was to find a qualified person to develop the industrial engineering function. Paul Green, an industrial engineer 31 years of age, was hired from the industrial engineering department of a large steel company in Pittsburgh. Green had an M.B.A., a good academic record, an honorable discharge from the military, and two years of relevant experience.

Green and Rider both felt that the company was in bad condition in relation to machine utilization, employee utilization, waste, and reject rates. On the basis of their first impressions of the production facilities, they estimated that production management and industrial engineering changes might be able to increase productivity at least 25 percent and reduce unit costs 35 percent.

Green wanted time to get acquainted with the processes and the supervisory personnel before recommending major improvements. Rider granted this wish, and Green spent two months getting acquainted with the supervisors. During this period, he recommended to Rider only minor changes, which the supervisors seemed to accept, with only minor disagreement. However, after this period, Simpson, Rider, and Green felt that major steps had to be taken to improve both production and quality. They decided that the first industrial engineering project should be a study of production processes, department by department. The study was to cover every operation done on the products. All processes were to be put in writing since many of the processes had developed without anyone's ever writing down just how they were to be performed. Several of the supervisors were the only ones who understood how certain operations were to be set up and performed, and any supervisor who left the company often took valuable knowledge that was difficult to replace.

At the next supervisory meeting (of all managerial personnel), Simpson announced the plan for the production study. No estimated completion date for the study was given. No comments were made by the production supervisors, but it was plain to Rider and Green that several of the older supervisors were not happy about the idea. Simpson tried to get across the idea that full cooperation was required and that the company had "to meet its competition or go out of business."

Green started the survey the following week. There was outward rebellion in some cases, but he smoothed this over by discussing with the supervisor the reasons for the survey and then leaving that department alone for a few days. Green thought he was convincing the people who objected, so he proceeded with the study without comment to either Rider or Simpson about the resistance.

About five weeks after Green started the study, he and Rider left town together on a business trip that kept them away from the plant for two days. On the night of the second day, one of the second-shift supervisors telephoned Simpson, who happened to be working late at the office. The supervisor said that a group of them would like to talk to Simpson. Since many of these supervisors had known Simpson for a long time and called him by his first name, he did not object and told them to "come on up."

The group that arrived consisted of all supervisors with more than one year's company seniority. First-shift supervisors were there, even though they had been off duty for three hours. As soon as the group arrived, it was apparent to Simpson that they were troubled about something and that this was no social call. All the supervisors entered his office, and

Charles Warren, an older man who had been supervisor for nine years, acted as speaker for the group.

"Frank," he said, "all of us here have been in this game for a good many years. We know more about this business than anyone else around here, and we don't like people standing around in our departments watching what we are doing. We also don't like the idea of some young guy telling us that we should do this and that to improve our production and quality. This industry is different, and those new ideas about industrial engineering just won't work for us. We want you to tell that new guy, Green, that his ideas won't work for a company like this." Warren then paused to give Simpson a chance to answer. The other supervisors stood there quietly.

Study Guides

1. If you were Simpson, what would you do now? What would you do later, if anything? What behavioral models and ideas are involved in your decisions?
2. Should Simpson have permitted the supervisors to see him, since they now report directly to Rider?
3. What kinds of changes are taking place in this case? What are the effects of these changes? What ideas about change would be helpful in dealing with this situation?
4. Do the three stages in change (unfreezing, changing, refreezing) apply in this case? Discuss.

Role-Playing Situations

1. You are Simpson. Reply to Warren and the other supervisors gathered in your office.
2. Have people play the roles of Simpson, Rider, and Green in a meeting in Simpson's office to discuss the situation on the day Rider and Green return from their trip.
3. Role-play the supervisory meeting in which Simpson announces to his supervisors the production process study. Include people in the roles of Rider and Green.

Case Nine

Elite Electric Company

Elite Electric Company is a moderately small manufacturing subsidiary of a large European conglomerate. The company manufactures electric components supplied to its parent company for sale to consumer retail outlets as well as for commercial distribution. Sales five years ago were approximately $10 million and grew to $35 million last year. Elite Electric Company has two plants, one in Pennsylvania and the other in Massachusetts. The plant in Pennsylvania is relatively new and can manufacture three times the number of units produced by the Massachusetts plant. The Massachusetts plant was established in the early 1920s and is on a large, beautifully manicured estate. The buildings are quite old, and the machinery is antiquated. However, the company headquarters is at the Massachusetts plant, and the company's president is insistent upon keeping both plants active. (See the table for the five-year production history of the plants.)

In order to cope with the growth of the company administratively, additional staff were hired. However, there was no organized plan to establish systems and procedures for training, mechanization, and so on, in anticipation of the increased workload and the specialization of activities and functions that would eventually arise. People who had been with the company for a long period of time knew their assignments and, by and large, carried the company through its day-to-day activities. When many of these people left suddenly during a personnel reduction, an information void was created because there was little in the way of written procedures to guide those who remained and the replacement staff who were hired.

Another significant factor in the company's history was employee turnover. An administrative employee organization chart shows that 40 percent of the people employed as of just two years ago are no longer associated with the company. Of those remaining, 90 percent have different assignments today. Many of the losses in staff were in important positions, and all levels were affected. (Figures 1 and 2 show the organization charts for the company and for the Massachusetts plant, respectively.)

THE MASSACHUSETTS PLANT

The president of the company, Mr. William White, originally came from LTV, which is located in Dallas, Texas. From there he was recruited to be plant operations manager in Massachusetts. When the original owners sold out to the European concern, White was made president. The next year, he opened the Pennsylvania plant.

This case was prepared by Barry R. Armandi, and is used with permission of the author and the publisher, Elsevier Science Publishing Co., Inc.

As president, White developed a six-item operational philosophy. The components of this philosophy are as follows:

1. Make product quality and customer service top priorities.
2. Foster a human-oriented working atmosphere.
3. Maximize communication, interaction, and involvement.
4. Minimize the layers of organizational structure, and control the growth of bureaucracy.
5. Value and respect our form of company organization.
6. Strive for excellence in our business performance.

Upon being appointed president, White promoted Peter Johnson to the position of plant operations manager from his previous position of production manager. White told Johnson that he (Johnson) had a lot to learn about running a plant and to go easy with changes until he got his feet wet. He also indicated that with the projected operation of the new plant the following year, Johnson should expect some reduction in production demand. But White felt this reduction would be temporary. Further, White emphatically reminded Johnson of the company's operational philosophy.

While White was plant operations manager, he initiated daily operations meetings with the following people: the purchasing manager (Paul Barbato), the production manager (Brian Campbell), the quality-control manager (Elizabeth Schultz), the engineering manager (David Arato), the safety manager (Martin Massell), the personnel manager (Jane Wieder), the customer service manager (Michael St. John), and one of the assistant controllers (Harvey Jones).

Five-Year Production History for Elite Electric Company (in units)

	Year 1	Year 2	Year 3*		Year 4		Year 5	
			Mass.	Penn.	Mass.	Penn.	Mass.	Penn.
Transistors (thousands)	800	600	500	400	475	535	452	629
Large integrated circuit boards (thousands)	475	479	325	201	300	227	248	325
Small integrated circuit boards (thousands)	600	585	480	175	250	212	321	438
Large-capacity chips (millions)	1.2	1.1	0.7	0.5	0.6	0.7	0.6	0.9
Small-capacity chips (millions)	1.8	2.0	0.5	1.3	0.2	2.0	0.3	2.7
Cathode-ray tubes (thousands)	325	250	210	22	126	46	147	63
Percent with defects	0.1	0.15	0.9	4.2	1.6	2.5	2.5	1.2

*New plant begins operations

When Johnson took over, he decided to continue the daily meetings. One day, after discussing problems of the company at an open meeting, it was decided that individuals from various other line and staff areas should attend the daily meetings. The transcript of a typical meeting follows.

Peter Johnson: Okay, everybody, it's 9:00, so let's get started. You all know what the agenda is, so let's start with safety first.

Martin Massell (Safety Manager): Well Peter, I have a number of things to go over. First, we should look into feedback from maintenance. The other day we had an incident where the maintenance crew was washing down the walls and water leaked into the electrical wiring. Nobody was told about this, and subsequently, seepage began Friday and smoke developed.

Peter Johnson: Okay, we will have maintenance look into it and they will get back to you. What else, Marty?

Martin Massell: We found out that the operators of the forklifts are operating them too fast in the plant. We are sending out a memo telling them to slow down.

David Arato (Engineering Manager): Why don't we just put some bumps in the floor so they can't speed over them?

Martin Massell: Well, we are looking at that. We may decide to do it, but we have to get some cost estimates and maintenance will have to fill us in.

Peter Johnson: By the way, where is the representative from maintenance? Well, I will have to contact Irving (Maintenance Manager). Anything else, Marty?

Martin Massell: Oh yeah, I forgot to tell you yesterday the entire loading dock has been cleaned. We shouldn't be having any more problems. By the way, Brian, make sure you contact Irv about the spill in the area.

Brian Campbell (Production Manager): Oh, I forgot to tell you, Peter. Irv said we would have to close down machines 1 and 6 to get at the leak that's causing the oil spill. I've already gone ahead with that.

Peter Johnson: Gee, Brian, I wish you would clear these things with me first. How badly will this affect our production?

FIGURE 1 Elite Electric Company Organization Chart

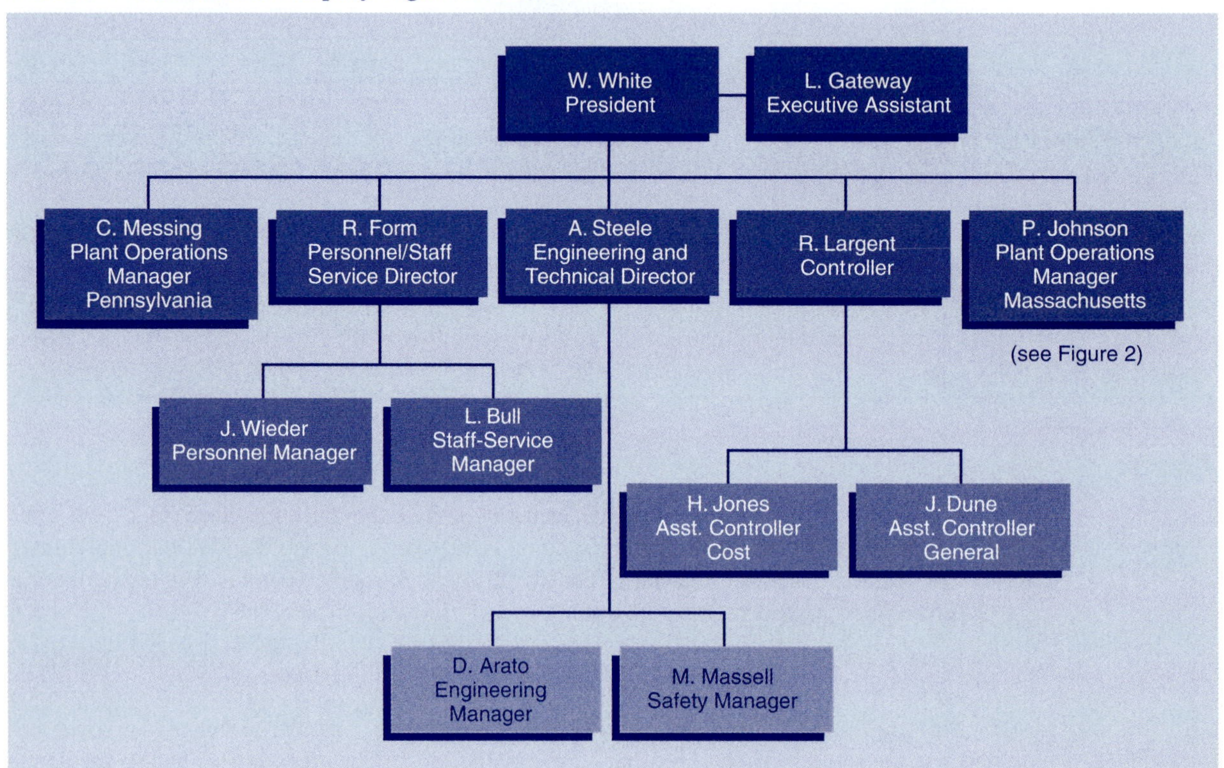

Brian Campbell: Not badly, we should be able to get away with a minimum of overtime this weekend.

Peter Johnson: Customer service is next. Mike, how are we doing with our parent company?

Michael St. John (Customer Service Manager): Nothing much new to report. We are starting to get flack for not taking that Japanese order, but the guys at the parent company understand. They may not like it, but they can deal with it. Oh, Paul, are you going to have enough transistors on hand to complete the order by next Tuesday?

Paul Barbato (Purchasing Manager): Sure, Mike, I sent you a memo on that yesterday.

Michael St. John: Sorry, but I haven't had a chance to get to my morning mail yet. I was too busy with some visitors from Europe.

Peter Johnson: Are these people being taken care of, Mike? Is there anything we can do to make their stay here more comfortable?

Michael St. John: No, everything is fine.

Peter Johnson: Okay. Let's move on to employee relations. Jane?

Jane Wieder (Personnel Manager): I would like to introduce two guests from Training Programs, Inc. As you know, we will be embarking upon our final training program

FIGURE 2 **Massachusetts Plant Organization Chart**

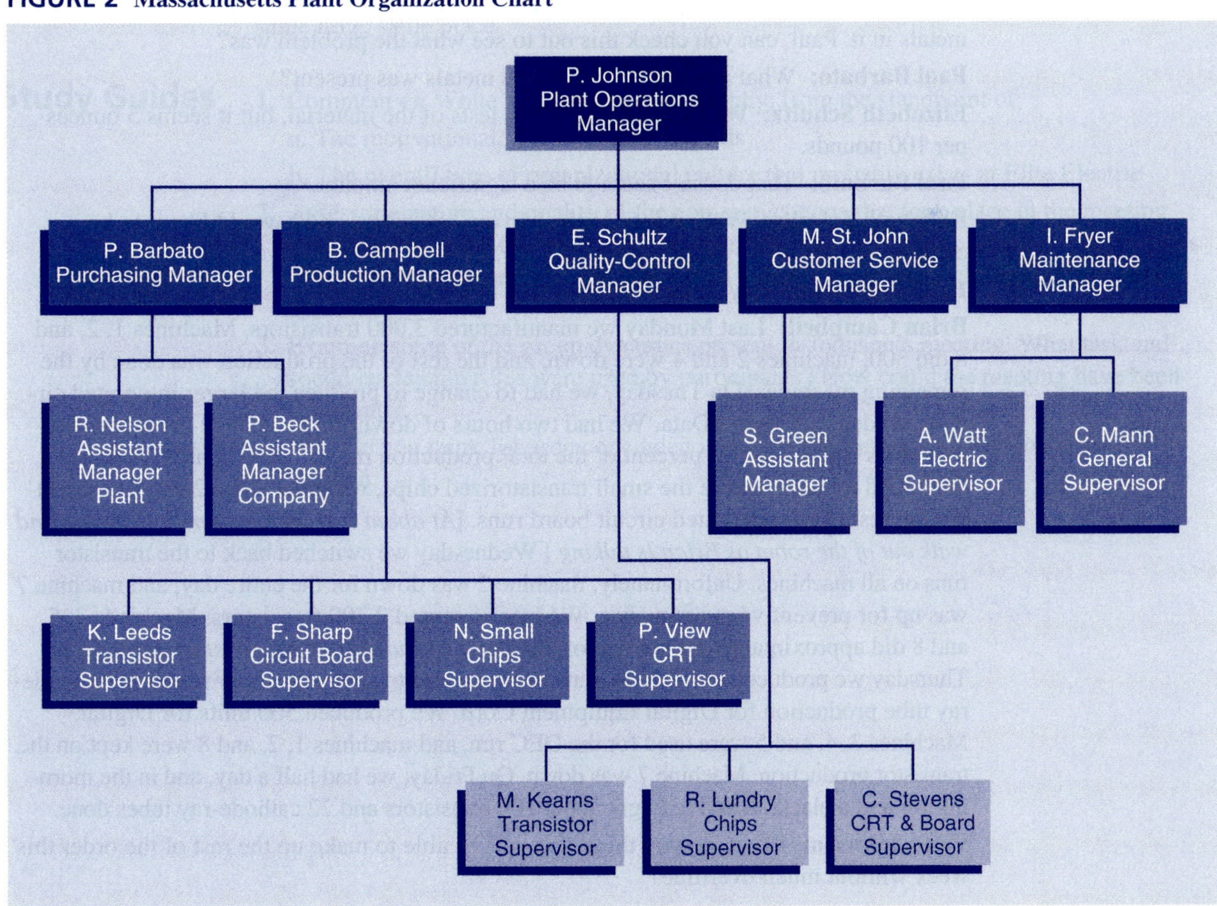

Case Eleven

TRW—Oilwell Cable Division

It was July 5, and Bill Russell had been expecting the phone call he had just received from the corporate office of TRW in Cleveland naming him general manager. Bill had been the acting general manager of the Oilwell Cable Division in Lawrence, Kansas, since January when Gino Strippoli left the division for another assignment. He had expected to be named general manager, but the second part of the call informing him that he must lay off 20 people or achieve an equivalent reduction in labor costs was greatly disturbing to him. It was now 8:00 A.M., and Bill had called a meeting of all plant personnel at 8:15 A.M. to announce his appointment and, now, to also announce the impending layoffs. He was wondering how to handle the tough decisions that lay before him.

TRW

TRW is a diversified multinational manufacturing firm that has sales approaching $5.5 billion. Its roots can be found in the Cleveland Cap Screw Company, which was founded in 1901 with a total investment of $2,500 and 29 employees. Today, through a growth strategy of acquisition and diversification, the company employs 88,000 employees at over 300 locations in 17 countries. The original shareholders' investment has grown to over $1.6 billion. As quoted from a company publication, "This growth reflects the company's ability to anticipate promising new fields and to pioneer in their development—automotive, industrial, aircraft, aerospace, systems, electronics, and energy. We grew with these markets and helped create them."

OILWELL CABLE DIVISION, LAWRENCE, KANSAS

The Oilwell Cable Division is part of the Industrial and Energy Segment of TRW. This segment of TRW's business represents 24 percent of its sales and 23 percent of its operating profits. The pumps, valves, and energy-services group, of which the Oilwell Cable Division is a part, accounts for 30 percent of the Industrial and Energy Segment's net sales.

The Oilwell Cable Division had its beginning as the Crescent Wire and Cable Company of Trenton, New Jersey. When TRW acquired Crescent, the company was losing money, occupied an outmoded plant, and had significant labor problems. In order to improve the profitability of the recent division, TRW decided to move its operations out of Trenton.

This case was prepared by Michael G. Kolchin, Thomas J. Hyclak, and Sheree Deming, and is used with permission of the authors and the publisher, Elsevier Science Publishing Co., Inc.

The first decision was to move Oilwell cable production to Lawrence, Kansas, about 10 years ago. The line was moved into a new building and all new equipment was purchased. Only Gino Strippoli, the plant manager, and three other employees made the move from Trenton to Lawrence.

The reason for choosing Lawrence as the new site for the Crescent division was fourfold. Most important, Lawrence was considerably closer to the customer base of the division, which was in northeast Oklahoma. Second, Kansas was a right-to-work state, and given the labor problems of the Trenton plant, TRW was looking for a more supportive labor environment for its new operations. Third, the wage rates for the Lawrence area were very reasonable compared with those in Trenton. Finally, there was an already existing building that could house the Oilwell cable production line in an industrial park in North Lawrence. In addition, considerable acreage next to the building would allow for future expansion.

By just moving the Oilwell cable line to Lawrence, TRW hoped to be able to focus in on this product and make it more profitable before moving the other products from the Crescent plant in Trenton. Soon thereafter, when the Oilwell cable plant had reached division status, no further consideration was given to moving the rest of the Trenton plant. The remaining operations in Trenton were sold.

Team Management at Lawrence

When Gino Strippoli was given the task of starting up operations in Lawrence, he saw a great opportunity to establish a new management system. With a new plant, new equipment, and almost all new employees, the time seemed perfect to test the value of team management. Gino had long been a supporter of team management, and now a golden opportunity was being presented to him to set up an experiment to test his ideas.

In the case of the TRW-Lawrence plant, 11 teams exist, ranging in size from 4 to 17 members. The titles of the teams and brief descriptions of their makeup are shown in the following table. Figure 1 depicts the current organization of the Oilwell Cable Division.

Team Structure

Team	Number of Teams	Composition
Management	1	Members of management
Resource	1	Management information systems, design engineering, process engineering, employment, accounting, etc.
Technical	1	Nonexempt laboratory personnel
Administration	1	
Maintenance	1	Boiler, electrical, and mechanical maintenance personnel
Shipping and receiving	1	
Production	5	Extruding, armoring, braiding

The five production teams are formed around the production process in use at TRW-Lawrence. Each team meets on a weekly basis or as needed, with the exception of the resource team, which meets every two weeks. The typical meeting lasts an hour and a half

Glossary

A

absences Employees who fail to show up for work as scheduled.

abusive supervision The actions, by some supervisors, to intentionally engage in repeated verbal and even nonverbal mistreatment of employees.

achievement motivation Drive to overcome challenges and obstacles in the pursuit of goals.

acquired immune deficiency syndrome (AIDS) Contagious viral disease of the human immune system.

action research Cyclical process of identifying system problems, gathering data, taking corrective action, assessing progress, making ongoing adjustments, and learning from the experience.

active listening Using a variety of principles and behaviors to receive both the factual and emotional message being sent by another person.

affiliation motivation Drive to relate to people on a social basis.

aggression Engaging in threatening behavior, verbal abuse, or dangerous actions against another employee.

alpha dogs Aggressive and domineering persons who ruthlessly use their personal characteristics, skills, or positions to intimidate others.

appraisal interview Session in which supervisors provide feedback to their employees on past performance, discuss problems, and invite a response.

appreciative inquiry An approach to organizational change that focuses on what is going well and what is valued most that can serve as a foundation for future improvements.

area of job freedom Area of discretion after all restraints have been applied.

assertiveness Process of expressing feelings, asking for legitimate changes, and giving and receiving honest feedback.

at-risk pay Amount of employee pay that will not be received if employee does not achieve certain individual performance targets.

attitudes Feelings and beliefs that largely determine how employees will perceive their environment, commit themselves to intended actions, and ultimately behave.

attribution Process by which people interpret the causes of their own and others' behavior.

authenticity The ability of managers to be honest, transparent with their feelings and emotions, and consistent in their words and actions ("walking the talk").

autocratic leaders People who centralize power and decision-making authority in themselves.

autocratic model Managerial view that power and formal authority are necessary to control employee behavior.

autonomy Policy of giving employees some discretion and control over job-related decisions.

B

bases of power Sources by which leaders gain and extend their influence over others; these bases include personal, legitimate, expert, reward, and coercive power.

behavioral bias Narrow viewpoint of some people that emphasizes satisfying employee experiences while overlooking the broader system of the organization in relation to all its publics.

behavioral intentions Employee plans and predispositions to act in a certain way (e.g., arrive late, skip work, slow down, be creative, or resign).

blogs Online Web logs (diaries or journals) created and updated frequently by individuals as a way of expressing their personal thoughts, musings, and commentaries on topics of interest to them.

body language Way in which people communicate meaning to others with their bodies in interpersonal interaction.

boundary roles Positions that require an ability to interact with different groups in order to keep a project successful.

boundary spanners Employees with strong communication links within their department, with people in other units, and often with the external community.

brainstorming Group structure that encourages creative thinking by deferring judgment on ideas generated.

burnout Condition in which employees are emotionally exhausted, become detached from their work, and feel helpless in accomplishing their goals.

bypassing Communication breakdowns caused by the definition and use of a word differently in different cultures.

C

chain-reaction effect Situation in which a change, or other condition, that directly affects only one or a few persons may lead to a reaction from many people, even hundreds or thousands, because of their mutual interest in it.

champions Persons who initiate and actively support change.

change Any alteration occurring in the work environment that affects the way in which employees must act.

change agents People whose roles are to stimulate, facilitate, and coordinate change within a system while remaining independent of it.

changing Learning new ideas and practices of thinking, reasoning, and performing.

charisma Leadership characteristic that inspires and influences employees to take early and sustained action to carry out a vision.

clarified thinking Removal of emotional blocks to rational and realistic thinking.

closed-end question A question presented in an interview or survey format that directs the respondent to simply select and mark the answer that best represents his or her own feelings.

closed question Question that focuses on a narrow topic and directs the receiver to provide a specific response.

cluster chain Grapevine chain in which one person tells several others, and a few of those tell more than one person.

coach Leadership role in which a leader prepares, guides, facilitates, cheers, and directs the team but does not play the game.

coercive power Capacity to punish other people (or to create the perceived threat to do so) so as to influence them.

cognitive dissonance Internal conflict and anxiety that occurs when people receive information incompatible with their value systems, prior decisions, or other information they may have.

cohesiveness Degree to which employees stick together, rely on one another, and desire to remain members of a group.

collectivism Process of placing heavy emphasis on the group and valuing harmony among its members.

collegial model Managerial view that teamwork is the way to build employee responsibility.

committee Specific type of group meeting in which members in their group role have been delegated authority with regard to the problem at hand.

communication Transfer of information and understanding from one person to another.

communication overload Condition in which employees receive more communication input than they can process, or more than they need.

communication process Steps by which a sender reaches a receiver with a message and receives feedback on it. See *Two-way communication process*.

comparable worth Attempt to give employees in comparable jobs—those of equal value to the employer—similar levels of pay.

compassion Genuine caring and concern for others, as reflected in their sensitivity to emotions and needs.

complete pay program Comprehensive reward system that uses different bases of pay to accomplish various objectives (e.g., retention, production, teamwork).

conceptual skill Ability to think in terms of models, frameworks, and broad relationships.

conditional strokes Strokes offered to employees if they perform correctly or avoid problems.

conflict Disagreement over the goals to attain or the methods to be used to accomplish them.

conformity Adaptation to the norms and expectations of others without independent thinking.

confronting Facing a conflict directly and working through it to a mutually satisfactory resolution. Also known as *problem solving* or *integrating*.

consensus Agreement of most of the members of a group and willingness to support the decision.

consideration Leader's employee orientation, which reflects concern about employees' human needs.

consultative leaders Managers who approach one or more employees and ask for inputs prior to making a decision.

contingency approach to OB Philosophy that different environments require different behavioral practices for effectiveness.

contingency model of leadership Model which states that the most appropriate leadership style depends on the favorableness of the situation, especially in relation to leader–member relations, task structure, and position power.

continuous reinforcement Reinforcement accompanying each correct behavior.

core dimensions Five factors of jobs—skill variety, task identity, task significance, autonomy, and feedback—identified in a job characteristics approach to job enrichment.

corrective discipline Action taken to discourage further infractions so that future acts will be in compliance with standards.

cost-benefit analysis Determination of net effects of an action that has both positive and negative impacts (financial and other).

cost-reward comparison Process in which employees identify and compare personal costs and rewards to determine the point at which they are approximately equal.

counseling Discussion of a problem that usually has emotional content with an employee in order to help the employee cope with it better.

counseling functions Six activities that may be performed by counseling: advice, reassurance, communication, release of emotional tension, clarified thinking, and reorientation.

organizational commitment Degree to which an employee identifies with the organization and wants to continue actively participating in it.

organizational culture The values, beliefs, and norms shared by an organization's members.

organizational identification The emotional state in which employees blend in so well and fit the organization's ethics and expectations that they experience a sense of oneness with the firm.

organizational politics Use of behaviors that enhance or protect a person's influence and self-interest.

organizational socialization Continuous process of transmitting key elements of an organization's culture to its employees.

organization development (OD) Systematic application of behavioral science knowledge at various levels (group, intergroup, and total organization) to bring about planned change.

outcomes Rewards employees perceive they get from their job and employer.

output restriction Situation in which workers choose to produce less than they could produce with normal effort.

outsourcing Contracting with suppliers in low-cost countries to produce products for an organization.

overparticipation Condition in which employees have more participation than they want.

P

paradigms Frameworks of possible explanations of how things work.

paradigm shift The release of an old model (way of thinking) and adoption of a new (and presumably better) one.

parochialism Seeing the situation around oneself from one's own perspective only.

partial reinforcement The act of encouraging learning by reinforcing some correct behaviors on one of four possible schedules.

participation Mental and emotional involvement of people in group situations that encourages them to contribute to group goals and share responsibility for them.

participative counseling Mutual counselor–counselee relationship that establishes a cooperative exchange of ideas to help solve a counselee's problems. Also known as *cooperative counseling*.

participative leaders Leaders who decentralize authority by consulting with followers.

participative management Use of programs that develop a substantial sense of empowerment among employees.

path-goal leadership Model that states that the leader's job is to create a work environment through structure, support, and rewards that helps employees reach the organization's goals.

perceived control Amount of control that employees believe they have over their work and working conditions.

perception Individual's own view of the world.

perceptual distortions The inaccurate mental records or interpretations of events that can detrimentally affect performance assessments.

perceptual set People's tendency to perceive what they expect to perceive.

performance appraisal Process of evaluating the performance of employees.

performance feedback Timely provision of data or judgment regarding task-related results.

performance management Procedures and systems designed to improve employee output and performance, often through the use of economic incentive systems.

performance monitoring Observing behavior, inspecting output, or studying documents of performance indicators.

performance-satisfaction-effort loop Flow model that shows the directional relationship between performance, satisfaction, and effort.

personal barriers Communication interferences that arise from human emotions, values, and poor listening habits.

personal power Ability of leaders to develop followers from the strength of their own personalities.

personal wellness Programs of preventive maintenance that help individuals reduce the causes of stress, cope with stressors that are beyond their direct control, or otherwise improve their health.

philosophy of OB Integrated set of explicit or implicit assumptions and beliefs about the way things are and the way they should be in organizations.

physical barriers Communication interferences that occur in the environment in which the communication takes place.

physical withdrawal Unauthorized absences, early departures, extended breaks, work slowdowns, or acts of aggression and retaliation.

piece rate Reward system that pays employees according to the number of acceptable pieces produced.

polarization Rigid and extreme position in one's attitudes.

polarized The situation that results when two parties take extreme positions or viewpoints on a subject.

political power Ability to work with people and social systems to gain their allegiance and support.

politics Ways that leaders and others gain and use power.

polygraph Instrument (lie detector) that attempts to measure the physiological changes when a person tells a significant lie.

positive affectivity A personal characteristic of employees that inclines them to be predisposed to be satisfied at work.

positive contagion The process of allowing an event or strong self-image to positively affect one's performance beliefs.

positive organizational behavior The emerging focus of OB on creating a workplace culture that fosters feelings of optimism, empathy, esteem, courage, and resilience.

positive reinforcement Favorable consequence that accompanies behavior and encourages repetition of the behavior.

positive strokes Recognition provided that feels good when received and contributes to another's sense of well-being.

post-traumatic stress disorder (PTSD) Residual stress-related consequences for an employee who has experienced sudden and dramatic negative incidents (e.g., violence or injury).

posturing Positioning oneself for visibility by making sure others know about your successes, and practicing skills of "one-upmanship" over others.

power Ability to influence other people and events.

power distance Belief that there are strong and legitimate decision-making rights separating managers and employees.

power motivation Drive to influence people and change situations.

practice Conscious application of conceptual models and research results with the goal of improving individual and organizational performance.

praise The provision of approval or admiration for an employee's positive qualities or worthwhile achievements.

prejudice Negative attitudes toward other individuals or groups.

presenteeism The act of employees persistently coming to work despite troublesome (and often recurring) physical and emotional health conditions that substantially affect their work performance.

preventive discipline Action taken to encourage employees to follow standards and rules so that infractions do not occur.

primary needs Basic physiological and security needs.

primary outcomes Rewards that employees receive directly as a result of their actions.

proactive Anticipating events, initiating change, and taking control of one's destiny.

procedural justice The assessment, by employees, of the fairness of the *process* by which rewards are administered. This evaluation focuses on two elements—interpersonal treatment and clarity of explanations.

process consultation Set of activities that helps others perceive, understand, and react constructively to current behavioral events around them.

processing Having a group examine what went well, what went poorly, and how the group's behavior could be improved in future sessions.

productivity Ratio that compares units of output with units of input.

profit sharing System that distributes to employees some portion of the profits of business.

progressive discipline Policy that provides stronger penalties for repeated offenses.

protégé Person who receives and accepts advice and examples from a trusted mentor.

proxemics Exploration of different practices and feelings about interpersonal space within and across cultures.

pseudoparticipation False attempts by managers to involve employees in decision making.

psychic costs Costs that affect a person's inner self or psyche.

psychological contract Unwritten agreement that defines the conditions of each employee's psychological involvement with the system—what they intend to give to it and receive from it.

psychological distance Feeling of being emotionally separated from another that acts as a personal barrier to effective communication.

psychological ownership A feeling of possessiveness, responsibility, identity, and sense of belongingness regarding an object, group, or organization.

psychological support Condition in which leaders stimulate people to want to do a particular job.

psychological withdrawal Emotional detachment from one's job, such as engaging in daydreaming.

punishment Unfavorable consequence that accompanies behavior and discourages repetition of the behavior.

Q

quality circles Voluntary groups that receive training in statistical techniques and problem-solving skills and then meet to produce ideas for improving productivity and working conditions.

quality of work life (QWL) Favorableness or unfavorableness of a total job environment for people.

quick fix Managerial use of a fad that addresses symptoms while ignoring underlying problems.

R

rapid-cycle decision making A participative process that is time-efficient, inclusive, genuine, transparent, and yields definitive outcomes.

rate setting Process of determining the standard output for each job.

reactive Responding to events, adapting to change, and tempering its consequences.

readability Degree to which writing and speech are understandable to receivers.

red teaming Using a subset of a group to challenge underlying assumptions, take an adversary's viewpoint, and propose different scenarios not previously considered.

reference group Group whose norms a person accepts.

refreezing Term applying to situations involving change and referring to the action of integrating what has been learned into actual practice.

reinforcement Behavior modification consequence that influences future behavior.

reinforcement schedules Frequency with which reinforcement accompanies a desired behavior.

relatedness needs Needs that involve the desire of an employee to be understood and accepted.

relaxation response Use of quiet concentrated inner thought in order to rest the body physically and emotionally, thus reducing symptoms of stress.

reliability Capacity of a survey instrument (or action) to produce consistent results.

reorientation Change in an employee's psychic self through a change in basic goals and values.

repatriation Return of an employee to the home country, smooth blending into the original culture, and effective utilization in the organization after working in another nation for several years.

repetitive change syndrome The paralyzing effect on individuals from continuous rounds of organizational change, resulting in overload and the inability to cope with new changes.

research Process of gathering and interpreting relevant and valid evidence that will either support a behavioral theory or help change it.

re-shoring The process of bringing previously outsourced work back to the homeland.

resilience A person's capacity to handle short-term tensions.

resistance to change Desire not to accept a change or to accept it only partially, often resulting in actions designed to discredit, delay, or prevent the implementation of a work change.

results orientation Placing a continuing emphasis on the achievement of relevant organizational goals and outcomes—human, social, and financial.

results-oriented approach to OB Emphasis on relevant organizational outcomes, often expressed in terms of productivity.

reverse cultural shock Difficulty experienced by expatriates in readjusting to the surroundings of their home country upon their reentry.

reverse mentoring The process of having new (or younger) employees share their (tech savvy) skills with more senior managers.

reward power Capacity to control and administer items that are valued by other people so as to influence them.

rights of privacy Freedom from organizational invasion of a person's private life and unauthorized release of confidential information about a person.

risky shift Act of a group becoming more willing to take chances when its members are dealing with the resources of others and cannot be held individually accountable.

role Pattern of actions expected of a person in activities involving others.

role ambiguity Feeling that arises when roles are inadequately defined or are substantially unknown.

role conflict Feeling that arises when others have different perceptions or expectations of a person's role.

role models Leaders who serve as examples for their followers.

role perceptions How people think they are supposed to act in their own roles and think others should act in their roles.

rule-bending The intentional interpretation of organizational policies to obtain personal gain.

rumor Grapevine information that is communicated without secure standards of evidence being present.

S

sabbatical leaves Provision to employees of paid or unpaid time off from work to encourage stress relief and personal education.

secondary needs Social and psychological needs.

secondary outcomes Rewards that employees receive indirectly, following their primary outcomes.

selective perception Act of paying attention to those features of the work environment that are consistent with or reinforce one's own expectations.

self-actualization Need to become all that one is capable of becoming.

self-appraisal Process of asking individuals to identify and assess their accomplishments, strengths, and weaknesses.

self-concept An employee's "face," or level of self-esteem.

self-efficacy Internal belief that one has the necessary capabilities and competencies to perform a task, fulfill role expectations, or meet a challenging situation successfully.

self-fulfilling prophecy Condition that exists when a manager's expectations for an employee cause the manager to treat the employee differently, and the employee responds in a way that confirms the initial expectations. Also known as the *Pygmalion effect*.

self-leadership Act of leading oneself to perform naturally motivating tasks and of managing oneself to do work that is required but not naturally rewarding.

self-managing teams Natural work groups that are given a large degree of decision-making autonomy and are expected to control their own behavior and results. Also known as *self-directing teams*, *self-reliant teams*, *socio-technical teams*, or *semi-autonomous work groups*.

self-monitors Persons who are concerned about their impression on others, sensitive to interpersonal cues, and adept at responding to signals they receive.

self-perceived task ability Degree of employee confidence in his or her potential to perform a task successfully.

self-serving bias Tendency to claim undue credit for one's own success and minimize personal responsibility for problems.

semantic barriers Communication limitations caused by the variety of meanings in the symbols used.

semantics Science of meaning.

sensemaking Process of finding order in complex or ambiguous situations.

servant leadership The process of placing the needs of others above one's own self-interest, while affirming their worth and contributions.

sexual harassment Process of making employment or promotion decisions contingent on sexual favors; also, any verbal or physical conduct that creates an offensive working environment.

shaping Systematic and progressive application of positive reinforcement as behavior comes closer to the desired behavior.

shared mental model A common understanding among team members of the nature or their task and how to accomplish it.

short-term orientation Cultural value that emphasizes valuing the past and accenting the present while respecting tradition and the need to fulfill historical social obligations.

signature experiences Clearly defined and dramatic devices that convey a key element of the firm's culture and vividly reinforce the values of the organization.

situational leadership model Theory of leadership that suggests a leader's style should be determined by matching it with the task-related development (maturity) level of each subordinate.

skill-based pay System that rewards individual employees for what they know how to do. Also known as *knowledge-based pay* or *multiskill pay*.

skill variety Policy of allowing employees to perform different operations that often require different skills.

social cues Positive or negative bits of information that employees receive from their social surroundings and that act to influence how they react to a communication.

social culture Social environment of human-created beliefs, customs, knowledge, and practices that defines conventional behavior in a society.

social equilibrium Dynamic working balance among the interdependent parts of a system.

social facilitation Process by which individuals often try harder to contribute to a task just because other people are present.

social information processing Recognition that social cues provided by peers and others affect employee perceptions of their jobs.

social intelligence Social awareness, encompassing empathy, presence, situational radar, clarity, and authenticity.

social screening The examination, by prospective employers, of information gleaned from social media so as to check on the validity of an applicants' qualifications.

socialization See *organizational socialization.*

social leader Person who helps restore and maintain group relationships.

social learning The vicarious process by which employees learn by observing the actions of others, understanding the consequences that others are experiencing, and using that new information to modify their own behavior.

social loafing Employee lessening of output when employees think their contributions to a group cannot be measured.

social networks Internet sites and software programs that allow people to link together into a virtual social community.

social norms The beliefs, actions, and expectations of comparable persons.

social responsibility Recognition that organizations have significant influence on the social system, which must be considered and balanced in all organizational actions.

social support Network of activities and relationships that satisfies an employee's perceived need to be cared for, esteemed, and valued.

social system Complex set of human relationships interacting in many ways.

spillover effect Impact of job satisfaction on life satisfaction, and vice versa.

spirit Harmony among all facets of life as guided by a higher (religious) power.

spirituality The desire for employees to know their deepest selves better, to grow personally, to make a meaningful contribution to society, and to demonstrate integrity in every action taken.

stages of team development Movement of a group through the evolutionary phases of forming, storming, norming, performing, and (possibly) adjourning.

status Social rank of a person in a group.

status anxiety Employees' feelings of being upset because of differences between their actual and desired status levels.

status deprivation Loss of status, or a level of insufficient status, for a person. Also known as *losing face*.

status symbols Visible external things that attach to a person or workplace and serve as evidence of social rank.

status systems Hierarchies of status that define employee rank relative to others in the group.

steward Leaders who view their roles as caretakers, guardians, and developers of employee talent.

storytelling The process of using memorable stories to help forge a culture and communicate key values to employees.

stress General term applied to the pressures people feel in life.

stress audit An anonymous survey that solicits employee opinions about a variety of working conditions.

stressors Conditions that tend to cause stress.

stress-performance model Visual portrait of the relationship between stress and job performance, illustrating different thresholds for different people.

stress threshold Level of stressors that one can tolerate before feelings of stress occur and adversely affect performance.

stroking Performing any act of recognition for another person.

structure Leader's task orientation that, at the extreme, ignores personal issues and emotions of employees.

substitutes for leadership Characteristics of the task, employees, or organization that may reduce the need for leadership behaviors.

sucker effect Lessening of output by a team member under the belief that others are doing so and that it would be foolish not to do the same thing.

suggestion programs Formal plans to encourage individual employees to recommend work improvements. A monetary award frequently is offered for acceptable suggestions.

superleadership Actively working to unleash the abilities of subordinates and encouraging them to become capable of self-leadership.

superordinate goal Goal that integrates the efforts of individuals or groups.

supportive approach to OB Philosophy of working with people in ways that seek to satisfy their needs and develop their potential.

supportive model Managerial view that leaders should support employees in their attempts to grow in their jobs and to perform them well.

surface agenda Official task of a group.

surveillance devices Equipment and procedures for observing employee actions (often done secretly).

sustainability The capacity of a system to endure over time while balancing environmental, social, and economic demands.

system model Managerial view that employees are concerned about finding meaning at work; having a work context infused with integrity, trust, and a sense of community; and receiving care and compassion from managers.

systems approach to OB Belief that there are many variables in organizations and that each of them affects all the others in a complex relationship.

T

tardiness Arriving late for work.

task identity Practice of allowing employees to perform a complete piece of work.

task leader Person who helps the group accomplish its objectives and stay on target.

task significance Amount of impact, as perceived by the worker, that the work has on other people.

task structure Degree to which one specific method is required to do the job (a variable in Fiedler's contingency model of leadership).

task support Condition in which leaders provide the resources, budgets, power, and other elements that are essential in getting the job done.

task team Cooperative small group in regular contact that is engaged in coordinated action.

taxonomy of leadership behaviors A conceptual classification of fifteen leadership acts into four major categories (task, relations, change, and external).

team building Process of making teams more effective by encouraging members to examine how they work together, identify their weaknesses, and develop more effective ways of cooperating.

team coaching A leader's interaction with a team to help its members make appropriate use of their collective resources by focusing on motivation of members, performance method improvements, or knowledge/skill deficiencies.

teamwork State that occurs when members know their objectives, contribute responsibly and enthusiastically to the task, and support one another.

technical skill Knowledge of, and ability in, any type of process or technique.

telecommuting Process of accomplishing all or part of an employee's work at home through computer links to the office. Also known as an *electronic cottage*.

theft Unauthorized removal of company resources by an employee.

theories Research-based explanations of how and why people think, feel, and act as they do.

Theory X Autocratic and traditional set of assumptions about people.

Theory Y Humanistic and supportive set of assumptions about people.

Theory Z Model that adapts the elements of Japanese management systems to the U.S. culture and emphasizes cooperation and consensus decision processes.

360-degree feedback Process of systematically gathering data on a person's skills, abilities, and behaviors from a variety of sources, such as their manager, peers, subordinates, and customers, so as to see where problems exist and improvements can be made.

total quality management (TQM) Process of getting every employee involved in the task of searching for continuous improvements in their operations.

traits Physical, intellectual, or personality characteristics that differentiate between leaders and nonleaders or between successful and unsuccessful leaders.

transcultural employees Employees who have learned to operate effectively in several cultures.

transformational leaders Managers who initiate bold strategic changes to position the organization for its future.

transparency Sharing meaningful information on an open, candid, clear, timely basis.

trauma Stress resulting from a severe threat to one's security.

triple bottom line The three P's that organizations attempt to be sensitive to—planet, people, and profits.

trust Capacity to depend on another's word and actions.

turnover Rate at which employees leave an organization.

twittering Expressing oneself in a brief message (a "Tweet") in real time to a network of interested persons.

two-factor model of motivation Motivational model developed by Frederick Herzberg, which concludes that one set of job conditions (motivators) primarily motivates an employee and produces satisfaction if they are adequate, while a different set (hygiene factors) primarily dissatisfies the employee if they are inadequate.

two-way communication process Eight-step process in which a sender develops, encodes, and transmits an idea, with the recipient receiving, decoding, accepting, and using it, followed by sending feedback to the sender.

type A people People who are aggressive and competitive, set high standards, and put themselves under constant time pressures.

type B people People who are relaxed and easygoing and accept situations readily.

U

uncertainty avoidance Lack of comfort with ambiguity that drives some employees to avoid it and seek clarity.

unconditional strokes Strokes presented without any connection to behavior.

underparticipation Condition in which employees want more participation than they have.

unfreezing Term applying to situations that involve change and referring to the act of casting aside old ideas and practices so new ones can be learned.

upward communication Flows of information from lower to higher levels in an organization.

V

valence Strength of a person's preference for receiving a reward.

validity Capacity of a survey instrument to measure what it claims to measure.

value premises Personal views of the desirability of certain goals and activities.

valuing diversity Philosophy and programs asserting that differences among people need to be recognized, acknowledged, appreciated, and used to collective advantage.

violence Various forms of verbal or physical aggression at work.

virtual offices Layouts in which physical office space and individual desks are replaced with an array of portable communication tools, allowing employees to work almost anywhere.

virtual teams Working groups that meet without all their members being in the same location; such teams often rely heavily on technology to achieve their communication and coordination needs.

vision Challenging and crystallized long-range portrait of what the organization and its members can and should be—a possible, and desirable, image of the future.

voice Discretionary verbal behaviors (challenging or supportive) by employees that are intended to be beneficial to the organization.

W

wage incentives Reward systems that provide more pay for more production.

whistle-blowing Disclosing alleged misconduct to an internal or external source.

wikipedia A collaboratively created and constantly updated collection of definitions and articles on the Internet.

willingness to accept the influence of others Contingency factor in the path-goal model of leadership that suggests a leader's choice of style is partially dependent on an employee's readiness to accept direction from others.

win–win outcome of conflict Outcome in which both parties perceive they are in a better position than they were before a conflict began.

workaholics People who immerse themselves in work activities and place high expectations on themselves and others and, as a result, experience difficulty achieving a desired work–life balance

work ethic Employee attitude of viewing (hard) work as a central life interest and desirable goal in life.

work-family conflict The dysfunctional result of competing demands placed on an employee from a variety of employment and non-work roles.

workplace incivility The failure of employees to exhibit concern and regard for others or—worse yet—one of many acts of disrespect shown toward each other on the job.

work moods Employees' feelings about their jobs that can change within a day, hour, or minute.

work motivation The result of a set of internal and external forces that cause an employee to choose a course of action and engage in certain behaviors.

workplace bullies Negative leaders who intimidate, ridicule, insult, and make unreasonable demands on others.

workplace trauma Disintegration of employee self-concepts and beliefs in their capabilities arising from dramatic negative factors or experiences at work.

workplace violence Dramatic action harming employees, their co-workers, managers, or company property.

X

xenophobia Fear and rejection of ideas and things foreign to a person.

References

Chapter 1

1. Jane Schmidt-Wilk, "Reflection: A Prerequisite for Developing the 'CEO' of the Brain," *Journal of Management Education*, vol. 33, no. 1, 2009, p. 3.
2. Ram Mudambi, Thomas J. Hannigan, and William Kline, "Advancing Science on the Knife's Edge: Integration and Specialization in Management Ph.D. Programs," *Academy of Management Perspectives*, August 2012, p. 103.
3. Larry Hirschhorn and Thomas Gilmore, "The New Boundaries of the 'Boundaryless' Company," *Harvard Business Review*, May–June 1992, pp. 104–15.
4. Excellent discussions of theory appear in Donald C. Hambrick, "The Field of Management's Devotion to Theory: Too Much of a Good Thing?" *Academy of Management Journal*, vol. 50, no. 6, 2007, pp. 1346–52; and John B. Miner, "The Rated Importance, Scientific Validity, and Practical Usefulness of Organizational Behavior Theories: A Quantitative Review," *Academy of Management Learning and Education*, vol. 2, no. 3, 2003, pp. 250–68.
5. This idea is discussed in Richard Klimoski and Benjamin Amos, "Practicing Evidence-Based Education in Leadership Development," *Academy of Management Learning and Education*, vol. 11, no. 4, 2012, pp. 685–702. See also Jeffrey Pfeffer and Robert I. Sutton, *Hard Facts, Dangerous Half-Truths, and Total Nonsense: Profiting from Evidence-Based Management*, Boston: Harvard Business School Press, 2006; and Denise M. Rousseau and Sharon McCarthy, "Educating Managers from an Evidence-Based Perspective," *Academy of Management Learning and Education*, vol. 6, no. 1, 2007, pp. 84–101.
6. One author suggests that a dozen different organizational behavior models all assume it is possible to achieve both employee satisfaction and organizational performance at the same time through this mutuality of interest. See Barry M. Staw, "Organizational Psychology and the Pursuit of the Happy/Productive Worker," *California Management Review*, Summer 1986, pp. 40–53.
7. Early emphasis on the human resources approach to organizational behavior is provided in Raymond E. Miles, "Human Relations or Human Resources?" *Harvard Business Review*, July–August 1965, pp. 148–63. A more recent treatment of the model appears in Kaifeng Jiang, David P. Lepak, Jia Hu, and Judith C. Baer, "How Does Human Resource Management Influence Organizational Outcomes? A Meta-Analytic Investigation of Mediating Mechanisms," *Acaedemy of Management Journal*, vol. 55, no. 6, 2012, pp. 1264–94.
8. Rebecca Vesely, "Top Workplace Distraction? Survey Says: That's Personal," *Workforce Management*, August 2012, p. 14.
9. Jay Forrester, the "father" of systems dynamics thinking in organizations, is interviewed in "The Loop You Can't Get Out Of," *Sloan Management Review*, Winter 2009, pp. 9–12.
10. Jack Gordon, "Microsoft's Leading Edge," *Training*, June 2007, pp. 30–33.
11. Jack Stack, *The Great Game of Business,* New York: Currency Doubleday, 1992, p. 203.
12. This discussion is adapted from Keith Davis, "A Law of Diminishing Returns in Organizational Behavior?" *Personnel Journal*, December 1975, pp. 616–19.
13. See, for example, John Carey, "Hugging the Tree-Huggers," *BusinessWeek*, March 12, 2007, pp. 66–68; and "Green is Good," *Fortune*, April 2, 2007, pp. 43–50.
14. Walter Kiechel III, "The Management Century," *Harvard Business Review*, November 2012, p. 75.
15. See, for example, John Micklethwait and Adrian Wooldridge, *The Witch Doctors: Making Sense of the Management Gurus*, New York: Times Business, 1996.

Chapter 2

1. Julian Birkinshaw and Jules Goddard, "What Is Your Management Model?" *Sloan Management Review*, Winter 2009, p. 81.
2. Herb Kelleher, in Jennifer Reingold, "Still Crazy After All These Years," *Fortune*, January 14, 2013, p. 97.
3. Andy Meisler, "Success, Scandinavian Style," *Workforce Management*, August 2004, pp. 27–32.
4. Theory X and Theory Y were first published in Douglas McGregor, "The Human Side of Enterprise," in *Proceedings of the Fifth Anniversary Convocation of the School of Industrial Management*, Cambridge, MA: Massachusetts Institute of Technology, April 9, 1957. Interested readers may wish to examine the conflicting viewpoints on McGregor's ideas presented by Gary Heil, Warren Bennis, and Deborah C. Stephens, *Douglas McGregor, Revisited: Managing the Human Side of the Enterprise*, New York: Wiley, 2000.
5. Joel Arthur Barker, *Paradigms: The Business of Discovering the Future*, New York: Harper Business, 1992.
6. The distinctions between the first four models of organizational behavior were originally published in Keith Davis, *Human Relations at Work: The Dynamics of Organizational Behavior*, 3rd ed., New York: McGraw-Hill, 1967, p. 480.
7. http://www.ihscslnews.org/view_article.php?id=162.
8. Caleb Hannan, "Management Secrets from the Meanest Company in America," *Bloomberg BusinessWeek*, January 7–13, 2013, pp. 46–51.

9. "The Law of the Hog: A Parable about Improving Employee Effectiveness," *Training*, March 1987, p. 67.

10. Dawn Anfuso, "Creating a Culture of Caring Pays Off," *Personnel Journal*, August 1995, pp. 70–77.

11. See, for example, programs at 3M Corporation and IBM, in "3M Offers Buyouts to 1,300 Employees," *Duluth News Tribune*, December 10, 1995, p. 5B; and Aaron Bernstein, Scott Ticer, and Jonathan B. Levine, "IBM's Fancy Footwork to Sidestep Layoffs," *BusinessWeek*, July 7, 1986, pp. 54–55.

12. Rensis Likert, *New Patterns of Management*, New York: McGraw-Hill, 1961, pp. 102–3. Italics in original.

13. An example of this early research is a study of the Prudential Insurance Company in Daniel Katz, Nathan Maccoby, and Nancy C. Morse, *Productivity, Supervision, and Morale in an Office Situation*, Part 1, Ann Arbor: Institute for Social Research, University of Michigan, 1950. The conclusion about job satisfaction and productivity is reported on p. 63.

14. Elton Mayo, *The Human Problems of an Industrial Civilization*, Cambridge, MA: Harvard University Press, 1933; F. J. Roethlisberger and W. J. Dickson, *Management and the Worker*, Cambridge, MA: Harvard University Press, 1939; and F. J. Roethlisberger, *The Elusive Phenomena: An Autobiographical Account of My Work in the Field of Organizational Behavior at the Harvard Business School*, Cambridge, MA: Harvard University Press, 1977. The symposium on the 50th anniversary of the Western Electric Company, Hawthorne Studies, is reported in Eugene Louis Cass and Frederick G. Zimmer (eds.), *Man and Work in Society*, New York: Van Nostrand Reinhold Company, 1975. Recollections of the participants are reported in Ronald G. Greenwood, Alfred A. Bolton, and Regina A. Greenwood, "Hawthorne a Half Century Later: Relay Assembly Participants Remember," *Journal of Management*, Fall–Winter 1983, pp. 217–31. The earliest general textbook on human relations was Burleigh B. Gardner and David G. Moore, *Human Relations in Industry*, Chicago: Irwin, 1945.

15. Frank Harrison, "The Management of Scientists: Determinants of Perceived Role Performance," *Academy of Management Journal*, June 1974, pp. 234–41.

16. See, for example, Carolyn M. Youssef and Fred Luthans, "Positive Organizational Behavior in the Workplace: The Impact of Hope, Optimism, and Resilience," *Journal of Management*, vol. 33, no. 5, 2007, pp. 774–800; and Fred Luthans, Carolyn M. Youssef, and Bruce J. Avolio, *Psychological Capital: Developing the Human Competitive Edge*, New York: Oxford University Press, 2007.

17. Karl Albrecht, *Social Intelligence: The New Science of Success*, San Francisco: Pfeiffer Publishing, 2006. See also Howard Gardner, *Five Minds for the Future*, Boston: Harvard Business Press, 2008.

18. Naomi Weiss, "How Starbucks Impassions Workers to Drive Growth," *Workforce*, August 1998, pp. 59–64.

19. Interested readers may wish to consult the history of organizational behavior, as traced by Keith Davis in "Human Relations, Industrial Humanism, and Organizational Behavior," in a presentation to the Southern Division of the Academy of Management, November 13, 1986.

Chapter 3

1. Patricia A. Muir, "Interaction: A Smarter Way to Network," *Harvard Business Review*, October 2011, p. 25.

2. Alex Pentland and Tracy Heibeck, "Understanding 'Honest Signals' in Business," *Sloan Management Review*, Fall 2008, p. 71.

3. Martin Delahoussaye, "Leadership in the 21st Century," *Training*, September 2001, pp. 60–72.

4. Jeanne M. Brett et al., "Sticks and Stones: Language, Face, and Online Dispute Resolution," *Academy of Management Journal*, vol. 50, no. 1, pp. 85–99.

5. Ethan R. Burris, "The Risks and Rewards of Speaking Up: Managerial Responses to Employee Voice," *Academy of Management Journal*, 2012, vol. 55, no. 4, pp. 851–75.

6. James M. Kouzes and Barry Z. Posner, "The Credibility Factor: What Followers Expect from Their Leaders," *Management Review*, January 1990, pp. 29–33; and Alan Farnham, "The Trust Gap," *Fortune*, December 4, 1989, pp. 57–78.

7. For a retrospective analysis of a classic study in misperception of employee needs by supervisors, see Stephen A. Rubenfeld, John W. Newstrom, and Thomas Duff, "Caveat Emptor: Avoiding Pitfalls in Data-Based Decision Making," *Review of Business*, Winter 1994, pp. 20–23.

8. James R. Larson Jr., "The Dynamic Interplay between Employees' Feedback-Seeking Strategies and Supervisors' Delivery of Performance Feedback," *Academy of Management Review*, July 1989, pp. 408–22. See also "Friendly Feedback," *Training*, May 2007, p. 11; and Fernando Bartolome and John Weeks, "Find the Gold in Toxic Feedback," *Harvard Business Review*, April 2007, pp. 24, 26.

9. "Communications: Key to Product Redesign at McDonnell Douglas," *Quality Digest*, July 1994, pp. 62–65.

10. Sandra L. Kirmeyer and Thung-Rung Lin, "Social Support: Its Relationship to Observed Communication with Peers and Superiors," *Academy of Management Journal*, March 1987, pp. 138–51.

11. Jennifer J. Laabs, "Interactive Sessions Further TQM Effort," *Personnel Journal*, March 1994, pp. 22–28.

12. "When Leaders Go Wrong," *Training*, August 2006, p. 11.

13. N. Anand and Jay A. Conger, "Capabilities of the Consummate Networker," *Organizational Dynamics*, vol. 36, no. 1, pp. 13–27. Also see Rob Cross and Robert Thomas, "A Smarter Way to Network," *Harvard Business Review*, July–August 2011, pp. 149–53.

14. Ron Alsop, *The Trophy Kids Grow Up: How the Millennial Generation Is Shaking up the Workplace*, San Francisco: Jossey-Bass, 2008; Don Tapscott, *Grown Up Digital: How the Net Generation Is Changing Your World*, New York: McGraw-Hill, 2008; and Lin Grensing-Pophal, "Maddened By Millennials?" *Workforce Management*, April 2013, p. 10.

15. Sarah Fister Gale, "Policies Must Score a Mutual Like," *Workforce Management*, August 2012, p. 18; and David Ferris, "From Neophytes to Socialites," *Workforce Management*, June 2012, pp. 32–34.

16. Edward Hallowell, *Crazy Busy: Overstretched, Overbooked, and About to Snap!*, New York: Ballantine Books, 2006; and Kristin Byron, "Carrying Too Heavy a Load? The Communication and Miscommunication of Emotion by Email," *Academy of Management Review*, vol. 33, no. 2, pp. 309–327.

17. William H. Ross, Jr., "What Every Human Resource Manager Should Know About Web Logs," *SAM Advanced Management Journal*, Summer 2005, pp. 4–14.

18. Adam Lashinsky, "The True Meaning of Twitter," *Fortune*, August 18, 2008, pp. 39–42; Stephen Baker and Heather Green, "Beyond Blogs," *BusinessWeek*, June 2, 2008, pp. 45–50; and Ed Frauenheim, "Technology Forcing Firms to Shed More Light on Layoffs," *Workforce Management*, January 19, 2009, pp. 7–8.

19. Employers are pushing telecommuting; see Michelle Conlin, "Home Offices: The New Math," *BusinessWeek*, March 9, 2009, pp. 66–68; John A. Pearce II, "Successful Corporate Telecommuting with Technology Considerations for Late Adopters," *Organizational Dynamics*, vol. 38, no. 1, 2009, pp. 16–25. However, telecommuting often results in longer work hours and a surprisingly diminished sense of flexibility; see Charles R. Stoner, Paul Stephens, and Matthew K. McGowan, "Connectivity and Work Dominance: Panacea or Pariah?" *Business Horizons*, vol. 52, 2009, pp. 67–78. For a discussion of the importance of family-friendly policies and gender diversity, see Sheelah Kolhatkar, "Why Mommy Can't Get Ahead," *Bloomberg BusinessWeek*, November 19–25, 2012, pp. 10–11.

Chapter 4

1. Ronald J. Alsop, "Cultural Awareness," *Workforce Management*, July 2011, p. 42.

2. Mark S. Schwartz, "Developing and Sustaining an Ethical Corporate Culture: The Core Elements," *Business Horizons*, January–February 2013, p. 40.

3. Milton Moskowitz and Robert Levering, "The 100 Best Companies to Work For," *Fortune*, February 4, 2013, pp. 85–96.

4. David Kiley, "The New Heat on Ford," *BusinessWeek*, June 4, 2007, pp. 32–38.

5. Denise Rousseau, "Psychological Contracts in the Workplace: Understanding the Ties that Motivate," *Academy of Management Executive*, vol. 18, no. 1, 2004, pp. 120–27.

6. Holly Dolezalek, "The Path to Inclusion," *Training*, May 2008, pp. 52–54; and Sylvia Ann Hewlett and Karen Sumberg, "For LGBT Workers, Being 'Out' Brings Advantages," *Harvard Business Review*, July–August 2011, p. 28.

7. For a discussion of diversity coverage, see Patricia A. Parham and Helen J. Muller, "Review of Workforce Diversity Content in Organizational Behavior Texts," *Academy of Management Learning and Education*, September 2008, pp. 424–28. See also Todd Henneman, "Making the Pieces Fit," *Workforce Management*, August 2011, pp. 12–18.

8. *Wipro Limited Annual Report 2004–2005*, Doddakannelli, Sarjapur Road, Bangalore, India, p. 11.

9. Thomas J. DeLong, John J. Gabarro, and Robert J. Lees, "Why Mentoring Matters in a Hypercompetitive World," *Harvard Business Review*, January 2008, pp. 115–21.

10. Kristina A. Bourne, Fiona Wilson, Scott W. Lester, and Jill Kickul, "Embracing the Whole Individual: Advantages of a Dual-centric Perspective of Work and Life," *Business Horizons*, July–August 2009, pp. 387–98.

11. Chester I. Barnard, "Functions and Pathology of Status Systems in Formal Organizations," in William F. Whyte (ed.), *Industry and Society*, New York: McGraw-Hill, 1946, p. 69.

12. Stephenie Overman, "A Company of Champions," *HRMagazine*, October 1990, pp. 58–60.

13. Elizabeth R. Moore, "Prudential Reinforces Its Business Values," *Personnel Journal*, January 1993, pp. 84–89.

14. Sushil Nifadkar, Anne S. Tsui, and Blake E. Ashforth, "The Way You Make Me Feel and Behave: Supervisor-Triggered Newcomer Affect and Approach-Avoidance Behavior," *Academy of Management Journal*, 2012, vol. 55, no. 5, pp. 1146–68.

15. Tamara J. Erickson and Lynda Gratton, "What It Means to Work Here," *Harvard Business Review*, March 2007, pp. 104–12.

16. "Storytelling," *ASTD Info-Line*, no. 0006, June 2000, pp. 1–16; and Beverly Kaye and Betsy Jacobson, "True Tales and Tall Tales: The Power of Organizational Storytelling," *Training and Development*, March 1999, pp. 45–50.

17. "Organizational Culture," *ASTD Info-Line*, no. 9304, April 1993, pp. 1–16.

18. Jon R. Katzenbach, Ilona Steffen, and Caroline Kronley, "Cultural Change That Sticks: Start with What's Already Working," *Harvard Business Review*, July–August 2012, pp. 110–17.

19. Jeffrey M. O'Brien, "Zappos Knows How to Kick It," *Fortune*, February 2, 2009, pp. 55–58. Other corporate examples of fun workplaces appear in Quy Huy and Andrew Shipilov, "The Key to Social Media Success Within Organizations," *Sloan Management Review*, Fall 20112, pp. 73–81; Meg McSherry Breslin, "Using Recess to Send Morale on an Upswing," *Workforce Management*, May 2012, p. 14; and Megan Garber, "Perks and Recreation," *The Atlantic*, December 2012, pp. 28–32.

20. Evren Esen, Robert Ford, John Newstrom, and Frank McLaughlin, *Fun Work Environment Survey*, Alexandria, VA: SHRM Research Department, 2002. The benefits and dangers of using humor are discussed in Jim Lyttle, "The Judicious Use and Management of Humor in the Workplace," *Business Horizons*, 2007, pp. 239–45.

Chapter 5

1. Verne Harnish, "Five Ways to Keep Employees Excited," *Fortune*, December 3, 2012, p. 40.

2. Nitin Nohria, Boris Groysberg, and Linda-Eling Lee, "Employee Motivation: A Powerful New Model," *Harvard Business Review*, July–August 2008, pp. 78–84.

3. Charlotte Fritz, Chak Fu Lam, and Gretchen M. Spreitzer, "It's the Little Things That Matter: An Examination of Knowledge Workers' Energy Management," *Academy of Management Perspectives*, August 2011, pp. 28–39.

4. The original work on achievement motivation is David C. McClelland, *The Achieving Society*, New York: Van Nostrand, 1961.

5. A. H. Maslow, "A Theory of Motivation," *Psychological Review*, vol. 50, 1943, pp. 370–96; and A. H. Maslow, *Motivation and Personality*, New York: Harper & Row, 1954. Although the model has been criticized by some, a strong defense of it is offered in Dennis O'Connor and Leodones Yballe, "Maslow Revisited: Constructing a Road Map of Human Nature," *Journal of Management Education*, December 2007, pp. 738–56.

6. Frederick Herzberg, Bernard Mausner, and Barbara Snyderman, *The Motivation to Work*, New York: John Wiley & Sons, 1959; Frederick Herzberg, *Work and the Nature of Man*, Cleveland: World Publishing Company, 1966; and Frederick Herzberg, *The Managerial Choice: To Be Efficient or to Be Human*, rev. ed., Salt Lake City: Olympus, 1982.

7. Nico W. Van Yperen and Mariët Hagedoorn, "Do High Job Demands Increase Intrinsic Motivation or Fatigue or Both? The Role of Job Control and Job Social Support," *Academy of Management Journal*, vol. 46, no. 3, 2003, pp. 339–48.

8. Early criticisms were in Martin G. Evans, "Herzberg's Two-Factor Theory of Motivation: Some Problems and a Suggested Test," *Personnel Journal*, January 1970, pp. 32–35; and Valerie M. Bockman, "The Herzberg Controversy," *Personnel Psychology*, Summer 1971, pp. 155–89. The latter article reports the first 10 years of research on the model. A study of the role of intrinsic satisfaction as a motivator of suggestion system participation is in Nigel Bassett-Jones and Geoffrey C. Lloyd, "Does Herzberg's Motivation Theory Have Staying Power?" *Journal of Management Development*, vol. 24, no. 10, pp. 929–43.

9. Clayton P. Alderfer, "An Empirical Test of a New Theory of Human Needs," *Organizational Behavior and Human Performance*, vol. 4, 1969, pp. 142–75.

10. B. F. Skinner, *Science and Human Behavior*, New York: Macmillan (Free Press), 1953; and B. F. Skinner, *Contingencies of Reinforcement*, New York: Appleton-Century-Crofts, 1969. OB Mod is discussed in Fred Luthans and Robert Kreitner, *Organizational Behavior Modification and Beyond: An Operant and Social Learning Approach*, Glenview, IL: Scott, Foresman, 1985.

11. Timothy R. Hinkin and Chester A. Schriesheim, "Performance Incentives for Tough Times," *Harvard Business Review*, March 2009, p. 26.

12. "Productivity Gains from a Pat on the Back," *BusinessWeek*, January 23, 1978, pp. 56–62.

13. Sara L. Rynes, Kenneth G. Brown, and Amy E. Colbert, "Seven Common Misconceptions about Human Resource Practices: Research Findings versus Practitioner Beliefs," *Academy of Management Executive*, vol. 16, no. 3, 2002, pp. 92–102. The debate about goal setting continues at the present time; see Lisa D. Ordonez, Maurice E. Schweitzer, Adam D. Galinsky, and Max H. Bazerman, "Goals Gone Wild: The Systematic Side Effects of Overprescribing Goal Setting," *Academy of Management Perspectives*, February 2009, pp. 6–16; and Edwin A. Locke and Gary P. Latham, "Has Goal Setting Gone Wild, or Have Its Attackers Abandoned Good Scholarship?" *Academy of Management Perspectives*, February 2009, pp. 17–23.

14. See, for example, Alexander D. Stajkovic and Fred Luthans, "Going beyond Traditional Motivational and Behavioral Approaches," *Organizational Dynamics*, Spring 1998, pp. 62–74. Also see John Newstrom, Don Gardner, and Jon Pierce, "A Neglected Supervisory Role: Building Self-Esteem at Work," *Supervision*, January 2004, pp. 18–21.

15. Nicholas Bloom, Raffaella Sadun, and John Van Reenen, "How Three Essential Practices Can Address Even the Most Complex Global Problems," *Harvard Business Review*, November 2012, pp. 77–82.

16. Victor H. Vroom, *Work and Motivation*, New York: John Wiley & Sons, 1964; and Lyman W. Porter and Edward E. Lawler III, *Managerial Attitudes and Performance*, Homewood, IL: Dorsey Press and Richard D. Irwin, 1968.

17. The original meaning of instrumentality, as offered by Victor Vroom, reflected the level of association between performance and reward and thus was a correlation that could range between 1 and +1. However, later interpretations and modifications to the expectancy model by other writers have generally limited the effective range of instrumentality to include only positive associations from 0 to +1. For a more thorough discussion, see Craig C. Pinder, "Valence-Instrumentality-Expectancy Theory," in Richard M. Steers and Lyman W. Porter (eds.), *Motivation and Work Behavior*, 4th ed., New York: McGraw-Hill Book Company, 1987, pp. 69–89.

18. J. S. Adams, "Inequity in Social Exchange," in L. Berkowitz (ed.), *Advances in Experimental Social Psychology*, vol. 2, New York: Academic Press, 1965, pp. 267–99. For a discussion of the impact of different cultural backgrounds, see Lynda M. Kilbourne and Anne M. O'Leary-Kelly, "A Reevaluation of Equity Theory: The Influence of Culture," *Journal of Management Inquiry*, June 1994, pp. 177–88.

19. Jerald Greenberg, "Employee Theft as a Reaction to Underpayment Inequity: The Hidden Cost of Pay Cuts," *Journal of Applied Psychology*, October 1990, pp. 561–68.

20. Richard C. Huseman, John D. Hatfield, and Edward W. Miles, "A New Perspective on Equity Theory: The Equity Sensitivity Construct," *Academy of Management Review*, April 1987, pp. 222–34.

21. See, for example, Piers Steel and Cornelious J. König, "Integrating Theories of Motivation," *Academy of Management Review*, vol. 31, no. 4, pp. 889–913; and Marc Anderson, "Why Are There So Many Theories?

A Classroom Exercise to Help Students Appreciate the Need for Multiple Theories of a Management Domain," *Journal of Management Education*, vol. 31, no. 6, December 2007, pp. 757–76.

22. Developed from an article by Liz Roman Gallese, "Stephen Jellen Builds Pianos Not for Money but for Satisfaction," *The Wall Street Journal* (Pacific Coast edition), September 6, 1973, pp. 1, 12.

Chapter 6

1. Charles Coy, "The Road to Total Compensation," Special Supplement to *Workforce Management*, 2008, p. S3.
2. Daniel Pink, in "Performance Management Guide," *Workforce Management*, July 2012, p. 22.
3. An example of a multilevel reward system can be found at Boeing, where they combine formal appreciation, cash awards, instant recognition, and service awards. See Bridget Mintz Testa, "Boeing Awards Taking Off in a New Direction," *Workforce Management*, April 24, 2006, pp. 37–39. Also see Alden M. Hayashi, "What's the Best Way to Pay Employees?" *Sloan Management Review*, Winter 2007, pp. 8–9.
4. Carolyn Wiley, "Incentive Plan Pushes Production," *Personnel Journal*, August 1993, pp. 86–91.
5. Three field tests of the underpaid/overpaid equity hypotheses support a curvilinear relationship with pay satisfaction in Paul D. Sweeney, "Distributive Justice and Pay Satisfaction: A Field Test of an Equity Theory Predication," *Journal of Business and Psychology*, Spring 1990, pp. 329–41.
6. This trade-off between extrinsic rewards and intrinsic satisfaction was originally proposed by Edward L. Deci, "Effects of Externally Mediated Rewards on Intrinsic Motivation," *Journal of Personality and Social Psychology*, vol. 18, 1971, pp. 105–15. Recent field-research support for his proposal appears in Paul C. Jordan, "Effects of an Extrinsic Reward on Intrinsic Motivation: A Field Experiment," *Academy of Management Journal*, June 1986, pp. 405–12.
7. Jackee McNitt, "In Good Company: An Employee Recognition Plan with Staying Power," *Compensation and Benefits Management*, Spring 1990, pp. 242–46.
8. Adrienne Colella et al., "Exposing Pay Secrecy," *Academy of Management Review*, 2007, vol. 32, no. 1, pp. 55–71.
9. Useful discussions are in Beth Hazels and Craig M. Sasse, "Forced Ranking: A Review," *SAM Advanced Management Journal*, Spring 2008, pp. 35–40; and Sarah Boehle, "Keeping Forced Ranking Out of Court," *Training*, June 2008, pp. 40–46.
10. Michal Lev-Ram, "Performance Review Remade," *Fortune*, October 29, 2012, p. 60; and Clive Fletcher, "Performance Appraisal and Management: The Developing Research Agenda," *Journal of Occupational and Organizational Psychology*, 2001, vol. 74, pp. 473–87.
11. Mary Carson, "Saying It Like It Isn't: The Pros and Cons of 360-Degree Feedback," *Business Horizons*, 2006, pp. 395–402.
12. Jena McGregor, "The Employee Is Always Right," *BusinessWeek*, November 19, 2007, pp. 80, 82.
13. Meg McSherry Breslin, "Properly Rewarding Workers Could Reward Employers, Too," *Workforce Management*, August 2012, p. 8. Also see Robert A. Eckert, "The Two Most Important Words (Thank You)." *Harvard Business Review*, April 2013, p. 38.
14. The attribution process was first presented in Fritz Heider, *The Psychology of Interpersonal Relations*, New York: John Wiley & Sons, Inc., 1958. It was elaborated upon in H. H. Kelley, "The Processes of Causal Attribution," *American Psychologist*, February 1973, pp. 107–28. Attributions are discussed in Michael J. Mauboussin, "The Success Equation: Untangling Skill and Luck in Business, Sports, and Investing," Boston: Harvard Business Review Press, 2012.
15. The self-fulfilling prophecy was initially presented in Robert K. Merton, "The Self-Fulfilling Prophecy," *Antioch Review*, vol. 8, 1948, pp. 193–210. Positive contagion is presented in Kelly Linkenberger, "You'll Get Better if You Think Tiger Woods Has Used Your Clubs," *Harvard Business Review*, July–August 2012, pp. 32–34.
16. Serguei Netessine and Valery Yakubovich, "The Darwinian Workplace," *Harvard Business Review*, May 2012, pp. 25–28; and Michael J. Mauboussin, "The True Measures of Success," *Harvard Business Review*, October 2012, pp. 46–56.
17. The Nucor system is described in "Nucor's Ken Iverson on Productivity and Pay," *Personnel Administrator*, October 1986, pp. 46 ff.
18. C. Bram Cadsby, Fei Song, and Francis Tapon, "Sorting and Incentive Effects of Pay for Performance: An Experimental Investigation," *Academy of Management Journal*, 2007, vol. 50, no. 2, pp. 387–405. Also see Herman Aguinis, Harry Joo, and Ryan K. Gottfredson, "What Monetary Rewards Can and Cannot Do: How to Show Employees the Money," *Business Horizons*, 2013, vol. 56, pp. 241–49.
19. Garry M. Ritzky, "Incentive Pay Programs that Help the Bottom Line," *HR Magazine*, April 1995, pp. 68–74.
20. Edward E. Lawler III, Gerald E. Ledford Jr., and Lei Chang, "Who Uses Skill-Based Pay, and Why," *Compensation and Benefits Review*, March–April 1993, pp. 22–26.

Chapter 7

1. Hao Ma, Ranjan Karri, and Kumar Chittipeddi, "The Paradox of Managerial Tyranny," *Business Horizons*, July–August 2004, p. 33.
2. Marcus Buckingham, "Leadership Development in the Age of the Algorithm," *Harvard Business Review*, June 2012, p. 90.
3. Jena McGregor, "Behind the List of Customer Service Champs," *BusinessWeek*, March 2, 2009, pp. 32–33.
4. The emphasis on influence in the definition of leadership is consistent with a review of 11 different approaches to leadership discussed in Jon L. Pierce and John W. Newstrom, "On the Meaning of Leadership," *Leaders and the Leadership Process: Readings, Self-Assessments, and*

Applications, 6th ed., New York: McGraw-Hill/Irwin, 2011, pp. 7–11. It is consistent with the former supreme commander of NATO's definition ("the art of persuading the other fellow to want to do what you want him to do") in General Wesley Clark, "The Potency of Persuasion," *Fortune*, November 12, 2007, p. 48.

5. Michael D. Watkins, "How Managers Become Leaders: The Seven Seismic Shifts of Perspective and Responsibility," *Harvard Business Review*, June 2012, pp. 65–72.
6. Shelley A. Kirkpatrick and Edwin A. Locke, "Leadership: Do Traits Matter?" *Academy of Management Executive*, May 1991, pp. 48–60; and R. J. House et al., *Leadership, Culture, and Organizations: The GLOBE Study of 62 Societies*, Thousand Oaks, CA: Sage, 2004.
7. Manfred Kets de Vries and Stanislav Shekshnia, "Vladimir Putin, CEO of Russia Inc.: The Legacy and the Future," *Organizational Dynamics*, vol. 37, no. 3, 2008, pp. 236–53.
8. Kate Ludeman and Eddie Erlandson, *Alpha Male Syndrome,* Boston: Harvard Business School, 2006; Bradley P. Owens and David R. Hekman, "Modeling How to Grow: An Inductive Examination of Humble Leader Behaviors, Contingencies, and Outcomes," *Academy of Management Journal,* 2012, vol. 55, no. 4, pp. 787–818.
9. Daniel Goleman and Richard Boyatzis, "Social Intelligence and the Biology of Leadership," *Harvard Business Review*, September 2008, pp. 74–81.
10. Richard Wellins and William Byham, "The Leadership Gap," *Training*, March 2001, pp. 98–106.
11. See, for useful illustrations, Jeffrey A. Sonnenfeld and Andrew J. Ward, "Firing Back: How Great Leaders Rebound After Career Disasters," *Harvard Business Review*, January 2007, pp. 77–84.
12. Discussions of followership are found in Barbara Kellerman, "What Every Leader Needs to Know About Followers," *Harvard Business Review*, December 2007, pp. 84–89; and Barbara Kellerman, *Followership: How Followers Are Creating Change and Changing Leaders*, Boston: Harvard Business Press, 2008.
13. Boris Groysberg and Michael Slind, "Leadership Is a Conversation," *Harvard Business Review*, June 2012, pp. 76–84.
14. Susan G. Hauser, "The Degeneration of Decorum," *Workforce Management,* January 2011, pp. 16–21.
15. Examples of early reports from each university are Daniel Katz et al., *Productivity, Supervision and Morale in an Office Situation*, Ann Arbor: University of Michigan Press, 1950; and E. A. Fleishman, *Leadership Climate and Supervisory Behavior*, Columbus: Personnel Research Board, Ohio State University Press, 1951.
16. Alice H. Eagly and Linda L. Carli, *Through the Labyrinth: The Truth About How Women Become Leaders*, Boston: Harvard Business School Press, 2007.
17. Fred E. Fiedler, *A Theory of Leadership Effectiveness*, New York: McGraw-Hill, 1967; and Fred E. Fiedler and Martin M. Chemers, *Leadership and Effective Management*, Glenview, IL: Scott, Foresman, 1974. A current application is cited in Stephen J. Sauer, "Why Bossy Is Better for Rookie Managers," *Harvard Business Review*, May 2012, p. 30. For a critique, see Arthur G. Jago and James W. Ragan, "The Trouble with Leader Match Is that It Doesn't Match Fiedler's Contingency Model," *Journal of Applied Psychology*, November 1986, pp. 555–59.
18. Paul Hersey and Kenneth H. Blanchard, *Management of Organizational Behavior*, 5th ed., Englewood Cliffs, NJ: Prentice Hall, 1988.
19. Robert J. House, "A Path Goal Theory of Leadership Effectiveness," *Administrative Science Quarterly*, September 1971, pp. 321–28. For the original explanation, see M. G. Evans, *The Effects of Supervisory Behavior upon Worker Perceptions of Their Path-Goal Relationships*, unpublished doctoral dissertation, New Haven, CT: Yale University, 1968. For a broad review of the path-goal literature, see J. C. Wofford and Laurie Z. Liska, "Path-Goal Theories of Leadership: A Meta-Analysis," *Journal of Management*, Winter 1993, pp. 857–76.
20. V. H. Vroom and P. W. Yetton, *Leadership and Decision Making*, Pittsburgh: University of Pittsburgh Press, 1973, contains both an individual (consultative) model and a similar one for group decision making. Subsequent research and modifications to the original model are reported in Victor H. Vroom and Arthur G. Jago, *The New Leadership: Managing Participation in Organizations*, Englewood Cliffs, NJ: Prentice Hall, 1988. Research supporting the importance of the problem attributes is reported in Richard H. G. Field, Peter C. Read, and Jordan J. Louviere, "The Effect of Situation Attributes on Decision Method Choice in the Vroom-Jago Model of Participation in Decision Making," *Leadership Quarterly*, Fall 1990, pp. 165–76. For an update, see Victor H. Vroom, "Leadership and the Decision-Making Process," *Organizational Dynamics*, vol. 28, no. 4, 2000, pp. 82–94.
21. Steven Kerr and J. M. Jermier, "Substitutes for Leadership: Their Meaning and Measurement," *Organizational Behavior and Human Performance*, December 1978, pp. 375–403.
22. Jon P. Howell et al., "Substitutes for Leadership: Effective Alternatives to Ineffective Leadership," *Organizational Dynamics*, Summer 1990, pp. 20–38.
23. Useful discussions of coaching are in Diane Coutu and Carol Kauffman, "What Can Coaches Do for You?" *Harvard Business Review*, January 2009, pp. 91–97; and Clinton O. Longenecker and Mitchell J. Neubert, "The Practices of Effective Managerial Coaching," *Business Horizons*, vol. 48, 2005, pp. 493–500.
24. Sensemaking is one of four interdependent managerial capabilities proposed in Debora Ancona, Thomas W. Malone, Wanda J. Orlikowski, and Peter M. Senge, "In Praise of the Incomplete Leader," *Harvard Business Review*, February 2007, pp. 92–100.

Chapter 8

1. Margaret Wheatley, quoted in John Hollon, "Leading Well is Simple," *Workforce Management*, November 6, 2006, p. 50.
2. Traci Fenton, "Democracy at Work," *Workforce Management*, December 2011, p. 13.

3. Manfred F. R. Kets de Vries, "The Dangers of Feeling Like a Fake," *Harvard Business Review*, September 2005, pp. 108–16.

4. Robert C. Ford and Myron D. Fottler, "Empowerment: A Matter of Degree," *Academy of Management Executive*, vol. 9, no. 3, 1995, pp. 21–31.

5. Gretchen M. Spreitzer, Mark A. Kizilos, and Stephen W. Nason, "A Dimensional Analysis of the Relationship between Psychological Empowerment and Effectiveness, Satisfaction, and Strain," *Journal of Management*, vol. 23, no. 5, 1997, pp. 679–704.

6. Adam Bryant, "What He Learned from the Boss Who Left at 5:30," *The New York Times*, December 23, 2012, p. B2.

7. F. J. Roethlisberger and W. J. Dickson, *Management and the Worker*, Cambridge, MA: Harvard University Press, 1939; and Lester Coch and John R. P. French Jr., "Overcoming Resistance to Change," *Human Relations*, vol. 1, no. 4, 1948, pp. 512–32.

8. John A. Wagner III, "Participation's Effects on Performance and Satisfaction: A Reconsideration of Research Evidence," *Academy of Management Review*, vol. 19, no. 2, 1994, pp. 312–30. Also see David J. Glew, Ricky W. Griffin, and David D. Van Fleet, "Participation in Organizations: A Review of the Issues and Proposed Framework for Future Analysis," *Journal of Management*, vol. 21, no. 3, 1995, pp. 395–421.

9. This interest is demonstrated by the wide popularity of books on management; see Jon L. Pierce and John W. Newstrom, *The Manager's Bookshelf: A Mosaic of Contemporary Views*, 9th ed., Upper Saddle River, NJ: Pearson Prentice Hall, 2010.

10. See, for example, "Companies Hit the Road Less Traveled," *BusinessWeek*, June 5, 1995, pp. 82–83; and Donald W. McCormick, "Spirituality and Management," *Spirit at Work*, Winter 1995, pp. 1–3.

11. Support for the participative process is in Carla S. Smith and Michael T. Brannick, "A Role and Expectancy Model of Participative Decision-Making: A Replication and Theoretical Extension," *Journal of Organizational Behavior*, March 1990, pp. 91–104; and Jeffrey L. Kerr, "The Limits of Organizational Democracy," *Academy of Management Journal*, vol. 18, no. 3, 2004, pp. 81–95.

12. Hollon, op cit.

13. This model was originally presented in F. Dansereau Jr., G. Graen, and W. J. Haga, "A Vertical Dyad Linkage Approach to Leadership within Formal Organizations: A Longitudinal Investigation of the Role Making Process," *Organizational Behavior and Human Performance*, vol. 13, 1975, pp. 46–68. Recent discussion appeared in Ceasar Douglas and Suzanne Zivnuska, "Developing Trust in Leaders: An Antecedent of Firm Performance," *Advanced Management Journal*, Winter 2008, pp. 20–28.

14. Scott W. Spreier, Mary H. Fontaine, and Ruth L. Malloy, "Leadership Run Amok: The Destructive Potential of Overachievers," *Harvard Business Review*, June 2006, pp. 72–82.

15. Andrea Jung, "Seek Frank Feedback," in "Leading by Feel," *Harvard Business Review*, January 2004, pp. 27–37; and Herminia Ibarra and Otilia Obodaru, "Women and the Vision Thing," *Harvard Business Review*, January 2009, pp. 62–70.

16. See Daniel Goleman, "What Makes a Leader?" *Harvard Business Review*, January 2004, pp. 82–91; and Peter J. Jordan, Neal M. Ashkanasy, and Charmine E. J. Hartel, "Emotional Intelligence as a Moderator of Emotional and Behavioral Reactions to Job Insecurity," *Academy of Management Review*, vol. 27, no. 3, 2002, pp. 361–72.

17. Mitchell Lee Marks et al., "Employee Participation in a Quality Circle Program: Impact on Quality of Work Life, Productivity, and Absenteeism," *Journal of Applied Psychology*, February 1986, pp. 61–69. A discussion of options for various levels of participation is in C. Philip Alexander, "Voluntary Participation," *Quality Digest*, October 1994, pp. 50–52.

18. Mark Van Kooy, "A New Path to Engagement," *Trustee*, November/December 2012, pp. 6–7.

19. Some have argued that it is necessary for employees to psychologically experience ownership before results can be expected from them. See Jon L. Pierce, Stephen A. Rubenfeld, and Susan Morgan, "Employee Ownership: A Conceptual Model of Process and Effects," *Academy of Management Review*, January 1991, pp. 121–44; the leap from actual stock ownership to a *feeling* of ownership is explored in Corey Rosen, John Case, and Martin Staubus, "Every Employee an Owner. [Really.]," *Harvard Business Review*, June 2005, pp. 123–30.

20. Lisa M. Leslie, Colleen Flaherty Manchester, Tae-Youn Park, and Si AhnMehng, "Flexible Work Practices: A Source of Career Premiums or Penalties?" *Academy of Management Journal*, 2012, vol. 55, no. 6, pp. 1407–28.

21. Max E. Douglas, "Service to Others," *Supervision*, March 2005, pp. 6–9.

Chapter 9

1. Daniel Gilbert, "The Science Behind the Smile," *Harvard Business Review*, January–February 2012, p. 87.

2. David Sturt, as quoted in Bridget Mintz Testa, "Early Engagement, Long Relationship?" *Workforce Management*, September 22, 2008, pp. 27–31.

3. Gretchen Spreitzer and Christine Porath, "Creating Sustainable Performance," *Harvard Business Review*, January–February 2012, pp. 93–102.

4. For a review of this relationship, see Remus Ilies, Kelly Schwind Wilson, and David T. Wagner, "The Spillover of Daily Job Satisfaction onto Employees' Family Lives: The Facilitating Role of Work-Family Integration," *Academy of Management Journal*, 2009, vol. 52, no. 1, pp. 87–102.

5. See, for example, the data reported in Joanne H. Gavin and Richard O. Mason, "The Virtuous Organization: The Value of Happiness in the Workplace," *Organizational Dynamics*,

vol. 33, no. 4, 2004, pp. 379–92; and Terence F. Shea, "For Many Employees, the Workplace Is Not a Satisfying Place," *HR Magazine*, October 2002, p. 28.

6. A review of the three forms of commitment appears in David Ozag, "The Relationship Between the Trust, Hope, and Normative and Continuance Commitment of Merger Survivors," *Journal of Management Development*, 2006, vol. 25, no. 9, pp. 870–83.
7. Charalambos A. Vlachoutsicos, "How to Cultivate Engaged Employees," *Harvard Business Review*, September 2012, pp. 123–26; and http://en.wikipedia.org/wiki/Employee_engagement.
8. C. Rusbult et al., "Impact of Exchange Variables on Exit, Voice, Loyalty, and Neglect: An Integrative Model of Responses to Declining Job Satisfaction," *Academy of Management Journal*, vol. 31, no. 3, 1988, pp. 599–627. See also Jacqueline Landau, "When Employee Voice Is Met by Deaf Ears," *Advanced Management Journal*, Winter 2009, pp. 4–12.
9. For a classic description of this relationship, see Edward E. Lawler III and Lyman W. Porter, "The Effect of Performance on Job Satisfaction," *Industrial Relations*, October 1967, pp. 20–28. Recent support, gathered from a study of 177 store managers, is in M. Christen, G. Iyler, and D. Soberman, "Job Satisfaction, Job Performance, and Effort: A Reexamination Using Agency Theory," *Journal of Marketing,* 2006, vol. 70, pp. 137–50.
10. W. H. Mobley, "Intermediate Linkages in the Relationship between Job Satisfaction and Employee Turnover," *Journal of Applied Psychology*, vol. 6, 1977, pp. 237–40. Also see Dmitry Khanin, "How to Reduce Turnover Intentions in the Family Business: Managing Centripetal and Centrifugal Forces," *Business Horizons*, 2013, vol. 56, pp. 63–73; and Anthony J. Nyberg and Robert E. Ployhart, "Context-Emergent Turnover (CET) Theory: A Theory of Collective Turnover," *Academy of Management Review*, 2013, vol. 38, no. 1, pp. 109–31.
11. "New Behavioral Study Defines Typical 'Turnover Personality,'" *Human Resource Measurements*, Supplement to *Personnel Journal*, April 1992, p. 4. The "turnover personality" is supported by Timothy A. Judge and Shinichiro Watanabe, "Is the Past Prologue? A Test of Ghiselli's Hobo Syndrome," *Journal of Management*, vol. 21, no. 2, 1995, pp. 211–29.
12. See "The 2009 List of Industry Stars," *Fortune*, March 16, 2009, pp. 81–88; and Robert Levering and Milton Moskowitz, "100 Best Companies to Work For," *Fortune*, February 2, 2009, pp. 67–78.
13. See, for example, Julie Bos, "Top Tips for Keeping Your Top Talent in Place," *Workforce Management*, April 21, 2008, pp. 28–30.
14. Brian R. Dineen, Raymond A. Noe, Jason D. Shaw, Michelle K. Duffy, and Carolyn Wiethoff, "Level and Dispersion of Satisfaction in Teams: Using Foci and Social Context to Explain the Satisfaction-Absenteeism Relationship," *Academy of Management Journal*, 2007, vol. 50, no. 3, pp. 623–43.
15. John Putzier and Frank T. Nowak, "Attendance Management and Control," *Personnel Administrator*, August 1989, pp. 58–60.
16. Paul Hemp, "Presenteeism: At Work—But Out of It," *Harvard Business Review*, October 2004, pp. 49–58, Claire Suddath, "Sick of This," *Bloomberg BusinessWeek*, February 4–10, 2013, p. 77; and Tammy Johns and Lynda Gratton, "The Third Wave of Virtual Work," *Harvard Business Review*, January–February 2013, pp. 66–73.
17. A comprehensive program that drastically reduced shrinkage (employee theft) at Trader Joe's grocery store is presented in Irwin Peizer, "Shopper's Special," *Workforce Management*, September 2004, pp. 51–54. A fascinating description of corporate loss-control programs is in John Colapinto, "Stop, Thief!" *The New Yorker*, September 1, 2008, pp. 74–83.
18. John F. Veiga, Timothy D. Golden, and Kathleen Dechant, "Why Managers Bend Company Rules," *Academy of Management Executive*, vol. 18, no. 2, 2004, pp. 84–90.
19. Kevin Dobbs, "The Lucrative Menace of Workplace Violence," *Training*, March 2000, pp. 55–62.
20. Dennis W. Organ, "Personality and Organizational Citizenship Behavior," *Journal of Management*, Summer 1994, pp. 465–78; and William H. Bommer, Erich C. Dierdorff, and Robert S. Rubin, "Does Prevalence Mitigate Relevance? The Moderating Effect of Group-Level OCB on Employee Performance," *Academy of Management Journal*, 2007, vol. 50, no. 6, pp. 1481–94.
21. Mark C. Bolino and William H. Turnley, "Going the Extra Mile: Cultivating and Managing Employee Citizenship Behavior," *Academy of Management Executive*, vol. 17, no. 3, 2003, pp. 60–71. An extension of this concept to the organizational level is found in Dirk Matten and Andrew Crane, "Corporate Citizenship: Toward an Extended Theoretical Conceptualization," *Academy of Management Review*, vol. 30, no. 1, 2005, pp. 166–79.
22. Elaine Hatfield, John T. Cacioppo, and Richard L Rapson, "Emotional Contagion," *Current Directions in Psychological Sciences*, 1993, vol. 2, pp. 96–99.

Chapter 10

1. Lew McCreary, "What Was Privacy?" *Harvard Business Review,* October 2008, p. 124.
2. Matthew Heller, "Supervisors Should Step In, Study Shows," *Workforce Management,* August 2012, p. 17.
3. Edgar H. Schein and J. Steven Ott, "The Legitimacy of Organizational Influence," *American Journal of Sociology,* May 1962, pp. 682–89; and Keith Davis, "Attitudes toward the Legitimacy of Management Efforts to Influence Employees," *Academy of Management Journal,* June 1968, pp. 153–62.
4. Paul Tolchinsky et al., "Employee Perceptions of Invasion of Privacy: A Field Simulation Experiment," *Journal of Applied Psychology,* June 1982, pp. 308–13.
5. James Sunshine, "How Companies Use Facebook to Hire and Fire Employees," *The Huffington Post,* August 4,

2011, in http://www.huffingtonpost.com/2011/08/04/new-infographic-shows-how-companies-target-unemployed_n_918816.html.

6. Stephen Baker, "The Next Net," *BusinessWeek,* March 9, 2009, pp. 42–46.

7. H. John Bernardin and Donna K. Cooke, "Validity of an Honesty Test in Predicting Theft among Convenience Store Employees," *Academy of Management Journal,* October 1993, pp. 1097–1108. Interestingly, some authors have noted that lying at work is not only common but even acceptable on some occasions; see Christopher Bonanos, "The Lies We Tell at Work," *Bloomberg BusinessWeek,* February 4–10, 2013, pp. 71–73.

8. Susan G. Hauser, "Companies Can Curb Cannabis Consumption," *Workforce Management,* January 2013, p. 9.

9. Timothy L. Baker, "Preventing Drug Abuse at Work," *Personnel Administrator,* July 1989, pp. 56–59.

10. Susan G. Hauser, "Sincerely Yours, GINA," *Workforce Management,* July 2011, pp. 16–22.

11. Cory R. Fine, "Video Tests Are the New Frontier in Drug Detection," *Personnel Journal,* July 1992, pp. 146–61.

12. J. Richard Hackman et al., "A New Strategy for Job Enrichment," *California Management Review,* Summer 1975, pp. 57–71. For a discussion of how personality traits act in concert with core job dimensions to produce feelings of meaningfulness, see Murray R. Barrick, Michael K. Mount, and Ning Li, "The Theory of Purposeful Work Behavior: The Role of Personality, Higher-Order Goals, and Job Characteristics," *Academy of Management Review,* 2013, vol. 38, no. 1, pp. 132–53.

13. "The Signature of Quality," *Management in Practice,* American Management Association, March–April 1977, pp. 2–3.

14. J. Richard Hackman and Greg R. Oldham, "Development of the Job Diagnostic Survey," *Journal of Applied Psychology,* April 1975, pp. 159–70.

15. Fred Luthans et al., "The Impact of a Job Redesign Intervention on Salespersons' Observed Performance Behaviors: A Field Experiment," *Group and Organization Studies,* March 1987, pp. 55–72.

16. See, for example, Hossam M. Abu Elanain, "The Five-Factor Model of Personality and Organizational Citizenship Behavior in United Arab Emirates," *Advanced Management Journal,* Summer 2007, pp. 47–57. Countering views are in Diane Bergeron, "The Potential Paradox of Organizational Citizenship Behavior: Good Citizens at What Cost?" *Academy of Management Review,* 2007, vol. 32, no. 4, pp. 1079–95; and Anthony C. Klotz and Mark C. Bolino, "Citizenship and Counterproductive Work Behavior: A Moral Licensing View," *Academy of Management Review,* 2012, vol. 38, no. 2, pp. 292–306.

17. Robert Ford and John Newstrom, "Dues-Paying: Managing the Costs of Recognition," *Business Horizons,* July–August 1999.

18. See Gary R. Weaver, Linda Klebe Trevino, and Bradley Agle, "Ethical Role Models in Organizations," *Organizational Dynamics,* 2005, vol. 34, no. 4, pp. 313–30; and Steven L. Grover, "The Truth, the Whole Truth, and Nothing but the Truth: The Causes and Management of Workplace Lying," *Academy of Management Executive,* 2005, vol. 19, no. 2, pp. 148–57. For an example of a "Hippocratic Oath for Managers," see Rakesh Khurana and Nitin Nohria, "It's Time to Make Management a True Profession," *Harvard Business Review,* October 2008, pp. 70–77.

19. Michael J. Gundlach, Mark J. Martinko, and Scott C. Douglas, "A New Approach to Examining Whistle-Blowing: The Influence of Cognitions and Anger," *Advanced Management Journal,* Autumn 2008, pp. 40–50; and Jeff Kehoe, "The Primacy of Personality," *Harvard Business Review,* December 2012, p. 130 (emphasis added).

20. Richard W. Stevenson, "A Whistle Blower to Get $7.5 Million in Big Fraud Case," *The New York Times,* July 15, 1992.

21. Susan Ladika, "Whistling While You Work," *Workforce Management,* April 2012, pp. 26–32.

Chapter 11

1. Rob Cross, Jeanne Liedtka, and Leigh Weiss, "A Practical Guide to Social Networks," *Harvard Business Review,* March 2005, p. 130.

2. Jeff Kehoe, "The Primacy of Personality," *Harvard Business Review*, December 2012, p. 130 (emphasis added).

3. Ellen Van Velsor and Jean Brittain Leslie, "Why Executives Derail: Perspectives Across Time and Cultures," *Academy of Management Executive*, vol. 9, no. 4, 1995, pp. 62–72.

4. Christine M. Pearson and Christine L. Porath, "On the Nature, Consequences, and Remedies of Workplace Incivility: Not Time for 'Nice'? Think Again," *Academy of Management Executive*, vol. 19, no. 1, 2005, pp. 7–18.

5. Christine Porath and Christine Pearson, "The Price of Incivility: Lack of Respect Hurts Morale—and the Bottom Line," *Harvard Business Review*, January–February 2013, pp. 115–21; and P. M. Forni, *Choosing Civility: The Twenty-Five Rules of Considerate Conduct*, New York, St. Martin's Press, 2002.

6. Joshua D. Margolis and Andrew Molinsky, "Navigating the Bind of Necessary Evils: Psychological Engagement and the Production of Interpersonally Sensitive Behavior," *Academy of Management Journal*, vol. 51, no. 5, 2008, pp. 847–72.

7. M. K. Mount and M. R. Barrick, "The Big Five Personality Dimensions: Implications for Research and Practice in Human Resources Management," *Research in Personnel and Human Resources Management*, 1995, pp. 153–200.

8. "Creating a Corporate Culture that Soars: Southwest Airlines and the Myers-Briggs Assessment," *Workforce Management*, December 11, 2006, p. 38.

9. W. L. Gardner and M. J. Martinko, "Using the Myers-Briggs Type Indicator to Study Managers: A Literature Review and Research Agenda," *Journal of Management*, vol. 22, 1996, pp. 45–83.

10. Robert R. Blake and Jane S. Mouton, *Managing Intergroup Conflict in Industry*, Houston: Gulf Publishing Co., 1964. Note that these authors and others often include an intermediate strategy called compromising.

11. Dean Tjosvold, "Constructive Controversy for Management Education: Developing Committed, Open-Minded Researchers," *Academy of Management Learning and Education*, vol. 7, no. 1, 2008, pp. 73–85.

12. Hong Ren and Barbara Gray, "Repairing Relationship Conflict: How Violation Types and Culture Influence the Effectiveness of Restoration Rituals," *Academy of Management Review*, vol. 34, no. 1, 2009, pp. 105–26; and Tammy Lenski, "Talk It Out," *Bloomberg BusinessWeek*, December 10–16, 2012, p. 85.

13. Useful strategies for conflict resolution are discussed in William Cottringer, "Adopting a Philosophy on Conflict," *Supervision*, March 2005, pp. 3–5; and Jeff Weiss and Jonathan Hughes, "Want Collaboration? Accept— and Actively Manage—Conflict," *Harvard Business Review*, March 2005, pp. 93–101. The importance of emotional awareness is examined in Kimberlyn Leary, Julianna Pillemer, and Michael Wheeler, "Negotiating with Emotion," *Harvard Business Review*, January–February 2013, pp. 96–103.

14. Useful components of this definition are found in F. David Schoorman, Roger C. Mayer, and James H. Davis, "An Integrative Model of Organizational Trust: Past, Present, and Future," *Academy of Management Review*, vol. 32, no. 2, 2007, pp. 344–54; and Roger C. Mayer and Mark B. Gavin, "Trust in Management and Performance: Who Minds the Shop While the Employees Watch the Boss?" *Academy of Management Journal*, vol. 48, no. 5, 2005, pp. 874–88.

15. Michele Williams, "Building Genuine Trust Through Interpersonal Emotion Management: A Threat Regulation Model of Trust and Collaboration Across Boundaries," *Academy of Management Review*, vol. 32, no. 2, 2007, pp. 595–621; and Melinda J. Moye and Alan B. Henkin, "Exploring Associations Between Employee Empowerment and Interpersonal Trust in Managers," *Journal of Management Development*, vol. 25, no. 2, 2006, pp. 101–17.

16. Paul W. B. Atkins and Sharon K. Parker, "Understanding Individual Compassion in Organizations: The Role of Appraisals and Psychological Flexibility," *Academy of Management Review*, 2012, vol. 37, no. 4, pp. 524–46.

17. J. R. P. French and B. H. Raven, "The Bases of Social Power," in D. Cartwright (ed.), *Studies in Social Power*, Ann Arbor: University of Michigan Press, 1959.

18. Christopher P. Parker, Robert L. Dipboye, and Stacey L. Jackson, "Perceptions of Organizational Politics: An Investigation of Antecedents and Consequences," *Journal of Management*, vol. 21, no. 5, 1995, pp. 891–912; Amos Drory and Tsilia Romm, "The Definition of Organizational Politics: A Review," *Human Relations*, November 1990, pp. 1133–54; and Pamela L. Perrewe and Debra L. Nelson, "The Facilitative Role of Political Skill," *Organizational Dynamics*, vol. 33, no. 4, 2004, pp. 366–78.

19. Jeffrey Gandz and Victor Murray, "The Experience of Workplace Politics," *Academy of Management Journal*, June 1980, p. 244.

20. Allen R. Cohen and David L. Bradford, *Influence without Authority*, New York: John Wiley & Sons, 1990.

21. Don Moyer, "Give to Get," *Harvard Business Review*, October 2005, p. 160.

22. Martin Kilduff and David V. Day, "Do Chameleons Get Ahead? The Effects of Self-Monitoring on Managerial Careers," *Academy of Management Journal*, vol. 37, no. 4, 1994, pp. 1047–60.

23. Sandy J. Wayne and Robert C. Liden, "Effects of Impression Management on Performance Ratings: A Longitudinal Study," *Academy of Management Journal*, vol. 38, no. 1, 1995, pp. 232–60.

Chapter 12

1. Thomas H. Davenport, "The Wisdom of Your In-House Crowd," *Harvard Business Review*, May 2012, p. 40.

2. Teresa M. Anabile and Mukti Khaire, "Creativity and the Role of the Leader," *Harvard Business Review*, October 2008, p. 103.

3. The idea that the informal organization's activities, interactions, and sentiments emerge from the formal organization is drawn from George C. Homans, *The Human Group*, New York: Harcourt Brace Jovanovich, 1950.

4. Stuart Drescher, Gary Burlingame, and Addie Fuhriman, "Cohesion: An Odyssey in Empirical Understanding," *Small Group Behavior*, February 1985, pp. 3–30. For discussion of a reliable instrument to measure cohesion, see Nancy J. Evans and Paul A. Jarvis, "The Group Attitude Scale: A Measure of Attraction to Group," *Small Group Behavior*, May 1986, pp. 203–16.

5. Four types of work group reactions (acceptance, avoidance, confrontation, and nurturance) are discussed by James W. Fairfield-Sonn, "Work Group Reactions to New Members: Tool or Trap in Making Selection Decisions?" *Public Personnel Management*, Winter 1984, pp. 485–93.

6. Daniel Feldman, "The Development and Enforcement of Group Norms," *Academy of Management Review*, January 1984, pp. 47–53.

7. Monika Henderson and Michael Argyle, "The Informal Rules of Working Relationships," *Journal of Occupational Behaviour*, vol. 7, 1986, pp. 259–75.

8. The saying "sent to Coventry" is derived from the following situation: The citizens of Coventry, England, so disliked soldiers that people seen talking to one were isolated from their social community, so those few citizens who felt like talking to soldiers did not dare do so. Hence, a soldier sent to Coventry was isolated from community interaction.

9. Steve Martin, "98% of HBR Readers Love This Article," *Harvard Business Review*, October 2012, pp. 23–25.

10. David Krackhardt and Jeffrey R. Hanson, "Informal Networks: The Company behind the Chart," *Harvard Business Review*, July–August 1993, pp. 104–11; and Rob Cross,

Nitin Noria, and Andrew Parker, "Six Myths about informal Networks—And How to Overcome Them," *Sloan Management Review*, Spring 2002, pp. 67–75; see also Tiziana Casciaro and Miguel Sousa Lobo, "Competent Jerks, Lovable Fools, and the Formation of Social Networks," *Harvard Business Review*, June 2005, pp. 92–99.

11. Jan van den Ende, "Nurturing Good Ideas," *Harvard Business Review*, April 2009, p. 24.

12. Practical suggestions from executives at Intel and McDonald's are in Jia Lynn Yang, "What's the Secret to Running Great Meetings?" *Fortune*, October 27, 2008, p. 26.

13. T. L. Stanley, "I Beg Your Pardon, This Meeting Is Not a Waste of Time," *Supervision*, April 2002, pp. 6–9; J. Robert Parkinson, "Meetings Are to Gather Ideas; Here's a Way They Can Succeed," *Sarasota Herald-Tribune*, March 2, 2013, p. 3D.

14. Task and social roles were originally presented by R. F. Bales, *Interaction Process Analysis*, Cambridge, MA: Addison-Wesley, 1950.

15. A fascinating discussion around the theme of "where you sit influences where you stand" is in Aili McConnon, "You Are Where You Sit," *BusinessWeek*, July 23, 2007, pp. 66–67.

16. Brainstorming was developed by Alex F. Osborn and is described in his book *Applied Imagination*, New York: Charles Scribner's Sons, 1953. An anecdotal critique of brainstorming appears in Jonah Lehrer, "Groupthink: The Brainstorming Myth," *The New Yorker*, January 30, 2012, pp. 22–27.

17. Greg Bachman, "Brainstorming Deluxe," *Training and Development*, January 2000, pp. 15–17.

18. R. Brent Gallupe, Lana M. Bastianutti, and William H. Cooper, "Unblocking Brainstorms," *Journal of Applied Psychology*, January 1991, pp. 137–42; for comparative results, see Alan R. Dennis and Joseph S. Valacich, "Group, Sub-Group, and Nominal Group Idea Generation: New Rules for a New Media?" *Journal of Management*, vol. 20, no. 4, 1994, pp. 723–36.

19. Gene E. Burton, "The 'Clustering Effect': An Idea-Generation Phenomenon during Nominal Grouping," *Small Group Behavior*, May 1987, pp. 224–38.

20. Recommendations ranging from two to five iterations of the Delphi process have been made. One study found that results stabilized after four rounds; see Robert C. Erffmeyer et al., "The Delphi Technique: An Empirical Evaluation of the Optimal Number of Rounds," *Group and Organization Studies*, March–June 1986, pp. 120–28. For a discussion of scenario-building through the Delphi technique, see Robert S. Duboff, "The Wisdom of (Expert) Crowds," *Harvard Business Review*, September 2007, p. 28.

21. Richard A. Cosier and Charles R. Schwenk, "Agreement and Thinking Alike: Ingredients for Poor Decisions," *The Executive*, February 1990, pp. 69–74; and David M. Schweiger, William R. Sandberg, and Paula L. Rechner, "Experiential Effects of Dialectical Inquiry, Devil's Advocacy, and Consensus Approaches to Strategic Decision Making," *Academy of Management Journal*, December 1989, pp. 745–72.

22. See, for example, discussions in Ed Frauenheim, "2022: A Workplace Odyssey," *Workforce Management*, December 2012, pp. 16–18; Allan Afuah and Christopher L. Tucci, "Crowdsourcing as a Solution to Distant Search," *Academy of Management Review*, 2012, vol. 37, no. 3, pp. 355–75; and Paul M. Healy and Karthik Ramanna, "When the Crowd Fights Corruption," *Harvard Business Review*, January–February 2013, pp. 122–29.

23. Thomas H. Davenport, "The Wisdom of Your In-House Crowd," *Harvard Business Review*, May 2012, p. 40; Gary Hamel, "First, Let's Fire All the Managers," *Harvard Business Review*, December 2011, pp. 49–60.

24. Larry Dressler, *Consensus Through Conversation*, San Francisco: Berrett-Koehler, 2006.

25. Steven Saint and James R. Lawson, *Rules for Reaching Consensus*, San Diego: Pfeiffer & Company, 1994.

26. Michael Wilkinson, *The Secrets of Facilitation: The S.M.A.R.T. Guide to Getting Results with Groups*, San Francisco: Jossey-Bass, 2004.

27. Rob Cross, Robert J. Thomas, and David A. Light, "How 'Who You Know' Affects What You Decide," *Sloan Management Review*, Winter 2009, pp. 35–42.

28. Mark Milian, "It's Not You, It's Meetings," *Bloomberg BusinessWeek*, June 11–17, 2012, pp. 51–52.

29. Irving L. Janis, *Victims of Groupthink*, Boston: Houghton-Mifflin, 1972; see also Glen Whyte, "Groupthink Reconsidered," *Academy of Management Review*, January 1989, pp. 40–56.

30. See Eric Bonabeau, "Decisions 2.0: The Power of Collective Intelligence," *Sloan Management Review*, Winter 2009, pp. 45–52; and Paul J. H. Schoemaker and George S. Day, "Why We Miss the Signs," *Sloan Management Review*, Winter 2009, pp. 43–44.

Chapter 13

1. Rich Karlgaard, "Teams Matter: Talent Is Not Enough," *Forbes,* March 25, 2013, p. 38.

2. Keith Ferrazzi, "Candor, Criticism, Teamwork," *Harvard Business Review,* January–February 2012, p. 40.

3. The five stages noted here were originally identified by B. W. Tuckman, "Developmental Sequence in Small Groups," *Psychological Bulletin,* vol. 63, 1965, pp. 384–99.

4. Lynn R. Offermann and Rebecca K. Spiros, "The Science and Practice of Team Development: Improving the Link," *Academy of Management Journal,* vol. 44, no. 2, 2001, pp. 376–92.

5. Miriam Erez and Anit Somech, "Is Group Productivity Loss the Rule or the Exception? Effects of Culture and Group-Based Motivation," *Academy of Management Journal,* December 1996, pp. 1513–37. See also Avan Jassawalla, Hemant Sashittal, and Avinash Malshe, "Students' Perceptions of Social Loafing: Its Antecedents and Consequences in Undergraduate Business Classroom Teams," *Academy of Management Learning and Education,* vol. 8, no. 1, 2009, pp. 42–54.

6. Jeffrey A. Lepine and Linn Van Dyne, "Peer Responses to Low Performers: An Attributional Model of Helping in the Context of Groups," *Academy of Management Review,* vol. 26, no. 1, 2001, pp. 67–84.
7. Patrick Lencioni, *The Five Dysfunctions of a Team,* San Francisco: Jossey-Bass, 2002.
8. Michael Mankins, Alan Bird, and James Root, "Making Star Teams Out of Star Players," *Harvard Business Review,* January–February 2013, pp. 74–78.
9. Russ Forester and Allan B. Drexler, "A Model for Team-Based Organization Performance," *Academy of Management Executive,* August 1999, pp. 36–49.
10. See, for example, Yochai Benkler, "The Unselfish Gene," *Harvard Business Review,* July–August 2011, pp. 77–82; and Adam M. Grant and Shefali V. Patil, "Challenging the Norm of Self-Interest: Minority Influence and Transitions to Helping Norms in Work Units," *Academy of Management Review,* 2012, vol. 37, no. 4, pp. 547–68; and Ferrazzi, op. cit.
11. Bradley L. Kirkman and Benson Rosen, "Powering Up Teams," *Organizational Dynamics,* Winter 2000, pp. 48–66.
12. S. Schulz-Hardt et al., "Group Decision Making in Hidden Profile Situations: Dissent as a Facilitator for Decision Quality," *Journal of Personality and Social Psychology,* vol. 91, no. 6, 2006, pp. 1080–93; and Bob Frisch, "When Teams Can't Decide," *Harvard Business Review,* November 2008, pp. 121–26.
13. J. Richard Hackman and Ruth Wageman, "A Theory of Team Coaching," *Academy of Management Review,* vol. 30, no. 2, 2005, pp. 269–87. For discussions of leader mood and "face" see N. W. Chi, Y. Y. Chung, and W. C. Tsai, "How Do Happy Leaders Enhance Team Success? The Mediating Roles of Transformational Leadership, Group Affective Tone, and Team Processes," *Journal of Applied Social Psychology,* vol. 64, no. 6, pp. 1421–54; and Sim B. Sitkin and J. Richard Hackman, "Developing Team Leadership: An Interview with Coach Mike Krzyzewski," *Academy of Management Learning and Education,* 2011, vol. 10, no. 3, pp. 494–501.
14. Edgar H. Schein, *Process Consultation Revisited: Building the Helping Relationship,* Reading, MA: Addison-Wesley Longman, 1998.
15. Steven Prokesch, "How GE Teaches Teams to Lead Change," *Harvard Business Review,* January 2009, pp. 99–106.
16. Jeff Pfeffer, "Why Employees Should Lead Themselves," Chapter 6 in *What Were They Thinking?* Boston: Harvard Business School Press, 2007, pp. 39–45.
17. Amy C. Edmndson, "Teamwork on the Fly," *Harvard Business Review,* April 2012, pp. 72–80; and Alex "Sandy" Pentland, "The New Science of Building Great Teams," *Harvard Business Review,* April 2012, pp. 61–70.
18. Vanessa Urch Druskat and Jane V. Wheeler, "How to Lead a Self-Managing Team," *Sloan Management Review,* Summer 2004, pp. 65–71; and Vanessa Urch Druskat and Jane V. Wheeler, "Managing from the Boundary: The Effective Leadership of Self-Managing Teams," *Academy of Management Journal,* vol. 46, no. 4, 2003, pp. 435–57.
19. Jack Gordon, "Do Your Virtual Teams Deliver Only Virtual Performance?" *Training,* June 2005, pp. 20–25; Bradley Kirkman et al., "Five Challenges to Virtual Team Success: Lessons from Sabre, Inc.," *Academy of Management Executive,* vol. 16, no. 3, 2002, pp. 67–79; and Ilze Zigurs, "Leadership in Virtual Teams: Oxymoron or Opportunity?" *Organizational Dynamics,* vol. 31, no. 4, 2002, pp. 339–51.
20. Jessica Marquez, "Accentuating the Positive," *Workforce Management,* September 22, 2008, pp. 1, 18–25.
21. Thorough discussion of virtual teams appear in Deborah L. Duarte and Nancy Tenant Snyder, *Mastering Virtual Teams: Strategies, Tools, and Techniques that Succeed,* New York: John Wiley & Sons, 2006; and Jessica Lipnack and Jeffrey Stamps, *Virtual Teams: Reaching Across Space, Time, and Organizations with Technology,* New York: John Wiley & Sons, 1997.

Chapter 14

1. Claire Suddath, "Business by the Bard," *Bloomberg BusinessWeek*, December 3–9, 2012, p. 85.
2. John Beeson, "On Leading Change: A Conversation With Bill Glavin of Oppenheimer Funds, Inc.," *Business Horizons*, January–February 2013, p. 24.
3. Leslie Kwoh, "Memo to Staff: Take More Risks," *The Wall Street Journal*, March 20, 2013, p. B8.
4. F. J. Roethlisberger, *Management and Morale*, Cambridge, MA: Harvard University Press, 1941, p. 10. See also F. J. Roethlisberger and William J. Dickson, *Management and the Worker*, Cambridge, MA: Harvard University Press, 1939. An update is Ronald G. Greenwood et al., "Hawthorne a Half Century Later: Relay Assembly Participants Remember," *Journal of Management*, Fall–Winter 1983, pp. 217–31.
5. John P. Kotter, "How to Save Good Ideas," *Harvard Business Review*, October 2010, pp. 129–32.
6. Jennifer J. Laabs, "Expert Advice on How to Move Forward with Change," *Personnel Journal*, July 1996, pp. 54–63.
7. Eric Abrahamson, "Avoiding Repetitive Change Syndrome," *Sloan Management Review*, Winter 2004, pp. 93–95.
8. David A. Garvin and Michael A. Roberto, "Change through Persuasion," *Harvard Business Review*, February 2005, pp. 104–12.
9. Clinton O. Longenecker, Mitchell J. Neubert, and Laurence S. Fink, "Causes and Consequences of Managerial Failure in Rapidly Changing Organizations," *Business Horizons*, March–April 2007, pp. 145–55.
10. John P. Kotter and Leonard A. Schlesinger, "Choosing Strategies for Change," *Harvard Business Review*, July–August 2008, pp. 130–39.

11. Gary Bradt, "Why Change Is So Hard—and What Leaders Can Do About It," *Supervision*, vol. 69, no. 8, August 2008, pp. 10–11. See also Gary Bradt, *The Ring in the Rubble: Dig Through Change and Find Your Next Golden Opportunity*, New York: McGraw-Hill, 2007.

12. Jeffrey D. Ford and Laurie W. Ford, "Decoding Resistance to Change," *Harvard Business Review*, April 2009, pp. 99–103. Also see Jeffrey D. Ford, Laurie W. Ford, and Angelo D'Amelio, "Resistance to Change: The Rest of the Story," *Academy of Management Review*, vol. 33, no. 2, 2008, pp. 362–77; and Robert Kegan and Lisa Laskow Lahey, *Immunity to Change: How To Overcome It and Unlock the Potential in Yourself and Your Organization*, Boston: Harvard Business School Press, 2009.

13. Linda Honold, "The Power of Learning at Johnsonville Foods," *Training*, April 1991, pp. 54–58.

14. Charismatic leadership was originally proposed in Robert J. House, "A 1976 Theory of Charismatic Leadership," in J. G. Hunt and L. L. Larson (eds.), *Leadership: The Cutting Edge*, Carbondale: Southern Illinois University Press, 1977. See also, John Antonakis, Marika Fenley, and Sue Liechti, "Learning Charisma," *Harvard Business Review*, June 2012, pp. 127–30. A countering view is presented in Christian Stadler and Davis Dyer, "Why Good Leaders Don't Need Charisma," *Sloan Management Review*, Spring 2013, pp. 96–97.

15. Peter Guber, "The Four Truths of the Storyteller," *Harvard Business Review*, December 2007, pp. 53–59; and Stephen Denning, "Telling Tales," *Harvard Business Review*, May 2004, pp. 122–29.

16. These ideas were originally presented in Chris Argyris, "The Executive Mind and Double-Loop Learning," *Organizational Dynamics*, Autumn 1982, pp. 4–22. A parallel set of ideas are first order change (single-loop learning) and second order change (double-loop learning); see Andrew H. Van De Ven and Marshall Scott Poole, "Explaining Development and Change in Organizations," *Academy of Management Review*, July 1995, pp. 510–40.

17. Kurt Lewin, "Frontiers in Group Dynamics: Concept, Method, and Reality in Social Sciences, Social Equilibria, and Social Change," *Human Relations*, vol. 1, 1947, pp. 4–51.

18. Sherman and Garland, op cit.

19. This is consistent with the "law of the few," which suggests that a few well-placed people can be extremely influential in shaping others' opinions. See Malcolm Gladwell, *The Tipping Point: How Little Things Can Make a Big Difference*, Boston: Little, Brown, 2000.

20. Dave Ulrich, "Are You a Change Agent?" *Workforce Management*, June 9, 2008, pp. 22–23.

21. Albert S. King, "Expectation Effects in Organizational Change," *Administrative Science Quarterly*, June 1974, pp. 221–30.

22. John P. Kotter, "Accelerate!" *Harvard Business Review*, November 2012, pp. 44–58. Also see Karen Golden-Biddle, "How to Change an Organization Without Blowing It Up," *Sloan Management Review*, Winter 2013, pp. 35–41.

23. David Dorsey, "Change Factory," *Fast Company*, June 2000, pp. 211–24.

24. A pioneering effort to identify causal variables in organizational systems was in Rensis Likert, *The Human Organization: Its Management and Value*, New York: McGraw-Hill, 1967; and Rensis Likert, *New Patterns of Management*, New York: McGraw-Hill, 1961. The critical role of broad consensus on cause-effect relationships is discussed in Clayton M. Christensen, Matt Marx, and Howard H. Stevenson, "The Tools of Cooperation and Change," *Harvard Business Review*, October 2006, pp. 73–80.

25. For a discussion of personal, social, and organizational assumptions about motivation and the ability to change, see Joseph Grenny, David Maxfield, and Andrew Shimberg, "How to Have Influence," *Sloan Management Review*, Fall 2008, pp. 47–532.

26. Jack and Suzy Welch, "What Change Agents Are Made Of," *BusinessWeek*, October 20, 2008, p. 96.

27. Ellen B. Van Oosten, "Intentional Change Theory at the Organizational Level: A Case Study," *Journal of Management Development*, vol. 25, no. 7, 2006, pp. 707–17.

28. Thea Sheldon, "Organizational Change and Growth: Focus on What Works Using 'Appreciative Inquiry,'" *Business North*, June 2003, p. 4B.

Chapter 15

1. Ed Frauenheim, "Stressed and Depressed," *Workforce Management*, January 2012, p. 22.

2. Marina Khidekel, "The Entrepreneurial Pursuit of Happiness," *Bloomberg BusinessWeek*, December 17–23, 2012, p. 79.

3. Lauren Weber and Sue Shellenbarger, "Office Stress: His vs. Hers," *Wall Street Journal,* March 4, 2013, pp. D1–2; Leslie Brooks Suzukamo, "Fed Up, Fired Up or (Gulp) Fired," *Duluth News-Tribune*, February 26, 1996, pp. 1B, 4B; and Jennifer J. Laabs, "Job Stress," *Personnel Journal*, April 1992, p. 43.

4. Jane McGonigal, "Building Resilience by Wasting Time," *Harvard Business Review*, October 2012, p. 38.

5. Hans Selye, *The Stress of Life*, rev. ed., New York: McGraw-Hill, 1976.

6. Cynthia L. Cordes and Thomas W. Dougherty, "A Review and an Integration of Research on Job Burnout," *Academy of Management Review*, October 1993, pp. 621–56; and Steven Berglas, "How to Keep a Players Productive," *Harvard Business Review*, September 2006, pp. 105–12.

7. A self-test for workaholism is in Jonathan D. Quick, Amy B. Henley, and James Campbell Quick, "The Balancing Act—At Work and at Home," *Organizational Dynamics*, vol. 33, no. 4, 2004, pp. 426–38. The positive side of workaholics is presented in Stewart D. Friedman and Sharon Lobel, "The Happy Workaholic: A Role Model for Employees," *Academy of Management Executive*, vol. 17, no. 3, 2003, pp. 87–98; the value of work-life balance is presented in Charles R. Stoner, Jennifer Robin, and Lori Russell-Chapin,

"On the Edge: Perceptions and Responses to Life Imbalance," *Business Horizons*, vol. 48, 2005, pp. 337–46.

8. Karen Lowry Miller, "Now Japan Is Admitting It: Work Kills Executives," *BusinessWeek*, August 3, 1992, p. 35.

9. Aneil K. Mishra, Karen E. Mishra, and Gretchen M. Spreitzer, "Downsizing the Company Without Downsizing Morale," *Sloan Management Review*, Spring 2009, pp. 39–44.

10. "Reflecting on Downsizing: What Have Managers Learned?" *Advanced Management Journal*, Spring 2008, pp. 46–55; and Mina Kimes, "Does Your Team Have PLSD?" *Fortune*, March 2, 2009, p. 24.

11. Comprehensive discussions of contributing factors are in Michael G. Harvey and Richard A. Cosier, "Homicides in the Workplace: Crisis or False Alarm?" *Business Horizons*, March–April 1995, pp. 11–20; and Romauld A. Stone, "Workplace Homicide: A Time for Action," *Business Horizons*, March–April 1995, pp. 3–10.

12. Samuel Greengard, "Zero Tolerance: Making It Work," *Workforce*, May 1999, pp. 28–34. See also Helen Frank Bensimon, "What to Do about Anger in the Workplace," *Training and Development*, September 1997, pp. 28–32.

13. Blake E. Ashforth, Glen E. Kreiner, Mark A. Clark, and Mel Fugate, "Normalizing Dirty Work: Managerial Tactics for Countering Occupational Taint," *Academy of Management Journal*, vol. 50, no. 1, 2007, pp. 149–74.

14. John M. Ivancevich, "Life Events and Hassles as Predictors of Health Symptoms, Job Performance, and Absenteeism," *Journal of Occupational Behaviour*, January 1986, pp. 39–51.

15. Bennett J. Tepper, "Consequences of Abusive Supervision," *Academy of Management Journal*, vol. 43, no. 2, 2000, pp. 178–90; David Wescott, "Field Guide to Office Bullies," *Bloomberg BusinessWeek*, November 26–December 2, 2012, pp. 94–95; and Dong Liu, Hui Liao, and Raymond Loi, "The Dark Side of Leadership: A Three-level Investigation of the Cascading Effect of Abusive Supervision on Employee Creativity," *Academy of Management Journal*, 2012, vol. 55, no. 5, pp. 1187–1212.

16. "Recession Weather-Proofed," *Training*, March/April 2009, p. 8.

17. "Employees Value Workplace Relationships," *Personnel Journal*, June 1996, p. 25.

18. Meyer Friedman and Ray H. Rosenman, *Type A Behavior and Your Heart*, New York: Alfred A. Knopf, 1974; see also Meyer Friedman and Diane Ulmer, *Treating Type A Behavior and Your Heart*, New York: Alfred A. Knopf, 1984.

19. A meta-analysis, or quantitative review and synthesis of previous research results, is provided by Stephanie Booth-Kewley and Howard S. Friedman, "Psychological Predictors of Heart Disease: A Quantitative Review," *Psychological Bulletin*, May 1987, pp. 343–62; a readable update is Joshua Fischman, "Type A on Trial," *Psychology Today*, February 1987, pp. 42–50, 64.

20. See, for example, the prescriptions in Kathryn Tyler, "Cut the Stress," *HR Magazine*, May 2003, pp. 101–6; and Jerald Greenberg, "Managing Workplace Stress by Promoting Organizational Justice," *Organizational Dynamics*, vol. 33, no. 4, 2004, pp. 352–65.

21. Mary Ann Hazen, "Grief and the Workplace," *Academy of Management Perspectives*, August 2008, pp. 78–86.

22. Monika Henderson and Michael Argyle, "Social Support by Four Categories of Work Colleagues: Relationships between Activities, Stress, and Satisfaction," *Journal of Occupational Behaviour*, July 1985, pp. 229–39; and Kossek and Hammer, op cit. Also see Shawn Achor, "Positive Intelligence," *Harvard Business Review*, January-February, 2012, pp. 100–102.

23. Susan G. Hauser, "'Mindfulness' Over Matter of Multitasking," *Workforce Management*, December 2012, p. 10; Timothy J. Vogus and Kathleen M. Sutcliffe, "Organizational Mindfulness and Mindful Organizing: A Reconciliation and Path Forward," *Academy of Management Learning and Education*, 2012, vol. 11, no. 4, pp. 722–735. Also see Maria Konnikova, *Mastermind: How to Think Like Sherlock Holmes*, New York: Viking, 2013, esp. p. 22.

24. Charlene Marmer Solomon, "Picture This: A Safer Workplace," *Workforce*, February 1998, pp. 82–86.

25. F. J. Roethlisberger and William J. Dickson, *Management and the Worker*, Cambridge, MA: Harvard University Press, 1939, pp. 189–205, 593–604; and William J. Dickson and F. J. Roethlisberger, *Counseling in an Organization: A Sequel to the Hawthorne Researches*, Boston: Harvard Business School, Division of Research, 1966.

Chapter 16

1. "Managing the Global Workforce," *Bloomberg BusinessWeek,* January 16, 2008 (http://www.businessweek.com/stories/2008-01-16/managing-the-global-workforce).

2. Christine Porath and Christine Pearson, "The Price of Incivility: Lack of Respect Hurts Morale—and the Bottom Line," *Harvard Business Review,* January–February 2013, p. 119.

3. Geert Hofstede, Gert Jan Hofstede, and Michael Minkov, *Cultures and Organizations: Software of the Mind,* 3rd ed., New York: McGraw-Hill, 2010, p. 6.

4. Geert Hofstede, "Cultural Constraints in Management Theories," *Academy of Management Executive,* February 1993, pp. 81–94. See also Michael H. Hoppe, "An Interview with Geert Hofstede," *Academy of Management Executive,* vol. 18, no. 1, 2004, pp. 75–79.

5. Andre Laurent, "The Cultural Diversity of Western Conceptions of Management," *International Studies of Management and Organization,* Spring–Summer 1983, pp. 75–96.

6. Robert E. Cole, "Work and Leisure in Japan," *California Management Review,* Spring 1992, pp. 52–63. Also see the discussion of face time by Moon Ihlwan and Kenji Hall, "New Tech, Old Habits," *BusinessWeek,* March 26, 2007, pp. 48–49.

7. Mina Kimes, "Fluor's Corporate Crime Fighter," *Fortune,* February 16, 2009, p. 26.

8. Mariann Jelinek and Nancy J. Adler, "Women: World-Class Managers for Global Competition," *Academy of Management Executive,* February 1988, pp. 11–19.
9. "Court Invalidates Airline's Policy for Transfers to Foreign Cities," *Japan Labor Bulletin,* November 1, 1974, p. 7.
10. Ben W. Heineman, "Why We Can All Stop Worrying about Offshoring and Outsourcing," *The Atlantic* (website), March 26, 2013.
11. Aaron Bernstein, Dan Cook, Pete Engardio, and Gregory L. Miles, "The Difference Japanese Management Makes," *BusinessWeek,* July 14, 1986, pp. 47–50.
12. Gary Bonvillian and William A. Nowlin, "Cultural Awareness: An Essential Element of Doing Business Abroad," *Business Horizons,* November–December 1994, pp. 44–50; and Mary Munter, "Cross-Cultural Communication for Managers," *Business Horizons,* May–June 1993, pp. 69–78.
13. Geocentric attitudes are discussed in Lennie Copeland and Lewis Griggs, "The Internationable Employee," *Management Review,* April 1988, pp. 52–53.
14. Geert Hofstede, "Motivation, Leadership, and Organization: Do American Theories Apply Abroad?" *Organizational Dynamics*, Summer 1980, pp. 42–63.
15. John I. Reynolds, "Developing Policy Responses to Cultural Differences," *Business Horizons,* August 1978, pp. 28–35.
16. As many as 40 percent of American expatriates return early from overseas assignments; see Juan I. Sanchez, Paul E. Spector, and Cary L. Cooper, "Adapting to a Boundaryless World: A Developmental Expatriate Model," *Academy of Management Executive,* vol. 14, no. 2, 2000, pp. 96–106. Useful pre-move and post-move suggestions for expatriates are in Mark Alan Clouse and Michael D. Watkins, "Three Keys to Getting an Overseas Assignment Right," *Harvard Business Review,* October 2009, pp. 115–19.
17. Kerri Anne Crowne, "What Leads to Cultural Intelligence?" *Business Horizons,* vol. 51, 2008, pp. 391–99; and P. Christopher Earley and Elaine Mosakowski, "Toward Culture Intelligence: Turning Cultural Differences into a Workplace Advantage," *Academy of Management Executive,* vol. 18, no. 3, 2004, pp. 151–57.
18. Hoon Park and J. Kline Harrison, "Enhancing Managerial Cross-Cultural Awareness and Sensitivity: Transactional Analysis Revisited," *Journal of Management Development,* vol. 12, no. 3, 1993, pp. 20–29.
19. Charlene Marmer Solomon, "Repatriation: Up, Down or Out?" *Personnel Journal,* January 1995, pp. 28–37; see also Avan Jassawalla, Traci Connolly, and Lindsay Slojkowski, "Issues of Effective Repatriation: A Model and Managerial Implications," *SAM Advanced Management Journal,* Spring 2004, pp. 38–46.
20. Justin Fox, "The Triumph of English," *Fortune,* September 18, 2000, pp. 209–12.
21. Two sharply contrasting views on how to achieve this are in George B. Graen, "In the Eye of the Beholder: Cross-Cultural Lesson in Leadership from Project GLOBE: A Response Viewed from the Third Culture Bonding (TCB) Model of Cross-Cultural Leadership," *Academy of Management Perspectives,* November 2006, pp. 95–101; and Robert J. House, Mansour Javidan, Peter W. Dorfman, and Mary Sully de Luque, "A Failure of Scholarship: Response to George Graen's Critique of GLOBE," *Academy of Management Perspectives,* November 2006, pp. 102–14.
22. F. O. Walumba, J. J. Lawler, and B. J. Avolio, "Leadership, Individual Differences, and Work-Related Attitudes: A Cross-Cultural Investigation," *Applied Psychology: An International Review,* vol. 56, no. 2, 2007, pp. 212–30.

Preface

1. John Miner, "The Rated Importance, Scientific Validity, and Practical Usefulness of Organizational Behavior Theories: A Quantitative Review," *Academy of Management Learning and Education*, vol. 2, no. 3, 2003, p. 262.
2. Saku Mantere and Mikko Ketokivi, "Reasoning in Organization Science," *Academy of Management Review*, 2013, vol. 38, no. 1, pp. 79–89; and Ian I. Mitroff, Can M. Alpaslan, and Richard O. Mason, "The Messy Business of Management," *Sloan Management Review*, Fall 2012, p. 96.
3. Justin Menkes, "Hiring for Smarts," *Harvard Business Review*, November 2005, p. 102.
4. Descriptive elements in reflection are drawn from Patricia Raber Hedberg, "Learning Through Reflective Classroom Practice: Applications to Educate the Reflective Manager," *Journal of Management Education*, vol. 33, no. 1, February 2009, pp. 10–36; and Fernanda Duarte, "Rekindling the Sociological Imagination as a Pedagogical 'Package' in Management Education," *Journal of Management Education*, vol. 33, no. 1, pp. 59–76.

Name Index

Subject Index

D

E

Q

R